LAW

and

BIOETHICS

An Introduction

Jerry Menikoff

GEORGETOWN UNIVERSITY PRESS / WASHINGTON, D.C.

Georgetown University Press, Washington, D.C.
©2001 by Georgetown University Press. All rights reserved.
Printed in the United States of America

10 9 8 7 6 5 4 3 2 1   2001

This volume is printed on acid-free offset book paper.

Library of Congress Cataloging-in-Publication Data
Menikoff, Jerry.
  Law and bioethics : an introduction/edited by Jerry Menikoff.
    p. cm.
  Includes index.
  ISBN 0-87840-838-X (cloth : alk. paper)
    1. Medical laws and legislation—United States. 2. Medical care—Law and
  legislation—United States. 3. Bioethics—United States. I. Title.
  KF3821 .M46 2001
  344.73'041—dc21   00-061023

To my parents,
Max and Gloria Menikoff,
for always being there

[C]ancer research did not depress Jenny Garp, who liked to
describe herself as her father had described a novelist.
"A doctor who sees only terminal cases."
In the world according to her father, Jenny Garp knew,
we must have energy. . . .
But in the world according to Garp, we are all terminal cases.
—John Irving, *The World According to Garp*

There are so many damned rules.
—Graham Greene, *The Honorary Consul*

TABLE OF CONTENTS

PART IV
END-OF-LIFE DECISIONS

PART V
NEW TECHNOLOGIES

PART VI
DEATH AND TRANSPLANTATION

Introduction

Ask the average person to tell you something about bioethics and, likely as not, the response will include a reference to Karen Ann Quinlan, Nancy Cruzan, or Baby M. For better or worse, the American legal system has played a major role in how the public perceives this field. And it is not merely the public that recognizes the crucial connection between law and matters bioethical. Both leading scholarly bioethics textbooks and major professional bioethics organizations correctly conclude that knowledge of the relevant law is one of the key elements in truly understanding the field of bioethics.

This is a text about *the law relating to bioethics*. The phrase "law and bioethics" is used in the commonly accepted sense in which "law and . . ." refers to new fields of law that have grown up around certain areas of nonlegal endeavor. While some "law and . . ." courses are convenient juxtapositions of unrelated legal doctrines that merely share a common subject matter, that is most assuredly *not* the case with law and bioethics. This area embodies certain consistent themes that make it well worth studying as a whole. This text is designed to illustrate those general themes, and to highlight the interconnections among doctrines that have come out of specific cases. Constitutional law scholar Laurence Tribe goes to great pains to convince his readers that American "constitutional law is [not] simply a mishmash."[1] Hopefully, the reader might reach a similar conclusion with respect to both the constitutional and non-constitutional aspects of the law relating to bioethics.

This text is designed to enable someone with an interest in bioethics—student or professional—to achieve a relatively sophisticated understanding of this body of law. It attempts to do this in a relatively compact space, aiming more at appropriate coverage of core concepts than at encyclopedic detail. While the underlying subject matter is not simple, no specific legal background is assumed of the reader. Background material is included to highlight any general legal principles with which some readers may not be familiar. In

1

addition, a brief glossary at the back of the volume highlights core terms and concepts.

At the outset, it must be noted that the language of the law is different from that of "traditional" bioethics. That difference can be somewhat jarring to a reader who has no familiarity with legal reasoning. To a great degree, the difference stems from the distinct concerns of the law. While it is currently in vogue to speak of "pragmatic" bioethics, *law* is the ultimate pragmatic discipline.

The law is designed to enable our society to function appropriately. Often, the controversies that the law must resolve do not easily divide along moral lines. There is nothing particularly moral about concluding that people should drive on a green light and stop at a red one; to ensure public safety it is merely necessary that a (perhaps arbitrary) choice be made so that people behave in accordance with that choice. Moreover, even where moral interpretations of a given behavior are appropriate, the law will not necessarily be concerned with them. Few of us would want to live in a society in which we are punished by the government for every indiscretion that conflicts with a particular notion of morality.

Thus, much of this text will be concerned with introducing the reader to the unique language and concerns of the law. There will be much emphasis on the United States Constitution and how it circumscribes the actions of the government, specifically through the Fourteenth Amendment and its equal protection and due process clauses.

Another area of emphasis will be on the very different legal rules that govern relationships between individuals. The law is very protective of individual autonomy. That protection is accorded to *all* individuals—not merely to patients—and so we will deal with conflicts between the autonomy of doctors and that of patients.

Almost by definition, the law is designed to regulate human behavior. A significant theme in this text is therefore how laws restrict individual autonomy, and what determines whether and when such restrictions are acceptable. Some cases legitimize restrictions on autonomy for either the benefit of society in general or the more specific benefit of the person whose autonomy is restricted. Governmental paternalism (as opposed to the much-maligned caregiver paternalism discussed in "classical" bioethics) will be revealed as very much a core concept of the laws relating to bioethics.

The standard way law is taught in the United States is the case method: subjecting the texts of judicial decisions to critical analysis. This time-honored technique is particularly appropriate in the field of law and bioethics, where the great bulk of the law was in fact created by a relatively small number of decisions. This volume is accordingly built around the texts of those decisions, many of which are "classic." Only by reading the actual language of the judges can one fully appreciate the nuances raised in these cases, and thus begin to understand which distinctions are relevant to a future case.

The notes and questions are designed to make this text somewhat like the kind of workbook you might encounter in studying a new foreign language or a new topic in mathematics: there are numerous opportunities to apply legal rules to particular fact patterns. Many questions in the law do in fact have answers—or if not answers at least standard ways to frame arguments. A reader who attempts to answer the questions posed in this volume should hopefully gain facility in dealing with the standard ways that problems in law and bioethics are analyzed.

At times, the legal principles discussed in this book may seem disconcerting. For example, consider the turn-of-the-century case of *Hurley v. Eddingfield* (59 N.E. 1058 [Ind. 1901]), where a doctor, for no good reason, refuses to come to the aid of a woman he had previously treated. She and the child she was about to give birth to die. The court finds that the doctor committed no legal wrong.

More surprising, perhaps, is that *Hurley* represents current law. The reader who is disgusted by *Hurley*, thinking it demonstrates that the law truly is an ass—and thus has nothing meaningful to contribute to bioethics—might nonetheless be pleased by the result in *In re A.C.* (573 A.2d 1235 [D.C. 1990]), where a court comes out strongly in favor of not forcing surgery upon a woman, even if it is needed to save the life of her fetus. Yet variations on the same principle—an unwillingness in the law to lightly create duties to others—lead to both outcomes.

If nothing else, it is hoped that these materials will challenge some of your existing ideas about what is "right" and what is "wrong." While there will be relatively few references to ethics per se in this volume, this is not to say that the concerns that move the legal system are somehow inappropriate or less important than the writings of ethicists. Those skeptical about the law as a force for what is "right" should remember that many, if not most, of the landmark social changes relating to bioethics have come not from the world of philosophy, but from judicial decisions.

Those decisions represent the efforts of many talented people of good will who are vested with a unique responsibility: their conclusions in any particular case will assuredly affect the participants in that case, and often many thousands of others, in a way that no recommendation from a hospital ethics committee is likely to do. Whether or not you conclude that any particular case was decided correctly or incorrectly, hopefully you can enjoy and benefit from the journey of discovery. For many of you, this will be an entry to a new kingdom, with its own unique language. Perhaps it is not quite as magical as Harry Potter's world, but you might be pleasantly surprised to find that it does indeed possess a magic of its own.

I very much welcome comments, criticisms, and corrections from readers. Feel free to ask a question, or just say hello! I can be reached by e-mail at *jam@post.harvard.edu.*

Acknowledgements: For putting me on the pathway that led to this book, I am enormously grateful to Dennis Thompson, Mark Siegler, and Richard Epstein. I am also indebted to my current and former students at the law schools of the University of Chicago, Hofstra University, and the University of Kansas, who persevered with good will and enthusiasm as I attempted to work through with them these ideas.

My debt to numerous colleagues at those institutions, and at Harvard's Center for Ethics and the Professions, is equally large. For providing me with the free time and resources that were essential to producing this work, I am particularly grateful to Rob Martensen and Mike Hoeflich. Very special thanks go to Janet Dolgin, for having graciously made her way through a draft of this manuscript.

Last, but certainly not least, I thank the members of the Ethics Club (particularly the "regulars," Don Marquis, Ron Stephens, and Dick Silverstein) both for their frequent patience in devoting their attention to my writings and for providing many good memories.

A Note to Teachers: I have prepared a *Teacher's Manual* that further discusses many of the issues covered in the text, gives guidance on how to use it in various types of courses (not only a full course devoted to law and bioethics, but also a standard survey course in bioethics), and suggests answers to the numerous questions the text poses. To obtain a copy, contact me at *jam@post. harvard.edu*.

A Note on Further Reading: In keeping with the goal of making this volume relatively concise and affordable, citations to the very rich legal literature have been minimized. Excellent supplementary sources are the many citations to other cases and secondary materials (law review articles and books) that appear in most court opinions. To save space and for ease of reading, these citations have been edited out of the opinions printed in this book. Thus, one of the first steps in researching a topic more extensively should be to find the unedited text of a case.

If you have access to the WestLaw or LEXIS electronic data services, those services will not only provide the complete case but will let you search, in a matter of seconds, a database containing the full text of almost all law review articles. Typing in the name of any case mentioned in this book, or even a few words describing the topic you are interested in, will almost always produce a useful result. Those unfamiliar with legal research will discover that if there is a legal issue, it is likely that at least one law review article (and probably more) has been written about it, complete with numerous footnotes.

If you do not have access to those systems, use the citation at the beginning of each case to find these judicial opinions in any law library. (The law librarian can also help you find the law reviews where legal commentary on the cases is published.) Many of these opinions, especially the more recent ones, are also available on the web. In particular, check out Cornell Law School's excellent Legal Information Institute, at *www.law.cornell.edu*. Other good web sites for obtaining court opinions and other legal materials are FindLaw (*www.findlaw.com*) and the official site of the Supreme Court of the United States (*www.supremecourtus.gov*).

A Note on Editing of Cases: Throughout this book, deletions from quoted material are indicated by ellipses. Brackets indicate inserted material, which may also be accompanied by deletions. Citations, footnotes, and concurring or dissenting opinions are usually omitted without notice.

Endnote

1. Laurence H. Tribe, *American Constitutional Law* at 32 (New York: Foundation Press, 3rd ed, vol. 1, 2000).

PART I

The American Constitutional Structure

1

Federalism and Bioethics

Imagine that the national government passed a law that said, in effect, "Thou shalt not commit physician-assisted suicide."[1] At least one state—Oregon—already has a law that says just the opposite: in appropriate cases, it is very much okay to "actively" help a patient into the great beyond by prescribing a lethal dose of medication. How are we to decide which of these mutually inconsistent laws wins out?

It is these sorts of struggles between government behemoths that form the backdrop for much of the law relating to bioethics. Understanding how such struggles are resolved depends little on discerning which course of action is the best public policy—and even less on determining how best to protect a patient. The answer lies in working logically through the structure of this nation's government. For readers with minimal or no background, this chapter provides a brief introduction to the somewhat dry subject of federalism.

As its very name demonstrates—the *United* States—our nation is structured as a union of distinct smaller units. The country is governed through a sharing of power between the national (also called the federal) government, and the governments of the individual states. Indeed, the word *federalism* itself refers to a governmental structure in which smaller political units come together and agree to give up some of their power to a centralized government. The framework for this sharing of power is the United States Constitution.

In allocating power between the national and state governments, the Constitution also indirectly plays a major role in providing power to a third group: the public. Often the Constitution will effectively deny certain powers to the national or the state government, or to both. For example, the Tenth Amendment to the Constitution notes that the "powers not delegated to the United States by the Constitution, nor prohibited by it to the States, are reserved to the States respectively, or to the people." This makes explicit the concept that the United

States government is one of enumerated (listed) powers: if a power is not mentioned somewhere in the Constitution, then the national government presumably cannot exercise it.

In point of fact, the Constitution grants a number of very broad powers to
the United States government. Most of our attention, however, will be directed
at the relatively few instances where the Constitution denies specific powers to
national or state government. It is these denials that create individual rights,
and effectively allocate power to the individual members of the public. Many of
the issues that crop up in the study of bioethics relate to important aspects of
people's lives—issues turning on life, death, and reproduction—and these are
exactly the sorts of rights created by the Constitution (and in some cases by state
constitutions). To understand the law relating to bioethics, you must therefore
understand the basic details of federalism.

We should first note that there are four prototypical arrangements of power
that may exist under the Constitution.[2]

How the Constitution Allocates Power

		To the States?	
		No	*Yes*
To the National Government?	*No*	A	C
	Yes	B	D

**(A) Neither the national government nor the state governments
may have been given the power to act in a particular area.** Effectively, in
such an area the people can do what they want. The classic "individual rights"
created by the Bill of Rights—the right to freedom of religion, to name one—
are good examples.

It is important to keep in mind, however, that denials of power are rarely
absolute. On the one hand, the actual scope of the conduct protected by a particular right may be less than crystal clear. We have the right of freedom of
speech, but that does not protect all speech. It does not give us the right to incorrectly shout "fire" in a crowded theatre. And some kinds of speech may be
more protected than others (e.g., political speech v. commercial speech). Similarly, most constitutionally-created rights have definitional problems.

Assume in a particular instance that we are clearly dealing with conduct
protected by a constitutional provision. A finding that a given law conflicts with
such a "right" usually does not end the discussion. Instead it raises a second
question: how important is the interest that the government is advancing, and
how significantly does the law impinge on the individual right in question? Even
constitutionally protected rights can be overridden. However, only extremely

important government interests—often described as "compelling"—are likely to prevail in such situations, and only when the law is written so as to minimize its effect on the constitutional right.

Deciding whether the government interest or the individual right wins out is far from straightforward. An appropriate metaphor might be determining what gives when the hypothetical irresistible force meets an immovable object.

(B) The power to regulate an area may have been given solely to the national government. While Congress could enact laws to regulate such an area, state legislatures could not. Of course, the national government could also choose not to legislate in this area, which would effectively leave private conduct as free of regulation as would be the case under category (A).

(C) The power to regulate an area might be given solely to the states. This is the flip side of category (B). Any limitations on individual conduct in this area would depend on the state you are in, and whether that state has passed laws in that area.

Not that long ago, many would have said that few areas would fall into this category. Recent decisions by the United States Supreme Court have brought new attention to this category. Many now consider it one of the most important areas of constitutional law. Previously the power to "regulate commerce" was routinely accepted by Supreme Courts as giving Congress the authority to regulate things that the ordinary person would not view as having much, if anything, to do with commerce. Since 1995, the Supreme Court has dramatically rethought this issue, substantially cutting back on the power of Congress to use "the regulation of commerce" as a justification for its authority to enact laws. Charles Fried, former Solicitor General and retired federal judge, has described this general issue as follows:[3]

> When, in 1995, the Supreme Court struck down the Gun-Free School Zones Act, which had been passed on the preposterous excuse that banning guns within 1,000 yards of a school somehow regulated interstate commerce, it made clear that Congress's power over the country is not unlimited. Congress may not legislate just because something seems like a good idea; there must be a connection to one of the topics the Constitution entrusted to the care of the national government. And the claim that these topics are so vague that in reality Congress may legislate about anything at all was emphatically rejected.

A recent and dramatic example of this change in thinking is *United States v. Morrison*, 120 S. Ct. 1740 (2000). Christy Brzonkala claimed that while she was a student at Virginia Polytechnic Institute, two members of the football team raped her. After that attack, she was treated for depression and dropped out of school. During a school investigation, one of the men admitted having had sexual contact with her despite her having said "no" twice. He was initially suspended for two semesters, but on subsequent review by the school, his offense was recategorized as "using abusive language" and the suspension was set aside as being excessive.

Ms. Brzonkala then sued him and the school under the federal Violence against Women Act, which allows a woman to sue for money damages in federal court if she has been subjected to a gender-based violent attack. The Supreme Court determined that no provision of the Constitution—including the commerce clause—gave Congress the power to pass such a law, and declared it unconstitutional. As the dissenters to this 5-4 decision noted, the Court had in 1964 upheld the constitutionality of the federal civil rights laws on just such a commerce clause argument; it remained unclear why racial discrimination has a more obvious impact on commerce than violence against women.

(D) The national and state governments may have concurrent jurisdiction: they both have the power to pass laws in certain areas. Possible conflicts between these laws are resolved by the Constitution (Article VI, paragraph 2): "This Constitution, and the Laws of the United States which shall be made in Pursuance thereof . . . shall be the supreme Law of the Land . . . any Thing in the Constitution or Laws of any State to the Contrary notwithstanding." This "supremacy clause" assures that national laws will always win out in a battle with state laws. Often the hardest question, however, is determining what the state and national laws do in fact mean, and whether there is any conflict.

Finally, in addition to these four categories, it should be noted that even if the United States Constitution does not prevent a state from passing laws regulating particular conduct, the state's own constitution may do so. It, too, may create individual rights that reserve powers to the people. If these rights are more expansive than those created by the United States Constitution, then that state constitution will effectively limit the powers wielded by its legislators.

To demonstrate the consequences of a particular issue ending up in one category as opposed to another, let us assume that Dr. X has been treating John Doe for end-stage AIDS. Both of them live in Oregon, where state law allows doctors to prescribe a lethal dose of medication for patients who request it. John is not complaining of pain but is disturbed by his growing loss of function: he is now blind, in addition to being bed-ridden and suffering from gastrointestinal difficulties as a result of AIDS-related conditions. John had concluded that his life "sucks big-time." If he were rich, and had lots of servants to help out with day-to-day activities, he might find it minimally palatable. But given his current circumstances, and the minimal social services provided by the state, he has decided to ask Dr. X for the life-ending prescription.

We will assume that at the time of this scenario, there is a national law that criminalizes the conduct of a doctor who writes a prescription for a lethal dose of medication knowing that the patient intends to use it to end his life. Where does this situation fit in our categories?

There is a possibility (admittedly slim) that John's situation might fall into category (A), with both the national and state governments being denied the power to prevent him from getting the life-ending prescription. As will be discussed later, the Supreme Court has rejected a broad constitutional right to physician-assisted suicide. However, a number of the Justices have acknowledged that in the appropriate (relatively narrow) situation, a person might be able to demonstrate a constitutionally protected right to actively end his life. If John's situation were found to be such a situation—if, perhaps, he was suffering in a unique manner for which existing forms of palliative care are inadequate, or if the wording of the national law inappropriately restricted his access to palliative care—then the national law denying him the right to the lethal drug could well be declared unconstitutional by the U.S. Supreme Court. Each state would similarly be prohibited from enforcing against him any of their own laws that were essentially equivalent to the national law that had been struck down.

On the other hand, based on the language of the Supreme Court's opinions about physician-assisted suicide (see chapter 11), it is plausible to conclude that John does not have any constitutionally protected right at stake. Were that conclusion made, we would not be in category (A). We might, however, be in a relatively rare category (C) situation in which power has been denied to the national government and given solely to the states. Here is Charles Fried's comment on a similar scenario:[4]

> So what in the Constitution makes doctor-assisted suicide any of Congress's business? . . . Imagine a different Congress passing a "Right to Life Protection Act of 2003," prohibiting any state from imposing the death penalty. How could that be defended? As a regulation of interstate commerce because some of the material used in carrying out an execution might have crossed a state line? . . . You need only imagine the speeches that many of those who voted for [national law against assisted suicide] would be making if death penalty opponents tried to introduce the bill I just described, and you will appreciate what a travesty of federalism [a bill banning assisted suicide nationwide would be].

If this scenario were under category (C), the national law would be a nullity; state law alone would govern. In John's situation, since Oregon allows Dr. X to prescribe the lethal medication, he would be permitted to end his life. On the other hand, were they in any state other than Oregon, Dr. X's conduct would probably be illegal because all other states ban such conduct.

Finally, it is possible that our scenario will come not under category (C), but under category (D). Whatever the recent attention being paid to situations where the national government has acted beyond its powers, the category (C) situation is still relatively rare. National legislation in areas that have no obvious relationship to a specific purpose mentioned in the Constitution has been upheld far more often than it has been struck down as unconstitutional.

If our assisted-suicide case winds up as a category (D) situation, both the national and state governments have the authority to legislate in this area. Since the national and the state laws are clearly inconsistent, under the supremacy clause, the national law wins out. John would be denied access to the medication.

As this example demonstrates, federalism is a complicated concept—and its application can play a pivotal role in determining what governments can or cannot do in a particular circumstance. Problems logically arise before, and to some extent apart from, a full consideration of the ultimate policy issues relating to what we might want a government to do in a particular situation. We will be revisiting federalism issues throughout this book, especially in discussions of the right to privacy, abortion, cloning, and the right to refuse care. But virtually any topic in bioethics has federalism implications.

Endnotes

1. This circumstance is far from hypothetical. The Pain Relief Promotion Act of 1999 (H.R. 2260) passed by the House of Representatives included a provision that would make it a federal crime to prescribe a federally controlled drug for the purpose of assisting someone to end his life. The Senate Judiciary committee later approved a similar bill, but as of July 2000 the entire Senate had not yet voted on it.
2. Geoffrey R. Stone, et al., *Constitutional Law,* 3d ed., 154 (Boston: Little, Brown & Co., 1996).
3. Charles Fried, "Leave the Personal to the States," *New York Times* (Oct. 29, 1999), A-31.
4. Ibid.

PART II

Reproduction

2

The Right to Privacy

Privacy would appear to be a relatively simple concept, understandable by even young children: "Leave me alone!" Yet in the realm of law and bioethics, it has taken on a life of its own, one very different from its usual meaning. How did this state of affairs come about? The landmark case is *Griswold v. Connecticut*, which follows. To make sense of *Griswold*, we must first delve more deeply into the thicket of federalism.

The first ten amendments to the United States Constitution, adopted as a group in 1791, are commonly referred to as the Bill of Rights. They embody some of the best-known and most fundamental freedoms in this nation:

- freedom of religion (first amendment)
- freedom of speech (first)
- freedom from unreasonable searches and seizures (fourth)
- the right to due process of law (fifth)
- freedom from double jeopardy (fifth)
- freedom from self-incrimination (fifth)
- the right to trial by jury, with representation by counsel, in criminal matters (sixth).

When these amendments were first adopted, they were understood to apply only to the national government, not to the actions of the *state governments* or *private individuals*. And, as was noted in Chapter 1, the Tenth Amendment highlighted special concerns about the actions of the national government, noting that if a power was not specifically given to the national government, then it was reserved for exercise by the state governments and the public.

Thus, as of the beginning of the nineteenth century, if Congress passed a law making it a federal crime to practice a non-Christian religion, that law would have been unconstitutional, since it would be inconsistent with the First Amendment. On the other hand, if Wal-Mart created a nationwide policy in its stores to hire only Christians, nothing in the Bill of Rights would prevent it from doing so. This would be merely private action. A similar result would have occurred if the state of New Jersey had passed a law criminalizing the practice of any religion except Judaism. While this would have been the action of a government, it was state action—not federal action—and the Bill of Rights did not limit the actions of state governments.

In 1868, the Fourteenth Amendment to the United States Constitution was adopted. It contained the following language: "nor shall any State deprive any person of life, liberty, or property, without due process of law; nor deny to any person within its jurisdiction the equal protection of the laws." Unlike the Bill of Rights, this provision was specifically intended to limit the power of the state governments. Its guarantees of "due process" and its assurance of "equal protection" have since been expansively interpreted. They form the basis for many important limitations on the power of state governments. Working with other provisions of the Constitution, both of these guarantees also effectively restrict the power of the national government.

As we now discuss the meaning of these two important clauses, do not forget that, even after the Fourteenth Amendment, constitutional guarantees still limit only the power of governments, *not* the actions of private individuals. True, if Wal-Mart were to discriminate in its hiring practices based on a person's religion, it would likely violate a number of federal and state civil rights laws that *do* apply to private actions—but nothing in the Constitution required the national or a state government to pass such laws. It would be perfectly consistent with the Constitution if there were no laws at all restricting private actions motivated by religious animus (or many other forms of bias we might otherwise find improper).

THE MEANING OF "DUE PROCESS"

The guarantee of due process of law might initially seem to be relatively narrow. Based on the words themselves—due *process*—we might expect this to relate only to *procedural* issues, not *substantive* matters. For example, for a criminal trial to be fair to the defendant, certain procedures should be followed. It would be inappropriate to not allow the defendant to have a lawyer, to not give the lawyer time to prepare a defense, and to not permit the defendant to be present during the trial. These all relate to procedures for doing things, and it makes sense that a guarantee of due process of law should address these concerns.

On the other hand, does due process provide any substantive guarantees? For example, should the state be limited, on due process grounds, in what activities it determines to be crimes? We might initially think that substantive matters dealing with the content of rights, not the procedures by which we assure the rights are protected, are beyond the reach of due process protection. However, the Supreme Court has over many decades determined that the due process clause of the Fourteenth Amendment does in fact embody substantive protections.

This rather confusing yet extremely important concept is commonly referred to as *substantive due process*. Specifically, the Court has held that among those substantive protections are the provisions in the first eight amendments to the Constitution that relate to "fundamental personal rights." In other words, as a result of the passage of the Fourteenth Amendment, some of the provisions of the Bill of Rights now restrict the power not just of the federal government but also of state governments.

Griswold required the Court to determine whether this concept of substantive due process in any way restricted a state's ability to ban the use of contraceptives. In doing so, the Court had a great deal to say about the right of privacy—even though the word "privacy" appears nowhere in the Constitution.

GRISWOLD V. CONNECTICUT
Supreme Court of the United States
381 U.S. 479 (1965)

OPINION BY JUSTICE DOUGLAS:

Appellant Griswold is Executive Director of the Planned Parenthood League of Connecticut. Appellant Buxton is a licensed physician and a professor at the Yale Medical School who served as Medical Director for the League at its Center in New Haven—a center open and operating from November 1 to November 10, 1961, when appellants were arrested.

They gave information, instruction, and medical advice to *married persons* as to the means of preventing conception. They examined the wife and prescribed the best contraceptive device or material for her use. Fees were usually charged, although some couples were serviced free.

The statutes whose constitutionality is involved in this appeal are §§ 53–32 and 54–196 of the General Statutes of Connecticut (1958 rev.). The former provides:

> "Any person who uses any drug, medicinal article or instrument for the purpose of preventing conception shall be fined not less than fifty dollars or imprisoned not less than sixty days nor more than one year or be both fined and imprisoned."

Section 54–196 provides:

> "Any person who assists, abets, counsels, causes, hires or commands another to commit any offense may be prosecuted and punished as if he were the principal offender."

The appellants were found guilty as accessories and fined $100 each, against the claim that the accessory statute as so applied violated the Fourteenth Amendment. . . .

Coming to the merits, we are met with a wide range of questions that implicate the Due Process Clause of the Fourteenth Amendment. . . . We do not sit as a super-legislature to determine the wisdom, need, and propriety of laws that touch economic problems, business affairs, or social conditions. This law, however, operates directly on an intimate relation of husband and wife and their physician's role in one aspect of that relation.

The association of people is not mentioned in the Constitution nor in the Bill of Rights. The right to educate a child in a school of the parents' choice—whether public or private or parochial—is also not mentioned. Nor is the right to study any particular subject or any foreign language. Yet the First Amendment has been construed to include certain of those rights. . . . [T]he right to educate one's children as one chooses is made applicable to the States by the force of the First and Fourteenth Amendments. . . . [T]he same dignity is given the right to study the German language in a private school. In other words, the State may not, consistently with the spirit of the First Amendment, contract the spectrum of available knowledge. The right of freedom of speech and press includes not only the right to utter or to print, but the right to distribute, the right to receive, the right to read and freedom of inquiry, freedom of thought, and freedom to teach—indeed the freedom of the entire university community. Without those peripheral rights the specific rights would be less secure. . . .

. . . [S]pecific guarantees in the Bill of Rights have penumbras, formed by emanations from those guarantees that help give them life and substance. Various guarantees create zones of privacy. The right of association contained in the penumbra of the First Amendment is one, as we have seen. The Third Amendment in its prohibition against the quartering of soldiers "in any house" in time of peace without the consent of the owner is another facet of that privacy. The Fourth Amendment explicitly affirms the "right of the people to be secure in their persons, houses, papers, and effects, against unreasonable searches and seizures." The Fifth Amendment in its Self-Incrimination Clause enables the citizen to create a zone of privacy which government may not force him to surrender to his detriment. The Ninth Amendment provides: "The enumeration in the Constitution, of certain rights, shall not be construed to deny or disparage others retained by the people."

The Fourth and Fifth Amendments were described . . . as protection against all governmental invasions "of the sanctity of a man's home and the privacies of life." We recently referred . . . to the Fourth Amendment as creating a "right to privacy, no less important than any other right carefully and particularly reserved to the people." . . .

The present case, then, concerns a relationship lying within the zone of privacy created by several fundamental constitutional guarantees. And it concerns a law which, in forbidding the use of contraceptives rather than regulating their manufacture or sale, seeks to achieve its goals by means having a maximum destructive impact upon that relationship. Such a law cannot stand in light of the familiar principle, so often applied by this Court, that a "governmental purpose to control or prevent activities constitutionally subject to state regulation may not be achieved by means which sweep unnecessarily broadly and thereby invade the area of protected freedoms." Would we allow the police to search the sacred precincts of marital bedrooms for telltale signs of the use of contraceptives? The very idea is repulsive to the notions of privacy surrounding the marriage relationship.

We deal with a right of privacy older than the Bill of Rights—older than our political parties, older than our school system. Marriage is a coming together for better or for worse, hopefully enduring, and intimate to the degree of being sacred. It is an association that promotes a way of life, not causes; a harmony in living, not political faiths; a bilateral loyalty, not commercial or social projects. Yet it is an association for as noble a purpose as any involved in our prior decisions.

Reversed.

DISSENTING OPINION BY JUSTICE BLACK:

. . . Had the doctor defendant here, or even the nondoctor defendant, been convicted for doing nothing more than expressing opinions to persons coming to the clinic that certain contraceptive devices, medicines or practices would do them good and would be desirable, or for telling people how devices could be used, I can think of no reasons at this time why their expressions of views would not be protected by the First and Fourteenth Amendments, which guarantee freedom of speech. But speech is one thing; conduct and physical activities are quite another. The two defendants here were active participants in an organization which gave physical examinations to women, advised them what kind of contraceptive devices or medicines would most likely be satisfactory for them, and then supplied the devices themselves, all for a graduated scale of fees, based on the family income. Thus these defendants admittedly engaged with others in a planned course of conduct to help people violate the Connecticut law. Merely because some speech was used in carrying on that conduct—just as in ordinary life some speech accompanies most kinds of conduct—we are not in my view justified in holding that the First Amendment forbids the State to punish their conduct. Strongly as I desire to protect all First Amendment freedoms, I am unable to stretch the Amendment so as to afford protection to the conduct of these defendants in violating the Connecticut law. What would be the constitutional fate of the law if hereafter applied to punish nothing but speech is, as I have said, quite another matter.

The Court talks about a constitutional "right of privacy" as though there is some constitutional provision or provisions forbidding any law ever to be passed which might abridge the "privacy" of individuals. But there is not. There are, of course, guarantees in certain specific constitutional provisions which are designed in part to protect privacy at certain times and places with respect to certain activities. Such, for example, is the Fourth Amendment's guarantee against "unreasonable searches and seizures." But I think it belittles that Amendment to talk about it as though it protects nothing but "privacy." To treat it that way is to give it a niggardly interpretation, not the kind of liberal reading I think any Bill of Rights provision should be given. The average man would very likely not have his feelings soothed any more by having his property seized openly than by having it seized privately and by stealth. He simply wants his property left alone. And a person can be just as much, if not more, irritated, annoyed and injured by an unceremonious public arrest by a policeman as he is by a seizure in the privacy of his office or home.

One of the most effective ways of diluting or expanding a constitutionally guaranteed right is to substitute for the crucial word or words of a constitutional guarantee another word or words, more or less flexible and more or less restricted in meaning. This fact is well illustrated by the use of the term "right of privacy" as a comprehensive substitute for the Fourth Amendment's guarantee against "unreasonable searches and seizures." "Privacy" is a broad, abstract and ambiguous concept which can easily be shrunken in meaning but which can also, on the other hand, easily be interpreted as a constitutional ban against many things other than searches and seizures. . . . For these reasons I get nowhere in this case by talk about a constitutional "right of privacy" as an emanation from one or more constitutional provisions. I like my privacy as well as the next one, but I am nevertheless compelled to admit that government has a right to invade it unless prohibited by some specific constitutional provision. For these reasons I cannot agree with the Court's judgment and the reasons it gives for holding this Connecticut law unconstitutional. . . .

DISSENTING OPINION BY JUSTICE STEWART:

Since 1879 Connecticut has had on its books a law which forbids the use of contraceptives by anyone. I think this is an uncommonly silly law. As a practical matter, the law is obviously unenforceable, except in the oblique context of the present case. As a philosophical matter, I believe the use of contraceptives in the relationship of marriage should be left to personal and private choice, based upon each individual's moral, ethical, and religious beliefs. As a matter of social policy, I think professional counsel about methods of birth control should be available to all, so that each individual's choice can be meaningfully made. But we are not asked in this case to say whether we think this law is unwise, or even asinine. We are asked to hold that it violates the United States Constitution. And that I cannot do.

In the course of its opinion the Court refers to no less than six Amendments to the Constitution: the First, the Third, the Fourth, the Fifth, the Ninth, and the Fourteenth. But the Court does not say which of these Amendments, if any, it thinks is infringed by this Connecticut law.

We *are* told that the Due Process Clause of the Fourteenth Amendment is not, as such, the "guide" in this case. With that much I agree. There is no claim that this law, duly enacted by the Connecticut Legislature, is unconstitutionally vague. There is no claim that the appellants were denied any of the elements of procedural due process at their trial, so as to make their convictions constitutionally invalid. And, as the Court says, the day has long passed since the Due Process Clause was regarded as a proper instrument for determining "the wisdom, need, and propriety" of state laws. . . .

As to the First, Third, Fourth, and Fifth Amendments, I can find nothing in any of them to invalidate this Connecticut law, even assuming that all those Amendments are fully applicable against the States. It has not even been argued that this is a law "respecting an establishment of religion, or prohibiting the free exercise thereof." And surely, unless the solemn process of constitutional adjudication is to descend to the level of a play on words, there is not involved here any abridgment of "the freedom of speech, or of the press; or the right of the people peaceably to assemble, and to petition the Government for a redress of grievances." No soldier has been quartered in any house. There has been no search, and no seizure. Nobody has been compelled to be a witness against himself. . . .

What provision of the Constitution, then, does make this state law invalid? The Court says it is the right of privacy "created by several fundamental constitutional guarantees." With all deference, I can find no such general right of privacy in the Bill of Rights, in any other part of the Constitution, or in any case ever before decided by this Court.

At the oral argument in this case we were told that the Connecticut law does not "conform to current community standards." But it is not the function of this Court to decide cases on the basis of community standards. We are here to decide cases "agreeably to the Constitution and laws of the United States." It is the essence of judicial duty to subordinate our own personal views, our own ideas of what legislation is wise and what is not. If, as I should surely hope, the law before us does not reflect the standards of the people of Connecticut, the people of Connecticut can freely exercise their true Ninth and Tenth Amendment rights to persuade their elected representatives to repeal it. That is the constitutional way to take this law off the books.

NOTES AND QUESTIONS:
Griswold v. Connecticut

1. Try to describe in some detail what is protected—and what is not protected—by the right of privacy that is referred to in *Griswold*. Does the Court's understanding of the right of privacy fit well with your own? Is the language of the Court clear enough to give you a specific sense of what this right is about?

Griswold has been the target of a great deal of criticism, largely on the ground that it created the right to privacy out of thin air. Indeed, this opinion is at the center of the debate about the legitimacy of creating "new" rights under the aegis of substantive due process. Do you agree with the dissents of Justices Black and Stewart? If we start concluding that certain rights are protected by the Constitution even though it does not mention them, will we have a hard time determining which unmentioned rights are or are not protected?

2. What specifically were the defendants accused of doing? What about these activities implicated the right of privacy?

3. What specifically was the State of Connecticut trying to accomplish with its statute? Do you think its case would have been weaker or stronger if the statute had banned the importation of contraceptive drugs or devices into the state?

4. What is the role of marriage in this decision? Does it appear very important to the majority opinion that the people counseled were married? Why might a state write a law that took into account the marital status of the people affected? Would any of the following laws be constitutional? (In each case, your analysis should determine the possible purpose of the law, including why a given act is being criminalized and why similar acts are not being criminalized.)

    a. It is a crime for a single man to use a condom while having sex with a married woman.

    b. It is a crime for a single man to use a condom while having sex with a single woman.

    c. It is a crime for a married man to use a condom while having sex with a single woman.

    d. It is a crime for a married man to use a condom while having sex with a married woman who is not his wife.

5. The right of privacy has remained as the bedrock of many subsequent court decisions in the bioethics area. As you read some of those cases later, ask yourself if the content of that right has changed over time. Are the later decisions consistent with *Griswold?* Or with each other?

6. Is the determination that a particular right is protected by the Constitution the end of the discussion? Are there circumstances under which a state might be able to do things that limit the exercise of that right? What does the Court (briefly) say about this possibility? Why didn't the *Griswold* Court spend much time on this issue?

    This is an issue we will be returning to often. As noted in chapter 1, few rights are absolute, and much of bioethics law relates to resolving the clash between individual rights protected by the Constitution and the "compelling" goals of a government.

7. Assume that a state passed a law requiring that every man and woman must be sterilized after they have produced two children. Give the argu-

ments for or against its constitutionality. (See Justice Goldberg's concurrence in *Griswold*, 381 U.S. at 496).

8. Are the following likely to be found constitutional or unconstitutional? On what grounds?

  a. The United States government passes a law that forbids all doctors from discussing contraception with any of their patients.

  b. The State of New York passes such a law, applicable to doctors practicing in that state.

  c. A religious order creates such a rule, and applies it to all doctors who work in the hospitals it owns.

For the Supreme Court's discussion of a related though somewhat different issue, see *Rust v. Sullivan*, 500 U.S. 173 (1991) (involving federal restrictions on abortion counseling in programs receiving federal funds).

THE MEANING OF "EQUAL PROTECTION"

Laws draw lines. A major aspect of many laws is to determine that people who fit on one side of a line can do *X*, while those on the other side of the line cannot.

We now turn to the other major provision of the Fourteenth Amendment—the requirement that "no State" shall "deny to any person . . . the equal protection of the laws." It is this provision that plays the greatest role in determining what types of line-drawing are permissible. Like the due process clause of the Fourteenth Amendment, the equal protection clause restricts the activities only of governments, not individuals. Moreover, the requirement to assure equal protection of the laws has been interpreted to apply not just to the states but also to the national government. *Bolling v. Sharpe*, 347 U.S. 497 (1954).

It has always been understood that the equal protection clause prevents the government from *arbitrarily* treating people differently. It would be improper, for example, to limit membership on a police force to only Caucasians because Caucasians, who control the legislature, want to favor their own kind.

Most forms of discrimination are not quite so blunt. More frequently, a law will attempt to treat different people differently for a particular reason related to the purposes of the legislation. In the early days of interpreting the clause, so long as the differences in treatment were reasonably related to a legitimate goal of the government, such a law would pass equal protection scrutiny. No especially burdensome tests were imposed with regard to how close the relationship was between the classification and the avowed legitimate purpose. This "rational basis" test is not very demanding. Thus, for example, it might have been possible under this view of equal protection to limit the hiring of firefighters to men: it is a legitimate goal to make sure that firefighters are large and strong, and generally men are more likely than women to be large and strong.

Over time, however, equal protection analysis has become far more complicated. The first step in this process was the creation of a second tier of analysis.

Certain types of classifications—most particularly, those based on race—are assumed to be "suspect." As a result, the government needs to demonstrate both a *compelling* reason for the classification, and also that the classification has been *narrowly* tailored to meet that need. These very demanding requirements are described as "strict scrutiny." Over time, they have been applied not just to suspect classifications, but also to instances in which a law might limit a person's ability to exercise a "fundamental" right. As you might imagine, it is far from clear what makes a right fundamental. Nonetheless, many of the rights that bioethics is concerned with are likely to be categorized as fundamental, thus eliciting strict scrutiny.

Finally, there is a category of review that is somewhat more demanding than the rational basis test but not quite so demanding as the strict scrutiny test. The best example of a classification requiring this intermediate level of review is one related to gender. This test requires that the classification must be related to "important governmental objectives and must be substantially related to achievement of those objectives," said the Supreme Court in *Craig v. Boren*, 492 U.S. 190 (1976). In *Craig*, an Oklahoma law that prohibited the sale of 3.2% beer to males under the age of 21 and to females under the age of 18 was struck down. Under the looser rational basis standard of review, this law might have been upheld, since statistics demonstrated that in the age 18 to 20 group, a male was ten times more likely to be drinking and driving than a female.

As you might guess, equal protection analysis is very complicated: first correctly determining which of the three levels of scrutiny to apply, and then correctly applying the standard of review appropriate for that level. Moreover, the Supreme Court is regularly rethinking and modifying these rules. Table 1, though simplified and necessarily incomplete, outlines the rules:

Level of Scrutiny	When Applicable	Test Applied
1. Ordinary	Default (if no reason for applying intermediate or strict scrutiny)	Rational basis for law
2. Intermediate	Gender classifications, for instance	Law substantially related to important state objective
3. Strict	Racial classifications, for example, or Law affects a fundamental right	Law necessary to achieve compelling state interest

The equal protection case of *Eisenstadt v. Baird* is an important opinion in further clarifying the limits of the right to privacy announced in *Griswold*. "[T]he superficially quite modest sounding Eisenstadt opinion is widely seen in retrospect as a crucial stepping point from the arguably narrow ruling in Griswold to the unmistakably broad one" in *Roe v. Wade*.[1]

Not only does a reading of *Eisenstadt* help explain the full extent of the right to privacy, it helps to clarify the somewhat elusive difference between a substantive due process violation and an equal protection violation. The *Eisenstadt* court claims that it is "merely" an equal protection case, but, as we shall see, the majority is perhaps not quite correct in that claim. Moreover, this very distinction may itself be responsible for paving the path from *Eisenstadt* to the Supreme Court's acknowledgment of a right to abortion in *Roe v. Wade*.

EISENSTADT V. BAIRD

Supreme Court of the United States

405 U.S. 438 (1972)

OPINION BY JUSTICE BRENNAN:

Appellee William Baird was convicted [under Massachusetts law] first, for exhibiting contraceptive articles in the course of delivering a lecture on contraception to a group of students at Boston University and, second, for giving a young woman a package of Emko vaginal foam at the close of his address. The Massachusetts Supreme Judicial Court unanimously set aside the conviction for exhibiting contraceptives on the ground that it violated Baird's First Amendment rights, but by a four-to-three vote sustained the conviction for giving away the foam. . . .

[Section 21 of the Massachusetts law] under which Baird was convicted, provides a maximum five-year term of imprisonment for "whoever . . . gives away . . . any drug, medicine, instrument or article whatever for the prevention of conception," except as authorized in § 21A. Under § 21A, "[a] registered physician may administer to or prescribe for any married person drugs or articles intended for the prevention of pregnancy or conception. [And a] registered pharmacist actually engaged in the business of pharmacy may furnish such drugs or articles to any married person presenting a prescription from a registered physician." As interpreted by the State Supreme Judicial Court, these provisions make it a felony for anyone, other than a registered physician or pharmacist acting in accordance with the terms of § 21A, to dispense any article with the intention that it be used for the prevention of conception. The statutory scheme distinguishes among three distinct classes of distributees—first, married persons may obtain contraceptives to prevent pregnancy, but only from doctors or druggists on prescription; second, single persons may not obtain contraceptives from anyone to prevent pregnancy; and, third, married or single persons may obtain contraceptives from anyone to prevent, not pregnancy, but the spread of disease. This construction of state law is, of course, binding on us.

The legislative purposes that the statute is meant to serve are not altogether clear. In *Commonwealth v. Baird*, the Supreme Judicial Court noted only the State's interest in protecting the health of its citizens: "The prohibition in § 21," the court declared, "is directly related to" the State's goal of "preventing the distribution of articles designed to prevent conception which may have undesirable, if not dangerous, physical consequences." In a subsequent decision, *Sturgis v. Attorney General* (1970), the court, however, found "a second and more compelling ground for upholding the statute"—namely, to protect morals through "regulating the private sexual lives of single persons." The Court of Appeals, for reasons that will appear, did not consider the promotion of health or the protection of morals through the deterrence of fornication to be the legislative aim. Instead, the court concluded that the statutory goal was to limit contraception in and of itself—a purpose that the court held conflicted "with fundamental human rights" under *Griswold v. Connecticut*, where this Court struck down Connecticut's prohibition against the use of contraceptives as an unconstitutional infringement of the right of marital privacy.

We agree that the goals of deterring premarital sex and regulating the distribution of potentially harmful articles cannot reasonably be regarded as legislative aims of §§ 21 and 21A. And we hold that the statute, viewed as a prohibition on contraception per se, violates the rights of single persons under the Equal Protection Clause of the Fourteenth Amendment. . . .

II

The basic principles governing application of the Equal Protection Clause of the Fourteenth Amendment are familiar. As the Chief Justice only recently explained . . . :

> "In applying that clause, this Court has consistently recognized that the Fourteenth Amendment does not deny to States the power to treat different classes of persons in different ways. The Equal Protection Clause of that amendment does, however, deny to States the power to legislate that different treatment be accorded to persons placed by a statute into different classes on the basis of criteria wholly unrelated to the objective of that statute. A classification 'must be reasonable, not arbitrary, and must rest upon some ground of difference having a fair and substantial relation to the object of the legislation, so that all persons similarly circumstanced shall be treated alike.'"

The question for our determination in this case is whether there is some ground of difference that rationally explains the different treatment accorded married and unmarried persons under [the Massachusetts law]. For the reasons that follow, we conclude that no such ground exists.

First. Section 21 stems from [an earlier law] which prohibited, without exception, distribution of articles intended to be used as contraceptives. In *Commonwealth v. Allison* (1917), the Massachusetts Supreme Judicial Court explained that the law's "plain purpose is to protect purity, to preserve chastity, to encourage continence and self restraint, to defend the sanctity of the home, and thus to engender in the State and nation a virile and virtuous race of men and women." Although the State clearly abandoned that purpose with the enactment of § 21A, at least insofar as the illicit sexual activities of married persons are concerned, the court reiterated in *Sturgis v. Attorney General*, that the object of the legislation is to discourage premarital sexual intercourse. Conceding that the State could, consistently with the Equal Protection Clause, regard the problems of extramarital and premarital sexual relations as "evils . . . of different dimensions and proportions, requiring different remedies," we cannot agree that the deterrence of premarital sex may reasonably be regarded as the purpose of the Massachusetts law.

It would be plainly unreasonable to assume that Massachusetts has prescribed pregnancy and the birth of an unwanted child as punishment for fornication, which is a misdemeanor under Massachusetts [law]. Aside from the scheme of values that assumption would attribute to the State, it is abundantly clear that the effect of the ban on distribution of contraceptives to unmarried persons has at best a marginal relation to the proffered objective. What Mr. Justice Goldberg said in *Griswold v. Connecticut*, concerning the effect of Connecticut's prohibition on the use of contraceptives in discouraging extramarital sexual relations, is equally applicable here. "The rationality of this justification is dubious, particularly in light of the admitted widespread availability to all persons in the State of Connecticut, unmarried as well as married, of birth-control devices for the prevention of disease, as distinguished from the prevention of conception." Like Connecticut's laws, §§ 21 and 21A do not at all regulate the distribution of contraceptives when they are to be used to prevent, not pregnancy, but the spread of disease. Nor, in making contraceptives available to married persons without regard to their intended use, does Massachusetts attempt to deter married persons from engaging in illicit sexual relations with unmarried persons. Even on the assumption that the fear of pregnancy operates as a deterrent to fornication, the Massachusetts statute is thus so riddled with exceptions that deterrence of premarital sex cannot reasonably be regarded as its aim.

Moreover, §§ 21 and 21A on their face have a dubious relation to the State's criminal prohibition on fornication. As the Court of Appeals explained, "Fornication is a misdemeanor [in Massachusetts], entailing a thirty dollar fine, or three months in jail. Violation of the present statute is a felony, punishable by five years in prison. We find it hard to believe that the legislature adopted a statute carrying a five-year penalty for its possible, obviously by no means fully effective, deterrence of the commission of a ninety-day misdemeanor." Even conceding the legislature a full measure of discretion in fashioning means to prevent fornication, and recognizing that the State may seek to deter prohibited conduct by punishing more severely those who facilitate than those who actually engage in its commission, we, like the Court of Appeals, cannot believe that in this instance Massachusetts has chosen to expose the aider and abetter who simply gives away a contraceptive to 20 times the 90-day sentence of the offender himself. The very terms of the State's criminal statutes, coupled with the de minimis effect of §§ 21 and 21A in deterring fornication, thus compel the conclusion that such deterrence cannot reasonably be taken as the purpose of the ban on distribution of contraceptives to unmarried persons.

Second. Section 21A was added to the Massachusetts General Laws [by a 1966 amendment]. The Supreme Judicial Court in *Commonwealth v. Baird* held that the purpose of the amendment was to serve the health needs of the community by regulating the distribution of potentially harmful articles. It is plain that Massachusetts had no such purpose in mind before the enactment of § 21A. As the Court of Appeals remarked, "Consistent with the fact that the statute was contained in a chapter dealing with 'Crimes against Chastity, Morality, Decency and Good Order,' it was cast only in terms of morals. A physician was forbidden to prescribe contraceptives even when needed for the protection of health." Nor did the Court of Appeals "believe that the legislature [in enacting § 21A] suddenly reversed its field and developed an interest in health. Rather, it merely made what it thought to be the precise accommodation necessary to escape the *Griswold* ruling." Again, we must agree with the Court of Appeals. If health were the rationale of § 21A, the statute would be both discriminatory and overbroad. Dissenting in *Commonwealth v. Baird*, Justices Whittemore and Cutter stated that they saw "in § 21 and § 21A, read together, no public health purpose. If there is need to have a physician prescribe (and a pharmacist dispense) contraceptives, that need is as great for unmarried persons as for married persons." The Court of Appeals added: "If the prohibition [on distribution to unmarried persons] . . . is to be taken to mean that the same physician who can prescribe for married patients does not have sufficient skill to protect the health of patients who lack a marriage certificate, or who may be currently divorced, it is illogical to the point of irrationality." Furthermore, we must join the Court of Appeals in noting that not all contraceptives are potentially dangerous. As a result, if the Massachusetts statute were a health measure, it would not only invidiously discriminate against the unmarried, but also be overbroad with respect to the married, a fact that the Supreme Judicial Court itself seems to have conceded in *Sturgis v. Attorney General*, where it noted that "it may well be that certain contraceptive medication and devices constitute no hazard to health, in which event it could be argued that the statute swept too broadly in its prohibition." "In this posture," as the Court of Appeals concluded, "it is impossible to think of the statute as intended as a health measure for the unmarried, and it is almost as difficult to think of it as so intended even as to the married." . . .

Third. If the Massachusetts statute cannot be upheld as a deterrent to fornication or as a health measure, may it, nevertheless, be sustained simply as a prohibition on contraception? The Court of Appeals analysis "led inevitably to the conclusion that, so far as morals are concerned, it is contraceptives per se that are considered immoral — to the extent that *Griswold* will permit such a declaration." The Court of Appeals went on to hold:

> "To say that contraceptives are immoral as such, and are to be forbidden to unmarried persons who will nevertheless persist in having intercourse, means that such persons must risk for themselves an unwanted pregnancy, for the child, illegitimacy, and for society, a possible obligation of support. Such a view of morality is not only the very mirror image of sensible legislation; we consider that it conflicts with fundamental human rights. In the absence of demonstrated harm, we hold it is beyond the competency of the state."

We need not and do not, however, decide that important question in this case because, whatever the rights of the individual to access to contraceptives may be, the rights must be the same for the unmarried and the married alike. If under *Griswold* the distribution of contraceptives to married persons cannot be prohibited, a ban on distribution to unmarried persons would be equally impermissible. It is true that in *Griswold* the right of privacy in question inhered in the marital relationship. Yet the marital couple is not an independent entity with a mind and heart of its own, but an association of two individuals each with a separate intellectual and emotional makeup. If the right of privacy means anything, it is the right of the individual, married or single, to be free from unwarranted governmental intrusion into matters so fundamentally affecting a person as the decision whether to bear or beget a child.

On the other hand, if *Griswold* is no bar to a prohibition on the distribution of contraceptives, the State could not, consistently with the Equal Protection Clause, outlaw distribution to unmarried but not to married persons. In each case the evil, as perceived by the State, would be identical, and the underinclusion would be invidious. Mr. Justice Jackson . . . made the point:

> "The framers of the Constitution knew, and we should not forget today, that there is no more effective practical guaranty against arbitrary and unreasonable government than to require that the principles of law which officials would impose upon a minority must be imposed generally. Conversely, nothing opens the door to arbitrary action so effectively as to allow those officials to pick and choose only a few to whom they will apply legislation and thus to escape the political retribution that might be visited upon them if larger numbers were affected. Courts can take no better measure to assure that laws will be just than to require that laws be equal in operation."

. . . We hold that by providing dissimilar treatment for married and unmarried persons who are similarly situated, [the provisions of the Massachusetts law] violate the Equal Protection Clause.

NOTES AND QUESTIONS:
Eisenstadt v. Baird

1. Note the difference between the issue in *Griswold* (regulation of a person's use of contraceptives) and the issue in *Eisenstadt* (regulation of the distribution of contraceptives). Might there be reasons for allowing one form of regulation and not the other? In fact, the *Griswold* court had specifically distinguished these two issues, observing that "[this case] concerns a law which, in forbidding the use of contraceptives rather than regulating their manufacture or sale, seeks to achieve its goals by means having a maximum destructive impact upon [a relationship within the zone of privacy]." Since contraceptives are usually used in a (hopefully) very private setting, whereas their sale takes place in a public setting (such as a drugstore), it is not unreasonable to think that a rule regulating use would have a much greater effect on privacy interests than one regulating sales.

   The *Eisenstadt* majority goes to some effort to suggest it is not really deciding whether or not *Griswold* would have prevented a state from adopting laws that restricted the distribution of contraceptives. (Can you find the passages where it does this?) That is the beauty of using an equal protection analysis: one need not decide whether or not burdens can be placed on the right of married persons to get contraceptives, for so long as a state has chosen to give married persons such a right, then a state might not be able to deny a similar right to unmarried persons.

   At least two of the Justices in *Eisenstadt*, however, did conclude that under *Griswold*, a state could not, without proof of health risks, regulate the access of married persons to contraceptives. Here is an excerpt from the opinion of Justice White (joined by Justice Blackmun), who agreed with the *result* of the majority opinion, but not its *reasoning*:

   > Given *Griswold v. Connecticut*, and absent proof of the probable hazards of using vaginal foam, we could not sustain appellee's conviction had it been for selling or giving away foam to a married person. Just as in *Griswold*, where the right of married persons to use contraceptives was "diluted or adversely affected" by permitting a conviction for giving advice as to its exercise, so here, to sanction a medical restriction upon distribution of a contraceptive not proved hazardous to health would impair the exercise of the constitutional right.

   White went on to point out that since the Massachusetts law applied to the distribution of contraceptives to both unmarried and married people—indeed, Baird could have been convicted if he had distributed the foam to a married person—then the law was "overbroad" in that it burdened the constitutionally protected sales to married persons. In this manner, White avoided any need to invoke equal protection arguments, or say anything about the rights of unmarried people. (Of course, if that reasoning is accepted as the sole ground for invalidating the law, what might the Massachusetts legislature do in response?)

2. In commenting on what the Massachusetts Supreme Judicial Court (the highest court in Massachusetts) had previously determined, the U.S. Supreme Court notes that "[t]his construction of state law is, of course, binding on us." This comment demonstrates one important aspect of federalism: each state has the ultimate authority both to enact its own laws and to determine what those laws mean. In this case, the U.S. Supreme Court was merely noting that it cannot redetermine the meaning of the Massachusetts law, but must accept as a given what the highest court of that state says the law means. (As the rest of the *Eisenstadt* opinion demonstrates, however, those laws must nonetheless be in conformity with the U.S. Constitution, and they will be struck down when they are found to be unconstitutional.)

3. Recall that there are three levels of equal protection review. Which level is the Supreme Court applying in *Eisenstadt*? Why does it end up applying that level? (Consider the comment made by the Court in a footnote: "Of course, if we were to conclude that the Massachusetts statute impinges upon fundamental freedoms under *Griswold*, the statutory classification would have to be not merely rationally related to a valid public purpose but necessary to the achievement of a compelling state interest. But . . . we do not have to address the statute's validity under that test because the law fails to satisfy even the more lenient equal protection standard.")

4. Under the level of review that the Court determines is appropriate, what test must be applied? Show how the Court applies that test to the facts in this case. Do you agree with its conclusions about how the law fails to meet that test?

5. In a footnote, the Court commented on one alleged purpose of the Massachusetts laws, "to promote marital fidelity as well as to discourage premarital sex." The Court rejected that as a plausible purpose, noting that "contraceptives may be made available to married persons without regard to whether they are living with their spouses or the uses to which the contraceptives are to be put. Plainly the legislation has no deterrent effect on extramarital sexual relations."

What if a legislature designed a law in a way that *did* serve to both promote marital fidelity and discourage premarital sex? Assume that the new law also plugged the loophole in the prior law that allowed all persons to get the vaginal foam without a prescription if they were using it to prevent disease, rather than for contraceptive purposes. For example, assume that these products would require a prescription in all cases, and that married individuals seeking the products for contraceptive purposes would need to provide a signed statement from their spouses acknowledging that the product would be used by the couple for contraceptive purposes. (Thus, a married person could not obtain it behind the back of the spouse for use in an extramarital relationship.) Would such a statute survive an equal protection challenge? Why or why not?

6. In the introduction to this case we suggested that *Eisenstadt* is perhaps best understood as a substantive due process case rather than as an equal protection case. Here is what one commentator has said about it:

> *Eisenstadt v. Baird* . . . is a good example of the confusion of due process with equal protection: if A and B both have a right to X, and A is allowed X but B is not, B's primary complaint is a due process one, and his inequality vis-à-vis A is not his primary complaint. . . . The litmus test for distinguishing due process cases from equal protection cases is whether the complainants would be satisfied with the equality of lowering the comparison group to their level.[2]

Applying that terminology to the facts of this case, who is A? Who is B? What, specifically, would "lowering of the comparison group to their level" mean?

7. Does it really matter if we adopt the equal protection or the due process view of *Eisenstadt*? Consider the following statements:
   a. Unmarried persons have a right to contraceptives because the law denying them that right fails to meet the equal protection standard of review.
   b. Unmarried persons have a right to contraceptives because that is a right included in the right to privacy and thus is a right of all persons.

If (a) is the true rationale of *Eisenstadt*, might there not be a way to revise the law so that equal protection requirements are not violated? What two options might the state take in revising its laws, based on the Supreme Court's comment that perhaps "*Griswold* is no bar to a prohibition on the distribution of contraceptives?"

The rights of everyone could be watered down; alternatively, a statute might water down the rights of unmarried persons alone in a way that nonetheless does not violate equal protection (a way that meets the test for justifying the distinct treatment of married and unmarried persons). Can you think of such a statute?

From the point of view of unmarried persons, interpretation (b) is preferable because it gives them a stronger right to contraceptives, one that can be infringed only by a compelling governmental interest.

Perhaps even more significantly, note the other consequence of interpretation (b): not only does it alter the treatment of unmarried persons with regard to contraceptives, it requires a reinterpretation of the meaning and scope of the right to privacy to make it clear that this right does not apply only to marriage-related activities.[3]

8. Is there any reason for thinking that the majority opinion in *Eisenstadt* is more than a straightforward equal protection analysis? Rather than that it is saying something highly significant about substantive due process (i.e., the scope of the right to privacy)? Consider this statement from the opinion: "If

the right of privacy means anything, it is the right of the individual, married or single, to be free from unwarranted governmental intrusion into matters so fundamentally affecting a person as the decision whether to bear or beget a child." Based on the language from *Griswold* alone (take another look at it!), would you have thought that the right to privacy extended beyond the marital couple? Can you appreciate how different (and how much narrower) a right to privacy that merely protects the marital relationship is from one that finds its core in a concept not related to that relationship?

If we conclude that the right to privacy is not specifically tied to that relationship, is it at all clear what the right then covers? Can you now better appreciate the comment in this chapter's lead-in that many people view *Eisenstadt* as a key substantive due process (right to privacy) decision in paving the road to the abortion decisions?

9. In *Carey v. Population Services International*, 431 U.S. 678 (1977), the Supreme Court struck down on equal protection grounds a New York law that prohibited the sale or distribution of contraceptives to persons under the age of 16. The reasoning of Justice Brennan's opinion (which garnered the support of only three other Justices) was that since the law infringed on the constitutionally protected right to make decisions about childbearing, the strict scrutiny level of equal protection analysis had to be applied. Under that test, Brennan determined that the government's interest in protecting the morality of young people was insufficient to justify the law.

10. Looking at *Griswold* and *Eisenstadt* together, can you now articulate what is encompassed in the right to privacy? Does it apply to intimate sexual activities related to reproduction, whether or not the participants are married? Or is the concept even broader?

Some additional guidance on this issue came from *Bowers v. Hardwick*, 478 U.S. 186 (1986), which addressed a Georgia statute that punished sodomy—defined as the performance of a sexual act involving the sex organs of one person and the mouth or anus of another—with up to twenty years in jail. The Supreme Court rejected the substantive due process argument that this law unconstitutionally infringed upon the rights of homosexuals:

> [W]e think it evident that none of the rights announced in [prior] cases bears any resemblance to the claimed constitutional right of homosexuals to engage in acts of sodomy that is asserted in this case. No connection between family, marriage, or procreation on the one hand and homosexual activity on the other has been demonstrated, either by the Court of Appeals or by respondent. Moreover, any claim that these cases nevertheless stand for the proposition that any kind of private sexual conduct between consenting adults is constitutionally insulated from state proscription is unsupportable. . . .
>
> Striving to assure itself and the public that announcing rights not readily identifiable in the Constitution's text involves much more than the imposition of the Justices' own choice of values on the States and the Federal Govern-

ment, the Court has sought to identify the nature of the rights qualifying for heightened judicial protection. In *Palko v. Connecticut*, it was said that this category includes those fundamental liberties that are "implicit in the concept of ordered liberty," such that "neither liberty nor justice would exist if [they] were sacrificed." A different description of fundamental liberties appeared in *Moore v. East Cleveland*, where they are characterized as those liberties that are "deeply rooted in this Nation's history and tradition."

It is obvious to us that neither of these formulations would extend a fundamental right to homosexuals to engage in acts of consensual sodomy. Proscriptions against that conduct have ancient roots. Sodomy was a criminal offense at common law and was forbidden by the laws of the original 13 States when they ratified the Bill of Rights. . . . In fact, until 1961, all 50 States outlawed sodomy, and today, 24 States and the District of Columbia continue to provide criminal penalties for sodomy performed in private and between consenting adults. Against this background, to claim that a right to engage in such conduct is "deeply rooted in this Nation's history and tradition" or "implicit in the concept of ordered liberty" is, at best, facetious.

11. *Bowers* has generated substantial criticism. Do you think there is a coherent view of the right to privacy that would protect the types of sexual encounters taking place in *Griswold, Eisenstadt,* and *Carey* but not that in *Bowers*? Might a state be able to constitutionally criminalize, on moral grounds, sexual activities (even "sex organ-to-sex organ") among the following groups:
   a. Two unmarried persons
   b. A married person and an unmarried person
   c. Two married persons who are not married to each other
   d. All of the above groups combined (perhaps there might be distinct equal protection problems in a law that targeted only one or another of the above groups?)

12. The debate about *Bowers* has heated up since the Supreme Court's decision in *Romer v. Evans*, 517 U.S. 620 (1996), where the Court struck down an amendment to the Colorado Constitution that prevented Colorado from passing any laws or regulations that gave homosexuals any legal rights relating to discrimination based on their status as homosexuals. In effect, the amendment had prevented the Colorado legislature from enacting laws, similar to those in a number of states, that included sexual orientation as a prohibited basis for discriminating against someone. For example, in some states, a place of "public accommodation," such as a restaurant, cannot refuse to serve a person solely because that person is homosexual. The constitutional amendment prevented the Colorado legislature from enacting *any* law that used homosexuality as a basis for a discrimination claim. The argument advanced in favor of the constitutional change was that it *furthered* equality, in that it merely denied homosexuals special rights, putting them in the same position as all other people.

The Supreme Court struck down the Colorado constitutional amendment using the lowest tier of equal protection analysis: it found that there was no rational basis for the amendment. The majority opinion did not even mention *Bowers*.

Here is part of Justice Scalia's dissent in *Romer*:

> The constitutional amendment before us here is not the manifestation of a "bare . . . desire to harm" homosexuals, but is rather a modest attempt by seemingly tolerant Coloradans to preserve traditional sexual mores against the efforts of a politically powerful minority to revise those mores through use of the laws. That objective, and the means chosen to achieve it, are not only unimpeachable under any constitutional doctrine hitherto pronounced . . . ; they have been specifically approved by the Congress of the United States and by this Court.
>
> In holding that homosexuality cannot be singled out for disfavorable treatment, the Court contradicts a decision, unchallenged here, pronounced only 10 years ago, see *Bowers v. Hardwick* (1986), and places the prestige of this institution behind the proposition that opposition to homosexuality is as reprehensible as racial or religious bias. Whether it is or not is precisely the cultural debate that gave rise to the Colorado constitutional amendment . . . . Since the Constitution of the United States says nothing about this subject, it is left to be resolved by normal democratic means, including the democratic adoption of provisions in state constitutions. This Court has no business imposing upon all Americans the resolution favored by the elite class from which the Members of this institution are selected, pronouncing that "animosity" toward homosexuals is evil.

Scalia goes on to point out that *Bowers* clearly indicates that a state can make homosexual conduct a crime, and if it can do that, why can't it take the lesser step of merely failing to redress discrimination against homosexuals?

Who has the best of these arguments, Scalia or the majority? Are *Romer* and *Bowers* inconsistent? Much has been written on this issue. Consider the comments of Akil Reed Amar:

> But *Bowers* does not remotely stand for [the proposition that states can make homosexual conduct a crime]. For starters, even where male-male anal sexual intercourse is involved, *Bowers* held only that criminalization did not offend substantive due process. The Court explicitly refused to address the equal protection issues at stake. This refusal renders *Bowers* highly dubious. To borrow from Yogi Berra, "when you reach a fork in the road, take it." Either male-female anal sex can be criminalized or it cannot. If it can, how exactly are the principles of *Eisenstadt* . . . to be distinguished away? If it cannot, then doesn't criminalization of male-male—but not male-female— sodomy constitute . . . sex discrimination, in the same way antimiscegenation laws constituted . . . race discrimination? . . .
>
> Even if *Bowers* could somehow stand as an anal sex case, what about oral sex? (Again, can male-female oral sex be criminalized? And if not, how can a

ban on only male-male and female-female oral sex survive a sex discrimination challenge?) And what about petting below the waist? Or above the waist? Or kissing? Or handholding and hugging? Or saying "I love you?" Did *Bowers* "unquestionably" apply to all this conduct?[4]

Endnotes

1. Gerald Gunther and Kathleen M. Sullivan, *Consitutional Law*, 528 (Westbury, NY: Foundation Press, Inc., 13ᵗʰ ed., 1997).
2. Larry Alexander, "Sometimes Better Boring and Correct: *Romer v. Evans* as an Exercise of Ordinary Equal Protection Analysis," 68 *U. Colo. L. Rev.* 335, 339 (1997).
3. See, e.g., Janet L. Dolgin, "The Family in Transition: From *Griswold* to *Eisenstadt* and Beyond," 82 *Geo. L. J.* 1519 (1994).
4. Akil Reed Amar, "Attainder and Amendment 2: *Romer's* Rightness," 95 *Michigan Law Review* 203, 231–32 (1996).

3

The Past and Present of Sterilization

"Have you read Malthus?"
Charles shook his head.
"For him the tragedy of *Homo sapiens* is that the least fit to survive breed the most."

John Fowles, *The French Lieutenant's Woman*

The law's response to the practice of involuntary sterilization underwent a dramatic reversal during the twentieth century. In 1927 the U.S. Supreme Court decided *Buck v. Bell*, approving the decision of the State of Virginia to involuntarily sterilize "mentally defective" persons who were housed in state institutions. While that case has never been formally repudiated by the Court, it is likely that it no longer represents current law, as the later cases in this chapter suggest. Many people consider *Buck v. Bell* one of the most reprehensible decisions of the Supreme Court.

The reversal of attitudes toward involuntary sterilization is at least partially due to events that took place in the two decades following the decision: the rise of Nazi Germany and the efforts of that society to implement a eugenics policy. In retrospect, the German efforts to produce a genetically purer society by exterminating Jews and other "inferior" races might have appeared uncomfortably analogous to this country's efforts to prevent the reproduction of the "mentally defective."

In the cases that follow, you will see that in spite of this turn of events, while such procedures are certainly less common than they used to be, they do occasionally take place. The reasons for allowing them have dramatically changed, however: instead of being imposed on a person by the government (allegedly on behalf of society), they now take place only when they can be justified as a way to further the autonomy of the person being sterilized.

As you read this chapter, try to separate two distinct themes: the impropriety of a government's attempt to override a person's autonomy, as by destroying the person's ability to reproduce, and the impropriety of actions based on a negative attitude toward disabled persons, such as the mentally retarded. The notes following the cases will return to these two themes and raise the possibility that the current legal protection of individual autonomy, together with greater scientific control of reproduction, may be validating a new type of eugenics practice in modern America.

BUCK V. BELL

Supreme Court of the United States

274 U.S. 200 (1927)

OPINION BY JUSTICE HOLMES:

This is a writ of error to review a judgment of the Supreme Court of Appeals of the State of Virginia, affirming a judgment of the Circuit Court of Amherst County, by which the defendant in error, the superintendent of the State Colony for Epileptics and Feeble Minded, was ordered to perform the operation of salpingectomy upon Carrie Buck, the plaintiff in error, for the purpose of making her sterile. The case comes here upon the contention that the statute authorizing the judgment is void under the Fourteenth Amendment as denying to the plaintiff in error due process of law and the equal protection of the laws.

Carrie Buck is a feeble minded white woman who was committed to the State Colony above mentioned in due form. She is the daughter of a feeble minded mother in the same institution, and the mother of an illegitimate feeble minded child. She was eighteen years old at the time of the trial of her case in the Circuit Court, in the latter part of 1924. An Act of Virginia, approved March 20, 1924, recites that the health of the patient and the welfare of society may be promoted in certain cases by the sterilization of mental defectives, under careful safeguard, &c.; that the sterilization may be effected in males by vasectomy and in females by salpingectomy, without serious pain or substantial danger to life; that the Commonwealth is supporting in various institutions many defective persons who if now discharged would become a menace but if incapable of procreating might be discharged with safety and become self-supporting with benefit to themselves and to society; and that experience has shown that heredity plays an important part in the transmission of insanity, imbecility, &c. The statute then enacts that whenever the superintendent of certain institutions including the above named State Colony shall be of opinion that it is for the best interests of the patients and of society that an inmate under his care should be sexually sterilized, he may have the operation performed upon any patient afflicted with hereditary forms of insanity, imbecility, &c., on complying with the very careful provisions by which the act protects the patients from possible abuse. . . .

The attack is not upon the procedure but upon the substantive law. It seems to be contended that in no circumstances could such an order be justified. It certainly is contended that the order cannot be justified upon the existing grounds. The judgment finds the facts that have been recited and that Carrie Buck "is the probable potential parent of socially inadequate offspring, likewise afflicted, that she may be sexually sterilized without detriment to her general health and that her welfare and that of society will be promoted by her sterilization," and thereupon makes the order. In view of the general declarations of the legislature and the specific findings of the Court, obviously we cannot say as matter of law that the grounds do not exist, and if they exist they justify the result. We have seen more than once that the public welfare may call upon the best citizens for their lives. It would be strange if it could not call upon those who already sap the strength of the State for these lesser sacrifices, often not felt to be such by those concerned, in order to prevent our being swamped with incompetence. It is better for all the world, if instead of waiting to execute degenerate offspring for crime, or to let them starve for their imbecility, society can prevent those who are manifestly unfit from continuing their kind. The principle that sustains compulsory vaccination is broad enough to cover cutting the Fallopian tubes. Three generations of imbeciles are enough.

But, it is said, however it might be if this reasoning were applied generally, it fails when it is confined to the small number who are in the institutions named and is not applied to the multitudes outside. It is the usual last resort of constitutional arguments to point out shortcomings of this sort. But the answer is that the law does all that is needed when it does all that it can, indicates a policy, applies it to all within the lines, and seeks to bring within the lines all similarly situated so far and so fast as its means allow. Of course so far as the operations enable those who otherwise must be kept confined to be returned to the world, and thus open the asylum to others, the equality aimed at will be more nearly reached.

Judgment affirmed.

NOTES AND QUESTIONS:
Buck v. Bell

1. Subsequent history demonstrated that Carrie Buck was in fact not mentally retarded, and so there is no reason to suspect that her children would have been mentally retarded.
2. As noted in the introduction to this chapter, many would argue that this case is no longer good law. The primary reason is that the rules for determining what constitutes a violation of the equal protection clause of the Fourteenth Amendment have changed since 1927. The three-tiered level

of analysis described in the previous chapter did not exist then. Indeed, the case that follows in this chapter, *Skinner v. Oklahoma*, was one of the later cases that began to create a more complicated equal protection analysis.

3. In order to have an equal protection violation, two groups of people must be treated differently. What two groups did Carrie Buck's lawyers claim were being treated differently?

   What standard of review do you think the Court was applying in determining that the equal protection clause was not violated? What, exactly, was it requiring that the State of Virginia demonstrate to justify the different treatment of the two groups in order to have its law upheld?

4. Based on what you know about current understanding of the equal protection clause, reevaluate Carrie Buck's claim under current law: explain the appropriate standard of justification required to authorize discrimination between two groups, and then determine whether that standard is likely to be met.

5. Justice Holmes's comment that "three generations of imbeciles is enough" is widely viewed as one of the most infamous lines in American jurisprudence, and at best a major embarrassment for an otherwise great jurist. Do you agree with that consensus? At the time Holmes wrote the *Buck* opinion, he was using "imbecile" as a technical description for a person with an I.Q. demonstrating a mental age of between three and seven years old, and not as a slang or derogatory term. For which of the following views could Holmes most appropriately be condemned:

   a. For thinking that, since it is reasonable for society to not want to pay for the care of the mentally disabled, society should be able to prevent such people from being born.

   b. For having a negative opinion with respect to the mentally disabled.

6. *Buck v. Bell* involves an attempt to involuntarily sterilize someone. Are the issues different if we add an element of voluntariness?

   In 1990, the FDA approved Norplant as a contraceptive method. Norplant consists of six match-stick-sized flexible rods that are inserted under the skin of a woman's upper arm in a fifteen-minute procedure using local anesthetic. It provides five years of contraception, and can be removed at any time, thus restoring fertility. Is it appropriate to condition a woman's release on parole, after conviction for child abuse, on her agreement to use Norplant? Or to require its use as a condition to getting welfare benefits? Consider:

   > Some state legislators have seen Norplant as a tool for reducing the number of children born into poverty, and, by extension, curbing welfare costs. A Kansas legislator proposed that welfare recipients who accepted Norplant be paid an extra $500, plus $50 a year. The bill was quickly voted down.[1]

   Should we be encouraging the use of Norplant in certain retarded people? How about people who are at high risk of having children with major congenital problems?

SKINNER V. OKLAHOMA
Supreme Court of the United States
316 U.S. 535 (1942)

OPINION BY JUSTICE DOUGLAS:

This case touches a sensitive and important area of human rights. Oklahoma deprives certain individuals of a right which is basic to the perpetuation of a race—the right to have offspring. Oklahoma has decreed the enforcement of its law against petitioner, overruling his claim that it violated the Fourteenth Amendment. Because that decision raised grave and substantial constitutional questions, we granted the petition for certiorari.

The statute involved is Oklahoma's Habitual Criminal Sterilization Act. That Act defines an "habitual criminal" as a person who, having been convicted two or more times for crimes "amounting to felonies involving moral turpitude," either in an Oklahoma court or in a court of any other State, is thereafter convicted of such a felony in Oklahoma and is sentenced to a term of imprisonment in an Oklahoma penal institution. Machinery is provided for the institution by the Attorney General of a proceeding against such a person in the Oklahoma courts for a judgment that such person shall be rendered sexually sterile. . . . The issues triable in such a proceeding are narrow and confined. If the court or jury finds that the defendant is an "habitual criminal" and that he "may be rendered sexually sterile without detriment to his or her general health," then the court "shall render judgment to the effect that said defendant be rendered sexually sterile" by the operation of vasectomy in case of a male, and of salpingectomy in case of a female. Only one other provision of the Act is material here, and that . . . provides that "offenses arising out of the violation of the prohibitory laws, revenue acts, embezzlement, or political offenses, shall not come or be considered within the terms of this Act."

Petitioner was convicted in 1926 of the crime of stealing chickens, and was sentenced to the Oklahoma State Reformatory. In 1929 he was convicted of the crime of robbery with firearms, and was sentenced to the reformatory. In 1934 he was convicted again of robbery with firearms, and was sentenced to the penitentiary. He was confined there in 1935 when the Act was passed. In 1936 the Attorney General instituted proceedings against him. . . . A judgment directing that the operation of vasectomy be performed on petitioner was affirmed by the Supreme Court of Oklahoma by a five to four decision.

Several objections to the constitutionality of the Act have been pressed upon us. It is urged that the Act cannot be sustained as an exercise of the police power, in view of the state of scientific authorities respecting inheritability of criminal traits. It is argued that due process is lacking because, under this Act, unlike the Act upheld in *Buck v. Bell*, the defendant is given no opportunity to be heard on the issue as to whether he is the probable potential parent of socially undesirable offspring. It is also suggested that the Act is penal in character and that the sterilization provided for is cruel and unusual punishment and violative of the Fourteenth Amendment. We pass those points without intimating an opinion on them, for there is a feature of the Act which clearly condemns it. That is, its failure to meet the requirements of the equal protection clause of the Fourteenth Amendment.

We do not stop to point out all of the inequalities in this Act. A few examples will suffice. . . . A clerk who appropriates over $20 from his employer's till and a stranger who steals the same amount are thus both guilty of felonies. If the latter repeats his act and is convicted three times, he may be sterilized. But the clerk is not subject to the pains and penalties of the Act no matter how large his embezzlements nor how frequent his convictions. A person who enters a chicken coop and steals chickens commits a felony; and he may be sterilized if he is thrice convicted. . . . Thus, the nature of the two crimes is intrinsically the same and they are punishable in the same manner. . . .

. . . Only recently we reaffirmed the view that the equal protection clause does not prevent the legislature from recognizing "degrees of evil" by our ruling . . . that "the Constitution does not require things which are different in fact or opinion to be treated in law as though they were the same." Thus, if we had here only a question as to a State's classification of crimes, such as embezzlement or larceny, no substantial federal question would be raised. For a State is not constrained in the exercise of its police power to ignore experience which marks a class of offenders or a family of offenses for special treatment. Nor is it prevented by the equal protection clause from confining "its restrictions to those classes of cases where the need is deemed to be clearest." As stated in *Buck v. Bell*, ". . . the law does all that is needed when it does all that it can, indicates a policy, applies it to all within the lines, and seeks to bring within the lines all similarly situated so far and so fast as its means allow."

But the instant legislation runs afoul of the equal protection clause, though we give Oklahoma that large deference which the rule of the foregoing cases requires. We are dealing here with legislation which involves one of the basic civil rights of man. Marriage and procreation are fundamental to the very existence and survival of the race. The power to sterilize, if exercised, may have subtle, far-reaching and devastating effects. In evil or reckless hands it can cause races or types which are inimical to the dominant group to wither and disappear. There is no redemption for the individual whom the law touches. Any experiment which the State conducts is to his irreparable injury. He is forever deprived of a basic liberty. We mention these matters not to reexamine the scope of the police power of the States. We advert to them merely in emphasis of our view that strict scrutiny of the classification which a State makes in a sterilization law is essential, lest unwittingly, or otherwise, invidious discriminations are made against groups or types of individuals in violation of the constitutional guaranty of just and equal laws. The guaranty of "equal protection of the laws is a pledge of the protection of equal laws." When the law lays an unequal hand on those who have committed intrinsically the same quality of offense and sterilizes one and not the other, it has made as invidious a discrimination as if it had selected a particular race or nationality for oppressive treatment. Sterilization of those who have thrice committed grand larceny, with immunity for those who are embezzlers, is a clear, pointed, unmistakable discrimination. Oklahoma makes no attempt to say that he who commits larceny by trespass or trick or fraud has biologically inheritable traits which he who commits embezzlement lacks. . . . We have not the slightest basis for inferring that that line has any significance in eugenics, nor that the inheritability of criminal traits follows the neat legal distinctions which the law has marked between those two offenses. In terms of fines and imprisonment, the crimes of larceny and embezzlement rate the same under the Oklahoma code. Only when it comes to sterilization are the pains and penalties of the law different. The equal protection clause would indeed be a formula of empty words if such conspicuously artificial lines could be drawn. In *Buck v. Bell*, the Virginia statute was upheld though it applied only to feeble-minded persons in institutions of the State. But it was pointed out that "so far as the operations enable those who otherwise must be kept confined to be returned to the world, and thus open the asylum to others, the equality aimed at will be more nearly reached." Here there is no such saving feature. Embezzlers are forever free. Those who steal or take in other ways are not. . . .

CONCURRING OPINION BY CHIEF JUSTICE STONE:

I concur in the result, but I am not persuaded that we are aided in reaching it by recourse to the equal protection clause.

If Oklahoma may resort generally to the sterilization of criminals on the assumption that their propensities are transmissible to future generations by inheritance, I seriously doubt that the equal protection clause requires it to apply the measure to all criminals in the first instance, or to none.

Moreover, if we must presume that the legislature knows—what science has been unable to ascertain—that the criminal tendencies of any class of habitual offenders are transmissible regardless of the varying mental characteristics of its individuals, I should suppose that we must likewise presume that the legislature, in its wisdom, knows that the criminal tendencies of some classes of offenders are more likely to be transmitted than those of others. And so I think the real question we have to consider is not one of equal protection, but whether the wholesale condemnation of a class to such an invasion of personal liberty, without opportunity to any individual to show that his is not the type of case which would justify resort to it, satisfies the demands of due process.

There are limits to the extent to which the presumption of constitutionality can be pressed, especially where the liberty of the person is concerned and where the presumption is resorted to only to dispense with a procedure which the ordinary dictates of prudence would seem to demand for the protection of the individual from arbitrary action. Although petitioner here was given a hearing to ascertain whether sterilization would be detrimental to his health, he was given none to discover whether his criminal tendencies are of an inheritable type. Undoubtedly a state may, after appropriate inquiry, constitutionally interfere with the personal liberty of the individual to prevent the transmission by inheritance of his socially injurious tendencies. *Buck v. Bell*. But until now we have not been called upon to say that it may do so without giving him a hearing and opportunity to challenge the existence as to him of the only facts which could justify so drastic a measure.

Science has found and the law has recognized that there are certain types of mental deficiency associated with delinquency which are inheritable. But the State does not contend—nor can there be any pretense—that either common knowledge or experience, or scientific investigation, has given assurance that the criminal tendencies of any class of habitual offenders are universally or even generally inheritable. In such circumstances, inquiry whether such is the fact in the case of any particular individual cannot rightly be dispensed with. . . .

CONCURRING OPINION BY JUSTICE JACKSON:

. . . I also think the present plan to sterilize the individual in pursuit of a eugenic plan to eliminate from the race characteristics that are only vaguely identified and which in our present state of knowledge are uncertain as to transmissibility presents other constitutional questions of gravity. This Court has sustained such an experiment with respect to an imbecile, a person with definite and observable characteristics, where the condition had persisted through three generations and afforded grounds for the belief that it was transmissible and would continue to manifest itself in generations to come. *Buck v. Bell*.

There are limits to the extent to which a legislatively represented majority may conduct biological experiments at the expense of the dignity and personality and natural powers of a minority—even those who have been guilty of what the majority define as crimes.

NOTES AND QUESTIONS:
Skinner v. Oklahoma

1. As noted previously, *Skinner* represents a step on the road to the Supreme Court's creation of the current multilevel structure for equal protection analysis. What part of the current rule is created in the *Skinner* opinion?
2. What would have happened if the members of the Court who wrote the opinion in *Buck v. Bell* had been presented with the facts of *Skinner*? Do you think they would have overturned the Oklahoma law? Why or why not?
3. Did the *Skinner* Court need a higher level of scrutiny to strike down the Oklahoma law? Can you make a decent argument that this law could have been struck down even under the rational basis standard of equal protec-

tion review? What other case, where a law was struck down under that standard, might this remind you of?

4. At the end of the opinion the Court specifically chooses not to overrule *Buck v. Bell* but rather attempts to distinguish it. (As was noted earlier, *Buck v. Bell* has yet to be formally repudiated by the Supreme Court.) On what grounds does it find that case to be different? Do you agree with its conclusion?

5. Assume that scientific research had demonstrated that people with certain genetic patterns were likely to give birth to children who had an exceptionally high likelihood of becoming criminals. Suppose the Oklahoma law applied its penalty of sterilization to all third-time criminals who tested positive for those genetic patterns, and also provided a hearing in which the criminal could contest that evidence. Would this be constitutional based on the majority opinion in *Skinner*? How would Chief Justice Stone likely vote?

6. Why confine this statute to criminals? Suppose the scientific research demonstrated that there was a 90 percent chance that the above-mentioned children would become criminals. Presumably, some current possessors of that genetic pattern would not be criminals. Could a state pass a law mandating testing of all residents, with a requirement that those who test positive must be sterilized? If not, why not?

CONSERVATORSHIP OF VALERIE N.

Supreme Court of California

707 P.2d 760 (Cal. 1985)

OPINION BY JUSTICE GRODIN:

Mildred and Eugene G., her mother and stepfather, are coconservators of the person of their adult developmentally disabled daughter Valerie. They appeal from a judgment of the probate court denying their petition for authorization to have a tubal ligation (salpingectomy) performed on Valerie. . . .

Valerie was born on July 13, 1955, apparently a victim of Downs Syndrome as a result of which she is severely retarded. Her IQ is estimated to be 30. She is now 29 years old. She lives with her mother and stepfather. Although she has no comprehension of the nature of these proceedings, she has expressed her wish to continue to have her parents care for her. Her parents' long range plan for Valerie is that she will move to a residential home should they become mentally or physically unable to care for her. She has received therapy and training for behavior modification which was not successful in eliminating her aggressive sexual advances toward men. Her parents are attempting to prepare her for the time when they can no longer care for her, and to broaden her social activities as an aspect of this preparation. They have concluded that other methods of birth control are inadequate in Valerie's case. . . .

Valerie's mother testified that Valerie had not been sexually active, apart from masturbation, because she had been closely supervised. She was aggressive and affectionate toward boys. On the street she approached men, hugged and kissed them, climbed on them, and wanted to sit on their laps. Valerie had been given birth control pills in her early teens, but she rejected them and became ill. Her doctor then recommended the tubal ligation. Valerie was unable to apply other methods of birth control such as a diaphragm, and would not cooperate in a pelvic examination for an intrauterine device which the witness believed was unsafe in any event. . . .

In 1909, California enacted this state's first statute permitting sterilization of developmentally disabled individuals. That authority extended only to persons committed to state institutions or prisons . . .

Twenty-two states enacted similar legislation and, as a "pioneer" in the field, California performed the greatest number of sterilization operations. One of the first legal commentaries on the practice noted that "[b]etween 1907 and 1921 California sterilized 2,558 of the 3,233 total for all United States in that period." . . .

During the 40-year period during which involuntary sterilization was permissible significant advances occurred both in understanding of the causes of mental retardation, and in public awareness that many developmentally disabled persons lead self-sufficient, fulfilling lives, and become loving, competent, and caring marriage partners and parents. In 1978 the California Law Revision Commission submitted to the Legislature a draft of a new guardianship-conservatorship law which expressly denied the probate court jurisdiction to grant conservators the power to cause their wards and conservatees to be sterilized. . . .

Before enacting the new Guardianship-Conservatorship Law recommended by the Law Revision Commission, however, the Legislature repealed Welfare and Institutions Code section 7254. That section, therefore, no longer afforded authorization for the sterilization of mentally retarded wards or conservatees, even if they were admitted to state institutions and were afforded the procedural protections contemplated by the commission. The intent of the Legislature is clear. Neither the probate court nor state hospital personnel were to retain authority to permit a nontherapeutic sterilization of a conservatee who is unable to personally consent to the procedure. . . .

Our conclusion regarding the present legislative scheme requires that we confront appellants' contention that the scheme is unconstitutional. Both appellants and counsel for Valerie pose the constitutional question in terms of the right of procreative choice. Appellants argue that subdivision (d) of section

2356 deprives Valerie of that right by precluding the only means of contraception realistically available to her, while counsel for Valerie contends that the legislation furthers that right by protecting her against sterilization forced upon her by the will of others. The sad but irrefragable truth, however, is that Valerie is not now nor will she ever be competent to choose between bearing or not bearing children, or among methods of contraception. The question is whether she has a constitutional right to have these decisions made for her, in this case by her parents as conservators, in order to protect her interests in living the fullest and most rewarding life of which she is capable. At present her conservators may, on Valerie's behalf, elect that she not bear or rear children. As means of avoiding the severe psychological harm which assertedly would result from pregnancy, they may choose abortion should she become pregnant; they may arrange for any child Valerie might bear to be removed from her custody; and they may impose on her other methods of contraception, including isolation from members of the opposite sex. They are precluded from making, and Valerie from obtaining the advantage of, the one choice that may be best for her, and which is available to all women competent to choose—contraception through sterilization. We conclude that the present legislative scheme, which absolutely precludes the sterilization option, impermissibly deprives developmentally disabled persons of privacy and liberty interests protected by the Fourteenth Amendment to the United States Constitution, and article I, section 1 of the California Constitution.

The right to marriage and procreation are now recognized as fundamental, constitutionally protected interests. So, too, is the right of a woman to choose not to bear children, and to implement that choice by use of contraceptive devices or medication, and, subject to reasonable restrictions, to terminate a pregnancy. These rights are aspects of the right of privacy which exists within the penumbra of the First Amendment to the United States Constitution and is expressed in section 1 of article I of the California Constitution which includes among the inalienable rights possessed by all persons in this state, that of "privacy." They are also within the concept of liberty protected against arbitrary restrictions by the Fourteenth Amendment. . . .

In its enactment of section 2356, subdivision (d), and the omission of any provision in other legislation authorizing sterilization of incompetent developmentally disabled persons, the Legislature has denied incompetent women the procreative choice that is recognized as a fundamental, constitutionally protected right of all other adult women. We realize that election of the method of contraception to be utilized, or indeed whether to choose contraception at all, cannot realistically be deemed a "choice" available to an incompetent since any election must of necessity be made on behalf of the incompetent by others. The interests of the incompetent which mandate recognition of procreative choice as an aspect of the fundamental right to privacy and liberty do not differ from the interests of women able to give voluntary consent to this procedure, however. That these interests include the individual's right to personal growth and development is implicit in decisions of both the United States Supreme Court and this court.

NOTES AND QUESTIONS:
Conservatorship of Valerie N.

1. In a footnote to the *Valerie N* opinion, Justice Grodin describes *Buck v. Bell* as representing the attitude toward the developmentally disabled that prevailed at the beginning of the twentieth century. Apparently in an attempt to explain the earlier attitude of Justice Holmes, he observes that during that period there was "limited knowledge of the nature of developmental disabilities then available." 707 P.2d at 765 n.8. To which of the following do you think he was referring, and why do you think so:
   a. Limited knowledge of how to determine whether or not a person really had a significant disability (as demonstrated by the incorrect views about Ms. Buck's intelligence)
   b. Limited knowledge of when a disability is transmitted from a parent to a child
   c. Limited knowledge of the value to society of a person with a particular type of developmental disability
   d. Limited knowledge of the underlying "worth," as a human being, of a person with a particular developmental disability (regardless of his or her value to society)
2. Based on *Valerie N*, when can a mentally disabled person be sterilized? Is the opinion in *Valerie N* consistent with the views of those who condemn *Buck v. Bell*?
3. Assume that a decision has to be made about sterilizing a mentally disabled woman. She comes from a wealthy family, so that there is no issue with regard to the ability of her child to be cared for at her home. However, unlike the true facts in *Buck v. Bell*, assume it is the case that all of her children would have significant mental retardation. Further assume that, when competent pregnant women learn that they are carrying a fetus with such a problem, they routinely choose to abort the fetus. Based on *Buck v. Bell* and *Valerie N*, make the arguments for and against sterilizing her.
4. One of the themes in *Buck v. Bell*—a concern about producing defective offspring—shows up even more frequently in discussions not about sterilization but about abortion. As is discussed in chapter 4, the Court has found a right to abortion granted by the United States Constitution. One of the most common and most acceptable uses (at least among those who are not opposed to abortion under any circumstances) is for aborting fetuses that are likely to have mental retardation.

   A common genetically based form of mental retardation is Down's syndrome (the apparent cause of Valerie N.'s retardation), which can be detected by prenatal testing of the mother. Children with Down's syndrome can have variable degrees of mental retardation, but in general the great majority of such children appear to have highly worthwhile lives. Indeed, following the birth of such a child, the mere fact of its having mental retardation would not be sufficient justification for arguing that it should be deprived of needed medical care and allowed to die. Causing a child's death in such a manner would likely constitute murder. (For more discussion of this, see the notes following *In re Conroy* in chapter 10.)

Nonetheless, the use of genetic screening techniques is no doubt making it likely that fewer and fewer people with Down's syndrome, and a variety of other genetic defects that cause mental retardation, will be born.[2] A recent editorial in the *New England Journal of Medicine* commented on a new type of prenatal test, one whose results would not be available as quickly as current tests: "We would find it clinically and ethically troubling not to tell a pregnant woman about a heightened risk of Down's syndrome at a time when she could have chorionic-villus sampling and undergo elective termination of the pregnancy in a discrete and safe way, should the results be abnormal."[3] Thus, the "right" to avoid having a child with mental retardation has attained not just legal but also ethical support.

Note that the medical profession does not yet give similar "ethical" support to the full extent of a woman's legal right to abort a fetus. For example, we might contrast this acceptance of the option of aborting a fetus with Down's syndrome with a different practice that is strongly condemned: aborting a healthy fetus where the sex is not what the parents desired. Critical stories abound in the U.S. media about the use of this technique by women in India, who may attempt to illegally gain access to ultrasonography so that they may abort a female fetus. As to practices here in this country, some would consider it unethical for a doctor to assist a couple in determining the sex of a fetus if the purpose was to allow them to decide to abort it. Does the acceptability of aborting a Down's syndrome fetus, and the fact that we nonetheless do condemn other reasons for having an abortion, say something about our attitudes toward the mentally disabled?

5. The current law with regard to involuntary sterilization is largely influenced by a reaction to the eugenics movement in Nazi Germany. That movement was motivated by a desire to "improve" the race by making sure that only people with desirable genes were allowed to reproduce. What do you think are the primary reasons for which people have condemned that movement?

6. Are the reasons for condemning the German eugenics movement fully consistent with the current legal and ethical framework with regard to sterilization? Given our near endorsement of practices such as the abortion of a fetus with Down's syndrome, should we be so quick to continue to criti-

cize Justice Holmes for complaining about multiple generations of imbeciles? To the extent we fault eugenics as an attempt to say that some people are more valuable than others, has our current society merely replaced social determinations of such values with determinations to be made by the individual parents-to-be? In other words, have we given too much legal protection to the autonomy of individuals to make decisions about their own lives in the context of procreative decision-making? (As to the possible constitutionality of laws that might attempt to restrict such autonomy, see the notes following *Planned Parenthood v. Casey*, 505 U.S. 833 (1992), in chapter 4.)

Endnotes

1. Tamar Lewin, "Wide Use Seen For an Implant In Birth Control," *New York Times*, 29 November 1991, A-1; see also Stuart Taylor, Jr., "The Norplant Option," *Legal Times*, 19 August 1996, 23.
2. See, e.g., Thomas C. Schelling, *Micromotives and Macrobehavior*, 193 (New York: W.W. Norton & Co., 1978).
3. Joshua A. Copel and Ray O. Bahado-Singh, "Prenatal Screening for Down's Syndrome—A Search for the Family's Values," 341 *New Eng. J. Med.* 521 (1999).

4

The Right to Abortion

As the discussion of federalism demonstrated, the balancing of constitution-ally-protected rights against important state interests plays a major role in re-solving many legal disputes. The law relating to abortion is an example of such a balancing—albeit a complicated and highly controversial balancing. Again, as in *Griswold*, we are dealing with a state law that tries to restrict the conduct of pri-vate individuals in a way that may involve the use of powers that are denied the state under the United States Constitution. In this case, the conduct is that of a woman who wants to be able to go to a doctor to get an abortion, and that of the doctor who wants to comply with her request.

In *Roe v. Wade* you will see two important issues debated. The first is whether the conduct of a woman in trying to get an abortion is supported by any constitutionally protected interest. The Court concludes it is: her right to pri-vacy. But finding that a constitutionally protected interest is involved does not end the inquiry, since few such interests are absolute. The Court then moves to a second level of inquiry: is there another interest, to be asserted by the state or some other party, that justifies limiting or overriding that pregnant woman's pri-vacy interest? The answer to that question requires analysis of what it means to be a "person" for purposes of the law, since "persons" are granted certain legal rights. In particular, is a fetus a person? The Supreme Court's answer to both of these questions continues to generate a great deal of controversy. Legal com-mentators generally consider *Roe v. Wade* a poorly reasoned opinion. Nonethe-less, it has remained the law for a significant period, and even as the member-ship on the Supreme Court changed, the Justices have been reluctant to overturn its basic conclusions, as you will see in reading *Planned Parenthood v. Casey.*

In thinking about the abortion cases, it might be helpful for you to keep in mind a relevant analogy, so that you can critically evaluate the discussion. Imag-ine that we were dealing not with a woman seeking an abortion, but with a woman who has just given birth to an infant a few seconds before. Do state laws restrict her ability to actively terminate the infant's life (such as by strangling it)? Obviously, yes: in every state this would constitute murder, and there would be a significant criminal sentence if she were convicted for that act. But assume, for the sake of argument, that a woman chose to challenge the constitutionality of such a state law. What would the flow of arguments be? Outlining the nature of such arguments, and comparing them with the abortion arguments, is not as easy as it might seem.

On the one hand, could she raise her right to privacy again? Does that interest change much in observing her status a few minutes before birth, to looking at her status a few minutes after birth? In answering this question, you will have to determine what it is that the privacy right is protecting. Is it her bodily integrity, i.e., her choice not to have a fetus inside her? If so, is that interest less important as she nears the moment of delivery? Or is the interest related more broadly to "family" and "reproduction," as the other privacy cases observed? If that is the case, perhaps the interest goes beyond that of carrying the fetus inside her to an interest in controlling (at a minimum) the next 18 years of her life without the burden of caring for a child. Ask yourself, too, how much that interest changes as we straddle the moment of delivery.

Ask similar questions about the interests of the fetus, as it too straddles that moment. Do its interests change very much? What, exactly, are those interests? How does the Constitution deal with those interests? The Supreme Court wrestles with the fetus's status as a person, but the Court also ends up saying something about the nature and weight of the fetus's interests irrespective of its personhood. We will revisit that issue after you have read *Roe v. Wade*.

ROE V. WADE
Supreme Court of the United States
410 U.S. 113 (1973)

OPINION BY JUSTICE BLACKMUN:

This Texas federal appeal . . . present[s] constitutional challenges to state criminal abortion legislation. The Texas statutes under attack here are typical of those that have been in effect in many States for approximately a century. . . .

We forthwith acknowledge our awareness of the sensitive and emotional nature of the abortion controversy, of the vigorous opposing views, even among physicians, and of the deep and seemingly absolute convictions that the subject inspires. One's philosophy, one's experiences, one's exposure to the raw edges of human existence, one's religious training, one's attitudes toward life and family and their values, and the moral standards one establishes and seeks to observe, are all likely to influence and to color one's thinking and conclusions about abortion. . . .

The Texas statutes that concern us here are Arts. 1191–1194 and 1196 of the State's Penal Code. These make it a crime to "procure an abortion," as therein defined, or to attempt one, except with respect to "an abortion procured or attempted by medical advice for the purpose of saving the life of the mother." Similar statutes are in existence in a majority of the States. . . .

Jane Roe, a single woman who was residing in Dallas County, Texas, instituted this federal action in March 1970 against the District Attorney of the county. She sought a declaratory judgment that the Texas criminal abortion statutes were unconstitutional on their face, and an injunction restraining the defendant from enforcing the statutes.

Roe alleged that she was unmarried and pregnant; that she wished to terminate her pregnancy by an abortion "performed by a competent, licensed physician, under safe, clinical conditions"; that she was unable to get a "legal" abortion in Texas because her life did not appear to be threatened by the continuation of her pregnancy; and that she could not afford to travel to another jurisdiction in order to secure a legal abortion under safe conditions. She claimed that the Texas statutes were unconstitutionally vague and that they abridged her right of personal privacy, protected by the First, Fourth, Fifth, Ninth, and Fourteenth Amendments. By an amendment to her complaint Roe purported to sue "on behalf of herself and all other women" similarly situated.

James Hubert Hallford, a licensed physician, sought and was granted leave to intervene in Roe's action. In his complaint he alleged that he had been arrested previously for violations of the Texas abortion statutes and that two such prosecutions were pending against him. He described conditions of patients who came to him seeking abortions, and he claimed that for many cases he, as a physician, was unable to determine whether they fell within or outside the exception recognized by Article 1196. He alleged that, as a consequence, the statutes were vague and uncertain, in violation of the Fourteenth Amendment, and that they violated his own and his patients' rights to privacy in the doctor-patient relationship and his own right to practice medicine, rights he claimed were guaranteed by the First, Fourth, Fifth, Ninth, and Fourteenth Amendments. . . .

The principal thrust of appellant's attack on the Texas statutes is that they improperly invade a right, said to be possessed by the pregnant woman, to choose to terminate her pregnancy. Appellant would discover this right in the concept of personal liberty embodied in the Fourteenth Amendment's Due Process Clause; or in personal, marital, familial, and sexual privacy said to be protected by the Bill of Rights or its penumbras. Before addressing this claim, we feel it desirable briefly to survey, in several aspects, the history of abortion, for such insight as that history may afford us, and then to examine the state purposes and interests behind the criminal abortion laws.

It perhaps is not generally appreciated that the restrictive criminal abortion laws in effect in a majority of States today are of relatively recent vintage. Those laws, generally proscribing abortion or its attempt at any time during pregnancy except when necessary to preserve the pregnant woman's life, are not of ancient or even of common-law origin. Instead, they derive from statutory changes effected, for the most part, in the latter half of the 19th century.

1. *Ancient attitudes.* These are not capable of precise determination. We are told that at the time of the Persian Empire abortifacients were known and that criminal abortions were severely punished. We are also told, however, that abortion was practiced in Greek times as well as in the Roman Era, and that "it was resorted to without scruple." . . .

2. *The Hippocratic Oath.* What then of the famous Oath that has stood so long as the ethical guide of the medical profession and that bears the name of the great Greek (460(?)-377(?) B. C.), who has been described as the Father of Medicine, the "wisest and the greatest practitioner of his art," and the "most important and most complete medical personality of antiquity," who dominated the medical schools of his time, and who typified the sum of the medical knowledge of the past? The Oath varies somewhat according to the particular translation, but in any translation the content is clear: "I will give no deadly medicine to anyone if asked, nor suggest any such counsel; and in like manner I will not give to a woman a pessary to produce abortion," or "I will neither give a deadly drug to anybody if asked for it, nor will I make a suggestion to this effect. Similarly, I will not give to a woman an abortive remedy."

. . . The Oath was not uncontested even in Hippocrates' day; only the Pythagorean school of philosophers frowned upon the related act of suicide. Most Greek thinkers, on the other hand, commended abortion, at least prior to viability. For the Pythagoreans, however, it was a matter of dogma. For them the embryo was animate from the moment of conception, and abortion meant destruction of a living being. The abortion clause of the Oath, therefore, "echoes Pythagorean doctrines," and "[I]n no other stratum of Greek opinion were such views held or proposed in the same spirit of uncompromising austerity." . . .

3. *The common law.* It is undisputed that at common law, abortion performed *before* "quickening"—the first recognizable movement of the fetus *in utero*, appearing usually from the 16th to the 18th week of pregnancy—was not an indictable offense. The absence of a common-law crime for pre-quickening abortion appears to have developed from a confluence of earlier philosophical, theological, and civil and canon law concepts of when life begins. These disciplines variously approached the question in terms of the point at which the embryo or fetus became "formed" or recognizably human, or in terms of when a "person" came into being, that is, infused with a "soul" or "animated." A loose consensus evolved in early English law that these events occurred at some point between conception and live birth. This was "mediate animation." Although Christian theology and the canon law came to fix the point of animation at 40 days for a male and 80 days for a female, a view that persisted until the 19th century, there was otherwise little agreement about the precise time of formation or animation. There was agreement, however, that prior to this point the fetus

was to be regarded as part of the mother, and its destruction, therefore, was not homicide. Due to continued uncertainty about the precise time when animation occurred, to the lack of any empirical basis for the 40–80-day view, and perhaps to Aquinas' definition of movement as one of the two first principles of life, Bracton focused upon quickening as the critical point. The significance of quickening was echoed by later common-law scholars and found its way into the received common law in this country.

Whether abortion of a *quick* fetus was a felony at common law, or even a lesser crime, is still disputed. Bracton, writing early in the 13th century, thought it homicide. But the later and predominant view, following the great common-law scholars, has been that it was, at most, a lesser offense. . . .

5. *The American law.* In this country, the law in effect in all but a few States until mid-19th century was the pre-existing English common law. Connecticut, the first State to enact abortion legislation, adopted in 1821 that part of Lord Ellenborough's Act that related to a woman "quick with child." The death penalty was not imposed. Abortion before quickening was made a crime in that State only in 1860. In 1828, New York enacted legislation that, in two respects, was to serve as a model for early anti-abortion statutes. First, while barring destruction of an unquickened fetus as well as a quick fetus, it made the former only a misdemeanor, but the latter second-degree manslaughter. Second, it incorporated a concept of therapeutic abortion by providing that an abortion was excused if it "shall have been necessary to preserve the life of such mother, or shall have been advised by two physicians to be necessary for such purpose." By 1840, when Texas had received the common law, only eight American States had statutes dealing with abortion. It was not until after the War Between the States that legislation began generally to replace the common law. Most of these initial statutes dealt severely with abortion after quickening but were lenient with it before quickening. Most punished attempts equally with completed abortions. While many statutes included the exception for an abortion thought by one or more physicians to be necessary to save the mother's life, that provision soon disappeared and the typical law required that the procedure actually be necessary for that purpose. . . .

6. *The position of the American Medical Association.* The anti-abortion mood prevalent in this country in the late 19th century was shared by the medical profession. Indeed, the attitude of the profession may have played a significant role in the enactment of stringent criminal abortion legislation during that period. . . .

VII

Three reasons have been advanced to explain historically the enactment of criminal abortion laws in the 19th century and to justify their continued existence.

It has been argued occasionally that these laws were the product of a Victorian social concern to discourage illicit sexual conduct. Texas, however, does not advance this justification in the present case, and it appears that no court or commentator has taken the argument seriously. The appellants and *amici* contend, moreover, that this is not a proper state purpose at all and suggest that, if it were, the Texas statutes are overbroad in protecting it since the law fails to distinguish between married and unwed mothers.

A second reason is concerned with abortion as a medical procedure. When most criminal abortion laws were first enacted, the procedure was a hazardous one for the woman. This was particularly true prior to the development of antisepsis. Antiseptic techniques, of course, were based on discoveries by Lister, Pasteur, and others first announced in 1867, but were not generally accepted and employed until about the turn of the century. Abortion mortality was high. Even after 1900, and perhaps until as late as the development of antibiotics in the 1940's, standard modern techniques such as dilation and curettage were not nearly so safe as they are today. Thus, it has been argued that a State's real concern in enacting a criminal abortion law was to protect the pregnant woman, that is, to restrain her from submitting to a procedure that placed her life in serious jeopardy.

Modern medical techniques have altered this situation. Appellants and various *amici* refer to medical data indicating that abortion in early pregnancy, that is, prior to the end of the first trimester, although not without its risk, is now relatively safe. Mortality rates for women undergoing early abortions, where the procedure is legal, appear to be as low as or lower than the rates for normal childbirth. Consequently, any interest of the State in protecting the woman from an inherently hazardous procedure, except when it would be equally dangerous for her to forgo it, has largely disappeared. Of course, important state interests in the areas of health and medical standards do remain. The State has a legitimate interest in seeing to it that abortion, like any other medical procedure, is performed under circumstances that insure maximum safety for the patient. This interest obviously extends at least to the performing physician and his staff, to the facilities involved, to the availability of after-care, and to adequate provision for any complication or emergency that might arise. The prevalence of high mortality rates at illegal "abortion mills" strengthens, rather than weakens, the State's interest in regulating the conditions under which abortions are performed. Moreover, the risk to the woman increases as her pregnancy continues. Thus, the State retains a definite interest in protecting the woman's own health and safety when an abortion is proposed at a late stage of pregnancy.

The third reason is the State's interest—some phrase it in terms of duty—in protecting prenatal life. Some of the argument for this justification rests on the theory that a new human life is present from the moment of conception. The State's interest and general obligation to protect life then extends, it is argued, to prenatal life. Only when the life of the pregnant mother herself is at stake, balanced against the life she carries within her, should the interest of the embryo or fetus not prevail. Logically, of course, a legitimate state interest in this area need not stand or fall on acceptance of the belief that life begins at conception or at some other point prior to live birth. In assessing the State's interest, recognition may be given to the less rigid claim that as long as at least potential life is involved, the State may assert interests beyond the protection of the pregnant woman alone. . . .

It is with these interests, and the weight to be attached to them, that this case is concerned.

VIII

The Constitution does not explicitly mention any right of privacy. In a line of decisions, however, . . . the Court has recognized that a right of personal privacy, or a guarantee of certain areas or zones of privacy, does exist under the Constitution. . . . This right of privacy, whether it be founded in the Fourteenth Amendment's concept of personal liberty and restrictions upon state action, as we feel it is, or, as the District Court determined, in the Ninth Amendment's reservation of rights to the people, is broad enough to encompass a woman's decision whether or not to terminate her pregnancy. The detriment that the State would impose upon the pregnant woman by denying this choice altogether is apparent. Specific and direct harm medically diagnosable even in early pregnancy may be involved. Maternity, or additional offspring, may force upon the woman a distressful life and future. Psychological harm may be imminent. Mental and physical health may be taxed by child care. There is also the distress, for all concerned, associated with the unwanted child, and there is the problem of bringing a child into a family already unable, psychologically and otherwise, to care for it. In other cases, as in this one, the additional difficulties and continuing stigma of unwed motherhood may be involved. All these are factors the woman and her responsible physician necessarily will consider in consultation.

On the basis of elements such as these, appellant and some *amici* argue that the woman's right is absolute and that she is entitled to terminate her pregnancy at whatever time, in whatever way, and for whatever reason she alone chooses. With this we do not agree. Appellant's arguments that Texas either has no valid interest at all in regulating the abortion decision, or no interest strong enough to support any limitation upon the woman's sole determination, are unpersuasive. The Court's decisions recognizing a right of privacy also acknowledge that some state regulation in areas protected by that right is appropriate. As noted above, a State may properly assert important interests in safeguarding health, in maintaining medical standards, and in protecting potential life. At some point in pregnancy, these respective interests become sufficiently compelling to sustain regulation of the factors that govern the abortion decision. The privacy right involved, therefore, cannot be said to be absolute. In fact, it is not clear to us that the claim asserted by some *amici* that one has an unlimited right to do with one's body as one pleases bears a close relationship to the right of privacy previously articulated in the Court's decisions. The Court has refused to recognize an unlimited right of this kind in the past.

We, therefore, conclude that the right of personal privacy includes the abortion decision, but that this right is not unqualified and must be considered against important state interests in regulation. . . .

Where certain "fundamental rights" are involved, the Court has held that regulation limiting these rights may be justified only by a "compelling state interest," and that legislative enactments must be narrowly drawn to express only the legitimate state interests at stake. . . .

IX

. . . Appellant, as has been indicated, claims an absolute right that bars any state imposition of criminal penalties in the area. Appellee argues that the State's determination to recognize and protect prenatal life from and after conception constitutes a compelling state interest. As noted above, we do not agree fully with either formulation.

A. The appellee and certain *amici* argue that the fetus is a "person" within the language and meaning of the Fourteenth Amendment. In support of this, they outline at length and in detail the well-known facts of fetal development. If this suggestion of personhood is established, the appellant's case, of course, collapses, for the fetus' right to life would then be guaranteed specifically by the Amendment. The appellant conceded as much on reargument. On the other hand, the appellee conceded on reargument that no case could be cited that holds that a fetus is a person within the meaning of the Fourteenth Amendment.

The Constitution does not define "person" in so many words. Section 1 of the Fourteenth Amendment contains three references to "person." The first, in defining "citizens," speaks of "persons born or naturalized in the United States." The word also appears both in the Due Process Clause and in the Equal Protection Clause. "Person" is used in other places in the Constitution . . . But in nearly all these instances, the use of the word is such that it has application only postnatally. None indicates, with any assurance, that it has any possible pre-natal application.

All this, together with our observation that throughout the major portion of the 19th century prevailing legal abortion practices were far freer than they are today, persuades us that the word "person," as used in the Fourteenth Amendment, does not include the unborn. . . .

This conclusion, however, does not of itself fully answer the contentions raised by Texas, and we pass on to other considerations.

B. The pregnant woman cannot be isolated in her privacy. She carries an embryo and, later, a fetus, if one accepts the medical definitions of the developing young in the human uterus. The situation therefore is inherently different from marital intimacy, or bedroom possession of obscene material, or marriage, or procreation, or education, with which *Eisenstadt* and *Griswold, Stanley, Loving, Skinner,* and *Pierce* and *Meyer* were respectively concerned. As we have intimated above, it is reasonable and appropriate for a State to decide that at some point in time another interest, that of health of the mother or that of potential human life, becomes significantly involved. The woman's privacy is no longer sole and any right of privacy she possesses must be measured accordingly.

Texas urges that, apart from the Fourteenth Amendment, life begins at conception and is present throughout pregnancy, and that, therefore, the State has a compelling interest in protecting that life from and after conception. We need not resolve the difficult question of when life begins. When those trained in the respective disciplines of medicine, philosophy, and theology are unable to arrive at any consensus, the judiciary, at this point in the development of man's knowledge, is not in a position to speculate as to the answer.

It should be sufficient to note briefly the wide divergence of thinking on this most sensitive and difficult question. There has always been strong support for the view that life does not begin until live birth. This was the belief of the Stoics. It appears to be the predominant, though not the unanimous, attitude of the Jewish faith. It may be taken to represent also the position of a large segment of the Protestant community, insofar as that can be ascertained; organized groups that have taken a formal position on the abortion issue have generally regarded abortion as a matter for the conscience of the individual and her family. As we have noted, the common law found greater significance in quickening. Physicians and their scientific colleagues have regarded that event with less interest and have tended to focus either upon conception, upon live birth, or upon the interim point at which the fetus becomes "viable," that is, potentially able to live outside the mother's womb, albeit with artificial aid. Viability is usually placed at about seven months (28 weeks) but may occur earlier, even at 24 weeks. The Aristotelian theory of "mediate animation," that held sway throughout the Middle Ages and the Renaissance in Europe, continued to be official Roman Catholic dogma until the 19th century, despite opposition to this "ensoulment" theory from those in the Church who would recognize the existence of life from the moment of conception. The latter is now, of course, the official belief of the Catholic Church. As one brief *amicus* discloses, this is a view strongly held by many non-Catholics as well, and by many physicians. Substantial problems for precise definition of this view are posed, however, by new embryological data that purport to indicate that conception is a "process" over time, rather than an event, and by new medical techniques such as menstrual extraction, the "morning-after" pill, implantation of embryos, artificial insemination, and even artificial wombs.

In areas other than criminal abortion, the law has been reluctant to endorse any theory that life, as we recognize it, begins before live birth or to accord legal rights to the unborn except in narrowly defined situations and except when the rights are contingent upon live birth. For example, the traditional rule of tort law denied recovery for prenatal injuries even though the child was born alive. That rule has been changed in almost every jurisdiction. In most States, recovery is said to be permitted only if the fetus was viable, or at least quick, when the injuries were sustained, though few courts have squarely so held. In a recent development, generally opposed by the commentators, some States permit the parents of a stillborn child to maintain an action for wrongful death because of prenatal injuries. Such an action, however, would appear to be one to vindicate the parents' interest and is thus consistent with the view that the fetus, at most, represents only the potentiality of life. Similarly, unborn children have been recognized as acquiring rights or interests by way of inheritance or other devolution of property, and have been represented by guardians *ad litem*. Perfection of the interests involved, again, has generally been contingent upon live birth. In short, the unborn have never been recognized in the law as persons in the whole sense.

X

In view of all this, we do not agree that, by adopting one theory of life, Texas may override the rights of the pregnant woman that are at stake. We repeat, however, that the State does have an important and legitimate interest in preserving and protecting the health of the pregnant woman, whether she be a resident of the State or a nonresident who seeks medical consultation and treatment there, and that it has still *another* important and legitimate interest in protecting the potentiality of human life. These interests are separate and distinct. Each grows in substantiality as the woman approaches term and, at a point during pregnancy, each becomes "compelling." With respect to the State's important and legitimate interest in the health of the mother, the "compelling" point, in the light of present medical knowledge, is at approximately the end of the first trimester. This is so because of the now-established medical fact . . . that until the end of the first trimester mortality in abortion may be less than mortality in normal childbirth. It follows that, from and after this point, a State may regulate the abortion procedure to the extent that the regulation reasonably relates to the preservation and protection of maternal health. Examples of permissible state regulation in this area are requirements as to the qualifications of the person who is to perform the abortion; as to the licensure of that person; as to the facility in which the procedure is to be performed, that is, whether it must be a hospital or may be a clinic or some other place of less-than-hospital status; as to the licensing of the facility; and the like.

This means, on the other hand, that, for the period of pregnancy prior to this "compelling" point, the attending physician, in consultation with his patient, is free to determine, without regulation by the State, that, in his medical judgment, the patient's pregnancy should be terminated. If that decision is reached, the judgment may be effectuated by an abortion free of interference by the State. With respect to the State's important and legitimate interest in potential life, the "compelling" point is at viability. This is so because the fetus then presumably has the capability of meaningful life outside the mother's womb. State regulation protective of fetal life after viability thus has both logical and biological justifications. If the State is interested in protecting fetal life after viability, it may go so far as to proscribe abortion during that period, except when it is necessary to preserve the life or health of the mother. Measured against these standards, Art. 1196 of the Texas Penal Code, in restricting legal abortions to those "procured or attempted by medical advice for the purpose of saving the life of the mother," sweeps too broadly. The statute makes no distinction between abortions performed early in pregnancy and those performed later, and it limits to a single reason, "saving" the mother's life, the legal justification for the procedure. The statute, therefore, cannot survive the constitutional attack made upon it here. . . .

NOTES AND QUESTIONS:
Roe v. Wade

1. For each of the three trimesters of a pregnancy,
   a. State the rule created by the Court for determining the extent to which a state can regulate the practice of abortion.
   b. Give an explanation of how the Court came up with that rule. (Determine what interests existed for each of the parties to the case, and how the Court balanced those interests against one another.)
2. The Supreme Court's opinion in *Roe* is actually less significant for providing an answer to the question of when a woman can get an abortion than in answering a more specific question: In what circumstances can a state choose to restrict the right of a woman to get an abortion?

   Which of the following laws could constitutionally be passed by a state? In each case, give the reasons for your answers.
   a. A law that bans the abortion of any third-trimester fetus
   b. A law that provides for various safety criteria that must be met by an abortion clinic for all abortions that take place in its facilities
   c. A law that says that a woman can obtain an abortion from a willing doctor at any stage of her pregnancy

   Would your answers be any different if it was the federal government, and not a state, that was passing the law? (Ask yourself which of the categories of federalism discussed in chapter 1 applies here.)
3. The opinion discusses whether or not a fetus is a person for purposes of the Constitution. Why is that issue discussed? What is its legal significance?

   Notice that because of federalism, there is nothing a state can do—through legislation or even through amending its own constitution—to override the determination that the U.S. Constitution does not deem a fetus to be a person. A state can pass a law (or amend its constitution) to say that a fetus is a person under the laws of that state. But federalism overrides state laws to the extent they are in conflict with the Constitution. Thus, the key issue with regard to such a law is whether, and in what circumstances, it might conflict with the Constitution. (See further discussion of this in the notes following *Whitner* in chapter 6.)

4. What if the Court had determined that (at some point) the fetus did indeed become a person? (At what point might this occur: at conception? At viability?) How would that have changed the outcome of the case: (a) with regard to what sorts of laws states could pass relating to the first and second trimesters of pregnancies, and (b) with regard to what sorts of laws states could pass relating to the third trimester?

   Justice Blackmun's answer to some of these questions appears in Part IX of his opinion. Do you agree with that answer? Is it as straightforward as he suggests? If a fetus is indeed a person, does a woman necessarily have a duty to not abort it (in the absence of state legislation addressing the issue)? Or does it merely mean that the state would have an ability to constitutionally pass a law that prevented such an abortion? (You might revisit this question after reading chapter 6 with its discussion of duties the law imposes on each of us to protect the lives of others.)

5. There are two general methods for categorizing things, and both are used in the law. One is to categorize things by status, the other by attributes. The first starts from a logical statement such as "because X has property A, then we will consider it to have property B." In the case of personhood, a status categorization might, for example, be a determination that all human beings, after they are born, are persons. Similar attempts at line-drawing through use of status would be declarations that all fertilized human eggs, and anything they develop into, are persons, or that all third-trimester human fetuses, and anything *they* develop into, are persons.

   A very different way to draw lines is to determine what attributes are relevant to being in one category or another, and then checking to see whether the item or entity has those attributes. Thus, for personhood, we would determine what it is that makes someone a person, and then check to see whether or not those attributes exist in a particular case.

6. Did the Supreme Court use either of these two methods? A combination of them?

7. What attributes do you think are relevant to personhood? Is the use of the attribute method helpful in resolving the abortion issue? Why or why not?

8. We are getting more and more skillful in genetic engineering. The possibility of increasing the intelligence of animals is readily within our capabilities, and is no longer the subject of adventure movies about sharks, or science fiction stories such as Harlan Ellison's classic "A Boy and His Dog."[1] In addition, there is the possibility that we might be visited by intelligent aliens. Would such beings be considered persons under the law? Does this question add anything to whether you think "status" categorization is better than "attribute" categorization?

9. Similar questions are likely to arise as computer scientists make more and more powerful machines. Some predict that it will only be a few decades before a computer can pass Alan Turing's famous test: Can a person communicating with either a human being or a computer by typing questions on a key-

board reliably determine who or what is on the other end of the line? Should a machine passing that test have personhood for legal purposes?

10. The future is likely to see more and more situations in which human beings have their genetic material modified by the insertion of genes from other organisms. This is referred to as creating a "chimera," in reference to the monster in Greek mythology that had the head of a lion, the body of a goat, and the tail of a serpent. (Well over half of our current vegetable crops have been modified by such foreign genetic material—some of it from animals.) If we rely on a status test for determining personhood, might there come a time when so much of a person's genetic material has been replaced by non-human genes that the person is no longer a human being? Might this not be a far more difficult problem—determining when a chimeric entity is no longer a human being—than the issue of cloning human beings? Clones are 100 percent human beings, at least from a genetic standpoint.

That such questions are no longer the realm of science fiction is demonstrated by a November 14, 1998, letter from President Clinton to his advisory group, the National Bioethics Advisory Commission, commenting on newspaper reports regarding the "creation of an embryonic stem cell that is part human and part cow." The President indicated that he was "deeply troubled by this news of experiments involving the mingling of human and non-human species." Part of the response of the Commission was to pose and then attempt to answer the following question:

> Does the fusion of a human cell and an egg from a non-human cell result in a human embryo?
>
> The common understanding of a human embryo includes, at least, the concept of an organism at its earliest stages of development, which has the potential, if transferred to a uterus, to develop in the normal course of events into a living human being. At this time, however, there is insufficient scientific evidence to be able to say whether the combining of a human cell and the egg of a non-human animal results in an embryo in this sense. In our opinion, if this combination does result in an embryo, important ethical concerns arise, as is the case with all research involving human embryos. These concerns will be made more complex and controversial by the fact that these hybrid cells will contain both human and non-human biological material. [2]

11. The majority opinion in *Roe* notes that it need not address the "most sensitive and difficult question about when life begins." Is this really such a difficult question? What do you think of the claim that the fetus is not alive until birth takes place? As a scientific matter, life is indeed a great mystery, and our current techniques do not enable us to "create" life.[3] But what aspects of "life" is the fetus lacking that makes this such a difficult question?

In any event, of what legal relevance is the answer to this question? Is the Court really asking a different question, such as when does "human life" begin? Is that question any more helpful? What question, if any, do you think should be asked other than the personhood question?

12. The Court determines in *Roe* that the right of privacy, which is a fundamental right protected by the United States Constitution, includes the right to get an abortion. How would the analysis in this case have changed if the Court concluded that the right to privacy did not include the right to get an abortion?

13. Evaluate the Court's determination that the right of privacy includes the right to get an abortion. Is this consistent with the Court's other decisions about the right to privacy? The right to privacy has been determined to include the right to contraception for married (*Griswold*) and unmarried (*Eisenstadt v. Baird*) people, and the right to marry a person of a different race (*Loving v. Virginia*), but not the right to have sexual relations with persons of the same sex (*Bowers*). In *Bowers*, the Court in rejecting this latter right stated: "Proscriptions against that conduct have ancient roots. . . . Against this background, to claim that a right to engage in such conduct is 'deeply rooted in this Nation's history and tradition' or 'implicit in the concept of ordered liberty' is, at best, facetious." Review the Court's discussion of the history of abortion rights in *Roe*. Does that discussion demonstrate to you that the right to an abortion is "deeply rooted in this Nation's history and tradition"—or merely that it has not always been consistently subjected to criminal penalties? Is the first statement equivalent to the second?

14. The Court observed that "[i]n areas other than criminal law, the law has been reluctant to endorse any theory that life, as we recognize it, begins before live birth or to accord legal rights to the unborn." However true that might have been when *Roe v. Wade* was decided, there has been a definite trend in the other direction. This raises a host of interesting issues.

    a. **Criminal Laws**. More and more jurisdictions are increasing the penalty for causing the death of a fetus. In some cases, those penalties are being categorized as murder. In other words, causing the death of a fetus can lead to the same jail sentence as causing the death of a "person." (Some of the state laws that do this merely redefine "person" for purposes of state law to include a fetus. If you are in a state that does this, is the result in *Roe v. Wade* altered by such a law? Why or why not? See note 3, above.) Assume, for example, that someone robs a liquor store without using a weapon and pushes aside a woman in her second month of pregnancy, who is not even "showing." If the woman miscarries, the robber may face a much larger penalty for the "murder" of the fetus than he would for the robbery itself.

    There have even been attempts to pass such laws at the national level. In 1999 the House of Representatives approved a bill under which someone who injured or killed a fetus while committing certain federal crimes could be convicted for having committed an additional crime against the fetus. "[A] person who assaults a pregnant woman on a military base could be prosecuted under the bill for murder or manslaughter if the fetus died but the woman survived. This is not the case today, because Federal homicide statutes reach only the killing of a human being, a person who has been born."[4]

In those states that have passed such laws, if the robber caused the death of a second-trimester fetus, is it relevant that state law would have permitted the woman to terminate the pregnancy (e.g., because having a child at this point would delay her ability to move up the corporate ladder)? Be very specific in your arguments about what we are doing when we say something is murder. What if the fetus were in the third trimester? Again, is it relevant whether or not the state law bans third-trimester abortions?

b. **Civil Laws**. Under state tort laws (discussed in chapter 7), people can sue for damages when they are wrongfully injured or killed. (In the latter situation, of course, someone else has to bring the action on their behalf.) Should these statutes give a fetus the right to sue? Imagine, for example, that a pregnant woman is beaten by her ex-husband. As the Court said in *Roe v. Wade*, "the traditional rule of tort law denied recovery for prenatal injuries even though the child was born alive. That rule has been changed in almost every jurisdiction." Allowing such an action is not a big stretch in doctrine, since there was then a "person" who was suing based on his own injuries. If, however, the fetus is never born alive, it is a bigger conceptual leap to say that the fetus had a right to sue. Some courts are allowing such actions, although many will only allow them in the case of a viable fetus. How do these developments fit into the Court's description of this area of the law as demonstrating that "the unborn have never been recognized in the law as persons in the whole sense"?

Does *Roe v. Wade* in any way limit the ability of states to shape their tort laws? Can a state choose to allow damage actions on behalf of both viable and non-viable fetuses that are not born alive? In either case, does it matter (a) what laws the state has passed with regard to abortion, and (b) what laws the state has passed with regard to criminal penalties for injuring a fetus?

The possible ability of a fetus to bring lawsuits when it has been injured must be distinguished from a very different cause of action known as "wrongful life." This type of action is based upon a situation in which the "wrong" relates to the fact that a child was permitted to be born. The standard fact pattern is that a doctor fails to give a woman relevant prenatal information (e.g., about an infection to which the fetus was exposed) that might have led her to abort the fetus. While it is clear that the woman would have a cause of action for the harm caused to herself, the question is sometimes raised whether the child has its own distinct cause of action. Most courts have said no, finding it troubling to hold that anyone can be harmed by merely being born. (Note that the alternative would have been not being born, since the injury to the child has not been caused by the doctor's actions. It is the failure to detect that injury, and inform the woman about it, that leads to the legal wrong.)[5]

15. A crucially important part of the Court's opinion is not only its determinations about the status of the fetus and the rights of the woman, but how it balances these interests. As we noted in chapter 1, a finding that a constitutional right is involved—in this case, the woman's right to privacy, which includes the right to abortion—does not mean that other interests cannot override that right. Note the consequences of the Court's determination that, in the third trimester, a state law can effectively restrict a woman's right to get an abortion. In other words, under certain circumstances a woman can be forced to continue a pregnancy against her will. This means that a variety of highly non-trivial things will be happening to her body, also against her will: a continuing gain of weight, changes in her appearance, significant feelings of discomfort, and various biochemical and other changes. Any or all of these changes might also affect her daily activities, including her job, and her interaction with family and friends. Moreover, there are post-delivery changes that do not relate directly to her body, namely the fact she will have extensive legal duties with regard to that child.

It is important to recognize how *Roe* permits a state to force a woman to "involuntarily" undergo these consequences, for we are later going to turn to other issues raised by the relationship between a woman and a fetus. We will see that women might refuse medical care or abuse themselves (by taking illegal drugs) and in each case might endanger a fetus. We will even deal with the case of a dead pregnant woman. We will then have to revisit the complexities of *Roe* to determine the extent to which a state can, consistent with the Constitution, tip the scales in favor of either the mother or the fetus in such conflicts.

PLANNED PARENTHOOD OF SOUTHEASTERN PENNSYLVANIA V. CASEY

Supreme Court of the United States

505 U.S. 833 (1992)

OPINION BY JUSTICES O'CONNOR, KENNEDY, AND SOUTER:

I

Liberty finds no refuge in a jurisprudence of doubt. Yet 19 years after our holding that the Constitution protects a woman's right to terminate her pregnancy in its early stages, that definition of liberty is still questioned. Joining the respondents as *amicus curiae*, the United States, as it has done in five other cases in the last decade, again asks us to overrule *Roe*.

At issue in these cases are five provisions of the Pennsylvania Abortion Control Act of 1982, as amended in 1988 and 1989. The Act requires that a woman seeking an abortion give her informed consent prior to the abortion procedure, and specifies that she be provided with certain information at least 24 hours before the abortion is performed. For a minor to obtain an abortion, the Act requires the informed consent of one of her parents, but provides for a judicial bypass option if the minor does not wish to or cannot obtain a parent's consent. Another provision of the Act requires that, unless certain exceptions apply, a married woman seeking an abortion must sign a statement indicating that she has notified her husband of her intended abortion. The Act exempts compliance with these three requirements in the event of a "medical emergency," which is defined in § 3203 of the Act. In addition to the above provisions regulating the performance of abortions, the Act imposes certain reporting requirements on facilities that provide abortion services. . . .

After considering the fundamental constitutional questions resolved by *Roe*, principles of institutional integrity, and the rule of *stare decisis*, we are led to conclude this: the essential holding of *Roe v. Wade* should be retained and once again reaffirmed.

It must be stated at the outset and with clarity that *Roe*'s essential holding, the holding we reaffirm, has three parts. First is a recognition of the right of the woman to choose to have an abortion before viability and to obtain it without undue interference from the State. Before viability, the State's interests are not strong enough to support a prohibition of abortion or the imposition of a substantial obstacle to the woman's effective right to elect the procedure. Second is a confirmation of the State's power to restrict abortions after fetal viability, if the law contains exceptions for pregnancies which endanger the woman's life or health. And third is the principle that the State has legitimate interests from the outset of the pregnancy in protecting the health of the woman and the life of the fetus that may become a child. These principles do not contradict one another; and we adhere to each.

II

. . . Our law affords constitutional protection to personal decisions relating to marriage, procreation, contraception, family relationships, child rearing, and education. Our cases recognize "the right of the individual, married or single, to be free from unwarranted governmental intrusion into matters so fundamentally affecting a person as the decision whether to bear or beget a child." *Eisenstadt v. Baird.* Our precedents "have respected the private realm of family life which the state cannot enter." These matters, involving the most intimate and personal choices a person may make in a lifetime, choices central to personal dignity and autonomy, are central to the liberty protected by the Fourteenth Amendment. At the heart of liberty is the right to define one's own concept of existence, of meaning, of the universe, and of the mystery of human life. Beliefs about these matters could not define the attributes of personhood were they formed under compulsion of the State.

These considerations begin our analysis of the woman's interest in terminating her pregnancy but cannot end it, for this reason: though the abortion decision may originate within the zone of conscience and belief, it is more than a philosophic exercise. Abortion is a unique act. It is an act fraught with consequences for others: for the woman who must live with the implications of her decision; for the persons who perform and assist in the procedure; for the spouse, family, and society which must confront the knowledge that these procedures exist, procedures some deem nothing short of an act of violence against innocent human life; and, depending on one's beliefs, for the life or potential life that is aborted. Though abortion is conduct, it does not follow that the State is entitled to proscribe it in all instances. That is because the liberty of the woman is at stake in a sense unique to the human condition and so unique to the law. The mother who carries a child to full term is subject to anxieties, to physical constraints, to pain that only she must bear. That these sacrifices have from the beginning of the human race been endured by woman with a pride that ennobles her in the eyes of others and gives to the infant a bond of love cannot alone be grounds for the State to insist she make the sacrifice. Her suffering is too intimate and personal for the State to insist, without more, upon its own vision of the woman's role, however dominant that vision has been in the course of our history and our culture. The destiny of the woman must be shaped to a large extent on her own conception of her spiritual imperatives and her place in society. . . .

IV

From what we have said so far it follows that it is a constitutional liberty of the woman to have some freedom to terminate her pregnancy. We conclude that the basic decision in *Roe* was based on a constitutional analysis which we cannot now repudiate. The woman's liberty is not so unlimited, however, that from the outset the State cannot show its concern for the life of the unborn, and at a later point in fetal development the State's interest in life has sufficient force so that the right of the woman to terminate the pregnancy can be restricted.

That brings us, of course, to the point where much criticism has been directed at *Roe*, a criticism that always inheres when the Court draws a specific rule from what in the Constitution is but a general standard. We conclude, however, that the urgent claims of the woman to retain the ultimate control over her destiny and her body, claims implicit in the meaning of liberty, require us to perform that function. Liberty must not be extinguished for want of a line that is clear. And it falls to us to give some real substance to the woman's liberty to determine whether to carry her pregnancy to full term.

We conclude the line should be drawn at viability, so that before that time the woman has a right to choose to terminate her pregnancy. We adhere to this principle for two reasons. First, as we have said, is the doctrine of *stare decisis*. Any judicial act of line-drawing may seem somewhat arbitrary, but *Roe* was a reasoned statement, elaborated with great care. . . .

The second reason is that the concept of viability, as we noted in *Roe*, is the time at which there is a realistic possibility of maintaining and nourishing a life outside the womb, so that the independent existence of the second life can in reason and all fairness be the object of state protection that now overrides the rights of the woman. Consistent with other constitutional norms, legislatures may draw lines which appear arbitrary without the necessity of offering a justification. But courts may not. We must justify the lines we draw. And there is no line other than viability which is more workable. To be sure, as we have said, there may be some medical developments that affect the precise point of viability, but this is an imprecision within tolerable limits given that the medical community and all those who must apply its discoveries will continue to explore the matter. The viability line also has, as a practical matter, an element of fairness. In some broad sense it might be said that a woman who fails to act before viability has consented to the State's intervention on behalf of the developing child.

The woman's right to terminate her pregnancy before viability is the most central principle of *Roe v. Wade*. It is a rule of law and a component of liberty we cannot renounce.

On the other side of the equation is the interest of the State in the protection of potential life. The *Roe* Court recognized the State's "important and legitimate interest in protecting the potentiality of human life." The weight to be given this state interest, not the strength of the woman's interest, was the difficult question faced in *Roe*. We do not need to say whether each of us, had we been Members of the Court when the valuation of the state interest came before it as an original matter, would have concluded, as the *Roe* Court did, that its weight is insufficient to justify a ban on abortions prior to viability even when it is subject to certain exceptions. The matter is not before us in the first instance, and coming as it does after nearly 20 years of litigation in *Roe*'s wake we are satisfied that the immediate question is not the soundness of *Roe*'s resolution of the issue, but the precedential force that must be accorded to its holding. And we have concluded that the essential holding of *Roe* should be reaffirmed.

Yet it must be remembered that *Roe v. Wade* speaks with clarity in establishing not only the woman's liberty but also the State's "important and legitimate interest in potential life." That portion of the decision in *Roe* has been given too little acknowledgment and implementation by the Court in its subsequent cases. Those cases decided that any regulation touching upon the abortion decision must survive strict scrutiny, to be sustained only if drawn in narrow terms to further a compelling state interest. Not all of the cases decided under that formulation can be reconciled with the holding in *Roe* itself that the State has legitimate interests in the health of the woman and in protecting the potential life within her. In resolving this tension, we choose to rely upon *Roe*, as against the later cases.

Roe established a trimester framework to govern abortion regulations. Under this elaborate but rigid construct, almost no regulation at all is permitted during the first trimester of pregnancy; regulations designed to protect the woman's health, but not to further the State's interest in potential life, are permitted during the second trimester; and during the third trimester, when the fetus is viable, prohibitions are permitted provided the life or health of the mother is not at stake. Most of our cases since *Roe* have involved the application of rules derived from the trimester framework.

The trimester framework no doubt was erected to ensure that the woman's right to choose not become so subordinate to the State's interest in promoting fetal life that her choice exists in theory but not in fact. We do not agree, however, that the trimester approach is necessary to accomplish this objective. A framework of this rigidity was unnecessary and in its later interpretation sometimes contradicted the State's permissible exercise of its powers.

Though the woman has a right to choose to terminate or continue her pregnancy before viability, it does not at all follow that the State is prohibited from taking steps to ensure that this choice is thoughtful and informed. Even in the earliest stages of pregnancy, the State may enact rules and regulations designed to encourage her to know that there are philosophic and social arguments of great weight that can be brought to bear in favor of continuing the pregnancy to full term and that there are procedures and institutions to allow adoption of unwanted children as well as a certain degree of state assistance if the mother chooses to raise the child herself. "The Constitution does not forbid a State or city, pursuant to democratic processes, from expressing a preference for normal childbirth." It follows that States are free to enact laws to provide a reasonable framework for a woman to make a decision that has such profound and lasting meaning. This, too, we find consistent with *Roe*'s central premises, and indeed the inevitable consequence of our holding that the State has an interest in protecting the life of the unborn.

We reject the trimester framework, which we do not consider to be part of the essential holding of *Roe*. Measures aimed at ensuring that a woman's choice contemplates the consequences for the fetus do not necessarily interfere with the right recognized in *Roe*, although those measures have been found to be inconsistent with the rigid trimester framework announced in that case. A logical reading of the central holding in *Roe* itself, and a necessary reconciliation of the liberty of the woman and the interest of the State in promoting prenatal life, require, in our view, that we abandon the trimester framework as a rigid prohibition on all previability regulation aimed at the protection of fetal life. The trimester framework suffers from these basic flaws: in its formulation it misconceives the nature of the pregnant woman's interest; and in practice it undervalues the State's interest in potential life, as recognized in *Roe*.

As our jurisprudence relating to all liberties save perhaps abortion has recognized, not every law which makes a right more difficult to exercise is, *ipso facto*, an infringement of that right. An example clarifies the point. We have held that not every ballot access limitation amounts to an infringement of the right to vote. Rather, the States are granted substantial flexibility in establishing the framework within which voters choose the candidates for whom they wish to vote.

The abortion right is similar. Numerous forms of state regulation might have the incidental effect of increasing the cost or decreasing the availability of medical care, whether for abortion or any other medical procedure. The fact that a law which serves a valid purpose, one not designed to strike at the right itself, has the incidental effect of making it more difficult or more expensive to procure an abortion cannot be enough to invalidate it. Only where state regulation imposes an undue burden on a woman's ability to make this decision does the power of the State reach into the heart of the liberty protected by the Due Process Clause.

These considerations of the nature of the abortion right illustrate that it is an overstatement to describe it as a right to decide whether to have an abortion "without interference from the State." All abortion regulations interfere to some degree with a woman's ability to decide whether to terminate her pregnancy. It is, as a consequence, not surprising that despite the protestations contained in the original *Roe* opinion to the effect that the Court was not recognizing an absolute right, the Court's experience applying the trimester framework has led to the striking down of some abortion regulations which in no real sense deprived women of the ultimate decision. Those decisions went too far because the right recognized by *Roe* is a right "to be free from unwarranted governmental intrusion into matters so fundamentally affecting a person as the decision whether to bear or beget a child." Not all governmental intrusion is of necessity unwarranted; and that brings us to the other basic flaw in the trimester framework: even in *Roe's* terms, in practice it undervalues the State's interest in the potential life within the woman.

Roe v. Wade was express in its recognition of the State's "important and legitimate interests in preserving and protecting the health of the pregnant woman [and] in protecting the potentiality of human life." The trimester framework, however, does not fulfill *Roe's* own promise that the State has an interest in protecting fetal life or potential life. *Roe* began the contradiction by using the trimester framework to forbid any regulation of abortion designed to advance that interest before viability. Before viability, *Roe* and subsequent cases treat all governmental attempts to influence a woman's decision on behalf of the potential life within her as unwarranted. This treatment is, in our judgment, incompatible with the recognition that there is a substantial state interest in potential life throughout pregnancy.

The very notion that the State has a substantial interest in potential life leads to the conclusion that not all regulations must be deemed unwarranted. Not all burdens on the right to decide whether to terminate a pregnancy will be undue. In our view, the undue burden standard is the appropriate means of reconciling the State's interest with the woman's constitutionally protected liberty. . . .

A finding of an undue burden is a shorthand for the conclusion that a state regulation has the purpose or effect of placing a substantial obstacle in the path of a woman seeking an abortion of a nonviable fetus. A statute with this purpose is invalid because the means chosen by the State to further the interest in potential life must be calculated to inform the woman's free choice, not hinder it. And a statute which, while furthering the interest in potential life or some other valid state interest, has the effect of placing a substantial obstacle in the path of a woman's choice cannot be considered a permissible means of serving its legitimate ends. . . .

Some guiding principles should emerge. What is at stake is the woman's right to make the ultimate decision, not a right to be insulated from all others in doing so. Regulations which do no more than create a structural mechanism by which the State, or the parent or guardian of a minor, may express profound respect for the life of the unborn are permitted, if they are not a substantial obstacle to the woman's exercise of the right to choose. Unless it has that effect on her right of choice, a state measure designed to persuade her to choose childbirth over abortion will be upheld if reasonably related to that goal. Regulations designed to foster the health of a woman seeking an abortion are valid if they do not constitute an undue burden . . . .

NOTES AND QUESTIONS:
Planned Parenthood of Southeastern Pennsylvania v. Casey

1. *Casey* replaces the trimester system of *Roe* with a framework that divides a pregnancy into only two segments. What are these two segments, and what rule applies to each segment?
2. How did the Court go from the trimester structure to the two-part structure? Did any of the elements in the trimester structure totally disappear? If so, which one was it?
3. What reasons motivated the Court's decision to scrap the trimester structure?
4. Discuss whether and why each of the following state laws is or is not constitutional, based on the reasoning in *Casey*:
   a. A law that bans the abortion of any third-trimester fetus
   b. A law that bans the abortion of any viable fetus
   c. A law that provides for various safety criteria that must be met by a clinic for all abortions that take place in its facilities
   d. A law that says that a woman can obtain an abortion from a willing doctor at any stage of her pregnancy
5. Assume that a state has passed a "Pregnant Woman Protection Act" providing that a pregnant woman under no circumstances had any duty to her fetus. Would such a law pass constitutional muster? How would it differ from

the law described in note 4(d)? What might a pregnant woman want to do that would endanger her fetus, apart from actually trying to abort it? (These questions will be revisited in chapter 6.)

6. In portions of the opinion not included here, the Court evaluated the specific mandates of the Pennsylvania statute and determined whether or not they imposed an undue burden on a woman's right to abortion. Among its conclusions:

a. The statute required the woman's physician, prior to performing an abortion, to "inform the woman of the nature of the procedure, the health risks of the abortion and of childbirth, and the 'probable gestational age of the unborn child.'" The physician also had to inform the woman of the availability of printed materials published by the state that described the fetus and discussed support available for mothers. The Court concluded that these requirements did not unduly burden the woman's right to get an abortion; given the "important interest in potential life," there is nothing wrong in a state's requiring a physician to give "truthful, nonmisleading information" to the woman:

> We would think it constitutional for the State to require that in order for there to be informed consent to a kidney transplant operation the recipient must be supplied with information about risks to the donor as well as risks to himself or herself . . . .
>
> Whatever constitutional status the doctor-patient relationship may have as a general matter, in the present context it is derivative of the woman's position. The doctor-patient relationship does not underlie or override the two more general rights under which the abortion right is justified: the right to make family decisions and the right to physical autonomy. On its own, the doctor-patient relationship is entitled to the same solicitude it receives in other contexts. . . .
>
> All that is left of petitioners' argument is an asserted First Amendment right of a physician not to provide information about the risks of abortion, and childbirth, in a manner mandated by the State. To be sure, the physician's First Amendment rights not to speak are implicated, but only as part of the practice of medicine, subject to reasonable licensing and regulation by the State. We see no constitutional infirmity in the requirement that the physician provide the information mandated by the State here.

b. Pennsylvania had imposed a 24-hour waiting period between the time the woman received the information and the time the abortion could take place. There was evidence that this would indeed be a burden to some women, who had to travel substantial distances to get to a doctor who performed abortions, since now they might have to make the trip twice. Nonetheless, the Court concluded that this did not constitute a sufficient burden so as to make the waiting period unconstitutional.

c. Pennsylvania required that the woman first notify her husband that she was getting an abortion. This notice requirement had a variety of exceptions, including where the woman "believes that notifying her husband will cause him or someone else to inflict bodily injury upon her." The court found that this requirement was indeed a constitutionally invalid undue burden, based upon evidence that many women are unwilling to report spousal abuse to state agencies.

   d. Pennsylvania required that an unemancipated woman under the age of 18 needed the consent of a parent or guardian in most circumstances. This requirement could be overridden if a judge determined that the woman was sufficiently mature. The Court found this requirement acceptable.

7. To what extent should a restriction on the information available to a woman be viewed as creating an undue (and thus unconstitutional) burden on the right to abortion? Consider the following possibilities:

   a. A state legislature, aware that a small but significant number of abortions are taking place because the parents want a child of the opposite sex, passes a law that prevents health care providers from revealing the sex of a fetus to the parents.

   b. A new prenatal blood test becomes available that detects certain types of genetically-caused homosexuality. The legislature again chooses to ban the use of such a test.

   c. The legislature is concerned about the large numbers of fetuses with Down's syndrome that are being aborted. It passes a law preventing health care providers from telling parents whether or not the fetus has Down's syndrome.

For a discussion of related issues, and citations to the literature, see the notes following Cloning in chapter 5.

Stenberg v. Carhart

Supreme Court of the United States

120 S.Ct. 2597 (2000)

OPINION BY JUSTICE BREYER:

We again consider the right to an abortion. We understand the controversial nature of the problem. Millions of Americans believe that life begins at conception and consequently that an abortion is akin to causing the death of an innocent child; they recoil at the thought of a law that would permit it. Other millions fear that a law that forbids abortion would condemn many American women to lives that lack dignity, depriving them of equal liberty and leading those with least resources to undergo illegal abortions with the attendant risks of death and suffering. Taking account of these virtually irreconcilable points of view, aware that constitutional law must govern a society whose different members sincerely hold directly opposing views, and considering the matter in light of the Constitution's guarantees of fundamental individual liberty, this Court, in the course of a generation, has determined and then predetermined that the Constitution offers basic protection to the woman's right to choose. We shall not revisit those legal principles. Rather, we apply them to the circumstances of this case.

Three established principles determine the issue before us. We shall set them forth in the language of the joint opinion in *Casey*. First, before "viability . . . the woman has a right to choose to terminate her pregnancy."

Second, "a law designed to further the State's interest in fetal life which imposes an undue burden on the woman's decision before fetal viability" is unconstitutional. An "undue burden is . . . shorthand for the conclusion that a state regulation has the purpose or effect of placing a substantial obstacle in the path of a woman seeking an abortion of a nonviable fetus."

Third, "'subsequent to viability, the State in promoting its interest in the potentiality of human life may, if it chooses, regulate, and even proscribe, abortion except where it is necessary, in appropriate medical judgment, for the preservation of the life or health of the mother.'"

We apply these principles to a Nebraska law banning "partial birth abortion." The statute reads as follows:

> "No partial birth abortion shall be performed in this state, unless such procedure is necessary to save the life of the mother whose life is endangered by a physical disorder, physical illness, or physical injury, including a life-endangering physical condition caused by or arising from the pregnancy itself." Neb. Rev. Stat. Ann. §28–328(1) (Supp. 1999)

The statute defines "partial birth abortion" as:

> "an abortion procedure in which the person performing the abortion partially delivers vaginally a living unborn child before killing the unborn child and completing the delivery." §28–326(9)

It further defines "partially delivers vaginally a living unborn child before killing the unborn child" to mean

> "deliberately and intentionally delivering into the vagina a living unborn child, or a substantial portion thereof, for the purpose of performing a procedure that the person performing such procedure knows will kill the unborn child and does kill the unborn child." . . .

Because Nebraska law seeks to ban one method of aborting a pregnancy, we must describe and then discuss several different abortion procedures. Considering the fact that those procedures seek to terminate a potential human life, our discussion may seem clinically cold or callous to some, perhaps horrifying to others. There is no alternative way, however, to acquaint the reader with the technical distinctions among different abortion methods and related factual matters, upon which the outcome of this case depends. For that reason, drawing upon the findings of the trial court, underlying testimony, and related medical texts, we shall describe the relevant methods of performing abortions in technical detail.

The evidence before the trial court, as supported or supplemented in the literature, indicates the following:

1. About 90% of all abortions performed in the United States take place during the first trimester of pregnancy, before 12 weeks of gestational age. During the first trimester, the predominant abortion method is "vacuum aspiration," which involves insertion of a vacuum tube (cannula) into the uterus to evacuate the contents. Such an abortion is typically performed on an outpatient basis under local anesthesia. Vacuum aspiration is considered particularly safe. The procedure's mortality rates for first trimester abortion are, for example, 5 to 10 times lower than those associated with carrying the fetus to term. Complication rates are also low. As the fetus grows in size, however, the vacuum aspiration method becomes increasingly difficult to use.

2. Approximately 10% of all abortions are performed during the second trimester of pregnancy (12 to 24 weeks). In the early 1970's, inducing labor through the injection of saline into the uterus was the predominant method of second trimester abortion. Today, however, the medical profession has switched from medical induction of labor to surgical procedures for most second trimester abortions. The most commonly used procedure is called "dilation and evacuation" (D&E). That procedure (together with a modified form of vacuum aspiration used in the early second trimester) accounts for about 95% of all abortions performed from 12 to 20 weeks of gestational age.

3. D&E "refers generically to transcervical procedures performed at 13 weeks gestation or later." The [American Medical Association] Report, adopted by the District Court, describes the process as follows.

Between 13 and 15 weeks of gestation:

> "D&E is similar to vacuum aspiration except that the cervix must be dilated more widely because surgical instruments are used to remove larger pieces of tissue. Osmotic dilators are usually used. Intravenous fluids and an analgesic or sedative may be administered. A local anesthetic such as a paracervical block may be administered, dilating agents, if used, are removed and instruments are inserted through the cervix into the uterus to removal fetal and placental tissue. Because fetal tissue is friable and easily broken, the fetus may not be removed intact. The walls of the uterus are scraped with a curette to ensure that no tissue remains."

After 15 weeks:

> "Because the fetus is larger at this stage of gestation (particularly the head), and because bones are more rigid, dismemberment or other destructive procedures are more likely to be required than at earlier gestational ages to remove fetal and placental tissue." . . .

There are variations in D&E operative strategy. However, the common points are that D&E involves (1) dilation of the cervix; (2) removal of at least some fetal tissue using nonvacuum instruments; and (3) (after the 15th week) the potential need for instrumental disarticulation or dismemberment of the fetus or the collapse of fetal parts to facilitate evacuation from the uterus.

4. When instrumental disarticulation incident to D&E is necessary, it typically occurs as the doctor pulls a portion of the fetus through the cervix into the birth canal. Dr. Carhart testified at trial as follows:

"Dr. Carhart: . . . 'The dismemberment occurs between the traction of . . . my instrument and the counter-traction of the internal os of the cervix . . . .

"Counsel: 'So the dismemberment occurs after you pulled a part of the fetus through the cervix, is that correct?

"Dr. Carhart: 'Exactly. Because you're using — The cervix has two strictures or two rings, the internal os and the external os . . . that's what's actually doing the dismembering. . . .

5. The D&E procedure carries certain risks. The use of instruments within the uterus creates a danger of accidental perforation and damage to neighboring organs. Sharp fetal bone fragments create similar dangers. And fetal tissue accidentally left behind can cause infection and various other complications. Nonetheless studies show that the risks of mortality and complication that accompany the D&E procedure between the 12th and 20th weeks of gestation are significantly lower than those accompanying induced labor procedures (the next safest midsecond trimester procedures).

6. At trial, Dr. Carhart and Dr. Stubblefield described a variation of the D&E procedure, which they referred to as an "intact D&E." Like other versions of the D&E technique, it begins with induced dilation of the cervix. The procedure then involves removing the fetus from the uterus through the cervix "intact," *i.e.*, in one pass, rather than in several passes. It is used after 16 weeks at the earliest, as vacuum aspiration becomes ineffective and the fetal skull becomes too large to pass through the cervix. The intact D&E proceeds in one of two ways, depending on the presentation of the fetus. If the fetus presents head first (a vertex presentation), the doctor collapses the skull; and the doctor then extracts the entire fetus through the cervix. If the fetus presents feet first (a breech presentation), the doctor pulls the fetal body through the cervix, collapses the skull, and extracts the fetus through the cervix. The breech extraction version of the intact D&E is also known commonly as "dilation and extraction," or D&X. . . .

8. The American College of Obstetricians and Gynecologists describes the D&X procedure in a manner corresponding to a breech-conversion intact D&E, including the following steps:

"1. deliberate dilatation of the cervix, usually over a sequence of days;

"2. instrumental conversion of the fetus to a footling breech;

"3. breech extraction of the body excepting the head; and

"4. partial evacuation of the intracranial contents of a living fetus to effect vaginal delivery of a dead but otherwise intact fetus."

Despite the technical differences we have just described, intact D&E and D&X are sufficiently similar for us to use the terms interchangeably.

9. Dr. Carhart testified he attempts to use the intact D&E procedure during weeks 16 to 20 because (1) it reduces the dangers from sharp bone fragments passing through the cervix, (2) minimizes the number of instrument passes needed for extraction and lessens the likelihood of uterine perforations caused by those instruments, (3) reduces the likelihood of leaving infection-causing fetal and placental tissue in the uterus, and (4) could help to prevent potentially fatal absorption of fetal tissue into the maternal circulation. The District Court made no findings about the D&X procedure's overall safety. The District Court concluded, however, that "the evidence is both clear and convincing that Carhart's D&X procedure is superior to, and safer than, the . . . other abortion procedures used during the relevant gestational period in the 10 to 20 cases a year that present to Dr. Carhart."

10. The materials presented at trial referred to the potential benefits of the D&X procedure in circumstances involving nonviable fetuses, such as fetuses with abnormal fluid accumulation in the brain (hydrocephaly). Others have emphasized its potential for women with prior uterine scars, or for women for whom induction of labor would be particularly dangerous.

11. There are no reliable data on the number of D&X abortions performed annually. Estimates have ranged between 640 and 5,000 per year.

II

The question before us is whether Nebraska's statute, making criminal the performance of a "partial birth abortion," violates the Federal Constitution, as interpreted in *Planned Parenthood of Southeastern Pa. v. Casey* and *Roe v. Wade*. We conclude that it does for at least two independent reasons. First, the law lacks any exception "'for the preservation of the . . . health of the mother.'" Second, it "imposes an undue burden on a woman's ability" to choose a D&E abortion, thereby unduly burdening the right to choose abortion itself. We shall discuss each of these reasons in turn.

A

The *Casey* joint opinion reiterated what the Court held in *Roe*; that "'subsequent to viability, the State in promoting its interest in the potentiality of human life may, if it chooses, regulate, and even proscribe, abortion *except where it is necessary, in appropriate medical judgment, for the preservation of the life or health of the mother.*'"

The fact that Nebraska's law applies both pre- and postviability aggravates the constitutional problem presented. The State's interest in regulating abortion previability is considerably weaker than postviability. Since the law requires a health exception in order to validate even a postviability abortion regulation, it at a minimum requires the same in respect to previability regulation.

The quoted standard also depends on the state regulations "promoting [the State's] interest in the potentiality of human life." The Nebraska law, of course, does not directly further an interest "in the potentiality of human life" by saving the fetus in question from destruction, as it regulates only a *method* of performing abortion. Nebraska describes its interests differently. It says the law "'shows concern for the life of the unborn,'" "prevents cruelty to partially born children," and "preserves the integrity of the medical profession." But we cannot see how the interest-related differences could make any difference to the question at hand, namely, the application of the "health" requirement.

Consequently, the governing standard requires an exception "where it is necessary, in appropriate medical judgment for the preservation of the life or health of the mother," *Casey*, for this Court has made clear that a State may promote but not endanger a woman's health when it regulates the methods of abortion. . . .

B

The Eighth Circuit found the Nebraska statute unconstitutional because, in *Casey*'s words, it has the "effect of placing a substantial obstacle in the path of a woman seeking an abortion of a nonviable fetus." It thereby places an "undue burden" upon a woman's right to terminate her pregnancy before viability. Nebraska does not deny that the statute imposes an "undue burden" *if* it applies to the more commonly used D&E procedure as well as to D&X. And we agree with the Eighth Circuit that it does so apply.

Our earlier discussion of the D&E procedure shows that it falls within the statutory prohibition. The statute forbids "deliberately and intentionally delivering into the vagina a living unborn child, or a substantial portion thereof, for the purpose of performing a procedure that the person performing such procedure knows will kill the unborn child." We do not understand how one could distinguish, using this language, between D&E (where a foot or arm is drawn through the cervix) and D&X (where the body up to the head is drawn through the cervix). Evidence before the trial court makes clear that D&E will often involve a physician pulling a "substantial portion" of a still living fetus, say, an arm or leg, into the vagina prior to the death of the fetus. Indeed D&E involves dismemberment that commonly occurs only when the fetus meets resistance that restricts the motion of the fetus: "The dismemberment occurs between the traction of . . . [the] instrument and the counter-traction of the internal os of the cervix." And these events often do not occur until after a portion of a living fetus has been pulled into the vagina.

Even if the statute's basic aim is to ban D&X, its language makes clear that it also covers a much broader category of procedures. The language does not track the medical differences between D&E and D&X—though it would have been a simple matter, for example, to provide an exception for the performance of D&E and other abortion procedures. Nor does the statute anywhere suggest that its application turns on whether a portion of the fetus' body is drawn into the vagina as part of a process to extract an intact fetus after collapsing the head as opposed to a process that would dismember the fetus. Thus, the dissenters' argument that the law was generally intended to bar D&X can be both correct and irrelevant. The relevant question is *not* whether the legislature wanted to ban D&X; it is whether the law was intended to apply *only* to D&X. The plain language covers both procedures. . . . Both procedures can involve the introduction of a "substantial portion" of a still living fetus, through the cervix, into the vagina—the very feature of an abortion that leads Justice Thomas to characterize such a procedure as involving "partial birth." . . .

In sum, using this law some present prosecutors and future Attorneys General may choose to pursue physicians who use D&E procedures, the most commonly used method for performing previability second trimester abortions. All those who perform abortion procedures using that method must fear prosecution, conviction, and imprisonment. The result is an undue burden upon a woman's right to make an abortion decision. We must consequently find the statute unconstitutional.

NOTES AND QUESTIONS:
Stenberg v. Carhart

1. The controversy about partial birth abortions was not solely related to the perhaps horrifying aspects of the procedure. The laws banning this procedure were unique in that they regulated the practice of medicine in a new manner: they told physicians how to perform a particular type of procedure. As we shall discuss in chapter 7, the law generally gives physicians, as members of a profession, a great deal of authority in setting their own legally binding standards for conducting themselves.
2. Presumably it was not an accident that the Nebraska law had an exception for the life of the mother, but not one for her health. Why do you think the law was written this way?
3. Justice Thomas, one of the dissenters in this 5–4 decision, argued that the "health exception" only applied where the pregnancy itself created a risk to the woman's health, and that this rule was irrelevant where the issue related to a risk created by the abortion procedure itself. Based on *Roe* and *Casey*, what do you think of this argument?
4. Nebraska raised a number of arguments as to why its law did not need an exception for the health of the woman. Provide a response to each of the following arguments:

a. The D&X procedure is rarely used.

b. The D&E procedure is always a safe alternative to that procedure.

5. Nebraska agreed with its opponents that if its law applied to the D&E procedure, then the law did indeed impose an "undue burden" on a woman's right to an abortion and would therefore be unconstitutional. Explain why this would be the case.

6. Discuss the constitutionality of each of the following state laws:

   a. A state law banning just the D&X procedure, when it is performed on a viable fetus. The law makes an exception for the life or health of the woman. (Should it matter whether or not another abortion procedure is legally available when the woman's life or health is not at risk? Assuming there is an alternative procedure, is it relevant that it creates a greater risk to the woman's health?)

   b. The same law, but modified to apply to all fetuses, viable or not.

7. Assume that Nebraska rewrote its law to specify that it applied only to the D&X procedure, and also added an exception for the health of the mother. Would that revised law be constitutional? What medical facts might you want to know?

Endnotes

1. See, e.g., Nicholas Wade, "Scientist Creates a Smarter Mouse," *New York Times,* 2 September 1999, A1.

2. This correspondence appears in the Commission's 1999 report on *Ethical Issues in Human Stem Cell Research.* That report, and other reports by the Commission, can be found in full text on the web at *bioethics.gov.* You can also order free printed copies at that site.

3. Recent scientific reports suggest that we may at some time in the near future be able to put chemicals together to "create life." The ethics of such an endeavor are discussed in Mildred K. Cho et al., "Ethical Considerations in Synthesizing a Minimal Genome," 286 *Science* 2087 (1999).

4. Robert Pear, "Led by Republicans, House Approves Bill Giving the Fetus Legal Protection," *New York Times,* 10 October 1999.

5. See, e.g., Mark Strasser, "Wrongful Life, Wrongful Birth, and the Right to Refuse Treatment: Can Reasonable Jurisdictions Recognize All But One?," 64 *Mo. L. Rev.* 29 (1999).

5

The Brave New World of Reproduction

The freedom to enter into private contracts is a foundation of American law. It is generally considered a good thing that people have great flexibility in structuring their arrangements with others. The ability to contractually bind ourselves, and to know that the courts will enforce those commitments, facilitates an enormous variety of useful transactions. The parties to contracts will usually directly benefit from such transactions voluntarily entered into. Indirectly, society will also generally benefit.

But there are limits to the freedom to contract. Even if the terms of a contract are beneficial to both parties, there may be "externalities," to use the economist's term: effects on others that need to be taken into account. If I am very unhappy with my next-door neighbor, I might contract with a hit man to have him executed. Having my neighbor disposed of could make me very happy, and the cash payment the hit man receives for doing the job would no doubt make him very happy. Presumably, my neighbor and the members of his family would be less than pleased. To protect the interests of persons who are not parties to the contract, society declares such a contract void and unenforceable.

Society may even intervene to protect the interests of one of the contracting parties. If I were dying of prostate cancer, I might hire that same hit man to end my own life. Such a contract would also be unenforceable: we are not permitted to consent to our own murders. One reason for this is that people often have "wrong" impulses, and society should protect them from those impulses. A separate reason may relate to protecting not the parties to this contract but society as a whole: a society in which people can actively end their lives may be a less meaningful society.

The debate about surrogate motherhood raises all of these issues squarely. It was first confronted in the *Baby M* case. Unlike cases in earlier chapters, here the concerns are less about limiting the power of a state government than about how the state should exercise its power to limit the ability of individuals to make private contracts about creating and raising children.

IN RE BABY M

Supreme Court of New Jersey

537 A.2d 1227 (N.J. 1988)

OPINION BY CHIEF JUSTICE WILENTZ:

. . . In February 1985, William Stern and Mary Beth Whitehead entered into a surrogacy contract. It recited that Stern's wife, Elizabeth, was infertile, that they wanted a child, and that Mrs. Whitehead was willing to provide that child as the mother with Mr. Stern as the father.

The contract provided that through artificial insemination using Mr. Stern's sperm, Mrs. Whitehead would become pregnant, carry the child to term, bear it, deliver it to the Sterns, and thereafter do whatever was necessary to terminate her maternal rights so that Mrs. Stern could thereafter adopt the child. Mrs. Whitehead's husband, Richard, was also a party to the contract; Mrs. Stern was not. Mr. Whitehead promised to do all acts necessary to rebut the presumption of paternity under the Parentage Act. Although Mrs. Stern was not a party to the surrogacy agreement, the contract gave her sole custody of the child in the event of Mr. Stern's death. Mrs. Stern's status as a nonparty to the surrogate parenting agreement presumably was to avoid the application of the baby-selling statute to this arrangement.

Mr. Stern, on his part, agreed to attempt the artificial insemination and to pay Mrs. Whitehead $10,000 after the child's birth, on its delivery to him. In a separate contract, Mr. Stern agreed to pay $7,500 to the Infertility Center of New York ("ICNY"). The Center's advertising campaigns solicit surrogate mothers and encourage infertile couples to consider surrogacy. ICNY arranged for the surrogacy contract by bringing the parties together, explaining the process to them, furnishing the contractual form, and providing legal counsel. . . .

The struggle over Baby M began when it became apparent that Mrs. Whitehead could not return the child to Mr. Stern. Due to Mrs. Whitehead's refusal to relinquish the baby, Mr. Stern filed a complaint seeking enforcement of the surrogacy contract. . . .

Invalidity and Unenforceability of Surrogacy Contract

We have concluded that this surrogacy contract is invalid. Our conclusion has two bases: direct conflict with existing statutes and conflict with the public policies of this State, as expressed in its statutory and decisional law.

One of the surrogacy contract's basic purposes, to achieve the adoption of a child through private placement, though permitted in New Jersey "is very much disfavored." Its use of money for this purpose— and we have no doubt whatsoever that the money is being paid to obtain an adoption and not, as the Sterns argue, for the personal services of Mary Beth Whitehead—is illegal and perhaps criminal. In addition to the inducement of money, there is the coercion of contract: the natural mother's irrevocable agreement, prior to birth, even prior to conception, to surrender the child to the adoptive couple. Such an agreement is totally unenforceable in private placement adoption. Even where the adoption is through an approved agency, the formal agreement to surrender occurs only after birth . . . , and then, by regulation, only after the birth mother has been offered counseling. Integral to these invalid provisions of the surrogacy contract is the related agreement, equally invalid, on the part of the natural mother to cooperate with, and not to contest, proceedings to terminate her parental rights, as well as her contractual concession, in aid of the adoption, that the child's best interests would be served by awarding custody to the natural father and his wife—all of this before she has even conceived, and, in some cases, before she has the slightest idea of what the natural father and adoptive mother are like.

The foregoing provisions not only directly conflict with New Jersey statutes, but also offend long-established State policies. These critical terms, which are at the heart of the contract, are invalid and unenforceable; the conclusion therefore follows, without more, that the entire contract is unenforceable.

A. CONFLICT WITH STATUTORY PROVISIONS

The surrogacy contract conflicts with: (1) laws prohibiting the use of money in connection with adoptions; (2) laws requiring proof of parental unfitness or abandonment before termination of parental rights is ordered or an adoption is granted; and (3) laws that make surrender of custody and consent to adoption revocable in private placement adoptions.

(1) Our law prohibits paying or accepting money in connection with any placement of a child for adoption. Violation is a high misdemeanor. Excepted are fees of an approved agency (which must be a non-profit entity) and certain expenses in connection with childbirth.

Considerable care was taken in this case to structure the surrogacy arrangement so as not to violate this prohibition. The arrangement was structured as follows: the adopting parent, Mrs. Stern, was not a party to the surrogacy contract; the money paid to Mrs. Whitehead was stated to be for her services—not for the adoption; the sole purpose of the contract was stated as being that "of giving a child to William Stern, its natural and biological father"; the money was purported to be "compensation for services and expenses and in no way . . . a fee for termination of parental rights or a payment in exchange for consent to surrender a child for adoption"; the fee to the Infertility Center ($7,500) was stated to be for legal representation, advice, administrative work, and other "services."

Nevertheless, it seems clear that the money was paid and accepted in connection with an adoption. . . .

Mr. Stern knew he was paying for the adoption of a child; Mrs. Whitehead knew she was accepting money so that a child might be adopted; the Infertility Center knew that it was being paid for assisting in the adoption of a child. The actions of all three worked to frustrate the goals of the statute. It strains credulity to claim that these arrangements, touted by those in the surrogacy business as an attractive alternative to the usual route leading to an adoption, really amount to something other than a private placement adoption for money.

The prohibition of our statute is strong. Violation constitutes a high misdemeanor, a third-degree crime, carrying a penalty of three to five years imprisonment. The evils inherent in baby-bartering are loathsome for a myriad of reasons. The child is sold without regard for whether the purchasers will be suitable parents. The natural mother does not receive the benefit of counseling and guidance to assist her in making a decision that may affect her for a lifetime. In fact, the monetary incentive to sell her child may, depending on her financial circumstances, make her decision less voluntary. Furthermore, the adoptive parents may not be fully informed of the natural parents' medical history.

Baby-selling potentially results in the exploitation of all parties involved. Conversely, adoption statutes seek to further humanitarian goals, foremost among them the best interests of the child. The negative consequences of baby-buying are potentially present in the surrogacy context, especially the potential for placing and adopting a child without regard to the interest of the child or the natural mother.

(2) The termination of Mrs. Whitehead's parental rights, called for by the surrogacy contract and actually ordered by the court, fails to comply with the stringent requirements of New Jersey law. Our law, recognizing the finality of any termination of parental rights, provides for such termination only where there has been a voluntary surrender of a child to an approved agency or to the Division of Youth and Family Services ("DYFS"), accompanied by a formal document acknowledging termination of parental rights, or where there has been a showing of parental abandonment or unfitness. A termination may ordinarily take one of three forms: an action by an approved agency, an action by DYFS, or an action in connection with a private placement adoption. The three are governed by separate statutes, but the standards for termination are substantially the same, except that whereas a written surrender is effective when made to an approved agency or to DYFS, there is no provision for it in the private placement context. . . .

(3) The provision in the surrogacy contract stating that Mary Beth Whitehead agrees to "surrender custody . . . and terminate all parental rights" contains no clause giving her a right to rescind. It is intended to be an irrevocable consent to surrender the child for adoption—in other words, an irrevocable commitment by Mrs. Whitehead to turn Baby M over to the Sterns and thereafter to allow termination of her parental rights. . . .

[That provision] conflicts with the settled interpretation of New Jersey statutory law. There is only one irrevocable consent, and that is the one explicitly provided for by statute: a consent to surrender of custody and a placement with an approved agency or with DYFS. [That provision] is one more indication of the essential nature of this transaction: the creation of a contractual system of termination and adoption designed to circumvent our statutes.

B. PUBLIC POLICY CONSIDERATIONS

The surrogacy contract's invalidity, resulting from its direct conflict with the above statutory provisions, is further underlined when its goals and means are measured against New Jersey's public policy. The contract's basic premise, that the natural parents can decide in advance of birth which one is to have custody of the child, bears no relationship to the settled law that the child's best interests shall determine custody. The fact that the trial court remedied that aspect of the contract through the "best interests" phase does not make the contractual provision any less offensive to the public policy of this State.

The surrogacy contract guarantees permanent separation of the child from one of its natural parents. Our policy, however, has long been that to the extent possible, children should remain with and be brought up by both of their natural parents. That was the first stated purpose of the previous adoption act. While not so stated in the present adoption law, this purpose remains part of the public policy of this State. This is not simply some theoretical ideal that in practice has no meaning. The impact of failure to follow that policy is nowhere better shown than in the results of this surrogacy contract. A child, instead of starting off its life with as much peace and security as possible, finds itself immediately in a tug-of-war between contending mother and father. . . .

Worst of all, however, is the contract's total disregard of the best interests of the child. There is not the slightest suggestion that any inquiry will be made at any time to determine the fitness of the Sterns as custodial parents, of Mrs. Stern as an adoptive parent, their superiority to Mrs. Whitehead, or the effect on the child of not living with her natural mother.

This is the sale of a child, or, at the very least, the sale of a mother's right to her child, the only mitigating factor being that one of the purchasers is the father. Almost every evil that prompted the prohibition on the payment of money in connection with adoptions exists here.

The differences between an adoption and a surrogacy contract should be noted, since it is asserted that the use of money in connection with surrogacy does not pose the risks found where money buys an adoption.

First, and perhaps most important, all parties concede that it is unlikely that surrogacy will survive without money. Despite the alleged selfless motivation of surrogate mothers, if there is no payment, there will be no surrogates, or very few. That conclusion contrasts with adoption; for obvious reasons, there remains a steady supply, albeit insufficient, despite the prohibitions against payment. The adoption itself, relieving the natural mother of the financial burden of supporting an infant, is in some sense the equivalent of payment.

Second, the use of money in adoptions does not produce the problem—conception occurs, and usually the birth itself, before illicit funds are offered. With surrogacy, the "problem," if one views it as such, consisting of the purchase of a woman's procreative capacity, at the risk of her life, is caused by and originates with the offer of money.

Third, with the law prohibiting the use of money in connection with adoptions, the built-in financial pressure of the unwanted pregnancy and the consequent support obligation do not lead the mother to the highest paying, ill-suited, adoptive parents. She is just as well-off surrendering the child to an approved agency. In surrogacy, the highest bidders will presumably become the adoptive parents regardless of suitability, so long as payment of money is permitted. . . .

The main difference, that the unwanted pregnancy is unintended while the situation of the surrogate mother is voluntary and intended, is really not significant. Initially, it produces stronger reactions of sympathy for the mother whose pregnancy was unwanted than for the surrogate mother, who "went into this with her eyes wide open." On reflection, however, it appears that the essential evil is the same, taking advantage of a woman's circumstances (the unwanted pregnancy or the need for money) in order to take away her child, the difference being one of degree.

In the scheme contemplated by the surrogacy contract in this case, a middle man, propelled by profit, promotes the sale. Whatever idealism may have motivated any of the participants, the profit motive predominates, permeates, and ultimately governs the transaction. The demand for children is great and the supply small. The availability of contraception, abortion, and the greater willingness of single mothers to bring up their children has led to a shortage of babies offered for adoption. The situation is ripe for the entry of the middleman who will bring some equilibrium into the market by increasing the supply through the use of money.

Intimated, but disputed, is the assertion that surrogacy will be used for the benefit of the rich at the expense of the poor. *See, e.g.*, Radin, "Market Inalienability," 100 *Harv. L. Rev.* 1849, 1930 (1987). In response it is noted that the Sterns are not rich and the Whiteheads not poor. Nevertheless, it is clear to us that it is unlikely that surrogate mothers will be as proportionately numerous among those women in the top twenty percent income bracket as among those in the bottom twenty percent. Put differently, we doubt that infertile couples in the low-income bracket will find upper income surrogates. . . .

The point is made that Mrs. Whitehead agreed to the surrogacy arrangement, supposedly fully understanding the consequences. Putting aside the issue of how compelling her need for money may have been, and how significant her understanding of the consequences, we suggest that her consent is irrelevant. There are, in a civilized society, some things that money cannot buy. In America, we decided long ago that merely because conduct purchased by money was "voluntary" did not mean that it was good or beyond regulation and prohibition. Employers can no longer buy labor at the lowest price they can bargain for, even though that labor is "voluntary," or buy women's labor for less money than paid to men for the same job, or purchase the agreement of children to perform oppressive labor, or purchase the agreement of workers to subject themselves to unsafe or unhealthful working conditions. There are, in short, values that society deems more important than granting to wealth whatever it can buy, be it labor, love, or life. Whether this principle recommends prohibition of surrogacy, which presumably sometimes results in great satisfaction to all of the parties, is not for us to say. We note here only that, under existing law, the fact that Mrs. Whitehead "agreed" to the arrangement is not dispositive.

The long-term effects of surrogacy contracts are not known, but feared— the impact on the child who learns her life was bought, that she is the offspring of someone who gave birth to her only to obtain money; the impact on the natural mother as the full weight of her isolation is felt along with the full reality of the sale of her body and her child; the impact on the natural father and adoptive mother once they realize the consequences of their conduct. Literature in related areas suggests these are substantial considerations, although, given the newness of surrogacy, there is little information.

The surrogacy contract is based on principles that are directly contrary to the objectives of our laws. It guarantees the separation of a child from its mother; it looks to adoption regardless of suitability; it totally ignores the child; it takes the child from the mother regardless of her wishes and her maternal fitness; and it does all of this, it accomplishes all of its goals, through the use of money.

Beyond that is the potential degradation of some women that may result from this arrangement. In many cases, of course, surrogacy may bring satisfaction, not only to the infertile couple, but to the surrogate mother herself. The fact, however, that many women may not perceive surrogacy negatively but rather see it as an opportunity does not diminish its potential for devastation to other women.

In sum, the harmful consequences of this surrogacy arrangement appear to us all too palpable. In New Jersey the surrogate mother's agreement to sell her child is void. Its irrevocability infects the entire contract, as does the money that purports to buy it. . . .

Constitutional Issues

Both parties argue that the Constitutions—state and federal—mandate approval of their basic claims. The source of their constitutional arguments is essentially the same: the right of privacy, the right to procreate, the right to the companionship of one's child, those rights flowing either directly from the fourteenth amendment or by its incorporation of the Bill of Rights, or from the ninth amendment, or through the penumbra surrounding all of the Bill of

Rights. They are the rights of personal intimacy, of marriage, of sex, of family, of procreation. Whatever their source, it is clear that they are fundamental rights protected by both the federal and state Constitutions. The right asserted by the Sterns is the right of procreation; that asserted by Mary Beth Whitehead is the right to the companionship of her child. We find that the right of procreation does not extend as far as claimed by the Sterns. As for the right asserted by Mrs. Whitehead, since we uphold it on other grounds (*i.e.*, we have restored her as mother and recognized her right, limited by the child's best interests, to her companionship), we need not decide that constitutional issue, and for reasons set forth below, we should not.

The right to procreate, as protected by the Constitution, has been ruled on directly only once by the United States Supreme Court. *See Skinner v. Oklahoma* (forced sterilization of habitual criminals violates equal protection clause of fourteenth amendment). Although *Griswold v. Connecticut* is obviously of a similar class, strictly speaking it involves the right not to procreate. The right to procreate very simply is the right to have natural children, whether through sexual intercourse or artificial insemination. It is no more than that. Mr. Stern has not been deprived of that right. Through artificial insemination of Mrs. Whitehead, Baby M is his child. The custody, care, companionship, and nurturing that follow birth are not parts of the right to procreation; they are rights that may also be constitutionally protected, but that involve many considerations other than the right of procreation. To assert that Mr. Stern's right of procreation gives him the right to the custody of Baby M would be to assert that Mrs. Whitehead's right of procreation does not give her the right to the custody of Baby M; it would be to assert that the constitutional right of procreation includes within it a constitutionally protected contractual right to destroy someone else's right of procreation.

We conclude that the right of procreation is best understood and protected if confined to its essentials, and that when dealing with rights concerning the resulting child, different interests come into play. There is nothing in our culture or society that even begins to suggest a fundamental right on the part of the father to the custody of the child as part of his right to procreate when opposed by the claim of the mother to the same child. We therefore disagree with the trial court: there is no constitutional basis whatsoever requiring that Mr. Stern's claim to the custody of Baby M be sustained. Our conclusion may thus be understood as illustrating that a person's rights of privacy and self-determination are qualified by the effect on innocent third persons of the exercise of those rights.

Mr. Stern also contends that he has been denied equal protection of the laws by the State's statute granting full parental rights to a husband in relation to the child produced, with his consent, by the union of his wife with a sperm donor. The claim really is that of Mrs. Stern. It is that she is in precisely the same position as the husband in the statute: she is presumably infertile, as is the husband in the statute; her spouse by agreement with a third party procreates with the understanding that the child will be the couple's child. The alleged unequal protection is that the understanding is honored in the statute when the husband is the infertile party, but no similar understanding is honored when it is the wife who is infertile.

It is quite obvious that the situations are not parallel. A sperm donor simply cannot be equated with a surrogate mother. The State has more than a sufficient basis to distinguish the two situations—even if the only difference is between the time it takes to provide sperm for artificial insemination and the time invested in a nine-month pregnancy—so as to justify automatically divesting the sperm donor of his parental rights without automatically divesting a surrogate mother. Some basis for an equal protection argument might exist if Mary Beth Whitehead had contributed her egg to be implanted, fertilized or otherwise, in Mrs. Stern, resulting in the latter's pregnancy. That is not the case here, however.

Mrs. Whitehead, on the other hand, asserts a claim that falls within the scope of a recognized fundamental interest protected by the Constitution. As a mother, she claims the right to the companionship of her child. This is a fundamental interest, constitutionally protected. Furthermore, it was taken away from her by the action of the court below. Whether that action under these circumstances would constitute a constitutional deprivation, however, we need not and do not decide. By virtue of our decision Mrs. Whitehead's constitutional complaint—that her parental rights have been unconstitutionally terminated—is moot. We have decided that both the statutes and public policy of this state require that that termination be voided and that her parental rights be restored. It therefore becomes unnecessary to decide whether that same result would be required by virtue of the federal or state Constitutions. Refraining from deciding such constitutional issues avoids further complexities involving the full extent of a parent's right of companionship, or questions involving the fourteenth amendment. . . .

Notes and Questions:
In re Baby M

1. What are the court's reasons for not enforcing the contract that the parties wrote?
2. Which of the court's reasons appear more compelling, and why: its arguments based on the New Jersey statutes, or those based on public policy?
3. Why did it matter to the Sterns that the contract was enforced? Which of their goals were dependent on the enforcement of the contract? Suppose, for example, that Mary Beth Whitehead had agreed, for the $10,000, merely to be artificially inseminated with Mr. Stern's sperm, but had not agreed to anything beyond that. What would have happened?
4. Note that the artificial insemination technique involved in this case need not require anything particularly high-tech. Indeed, all we are talking about is a way to get a man's sperm into the surrogate mother. This can easily be

done without any assistance by medical personnel. The man need merely produce sperm by masturbation, as is done in sperm donation, and the sperm can be placed into the surrogate's vagina by something as low-tech as a turkey baster.

Indeed, apart from possible ethical qualms (and a likely argument from the wife!), there is nothing to prevent this from taking place by the natural method. This tried and true technique going back to biblical times is still used, though one might wonder about the wisdom of the parties using it. For example, when Joe and Jean Kaplan had difficulty conceiving a child, they made an informal arrangement with family friend Susan Chamberlain to have her act as a surrogate mother. One of the women— there is some disagreement on who said what—suggested using the natural way to deliver the sperm, and that is what in fact took place—on a number of occasions.[1]

5. You might think that Mrs. Stern was not able to become pregnant. In fact, that was not the case. She—incorrectly—believed that because of a medical condition (multiple sclerosis), she might have been risking her health by having a child. She was actually mistaken about the medical facts. Assuming she was correct, however, does this change your view of the ethical aspects of what the Sterns were trying to accomplish? Does it matter how much of a risk to Mrs. Stern's health the pregnancy would have been?

6. Notice how a court decision will usually accomplish two things at once: it will settle the dispute between the parties, and it will also create a precedent to be (perhaps) followed by future cases. These distinct aspects of a court's decision may conflict. This court, for example, ended up granting custody of the child to Mr. Stern, on the ground that this was in the best interests of the child. Do you agree with that determination? Do you think this might encourage future couples to perhaps enter into similar contractual arrangements, on the theory that even if the contract is not enforced, they have a good chance of keeping the child if a best interests standard is applied? What might the court have done to the Sterns to discourage future couples? What might the legislature do?

7. The court is very concerned about the use of money in the surrogacy arrangement. Which of its complaints are specifically related to the use of money? Should it be willing to allow uncompensated surrogacy arrangements, such as where the sister of the infertile woman becomes the surrogate?

8. There is an extensive literature about what things (if any) a society should not allow to be sold: babies, human organs, the obligation to fight in a war, one's freedom. Of course, it is not always clear what constitutes the "impermissible" sale of something—what makes someone a slave rather than an employee in a very menial job? Nor is there agreement about what might be wrong about making a market in (the "commodification" of) such things.

One of the most famous law review articles ever written concerns the possible benefits from a market in newborn infants.[2] This fascinating article by Elizabeth Landes and Richard Posner is replete with extensive supply-and-demand diagrams and discussion of such issues as the fact that white babies are likely to bring higher prices in this market than non-white babies. (Some say that his co-authorship of this article is itself a significant reason why Posner, now a prominent federal judge and considered by many to possess one of this nation's greatest legal minds, will never be appointed to the Supreme Court.)

What problems does the *Baby M* court say are caused by baby-selling? Are the primary concerns harm to society in general, or harms to the child? Do you agree with the court's conclusions about those possible harms? Does this case really involve baby-selling?

9. In *Baby M* there is no dispute about the fact that William Stern is the father of the child. Why not? Is it obvious that he is the father? If so, why? To determine fatherhood, do we just look to genetics? Consider the following scenarios:

a. Tom regularly donates sperm to a sperm bank, and gets paid $50 per donation. A married couple uses this sperm in order to have a child. Should Tom be considered the legal father of that child?

b. Fred and Wilma have been trying unsuccessfully to have a child. Their doctor has determined Fred's sperm are not very good at swimming, and that Wilma's likelihood of becoming pregnant can be increased by directly inserting Fred's sperm deep into Wilma's uterus.

   On the day they go to the doctor's office to do this procedure, Fred is accompanied by his best friend, Barney, who covertly switches the vial of Fred's sperm with one containing his own sperm. (Barney and his wife Betty were themselves trying to have children, and they always admired Fred's tall and manly physique.) Barney goes home and impregnates Betty with Fred's sperm using the reliable turkey baster technique. Oddly enough, Betty becomes pregnant, in spite of the motility problem with Fred's sperm. Wilma also becomes pregnant.

   Assuming these facts become public at the time of the births of the two children, who should be considered the father of the child born to Wilma? Who should be considered the father of the child born to Betty?

Almost all states have statutes dealing with at least some aspects of the newer forms of reproductive technologies. Consider, for example, the following excerpt from the California Family Code (1999):

§ 7613 **Artificial Insemination**

(a) If, under the supervision of a licensed physician and surgeon and with the consent of her husband, a wife is inseminated artificially with semen donated by a man not her husband, the husband is treated in law as if he were the natural father of a child thereby conceived. The husband's consent must be in writing and signed by him and his wife. . . .

(b) The donor of semen provided to a licensed physician and surgeon for use in artificial insemination of a woman other than the donor's wife is treated in law as if he were not the natural father of a child thereby conceived.

Does this law help you resolve scenario (a)? (And what if the doctor had forgotten to get the husband's written consent?) How about scenario (b) (with regard to either of the children)?

Although there are a variety of state laws responding to these issues, they typically deal with only the most common scenarios such as the straightforward artificial insemination using a donor's sperm at a doctor's office. When the statute does not apply to the facts, there may be real uncertainty as to who the father is; a court may have to resolve the situation.

The National Conference of Commissioners on Uniform State Laws, which is comprised of more than 300 lawyers, judges, and law professors appointed by the states, attempts to draft model laws and then encourages states to adopt these laws, or variations of them, as their own. The California law excerpted above is a version of part of that group's Uniform Parentage Act. (This act will be discussed with the next case.) The Conference's Web site lists all the Uniform Laws, including changes over time and comments made by the drafters (*www.law.upenn.edu/bll/ulc/ulc_frame.htm*). In some areas, such as organ donation, there is notable uniformity among state laws precisely because virtually all states have adopted a version of the model law. That is not so with regard to parenthood, where there is still significant variety in state statutes. Nonetheless, examining the current version of a uniform law and the comments being discussed by the drafters can give you valuable insight into unresolved issues in that area of the law.

10. Do you agree with the court's analysis of the constitutional issues? Is there a constitutionally protected "right to procreate"? If there is, what is protected by that right? What do you think of the court's distinction between the right to procreate and the right to have contact with the resulting child? Does the former right have much importance if not linked to the latter right? (For more on the constitutional right to procreate, see the discussion of Cloning later in this chapter.)

11. Even if there is a constitutionally protected right to procreate, is it relevant to this case? Constitutional protections are usually limits on the actions of governments, not private persons. Does *Baby M* involve any laws restricting anyone's ability to procreate?

GESTATIONAL SURROGACY

The next case involves a type of reproductive technique different from what took place between the Sterns and Mary Beth Whitehead. "Gestational surrogacy" does require the use of relatively new medical technology. Here is how it is described by Justice Kennard, in her dissent in *Johnson v. Calvert*:

Recent advances in medical technology have dramatically expanded the means of human reproduction. Among the new technologies are in vitro fertilization, embryo and gamete freezing and storage, gamete intra-fallopian transfer, and embryo transplantation. Gestational surrogacy is the result of two of these techniques: in vitro fertilization and embryo transplantation.

In vitro fertilization or IVF is the fertilization of a human egg outside the human body in a laboratory. Children that have been conceived this way are often called "test tube babies," because their actual conception took place in a petri dish. The first live birth of a child conceived in vitro occurred in 1979 in Great Britain after 20 years of research by a British team.

To facilitate the retrieval or "harvesting" of eggs for in vitro fertilization, a woman ingests fertility hormones to induce "superovulation" or the production of multiple eggs. The eggs are then removed through aspiration, a nonsurgical technique, or through an invasive surgical procedure known as laparoscopy. (See generally *Developments in the Law: Medical Technology and the Law* (1990), 103 Harv. L. Rev. 1519, 1537-1542.) To undergo superovulation and egg retrieval is taxing, both physically and emotionally; the hormones used for superovulation produce bodily changes similar to those experienced in pregnancy, while the surgical removal of mature eggs has been likened to caesarian-section childbirth.

After removal, eggs are exposed to live sperm in a petri dish. If an egg is fertilized, the resulting zygote is allowed to divide and become multicellular before uterine implantation. The expense and low success rate of in vitro fertilization demonstrate just how much prospective parents are willing to endure to achieve biological parenthood.

Generally, an egg fertilized in vitro is implanted in the uterus of the woman who produced it. The technique, however, allows for embryo transplantation, which is the transfer of an embryo formed from one woman's egg to the uterus of another woman who will gestate the fetus to term. This can take place in at least three different situations: (1) a woman may donate an egg that, when fertilized, will be implanted in the uterus of a woman who intends to raise the child; (2) the woman who provides the egg may herself intend to raise the child carried to term by a gestational surrogate; or (3) a couple desiring a child may arrange for a surrogate to gestate an embryo produced from an egg and sperm, both donated (perhaps by close relatives of the couple).

In reading *Johnson v. Calvert*, you will note that, as in *Baby M*, there was a detailed contract that laid out what the parties intended to happen. And, as in the *Baby M* case, the surrogate mother again ended up wanting to keep the child, in violation of the terms of the contract. Yet, as you will now see, there is remarkably little discussion of the contract in this opinion. Why?

JOHNSON V. CALVERT
Supreme Court of California
851 P.2d 776 (Cal. 1993)

OPINION BY JUSTICE PANELLI:

In this case we address several of the legal questions raised by recent advances in reproductive technology. When, pursuant to a surrogacy agreement, a zygote formed of the gametes of a husband and wife is implanted in the uterus of another woman, who carries the resulting fetus to term and gives birth to a child not genetically related to her, who is the child's "natural mother" under California law? Does a determination that the wife is the child's natural mother work a deprivation of the gestating woman's constitutional rights? And is such an agreement barred by any public policy of this state?

We conclude that the husband and wife are the child's natural parents, and that this result does not offend the state or federal Constitution or public policy.

Facts

Mark and Crispina Calvert are a married couple who desired to have a child. Crispina was forced to undergo a hysterectomy in 1984. Her ovaries remained capable of producing eggs, however, and the couple eventually considered surrogacy. In 1989 Anna Johnson heard about Crispina's plight from a coworker and offered to serve as a surrogate for the Calverts.

On January 15, 1990, Mark, Crispina, and Anna signed a contract providing that an embryo created by the sperm of Mark and the egg of Crispina would be implanted in Anna and the child born would be taken into Mark and Crispina's home "as their child." Anna agreed she would relinquish "all parental rights" to the child in favor of Mark and Crispina. In return, Mark and Crispina would pay Anna $10,000 in a series of installments, the last to be paid six weeks after the child's birth. Mark and Crispina were also to pay for a $200,000 life insurance policy on Anna's life.

The zygote was implanted on January 19, 1990. Less than a month later, an ultrasound test confirmed Anna was pregnant.

Unfortunately, relations deteriorated between the two sides. . . .

In July 1990, Anna sent Mark and Crispina a letter demanding the balance of the payments due her or else she would refuse to give up the child. The following month, Mark and Crispina responded with a lawsuit, seeking a declaration they were the legal parents of the unborn child. Anna filed her own action to be declared the mother of the child, and the two cases were eventually consolidated. The parties agreed to an independent guardian ad litem for the purposes of the suit.

The child was born on September 19, 1990, and blood samples were obtained from both Anna and the child for analysis. The blood test results excluded Anna as the genetic mother. The parties agreed to a court order providing that the child would remain with Mark and Crispina on a temporary basis with visits by Anna.

At trial in October 1990, the parties stipulated that Mark and Crispina were the child's genetic parents. After hearing evidence and arguments, the trial court ruled that Mark and Crispina were the child's "genetic, biological and natural" father and mother, that Anna had no "parental" rights to the child, and that the surrogacy contract was legal and enforceable against Anna's claims. The court also terminated the order allowing visitation. Anna appealed from the trial court's judgment. The Court of Appeal for the Fourth District, Division Three, affirmed. We granted review.

Discussion

DETERMINING MATERNITY UNDER THE UNIFORM PARENTAGE ACT

The Uniform Parentage Act (the Act) was part of a package of legislation introduced in 1975 as Senate Bill No. 347. The legislation's purpose was to eliminate the legal distinction between legitimate and illegitimate children. The Act followed in the wake of certain United States Supreme Court decisions mandating equal treatment of legitimate and illegitimate children. . . .

Civil Code sections 7001 and 7002 replace the distinction between legitimate and illegitimate children with the concept of the "parent and child relationship." The "parent and child relationship" means "the legal relationship existing between a child and his natural or adoptive parents incident to which the law confers or imposes rights, privileges, duties, and obligations. It includes the mother and child relationship and the father and child relationship." . . . The "parent and child relationship" is thus a legal relationship encompassing two kinds of parents, "natural" and "adoptive."

Passage of the Act clearly was not motivated by the need to resolve surrogacy disputes, which were virtually unknown in 1975. Yet it facially applies to any parentage determination, including the rare case in which a child's maternity is in issue. We are invited to disregard the Act and decide this case according to other criteria, including constitutional precepts and our sense of the demands of public policy. We feel constrained, however, to decline the invitation. . . .

These contentions are readily summarized. Anna, of course, predicates her claim of maternity on the fact that she gave birth to the child. The Calverts contend that Crispina's genetic relationship to the child establishes that she is his mother. Counsel for the minor joins in that contention and argues, in addition, that several of the presumptions created by the Act dictate the same result. As will appear, we conclude that presentation of blood test evidence is one means of establishing maternity, as is proof of having given birth, but that the presumptions cited by minor's counsel do not apply to this case.

We turn to those few provisions of the Act directly addressing the determination of maternity. "Any interested party," presumably including a genetic mother, "may bring an action to determine the existence . . . of a mother and child relationship." Civil Code section 7003 provides, in relevant part, that between a child and the natural mother a parent and child relationship "may be established by proof of her having given birth to the child, or under [the Act]." Apart from Civil Code section 7003, the Act sets forth no specific means by which a natural mother can establish a parent and child relationship. However, it declares that, insofar as practicable, provisions applicable to the father and child relationship apply in an action to determine the existence or nonexistence of a mother and child relationship. Thus, it is appropriate to examine those provisions as well. . . .

Significantly for this case, Evidence Code section 892 provides that blood testing may be ordered in an action when paternity is a relevant fact. When maternity is disputed, genetic evidence derived from blood testing is likewise admissible. The Evidence Code further provides that if the court finds the conclusions of all the experts, as disclosed by the evidence based on the blood tests, are that the alleged father is not the father of the child, the question of paternity is resolved accordingly. By parity of reasoning, blood testing may also be dispositive of the question of maternity. Further, there is a rebuttable presumption of paternity (hence, maternity as well) on the finding of a certain number of genetic markers.

Disregarding the presumptions of paternity that have no application to this case, then, we are left with the undisputed evidence that Anna, not Crispina, gave birth to the child and that Crispina, not Anna, is genetically related to him. Both women thus have adduced evidence of a mother and child relationship as contemplated by the Act. Yet for any child California law recognizes only one natural mother, despite advances in reproductive technology rendering a different outcome biologically possible.

We see no clear legislative preference in Civil Code section 7003 as between blood testing evidence and proof of having given birth. "May" indicates that proof of having given birth is a permitted method of establishing a mother and child relationship, although perhaps not the exclusive one. The disjunctive "or" indicates that blood test evidence, as prescribed in the Act, constitutes an alternative to proof of having given birth. It may be that the language of the Act merely reflects "the ancient dictum *mater est quam [gestatio] demonstrat* (by gestation the mother is demonstrated). This phrase, by its use of the word 'demonstrated,' has always reflected an ambiguity in the meaning of the presumption. It is arguable that, while gestation may demonstrate maternal status, it is not the sine qua non of motherhood. Rather, it is possible that the common law viewed genetic consanguinity as the basis for maternal rights. Under this latter interpretation, gestation simply would be irrefutable evidence of the more fundamental genetic relationship." This ambiguity, highlighted by the problems arising from the use of artificial reproductive techniques, is nowhere explicitly resolved in the Act.

Because two women each have presented acceptable proof of maternity, we do not believe this case can be decided without enquiring into the parties' intentions as manifested in the surrogacy agreement. Mark and Crispina are a couple who desired to have a child of their own genes but are physically unable to do so without the help of reproductive technology. They affirmatively intended the birth of the child, and took the steps necessary to effect in vitro fertilization. But for their acted-on intention, the child would not exist.

Anna agreed to facilitate the procreation of Mark's and Crispina's child. The parties' aim was to bring Mark's and Crispina's child into the world, not for Mark and Crispina to donate a zygote to Anna. Crispina from the outset intended to be the child's mother. Although the gestative function Anna performed was necessary to bring about the child's birth, it is safe to say that Anna would not have been given the opportunity to gestate or deliver the child had she, prior to implantation of the zygote, manifested her own intent to be the child's mother. No reason appears why Anna's later change of heart should vitiate the determination that Crispina is the child's natural mother.

We conclude that although the Act recognizes both genetic consanguinity and giving birth as means of establishing a mother and child relationship, when the two means do not coincide in one woman, she who intended to procreate the child—that is, she who intended to bring about the birth of a child that she intended to raise as her own—is the natural mother under California law. . . .

In deciding the issue of maternity under the Act we have felt free to take into account the parties' intentions, as expressed in the surrogacy contract, because in our view the agreement is not, on its face, inconsistent with public policy. . . .

Anna urges that surrogacy contracts violate several social policies. Relying on her contention that she is the child's legal, natural mother, she cites the public policy embodied in Penal Code section 273, prohibiting the payment for consent to adoption of a child. She argues further that the policies underlying the adoption laws of this state are violated by the surrogacy contract because it in effect constitutes a prebirth waiver of her parental rights.

We disagree. Gestational surrogacy differs in crucial respects from adoption and so is not subject to the adoption statutes. The parties voluntarily agreed to participate in in vitro fertilization and related medical procedures before the child was conceived; at the time when Anna entered into the contract, therefore, she was not vulnerable to financial inducements to part with her own expected offspring. As discussed above, Anna was not the genetic mother of the child. The payments to Anna under the contract were meant to compensate her for her services in gestating the fetus and undergoing labor, rather than for giving up "parental" rights to the child. Payments were due both during the pregnancy and after the child's birth. We are, accordingly, unpersuaded that the contract used in this case violates the public policies embodied in Penal Code section 273 and the adoption statutes. For the same reasons, we conclude these contracts do not implicate the policies underlying the statutes governing termination of parental rights.

It has been suggested that gestational surrogacy may run afoul of prohibitions on involuntary servitude. Involuntary servitude has been recognized in cases of criminal punishment for refusal to work. We see no potential for that evil in the contract at issue here, and extrinsic evidence of coercion or duress is utterly lacking. We note that although at one point the contract purports to give Mark and Crispina the sole right to determine whether to abort the pregnancy, at another point it acknowledges: "All parties understand that a pregnant woman has the absolute right to abort or not abort any fetus she is carrying. Any promise to the contrary is unenforceable." We therefore need not determine the validity of a surrogacy contract purporting to deprive the gestator of her freedom to terminate the pregnancy.

Finally, Anna and some commentators have expressed concern that surrogacy contracts tend to exploit or dehumanize women, especially women of lower economic status. Anna's objections center around the psychological harm she asserts may result from the gestator's relinquishing the child to whom she has given birth. Some have also cautioned that the practice of surrogacy may encourage society to view children as commodities, subject to trade at their parents' will.

We are all too aware that the proper forum for resolution of this issue is the Legislature, where empirical data, largely lacking from this record, can be studied and rules of general applicability developed. However, in light of our responsibility to decide this case, we have considered as best we can its possible consequences.

We are unpersuaded that gestational surrogacy arrangements are so likely to cause the untoward results Anna cites as to demand their invalidation on public policy grounds. Although common sense suggests that women of lesser means serve as surrogate mothers more often than do wealthy women, there has been no proof that surrogacy contracts exploit poor women to any greater degree than economic necessity in general exploits them by inducing them to accept lower-paid or otherwise undesirable employment. We are likewise unpersuaded by the claim that surrogacy will foster the attitude that children are mere commodities; no evidence is offered to support it. The limited data available seem to reflect an absence of significant adverse effects of surrogacy on all participants.

The argument that a woman cannot knowingly and intelligently agree to gestate and deliver a baby for intending parents carries overtones of the reasoning that for centuries prevented women from attaining equal economic rights and professional status under the law. To resurrect this view is both to foreclose a personal and economic choice on the part of the surrogate mother, and to deny intending parents what may be their only means of procreating a child of their own genes. Certainly in the present case it cannot seriously be argued that Anna, a licensed vocational nurse who had done well in school and who had previously borne a child, lacked the intellectual wherewithal or life experience necessary to make an informed decision to enter into the surrogacy contract.

CONSTITUTIONALITY OF THE DETERMINATION THAT
ANNA JOHNSON IS NOT THE NATURAL MOTHER

Anna argues at length that her right to the continued companionship of the child is protected under the federal Constitution. . . .

. . . [N]either Anna nor amicus curiae ACLU articulates a claim under the equal protection clause, and we are unable to discern in these facts the necessary predicate to its operation. This is because a woman who voluntarily agrees to gestate and deliver for a married couple a child who is their genetic offspring is situated differently from the wife who provides the ovum for fertilization, intending to mother the resulting child.

Anna relies mainly on theories of substantive due process, privacy, and procreative freedom, citing a number of decisions recognizing the fundamental liberty interest of natural parents in the custody and care of their children. Most of the cases Anna cites deal with the rights of unwed fathers in the face of attempts to terminate their parental relationship to their children. These cases do not support recognition of parental rights for a gestational surrogate. Although Anna quotes language stressing the primacy of a developed parent-child relationship in assessing unwed fathers' rights, certain language in the cases reinforces the importance of genetic parents' rights. (*Lehr v. Robertson* ["The significance of the biological connection is that it offers the natural father an opportunity that no other male possesses to develop a relationship with his offspring. If he grasps that opportunity and accepts some measure of responsibility for the child's future, he may enjoy the blessings of the parent-child relationship and make uniquely valuable contributions to the child's development."])

Anna's argument depends on a prior determination that she is indeed the child's mother. Since Crispina is the child's mother under California law because she, not Anna, provided the ovum for the in vitro fertilization procedure, intending to raise the child as her own, it follows that any constitutional interests Anna possesses in this situation are something less than those of a mother. As counsel for the minor points out, the issue in this case is not whether Anna's asserted rights as a natural mother were unconstitutionally violated, but rather whether the determination that she is not the legal natural mother at all is constitutional.

Anna relies principally on the decision of the United States Supreme Court in *Michael H. v. Gerald D.* to support her claim to a constitutionally protected liberty interest in the companionship of the child, based on her status as "birth mother." In that case, a plurality of the court held that a state may constitutionally deny a man parental rights with respect to a child he fathered during a liaison with the wife of another man, since it is the marital family that traditionally has been accorded a protected liberty interest, as reflected in the historic presumption of legitimacy of a child born into such a family. The reasoning of the plurality in *Michael H.* does not assist Anna. Society has not traditionally protected the right of a woman who gestates and delivers a baby pursuant to an agreement with a couple who supply the zygote from which the baby develops and who intend to raise the child as their own; such arrangements are of too recent an origin to claim the protection of tradition. To the extent that tradition has a bearing on the present case, we believe it supports the claim of the couple who exercise their right to procreate in order to form a family of their own, albeit through novel medical procedures. Moreover, if we were to conclude that Anna enjoys some sort of liberty interest in the companionship of the child, then the liberty interests of Mark and Crispina, the child's natural parents, in their procreative choices and their relationship with the child would perforce be infringed. Any parental rights Anna might successfully assert could come only at Crispina's expense. As we have seen, Anna has no parental rights to the child under California law, and she fails to persuade us that sufficiently strong policy reasons exist to accord her a protected liberty interest in the companionship of the child when such an interest would necessarily detract from or impair the parental bond enjoyed by Mark and Crispina.

CONCURRING OPINION BY JUSTICE ARABIAN:

I concur in the decision to find under the Uniform Parentage Act that Crispina Calvert is the natural mother of the child she at all times intended to parent and raise as her own with her husband Mark, the child's natural father. That determination answers the question on which this court granted review, and in my view sufficiently resolves the controversy between the parties to warrant no further analysis. I therefore decline to subscribe to the dictum in which the majority find surrogacy contracts "not . . . inconsistent with public policy." . . .

DISSENTING OPINION BY JUSTICE KENNARD:

When a woman who wants to have a child provides her fertilized ovum to another woman who carries it through pregnancy and gives birth to a child, who is the child's legal mother? Unlike the majority, I do not agree that the determinative consideration should be the intent to have the child that originated with the woman who contributed the ovum. In my view, the woman who provided the fertilized ovum and the woman who gave birth to the child both have substantial claims to legal motherhood. Pregnancy entails a unique commitment, both psychological and emotional, to an unborn child. No less substantial, however, is the contribution of the woman from whose egg the child developed and without whose desire the child would not exist.

For each child, California law accords the legal rights and responsibilities of parenthood to only one "natural mother." When, as here, the female reproductive role is divided between two women, California law requires courts to make a decision as to which woman is the child's natural mother, but provides no standards by which to make that decision. The majority's resort to "intent" to break the "tie" between the genetic and gestational mothers is unsupported by statute, and, in the absence of appropriate protections in the law to guard against abuse of surrogacy arrangements, it is ill-advised. To determine who is the legal mother of a child born of a gestational surrogacy arrangement, I would apply the standard most protective of child welfare— the best interests of the child. . . .

IV. Policy Considerations

The ethical, moral and legal implications of using gestational surrogacy for human reproduction have engendered substantial debate. A review of the scholarly literature that addresses gestational surrogacy reveals little consensus on the desirability of surrogacy arrangements, particularly those involving paid surrogacy, or on how best to decide questions of the parentage of children born of such arrangements.

Surrogacy proponents generally contend that gestational surrogacy, like the other reproductive technologies that extend the ability to procreate to persons who might not otherwise be able to have children, enhances "individual freedom, fulfillment and responsibility." Under this view, women capable of bearing children should be allowed to freely agree to be paid to do so by infertile couples desiring to form a family. The "surrogate mother" is expected "to weigh the prospective investment in her birthing labor" before entering into the arrangement, and, if her "autonomous reproductive decision" is "voluntary," she should be held responsible for it so as "to fulfill the expectations of the other parties . . . ."

One constitutional law scholar argues that the use of techniques such as gestational surrogacy is constitutionally protected and should be restricted only on a showing of a compelling state interest. Professor Robertson reasons that procreation is itself protected under decisions of the United States Supreme Court that affirm the basic civil right to marry and raise children. From this premise, he argues that the right to procreate should extend to persons who cannot conceive or bear children. . . .

Surrogacy critics, however, maintain that the payment of money for the gestation and relinquishment of a child threatens the economic exploitation of poor women who may be induced to engage in commercial surrogacy arrangements out of financial need. Some fear the development of a "breeder" class of poor women who will be regularly employed to bear children for the economically advantaged. Others suggest that women who enter into surrogacy arrangements may underestimate the psychological impact of relinquishing a child they have nurtured in their bodies for nine months.

Gestational surrogacy is also said to be "dehumanizing" and to "commodify" women and children by treating the female reproductive capacity and the children born of gestational surrogacy arrangements as products that can be bought and sold. The commodification of women and children, it is feared, will reinforce oppressive gender stereotypes and threaten the well-being of all children. Some critics foresee promotion of an ever-expanding "business of surrogacy brokerage."

Whether surrogacy contracts are viewed as personal service agreements or agreements for the sale of the child born as the result of the agreement, commentators critical of contractual surrogacy view these contracts as contrary to public policy and thus not enforceable. . . .

Proponents and critics of gestational surrogacy propose widely differing approaches for deciding who should be the legal mother of a child born of a gestational surrogacy arrangement. Surrogacy advocates propose to enforce pre-conception contracts in which gestational mothers have agreed to relinquish parental rights, and, thus, would make "bargained-for intentions determinative of legal parenthood." Professor Robertson, for instance, contends that "The right to noncoital, collaborative reproduction also includes the right of the parties to agree how they should allocate their obligations and entitlements with respect to the child. Legal presumptions of paternity and maternity would be overridden by this agreement of the parties."

Surrogacy critics, on the other hand, consider the unique female role in human reproduction as the determinative factor in questions of legal parentage. They reason that although males and females both contribute genetic material for the child, the act of gestating the fetus falls only on the female. Accordingly, in their view, a woman who, as the result of gestational surrogacy, is not genetically related to the child she bears is like any other woman who gives birth to a child. In either situation the woman giving birth is the child's mother. Under this approach, the laws governing adoption should govern the parental rights to a child born of gestational surrogacy. Upon the birth of the child, the gestational mother can decide whether or not to relinquish her parental rights in favor of the genetic mother. . . .

VII. Analysis of the Majority's "Intent" Test

. . . [I]n making the intent of the genetic mother who wants to have a child the dispositive factor, the majority renders a certain result preordained and inflexible in every such case: as between an intending genetic mother and a gestational mother, the genetic mother will, under the majority's analysis, always prevail. The majority recognizes no meaningful contribution by a woman who agrees to carry a fetus to term for the genetic mother beyond that of mere employment to perform a specified biological function.

The majority's approach entirely devalues the substantial claims of motherhood by a gestational mother such as Anna. True, a woman who enters into a surrogacy arrangement intending to raise the child has by her intent manifested an assumption of parental responsibility in addition to her biological contribution of providing the genetic material. But the gestational mother's biological contribution of carrying a child for nine months and giving birth is likewise an assumption of parental responsibility. A pregnant woman's commitment to the unborn child she carries is not just physical; it is psychological and emotional as well. The United States Supreme Court made a closely related point in *Lehr v.*

Robertson (1983), explaining that a father's assertion of parental rights depended on his having assumed responsibility for the child after its birth, whereas a mother's "parental relationship is clear" because she "carries and bears the child." . . . A pregnant woman intending to bring a child into the world is more than a mere container or breeding animal; she is a conscious agent of creation no less than the genetic mother, and her humanity is implicated on a deep level. Her role should not be devalued.

I find the majority's reliance on "intent" unsatisfactory for yet another reason. By making intent determinative of parental rights to a child born of a gestational surrogacy arrangement, the majority would permit enforcement of a gestational surrogacy agreement without requiring any of the protections that would be afforded by the Uniform Status of Children of Assisted Conception Act. Under that act, the granting of parental rights to a couple that initiates a gestational surrogacy arrangement would be conditioned upon compliance with the legislation's other provisions. They include court oversight of the gestational surrogacy arrangement before conception, legal counsel for the woman who agrees to gestate the child, a showing of need for the surrogacy, medical and mental health evaluations, and a requirement that all parties meet the standards of fitness of adoptive parents. . . .

VIII. The Best Interests of the Child

As I have discussed, in California the existing statutory law applicable to this case is the UPA, which was never designed to govern the new reproductive technology of gestational surrogacy. Under the UPA, both the genetic mother and the gestational mother have an equal right to be the child's natural mother. But the UPA allows one natural mother for each child, and thus this court is required to make a choice. To break this "tie" between the genetic mother and the gestational mother, the majority uses the legal concept of intent. In so doing, the majority has articulated a rationale for using the concept of intent that is grounded in principles of tort, intellectual property and commercial contract law.

But, as I have pointed out, we are not deciding a case involving the commission of a tort, the ownership of intellectual property, or the delivery of goods under a commercial contract; we are deciding the fate of a child. In the absence of legislation that is designed to address the unique problems of gestational surrogacy, this court should look not to tort, property or contract law, but to family law, as the governing paradigm and source of a rule of decision.

The allocation of parental rights and responsibilities necessarily impacts the welfare of a minor child. And in issues of child welfare, the standard that courts frequently apply is the best interests of the child. Indeed, it is highly significant that the UPA itself looks to a child's best interests in deciding another question of parental rights. This "best interests" standard serves to assure that in the judicial resolution of disputes affecting a child's well-being, protection of the minor child is the foremost consideration. Consequently, I would apply "the best interests of the child" standard to determine who can best assume the social and legal responsibilities of motherhood for a child born of a gestational surrogacy arrangement.

The determination of a child's best interests does not depend on the parties' relative economic circumstances, which in a gestational surrogacy situation will usually favor the genetic mother and her spouse. As this court has recognized, however, superior wealth does not necessarily equate with good parenting.

Factors that are pertinent to good parenting, and thus that are in a child's best interests, include the ability to nurture the child physically and psychologically, and to provide ethical and intellectual guidance. Also crucial to a child's best interests is the "well recognized right" of every child "to stability and continuity." The intent of the genetic mother to procreate a child is certainly relevant to the question of the child's best interests; alone, however, it should not be dispositive.

Here, the child born of the gestational surrogacy arrangement between Anna Johnson and Mark and Crispina Calvert has lived continuously with Mark and Crispina since his birth in September 1990. The trial court awarded parental rights to Mark and Crispina, concluding that as a matter of law they were the child's "genetic, biological and natural" parents. In reaching that conclusion, the trial court did not treat Anna's statutory claim to be the child's legal mother as equal to Crispina's, nor did the trial court consider the child's best interests in deciding between those two equal statutory claims. Accordingly, I would remand the matter to the trial court to undertake that evaluation. . . .

NOTES AND QUESTIONS:
Johnson v. Calvert

1. What were the terms of the contract that was signed by the parties to this case?
2. Which of the goals of the Calverts, as stated in that contract, were accomplished as a result of the court's decision?
3. Why does most of this court's opinion (and even the dissenter's comments) not even mention the contract? Would the outcome have changed if there had been no contractual agreement regarding parental rights? (Assume, for example, that when Anna had been told about the arrangement, she had not agreed about who would get custody of the child, but instead said they should all talk about that after the child was born, and the Calverts agreed to that arrangement.) Note that the court would still have to determine who is the child's legal mother.
4. Recalling the *Baby M* case, could the Sterns have done what was done in this case? Should they have?
5. Assuming that all of the participants in this case lived in New Jersey, and this case was argued in a New Jersey court after the *Baby M* decision, what do you think the outcome would have been? Why?

6. The majority opinion indicates that the contract was not inconsistent with public policy. Do you agree? In any event, does it matter in terms of the resolution of the case whether the contract was consistent with public policy? What do you think about the views of Justice Arabian, who concurs with the majority opinion, yet criticizes the comments about what California's public policy is?

7. The American Civil Liberties Union argued in this case in favor of concluding that the child has two mothers. What do you think of that as a resolution? You should revisit this "two parent" idea after reading the next case, *Michael H. v. Gerald D.*

8. What do you think of Justice Kennard's criticisms of the majority's "intent" test?

9. If we apply an "intent" test to resolve the question of who is the mother, how different is that from saying that we are enforcing the contract? In spite of the lack of language about enforcing the contract, did the majority opinion end up enforcing the contract? (What was your answer to the question posed in note 3?)

10. A later California case, *In re Marriage of Buzzanca*, 72 Cal. Rptr. 2d 280 (Cal. Ct. App. 1998), added a permutation to this line of cases. The appellate court said:

> Jaycee was born because Luanne and John Buzzanca agreed to have an embryo genetically unrelated to either of them implanted in a woman—a surrogate—who would carry and give birth to the child for them. After the fertilization, implantation and pregnancy, Luanne and John split up, and the question of who are Jaycee's lawful parents came before the trial court.
>
> Luanne claimed that she and her erstwhile husband were the lawful parents, but John disclaimed any responsibility, financial or otherwise. The woman who gave birth also appeared in the case to make it clear that she made no claim to the child.
>
> The trial court then reached an extraordinary conclusion: Jaycee had no lawful parents. First, the woman who gave birth to Jaycee was not the mother; the court had—astonishingly—already accepted a stipulation that neither she nor her husband were the "biological" parents. Second, Luanne was not the mother. According to the trial court, she could not be the mother because she had neither contributed the egg nor given birth. And John could not be the father, because, not having contributed the sperm, he had no biological relationship with the child.
>
> We disagree. Let us get right to the point: Jaycee never would have been born had not Luanne and John both agreed to have a fertilized egg implanted in a surrogate.
>
> The trial judge erred because he assumed that legal motherhood, under the relevant California statutes, could only be established in one of two ways, either by giving birth or by contributing an egg. He failed to consider the substantial and well-settled body of law holding that there are times when fatherhood can be established by conduct apart from giving birth or being genetically related to a child. The typical example is when an infertile husband consents to allowing his wife to be artificially inseminated. As our Supreme Court noted in

such a situation over 30 years ago, the husband is the "lawful father" because he consented to the procreation of the child.

The same rule which makes a husband the lawful father of a child born because of his consent to artificial insemination should be applied here—by the same parity of reasoning that guided our Supreme Court in the first surrogacy case, *Johnson v. Calvert*—to both husband and wife. Just as a husband is deemed to be the lawful father of a child unrelated to him when his wife gives birth after artificial insemination, so should a husband and wife be deemed the lawful parents of a child after a surrogate bears a biologically unrelated child on their behalf. In each instance, a child is procreated because a medical procedure was initiated and consented to by intended parents. The only difference is that in this case—unlike artificial insemination—there is no reason to distinguish between husband and wife. We therefore must reverse the trial court's judgment and direct that a new judgment be entered, declaring that both Luanne and John are the lawful parents of Jaycee.

Do you agree with this court's analysis? Certainly, the lower court was wrong in concluding that John was not the legal father. As discussed in the notes after the *Baby M* case, it is common for states to pass laws stating that sperm donors are never to be considered the fathers of the resulting children, and that the "intended" father is to be recognized as the father. This analysis should no doubt apply in a standard egg donation, where a woman desiring to be a mother but who cannot supply her own eggs becomes impregnated with an egg supplied by an anonymous donor.

Those are not the facts of the *Buzzanca* case. In *Johnson v. Calvert*, even accepting the correctness of the intent test, it was applied to break a tie where each of two women had biological grounds for claiming their motherhood. Does a similar situation exist with regard to Luanne, the mother "by intent," compared to the woman who gestated the child? Is Luanne's intent doing double duty here?

11. As the following case will indirectly suggest, the Constitution imposes few constraints on state surrogacy laws. There is accordingly great diversity in state surrogacy arrangements, both "traditional" (as in *Baby M*) and gestational (as in *Johnson v. Calvert*). This diversity relates not only to whether such agreements are enforceable, but also to who will be considered the parent. (This issue is discussed further in the Cloning section of this chapter.) Nonetheless, the recent announcement by 52-year-old supermodel Cheryl Tiegs that she and her husband will have twins using a gestational surrogate may indicate the growing acceptability of these arrangements.[3]

PARENTHOOD AND THE UNITED STATES CONSTITUTION

Both *Baby M* and *Johnson v. Calvert* touch on the relevance of the United States Constitution to surrogacy arrangements. As we have seen, the right to privacy announced in *Griswold* would seem to have some bearing on issues relating to determining who is a parent. The right to privacy has been interpreted to embody a variety of rights that go far beyond the concept of being left alone, and to specifically protect relationships centering on reproductive rights. Certainly, if the Constitutional right to privacy impinges on the ability of a state to control a person's right to contraceptives or to an abortion, it should say something about the fundamental purpose of the reproductive process: producing and raising a child.

In fact, the Supreme Court has spoken on this issue in an opinion discussed briefly by both the majority and the dissent in *Johnson v. Calvert*. The case of *Michael H. v. Gerald D.* had very little to do with surrogacy per se. In fact, it sprang from a rather mundane situation of infidelity. Nonetheless, because of the unusual California law that was at issue, the Supreme Court had to address very complex issues regarding the role of genetics in determining parenthood.

The Court's conclusions in this case remain controversial. The opinion, however, is over a decade old, and no Supreme Court rulings since have cast any doubt on it. Indeed, the most surprising thing about this case, given its enormous importance, is how little public attention it has gotten. While significant segments of the public are very familiar with *Baby M* and with *Johnson v. Calvert*, *Michael H.* is largely unheard of outside the legal profession.

MICHAEL H. V. GERALD D.

Supreme Court of the United States

491 U.S. 110 (1989)

OPINION BY JUSTICE SCALIA:

. . . The facts of this case are, we must hope, extraordinary. On May 9, 1976, in Las Vegas, Nevada, Carole D., an international model, and Gerald D., a top executive in a French oil company, were married. The couple established a home in Playa del Rey, California, in which they resided as husband and wife when one or the other was not out of the country on business. In the summer of 1978, Carole became involved in an adulterous affair with a neighbor, Michael H. In September 1980, she conceived a child, Victoria D., who was born on May 11, 1981. Gerald was listed as father on the birth certificate and has always held Victoria out to the world as his daughter. Soon after delivery of the child, however, Carole informed Michael that she believed he might be the father.

In the first three years of her life, Victoria remained always with Carole, but found herself within a variety of quasifamily units. In October 1981, Gerald moved to New York City to pursue his business interests, but Carole chose to remain in California. At the end of that month, Carole and Michael had blood tests of themselves and Victoria, which showed a 98.07% probability that Michael was Victoria's father. In January 1982, Carole visited Michael in St.

Thomas, where his primary business interests were based. There Michael held Victoria out as his child. In March, however, Carole left Michael and returned to California, where she took up residence with yet another man, Scott K. Later that spring, and again in the summer, Carole and Victoria spent time with Gerald in New York City, as well as on vacation in Europe. In the fall, they returned to Scott in California.

In November 1982, rebuffed in his attempts to visit Victoria, Michael filed a filiation action in California Superior Court to establish his paternity and right to visitation. In March 1983, the court appointed an attorney and guardian ad litem to represent Victoria's interests. Victoria then filed a cross-complaint asserting that if she had more than one psychological or *de facto* father, she was entitled to maintain her filial relationship, with all of the attendant rights, duties, and obligations, with both. In May 1983, Carole filed a motion for summary judgment. During this period, from March through July 1983, Carole was again living with Gerald in New York. In August, however, she returned to California, became involved once again with Michael, and instructed her attorneys to remove the summary judgment motion from the calendar.

For the ensuing eight months, when Michael was not in St. Thomas he lived with Carole and Victoria in Carole's apartment in Los Angeles and held Victoria out as his daughter. In April 1984, Carole and Michael signed a stipulation that Michael was Victoria's natural father. Carole left Michael the next month, however, and instructed her attorneys not to file the stipulation. In June 1984, Carole reconciled with Gerald and joined him in New York, where they now live with Victoria and two other children since born into the marriage.

In May 1984, Michael and Victoria, through her guardian ad litem, sought visitation rights for Michael *pendente lite* ["while the litigation is taking place"]. To assist in determining whether visitation would be in Victoria's best interests, the Superior Court appointed a psychologist to evaluate Victoria, Gerald, Michael, and Carole. The psychologist recommended that Carole retain sole custody, but that Michael be allowed continued contact with Victoria pursuant to a restricted visitation schedule. The court concurred and ordered that Michael be provided with limited visitation privileges *pendente lite*.

On October 19, 1984, Gerald, who had intervened in the action, moved for summary judgment on the ground that under Cal. Evid. Code § 621 there were no triable issues of fact as to Victoria's paternity. This law provides that "the issue of a wife cohabiting with her husband, who is not impotent or sterile, is conclusively presumed to be a child of the marriage." The presumption may be rebutted by blood tests, but only if a motion for such tests is made, within two years from the date of the child's birth, either by the husband or, if the natural father has filed an affidavit acknowledging paternity, by the wife.

On January 28, 1985, having found that affidavits submitted by Carole and Gerald sufficed to demonstrate that the two were cohabiting at conception and birth and that Gerald was neither sterile nor impotent, the Superior Court granted Gerald's motion for summary judgment, rejecting Michael's and Victoria's challenges to the constitutionality of § 621. The court also denied their motions for continued visitation pending the appeal . . . [finding] that allowing such visitation would "violat[e] the intention of the Legislature by impugning the integrity of the family unit." . . .

We address first the claims of Michael. At the outset, it is necessary to clarify what he sought and what he was denied. California law, like nature itself, makes no provision for dual fatherhood. Michael was seeking to be declared *the* father of Victoria. The immediate benefit he evidently sought to obtain from that status was visitation rights. But if Michael were successful in being declared the father, other rights would follow—most importantly, the right to be considered as the parent who should have custody, a status which "embrace[s] the sum of parental rights with respect to the rearing of a child, including the child's care; the right to the child's services and earnings; the right to direct the child's activities; the right to make decisions regarding the control, education, and health of the child; and the right, as well as the duty, to prepare the child for additional obligations, which includes the teaching of moral standards, religious beliefs, and elements of good citizenship." All parental rights, including visitation, were automatically denied by denying Michael status as the father. . . .

Michael contends as a matter of substantive due process that, because he has established a parental relationship with Victoria, protection of Gerald's and Carole's marital union is an insufficient state interest to support termination of that relationship. This argument is, of course, predicated on the assertion that Michael has a constitutionally protected liberty interest in his relationship with Victoria. It is an established part of our constitutional jurisprudence that the term "liberty" in the Due Process Clause extends beyond freedom from physical restraint. Without that core textual meaning as a limitation, defining the scope of the Due Process Clause "has at times been a treacherous field for this Court," giving "reason for concern lest the only limits to . . . judicial intervention become the predilections of those who happen at the time to be Members of this Court." . . . In an attempt to limit and guide interpretation of the Clause, we have insisted not merely that the interest denominated as a "liberty" be "fundamental" (a concept that, in isolation, is hard to objectify), but also that it be an interest traditionally protected by our society. As we have put it, the Due Process Clause affords only those protections "so rooted in the traditions and conscience of our people as to be ranked as fundamental." Our cases reflect "continual insistence upon respect for the teachings of history [and] solid recognition of the basic values that underlie our society . . . ." *Griswold v. Connecticut.*

This insistence that the asserted liberty interest be rooted in history and tradition is evident, as elsewhere, in our cases according constitutional protection to certain parental rights. Michael reads the landmark case of *Stanley v. Illinois* and the subsequent cases of *Quilloin v. Walcott*, *Caban v. Mohammed*, and *Lehr v. Robertson* as establishing that a liberty interest is created by biological fatherhood plus an established parental relationship—factors that exist in the present case as well. We think that distorts the rationale of those cases. As we view them, they rest not upon such isolated factors but upon the historic respect—indeed, sanctity would not be too strong a term—traditionally accorded to the relationships that develop within the unitary family. In *Stanley*, for example, we forbade the destruction of such a family when, upon the death of the mother, the State had sought to remove children from the custody of a father who had lived with and supported them and their mother for 18 years. As Justice Powell stated for the plurality in *Moore v. East Cleveland*: "Our decisions establish that the Constitution protects the sanctity of the family precisely because the institution of the family is deeply rooted in this Nation's history and tradition."

Thus, the legal issue in the present case reduces to whether the relationship between persons in the situation of Michael and Victoria has been treated as a protected family unit under the historic practices of our society, or whether on any other basis it has been accorded special protection. We think it impossible to find that it has. In fact, quite to the contrary, our traditions have protected the marital family (Gerald, Carole, and the child they acknowledge to be theirs) against the sort of claim Michael asserts.

The presumption of legitimacy was a fundamental principle of the common law. Traditionally, that presumption could be rebutted only by proof that a husband was incapable of procreation or had had no access to his wife during the relevant period. As explained by Blackstone, nonaccess could only be proved "if the husband be out of the kingdom of England . . . for above nine months . . . ." And, under the common law both in England and here, "neither husband nor wife [could] be a witness to prove access or nonaccess." The primary policy rationale underlying the common law's severe restrictions on rebuttal of the presumption appears to have been an aversion to declaring children illegitimate, thereby depriving them of rights of inheritance and succession, and likely making them wards of the state. A secondary policy concern was the interest in promoting the "peace and tranquillity of States and families," a goal that is obviously impaired by facilitating suits against husband and wife asserting that their children are illegitimate. Even though, as bastardy laws became less harsh, "[j]udges in both [England and the United States] gradually widened the acceptable range of evidence that could be offered by spouses, and placed restraints on the 'four seas rule' . . . [,] the law retained a strong bias against ruling the children of married women illegitimate."

We have found nothing in the older sources, nor in the older cases, addressing specifically the power of the natural father to assert parental rights over a child born into a woman's existing marriage with another man. Since it is Michael's burden to establish that such a power (at least where the natural father has established a relationship with the child) is so deeply embedded within our traditions as to be a fundamental right, the lack of evidence alone might defeat his case. But the evidence shows that even in modern times—when, as we have noted, the rigid protection of the marital family has in other respects been relaxed—the ability of a person in Michael's position to claim paternity has not been generally acknowledged. . . .

. . . What Michael asserts here is a right to have himself declared the natural father and thereby to obtain parental prerogatives. What he must establish, therefore, is not that our society has traditionally allowed a natural father in his circumstances to establish paternity, but that it has traditionally accorded such a father parental rights, or at least has not traditionally denied them. Even if the law in all States had always been that the entire world could challenge the marital presumption and obtain a declaration as to who was the natural father, that would not advance Michael's claim. Thus, it is ultimately irrelevant, even for purposes of determining current social attitudes towards the alleged substantive right Michael asserts, that the present law in a number of States appears to allow the natural father—including the natural father who has not established a relationship with the child—the theoretical power to rebut the marital presumption. What counts is whether the States in fact award substantive parental rights to the natural father of a child conceived within, and born into, an extant marital union that wishes to embrace the child. We are not aware of a single case, old or new, that has done so. This is not the stuff of which fundamental rights qualifying as liberty interests are made. . . .

It is a question of legislative policy and not constitutional law whether California will allow the presumed parenthood of a couple desiring to retain a child conceived within and born into their marriage to be rebutted.

We do not accept Justice Brennan's criticism that this result "squashes" the liberty that consists of "the freedom not to conform." It seems to us that reflects the erroneous view that there is only one side to this controversy—that one disposition can expand a "liberty" of sorts without contracting an equivalent "liberty" on the other side. Such a happy choice is rarely available. Here, to *provide* protection to an adulterous natural father is to *deny* protection to a marital father, and vice versa. If Michael has a "freedom not to conform" (whatever that means), Gerald must equivalently have a "freedom to conform." One of them will pay a price for asserting that "freedom"—Michael by being unable to act as father of the child he has adulterously begotten, or Gerald by being unable to preserve the integrity of the traditional family unit he and Victoria have established. Our disposition does not choose between these two "freedoms," but leaves that to the people of California. Justice Brennan's approach chooses one of them as the constitutional imperative, on no apparent basis except that the unconventional is to be preferred.

IV

We have never had occasion to decide whether a child has a liberty interest, symmetrical with that of her parent, in maintaining her filial relationship. We need not do so here because, even assuming that such a right exists, Victoria's claim must fail. Victoria's due process challenge is, if anything, weaker than Michael's. Her basic claim is not that California has erred in preventing her from establishing that Michael, not Gerald, should stand as her legal father. Rather, she claims a due process right to maintain filial relationships with both Michael and Gerald. This assertion merits little discussion, for, whatever the merits of the guardian ad litem's belief that such an arrangement can be of great psychological benefit to a child, the claim that a State must recognize multiple fatherhood has no support in the history or traditions of this country. Moreover, even if we were to construe Victoria's argument as forwarding the lesser proposition that, whatever her status vis-a-vis Gerald, she has a liberty interest in maintaining a filial relationship with her natural father, Michael, we find that, at best, her claim is the obverse of Michael's and fails for the same reasons. . . .

NOTES AND QUESTIONS:
Michael H. v. Gerald D.

1. The opinion by Justice Scalia is unusual in that it is a plurality opinion. Since there are nine members of the Supreme Court voting on most cases, normally there will be a majority opinion, meaning that at least five Justices agree with what is said in that opinion (presumably, the person who wrote the opinion, with four or more others). In this case, only three Justices concurred in Scalia's opinion—Rehnquist, O'Connor and Kennedy, and the latter two even disagreed with a footnote in the opinion (discussed below in item 7).

   Justice Stevens provided the fifth and deciding vote, but he concurred "in the judgment" only. In other words, he agreed that Michael should lose, but not for the reasons stated in Scalia's opinion. Stevens felt that Michael might indeed have a constitutionally protected interest in having a relationship with his biological daughter. He felt, however, that such an interest was adequately protected by the California laws, since a provision of those laws allowed a judge to grant visitation rights not only to parents, but to "any other person having an interest in the welfare of the child." None of the other Justices accepted this interpretation of the California law.

   Justice Brennan wrote a dissenting opinion, in which Justices Marshall and Blackmun joined, and which is discussed below. Justice White wrote a separate dissenting opinion, in which Justice Brennan joined.

2. Wife cheats on husband, has a child with her lover, who then wishes to be involved in raising that child. What, exactly, does Justice Scalia believe to be "extraordinary" about the facts of this case?

3. The evidentiary rules at issue in this case came into being at a time when there were no reliable scientific tests for fatherhood. Thus, instead of having a legal battle between two candidates for fatherhood, with no way of resolving that battle in a very conclusive way, state laws often opted just to assume that the husband of the mother was the father. At a minimum, this prevented legal fights that might disrupt families, and in addition it had a decent chance of producing the right outcome, since often the father might indeed be the husband.

4. In determining whether or not a particular law is constitutional, it is often crucial to determine the legislature's purpose in passing the law. A possible purpose of this statute was to diminish family discord resulting from paternity suits when there was no way to definitively resolve those lawsuits. Given current reliable tests of paternity, why did the Court not merely de-

termine that the law violated the due process rights of fathers? In a pre-genetic testing world, it made sense to have a procedure that arbitrarily designates one person as the father. Once there are reliable genetic tests, the continued use of such an "arbitrary" procedure would certainly seem constitutionally suspect—at least, if the purpose of the statute was to determine the genetic father. (Indeed, after the *Michael H.* case, California did somewhat broaden its evidentiary rules to allow the Michaels of the world greater ability to demonstrate their parenthood.)

5. The Court bypasses such arguments by restating the purpose of the California statute: California is not trying to figure out who the genetic father is; it doesn't care. Rather, the legislature was allegedly saying that regardless of who the genetic father is, the husband should be treated as the father under the law, because by doing so the integrity of families will be preserved. Indeed, the importance of the outcome in *Michael H.* is precisely that in evaluating the acceptability of this purpose, the plurality has to decide whether or not Michael did have a fundamental liberty interest in maintaining a relationship with his daughter.

Do you think the Court was correct in its description of the purpose of the California law? Given the history of such statutes, is it likely that the California legislature (or any other legislature) had specifically determined that men in Michael's situation were uniformly to be denied contact with their children?

6. Do you agree with the plurality's conclusions about Michael's liberty interest? Do you think that the right of a father to have a relationship with his biological offspring is less fundamental than other rights that have been determined to be fundamental? (Recall *Eisenstadt v. Baird.*)

7. Perhaps whether an interest is "fundamental" depends on whether you phrase it in a general or a specific way. Consider Justice Brennan's comments in his dissent (491 U.S. at 139-42):

> Today's plurality, however, does not ask whether parenthood is an interest that historically has received our attention and protection; the answer to that question is too clear for dispute. Instead, the plurality asks whether the specific variety of parenthood under consideration—a natural father's relationship with a child whose mother is married to another man—has enjoyed such protection.
>
> If we had looked to tradition with such specificity in past cases, many a decision would have reached a different result. Surely the use of contraceptives by unmarried couples, *Eisenstadt v. Baird* (1972), or even by married couples, *Griswold v. Connecticut* (1965); the freedom from corporal punishment in schools, *Ingraham v. Wright* (1977); the freedom from an arbitrary transfer from a prison to a psychiatric institution, *Vitek v. Jones* (1980); and even the right to raise one's natural but illegitimate children, *Stanley v. Illinois* (1972), were not "interest[s] traditionally protected by our society," at the time of their consideration by this Court. If we had asked, therefore, in *Eisenstadt, Griswold, Ingraham, Vitek,* or *Stanley* itself whether the specific interest under consideration had been traditionally protected, the answer would have been a resounding "no." That we did not ask this question in those cases high-

lights the novelty of the interpretive method that the plurality opinion employs today.

The plurality's interpretive method is more than novel; it is misguided. It ignores the good reasons for limiting the role of "tradition" in interpreting the Constitution's deliberately capacious language. In the plurality's constitutional universe, we may not take notice of the fact that the original reasons for the conclusive presumption of paternity are out of place in a world in which blood tests can prove virtually beyond a shadow of a doubt who sired a particular child and in which the fact of illegitimacy no longer plays the burdensome and stigmatizing role it once did. Nor, in the plurality's world, may we deny "tradition" its full scope by pointing out that the rationale for the conventional rule has changed over the years, as has the rationale for [the California rule of evidence]; instead, our task is simply to identify a rule denying the asserted interest and not to ask whether the basis for that rule—which is the true reflection of the values undergirding it—has changed too often or too recently to call the rule embodying that rationale a "tradition." Moreover, by describing the decisive question as whether Michael's and Victoria's interest is one that has been "traditionally *protected by* our society," rather than one that society traditionally has thought important (with or without protecting it), and by suggesting that our sole function is to "*discern* the society's views," the plurality acts as if the only purpose of the Due Process Clause is to confirm the importance of interests already protected by a majority of the States. Transforming the protection afforded by the Due Process Clause into a redundancy mocks those who, with care and purpose, wrote the Fourteenth Amendment. . . .

Thus, to describe the issue in this case as whether the relationship existing between Michael and Victoria "has been treated as a protected family unit under the historic practices of our society, or whether on any other basis it has been accorded special protection," is to reinvent the wheel. The better approach—indeed, the one commanded by our prior cases and by common sense—is to ask whether the specific parent-child relationship under consideration is close enough to the interests that we already have protected to be deemed an aspect of "liberty" as well. On the facts before us, therefore, the question is not what "level of generality" should be used to describe the relationship between Michael and Victoria, see *ante*, n. 6, but whether the relationship under consideration is sufficiently substantial to qualify as a liberty interest under our prior cases.

Justice Scalia responded to these criticisms in footnote 6 of his opinion, which reads, in part:

We do not understand why, having rejected our focus upon the societal tradition regarding the natural father's rights vis-a-vis a child whose mother is married to another man, Justice Brennan would choose to focus instead upon "parenthood." Why should the relevant category not be even more general—perhaps "family relationships"; or "personal relationships"; or even "emotional attachments in general"? Though the dissent has no basis for the level of generality it would select, we do: We refer to the most specific level at which a relevant tradition protecting, or denying protection to, the asserted right can be identified. If, for example, there were no societal tradition, either way, regarding the rights of the natural father of a child adulterously conceived, we would have to consult, and (if possible) reason from, the traditions regarding natural fathers in general. But there is such a more specific tradition, and it unqualifiedly denies protection to such a parent.

8. What would have happened if the Supreme Court had instead determined that Michael did have a fundamental interest in a relationship with his child? Would that have resolved the case? What other issues would then have to be discussed to determine the outcome?

9. Assume that California passed another statute: "The issue resulting from intercourse between an unmarried woman and a married man shall conclusively be presumed to be a child of the married man and his wife." Assume that the California legislature stated as its purpose the desire that children be raised in family units, where possible. Would this statute be constitutional, based on the reasoning of the plurality in *Michael H.*?

10. If you found the statute given in note 9 to be unconstitutional, does that mean that there was perhaps an equal protection problem with the original statute? Can a state deny men the right to have a relationship with their out-of-wedlock children, yet provide such a right to women? What arguments might justify this distinction? Would a state have to have an especially important purpose in mind to make this difference constitutionally permissible? (Determine what category of equal protection review would take place, based on what the Supreme Court says in *Michael H.*) Michael in fact tried to raise an equal protection argument before the Supreme Court, but because that argument was not made in the lower court proceedings, the Supreme Court did not address it.

11. Does the outcome in the *Michael H.* case tell you anything about the scope of the discretion that states have in passing laws that deal with surrogacy issues, such as those raised in the *Baby M* and *Johnson v. Calvert* cases? What role is the United States Constitution likely to play in controlling the nature of such laws?

CLONING

In February of 1997, it was announced that scientist Ian Wilmut had cloned a sheep. The technique he used needs to be distinguished from an older and very different technique known as "embryo splitting" or "twinning." Imagine that a human sperm fertilizes a human egg, and the resulting fertilized egg begins to divide. For the first few divisions, all of the cells are essentially identical. Thus, if you took the fertilized egg when it was in the two-cell stage (i.e., after one division), and split the cells apart, each one could theoretically continue to divide on its own and become a separate embryo. Indeed, this is exactly what happens naturally when identical twins are created. The two resulting individuals are genetically identical. It has been somewhat difficult to duplicate this process in the laboratory. The main purpose for this endeavor would be to increase the number of embryos available to implant in a woman undergoing infertility treatment.

What Dr. Wilmut did in creating the sheep named Dolly was very different, both in its science and in its effect. He took a non-reproductive cell from an adult sheep (called a "somatic" cell), and in effect took its nucleus, with the genetic instructions contained in the DNA, and inserted it into an egg cell of a different sheep from which the nucleus had been removed. He then was able to stimulate the resulting cell and get it to begin dividing. The eventual result of those divisions, after implanting this cell in a sheep's uterus, was Dolly. Dolly was nearly genetically identical to the original adult sheep whose nucleus had been removed. (Almost, but not quite, since the power plants of a cell, the mitochondria, contain their own DNA, and are not formed by the instructions contained in the nuclear DNA.) Wilmut's technique is known as "somatic cell nuclear transfer." It results in a delayed twin: Dolly is a newborn sheep, whereas the sheep from which she was cloned was already an adult. This is very different from the result of the embryo-splitting technique, which creates a clone of an embryo, with the two resulting animals the same age.

After the announcement of Dolly's creation, President Clinton asked the National Bioethics Advisory Commission, a group which advised him on bioethics matters, to study the cloning issue. Its report determined, among other things, that it would be "morally unacceptable" to attempt to create a human being using Wilmut's technique, either for research purposes or to help someone have a child.[4] The major reason for this conclusion was the unknown risks to the child, since the technique was new and had not yet been used on human cells. Accordingly, the Commission recommended that federal legislation be enacted to prevent anyone from attempting to do this for at least the next several years. While a number of bills were introduced on this subject, no single bill has yet won a majority, so there is not yet a ban. President Clinton did implement a ban on using federal funding for purposes of human cloning research, since that did not require legislation.

As an aid to its deliberations, the Commission asked experts to produce background papers. What follows is a brief excerpt from the executive summary portion of a paper discussing legal issues raised by cloning.[5]

THE CURRENT AND FUTURE
LEGAL STATUS OF CLONING
By Lori B. Andrews

B. CONSTITUTIONAL CONCERNS

If the federal government chooses to regulate or even ban cloning, that action might be challenged on a number of constitutional grounds—as not being justified under the commerce clause, as violating scientists' First Amendment freedom of inquiry, or as violating a couple's or individual's constitutional right of privacy or liberty to make reproductive decisions.

1. Reach of the Commerce Clause

Congress has the power to regulate interstate commerce, but states maintain the power to regulate intrastate activities that have little impact on interstate commerce. In 1995, [in *U.S. v. Lopez*, 514 U.S. 549,] the U.S. Supreme Court held, for the first time in almost 60 years, that Congress had adopted legislation that exceeded its authority under the commerce clause. The facts at issue in that case, however, are distinguishable from the case of cloning. In that case, Congress had banned the possession of a firearm within 1,000 feet of a schoolyard. The U.S. Supreme Court held that the law was not a proper exercise of federal power because the activity at issue did not affect interstate commerce, interfered with a traditional state activity (education), and had already been addressed by state laws in most states. There is much more leeway for the federal government to regulate cloning. It is likely that some of the equipment or materials used in the cloning procedure will have moved in interstate commerce, some of the individuals seeking cloning services will have traveled interstate to obtain those services, some funding will have come from out of state, some of the personnel may have been hired from out of state, and some of the researchers may attend related conferences and classes out of state. Moreover, if the federal government were to adopt a law on cloning, Congress could address the commerce clause concerns in the legislative history, which it failed to do in connection with the firearm ban at issue in *Lopez*. Congress' power to regulate cloning under the commerce clause would include a power to ban it.

2. Right to Scientific Inquiry

Certain commentators have speculated that there might be a right of scientific inquiry protected by the First Amendment right to free speech. If the First Amendment protects a marketplace of ideas, it seems likely it would protect the generation of information that would be included in that marketplace. The U.S. Supreme Court has not directly addressed the right of scientific inquiry, but a lower federal court has suggested . . . that scholars have a "right . . . to do research and advance the state of man's knowledge." Other federal courts, however, have refused to recognize a First Amendment right of scientific inquiry. And even if the First Amendment were found to be applicable to scientific inquiry, there is widespread agreement that the method of research could be regulated to prevent harms.

3. Right to Make Reproductive Decisions

The right to make decisions about whether to bear children is constitutionally protected under the constitutional right to privacy and the constitutional right to liberty. The U.S. Supreme Court in 1992 reaffirmed the "recognized protection accorded to liberty relating to intimate relationships, the family, and decisions about whether to bear and beget a child." Early decisions protected married couples' right to privacy to make procreative decisions, but later decisions focused on the individual's rights. The U.S. Supreme Court, in *Eisenstadt v. Baird*, stated, "[i]f the right of privacy means anything, it is the right of the individual, married or single, to be free from unwarranted governmental intrusion into matters so fundamentally affecting a person as the decision whether to bear or beget a child."

A federal district court has indicated that the right to make procreative decisions encompasses the right of an infertile couple to undergo medically assisted reproduction, including in vitro fertilization and the use of a donated embryo. Some legal analysts have suggested that the constitutional right to make reproductive decisions free from unnecessary governmental intrusion covers the decision of a couple to undergo cloning. However, other legal analysts have noted that the unprecedented step of creating a child with only one genetic progenitor would be such a fundamental change in the way humans "reproduce" that it would not be constitutionally protected.

Even if a restriction on cloning were found to infringe upon an individual's or a couple's right to make reproductive decisions, the government could justify the restriction if it had a compelling state interest and the restriction furthered that interest in the least restrictive manner possible. The potential physical and psychological risks of cloning an entire individual are sufficiently compelling to justify banning the procedure. Moreover, certain uses of cloning—such as creation of a clone as a source of spare organs—would likely be banned by the Thirteenth Amendment prohibition of slavery and involuntary servitude.

The use of cloned cells and tissue for research purposes other than the creation of a child would not be protected by the constitutional rights of privacy and liberty that protect reproductive decisions. Consequently, a governmental regulation or ban of such research would not have to have such stringent justification. It would be constitutional so long as it was rationally related to an important government purpose. Under such an analysis, a court could uphold restrictions that require sufficient animal research be done in advance. Moreover, it would be permissible to require the scientists proposing the research to have "the burden of proving that the research is vital, cannot be conducted any other way, and is unlikely to produce harm to society."

C. PARENTHOOD ISSUES

Current state laws addressing parentage, including paternity acts, surrogacy statutes, and egg donation statutes, are not broad enough to address the multitude of parentage issues raised by the process of cloning through nuclear transfer. The process of cloning will result in a child having genetic material from as many as four individuals: the person from whom the cell nucleus was derived, that individual's biological parents, and the woman contributing the enucleated egg cell which contains a tiny fraction of DNA in the mitochondria. In addition, if the egg with the transferred genetic material is implanted in a surrogate gestational mother, the child will have two other potential parents—the gestator and, if she is married, her husband. The latter will have rights (even though no biological connection to the child) based on the common law presumption that if a woman gives birth within marriage, her husband is the child's legal father, or in some states, based on specific statutes holding that the surrogate and her husband are the legal parents of a child she gestated, regardless of their genetic contribution. There may also be intended rearing parents unrelated to the individual who is cloned; this may occur when the cloned individual is deceased, a celebrity, or a favorite relative.

Various contributors in the cloning arrangements will have legal rights and responsibilities with respect to the resulting child. Since the clone is a twin to the cloned individual, the latter's parents could be recognized as legal parents. They certainly would be identified as the parents under DNA paternity testing. Yet, given that they will likely have not made the decision to create offspring (in fact, they may be dead at the time their own offspring is cloned), it seems unfair to designate them as the legal parents. It is also not in keeping with a perspective that considers preconception intention as a relevant factor for determining parenthood in the context of assisted reproduction.

In many states, the woman who gives birth is considered to be the legal mother and her husband the legal father of any resulting child. Under statutes in Arizona and Utah, this holds true even when the surrogate is gestating an embryo with no genetic relationship to her. Only in Florida, New Hampshire, North Dakota, and Virginia do court-approved gestational surrogacy arrangements result in the intended parents—not the surrogate—being viewed as the legal parents. However, these four states have leeway for denial of parenthood to people who clone. The laws allow only married individuals to contract with gestational surrogates (thus not applying to the unmarried individual who clones himself or herself). Virginia also allows judges the leeway to deny gestational surrogacy based on psychological examination of the intended parents. Some would argue that the desire to clone oneself is evidence of psychological disturbance.

The person who clones himself or herself could try to establish paternity (or maternity) under the state paternity statute. If such individuals are denied use of the provisions allowing "mothers" and "fathers" (because they do not seem to fit traditional conceptions of that role), they might be able nonetheless to go forward under the provisions in at least 13 states that allow "interested persons" to bring a paternity action. Such an action could be challenged by one of the other rights holders, though, such as the cloned individual's parents or the gestational surrogate.

The state laws for blood testing to prove paternity may or may not be useful to the individual who wishes to prove he or she is the "parent" of his or her clone. The laws provide for a wide range of such tests—from HLA typing to

DNA tests. If one of the less precise tests were used, the individual whose nucleic material were used might have a match that makes it apparent that he or she is the "parent" and might be declared the legal parent on those grounds. However, if DNA testing were used, the nucleus provider would clearly have a pattern closer to that of a twin (a nearly 100% match) rather than a parent (a 50% match). It is not clear what a judge would make of such information. The legal standard for paternity is often a particular probability of being a parent. For example, in Mississippi, the blood tests must show that there is a statistical probability of paternity of 98% or greater. So, the judge's ideas about paternity and parenthood, rather than the DNA test, would be determinative of whether the nucleus provider was declared the parent of the clone. The nucleus donor's claim to the rights and responsibilities of parenthood would be bolstered under doctrines and cases that give weight to preconception intent in recognizing legal parenthood.

If a couple creates a child who is the clone of a loved one or an unrelated individual chosen for that person's valued traits, parenting rights would also be dispersed across individuals. If the wife carried the clone to term, the couple would be protected by legal presumptions assigning parenthood to the birth mother and her husband. If paternity testing were done, however, the parents of the cloned individual (and maybe the cloned individual himself or herself) might be able to assert rights to the child.

NOTES AND QUESTIONS:
Cloning

1. The excerpt by Lori Andrews discusses the possibility of federal regulation of cloning. States, too, have been attempting to regulate this technology. Assume that Congress enacts a law banning cloning, and that the law is later struck down as unconstitutional by the Supreme Court. Given your knowledge of the U.S. Constitution and federalism, you should be able to understand how the Court's rationale for its decision might be very important. In particular, in each of the following circumstances, determine whether a state might be able to pass a law banning cloning:
   a. The Supreme Court struck down the national law based on a commerce clause argument.
   b. The Supreme Court struck down the national law based on a right to scientific inquiry.
   c. The Supreme Court struck down the national law based on a right to make reproductive decisions.
2. As Andrews notes, issues relating to the regulation of cloning are actually a sub-category of the broader issues relating to what the federal or state governments can constitutionally do to regulate assisted reproductive technol-

ogies. We briefly addressed this issue in the discussion following the *Baby M* opinion, where the court concluded that "the right to procreate very simply is the right to have natural children, whether through sexual intercourse or artificial insemination."

Based on your understanding of the right to privacy under the U.S. Constitution, give specific arguments for and against the constitutionality of the following possible state laws:[6]

a. A law that bans all reproductive technologies in which an egg is first removed from a woman. (This would include a ban on in vitro fertilization.) The legislature notes that these technologies have led to increasing social uncertainty about what it means to be a parent, and a resulting diminution in moral values.

b. A law that bans cloning. The legislative history of the law mentions concerns about both the physical health of the resulting children and the consequences for the moral values of our society.

c. A law that criminalizes reproductive procedures involving the use of a surrogate mother (such as took place in *Baby M*), whether or not the mother is genetically related to the child. Note that *Baby M* seems to suggest that there may be a constitutionally protected right to have a child, but not to be able to be its parent. Do you agree with that distinction? What, exactly, is the court saying about the ability of the state to ban what took place in *Baby M*?

d. A law that criminalizes reproductive procedures in which a woman gestates a fetus that is not genetically related to her (as in *Johnson v. Calvert*).

3. The federal court opinion discussing the constitutionality of restrictions on assisted reproductive technologies that was mentioned by Andrews is *Lifchez v. Hartigan*, 735 F. Supp. 1361 (N.D. Ill. 1990). That case interpreted a section of the Illinois Abortion Law providing that "[n]o person shall sell or experiment upon a fetus produced by the fertilization of a human ovum by a human sperm unless such experimentation is therapeutic to the fetus thereby produced. . . . Nothing in this subsection (7) is intended to prohibit the performance of in vitro fertilization." Here is an excerpt from the opinion:

> Section 6(7) of the Illinois Abortion Law is also unconstitutional because it impermissibly restricts a woman's fundamental right of privacy, in particular, her right to make reproductive choices free of governmental interference with those choices. Various aspects of this reproductive privacy right have been articulated in a number of landmark Supreme Court cases, including *Griswold v. Connecticut*, *Eisenstadt v. Baird*, *Roe v. Wade*, and *Planned Parenthood of Missouri v. Danforth* (1976) (striking down provisions of abortion statute requiring spousal consent and parental consent). . . .
>
> Section 6(7) intrudes upon this "cluster of constitutionally protected choices." Embryo transfer and chorionic villi sampling are illustrative. Both

procedures are "experimental" by most definitions of that term. Both are performed directly, and intentionally, on the fetus. Neither procedure is necessarily therapeutic to the fetus. In embryo transfer, it is not therapeutic to remove the embryo from a woman's uterus after it has been fertilized and expose it to the high risk associated with trying to implant it in the infertile woman. In chorionic villi sampling, it is not therapeutic to the fetus to invade and snip off some of its surrounding tissue. Both embryo transfer and chorionic villi sampling violate any reasonable interpretation of § 6(7).

Both procedures, however, fall within a woman's zone of privacy . . . . Embryo transfer is a procedure designed to enable an infertile woman to bear her own child. It takes no great leap of logic to see that within the cluster of constitutionally protected choices that includes the right to have access to contraceptives, there must be included within that cluster the right to submit to a medical procedure that may bring about, rather than prevent, pregnancy. Chorionic villi sampling is similarly protected. The cluster of constitutional choices that includes the right to abort a fetus within the first trimester must also include the right to submit to a procedure designed to give information about that fetus which can then lead to a decision to abort. Since there is no compelling state interest sufficient to prevent a woman from terminating her pregnancy during the first trimester, . . . there can be no such interest sufficient to intrude upon these other protected activities during the first trimester.

Do you agree? Does the existence of a right to prevent an unwanted pregnancy necessarily lead to a right to use reproductive technologies?

4. In the notes after *Casey* in chapter 4 we asked about the constitutionality of laws denying a pregnant woman information she might use to make "discriminatory" abortion decisions. A couple might achieve the same goal by using newer technologies:

   a. A new technique allows preselection of sperm prior to fertilization so as to maximize the likelihood of having a child of a certain sex.

   b. A clinic offering in vitro fertilization agrees to screen the fertilized eggs and to implant only those that are of the desired sex.

   c. The clinic described in (b) claims to be able to detect a genetic mutation that leads to homosexuality, and offers to screen out such fertilized eggs.

   d. The same clinic also offers to screen out fertilized eggs that indicate the existence of Down's syndrome.

   Would a state law banning any of these practices be constitutional? Does it make a difference that technique (a) deals with pre-fertilization events, as opposed to the other three techniques?[7]

5. Assuming that it was constitutional for either the state or federal government to regulate cloning, is such regulation appropriate? A major reason that the National Bioethics Advisory Commission recommended at least a temporary ban against cloning human beings was the risk that the resulting child might have medical problems.

   Given that rationale, it is interesting to note that new reproductive techniques—more specifically, "assisted reproductive technologies" used to help infertile couples have children—have thus far been subject to minimal regulation. Such well-used technologies are far from being risk-free with regard to the children that are conceived. In particular, current techniques have led to large increases in "multiple gestation": pregnancies with three or more fetuses. The children, assuming they survive, have a substantial likelihood of suffering from life-long medical problems.[8]

While this issue has been discussed extensively, legislatures and the public have yet to take a hard look at it. Indeed, quite the opposite tends to take place, as is best exemplified by the public and the media's exceptionally positive response to the birth of Bobbi McCaughey's septuplets in November 1997. Her appearances on the television news shows and the cover of major newsmagazines, announcing her belief that God told her to proceed with the risky pregnancy, dwarfed the few critical articles that raised ethical issues about allowing her to proceed with this pregnancy and highlighted the far more numerous "bad" outcomes from multiple pregnancies.

6. Apart from the constitutional issues, what is an appropriate governmental response to multiple pregnancies? If we know that, e.g., the gestation of quadruplets or more is very likely to produce one or more children with severe disabilities, is it proper to regulate the technology that leads to multiple-gestation situations?[9] Or should it be solely a choice of the mother and the doctor—or the mother alone—to take the risk? Why should it be acceptable to allow a mother to accept this known high risk of producing very disabled children, yet be concerned about the unknown risk of cloning?

A distinct issue raised by the multiple gestation cases is the possibility of selective reduction, a procedure in which some of the fetuses are destroyed so that the remaining fetuses are likely to become healthy children. (A common analogy is a lifeboat with too many people aboard that is very likely to sink unless the number of passengers is reduced.[10]) Assuming that there is no way to know ahead of time which women using a particular assisted reproductive technology are likely to have multiple gestations, is it appropriate to condition the use of such technology on the woman's agreement ahead of time to consent to selective reduction, if needed? (As you can imagine, this type of forced abortion is very controversial.)[11]

Endnotes

1. *Dateline NBC*, 3 August 1999.
2. Elizabeth Landes and Richard Posner, "The Economics of the Baby Shortage," 7 *J. Legal Studies* 323 (1978).
3. Brent Begun, "Parenthood at 50-Plus," *Newsweek*, 12 June 2000, 82. For more details on surrogacy laws in specific states, see, e.g., Barry Furrow et al., *Health Law* at 968–75 (St. Paul: West Group, 2d ed., 2000).
4. The full 1997 report, *Cloning Human Beings: Report and Recommendations of the National Bioethics Advisory Commission*, is on the web at *bioethics.gov*.

5. Written by law professor Lori B. Andrews. The full text of her paper is available on the web at *bioethics.gov*. This report is a product of the U.S. federal government; therefore, it is not protected by the Copyright Act, and copyright ownership cannot be transferred.

6. For an argument that the Constitution does indeed provide broad access to reproductive technologies, see John A. Robertson, *Children of Choice: Freedom and the New Reproductive Technologies* (Princeton: Princeton University Press, 1994).

7. For further discussion, see, e.g., Joni Danis, "Sexism and 'the Superfluous Female': Arguments for Regulating Pre-implantation Sex Selection," 18 *Harv. Women's L. J.* 219 (1995); Owen D. Jones, "Sex Selection: Regulating Technology enabling the Predetermination of a Child's Gender," 6 *Harv. J. L. & Tech.* 1 (1992).

8. See, e.g., Gina Kolata, "Many Specialists Are Left in No Mood for Celebration," *New York Times*, 21 November 1997, A32; Pam Belluck, "Heartache Frequently Visits Parents with Multiple Births," *New York Times*, 3 January 1998, A1; Arlene Judith Klotzko, "Medical Miracle or Medical Mischief?: The Saga of the McCaughey Septuplets," 28 (3) *Hastings Center Report* 5 (1998). Indeed, there have even been anti-ethicist backlash articles: Cal Thomas, "Medical Ethicists Take a Long Slide down Slippery Slope to Infanticide," *Newsday*, 27 November 1997, A38.

9. It may in fact not be easy for clinical medicine to modify reproductive technologies so as to limit the number of multiple births. See Siladitya Bhattacharya and Allan Templeton, "In Treating Infertility, Are Multiple Pregnancies Unavoidable?" 343 *New Eng. J. Med.* 58 (2000).

10. Such situations have actually come before courts. See *United States v. Holmes*, 26 F. Cas. 360 (E.D. Pa. 1842) (No. 15,383); Eric Rakowski, "Taking and Saving Lives," 93 *Colum. L. Rev.* 1063 (1993). A very famous law review article sets out a similar fictional situation, with a group of cave explorers trapped but in radio contact with the rescuers. Lon L. Fuller, "The Case of the Speluncean Explorers," 62 *Harv. L. Rev.* 616 (1949). Another much-discussed fictional dilemma dealing with somewhat related issues is the "trolley problem," involving a choice of whom to save when a train about to hit a group of people can be diverted to hit a different group. See, e.g., Judith Jarvis Thomson, "The Trolley Problem," 94 *Yale L. J.* 1395 (1985).

11. One of the most thorough discussions of the full range of legal and ethical issues raised by new reproductive technologies is the report by the New York State Task Force on Life and the Law, *Assisted Reproductive Technologies: Analysis and Recmmendations for Public Policy* (1998). Information on buying this 474-page report (for $12) can be found at the Task Force web page, *www.health.state.ny.us/nysdoh/taskfce/index.htm*.

6

Beyond Abortion:
The Interests of Women and Fetuses

The interests of a woman and those of her fetus do not always coincide. The most obvious area of conflict has already been discussed: a woman may actively desire, for various reasons, to terminate a pregnancy through an abortion. Often, though, a woman may very much want to have a child, yet to further other of her own interests she may be doing things that might harm the fetus (and thus the child that it would ultimately become). This area is sometimes referred to as "maternal-fetal conflicts." As we shall see, though they overlap, the issues it raises are somewhat different from those discussed in the analysis of the right to abortion.

At the outset, it is important to understand how the American legal tradition views the basic duty that an individual has to someone else. Absent a specific relationship between two individuals, in general no one has any special obligation to do anything to help out anyone else. This concept is firmly ingrained in the individualistic streak that this nation has inherited from English common law traditions. It is, however, a concept that may seem alien to persons who come to bioethics from a more ethics-centered tradition. Although "beneficence"—the concept of altruistically looking out for the interests of others—plays a powerful role in ethics, its role in the law is much more limited.

The key to applying the relevant legal concepts lies in determining when a special relationship might override the general "no duty" rule. Such a relationship can occur due to a person's role or status or due to actions the person has taken. Some examples may clarify this:

1. Walking by the side of a lake, I notice a toddler playing at the edge of the lake. No one else is around. As I watch, the toddler stumbles and falls into the lake. His head is underwater, and it is clear that he will drown if nothing is done. I could easily reach in, with no risk to myself, and pull the child out. Nonetheless, I choose not to do so. I have never witnessed a child drowning, and am curious to see what actually happens. The child does in fact drown.

It is highly unlikely that I would be considered to have done anything wrong under the law. I had no obligation to help this child. Even the "good Samaritan" laws that most states have passed would rarely alter this result. The only thing the great majority of such statutes do is to encourage a rescue by immunizing a good Samaritan from liability if he attempts a rescue in good faith. Thus, assume that I attempt to rescue the child and incorrectly apply cardiopulmonary resuscitation, with the result that the child ends up with severe brain damage. As a result of a good Samaritan law, the parents of the child would be unable to sue me for my negligent attempt to save their child. These laws therefore encourage rescue but usually do not require it; nor do they punish a person's failure to rescue. It is accepted that the notion of going to the aid of a stranger is somewhat alien to the American legal tradition.[1]

A compelling example is the case of David Cash, who stood by and did nothing while his best friend, Jeremy Strohmeyer, took seven-year-old Sherrice Iverson into a bathroom at a Las Vegas casino to rape and murder her. Although the University of California at Berkeley was less than thrilled at learning how Cash had behaved immediately before enrolling at the school, the local district attorney acknowledged that Cash had not committed a crime: "Moral reprehensibility isn't a crime. You have to participate—do something affirmatively—to assist in the commission of a crime. Watching and failing to report, regrettably, is not a crime."[2]

2. Again walking by the side of the lake, I see the child fall in. This child, however, is my son. Because of the relationship between the two of us, I am under a clear legal duty to protect him. My failure to rescue him would be an abrogation of that duty.

3. Again walking by the side of the lake, I see the child playing at the edge. Seen in profile, the child has an amazing resemblance to a football, and I follow through with my urge to practice kicking a field goal. I send the child on a parabolic course into the center of the lake. In this instance, I have created the danger to the child, and I have an obligation to rescue him. The fact that we had no prior relationship is irrelevant. My actions have created a relationship.

4. I am at the same lake with my toddler son, who is a few feet away from me. A stranger, acting more quickly than I can respond, picks my son up and drop-kicks him into the center of the lake. I know that this lake is greater than 20 feet deep at the center, and I happen to be a poor swimmer. If I choose not to try to rescue my son, I would not be violating any laws. Even though I had a pre-existing duty to protect my son, that duty has limits. In particular, in circumstances where I have not created the risk to my child, it is unlikely that my duty would require that I expose myself to significant personal harm on my son's behalf.

Keep the differences among these scenarios in mind as you read the cases in this section, in particular *In re A.C.* Into which of these categories do you think that case falls? That determination may alter how you believe the holding of the case will apply to other fact patterns. In addition, it will be helpful to think about how these cases, and these categories, relate to the abortion issues discussed in chapter 4. In particular, which category fits the case of a woman who chooses an abortion in order to prevent marital discord? How about a woman who chooses abortion when continuing the pregnancy might harm her health?

In re A.C.

District of Columbia Court of Appeals

573 A.2d 1235 (D.C. 1990)

OPINION BY JUDGE TERRY:

. . . We are confronted here with two profoundly difficult and complex issues. First, we must determine who has the right to decide the course of medical treatment for a patient who, although near death, is pregnant with a viable fetus. Second, we must establish how that decision should be made if the patient cannot make it for herself—more specifically, how a court should proceed when faced with a pregnant patient, *in extremis*, who is apparently incapable of making an informed decision regarding medical care for herself and her fetus. We hold that in virtually all cases the question of what is to be done is to be decided by the patient — the pregnant woman — on behalf of herself and the fetus. If the patient is incompetent or otherwise unable to give an informed consent to a proposed course of medical treatment, then her decision must be ascertained through the procedure known as substituted judgment. Because the trial court did not follow that procedure, we vacate its order and remand the case for further proceedings.

I

This case came before the trial court when George Washington University Hospital petitioned the emergency judge in chambers for declaratory relief as to how it should treat its patient, A.C., who was close to death from cancer and was twenty-six and one-half weeks pregnant with a viable fetus. After a hearing lasting approximately three hours, which was held at the hospital (though not in A.C.'s room), the court ordered that a caesarean section be performed on A.C. to deliver the fetus. Counsel for A.C. immediately sought a stay in this court, which was unanimously denied by a hastily assembled division of three judges. The caesarean was performed, and a baby girl, L.M.C., was delivered. Tragically, the child died within two and one-half hours, and the mother died two days later. . . .

II

A.C. was first diagnosed as suffering from cancer at the age of thirteen. In the ensuing years she underwent major surgery several times, together with multiple radiation treatments and chemotherapy. A.C. married when she was twenty-seven, during a period of remission, and soon thereafter she became pregnant. She was excited about her pregnancy and very much wanted the child. Because of her medical history, she was referred in her fifteenth week of pregnancy to the high-risk pregnancy clinic at George Washington University Hospital.

On Tuesday, June 9, 1987, when A.C. was approximately twenty-five weeks pregnant, she went to the hospital for a scheduled check-up. Because she was experiencing pain in her back and shortness of breath, an x-ray was taken, revealing an apparently inoperable tumor which nearly filled her right lung. On Thursday, June 11, A.C. was admitted to the hospital as a patient. By Friday her condition had temporarily improved, and when asked if she really wanted to have her baby, she replied that she did.

Over the weekend A.C.'s condition worsened considerably. Accordingly, on Monday, June 15, members of the medical staff treating A.C. assembled, along with her family, in A.C.'s room. The doctors then informed her that her illness was terminal, and A.C. agreed to palliative treatment designed to extend her life until at least her twenty-eighth week of pregnancy. The "potential outcome [for] the fetus," according to the doctors, would be much better at twenty-eight weeks than at twenty-six weeks if it were necessary to "intervene." A.C. knew that the palliative treatment she had chosen presented some increased risk to the fetus, but she opted for this course both to prolong her life for at least another two weeks and to maintain her own comfort. When asked if she still wanted to have the baby, A. C. was somewhat equivocal, saying "something to the effect of 'I don't know, I think so.'" As the day moved toward evening, A.C.'s condition grew still worse, and at about 7:00 or 8:00 p.m. she consented to intubation to facilitate her breathing.

The next morning, June 16, the trial court convened a hearing at the hospital in response to the hospital's request for a declaratory judgment. The court appointed counsel for both A.C. and the fetus, and the District of Columbia was permitted to intervene for the fetus as *parens patriae*. The court heard testimony on the facts as we have summarized them, and further testimony that at twenty-six and a half weeks the fetus was viable, i.e., capable of sustained life outside of the mother, given artificial aid. A neonatologist, Dr. Maureen Edwards, testified that the chances of survival for a twenty-six-week fetus delivered at the hospital might be as high as eighty percent, but that this particular fetus, because of the mother's medical history, had only a fifty to sixty percent chance of survival. Dr. Edwards estimated that the risk of substantial impairment for the fetus, if it were delivered promptly, would be less than twenty percent. However, she noted that the fetus' condition was worsening appreciably at a rapid rate, and another doctor—Dr. Alan Weingold, an obstetrician who was one of A.C.'s treating physicians—stated that any delay in delivering the child by caesarean section lessened its chances of survival.

Regarding A.C.'s ability to respond to questioning and her prognosis, Dr. Louis Hamner, another treating obstetrician, testified that A.C. would probably die within twenty-four hours "if absolutely nothing else is done . . . . As far as her ability to interact, she has been heavily sedated in order to maintain her ventilatory function. She will open her eyes sometimes when you are in the room, but as far as her being able to . . . carry on a meaningful-type conversation . . . at this point, I don't think that is reasonable." When asked whether reducing her medication to "permit recovery of enough cognitive function on her part that we could get any sense from her as to what her preference would be as to therapy," Dr. Hamner replied, "I don't think so. I think her respiratory status has deteriorated to the point where she is [expending] an enormous amount of energy just to keep the heart going." Dr. Weingold, asked the same question, gave a similar answer: that A.C.'s few remaining hours of life "will be shortened by attempting to raise her level of consciousness because that is what is keeping her, in a sense, physiologically compliant with the respirator. If you remove that, then I think that will shorten her survival."

There was no evidence before the court showing that A.C. consented to, or even contemplated, a caesarean section before her twenty-eighth week of pregnancy. There was, in fact, considerable dispute as to whether she would have consented to an immediate caesarean delivery at the time the hearing was held. A.C.'s mother opposed surgical intervention, testifying that A.C. wanted "to live long enough to hold that baby" and that she expected to do so, "even though she knew she was terminal." . . .

After hearing this testimony and the arguments of counsel, the trial court made oral findings of fact. It found, first, that A.C. would probably die, according to uncontroverted medical testimony, "within the next twenty-four to forty-eight hours"; second, that A.C. was "pregnant with a twenty-six and a half week viable fetus who, based upon uncontroverted medical testimony, has approximately a fifty to sixty percent chance to survive if a caesarean section is performed as soon as possible"; third, that because the fetus was viable, "the state has [an] important and legitimate interest in protecting the potentiality of human life"; and fourth, that there had been some testimony that the operation "may very well hasten the death of [A.C.]," but that there had also been testimony that delay would greatly increase the risk to the fetus and that "the prognosis is not great for the fetus to be delivered post-mortem. . . ." Most significantly, the court found:

> The court is of the view that it does not clearly know what [A.C.'s] present views are with respect to the issue of whether or not the child should live or die. She's presently unconscious. As late as Friday of last week, she wanted the baby to live. As late as yesterday, she did not know for sure.

Having made these findings of fact and conclusions of law, . . . the court ordered that a caesarean section be performed to deliver A.C.'s child. . . .

IV

A. *Informed Consent and Bodily Integrity*

A number of learned articles have been written about the propriety or impropriety of court-ordered caesarean sections. *E.g.,* . . . Rhoden, *The Judge in the Delivery Room: The Emergence of Court-Ordered Cesareans,* 74 Cal. L. Rev. 1951 (1986); Robertson, *Procreative Liberty and the Control of Conception, Pregnancy and Childbirth,* 69 Va. L. Rev. 405 (1983). Commentators have also considered how medical decisions for incompetent persons which may involve some detriment or harm to them should be made. These and other articles demonstrate the complexity of medical intervention cases, which become more complex with the steady advance of medical technology. From a recent national survey, it appears that over the five years preceding the survey there were thirty-six attempts to override maternal refusals of proposed medical treatment, and that in fifteen instances where court orders were sought to authorize caesarean interventions, thirteen such orders were granted. . . .

Thus our analysis of this case begins with the tenet common to all medical treatment cases: that any person has the right to make an informed choice, if competent to do so, to accept or forego medical treatment. The doctrine of informed consent, based on this principle and rooted in the concept of bodily integrity, is ingrained in our common law. Under the doctrine of informed consent, a physician must inform the patient, "at a minimum," of "the nature of the proposed treatment, any alternative treatment procedures, and the nature and degree of risks and benefits inherent in undergoing and in abstaining from the proposed treatment." To protect the right of every person to bodily integrity, courts uniformly hold that a surgeon who performs an operation without the patient's consent may be guilty of a battery, or that if the surgeon obtains an insufficiently informed consent, he or she may be liable for negligence. Furthermore, the right to informed consent "also encompasses a right to informed refusal."

In the same vein, courts do not compel one person to permit a significant intrusion upon his or her bodily integrity for the benefit of another person's health. *See, e.g., McFall v. Shimp* (Allegheny County Ct. 1978). In *McFall* the court refused to order Shimp to donate bone marrow which was necessary to save the life of his cousin, McFall:

> The common law has consistently held to a rule which provides that one human being is under no legal compulsion to give aid or to take action to save another human being or to rescue. . . . For our law to *compel* defendant to submit to an intrusion of his body would change every concept and

principle upon which our society is founded. To do so would defeat the sanctity of the individual, and would impose a rule which would know no limits, and one could not imagine where the line would be drawn.

Even though Shimp's refusal would mean death for McFall, the court would not order Shimp to allow his body to be invaded. It has been suggested that fetal cases are different because a woman who "has chosen to lend her body to bring [a] child into the world" has an enhanced duty to assure the welfare of the fetus, sufficient even to require her to undergo caesarean surgery. Surely, however, a fetus cannot have rights in this respect superior to those of a person who has already been born.

Courts have generally held that a patient is competent to make his or her own medical choices when that patient is capable of "the informed exercise of a choice, and that entails an opportunity to evaluate knowledgeably the options available and the risks attendant upon each." Thus competency in a case such as this turns on the patient's ability to function as a decision-maker, acting in accordance with her preferences and values.

This court has recognized as well that, above and beyond common law protections, the right to accept or forego medical treatment is of constitutional magnitude. Other courts also have found a basis in the Constitution for refusing medical treatment. . . .

This court and others, while recognizing the right to accept or reject medical treatment, have consistently held that the right is not absolute. In some cases, especially those involving life-or-death situations or incompetent patients, the courts have recognized four countervailing interests that may involve the state as *parens patriae*: preserving life, preventing suicide, maintaining the ethical integrity of the medical profession, and protecting third parties. Neither the prevention of suicide nor the integrity of the medical profession has any bearing on this case. Further, the state's interest in preserving life must be truly compelling to justify overriding a competent person's right to refuse medical treatment. This is equally true for incompetent patients, who have just as much right as competent patients to have their decisions made while competent respected, even in a substituted judgment framework. . . .

We think it is incumbent on any trial judge in a case like this, unless it is impossible to do so, to ascertain whether a patient is competent to make her own medical decisions. Whenever possible, the judge should personally attempt to speak with the patient and ascertain her wishes directly, rather than relying exclusively on hearsay evidence, even from doctors. It is improper to presume that a patient is incompetent. We have no reason to believe that, if competent, A.C. would or would not have refused consent to a caesarean. We hold, however, that without a competent refusal from A.C. to go forward with the surgery, and without a finding through substituted judgment that A.C. would not have consented to the surgery, it was error for the trial court to proceed to a balancing analysis, weighing the rights of A.C. against the interests of the state. . . .

B. Substituted Judgment

In the previous section we discussed the right of an individual to accept or reject medical treatment. We concluded that if a patient is competent and has made an informed decision regarding the course of her medical treatment, that decision will control in virtually all cases. Sometimes, however, as our analysis presupposes here, a once competent patient will be unable to render an informed decision. In such a case, we hold that the court must make a substituted judgment on behalf of the patient, based on all the evidence. This means that the duty of the court, "as surrogate for the incompetent, is to determine as best it can what choice that individual, if competent, would make with respect to medical procedures." . . .

OPINION BY JUDGE BELSON,
CONCURRING IN PART AND DISSENTING IN PART:

I agree with much of the majority opinion, but I disagree with its ultimate ruling that the trial court's order must be set aside, and with the narrow view it takes of the state's interest in preserving life and the unborn child's interest in life. . . .

I think it appropriate, nevertheless, to state my disagreement with the very limited view the majority opinion takes of the circumstances in which the interests of a viable unborn child can afford such compelling reasons. The state's interest in preserving human life and the viable unborn child's interest in survival are entitled, I think, to more weight than I find them assigned by the majority when it states that "in virtually all cases the decision of the patient . . . will control." I would hold that in those instances, fortunately rare, in which the viable unborn child's interest in living and the state's parallel interest in protecting human life come into conflict with the mother's decision to forgo a procedure such as a caesarean section, a balancing should be struck in which the unborn child's and the state's interests are entitled to substantial weight.

It was acknowledged in *Roe v. Wade* that the state's interest in potential human life becomes compelling at the point of viability. Even before viability, the state has an "important and legitimate interest in protecting the potentiality of human life." When approximately the third trimester of pregnancy is reached (roughly the time of viability, although with advances in medical science the time of viability is being reached sooner and sooner), the state's interest becomes sufficiently compelling to justify what otherwise would be unduly burdensome state interference with the woman's constitutionally protected privacy interest. Once that stage is reached, the state "may, if it chooses, regulate, and even proscribe, abortion except where it is necessary, in appropriate medical judgment, for the preservation of the life or health of the mother." In addressing this issue, it is important to emphasize, as does the majority opinion, that this case is not about abortion; we are not discussing whether a woman has the legal right to terminate her pregnancy in its early stages. Rather, we are dealing with the situation that exists when a woman has carried an unborn child to viability. When the unborn child reaches the state of viability, the child becomes a party whose interests must be considered. . . .

The balancing test should be applied in instances in which women become pregnant and carry an unborn child to the point of viability. This is not an unreasonable classification because, I submit, a woman who carries a child to viability is in fact a member of a unique category of persons. Her circumstances differ fundamentally from those of other potential patients for medical procedures that will aid another person, for example, a potential donor of bone marrow for transplant. This is so because she has undertaken to bear another human being, and has carried an unborn child to viability. Another unique feature of the situation we address arises from the singular nature of the dependency of the unborn child upon the mother. A woman carrying a viable unborn child is not in the same category as a relative, friend, or stranger called upon to donate bone marrow or an organ for transplant. Rather, the expectant mother has placed herself in a special class of persons who are bringing another person into existence, and upon whom that other person's life is totally dependent. Also, uniquely, the viable unborn child is literally captive within the mother's body. No other potential beneficiary of a surgical procedure on another is in that position.

For all of these reasons, a balancing becomes appropriate in those few cases where the interests we are discussing come into conflict. To so state is in no sense to fail to recognize the extremely strong interest of each individual person, including of course the expectant mother, in her bodily integrity, her privacy, and, where involved, her religious beliefs. . . .

NOTES AND QUESTIONS:
In re A.C.

1. Judge Terry is certainly correct is noting that, *in general*, "one human being is under no legal compulsion to give aid or take action to save another human being." But should this general rule of "no duty" apply to the relationship between a woman and her fetus? Why or why not? Is the relationship essentially the same as that between two cousins? Into which of the four categories listed on pp. 128–29 would you place the mother-fetus relationship? (Or do you perhaps want to further subcategorize those based on what the woman is trying to do—e.g., does it make a difference if the woman has made a decision to continue with the pregnancy, rather than getting an abortion?)

2. Do you think that the Supreme Court decisions in *Roe v. Wade* and *Casey* say anything about how that Court would answer the questions in item 1? Do the abortion cases lay out parameters under which a state can pass laws that determine when a woman has a duty to her fetus?

3. One of the most famous analogies about the relationship between a woman and her fetus was written by Judith Jarvis Thomson:

> You wake up in the morning and find yourself back to back in bed with an unconscious violinist. He has been found to have a fatal kidney ailment, and the Society of Music Lovers has canvassed all the available medical records and found that you alone have the right blood type to help. They have therefore kidnapped you, and last night the violinist's circulatory system was plugged into yours, so that your kidneys can be used to extract poisons from his blood as well as your own. The director of the hospital now tells you, "Look, we're sorry the Society of Music Lovers did this to you—we would never have permitted it if we had known. But still, they did it, and the violinist is now plugged into you. To unplug you would be to kill him. But never mind, it's only for nine months. By then he will have recovered from his ailment, and can safely be unplugged from you." Is it morally incumbent upon you to accede to this situation? No doubt it would be very nice if you did, a great kindness. But do you have to accede to it? What if it were not nine months, but nine years? Or longer still? What if the director of the hospital says, "Tough luck, I agree, but you've now got to stay in bed, with the violinist plugged into you, for the rest of your life. Because remember this. All persons have a right to life, and violinists are persons. . . . [A] person's right to life outweighs your right to decide what happens in and to your body."[3]

Is this analogy convincing? Some say that Thomson's scenario works best in the case of a truly involuntary pregnancy, such as where a woman has been raped. In other contexts, is it appropriate to view the pregnant woman as having been arbitrarily chosen to help an unrelated person? Does the fact that we are biological beings, and that reproduction is a natural process, suggest we should view this situation in a special way? If so, should the degree of involuntariness of the pregnancy matter? Is a woman who used "good" birth control in a different situation from a woman who used no birth control?

4. Others suggest that analogies like Thomson's are unhelpful in that they resemble science fiction more than the day-to-day realities with which we are concerned. Richard Posner asks how our reaction might change if, in order to effectively detach the violinist from the woman, you had to run his body through a giant blender: "the abortion doctor doesn't merely 'pull the plug' on the fetus; he chops it up or sucks it out of its mother's womb."[4]

5. Judge Terry did have a response to the claim that "fetal cases are different." He said that "a fetus cannot have rights in this respect superior to those of a person who has already been born." One response might be: Why not? Could the unique biological relationship between a woman and a fetus impose special duties on the woman during the pregnancy?

6. If Judge Terry is correct in claiming that a fetus cannot have "superior" rights, can the Supreme Court's abortion decisions still stand? No "person who has already been born" has the right to hook himself up to anyone

else's bloodstream if that other person does not consent. Yet the abortion decisions indicate that, assuming a state wishes to pass a law protecting the interests of viable fetuses, it is constitutionally acceptable to force the woman to have such "parasitism" forced upon her, so long as her health is not endangered. Does Judge Terry's claim need modification? Is it correct if he is merely saying that, in the District of Columbia, laws have not yet been passed that favor the interests of a fetus in a situation like that in *A.C.*? Does that mean that a state *could not*, consistent with the Constitution, pass such a law?

7. How important is it to the outcome in *A.C.* that the surgery actually was going to harm the woman? The majority opinion makes nothing of this point. Yet even under *Roe v. Wade* and *Casey*, a state cannot constitutionally prevent a woman from seeking an abortion when continuing the pregnancy might endanger her health. If that is true, why should it not follow that no state can force a woman, for the sake of the fetus, to take actions (including undergoing surgery) that will endanger her health?

On the other hand, if the actions at issue would not endanger the woman's health, why could not the state, should it so desire, choose to force them upon the woman?

8. Assume a woman, Kathy, is within hours of delivering a child. She is in a state that does not allow an abortion unless the health of the mother is at stake. Recently, her husband has separated from her, since he does not want to have a child at this time of his life, and he is angry that she never agreed to an abortion. Kathy is now desperate to reconcile with him.

While she is at the hospital having contractions, the doctors tell her that it appears the baby's head is too large for her to undergo a natural vaginal delivery. She needs to have a Caesarean section. She asks what will happen if she does not have it. The doctors indicate that the fetus will die. She refuses to allow the operation.

Should a court reach the same outcome as in *A.C.*? Assuming that you believe it is inappropriate to force an operation on a pregnant woman under any circumstances, would it be constitutional for the state to nonetheless impose a criminal penalty on Kathy's refusal of the surgery?

9. Note that a woman can take a variety of actions that may impact the health of her fetus. For example, she might:
   a. actively try to end the existence of the fetus (as by getting an abortion);
   b. avoid doing things that might be harmful to her health though beneficial to the health of the fetus (like the operation in *A.C.*);
   c. avoid doing things that are not harmful to her but might be beneficial to the health of the fetus (like taking prenatal vitamins);
   d. do things that she wants to do, but which might harm her own health and incidentally that of her fetus (as will be discussed below and in the *Whitner* case).

Presumably the permissibility of these actions will depend on the interests at stake: those of the woman, on the one hand, and those of the state, which may or may not be trying to protect the fetus. Thus, will one side of the "balancing" depend on the existing state law? What if a state passed a "Pregnant Woman Protection Act" (see notes following *Casey* in chapter 4) that declared a woman had no duty to her fetus? Would there be any question about her right to legally do any of the above?

On the other hand, what if a state passed a law that tried to maximally protect the interests of the fetus, consistent with any constitutional limitations imposed by the Constitution? Then we would have to balance the two opposing interests, as the Supreme Court did in *Roe*. Do any of these situations involve a woman's exercise of a right that, alone or with other rights, outweighs the state interest—assuming the fetus was viable?

10. A case on which the trial court relied in ordering the Caesarean section was *In re Madyun*. (The *Madyun* opinion is reprinted in full as an appendix to the *A.C.* opinion, at 573 A.2d 1259–64.) Ayesha Madyun was a 19-year-old pregnant Muslim woman whose water had broken. As the hours pass after such an event, there is increasing risk of infection that may lead to the death of the child. Accordingly, the doctors were strongly advising Mrs. Madyun to undergo a Caesarean section. She refused, preferring to wait for a natural delivery. She noted that "a Muslim woman has the right to decide whether or not to risk her own health to eliminate a possible risk to the life of her undelivered fetus." The hospital took this dispute to court, and the court ordered that the surgery take place, with the following explanation of its decision:

> The Court had before it parents who, in part, refused a Caesarean section on the basis of religious beliefs. Although both parents impressed the Court as sincere, it was evident that the stronger basis for their individual decisions was the belief that the surgical procedure was not necessary and that additional steps could be taken to enhance the possibility of a vaginal delivery. Neither parent, however, is a trained physician. To ignore the undisputed opinion of a skilled and trained physician to indulge the desires of the patient where, as here, there is a substantial risk to the unborn infant, is something the Court cannot do. Indeed, even if the religious beliefs of the parents were the primary or sole reason for refusing a Caesarean, the state had a compelling interest in ensuring this infant could be born.

The *A.C.* court distinguished *Madyun* (and a case on which the *Madyun* court had relied, *Jefferson v. Griffin Spalding County Hospital Authority*, 274 S.E.2d 457 (Ga. 1981)) on the ground that in those cases, "there was no real conflict between the interests of the mother and fetus; on the contrary, there was strong evidence that the proposed caesarean would be beneficial to both."

Do you agree with this attempt to distinguish the cases? If Mrs.
Madyun was refusing on religious grounds, is it appropriate to conclude
that having the surgery was in her best interests? (As we will discuss in
chapter 10, it is generally acknowledged that a competent person can refuse medical treatment for a variety of reasons, whether or not doing so will
cause the person's medical condition to worsen.)

11. A more recent case of a pregnant woman's refusal of care on religious
grounds is *In re Fetus Brown*, 689 N.E.2d 397 (Ill. App. Ct. 1997):

> The issue before this court is whether a competent, pregnant woman's right to
> refuse medical treatment, which in this case involves religiously offensive
> blood transfusions, may be overridden by the State's substantial interest in the
> welfare of the viable fetus. . . .
>
> On June 26, 1996, Darlene Brown, then 26 years old, was 34-3/7 weeks
> pregnant. After consulting with her treating physician, Dr. Robert Walsh,
> Brown was admitted into Ingalls Memorial Hospital in Harvey, Illinois, to have
> a cystoscopy and then to remove a urethral mass. Brown was anticipated to lose
> 100 cubic centimeters of blood due to the procedure. Before the surgery,
> Brown did not discuss with Dr. Walsh that she was a Jehovah's Witness.
>
> During the surgery, Brown lost more blood than anticipated. . . . Dr. Walsh
> ordered three units of blood for transfusion. Once the blood arrived in the op-
> erating room, Brown, who was fully conscious and alert during the procedure,
> refused the blood, explaining that she was a Jehovah's Witness. The doctors be-
> lieved Brown was competent to refuse the blood and they completed the sur-
> gery using other techniques to control her bleeding. . . .
>
> After the surgery, . . . Brown's hemoglobin level continued to drop. . . .
> Brown's low hemoglobin level and the abrupt change in that level posed a sig-
> nificant, life-threatening risk to both Brown and to the fetus.

The State of Illinois went to court, on behalf of the fetus, to force Brown to
undergo a blood transfusion.

Assuming that Brown indeed had the right to refuse blood, had she not
been pregnant, does the pregnancy alter the outcome? Is it relevant to what
extent Illinois law does or does not impose duties upon pregnant women to
protect a viable fetus?

12. As will be discussed in chapter 10, one way for people to protect their autonomy and to make sure that their wishes with regard to refusing care are
followed if they become incompetent is to sign ahead of time a written document known as an advance directive. Every state has at least some statutory provisions authorizing the use of such documents. However, many of
these statutes allow for circumstances when an advance directive cannot be
applied. Consider, for example, the following Ohio statute, Ohio Rev. Code
Ann. § 2133.06(B) (Anderson 1999):

> Life-sustaining treatment shall not be withheld or withdrawn from a declarant
> pursuant to a declaration if she is pregnant and if the withholding or with-
> drawal of the treatment would terminate the pregnancy, unless the declarant's

attending physician and one other physician who has examined the declarant determine, to a reasonable degree of medical certainty and in accordance with reasonable medical standards, that the fetus would not be born alive.

This and similar limitations from other states would appear to apply to situations involving both viable and non-viable fetuses. (Note that a fetus might be capable of being born alive, but nonetheless might be virtually certain to die shortly thereafter, and thus be non-viable.) If we assume that a woman's right to refuse care by completing an advance directive is legally equivalent to her right to refuse care while she is competent, is the Ohio provision constitutional when applied to a woman whose fetus is non-viable? Is the answer any different if the fetus is viable?[5]

13. Sometimes a pregnant woman may end up "brain dead": her whole brain is permanently non-functional, though her body is being kept alive through the use of a ventilator. (Brain death is discussed in chapter 15.) Suppose the state had a law that required that such life-support be continued, regardless of the previously expressed views of the woman. Would the fact that such a person is considered legally dead perhaps lead to different answers about this law's constitutionality than you reached in the questions posed in the previous item?[6]

WHITNER V. STATE
Supreme Court of South Carolina
492 S.E.2d 777 (S.C. 1997)

OPINION BY JUSTICE TOAL:

This case concerns the scope of the child abuse and endangerment statute in the South Carolina Children's Code. We hold the word "child" as used in that statute includes viable fetuses.

Facts

On April 20, 1992, Cornelia Whitner (Whitner) pled guilty to criminal child neglect for causing her baby to be born with cocaine metabolites in its system by reason of Whitner's ingestion of crack cocaine during the third trimester of her pregnancy. The circuit court judge sentenced Whitner to eight years in prison. . . .

Law/Analysis

. . . [Section 20-7-50 of the South Carolina statutes] provides:

Any person having the legal custody of any *child* or helpless person, who shall, without lawful excuse, refuse or neglect to provide, as defined in § 20-7-490, the proper care and attention for such *child* or helpless person, so that the life, health or comfort of such *child* or helpless person is endangered or is likely to be endangered, shall be guilty of a misdemeanor and shall be punished within the discretion of the circuit court (emphasis added).

The State contends this section encompasses maternal acts endangering or likely to endanger the life, comfort, or health of a viable fetus.

Under the Children's Code, "child" means a "person under the age of eighteen." The question for this Court, therefore, is whether a viable fetus is a "person" for purposes of the Children's Code.

In interpreting a statute, this Court's primary function is to ascertain the intent of the legislature. . . .

South Carolina law has long recognized that viable fetuses are persons holding certain legal rights and privileges. In 1960, this Court decided *Hall v. Murphy*. That case concerned the application of South Carolina's wrongful death statute to an infant who died four hours after her birth as a result of injuries sustained prenatally during viability. The Appellants argued that a viable fetus was not a person within the purview of the wrongful death statute, because, *inter alia*, a fetus is thought to have no separate being apart from the mother.

We found such a reason for exclusion from recovery "unsound, illogical and unjust," and concluded there was "no medical or other basis" for the "assumed identity" of mother and viable unborn child. In light of that conclusion, this Court unanimously held: "We have no difficulty in concluding that a fetus having reached that period of prenatal maturity where it is capable of independent life apart from its mother *is a person*."

Four years later . . . we interpreted *Hall* as supporting a finding that a viable fetus injured while still in the womb need not be born alive for another to maintain an action for the wrongful death of the fetus. . . .

More recently, we held the word "person" as used in a *criminal* statute includes viable fetuses. *State v. Horne* concerned South Carolina's murder statute. The defendant in that case stabbed his wife, who was nine months' pregnant, in the neck, arms, and abdomen. Although doctors performed an emergency caesarean section to deliver the child, the child died while still in the womb. The defendant was convicted of voluntary manslaughter and appealed his conviction on the ground South Carolina did not recognize the crime of feticide.

This Court disagreed. In a unanimous decision, we held it would be "grossly inconsistent . . . to construe a viable fetus as a 'person' for the purposes of imposing civil liability while refusing to give it a similar classification in the criminal context." Accordingly, the Court recognized the crime of feticide with respect to viable fetuses.

Similarly, we do not see any rational basis for finding a viable fetus is not a "person" in the present context. Indeed, it would be absurd to recognize the viable fetus as a person for purposes of homicide laws and wrongful death statutes but not for purposes of statutes proscribing child abuse. Our holding in *Hall* that a viable fetus is a person rested primarily on the plain meaning of the word "person" in light of existing medical knowledge concerning fetal development. We do not believe that the plain and ordinary meaning of the word "person" has changed in any way that would now deny viable fetuses status as persons.

The policies enunciated in the Children's Code also support our plain meaning reading of "person." S.C. Code Ann. § 20-7-20(C) (1985), which describes South Carolina's policy concerning children, expressly states: "It shall be the policy of this State to concentrate on the *prevention of children's problems* as the most important strategy which can be planned and implemented on behalf of children and their families." (emphasis added). The abuse or neglect of a child at any time during childhood can exact a profound toll on the child herself as well as on society as a whole. However, the consequences of abuse or neglect which takes place after birth often pale in comparison to those resulting from abuse suffered by the viable fetus before birth. This policy of prevention supports a reading of the word "person" to include viable fetuses. Furthermore, the scope of the Children's Code is quite broad. It applies "to *all* children who have need of services." When coupled with the comprehensive remedial purposes of the Code, this language supports the inference that the legislature intended to include viable fetuses within the scope of the Code's protection. . . .

C. CONSTITUTIONAL ISSUES . . .

2. Right to Privacy

Whitner argues that prosecuting her for using crack cocaine after her fetus attains viability unconstitutionally burdens her right of privacy, or, more specifically, her right to carry her pregnancy to term. We disagree. . . .

First, the State's interest in protecting the life and health of the viable fetus is not merely legitimate. It is compelling. *See, e.g., Roe v. Wade; Planned Parenthood v. Casey.* The United States Supreme Court in *Casey* recognized that the State possesses a profound interest in the potential life of the fetus, not only after the fetus is viable, but *throughout* the expectant mother's pregnancy.

Even more importantly, however, we do not think any fundamental right of Whitner's—or any right at all, for that matter—is implicated under the present scenario. It strains belief for Whitner to argue that using crack cocaine during pregnancy is encompassed within the constitutionally recognized right of privacy. Use of crack cocaine is illegal, period. No one here argues that laws criminalizing the use of crack cocaine are themselves unconstitutional. If the State wishes to impose additional criminal penalties on pregnant women who engage in this already illegal conduct because of the effect the conduct has on

the viable fetus, it may do so. We do not see how the fact of pregnancy elevates
the use of crack cocaine to the lofty status of a fundamental right.

NOTES AND QUESTIONS:
Whitner v. South Carolina

1. The United States Supreme Court chose not to review this decision (technically, it denied a "writ of certiorari"). Because the Supreme Court has
   some flexibility with regard to most cases it reviews, it is usually difficult to
   read very much into the Court's refusal to review a case. It might mean, for
   example, that not enough Justices think an issue is important enough for
   them to spend their limited time on. Thus, the denial of certiorari should
   not necessarily be viewed as an endorsement of the opinion of the South
   Carolina Supreme Court.
2. Federalism is very relevant to the *Whitner* case. The South Carolina court
   is interpreting a South Carolina law, and the court's opinion on that issue is
   final. Each state has the ultimate authority to interpret its own laws. Thus,
   even if the United States Supreme Court had chosen to review this case, it
   could not have reversed the South Carolina court's conclusion that the term
   "child" in the state law was meant by the state legislature to include a fetus.
   The U.S. Supreme Court would have had to take this finding as a given.
   (We commented on a similar circumstance in discussing *Eisenstadt v.
   Baird* in chapter 2.)
       Of course, such state laws can still be found inconsistent with the
   United States Constitution, and possibly declared unconstitutional. For example, some states have passed laws that define a fetus to be a person.
   While it is permissible for a state to do this, it does not change the balancing
   of interests that takes place in, for example, determining a woman's right to
   an abortion . The importance of the state's interest in protecting fetal rights
   does not change just because of a change in state law.
       Thus, while in the context of the *Whitner* case, South Carolina law has
   been definitely determined to apply to fetuses, it may still conflict with the
   U.S. Constitution. It might be, for example, that forcing a pregnant woman
   to go to jail under the facts of this case does indeed unconstitutionally burden her right to privacy.
3. Is the *Whitner* court correct in saying that no privacy interest of the woman
   is at issue here? If a privacy interest was at stake, is the state interest sufficient to override that interest, based on *Roe* and *Casey*?
4. Is the *Whitner* decision consistent with the *A.C.* opinion?
5. Should it make a difference if the fetus is not yet viable? Under *Casey*, in
   such a case a woman has a right to have an abortion. Is there any inconsistency in sending her to jail on the ground that she is harming the fetus, even
   though she has a right to terminate the existence of the fetus for any reason

she might choose? Recall the discussion in chapter 4 of state laws that categorize the "killing" of a fetus as homicide. Is the *Whitner* law more or less justifiable than such feticide laws?

6. The law that the *Whitner* court upheld had been used as part of a drug treatment program established at the Medical University of South Carolina (MUSC).[7] That program was the subject of a segment on the *60 Minutes* CBS news television show (first aired on November 20, 1994, and then updated on May 31, 1998). When the federal government threatened to withhold funding for the treatment program, claiming that it had not been properly approved, MUSC terminated it. In the meantime, several pregnant women who had participated in the program sued the university, claiming, among other things, that the program violated their right to be free from unconstitutional searches and seizures, and that it discriminated against African-Americans. Those claims were rejected by a federal district court in a decision that was upheld by an appellate court. The appellate opinion, *Ferguson v. Charleston*, 186 F.3d 469 (4th Cir. 1999), stated:

> In the fall of 1989, MUSC instituted a policy providing for the testing of the urine of pregnant women suspected of cocaine use and for the reporting, under certain circumstances, of test results to law enforcement officials. The impetus behind the policy came from Nurse Shirley Brown, a case manager in the obstetrics department at MUSC. Brown was concerned about a perceived rise in cocaine use among pregnant women and the consequences for the health of the users' children. Brown spoke with the General Counsel for MUSC, who in turn contacted the Ninth Circuit Solicitor (chief prosecuting attorney) concerning the development of a policy to address the problem. Eventually, a task force was formed that included Nurse Brown, the Solicitor, the Chief of [Police], and doctors from various departments involved in perinatal care at MUSC. During the course of task force meetings, the Solicitor informed the participants that because a viable fetus was a "person" under South Carolina law, a woman who ingested cocaine after the 24th week of pregnancy was guilty of the crime of distributing a controlled substance to a person under the age of eighteen.
>
> Pursuant to the policy formulated by the task force and implemented in late October or early November 1989, urine drug screens to detect evidence of cocaine use were given to all MUSC maternity patients when certain indicia of cocaine use were present. . . . When a patient tested positive, the test result was reported . . . and the patient was arrested for distributing cocaine to a minor. In early 1990, the policy was amended so that a patient who tested positive for cocaine use was given a choice between being arrested and receiving drug treatment. Positive test results of a patient who elected drug treatment were not forwarded to [the police], and the patient was not arrested, unless she tested positive for cocaine use a second time or failed to comply with treatment obligations. A patient who was arrested could avoid prosecution by completing a drug treatment program. Upon successful completion of such a program, the charges would be dismissed.

Implementation of the policy by MUSC involved substantial record keeping and educational efforts. A maternity patient whose urine tested positive for cocaine use was shown an educational video concerning the harmful effects of cocaine use during pregnancy and was given letters from the Solicitor's Office and the hospital staff relating to the policy. In addition, MUSC personnel advised the patient of the need to obtain substance abuse counseling and scheduled an initial appointment for such counseling. The patient then was given a document noting the date and time of the appointment. Additionally, MUSC maintained records on patients whose urine tested positive for cocaine use as a means of tracking them to ensure that they complied with the requirements of the policy. . . .

[T]he question presented is whether a balancing of MUSC's interest in protecting the health of children whose mothers use cocaine during pregnancy, the effectiveness of the policy to identify and treat women who use cocaine during pregnancy, and the degree of intrusion experienced by women whose urine was tested for evidence of cocaine use results in a conclusion that the searches violated the Fourth Amendment [of the U.S. Constitution, which protects against "unreasonable governmental searches and seizures"]. . . .

The policy at issue here was developed after medical personnel at MUSC noticed an alarming increase in the number of pregnancies affected by cocaine use. Maternal cocaine use is associated with a number of pregnancy complications, including low birth weight, premature labor, birth defects, and neurobehavioral problems. Even a single use of cocaine during pregnancy may result in separation of the placenta from the uterine wall—a condition that may threaten the life of the mother and the fetus—or a stroke in the fetus. Moreover, costs related to caring for infants exposed to cocaine in utero are substantial, as evidenced by the testimony of an expert for Appellants who testified that he had estimated in the late 1980s that such expenses nationwide might exceed three billion dollars annually over the next ten years. In light of the documented health hazards of maternal cocaine use and the resulting drain on public resources, MUSC officials unquestionably possessed a substantial interest in taking steps to reduce cocaine use by pregnant women. . . .

In sum, the rising use of cocaine by pregnant women among MUSC's patient base and the public health problems associated with maternal cocaine use created a special need beyond normal law enforcement goals; the method chosen to address that need—testing the urine of pregnant women when indicia of possible cocaine use were present—effectively advanced the public interest; and the intrusion suffered by Appellants was minimal. Therefore, a balancing of these factors clearly demonstrates that the searches conducted were reasonable and thus not violative of the Fourth Amendment. . . .

Pursuant to Title VI [a federal civil rights law], Appellants challenged MUSC's policy of testing for and reporting cocaine use by pregnant women, maintaining that it disparately impacted African-American women.

In order to succeed on a Title VI disparate impact claim, a plaintiff first must establish a prima facie case of discrimination by showing "that a facially neutral practice has a disproportionate adverse effect on a group protected by Title VI." The burden then "shifts to the defendant to demonstrate the existence of a substantial legitimate justification for the allegedly discriminatory practice."

If the defendant succeeds in doing so, the plaintiff nevertheless will prevail by showing "that other less discriminatory means would serve the same objective."

Here, Appellants maintained that the policy disproportionately affected African-Americans in several ways. Specifically, Appellants argued that African-Americans were disproportionately affected by application of the policy (1) only at MUSC; (2) only to certain departments at MUSC; and (3) only to cocaine. Appellants further asserted that the application of the factors utilized to determine which patients would be tested for cocaine use disproportionately affected African-Americans. The district court concluded that Appellants had failed to establish a prima facie case of discrimination with respect to any of the challenged practices. Additionally, the district court determined that even if a prima facie case of discrimination had been established, MUSC had offered a legitimate justification for the policy—that it identified pregnant women who abused cocaine so that they could be referred for treatment. Further, the court held that Appellants had failed to carry their burden of establishing the existence of an equally effective practice that would have a less disparate impact because the alternative practices offered by Appellants would have been prohibitively expensive. . . .

We therefore conclude that the district court correctly granted judgment to Appellees on the Title VI claim.

The United States Supreme Court has agreed to review this case (certiorari was granted on February 28, 2000, 120 S. Ct. 1239) on the issue of whether subjecting the women to drug tests violated their Fourth Amendment rights against unreasonable searches and seizures. Oral argument will take place in October of 2000.

7. One criticism of the law in *Whitner* relates to the possibility of a "slippery slope": once it is permissible to criminalize a pregnant woman's behavior on the ground that it might injure her fetus, how do you determine *what* behaviors should be criminalized? Do you think there is a viable line, as drawn by the *Whitner* court, at least limiting the statute to behaviors that would be criminal whether or not the woman is pregnant? Would the application of the *Whitner* law to non-criminal maternal behaviors—such as smoking or drinking moderate to high amounts of alcohol—raise more substantial constitutional questions?

Endnotes

1. See, e.g., Sungeeta Jain, "How Many People Does It Takes to Save a Drowning Baby? A Good Samaritan Statute in Washington State," 74 *Wash. L. Rev.* 1181 (1999).
2. "The Bad Samaritan," *60 Minutes*, CBS News, 29 August 1999.
3. Judith Jarvis Thomson, "A Defense of Abortion," 1 *Phil. & Pub. Aff.* 47, 48–49 (1971).
4. Richard Posner, "The Problematics of Moral and Legal Theory," 111 *Harv. L. Rev.* 1637, 1675–76 (1998).

5. For further discussion see Timothy J. Burch, "Incubator or Individual: The Legal and Policy Deficiencies of Pregnancy Clauses in Living Will and Advance Health Care Directive Statutes," 54 *Md. L. Rev.* 528 (1995).
6. For further discussion see John A. Robertson, "Posthumous Reproduction," 69 *Ind. L. J.* 1027 (1994).
7. For discussion of the policy aspects of these sorts of responses to the problem of addiction among pregnant women, see, e.g., C. Antoinette Clarke, "FINS, PINS, CHIPS & CHINS: A Reasoned Approach to the Problem of Drug Use during Pregnancy," 29 *Seton Hall L. Rev.* 643 (1998); Janet L. Dolgin, "The Law's Response to Parental Alcohol and 'Crack' Abuse," 56 *Brook. L. Rev.* 1213 (1991).

PART III

Doctors, Patients, and Standards of Care

7

The Doctor-Patient Relationship

He was beginning to live in the region of truth.

Graham Greene, *The Honorary Consul*

One of the classic skits from the early years of the Saturday Night Live television show had Steve Martin playing "Theodoric of York, Medieval Barber," with Theodoric "treating" a number of his patients by bleeding them. When her daughter dies as a result of such a bleeding, Joan, wife of Simkin, the Miller (Jane Curtin) erupts in anger, criticizing Theodoric for having killed the child: "You charlatan! . . . You don't know what you're doing!" Theodoric then turns to the camera, giving a soliloquy in which he questions the then-current (circa 1300s) techniques used by medieval barbers, and asks whether he should perhaps "begin a renaissance" by introducing scientific techniques:

> Wait a minute! Perhaps she's right. Perhaps I've been wrong to blindly follow the medical traditions. . . . Maybe we barbers should test those assumptions analytically, through experimentation and the scientific method. . . . Perhaps I could lead the way to a new age, an age of rebirth, a renaissance!

Since this was, after all, a comedy show, he concluded with a brief, obviously heartfelt, "Nah!"

The Theodoric skit provides a compelling lesson about the laws governing the relationship between patients and doctors. Although we sympathize with Joan's anguish, we might well ask, what has Theodoric done wrong? As played by Steve Martin, he appears to be very intelligent and thoughtful. We have no reason to suspect that he is not a good barber, in the sense of properly following the techniques of his profession. The major problem is that those techniques were relatively poor ones, and rarely led to favorable outcomes.

Curiously enough, if we applied modern law to the Theodoric skit, there is a decent chance—depending on which state's law we applied—that Theodoric would not be found to have done anything wrong. To understand why, we must take a detour into the somewhat intricate rules governing the relationships between doctors and patients. While these rules may have weaknesses, they also have not-inconsiderable strengths. Indeed, they play a major role in establishing the "right to refuse care" that will be discussed in chapter 10.

The doctor-patient relationship is governed by a number of different legal doctrines: contract, tort, and fiduciary law. Of these three, contract law has the smallest role. It is mainly relevant in determining whether or not a doctor-patient relationship has been formed. Once such a relationship exists, tort and fiduciary law, recognizing that patients are often in a weak bargaining situation, substantially limit the freedom of doctors and patients to define the nature of the doctor-patient relationship.

Our starting point in this chapter is straightforward contract law as we determine when a doctor-patient relationship has been formed.

HURLEY V. EDDINGFIELD

Supreme Court of Indiana

59 N.E. 1058 (Ind. 1901)

OPINION BY JUDGE BAKER:

. . . The material facts alleged may be summarized thus: At and for years before decedent's death appellee was a practicing physician at Mace in Montgomery county, duly licensed under the laws of the state. He held himself out to the public as a general practitioner of medicine. He had been decedent's family physician. Decedent became dangerously ill and sent for appellee. The messenger informed appellee of decedent's violent sickness, tendered him his fees for his services, and stated to him that no other physician was procurable in time and that decedent relied on him for attention. No other physician was procurable in time to be of any use, and decedent did rely on appellee for medical assistance. Without any reason whatever, appellee refused to render aid to decedent. No other patients were requiring appellee's immediate service, and he could have gone to the relief of decedent if he had been willing to do so. Death ensued, without decedent's fault, and wholly from appellee's wrongful act.

The alleged wrongful act was appellee's refusal to enter into a contract of employment. Counsel do not contend that, before the enactment of the law regulating the practice of medicine, physicians were bound to render professional service to every one who applied. The act regulating the practice of medicine provides for a board of examiners, standards of qualification, examinations, licenses to those found qualified, and penalties for practicing without license. The act is a preventive, not a compulsive, measure. In obtaining the state's license (permission) to practice medicine, the state does not require, and the licensee does not engage, that he will practice at all or on other terms than he may choose to accept. Counsel's analogies, drawn from the obligations to the public on the part of innkeepers, common carriers, and the like, are beside the mark.

Judgment affirmed.

NOTES AND QUESTIONS:
Hurley v. Eddingfield

1. The decedent in *Hurley* was Charlotte Burk, who was having difficulty in childbirth. Both she and the unborn child died when her husband was unable to get Dr. Eddingfield to come to their aid.
2. The opinion notes that the doctor had been Mrs. Burk's family physician. You might even assume that he had treated her during a prior pregnancy. Yet the court finds that Dr. Eddingfield is nonetheless not responsible for her death. On what ground does it base its conclusion? What rule does it create with respect to previous dealings between a doctor and a patient, and how they affect whether there is a current doctor-patient relationship? (This rule is followed even today.) What do you think would have been the outcome if Dr. Eddingfield had been treating Mrs. Burk for this pregnancy? Do you think the court's conclusions on this issue are correct?
3. Note the court's rejection of the analogy between physicians and other groups (such as innkeepers and common carriers) who are required to serve everyone who comes to their door. This is a distinction that persists to some extent even today: there is an understanding that the doctor's office is private in a way that is not true of the hotel or the bus station. Should we rewrite the law to change that understanding? Should a doctor be required to accept any patient who has sufficient money to pay the bill? Or, perhaps, any patient, with or without sufficient money?

   Of course, many modern contractual arrangements have altered the ability of the doctor to choose her patients. For example, a doctor's agreement with a managed care company will likely require the doctor to treat all of that company's patients who show up at the door.
4. A separate aspect of the case is that this was an emergency, and no other doctor could be obtained in time. Whatever you think of the general rule created by the court, should there be a different rule in emergencies? Note the similarity of the *Hurley* rule to the general rules about when people are required to aid others to whom they have no pre-existing duty, as discussed at the beginning of chapter 6.

5. The *Hurley* case is essentially still a correct statement of the law with regard to the formation of a doctor-patient relationship. It is not very different from the ethical standards adopted by organized medicine, which do require treatment in emergencies but otherwise preserve the underlying contract-based freedom of doctors to choose whom they treat. Consider American Medical Association, *Code of Medical Ethics*, 1996-1997 ed., Opinion 8.11: "Physicians are free to choose whom they will serve. The physician should, however, respond to the best of his or her ability in cases of emergency when first-aid treatment is essential." And Opinion 9.06: "Free choice of physicians is the right of every individual. One may select and change at will one's physicians. . . . Although the concept of free choice assures that an individual can generally choose a physician, likewise a physician may decline to accept that individual as a patient."

6. Just as the creation of a doctor-patient relationship requires the consent of both parties to the relationship, the termination of either party's consent will end the relationship. Thus, a patient can at any time choose to find another caregiver.

   As for the doctor, it is relatively difficult for a doctor to be found legally liable for abandoning a patient. If a doctor wishes to terminate a relationship with a patient, all he need do is provide notice and give the patient an opportunity to find another doctor. (We are excluding the circumstance where the doctor's motivation is inconsistent with a specific law, such as one preventing discrimination against certain classes of individuals.) Consistent with the contractual approach to doctor-patient relationships, the rule does not appear to impose an obligation on the doctor to make sure the patient has the money or other resources to obtain alternative services. To impose such a duty would seem inconsistent with the fact that under U.S. law there is no general "right" to health care (as is further discussed in chapter 9). Abandonment is only likely to be an issue where the patient needs urgent care and the doctor has already begun to provide that care. The most famous case discussing abandonment is *Payton v. Weaver*, 182 Cal. Rptr. 225 (Cal. Ct. App. 1982), where a doctor went to great lengths to avoid abandoning a patient.

THE LAW OF TORTS: FROM BATTERY TO INFORMED CONSENT

Tort law has probably had a greater impact on doctor-patient relations in this country than virtually any other branch of the law. It has had an equally powerful impact in shaping core aspects of American bioethics, having played a major role in elevating "autonomy" to its current position of importance in ethical thinking, and in creating the constitutional protections recognized in the "right to refuse care" jurisprudence.

Tort law is very old. Most of this nation's tort law is derived from our English *common law* ancestry: laws that were created by courts, over time, as judges gradually refined principles of law from decision to decision. This is in contrast to *statutory law*, where a legislature passes a statute. Often, what begins as common law ends up, after the passage of much time, as statutory law: the legislature collects all the principles contained in numerous court decisions, perhaps revising them or making them more internally consistent, and then passes a set of laws, a code, dealing with an entire area of conduct.

Tort law is a broad area of law governing *civil* wrongs: things we do to each other that are considered wrongful, so that the law allows someone to sue the wrongdoer and get damages, or to stop the wrongful conduct. Many of the wrongs covered by tort law are also violations of *criminal* law: someone who shot me might be guilty of the crime of assault and battery (the "assault" part relates to threatening me with harm, and the "battery" to the actual shooting). But the purpose of criminal law is not to compensate injured parties, so I would have my own right, under tort law, to sue the shooter for compensation for having committed the *torts* of assault and battery on me. The same names are used for both, but one is a criminal violation and the other involves a tort cause of action.

For purposes of bioethics, it is important to understand two distinct categories of tort law: *intentional torts* and *negligence*. Intentional torts are what the name suggests: the person committing the tort intended to do it. One of the classic intentional torts is battery—a touching that has not been consented to. In battery we see the earliest suggestions of what would become the right to refuse care (and its ultimate embodiment in the constitutional right to privacy). One of the most famous, and earliest, quotations about this right appears in Justice Cardozo's 1914 opinion for the New York Court of Appeals in *Schloendorff v. New York Hospital*. When Cardozo speaks about "trespass" in the following excerpt, he is merely using another name for battery, since touching a person without permission is similar to nonconsensually going onto a person's property:

> In the year 1771, by royal charter of George III, the Society of the New York Hospital was organized for the care and healing of the sick. During the century and more which has since passed, it has devoted itself to that high task. It has no capital stock; it does not distribute profits; and its physicians and surgeons, both the visiting and the resident staff, serve it without pay. Those who seek it in search of health, are charged nothing, if they are needy, either for board or for treatment. The well-to-do are required by its by-laws to pay $7 a week for board, an amount insufficient to cover the per capita cost of maintenance. Whatever income is thus received, is added to the income derived from the hospital's foundation, and helps to make it possible for the work to go on. The purpose is not profit, but charity, and the incidental revenue does not change the defendant's standing as a charitable institution.
>
> To this hospital the plaintiff came in January, 1908. She was suffering from some disorder of the stomach. She asked the superintendent or one of

his assistants what the charge would be and was told that it would be $7 a week. She became an inmate of the hospital, and after some weeks of treatment the house physician, Dr. Bartlett, discovered a lump, which proved to be a fibroid tumor. He consulted the visiting surgeon, Dr. Stimson, who advised an operation. The plaintiff's testimony is that the character of the lump could not, so the physicians informed her, be determined without an ether examination. She consented to such an examination, but notified Dr. Bartlett, as she says, that there must be no operation. She was taken at night from the medical to the surgical ward and prepared for an operation by a nurse. On the following day ether was administered, and while she was unconscious a tumor was removed. Her testimony is that this was done without her consent or knowledge. She is contradicted both by Dr. Stimson and by Dr. Bartlett, as well as by many of the attendant nurses. For the purpose of this appeal, however, since a verdict was directed in favor of the defendant, her narrative, even if improbable, must be taken as true. Following the operation, and, according to the testimony of her witnesses, because of it, gangrene developed in her left arm; some of her fingers had to be amputated; and her sufferings were intense. She now seeks to charge the hospital with liability for the wrong. . . .

In the case at hand, the wrong complained of is not merely negligence. It is trespass. *Every human being of adult years and sound mind has a right to determine what shall be done with his own body; and a surgeon who performs an operation without his patient's consent, commits an assault, for which he is liable in damages.* This is true except in cases of emergency where the patient is unconscious and where it is necessary to operate before consent can be obtained. The fact that the wrong complained of here is trespass rather than negligence, distinguishes this case from most of the cases that have preceded it. . . . She had never consented to become a patient for any purpose other than an examination under ether. She had never waived the right to recover damages for any wrong resulting from this operation, for she had forbidden the operation. (105 N.E. 92, 92–94, emphasis added.)

Although the italicized language appears definitive, the tort of battery plays a relatively minor role in modern doctor-patient relations. When Cardozo talks about performing an operation "without consent," he is not referring to a failure to adequately explain the risks and benefits of the procedure. Rather, battery takes place only when something happens to a patient other than what the patient expected. Examples of battery are doing a procedure that the patient did not want done (as in Ms. Schloendorff's case), having a different surgeon operate than the one you wanted, or having a surgeon operate on the wrong part of your body (e.g., amputating your good leg instead of the gangrenous one). Even today, it is, hopefully, relatively rare that physicians behave in a way that would make them liable for having committed a battery. Going ahead with an operation that the patient said "yes" to, even though the patient was not advised of substantial (perhaps life-threatening) risks, would *not* be a battery.

While battery has ancient origins dating back to English common law, the modern notion of informed consent did not come into being until at least the 1950s. It evolved as part of negligence law, which, as we shall see, is far more favorable to physicians than is the law of battery. Negligence, unlike the law of intentional torts, deals with situations where people make mistakes. Malpractice is the branch of negligence law that deals with mistakes by medical professionals.

Of course, mistakes are a part of life. Thus, the question arises as to who should bear the hardship when a doctor makes a mistake in treating a patient. The way this issue is resolved by negligence law generally is that we are all required to be reasonably careful in our day-to-day lives: in legal terms, we must act with the level of care (the *standard* of care) that others would use. If something goes wrong while you are being adequately careful, then the injured person must bear the loss. On the other hand, if you failed to follow the appropriate standard of care, then, because you were negligent, you must pay. In effect, negligence law assures the patient that the health care provider will exercise at least the average care and skill of her colleagues.

It is generally not open to the doctor and patient to bargain away this "guaranteed" level of competence. In effect, society paternalistically prevents us from choosing to obtain substandard care, even if that should be what we knowingly wanted. This is not unusual in the law. Many laws—standards for home construction or building cars, rules requiring the use of bicycle or motorcycle helmets—require us to do things for our own good. Nonetheless, given the bad rap that paternalism has gotten in bioethics (at least when a doctor overrides a patient's wishes), it is somewhat ironic to recognize the unabashedly paternalistic stance of the major legal rules governing doctor-patient relationships.

The case that follows, *Canterbury v. Spence*, demonstrates three key concepts: how professionals can define for themselves the standard of care, how the concept of informed consent became an element of negligence law, and how that led to two very different views of what informed consent should mean.

CANTERBURY V. SPENCE

United States Court of Appeals for the District of Columbia Circuit

464 F.2d 772 (D.C. 1969)

OPINION BY JUDGE ROBINSON:

. . . The record we review tells a depressing tale. A youth troubled only by back pain submitted to an operation without being informed of a risk of paralysis incidental thereto. A day after the operation he fell from his hospital bed after having been left without assistance while voiding. A few hours after the fall, the lower half of his body was paralyzed, and he had to be operated on again. Despite extensive medical care, he has never been what he was before. Instead of the back pain, even years later, he hobbled about on crutches, a victim of paralysis of the bowels and urinary incontinence. In a very real sense this lawsuit is an understandable search for reasons.

At the time of the events which gave rise to this litigation, appellant was nineteen years of age, a clerk-typist employed by the Federal Bureau of Investigation. In December, 1958, he began to experience severe pain between his shoulder blades. He consulted two general practitioners, but the medications they prescribed failed to eliminate the pain. Thereafter, appellant secured an appointment with Dr. Spence, who is a neurosurgeon.

Dr. Spence examined appellant in his office at some length but found nothing amiss. On Dr. Spence's advice appellant was x-rayed, but the films did not identify any abnormality. Dr. Spence then recommended that appellant undergo a myelogram—a procedure in which dye is injected into the spinal column and traced to find evidence of disease or other disorder—at the Washington Hospital Center.

Appellant entered the hospital on February 4, 1959. The myelogram revealed a "filling defect" in the region of the fourth thoracic vertebra. Since a myelogram often does no more than pinpoint the location of an aberration, surgery may be necessary to discover the cause. Dr. Spence told appellant that he would have to undergo a laminectomy—the excision of the posterior arch of the vertebra—to correct what he suspected was a ruptured disc. Appellant did not raise any objection to the proposed operation nor did he probe into its exact nature. . . .

Dr. Spence performed the laminectomy on February 11 at the Washington Hospital Center. . . . The laminectomy revealed several anomalies: a spinal cord that was swollen and unable to pulsate, an accumulation of large tortuous and dilated veins, and a complete absence of epidural fat which normally surrounds the spine. A thin hypodermic needle was inserted into the spinal cord to aspirate any cysts which might have been present, but no fluid emerged. In suturing the wound, Dr. Spence attempted to relieve the pressure on the spinal cord by enlarging the dura—the outer protective wall of the spinal cord—at the area of swelling.

For approximately the first day after the operation appellant recuperated normally, but then suffered a fall and an almost immediate setback. . . .

Several hours later, appellant began to complain that he could not move his legs and that he was having trouble breathing; paralysis seems to have been virtually total from the waist down. . . . The surgical wound was reopened and Dr. Spence created a gusset to allow the spinal cord greater room in which to pulsate.

Appellant's control over his muscles improved somewhat after the second operation but he was unable to void properly. . . . At the time of the trial in April,

1968, appellant required crutches to walk, still suffered from urinal incontinence and paralysis of the bowels, and wore a penile clamp. . . .

II

At the close of appellant's case in chief, each defendant moved for a directed verdict and the trial judge granted both motions. The basis of the ruling, he explained, was that appellant had failed to produce any medical evidence indicating negligence on Dr. Spence's part in diagnosing appellant's malady or in performing the laminectomy; that there was no proof that Dr. Spence's treatment was responsible for appellant's disabilities; and that notwithstanding some evidence to show negligent post-operative care, an absence of medical testimony to show causality precluded submission of the case against the hospital to the jury. The judge did not allude specifically to the alleged breach of duty by Dr. Spence to divulge the possible consequences of the laminectomy.

We reverse. The testimony of appellant and his mother that Dr. Spence did not reveal the risk of paralysis from the laminectomy made out a prima facie case of violation of the physician's duty to disclose which Dr. Spence's explanation did not negate as a matter of law. . . .

III

Suits charging failure by a physician adequately to disclose the risks and alternatives of proposed treatment are not innovations in American law. They date back a good half-century, and in the last decade they have multiplied rapidly. There is, nonetheless, disagreement among the courts and the commentators on many major questions, and there is no precedent of our own directly in point. For the tools enabling resolution of the issues on this appeal, we are forced to begin at first principles.

The root premise is the concept, fundamental in American jurisprudence, that "every human being of adult years and sound mind has a right to determine what shall be done with his own body. . . ." True consent to what happens to one's self is the informed exercise of a choice, and that entails an opportunity to evaluate knowledgeably the options available and the risks attendant upon each. The average patient has little or no understanding of the medical arts, and ordinarily has only his physician to whom he can look for enlightenment with which to reach an intelligent decision. From these almost axiomatic considerations springs the need, and in turn the requirement, of a reasonable divulgence by physician to patient to make such a decision possible.

A physician is under a duty to treat his patient skillfully but proficiency in diagnosis and therapy is not the full measure of his responsibility. The cases demonstrate that the physician is under an obligation to communicate specific information to the patient when the exigencies of reasonable care call for it. Due care may require a physician perceiving symptoms of bodily abnormality to alert the patient to the condition. It may call upon the physician confronting an ailment which does not respond to his ministrations to inform the patient thereof. It may command the physician to instruct the patient as to any limitations to be presently observed for his own welfare, and as to any precautionary therapy he should seek in the future. It may oblige the physician to advise the patient of the need for or desirability of any alternative treatment promising greater benefit than that being pursued. Just as plainly, due care normally demands that the physician warn the patient of any risks to his well-being which contemplated therapy may involve.

The context in which the duty of risk-disclosure arises is invariably the occasion for decision as to whether a particular treatment procedure is to be undertaken. To the physician, whose training enables a self-satisfying evaluation, the answer may seem clear, but it is the prerogative of the patient, not the physician, to determine for himself the direction in which his interests seem to lie. To enable the patient to chart his course understandably, some familiarity with the therapeutic alternatives and their hazards becomes essential.

A reasonable revelation in these respects is not only a necessity but, as we see it, is as much a matter of the physician's duty. It is a duty to warn of the dangers lurking in the proposed treatment, and that is surely a facet of due care. It is, too, a duty to impart information which the patient has every right to expect. The patient's reliance upon the physician is a trust of the kind which traditionally has exacted obligations beyond those associated with arms-length transactions. His dependence upon the physician for information affecting his well-being, in terms of contemplated treatment, is well-nigh abject. As earlier noted, long before the instant litigation arose, courts had recognized that the physician had the responsibility of satisfying the vital informational needs of the patient. More recently, we ourselves have found "in the fiducial qualities of [the physician-patient] relationship the physician's duty to reveal to the patient that which in his best interests it is important that he should know." We now find, as a part of the physician's overall obligation to the patient, a similar duty of reasonable disclosure of the choices with respect to proposed therapy and the dangers inherently and potentially involved.

This disclosure requirement, on analysis, reflects much more of a change in doctrinal emphasis than a substantive addition to malpractice law. It is well established that the physician must seek and secure his patient's consent before commencing an operation or other course of treatment. It is also clear that the consent, to be efficacious, must be free from imposition upon the patient. It is the settled rule that therapy not authorized by the patient may amount to a tort—a common law battery—by the physician. And it is evident that it is normally impossible to obtain a consent worthy of the name unless the physician first elucidates the options and the perils for the patient's edification. Thus the physician has long borne a duty, on pain of liability for unauthorized treatment, to make adequate disclosure to the patient. The evolution of the obligation to communicate for the patient's benefit as well as the physician's protection has hardly involved an extraordinary restructuring of the law.

IV

Duty to disclose has gained recognition in a large number of American jurisdictions, but more largely on a different rationale. The majority of courts dealing with the problem have made the duty depend on whether it was the custom of physicians practicing in the community to make the particular disclosure to the patient. If so, the physician may be held liable for an unreasonable and injurious failure to divulge, but there can be no recovery unless the omission forsakes a practice prevalent in the profession. We agree that the physician's noncompliance with a professional custom to reveal, like any other departure from prevailing medical practice, may give rise to liability to the patient. We do not agree that the patient's cause of action is dependent upon the existence and nonperformance of a relevant professional tradition.

There are, in our view, formidable obstacles to acceptance of the notion that the physician's obligation to disclose is either germinated or limited by medical practice. To begin with, the reality of any discernible custom reflecting a professional consensus on communication of option and risk information to patients is open to serious doubt. We sense the danger that what in fact is no custom at all may be taken as an affirmative custom to maintain silence, and that physician-witnesses to the so-called custom may state merely their personal opinions as to what they or others would do under given conditions. We cannot gloss over the inconsistency between reliance on a general practice respecting divulgence and, on the other hand, realization that the myriad of variables among patients makes each case so different that its omission can rationally be justified only by the effect of its individual circumstances. Nor can we ignore the fact that to bind the disclosure obligation to medical usage is to arrogate the decision on revelation to the physician alone. Respect for the patient's right of self-determination on particular therapy demands a standard set by law for physicians rather than one which physicians may or may not impose upon themselves.

More fundamentally, the majority rule overlooks the graduation of reasonable-care demands in Anglo-American jurisprudence and the position of professional custom in the hierarchy. The caliber of the performance exacted by the reasonable-care standard varies between the professional and non-professional worlds, and so also the role of professional custom. "With but few exceptions," we recently declared, "society demands that everyone under a duty to use care observe minimally a general standard." "Familiarly expressed judicially," we added, "the yardstick is that degree of care which a reasonably prudent person would have exercised under the same or similar circumstances." "Beyond this," however, we emphasized, "the law requires those engaging in activities requiring unique knowledge and ability to give a performance commensurate with the undertaking." Thus physicians treating the sick must perform at higher levels than non-physicians in order to meet the reasonable care standard in its special application to physicians—"that degree of care and skill ordinarily exercised by the profession in [the physician's] own or similar localities." And practices adopted by the profession have indispensable value as evidence tending to establish just what that degree of care and skill is.

We have admonished, however, that "the special medical standards are but adaptations of the general standard to a group who are required to act as reasonable men possessing their medical talents presumably would." There is, by the same token, no basis for operation of the special medical standard where the physician's activity does not bring his medical knowledge and skills peculiarly into play. And where the challenge to the physician's conduct is not to be gauged by the special standard, it follows that medical custom cannot furnish the test of its propriety, whatever its relevance under the proper test may be. The decision to unveil the patient's condition and the chances as to remediation, as we shall see, is ofttimes a non-medical judgment and, if so, is a decision outside the ambit of the special standard. Where that is the situation, professional custom hardly furnishes the legal criterion for measuring the physician's responsibility to reasonably inform his patient of the options and the hazards as to treatment. . . .

Thus we distinguished, for purposes of duty to disclose, the special and general-standard aspects of the physician-patient relationship. When medical judgment enters the picture and for that reason the special standard controls, prevailing medical practice must be given its just due. In all other instances, however, the general standard exacting ordinary care applies, and that standard is set by law. In sum, the physician's duty to disclose is governed by the same legal principles applicable to others in comparable situations, with modifications only to the extent that medical judgment enters the picture. We hold that the standard measuring performance of that duty by physicians, as by others, is conduct which is reasonable under the circumstances.

V

Once the circumstances give rise to a duty on the physician's part to inform his patient, the next inquiry is the scope of the disclosure the physician is legally obliged to make. The courts have frequently confronted this problem but no uniform standard defining the adequacy of the divulgence emerges from the decisions. Some have said "full" disclosure, a norm we are unwilling to adopt literally. It seems obviously prohibitive and unrealistic to expect physicians to discuss with their patients every risk of proposed treatment—no matter how small or remote—and generally unnecessary from the patient's viewpoint as well. Indeed, the cases speaking in terms of "full" disclosure appear to envision something less than total disclosure, leaving unanswered the question of just how much.

The larger number of courts, as might be expected, have applied tests framed with reference to prevailing fashion within the medical profession.

Some have measured the disclosure by "good medical practice," others by what a reasonable practitioner would have bared under the circumstances, and still others by what medical custom in the community would demand. We have explored this rather considerable body of law but are unprepared to follow it. The duty to disclose, we have reasoned, arises from phenomena apart from medical custom and practice. The latter, we think, should no more establish the scope of the duty than its existence. Any definition of scope in terms purely of a professional standard is at odds with the patient's prerogative to decide on projected therapy himself. That prerogative, we have said, is at the very foundation of the duty to disclose, and both the patient's right to know and the physician's correlative obligation to tell him are diluted to the extent that its compass is dictated by the medical profession.

In our view, the patient's right of self-decision shapes the boundaries of the duty to reveal. That right can be effectively exercised only if the patient possesses enough information to enable an intelligent choice. The scope of the physician's communications to the patient, then, must be measured by the patient's need, and that need is the information material to the decision. Thus the test for determining whether a particular peril must be divulged is its materiality to the patient's decision: all risks potentially affecting the decision must be unmasked. And to safeguard the patient's interest in achieving his own determination on treatment, the law must itself set the standard for adequate disclosure.

Optimally for the patient, exposure of a risk would be mandatory whenever the patient would deem it significant to his decision, either singly or in combination with other risks. Such a requirement, however, would summon the physician to second-guess the patient, whose ideas on materiality could hardly be known to the physician. That would make an undue demand upon medical practitioners, whose conduct, like that of others, is to be measured in terms of reasonableness. Consonantly with orthodox negligence doctrine, the physician's liability for nondisclosure is to be determined on the basis of foresight, not hindsight; no less than any other aspect of negligence, the issue on nondisclosure must be approached from the viewpoint of the reasonableness of the physician's divulgence in terms of what he knows or should know to be the patient's informational needs. If, but only if, the fact-finder can say that the physician's communication was unreasonably inadequate is an imposition of liability legally or morally justified.

Of necessity, the content of the disclosure rests in the first instance with the physician. Ordinarily it is only he who is in position to identify particular dangers; always he must make a judgment, in terms of materiality, as to whether and to what extent revelation to the patient is called for. He cannot know with complete exactitude what the patient would consider important to his decision, but on the basis of his medical training and experience he can sense how the average, reasonable patient expectably would react. Indeed, with knowledge of, or ability to learn, his patient's background and current condition, he is in a position superior to that of most others—attorneys, for example—who are called upon to make judgments on pain of liability in damages for unreasonable miscalculation.

From these considerations we derive the breadth of the disclosure of risks legally to be required. The scope of the standard is not subjective as to either the physician or the patient; it remains objective with due regard for the patient's informational needs and with suitable leeway for the physician's situation. In broad outline, we agree that "[a] risk is thus material when a reasonable person, in what the physician knows or should know to be the patient's position, would be likely to attach significance to the risk or cluster of risks in deciding whether or not to forego the proposed therapy."

The topics importantly demanding a communication of information are the inherent and potential hazards of the proposed treatment, the alternatives to that treatment, if any, and the results likely if the patient remains untreated. The factors contributing significance to the dangerousness of a medical technique are, of course, the incidence of injury and the degree of the harm threatened. A very small chance of death or serious disablement may well be significant; a potential disability which dramatically outweighs the potential benefit of the therapy or the detriments of the existing malady may summons discussion with the patient.

There is no bright line separating the significant from the insignificant; the answer in any case must abide a rule of reason. Some dangers—infection, for example—are inherent in any operation; there is no obligation to communicate those of which persons of average sophistication are aware. Even more clearly, the physician bears no responsibility for discussion of hazards the patient has already discovered, or those having no apparent materiality to patients' decision on therapy. The disclosure doctrine, like others marking lines between permissible and impermissible behavior in medical practice, is in essence a requirement of conduct prudent under the circumstances. Whenever nondisclosure of particular risk information is open to debate by reasonable-minded men, the issue is for the finder of the facts.

VI

Two exceptions to the general rule of disclosure have been noted by the courts. Each is in the nature of a physician's privilege not to disclose, and the reasoning underlying them is appealing. Each, indeed, is but a recognition that, as important as is the patient's right to know, it is greatly outweighed by the magnitudinous circumstances giving rise to the privilege. The first comes into play when the patient is unconscious or otherwise incapable of consenting, and harm from a failure to treat is imminent and outweighs any harm threatened by the proposed treatment. When a genuine emergency of that sort arises, it is settled that the impracticality of conferring with the patient dispenses with need for it. Even in situations of that character the physician should, as current law requires, attempt to secure a relative's consent if possible. But if time is too short to accommodate discussion, obviously the physician should proceed with the treatment.

The second exception obtains when risk-disclosure poses such a threat of detriment to the patient as to become unfeasible or contraindicated from a medical point of view. It is recognized that patients occasionally become so ill or emotionally distraught on disclosure as to foreclose a rational decision, or complicate or hinder the treatment, or perhaps even pose psychological damage to the patient. Where that is so, the cases have generally held that the physician is armed with a privilege to keep the information from the patient, and we think it clear that portents of that type may justify the physician in action he deems medically warranted. The critical inquiry is whether the physician responded to a sound medical judgment that communication of the risk information would present a threat to the patient's well-being.

The physician's privilege to withhold information for therapeutic reasons must be carefully circumscribed, however, for otherwise it might devour the disclosure rule itself. The privilege does not accept the paternalistic notion that the physician may remain silent simply because divulgence might prompt the patient to forego therapy the physician feels the patient really needs. That attitude presumes instability or perversity for even the normal patient, and runs counter to the foundation principle that the patient should and ordinarily can make the choice for himself. Nor does the privilege contemplate operation save where the patient's reaction to risk information, as reasonably foreseen by the physician, is menacing. And even in a situation of that kind, disclosure to a close relative with a view to securing consent to the proposed treatment may be the only alternative open to the physician.

VII

No more than breach of any other legal duty does nonfulfillment of the physician's obligation to disclose alone establish liability to the patient. An unrevealed risk that should have been made known must materialize, for otherwise the omission, however unpardonable, is legally without consequence. Occurrence of the risk must be harmful to the patient, for negligence unrelated to injury is nonactionable. And, as in malpractice actions generally, there must be a causal relationship between the physician's failure to adequately divulge and damage to the patient.

A causal connection exists when, but only when, disclosure of significant risks incidental to treatment would have resulted in a decision against it. The patient obviously has no complaint if he would have submitted to the therapy notwithstanding awareness that the risk was one of its perils. On the other hand, the very purpose of the disclosure rule is to protect the patient against consequences which, if known, he would have avoided by foregoing the treatment. The more difficult question is whether the factual issue on causality calls for an objective or a subjective determination.

It has been assumed that the issue is to be resolved according to whether the fact-finder believes the patient's testimony that he would not have agreed to the treatment if he had known of the danger which later ripened into injury. We think a technique which ties the factual conclusion on causation simply to the assessment of the patient's credibility is unsatisfactory. To be sure, the objective of risk-disclosure is preservation of the patient's interest in intelligent self-choice on proposed treatment, a matter the patient is free to decide for any reason that appeals to him. When, prior to commencement of therapy, the patient is sufficiently informed on risks and he exercises his choice, it may truly be said that he did exactly what he wanted to do. But when causality is explored at a postinjury trial with a professedly uninformed patient, the question whether he actually would have turned the treatment down if he had known the risks is purely hypothetical: "Viewed from the point at which he had to decide, would the patient have decided differently had he known something he did not know?" And the answer which the patient supplies hardly represents more than a guess, perhaps tinged by the circumstance that the uncommunicated hazard has in fact materialized.

In our view, this method of dealing with the issue on causation comes in second-best. It places the physician in jeopardy of the patient's hindsight and bitterness. It places the fact-finder in the position of deciding whether a speculative answer to a hypothetical question is to be credited. It calls for a subjective determination solely on testimony of a patient-witness shadowed by the occurrence of the undisclosed risk.

Better it is, we believe, to resolve the causality issue on an objective basis: in terms of what a prudent person in the patient's position would have decided if suitably informed of all perils bearing significance. If adequate disclosure could reasonably be expected to have caused that person to decline the treatment because of the revelation of the kind of risk or danger that resulted in harm, causation is shown, but otherwise not. The patient's testimony is relevant on that score of course but it would not threaten to dominate the findings. And since that testimony would probably be appraised congruently with the fact-finder's belief in its reasonableness, the case for a wholly objective standard for passing on causation is strengthened. Such a standard would in any event ease the fact-finding process and better assure the truth as its product. . . .

NOTES AND QUESTIONS:
Canterbury v. Spence

1. To prove that a battery has been committed, one of the key parts of the plaintiff's case is demonstrating that she did not consent to what happened. Does this require any testimony by medical experts? Recall Ms. Schloendorff's situation. What would she have had to show to the jury?
2. In contrast, in an action for medical malpractice, the plaintiff must demonstrate that there has been a failure to meet the standard of care. And since

we are dealing with a profession, that standard of care is determined by the members of the profession itself. Can you see how that gives the profession substantial control in determining its own legal liability? Is it appropriate to have such a standard of care set by the profession? Should there be limits on this?

3. In an actual malpractice lawsuit, to demonstrate that there has been a failure to follow the standard of care, the plaintiff must first demonstrate what that standard of care is. What kind of evidence must be introduced by the plaintiff to establish the standard? What types of experts will have to be put on the stand to present this evidence? Can you see how the negligence action is much harder to prove than a battery action such as Ms. Schloendorff's?

4. Returning to the Theodoric of York skit that began this chapter, do you think Theodoric committed malpractice (in the traditional sense, ignoring failure to get informed consent)? Why or why not? Note that performing "unproven" medical treatments is not confined to the Middle Ages. Commentators have suggested that up to 80 percent of the treatments provided by modern medicine are unproven, in the sense that they have not undergone double-blind, randomized testing. Moreover, many such treatments (particularly, many forms of chemotherapy used to treat cancer) are at least as harmful as bloodletting might have been.

5. Ignoring the informed consent issue, did the trial court find that Dr. Spence had committed malpractice? Does this tell you anything about the relationship between bad outcomes and liability for malpractice?

6. *Canterbury v. Spence* is a landmark opinion, in that it adopts a new view of informed consent. What was the old view of informed consent that it rejected? How did that old view—which itself was a relatively modern development in this century—logically flow from the law of negligence? If you view negligence as a failure to follow the standards set by the members of a profession, what rule might you reasonably come up with regarding how much to tell a patient?[1]

7. What was the new informed consent rule adopted by the *Canterbury* court? How do you determine what must be disclosed under that rule?

8. What reasoning did the court use to justify the need for the new rule? Do you agree with the court's decision to switch to the new rule?

9. Even today, only about half the states follow the "reasonable patient" standard articulated in *Canterbury*. The remainder still use a "professional" standard for determining the scope of disclosure, as is used for any other element of a malpractice case.

10. Under each of the two rules for informed consent, determine if Theodoric could have been found liable for failure to get consent.

11. The court describes two situations in which a doctor need not get informed consent. What are they? The second of these rules, the so-called "therapeu-

tic privilege," is rarely invoked, and only a foolish physician would rely on it. What does the court say that demonstrates the problems with this exception to informed consent?

12. The *Canterbury* court talks about the requirement that a physician "seek and secure his patient's consent before commencing an operation or other course of treatment." What if a doctor does not commence an operation or other treatment because the patient refuses it? Could he nonetheless be liable for inadequately informing the patient of the applicable risks, benefits, and alternatives? Is it consistent with negligence law (as opposed to the narrower law of battery, which only protects the patient when the doctor actually physically does something to the patient) that the doctor be liable whenever he wrongly deprives the patient of the opportunity to choose an appropriate course of treatment?

Rena Truman went to Dr. Claude Thomas for medical care over a six-year period in the 1960s. Allegedly he would usually tell her, "You should have a Pap smear," but she always refused. In 1969, she went to another doctor, who discovered she had advanced cervical cancer, which would likely have been detected at a treatable stage had she previously undergone a Pap smear. After her death, her children sued the doctor for causing her death. The major issue in the case was the adequacy of the information he gave her. *Truman v. Thomas*, 611 P.2d 902 (Cal. 1980). Assuming that other doctors would have told Mrs. Truman exactly what Dr. Thomas told her, what outcome would you expect if California followed the "professional" standard? What if it followed the "reasonable patient" standard? In the latter instance, what would the children's lawyer be claiming their mother needed to be told?

13. The special rules for getting informed consent in an emergency allow a health care provider to treat when there is no ability to get actual consent. Should they permit a provider to ignore an explicit refusal of consent by a competent patient? Catherine Shine was an asthmatic who arrived at the emergency room of Massachusetts General Hospital asking only for oxygen and medication; she refused to be put on a ventilator. When it appeared that the doctors were likely to do just that, she and her sister "ran down the corridor to the emergency room exit doors, where they were forcibly apprehended by a physician and a security guard." She was placed in four-point restraints and put on the ventilator. When she died two years later after refusing to go to a hospital during an asthma attack, her father sued the emergency room doctors, claiming that their treatment traumatized her and indirectly led to her death. The highest court in Massachusetts subsequently reversed a trial judge's determination that "no patient has a right to refuse medical treatment in a life-threatening emergency." *Shine v. Vega*, 709 N.E.2d 58 (Mass. 1999).

14. A patient presumably has at least some right to *not* be given information. Suppose Judy has just learned that she has cancer, and the doctor starts tell-

ing her about the survival statistics. She emphatically says, "Shut up! I don't want to know!" Her doctor works out with her an agreement to treat her with the best available chemotherapy, but not to tell her how much time she has left until there are likely only a few weeks. Is such an agreement consistent with the rules relating to informed consent? See *Arato v. Avedon*, 858 P.2d 598 (Cal. 1993).

15. Leah is an 18-year-old Israeli (which makes her legally an adult in Illinois) being examined by oncologists at the University of Chicago. She is from a very orthodox Jewish community in which important decisions in a young woman's life are often made by her father. She is engaged to be married very soon. However, she has a malignant tumor in her vagina, which should be treated with a hysterectomy. Her father has been dealing with the doctors, insisting that she not be told the details of her condition, nor of the treatment. If she gets the hysterectomy, it is likely that her engagement would fall apart because she would no longer be fertile, which would make her an inappropriate bride for a fertile man under Jewish teachings. Her father insisted that she could not deal with all of this. He accordingly wanted her to get the surgery without being told exactly what it involved. She told the doctors she was perfectly willing to go along with this arrangement.[2]

    Should the doctors do the surgery without telling her what it involves? Is there a limit to what a person can consent to, assuming they are unwilling to know the full details? While we might permit a consent that is not "fully" informed, is there a point beyond which a consent might be insufficiently informed?

16. Examining a Japanese patient for rectal bleeding, you have determined that he has a malignant colon cancer. Before you can discuss this with him, his wife takes you aside and tells you that she suspects that he has cancer, but that you must not tell him so. She points out that it is common in Japan to not tell patients about terminal cancers.

    Assuming that she is right about the practice in Japan, are you legally bound to tell him about the cancer, since you are in the U.S.? Apart from the law, is the right thing to tell him or not to tell him? Would it matter if there were statistics from Japan showing that 90 percent of patients would not want to be told? What if that number were 70 percent? 50 percent? 10 percent? How do the statistics change the issue of dealing with a particular patient whose views about being told you do not know? How different is this patient's situation from that of the average patient, who, even apart from ethnicity, might not want to know?

    Is there a way to individualize the informed consent process for each person? How might you deal with such situations ahead of time, before you diagnose a cancer?

17. Under either of the disclosure rules, there is a final element that a plaintiff must prove to win: that had the appropriate disclosure been made, the

plaintiff would have changed his behavior (e.g., would not have gone through with the operation). This is known as proving causation, for someone is only civilly liable for wrongful conduct if it caused an injury to someone else. What standard does the *Canterbury* court come up with for determining causation? Is it correct in accepting that standard? Is not the very purpose of requiring informed consent to allow each patient to make her *own* choice about what she wants to do? So is not the injury the very denial of the right to choose?

If we instead look to what the reasonable person would have done, have we effectively thrown out the patient's ability to exercise that element of choice? In the *Canterbury* case, Mr. Canterbury did lose in the trial that took place after remand because it was determined that a "prudent person" in his situation would still have opted to go ahead with the operation.

HELLING V. CAREY

Supreme Court of Washington

519 P.2d 981 (Wash. 1974)

OPINION BY JUSTICE HUNTER:

[Barbara Helling] suffers from primary open angle glaucoma. Primary open angle glaucoma is essentially a condition of the eye in which there is an interference in the ease with which the nourishing fluids can flow out of the eye. Such a condition results in pressure gradually rising above the normal level to such an extent that damage is produced to the optic nerve and its fibers with resultant loss in vision. The first loss usually occurs in the periphery of the field of vision. The disease usually has few symptoms and, in the absence of a pressure test, is often undetected until the damage has become extensive and irreversible.

The defendants (respondents), Dr. Thomas F. Carey and Dr. Robert C. Laughlin, are partners who practice the medical specialty of ophthalmology. Ophthalmology involves the diagnosis and treatment of defects and diseases of the eye.

The plaintiff first consulted the defendants for myopia, nearsightedness, in 1959. At that time she was fitted with contact lenses. She next consulted the defendants in September 1963, concerning irritation caused by the contact lenses. Additional consultations occurred in October 1963; February 1967; September 1967; October 1967; May 1968; July 1968; August 1968; September 1968; and October 1968. Until the October 1968 consultation, the defendants considered the plaintiff's visual problems to be related solely to complications associated with her contact lenses. On that occasion, the defendant, Dr. Carey, tested the plaintiff's eye pressure and field of vision for the first time. This test indicated that the plaintiff had glaucoma. The plaintiff, who was then 32 years of age, had essentially lost her peripheral vision and her central vision was reduced to approximately 5 degrees vertical by 10 degrees horizontal.

Thereafter, in August of 1969, after consulting other physicians, the plaintiff filed a complaint against the defendants alleging, among other things, that she sustained severe and permanent damage to her eyes as a proximate result of the defendants' negligence. During trial, the testimony of the medical experts for both the plaintiff and the defendants established that the standards of the profession for that specialty in the same or similar circumstances do not require routine pressure tests for glaucoma upon patients under 40 years of age. The reason the pressure test for glaucoma is not given as a regular practice to patients under the age of 40 is that the disease rarely occurs in this age group. Testimony indicated, however, that the standards of the profession do require pressure tests if the patient's complaints and symptoms reveal to the physician that glaucoma should be suspected.

The trial court entered judgment for the defendants following a defense verdict. The plaintiff thereupon appealed to the Court of Appeals, which affirmed the judgment of the trial court. The plaintiff then petitioned this court for review, which we granted.

In her petition for review, the plaintiff's primary contention is that under the facts of this case the trial judge erred in giving certain instructions to the jury and refusing her proposed instructions defining the standard of care which the law imposes upon an ophthalmologist. As a result, the plaintiff contends, in effect, that she was unable to argue her theory of the case to the jury that the standard of care for the specialty of ophthalmology was inadequate to protect the plaintiff from the incidence of glaucoma, and that the defendants, by reason of their special ability, knowledge and information, were negligent in failing to give the pressure test to the plaintiff at an earlier point in time which, if given, would have detected her condition and enabled the defendants to have averted the resulting substantial loss in her vision.

We find this to be a unique case. The testimony of the medical experts is undisputed concerning the standards of the profession for the specialty of ophthalmology. It is not a question in this case of the defendants having any greater special ability, knowledge and information than other ophthalmologists which would require the defendants to comply with a higher duty of care than "that degree of care and skill which is expected of the average practitioner in the class to which he belongs, acting in the same or similar circumstances." The issue is whether the defendants' compliance with the standard of the profession of ophthalmology, which does not require the giving of a routine pressure test to persons under 40 years of age, should insulate them from liability under the facts in this case where the plaintiff has lost a substantial amount of her vision due to the failure of the defendants to timely give the pressure test to the plaintiff.

The defendants argue that the standard of the profession, which does not require the giving of a routine pressure test to persons under the age of 40, is adequate to insulate the defendants from liability for negligence because the risk of glaucoma is so rare in this age group. The testimony of the defendant, Dr. Carey, however, is revealing as follows:

Q. Now, when was it, actually, the first time any complaint was made to you by her of any field or visual field problem? A. Really, the first time that she really complained of a visual field problem was the August 30th date. Q. And how soon before the diagnosis was that? A. That was 30 days. We made it on October 1st. Q. And in your opinion, how long, as you now have the whole history and analysis and the diagnosis, how long had she had this glaucoma? A. I would think she probably had it ten years or longer. Q. Now, Doctor, there's been some reference to the matter of taking pressure checks of persons over 40. What is the incidence of glaucoma, the statistics, with persons under 40? A. In the instance of glaucoma under the age of 40, is less than 100 to one per cent. The younger you get, the less the incidence. It is thought to be in the neighborhood of one in 25,000 people or less. Q. How about the incidence of glaucoma in people over 40? A. Incidence of glaucoma over 40 gets into the two to three per cent category, and hence, that's where there is this great big difference and that's why the standards around the world has been to check pressures from 40 on.

The incidence of glaucoma in one out of 25,000 persons under the age of 40 may appear quite minimal. However, that one person, the plaintiff in this instance, is entitled to the same protection, as afforded persons over 40, essential for timely detection of the evidence of glaucoma where it can be arrested to avoid the grave and devastating result of this disease. The test is a simple pressure test, relatively inexpensive. There is no judgment factor involved, and there is no doubt that by giving the test the evidence of glaucoma can be detected. The giving of the test is harmless if the physical condition of the eye permits. The testimony indicates that although the condition of the plaintiff's eyes might have at times prevented the defendants from administering the pressure test, there is an absence of evidence in the record that the test could not have been timely given. . . .

Under the facts of this case reasonable prudence required the timely giving of the pressure test to this plaintiff. The precaution of giving this test to detect the incidence of glaucoma to patients under 40 years of age is so imperative that irrespective of its disregard by the standards of the ophthalmology profession, it is the duty of the courts to say what is required to protect patients under 40 from the damaging results of glaucoma.

We therefore hold, as a matter of law, that the reasonable standard that should have been followed under the undisputed facts of this case was the timely giving of this simple, harmless pressure test to this plaintiff and that, in failing to do so, the defendants were negligent, which proximately resulted in the blindness sustained by the plaintiff for which the defendants are liable. . . .

CONCURRING OPINION BY JUSTICE UTTER:

I concur in the result reached by the majority. I believe a greater duty of care could be imposed on the defendants than was established by their profession. The duty could be imposed when a disease, such as glaucoma, can be detected by a simple, well-known harmless test whose results are definitive and the disease can be successfully arrested by early detection, but where the effects of the disease are irreversible if undetected over a substantial period of time. . . .

Although the incidence of glaucoma in the age range of the plaintiff is approximately one in 25,000, this alone should not be enough to deny her a claim. Where its presence can be detected by a simple, well-known harmless test, where the results of the test are definitive, where the disease can be successfully arrested by early detection and where its effects are irreversible if undetected over a substantial period of time, liability should be imposed upon defendants even though they did not violate the standard existing within the profession of ophthalmology. . . .

NOTES AND QUESTIONS:
Helling v. Carey

1. The doctors in this case saw Ms. Helling quite a few times before they thought about giving her a test for glaucoma. As the court noted, "the standards of the profession do require pressure tests if the patient's complaints and symptoms reveal to the physician that glaucoma should be suspected." Whether or not it was standard practice to give pressure tests to all people under age 40, do you think that Ms. Helling's complaints should have led the doctors to test her sooner? What evidence about the standard of care would Ms. Helling's lawyers have had to introduce in order to allow a jury to find in her favor on this point? Given that the court changed the standard of care as it did, what can you guess about what other ophthalmologists would have done if presented with Ms. Helling's case? (Note that glaucoma is usually a symptom-less disease, much like high blood pressure, and a person's complaints about visual problems are not likely to suggest that she has glaucoma.)

2. *Helling v. Carey* has had little direct impact on the law. There is no other reported case in which a court has chosen to override the medical profession's own determination of what constitutes standard care.[3] Nonetheless, the case has generated a huge amount of discussion, particularly in academic circles, because it raises very interesting questions about how a standard of care should be determined and by whom.

3. Malpractice law is a branch of negligence law, so one might suspect that issues relating to how a standard of care is determined can be answered by looking for guidance in negligence law. One of the most famous theories about determining liability for purposes of negligence comes from Judge

Learned Hand's opinion in *United States v. Carroll Towing Co.*, 159 F.2d 169 (2d Cir. 1947). In that case a barge broke away from its moorings and caused damage to property. Judge Hand concluded that the test for whether the barge owner had been negligent, and thus was liable for the damage, was "a function of three variables: (1) the probability that [the barge] will break away; (2) the gravity of the resulting injury, if she does; [and] (3) the burden of adequate precautions. . . . [I]f the probability be called P; the injury, L; and the burden, B; liability depends upon whether B is less than L multiplied by P." In effect, Hand is saying that you must balance the benefits of an action against its costs.

Since the determination of the standard of care in the malpractice realm is traditionally delegated to the medical profession, we might ask whether this sort of rule should be applied in medical malpractice. Is it appropriate to be balancing costs and benefits when we are talking about someone's health? What kinds of costs and benefits should we be looking at if it is appropriate? Costs and benefits to whom?

4. Whether or not you think the *Carroll Towing* rule should be applied in determining malpractice standards, there is a separate question of how the medical profession does in fact determine the standard of care. Do you think that the only question—presumably a scientific one—is whether or not a treatment "works"? Or do you think that medical professionals do in fact balance risks and benefits (either explicitly or implicitly) in determining standards of care? Note the difference between these two types of statements:

    a. Treatment *A*, when given to a patient with condition *B*, leads to result *C*.
    b. Treatment *A* should be given to a patient with condition *B*.

    What should the legal system be requiring (or permitting) doctors to think about in going from statement (a) to statement (b)?

5. Are monetary costs appropriately included in the "costs" side of the equation? Or should we only be talking about health costs (e.g., the side effects of a treatment)? What did the *Helling* court appear to say about this factor? Was it willing to look at the monetary costs of the pressure test?

6. Much of the criticism of *Helling* is directed not at the concept of a court overriding the medical profession's determination of the standard of care, but at how that court went about doing so. Is it obvious to you that the *Helling* court was correct in its determination that the glaucoma test should be given to everyone under the age of 40? Given the relative rarity of glaucoma, and the fact that additional (extensive) testing is required to evaluate a high pressure reading in a patient, it is not clear that routine testing is so obviously beneficial as the *Helling* court suggested.[4]

7. To properly do the type of balancing described in note 6, it is necessary to put a value on intangibles, such as the loss of part of one's vision. How do you think we (or the medical profession) determine such values? Presumably, there is no objective standard. Nonetheless, is it not the case that vir-

tually any medical standard of care requires making such calculations, and weighing benefits against costs? The answers may have been obvious when a dose of antibiotics saved someone's life, but they are likely to be far less obvious today, when we give expensive, high-tech treatments to people with chronic, incurable diseases.

8. Is there any suggestion in the *Helling* court's opinion that the costs and benefits should be balanced based on the subjective values of a particular patient? In other words, can the standard of care vary from patient to patient, with the doctor being required to determine each patient's values? Would such a concept be consistent with the very notion of a "standard" of care, a consistent floor set by the legal system to uniformly guarantee everyone a minimum level of care?

This issue will be of major importance in our analysis in chapter 12 of "medical futility," where patients are demanding care that is not included within the standard of care.[5]

9. It is not just the judicial system that has at times tried to dictate what constitutes standard care. Legislatures have in effect addressed similar issues by requiring insurers to pay for certain types of care. Thus, for example, federal law requires that insurers must provide women with at least a 48-hour stay in the hospital after an uncomplicated childbirth.[6] How can we determine whether a 48-hour stay in the hospital is more appropriate than a 24-hour stay? Presumably, having all women and children stay for the extra day will improve their health, and we may even be relatively sure that we can save some lives. Does that answer the question? Is that like the *Helling* court's determination that even though only one person in 25,000 under the age of 40 has glaucoma, "that one person . . . is entitled to the same protection as afforded persons over 40"?

Does it matter how much it costs to keep all women and children in the hospital for a second day (as opposed to just those for whom we know in advance that there is a greater likelihood of a risk to the mother or the child)? Would it be relevant to also determine how many women and children will die if we opt for the 24-hour rule instead of the 48-hour rule? Do you think that at any point members of Congress publicly debated how much they would spend to save the life of a newborn child?

CONFIDENTIALITY

The third prong of duties (in addition to contract and tort) that make up the doctor-patient relationship is a rather poorly defined set of obligations that come under the rubric of "fiduciary duties."

The concept of a fiduciary dates back to the beginnings of the law of trusts, which dealt with someone entrusting money or other property to another person. The person entrusted with the money would be under special duties to look out for the interests of the person for whom he held the property. Thus, for example, he would be under an obligation to avoid any conflicts in interest. If he was supposed to invest the money for the benefit of the owner, he would have to avoid investing it in his own business, since he might likely have a bias in determining whether or not that is as good an investment as other available investments.

The classic fiduciary duty imposed on doctors is the requirement to keep information about the patient confidential. Most states have passed laws that describe the scope of this duty.

The complicated part of confidentiality relates less to the duty than to understanding that there are times when a doctor may be permitted, even required, to breach confidentiality. In general, these relate to situations in which the patient, an identified third party, or the public generally, will be harmed if confidentiality is maintained. In essence, a balancing has been done, and it has been determined that the harm that comes from breaching confidentiality in a particular situation is less than the harm that would come from maintaining it. Thus, for example, doctors are typically required to report the name of patients with certain contagious diseases to public health authorities, regardless of whether the patient objects. (In Kansas, there are approximately 40 reportable diseases.)

The most famous confidentiality case is *Tarasoff*, which follows. Although formally it is indeed about confidentiality, the legal issue it raises is actually very different, one with which you are already familiar: when does someone have a duty to protect someone else? As you read *Tarasoff*, ask yourself if any of the parties really was ever claiming that there was an absolute duty to keep everything confidential.

TARASOFF V. REGENTS OF THE UNIVERSITY OF CALIFORNIA

Supreme Court of California

551 P.2d 334 (Cal. 1976)

OPINION BY JUSTICE TOBRINER:

On October 27, 1969, Prosenjit Poddar killed Tatiana Tarasoff. Plaintiffs, Tatiana's parents, allege that two months earlier Poddar confided his intention to kill Tatiana to Dr. Lawrence Moore, a psychologist employed by the Cowell Memorial Hospital at the University of California at Berkeley. They allege that on Moore's request, the campus police briefly detained Poddar, but released him when he appeared rational. They further claim that Dr. Harvey Powelson, Moore's superior, then directed that no further action be taken to detain Poddar. No one warned plaintiffs of Tatiana's peril. . . .

We shall explain that defendant therapists cannot escape liability merely because Tatiana herself was not their patient. When a therapist determines, or pursuant to the standards of his profession should determine, that his patient presents a serious danger of violence to another, he incurs an obligation to use reasonable care to protect the intended victim against such danger. The discharge of this duty may require the therapist to take one or more of various steps, depending upon the nature of the case. Thus it may call for him to warn the intended victim or others likely to apprise the victim of the danger, to notify the police, or to take whatever other steps are reasonably necessary under the circumstances.

In the case at bar, plaintiffs admit that defendant therapists notified the police, but argue on appeal that the therapists failed to exercise reasonable care to protect Tatiana in that they did not confine Poddar and did not warn Tatiana or others likely to apprise her of the danger. Defendant therapists, however, are public employees. Consequently, to the extent that plaintiffs seek to predicate liability upon the therapists' failure to bring about Poddar's confinement, the therapists can claim immunity under Government Code section 856. No specific statutory provision, however, shields them from liability based upon failure to warn Tatiana or others likely to apprise her of the danger. . . .

Plaintiffs therefore can amend their complaints to allege that, regardless of the therapists' unsuccessful attempt to confine Poddar, since they knew that Poddar was at large and dangerous, their failure to warn Tatiana or others likely to apprise her of the danger constituted a breach of the therapists' duty to exercise reasonable care to protect Tatiana. . . .

The . . . cause of action can be amended to allege that Tatiana's death proximately resulted from defendants' negligent failure to warn Tatiana or others likely to apprise her of her danger. Plaintiffs contend that as amended, such allegations of negligence and proximate causation, with resulting damages, establish a cause of action. Defendants, however, contend that in the circumstances of the present case they owed no duty of care to Tatiana or her parents and that, in the absence of such duty, they were free to act in careless disregard of Tatiana's life and safety. . . .

Although, as we have stated above, under the common law, as a general rule, one person owed no duty to control the conduct of another, nor to warn those endangered by such conduct, the courts have carved out an exception to this rule in cases in which the defendant stands in some special relationship to either the person whose conduct needs to be controlled or in a relationship to the foreseeable victim of that conduct. Applying this exception to the present case, we note that a relationship of defendant therapists to either Tatiana or Poddar will suffice to establish a duty of care; . . . a duty of care may arise from either "(a) a special relation . . . between the actor and the third person which imposes a duty upon the actor to control the third person's conduct, or (b) a special relation . . . between the actor and the other which gives to the other a right of protection."

Although plaintiffs' pleadings assert no special relation between Tatiana and defendant therapists, they establish as between Poddar and defendant therapists the special relation that arises between a patient and his doctor or psychotherapist. Such a relationship may support affirmative duties for the benefit of third persons. Thus, for example, a hospital must exercise reasonable care to control the behavior of a patient which may endanger other persons. A doctor must also warn a patient if the patient's condition or medication renders certain conduct, such as driving a car, dangerous to others.

Although the California decisions that recognize this duty have involved cases in which the defendant stood in a special relationship *both* to the victim and to the person whose conduct created the danger, we do not think that the duty should logically be constricted to such situations. Decisions of other jurisdictions hold that the single relationship of a doctor to his patient is sufficient to support the duty to exercise reasonable care to protect others against dangers emanating from the patient's illness. The courts hold that a doctor is liable to persons infected by his patient if he negligently fails to diagnose a contagious disease, or, having diagnosed the illness, fails to warn members of the patient's family. . . .

Defendants contend, however, that imposition of a duty to exercise reasonable care to protect third persons is unworkable because therapists cannot accurately predict whether or not a patient will resort to violence. In support of this argument amicus representing the American Psychiatric Association and other professional societies cites numerous articles which indicate that therapists, in the present state of the art, are unable reliably to predict violent acts; their forecasts, amicus claims, tend consistently to overpredict violence, and indeed are more often wrong than right. Since predictions of violence are often erroneous, amicus concludes, the courts should not render rulings that predicate the liability of therapists upon the validity of such predictions.

The role of the psychiatrist, who is indeed a practitioner of medicine, and that of the psychologist who performs an allied function, are like that of the physician who must conform to the standards of the profession and who must often make diagnoses and predictions based upon such evaluations. Thus the judgment of the therapist in diagnosing emotional disorders and in predicting whether a patient presents a serious danger of violence is comparable to the judgment which doctors and professionals must regularly render under accepted rules of responsibility.

We recognize the difficulty that a therapist encounters in attempting to forecast whether a patient presents a serious danger of violence. Obviously, we do not require that the therapist, in making that determination, render a perfect performance; the therapist need only exercise "that reasonable degree of skill, knowledge, and care ordinarily possessed and exercised by members of [that professional specialty] under similar circumstances." Within the broad range of reasonable practice and treatment in which professional opinion and judgment may differ, the therapist is free to exercise his or her own best judgment without liability; proof, aided by hindsight, that he or she judged wrongly is insufficient to establish negligence.

In the instant case, however, the pleadings do not raise any question as to failure of defendant therapists to predict that Poddar presented a serious danger of violence. On the contrary, the present complaints allege that defendant therapists did in fact predict that Poddar would kill, but were negligent in failing to warn.

Amicus contends, however, that even when a therapist does in fact predict that a patient poses a serious danger of violence to others, the therapist should be absolved of any responsibility for failing to act to protect the potential victim. In our view, however, once a therapist does in fact determine, or under applicable professional standards reasonably should have determined, that a patient poses a serious danger of violence to others, he bears a duty to exercise reasonable care to protect the foreseeable victim of that danger. While the discharge of this duty of due care will necessarily vary with the facts of each case, in each instance the adequacy of the therapist's conduct must be measured against the traditional negligence standard of the rendition of reasonable care under the circumstances. . . .

The risk that unnecessary warnings may be given is a reasonable price to pay for the lives of possible victims that may be saved. We would hesitate to hold that the therapist who is aware that his patient expects to attempt to assassinate the President of the United States would not be obligated to warn the authorities because the therapist cannot predict with accuracy that his patient will commit the crime. . . .

We recognize the public interest in supporting effective treatment of mental illness and in protecting the rights of patients to privacy, and the consequent public importance of safeguarding the confidential character of psychotherapeutic communication. Against this interest, however, we must weigh the public interest in safety from violent assault. The Legislature has undertaken the difficult task of balancing the countervailing concerns. . . . [T]he Legislature created a specific and limited exception to the psychotherapist-patient privilege: "There is no privilege . . . if the psychotherapist has reasonable cause to believe that the patient is in such mental or emotional condition as to be dangerous to himself or to the person or property of another and that disclosure of the communication is necessary to prevent the threatened danger."

We realize that the open and confidential character of psychotherapeutic dialogue encourages patients to express threats of violence, few of which are ever executed. Certainly a therapist should not be encouraged routinely to reveal such threats; such disclosures could seriously disrupt the patient's relationship with his therapist and with the persons threatened. To the contrary, the therapist's obligations to his patient require that he not disclose a confidence unless such disclosure is necessary to avert danger to others, and even then that he do so discreetly, and in a fashion that would preserve the privacy of his patient to the fullest extent compatible with the prevention of the threatened danger. The revelation of a communication under the above circumstances is not a breach of trust or a violation of professional ethics; as stated in the Principles of Medical Ethics of the American Medical Association (1957), section 9: "A physician may not reveal the confidence entrusted to him in the course of medical attendance . . . *unless he is required to do so by law or unless it becomes necessary in order to protect the welfare of the individual or of the community.*" We conclude that the public policy favoring protection of the confidential character of patient-psychotherapist communications must yield to the extent to which disclosure is essential to avert danger to others. The protective privilege ends where the public peril begins.

Our current crowded and computerized society compels the interdependence of its members. In this risk-infested society we can hardly tolerate the further exposure to danger that would result from a concealed knowledge of the therapist that his patient was lethal. If the exercise of reasonable care to protect the threatened victim requires the therapist to warn the endangered party or those who can reasonably be expected to notify him, we see no sufficient societal interest that would protect and justify concealment. The containment of such risks lies in the public interest. . . .

CONCURRING AND DISSENTING OPINION BY JUSTICE MOSK:

I concur in the result in this instance only because the complaints allege that defendant therapists did in fact predict that Poddar would kill and were therefore negligent in failing to warn of that danger. Thus the issue here is very narrow: we are not concerned with whether the therapists, pursuant to the standards of their profession, "should have" predicted potential violence; they allegedly did so in actuality. Under these limited circumstances I agree that a cause of action can be stated.

Whether plaintiffs can ultimately prevail is problematical at best. As the complaints admit, the therapists *did* notify the police that Poddar was planning to kill a girl identifiable as Tatiana. While I doubt that more should be required, this issue may be raised in defense and its determination is a question of fact.

I cannot concur, however, in the majority's rule that a therapist may be held liable for failing to predict his patient's tendency to violence if other practitioners, pursuant to the "standards of the profession," would have done so. The question is, what standards? Defendants and a responsible amicus curiae, supported by an impressive body of literature . . . , demonstrate that psychiatric predictions of violence are inherently unreliable. . . .

I would restructure the rule designed by the majority to eliminate all reference to conformity to standards of the profession in predicting violence. If a psychiatrist does in fact predict violence, then a duty to warn arises. The majority's expansion of that rule will take us from the world of reality into the wonderland of clairvoyance.

NOTES AND QUESTIONS:
Tarasoff v. Regents of the University of California

1. What general rules about when someone has a duty to someone else does the court state? In what other cases did you come across these rules? Is the court's description of the rules consistent with what you previously learned?
2. Assume that the court determined that there was no special duty to the person who is endangered by a doctor's patient. In other words, assume that the legal system did not allow that endangered person to sue the doctor. Does that necessarily mean that the doctor must nonetheless maintain complete confidentiality? Might not the law require a breach of confidentiality, and punish the doctor (perhaps by a fine or a criminal penalty) for not appropriately disclosing the information? Can you see how there is a difference between creating liability toward someone (i.e., allowing the victim to be able to sue the doctor) and nonetheless requiring that confidentiality be breached without allowing such lawsuits?
3. Do you agree with the court that a duty should be created between the therapist and the intended victim? Give the arguments in favor of and against the creation of such a duty.
4. In creating duties, we are generally more likely to find a duty to someone else when the person has created the risk to the other person rather than merely standing by and failing to alleviate a risk. This is the difference between *malfeasance* and *nonfeasance*. Using that distinction, which of these cases presents the strongest argument for finding the doctor owes a duty to the person who is injured:
   a. A doctor gives a patient an antihistamine for her allergies, but fails to warn her about its sedative properties. Falling asleep while driving, she severely injures a pedestrian.
   b. A doctor diagnoses a patient's epilepsy, but fails to warn him about driving. He has a seizure while driving and severely injures a pedestrian.
5. In creating a duty, should it matter whether the victim is identifiable ahead of time? In the examples given in note 4, neither pedestrian was identifiable. Does that mean neither can sue the doctor? Why or why not?
   How would that rule apply in the *Tarasoff* case? What if Poddar was threatening to kill not his girlfriend but the next girl he saw who resembled his girlfriend? Should that girl's family (after he kills her) be able to bring the same type of lawsuit that Tarasoff's family was permitted to bring?

6. Did Dr. Moore maintain complete confidentiality? Who did he tell about his patient? Do you think he was right to divulge the information in that way? Why or why not?
7. The *Tarasoff* decision is viewed by many members of the medical profession as requiring that the intended victim of a therapist's patient be warned about the threat. What does the court actually say about what a therapist needs to do?
8. It is sometimes said that there is a need for *complete* confidentiality in the relationship between health care professional and patient, and that the possibility of disclosure of confidential information might cause patients to be less open in talking about their problems, thus impeding their treatment. If you assume that a therapist does have a responsibility to divulge confidential information under certain circumstances, does it matter to the treatment relationship who must be given that information, and whether an injured party can sue or not? Are patients going to be more truthful if they know the therapist can only report them to the police (who can then assist the therapist in detaining them and locking them up) but not directly warn an intended victim?
9. Justice Mosk suggests a distinction between instances in which a therapist does in fact determine that a patient presents a risk, and what other circumstance? Do you agree with him about the need for a narrower rule than that created by the majority? How does the accuracy of predictions about violent behavior fit into this analysis?
10. David Spaulding is a passenger in a car driven by John Zimmerman that is involved in an accident. Spaulding sues Zimmerman for assorted injuries, including a concussion and rib fractures. The lawyers defending Zimmerman are allowed to make their own determination of how serious Spaulding's injuries are, and they hire Dr. Hewitt Hannah to examine him. As a result of that examination, Dr. Hannah determines that Spaulding is suffering from an aortic aneurysm, which is in essence a "ballooning out" of a weakened part of the wall of the largest artery. This might have resulted from the accident, although there is no way to be sure. It is a very serious condition, since it might rupture at any point, leading to Spaulding's sudden death.

Spaulding's doctors have apparently failed to discover the aneurysm. His lawyers are proposing to settle the case for $6,500. If they knew of the aneurysm, they would likely settle only for a much higher sum. Should Dr. Hannah disclose the existence of the aneurysm to Spaulding? If so, what rule would you create to govern the scope of such disclosure? Would you differentiate, for instance, between life-threatening and non-life-threatening conditions? Recall that the very purpose of bringing in Dr. Hannah was to help Zimmerman's defense, and that in examining Spaulding Dr. Hannah was not acting in the role of his doctor. *Spaulding v. Zimmerman*, 116 N.W.2d 704 (Minn. 1962).

11. One of the classic situations in which the law has required a breach of confidentiality is contagious diseases. Oddly enough, the legal response to the most prominent such disease of modern times—AIDS—has been very different. Soon after the outbreak of the AIDS epidemic, many state laws were passed to protect AIDS patients. Thus, for example, not only would there be no reporting of the name of the patient to health authorities, but a doctor might be prevented from revealing the patient's disease to a known sexual partner of the patient. These laws were justified largely on the ground that revealing a person's HIV status had compelling social consequences.

This initial legal response to AIDS was frequently referred to as AIDS "exceptionalism," highlighting how its near-absolute protection of the individual rights of the patients differed from the usual balancing of such rights against the needs of society. Over time, as both public discrimination against those who were HIV positive diminished and as treatments improved, the laws have gradually changed. Now they often require or at least permit health care providers to disclose a patient's status to appropriate parties.[7]

One of the more interesting aspects of this situation is the HIV testing of newborn infants. For a time, the federal government routinely performed such testing but the results were so coded that it was impossible to determine the test results for any specific child. This was done to protect the mother, who might not want to know her HIV status. (A positive test result in a child demonstrated that the mother was HIV positive.) Is such a policy reasonable if there is no treatment to be given to the child? Assuming there is a form of treatment, is this policy nonetheless still appropriate? Why or why not?[8]

Endnotes

1. For more on the doctrine of informed consent, see, e.g., Jay Katz, *The Silent World of Doctor and Patient* (New York: Free Press, 1986); Paul S. Appelbaum, Charles Lidz, and Alan Meisel, *Informed Consent: Legal Theory and Clinical Practice* (New York: Oxford University Press, 1987).
2. John D. Lantos, "The Case: What Should Leah Be Told?," 18 *Second Opinion* 81 (1993).
3. For a view that takes issue with conventional understanding, claiming that courts often reject the medical profession's own standard of care, see Philip G. Peters, Jr., "The Quiet Demise of Deference to Custom: Malpractice Law at the Millennium," 57 *Wash. & Lee L. Rev.* 163 (2000).
4. For a detailed analysis of how the cost-benefit balancing might be done, see Eric E. Fortess and Marshall B. Kapp, "Medical Uncertainty, Diagnostic Testing, and Legal Liability," 13 *Law, Med. & Health Care* 213 (1985).
5. For further discussion of the issues raised in these notes, see Jerry Menikoff, "Demanded Medical Care," 30 *Ariz. St. L. J.* 1091, 1100–08 (1998).

6. See, e.g., George J. Annas, "Women and Children First," 333 *New Eng. J. Med.* 1647 (1995).
7. See, e.g., Ronald Bayer, "Public Health Policy and the AIDS Epidemic: An End to HIV Exceptionalism," 324 *New Eng. J. Med.* 1500 (1991); Lawrence O. Gostin et al., "National HIV Case Reporting for the United States: A Defining Moment in the History of the Epidemic," 337 *New Eng. J. Med.* 1162 (1997).
8. See, e.g., Martha A. Field, "Pregnancy and AIDS," 52 *Md. L. Rev.* 402 (1993); Juliet J. McKenna, "Where Ignorance Is not Bliss: A Proposal for Mandatory HIV Testing of Pregnant Women," 7 *Stan. L. & Pol'y Rev.* 133 (1996).

8

The Outer Limits
of Informed Consent

This chapter includes two cases that, though they deal with very different aspects of informed consent, have a number of things in common. First, both represent relatively new developments in the law. The first, *Johnson v. Kokemoor*, deals with the extent to which informed consent requires the disclosure of "doctor-specific" information. Although your reading of the cases in chapter 7 might suggest this should be a straightforward and well recognized aspect of informed consent (particularly under "reasonable patient" laws), it is not. *Johnson* is a cutting-edge case. Moreover, beyond the informed consent issues, it further explores the role of paternalism in the law. To what extent should a particularly risky medical option be something that a patient is merely warned about (through informed consent), rather than being prevented from choosing? This theme will be followed through in the next chapter, where we move on to medical treatments that are not standard care.

The second case, *Herdrich v. Pegram*, even more directly addresses the conflict between informing patients of risks and preventing them from choosing to subject themselves to such risks. The conflict is raised in the context of managed care and the financial incentives that may encourage doctors to act less like the fiduciaries they are required to be, and to skimp on the care that patients are given. The applicable law, ERISA, is no doubt the most important federal statute regulating employer-provided health insurance. As you will see, the majority and dissent in this case have very different views about how that powerful law should apply to the new arrangements being created by managed care.

JOHNSON V. KOKEMOOR
Supreme Court of Wisconsin
545 N.W.2d 495 (Wis. 1996)

OPINION BY JUDGE ABRAHAMSON:

. . . Donna Johnson (the plaintiff) brought an action against Dr. Richard Kokemoor (the defendant) alleging his failure to obtain her informed consent to surgery. . . . The jury found that the defendant failed to adequately inform the plaintiff regarding the risks associated with her surgery. The jury also found that a reasonable person in the plaintiff's position would have refused to consent to surgery by the defendant if she had been fully informed of its attendant risks and advantages. . . .

This case presents the issue of whether the circuit court erred in admitting evidence that the defendant, in undertaking his duty to obtain the plaintiff's informed consent before operating to clip an aneurysm, failed (1) to divulge the extent of his experience in performing this type of operation; (2) to compare the morbidity and mortality rates for this type of surgery among experienced surgeons and inexperienced surgeons like himself; and (3) to refer the plaintiff to a tertiary care center staffed by physicians more experienced in performing the same surgery. The admissibility of such physician-specific evidence in a case involving the doctrine of informed consent raises an issue of first impression in this court and is an issue with which appellate courts have had little experience. . . .

We conclude that all three items of evidence were material to the issue of informed consent in this case. As we [previously] stated, "a patient cannot make an informed, intelligent decision to consent to a physician's suggested treatment unless the physician discloses what is material to the patient's decision, i.e., all of the viable alternatives and risks of the treatment proposed." In this case information regarding a physician's experience in performing a particular procedure, a physician's risk statistics as compared with those of other physicians who perform that procedure, and the availability of other centers and physicians better able to perform that procedure would have facilitated the plaintiff's awareness of "all of the viable alternatives" available to her and thereby aided her exercise of informed consent. We therefore conclude that under the circumstances of this case, the circuit court did not erroneously exercise its discretion in admitting the evidence.

I.

. . . On the advice of her family physician, the plaintiff underwent a CT scan to determine the cause of her headaches. Following the scan, the family physician referred the plaintiff to the defendant, a neurosurgeon in the Chippewa Falls area. The defendant diagnosed an enlarging aneurysm at the rear of the plaintiff's brain and recommended surgery to clip the aneurysm. The defendant performed the surgery in October of 1990.

The defendant clipped the aneurysm, rendering the surgery a technical success. But as a consequence of the surgery, the plaintiff, who had no neurological impairments prior to surgery, was rendered an incomplete quadriplegic. She remains unable to walk or to control her bowel and bladder movements. Furthermore, her vision, speech and upper body coordination are partially impaired.

At trial, the plaintiff introduced evidence that the defendant overstated the urgency of her need for surgery and overstated his experience with performing the particular type of aneurysm surgery which she required. According to testimony introduced during the plaintiff's case in chief, when the plaintiff questioned the defendant regarding his experience, he replied that he had performed the surgery she required "several" times; asked what he meant by "several," the defendant said "dozens" and "lots of times."

In fact, however, the defendant had relatively limited experience with aneurysm surgery. He had performed thirty aneurysm surgeries during residency, but all of them involved anterior circulation aneurysms. According to the plaintiff's experts, operations performed to clip anterior circulation aneurysms are significantly less complex than those necessary to clip posterior circulation aneurysms such as the plaintiff's. Following residency, the defendant had performed aneurysm surgery on six patients with a total of nine aneurysms. He had operated on basilar bifurcation aneurysms only twice and had never operated on a large basilar bifurcation aneurysm such as the plaintiff's aneurysm.

The plaintiff also presented evidence that the defendant understated the morbidity and mortality rate associated with basilar bifurcation aneurysm surgery. According to the plaintiff's witnesses, the defendant had told the plaintiff that her surgery carried a two percent risk of death or serious impairment and that it was less risky than the angiogram procedure she would have to undergo in preparation for surgery. The plaintiff's witnesses also testified that the defendant had compared the risks associated with the plaintiff's surgery to those associated with routine procedures such as tonsillectomies, appendectomies and gall bladder surgeries.

The plaintiff's neurosurgical experts testified that even the physician considered to be one of the world's best aneurysm surgeons, who had performed hundreds of posterior circulation aneurysm surgeries, had reported a morbidity and mortality rate of ten-and-seven-tenths percent when operating upon basilar bifurcation aneurysms comparable in size to the plaintiff's aneurysm. Furthermore, information in treatises and articles which the defendant reviewed in preparation for the plaintiff's surgery set the morbidity and mortality rate at approximately fifteen percent for a basilar bifurcation aneurysm. The plaintiff also introduced expert testimony that the morbidity and mortality rate for basilar bifurcation aneurysm operations performed by one with the defendant's relatively limited experience would be between twenty and thirty percent, and "closer to the thirty percent range."

Finally, the plaintiff introduced into evidence testimony and exhibits stating that a reasonable physician in the defendant's position would have advised the plaintiff of the availability of more experienced surgeons and would have referred her to them. The plaintiff also introduced evidence stating that patients with basilar aneurysms should be referred to tertiary care centers—such as the Mayo Clinic, only 90 miles away—which contain the proper neurological intensive care unit and microsurgical facilities and which are staffed by neurosurgeons with the requisite training and experience to perform basilar bifurcation aneurysm surgeries.

In his testimony at trial, the defendant denied having suggested to the plaintiff that her condition was urgent and required immediate care. He also denied having stated that her risk was comparable to that associated with an angiogram or minor surgical procedures such as a tonsillectomy or appendectomy. While he acknowledged telling the plaintiff that the risk of death or serious impairment associated with clipping an aneurysm was two percent, he also claims to have told her that because of the location of her aneurysm, the risks attending her surgery would be greater, although he was unable to tell her precisely how much greater. In short, the defendant testified that his disclosure to the plaintiff adequately informed her regarding the risks that she faced.

The defendant's expert witnesses testified that the defendant's recommendation of surgery was appropriate, that this type of surgery is regularly undertaken in a community hospital setting, and that the risks attending anterior and posterior circulation aneurysm surgeries are comparable. They placed the risk accompanying the plaintiff's surgery at between five and ten percent, although one of the defendant's experts also testified that such statistics can be misleading. The defendant's expert witnesses also testified that when queried by a patient regarding their experience, they would divulge the extent of that experience and its relation to the experience of other physicians performing similar operations.

II.

We now turn to a review of Wisconsin's law of informed consent. The common-law doctrine of informed consent arises from and reflects the fundamental notion of the right to bodily integrity. Originally, an action alleging that a physician had failed to obtain a patient's informed consent was pled as the intentional tort of assault and battery. In the typical situation giving rise to an informed consent action, a patient-plaintiff consented to a certain type of operation but, in the course of that operation, was subjected to other, unauthorized operative procedures.

The court further developed the doctrine of informed consent in [1972], stating for the first time that a plaintiff-patient could bring an informed consent action based on negligence rather than as an intentional tort. . . .

The concept of informed consent is based on the tenet that in order to make a rational and informed decision about undertaking a particular treatment or undergoing a particular surgical procedure, a patient has the right to know about significant potential risks involved in the proposed treatment or surgery. In order to insure that a patient can give an informed consent, a "physician or surgeon is under the duty to provide the patient with such information as may be necessary under the circumstances then existing" to assess the significant potential risks which the patient confronts.

The information that must be disclosed is that information which would be "material" to a patient's decision. . . . The *Canterbury* court defined as material and therefore "demanding a communication" from a physician to a patient all information regarding "the inherent and potential hazards of the proposed treatment, the alternatives to that treatment, if any, and the results likely if the patient remains untreated." . . .

What constitutes informed consent in a given case emanates from what a reasonable person in the patient's position would want to know. This standard regarding what a physician must disclose is described as the prudent patient standard; it has been embraced by a growing number of jurisdictions since the *Canterbury* decision. . . .

IV.

The defendant contends that the circuit court erred in allowing the plaintiff to introduce evidence regarding the defendant's limited experience in operating upon aneurysms comparable to the plaintiff's aneurysm. Wisconsin's law of informed consent, the defendant continues, requires a physician to reveal only those risks inherent in the treatment. Everyone agrees, argues the defendant, that he advised the plaintiff regarding those risks: the potential perils of death, a stroke or blindness associated with her surgery.

The defendant argues that the circuit court's decision to admit evidence pertaining to his surgical experience confused relevant information relating to treatment risks with irrelevant and prejudicial information that the defendant did not possess the skill and experience of the very experienced aneurysm surgeons. Therefore, according to the defendant, the jury's attention was diverted from a consideration of whether the defendant made required disclosures regarding treatment to the question of who was performing the plaintiff's operation. Thus, the defendant contends, the circuit court transformed a duty to reasonably inform into a duty to reasonably perform the surgery, even though the plaintiff was not alleging negligent treatment.

The doctrine of informed consent should not, argues the defendant, be construed as a general right to information regarding possible alternative procedures, health care facilities and physicians. Instead, urges the defendant, the doctrine of informed consent should be viewed as creating a "bright line" rule requiring physicians to disclose only significant complications intrinsic to the contemplated procedure. . . .

We reject the defendant's proposed bright line rule. . . .

In this case, the plaintiff introduced ample evidence that had a reasonable person in her position been aware of the defendant's relative lack of experience in performing basilar bifurcation aneurysm surgery, that person would not have undergone surgery with him. According to the record the plaintiff had made inquiry of the defendant's experience with surgery like hers. In response to her direct question about his experience he said that he had operated on aneurysms comparable to her aneurysm "dozens" of times. The plaintiff also introduced evidence that surgery on basilar bifurcation aneurysms is more difficult than any other type of aneurysm surgery and among the most difficult in all of neurosurgery. We conclude that the circuit court did not erroneously exercise its discretion in admitting evidence regarding the defendant's lack of experience and the difficulty of the proposed procedure. A reasonable person in the plaintiff's position would have considered such information material in making an intelligent and informed decision about the surgery. . . .

NOTES AND QUESTIONS:
Johnson v. Kokemoor

1. Which of the two types of informed consent rules—"professional standard" or "reasonable patient"—was the law in Wisconsin?
2. What would the outcome of this lawsuit have been if the other standard had been the law? What additional element of proof would have had to be introduced? Was any evidence on that point introduced in this case? How likely do you think it is that such evidence will exist in similar cases?
3. Why are the parties to the case arguing about the information given to Ms. Johnson, and not about the actual surgery? What can you conclude about whether, apart from the informed consent issue, Dr. Kokemoor had actually committed malpractice?

   Recall that the medical profession determines the standard of care for purposes of malpractice. (As you saw from the discussion of *Helling v. Carey*, it is extraordinarily rare for courts to modify the standard set by the profession.) As long as a particular type of conduct by a doctor does not constitute malpractice, it is acceptable for a patient to be subjected to that conduct. Should the medical profession be permitting Dr. Kokemoor to operate on the next person who walks into his office with a posterior circulation aneurysm, assuming he does in fact inform that patient adequately about the risks and the person chooses to allow him to operate? Is this an issue to be decided by patient choice?
4. *Johnson v. Kokemoor* represents the cutting edge of informed consent cases. As the court itself notes, few courts have commented on the need to disclose what might be referred to as "physician-specific" risks: not just the training issues discussed in this case, but related issues such as whether the physician is an alcoholic or has AIDS, either of which might, in certain cir-

cumstances, be relevant in determining how much risk patients might encounter in accepting such a person as their physician.

Up to now, it has generally been the rule—and probably continues to be the rule in most states—that a physician is under no obligation to divulge such types of information. Consider the case of Rosetta Whiteside, who went to see Dr. Robert Lukson for the removal of her gallbladder. At the time he obtained her consent, he had recently attended a two-day class on how to remove gallbladders using an endoscope, in which he performed the procedure on three pigs. He had not yet performed it on any human beings. He mentioned none of this to the patient. The Washington state court noted that "[f]ollowing [the] traditional approach, we conclude that a surgeon's lack of experience in performing a surgical procedure is not a material fact for purposes of finding liability predicated on failure to secure an informed consent." *Whiteside v. Lukson*, 947 P.2d 1263 (Wash. Ct. App. 1997).

Even more emphatic (though clearly an overstatement) are the words of the Hawaii Supreme Court in *Ditto v. McCurdy*, 947 P.2d 952, 958 (Haw. 1997): "No state court has ever held that the doctrine of informed consent requires disclosure of information concerning the personal characteristics of the physician. In fact, informed consent has been held not to require disclosure of: (1) the physician's lack of experience in performing the disputed procedure; (2) the physician's incompetence; nor (3) the qualifications of persons providing treatment."[1]

5. Even under the rule applied by most courts, a direct lie or misstatement by a doctor in answering a patient's question may itself, if material, lead to a finding of lack of informed consent. This may have been an additional issue in this case, since Dr. Kokemoor apparently distorted the facts in answering Ms. Johnson's questions. Do you find this source of possible physician liability adequate?[2]

6. Should a patient have to be savvy enough to know the right questions to ask? Or should the doctor be under an affirmative obligation to discuss issues such as her own training and experience? How might such an obligation impact on a doctor in training, doing a procedure for the first time?

In thinking about these questions, be aware that the legal system has in many areas eroded the concept of *caveat emptor* ("let the buyer beware") that has traditionally applied to two parties entering into an agreement. For example, it is now generally the rule in house sales that a seller must disclose to the buyer known defects in the house. The law changed because it appeared unjust, and served no useful purpose, to allow an inexperienced buyer effectively to be cheated on such a major transaction.

A person selling a house has no special relationship to the buyer, yet the law imposes this duty to disclose defects. In contrast, a doctor *does* have a special relationship to the patient, as we saw in chapter 7. While the exact nature of the duties created by this "fiduciary" relationship remains unclear, its intent is to require the doctor to look out in some special way for the interests of the patient. Given that special relationship, how would you characterize the traditional rule regarding disclosure of physician incompetence (which one might consider a form of doctor "defect")?

THE CONFLICTED WORLD OF MANAGED CARE

As we saw in chapter 7, state laws in general impose on physicians a duty to act as fiduciaries in dealing with their patients. The exact meaning of that obligation is far from clear. At the heart of the classic fiduciary relationship, however, has been a requirement that the fiduciary not put himself in a situation where he has a conflict of interest that encourages him to take actions that do not represent what is best for his patient.

An obvious issue for doctors is how they are compensated. Historically, doctors were compensated on a fee for service basis: the more things they did, the more they got paid. This in itself created a conflict of interest. A surgeon who is contemplating whether a patient with borderline vision needs cataract surgery might be pushed over the line in recommending it when he thinks about his bank balance. In spite of such obvious conflicts, the law has usually not imposed special rules designed to protect patients in such situations. (Most of the relevant laws were designed to protect the payers—such as Medicare—from having to pay for care that is not medically necessary.)

With the growing concerns about the cost of medical care we are now seeing financial arrangements that flip the previous incentives. Doctors are now often paid under a capitated ("by the head") arrangement, in which they get a fixed amount of money to provide services to each patient, no matter how sick a patient is. The doctor who operates on the person with the borderline cataract not only does not get any extra fee but may have to absorb some or all of the costs of providing the surgery. In other words, the doctor who provides more care to patients may actually be financially worse off.

One of the primary issues raised by this new conflict of interest relates to informed consent: Should a patient be informed when the doctor is subject to such financial conflicts of interests? If we acknowledge that there should be some sort of disclosure, how should we implement that requirement? Is it enough if the managed care plan discloses these rules when the patient joins the plan? Or must the doctor tell the patient every time he makes a decision to withhold care that is likely to impact his own wallet by more than $X, so that the patient can decide whether to scrutinize the decision?

The case that follows is unusual in that it involves the possible impact of a federal law, commonly known as ERISA, on this issue. ERISA, the Employee Retirement Income Security Act of 1974, was passed to regulate "employee benefits," particularly pension plans. Employers were sitting on huge pots of money that represented the contributions of their employees. ERISA imposed restrictions to make sure that the employers properly took care of this money.

Here the employer was in a classic fiduciary relationship: it was under a duty to take care of someone else's property, and to avoid conflicts of interest.

Most private health insurance in this country is provided by employers to their employees—a type of employee benefit. It therefore comes under ERISA (or so at least the courts have determined). Unfortunately, since ERISA was primarily designed to regulate pension plans, not health care insurance, applying ERISA in this area has produced results that are unusual, to say the least. (It would appear that Congress never really contemplated these results when it passed ERISA.)

Congress felt it was inappropriate to both impose lots of new regulations on employers and at the same time require them to comply with many separate rules imposed by state laws. As a result, ERISA has a very broad "preemption" provision that effectively overrides many state laws that would otherwise allow an employee to sue an employer, a pension company, or a health care organization. This is a straightforward application of federalism: in an area where both the states and the national government have authority to enact laws (category D from chapter 1), a national law overrides state laws.

When applied to employer-based health plans, this preemption provision has made it impossible in some cases for people to sue their health care providers. The reason is that one of the types of state law pre-empted by ERISA is tort law. A number of courts have held that when a health care provider makes an incorrect coverage decision, that decision can only be challenged under specific ERISA remedies, in a federal court of law.

The remedies under ERISA are relatively narrow; they usually do not allow the injured party to sue for the large damages they might get in a tort action under state law. Assume, for example, that Joan's managed care organization told her that she was not entitled to stress testing to evaluate her chest pain. Shortly thereafter she dies of a heart attack. Under ERISA, her family could sue only for the cost of the stress tests that were wrongfully withheld (maybe a few hundred dollars). Under state tort law, they could probably sue for millions of dollars, claiming that the organization wrongfully caused her death.

Proposals to change this are being addressed by a House-Senate conference committee as it debates legislation relating to a "Patient Bill of Rights." Oddly enough, the federalism at the heart of this issue has been largely (perhaps intentionally) ignored by many politicians. Thus, many politicians opposed to allowing managed care organizations to be sued are vehement supporters of states' rights, and the proposition that states should generally have the right to shape their own laws. Yet the only reason many managed care organizations cannot be sued is precisely because the federal government, through ERISA, has prevented the states from enforcing their own laws that would allow such lawsuits.[3]

The case that follows presents a very different issue that has recently been raised by ERISA. While ERISA has usually tended to cut back on patients' rights, *Herdrich v. Pegram* shows how an argument might be made that, given its emphasis on fiduciary obligations, ERISA's rules might make certain managed care arrangements illegal.

HERDRICH V. PEGRAM

United States Court of Appeals for the Seventh Circuit

154 F.3d 362 (7th Cir. 1998)

OPINION BY JUDGE COFFEY:

. . . This appeal arises out of a complaint filed by [Cynthia] Herdrich in the Circuit Court of McLean County, Illinois, on October 21, 1992, against Lori Pegram, M.D. and Carle Clinic Association. Counts I and II of the plaintiff's complaint were based upon a theory of professional medical negligence. Specifically, Herdrich alleged that she suffered a ruptured appendix and, in turn, contracted peritonitis due to Pegram's negligence in failing to provide her with timely and adequate medical care. . . . In [an amended complaint], she averred that the defendants breached their fiduciary duty [under ERISA] to plan beneficiaries by depriving them of proper medical care and retaining the savings resulting therefrom for themselves. . . .

On appeal, Herdrich contends that the district court erred in dismissing the amended count III of her complaint for failing to sufficiently state a claim for breach of a fiduciary duty under ERISA. . . .

2. Breach of Fiduciary Duty

Having determined that the defendants are fiduciaries under ERISA, we next consider whether the direct and inferential allegations contained in Herdrich's complaint are sufficient to establish the requisite breach of a fiduciary duty. . . .

A fiduciary breaches its duty of care under [the statute] whenever it acts to benefit its own interests. For example, ERISA expressly prohibits fiduciaries from "dealing with the assets of the plan in his own interest or for his own account," or "receiving any consideration for his own personal account from any party dealing with such plan in connection with a transaction involving the assets of the plan." The requirement that an ERISA fiduciary act "with an eye single to the interests of the participants and beneficiaries," is the most fundamental of his or her duties, and "must be enforced with uncompromising rigidity." . .

. . . Herdrich sets forth, in the amended third count of her complaint, the intricacies of the defendants' incentive structure. The Plan dictated that the very same HMO administrators vested with the authority to determine whether health care claims would be paid, and the type, nature, and duration of care to be given, were those physicians who became eligible to receive year-end bonuses as a result of cost-savings. Because the physician/administrators' year-end bonuses were based on the difference between total plan costs (i.e., the costs of providing medical services) and revenues (i.e., payments by plan beneficiaries), an incentive existed for them to limit treatment and, in turn, HMO costs so as to ensure larger bonuses. With a jaundiced eye focused firmly on year-end bonuses, it is not unrealistic to assume that the doctors rendering care under the Plan were swayed to be most frugal when exercising their discretionary authority to the detriment of their membership. . . .

The dissent disagrees with this aspect of today's holding, which it characterizes as concluding that "the mere existence of this asserted conflict [i.e., the conflict between the incentive scheme for Carle doctors to limit medical care and treatment, on the one hand, and the fiduciary duty of Carle to the beneficiaries, on the other], without more, gives rise to a cause of action for breach of fiduciary duty under ERISA." That is not the conclusion we reach. Our decision does not stand for the proposition that the existence of incentives automatically gives rise to a breach of fiduciary duty. Rather, we hold that incentives can rise to the level of a breach where, as pleaded here, the fiduciary trust between plan participants and plan fiduciaries no longer exists (i.e., where physicians delay providing necessary treatment to, or withhold administering proper care to, plan beneficiaries for the sole purpose of increasing their bonuses).

The dissent admittedly does "not rule out the possibility that the imposition of incentives to limit care could support a claim of breach of fiduciary duty." In its view, such a claim might very well be viable when "there is a serious flaw in the manner in which the incentive arrangement is established . . . ." Having said this, we fail to see how it can conclude that Herdrich did not plead such a flaw in the structure of the incentive program at issue. . . .

The dissent also stresses that ERISA allows fiduciaries to adopt dual loyalties, and that maintaining dual loyalties does not in itself constitute a breach of fiduciary duty. We do not disagree with this contention, for it is well established that dual loyalties are tolerated under ERISA. Our point is not that a fiduciary may not have dual loyalties; it is that the tolerance of dual loyalties does not extend to the situation like the case before us where a fiduciary jettisons his responsibility to the physical well-being of beneficiaries in favor of "loyalty" to his own financial interests. Tolerance, in other words, has its limits. . . .

. . . [The dissent] seems to argue that dual loyalties, and incentive schemes generally, are per se valid almost without limitation, and that only when there is a "breakdown in the market," or some "serious flaw" in the manner in which the incentive arrangement in question is established, can there possibly be a breach of fiduciary duty. Specifically, the dissent notes, without citation to any authority, that "plan sponsors are likely to take their business elsewhere if they perceive that incentives are working to the detriment of beneficiaries or the plan itself, and thus market forces go a long way towards ensuring that incentives do not rise to dangerous or undesirable levels."

To our way of thinking, the dissent's market theory flies in the face of the facts as set forth in the very record before us. On March 7, 1991, Pegram, Herdrich's doctor, discovered a six by eight centimeter "mass" (later determined to be her appendix) in Herdrich's abdomen. Although the mass was inflamed on March 7, Pegram delayed instituting an immediate treatment of Herdrich, and forced her to wait more than one week (eight days) to obtain the accepted diagnostic procedure (ultrasound) used to determine the nature, size and exact location of the mass. Ideally, Herdrich should have had the ultrasound administered with all speed after the inflamed mass was discovered in her abdomen in order that her condition could be diagnosed and treated before deteriorating as it did, but Carle's policy requires plan participants to receive medical care from Carle-staffed facilities in what they classify as "non-emergency" situations. Because Herdrich's treatment was considered to be "non-emergency," she was forced to wait the eight days before undergoing the ultrasound at a Carle facility in Urbana, Illinois. During this unnecessary waiting period, Herdrich's health problems were exacerbated and the situation rapidly turned into an "emergency"—her appendix ruptured, resulting in the onset of peritonitis. In an effort to defray the increased costs associated with the surgery required to drain and cleanse Herdrich's ruptured appendix, Carle insisted that she have the procedure performed at its own Urbana facility, necessitating that Herdrich travel more than fifty miles from her neighborhood hospital in Bloomington, Illinois. The "market forces" the dissent refers to hardly seem to have produced a positive result in this case—Herdrich suffered a life-threatening illness (peritonitis), which necessitated a longer hospital stay and more serious surgery at a greater cost to her and the Plan. And, as discussed below, we are far from alone in our belief that market forces are insufficient to cure the deleterious affects of managed care on the health care industry.

Across the country, health care critics and consumers are complaining that the quality of medical treatment in this nation is rapidly declining, leaving "a fear that the goal of managing care has been replaced by the goal of managing costs." Jan Greene, *Has Managed Care Lost Its Soul? Health Maintenance Organizations Focus More on Finances, Less on Care*, Am. Hosp. Publishing Inc., May 20, 1997.

An increasing number of Americans believe that dollars are more important than people in the evolving [HMO] system. Whether justified or not, this assumption needs to be taken seriously, according to keepers of the industry's conscience. University of Pennsylvania bioethicist Arthur Caplan argues that managed care should take a lesson from professional sports, which has alienated some fans because money and profits have eclipsed the reasons why fans care about the games: hero worship and the virtues of teamwork, loyalty and trustworthiness. The same goes for doctors. "People go to their doctor not because he's a good businessman . . . but because he's a good advocate, someone we can admire," says Caplan. "If we have to struggle with him to get what we want, we will have no trust anymore."

To regain trust, HMOs need to be more sensitive to the doctor-patient relationship and remove the physician from direct financial interest in patient care, says Caplan. Instead, doctors should have a predetermined budget and be able to advocate for patients without direct personal gain or loss.

Another hot-button issue for HMO members is the fear that a lifesaving experimental procedure will be denied because of its cost. Caplan says the industry should follow the lead of the handful of HMOs that have established outside, independent panels to make final decisions.

Even care providers fear that they "have become somewhat preoccupied with [their] ownership status and consequently have not paid as much attention as [they] should have to improving [their] basic core competencies." The specter of money concerns driving the health care system, says a group of Massachusetts physicians and nurses, "threatens to transform healing from a covenant into a business contract. Canons of commerce are displacing dictates of healing, trampling our professions' most sacred values. Market medicine treats patients as profit centers." As one professional stated, "It's too bad. We used to spend most of our time worrying about how to do a better job. Now we worry about doing a better job at a lower price." . . .

Sixty percent of all managed-care plans, including HMOs and preferred-provider organizations, now pay their primary-care doctors through some sort of "capitation" system, according to the Physician Payment Review Commission in Washington, D.C. That is, rather than simply pay any bill presented to them by your doctor, most HMOs pay their physicians a set amount every month—a fee for including you among their patients. At Chicago's GIA Primary Care Network, for instance, physicians get $8.43 each month for every male patient . . . and $10.09 for every female patient. . . . Some HMOs, such as Oxford Health Plans, Cigna and Aetna, have "withhold" systems, in which a percentage of the doctors' monthly fees are withheld and then reimbursed if they keep their referral rates low enough. Others, like U.S. Healthcare, pay bonuses for low referral rates.

Many physicians, frustrated with the cost pressures of managed care, including those attributable to unnecessary HMO, insurance company, and governmental regulations, have attempted to counter the influence of large, regional health care providers by organizing into unions. Collective bargaining provides unionized doctors with the ability to wield greater leverage when faced with an HMO's efforts to reduce physicians' incomes. Doctors who are dissatisfied with the corporate, profit-driven nature of HMOs, as well as the loss of independence in the doctor-patient relationship, are also considering competing head-on and are forming their own HMOs, just as was done here. Many of these physicians and surgeons have joined their respective specialty practices and linked up with local hospitals to compete with regional HMOs for managed care contracts. But in these circumstances, as in our case, doctors often assume the dual role of care-provider and HMO administrator, and are ultimately held accountable for breaches of fiduciary duty.

This court has previously addressed the costsaving pressures currently being exerted on medical-care providers. In *State of Wis., Dep't of Health and Soc. Servs. v. Bowen*, 797 F.2d 391 (7th Cir. 1986), the author of this majority opinion addressed the Secretary of Health's control over Medicaid's patient care costs.

> A nursing practitioner or physician's assistant is not adequately trained to make the all-important decision dealing with levels of care. It is shocking in our day of advanced medical research, techniques and surgery, when organ transplants and space medicine research are routinely-accepted medical procedures, that we seem to be forgetting and casting aside the all-important human and personal element in medical care. It is equally shocking that we are in effect turning the medical transfer decisions over to the paper shuffling bureaucrat for a review of an inadequately trained medical support assistant. Nursing practitioners and physician's assistants are incapable of making this life-threatening judgment, because they lack both the personal contact with the patient and his family over a period of time, and most frequently lack the necessary expertise, training and experience in psychology, psychiatry and geriatrics required to properly interpret and knowledgeably assess the dangers of transfer trauma.

We must remember that doctors, not insurance executives, are qualified experts in determining what is the best course of treatment and therapy for their patients. Trained physicians, and they alone, should be allowed to make care-related decisions (with, of course, input from the patient). Medical care should not be subject to the whim of the new layer of insurance bureaucracy now dictating the most basic, as well as the important, medical policies and procedures from the boardroom. . . .

A response to the crisis in market-based care has come to roost in Washington, D.C., as a result of constituent sentiment from across the country. Legislation has been introduced that would place restraints on HMOs, provide a "bill of rights" to unhappy health care consumers, and even extend to HMO participants the power to individually sue their health plans for damages. This ability to sue may possibly serve in some measure to rectify the troubling state of affairs which currently exists, where patients can be without a remedy for medical malpractice. These proposals are still being debated in the committee hearing stage of the legislative process, and as yet have not been enacted to control the accelerated decline of our health care system.

Along the same lines as its "market forces" argument, the dissent submits that the defendants' plan "encouraged physicians to use resources more efficiently." Although we agree, at least in principle, with the idea that financial incentives may very well bring about a more effective use of plan assets, we certainly are far from confident that it was at work in this particular case. The Carle health plan at issue was not used as efficiently as it should have been. Indeed, the eight-day delay in medical care, and the onset of peritonitis Herdrich incurred as a result of such delay in diagnosis, subjected her to a life threatening illness, a longer period of hospitalization and treatment, more extensive, invasive and dangerous surgery, increased hospitalization costs, and a greater ingestion of prescription drugs. . . .

In summary, we hold that the language of the plaintiff's complaint is sufficient in alleging that the defendants' incentive system depleted plan resources so as to benefit physicians who, coincidentally, administered the Plan, possibly to the detriment of their patients. The ultimate determination of whether the defendants violated their fiduciary obligations to act solely in the interest of the Plan participants and beneficiaries must be left to the trial court. . . .

DISSENTING OPINION BY JUDGE FLAUM:

This is a case of first impression in which the plaintiff alleges that the imposition of financial incentives designed to limit the provision of health care benefits constitutes a breach of fiduciary duty under ERISA. The plaintiff's complaint alleges that there is a conflict of interest built into the compensation structure of the health plan in question. I fully accept the Majority's conclusion that, taking the allegations of the complaint as true, "an incentive existed for [the defendants] to limit treatment and, in turn, HMO costs so as to ensure larger bonuses." I disagree with the Majority's holding, however, that the mere existence of this asserted conflict, without more, gives rise to a cause of action for breach of fiduciary duty under ERISA. I respectfully dissent.

As described in the complaint, the defendants occupy two different roles in the health plan. The defendants are the plan's doctors, who provide medical care to the plan beneficiaries, and they are also the plan administrators, who (as fiduciaries) make decisions about what claims and conditions are covered under the plan. The complaint alleges that the defendants have breached their fiduciary duty in two ways. First, according to the complaint, the defendants have hired CARLE owner/physicians (*i.e.*, themselves) to provide medical services under the plan while cutting costs by minimizing the resources expended on each patient. By minimizing these expenditures, the defendants preserve funds to be distributed to themselves as year-end bonuses. Second, the complaint alleges that the defendants have administered disputed and non-routine claims. Again, the implication is that these claims are administered with an eye towards denying these claims to augment the defendants' year-end bonuses. Thus, the complaint alleges a structural incentive to deny care both at the point of delivery (*i.e.*, the treatment decisions affecting patient care) and at the point of entry (*i.e.*, the coverage decisions). In my view, however, merely pointing out the existence of these structural incentives does not suffice to make out a cause of action for breach of fiduciary duty under ERISA. . . .

The complaint could be read to imply . . . that the defendants' incentives to limit care are so high that they work to the detriment of the plan and plan beneficiaries. When health plans provide physicians with incentives to internalize costs and maximize efficiency, as appears to be the case here, there is a serious concern that patient care will suffer if the incentives to limit care are set too high. The task of identifying appropriate limits for incentives is an important item on the legislative and regulatory agenda. . . . If the complaint is indeed asserting that the incentives in this case are excessive, then the plaintiffs in effect are inviting the court to make its own determination about appropriate incentive levels in managed care.

In reversing the dismissal of the plaintiff's complaint, the Majority appears to accept this invitation. In my view, however, judicial efforts to determine permissible levels of financial incentives through the vehicle of ERISA's fiduciary rules are unnecessary and ill-advised. No standards for conducting such an inquiry exist. Such a move would preempt legislative and regulatory efforts in this area and could seriously disrupt the ability of plan sponsors and beneficiaries to manage plan assets by agreeing to incentives that encourage cost-conscious medical decisionmaking. The Majority's decision provides little guidance for the district court on remand, and I fear that the decision today could lead, both in this case and in the future, to untethered judicial assessments of permissible incentive levels in health care plans.

Although I cannot join the Majority's decision in this case, I share the Majority's concern about the possibility of incentives that may harm plan beneficiaries, and I believe that courts have a role in ensuring that incentives are implemented in accordance with the fiduciary duties imposed by ERISA. In my judgment, this role is triggered when the market fails to ensure that the interests of sponsors, administrators, and beneficiaries are in alignment. As noted above, plan sponsors are likely to take their business elsewhere if they perceive that incentives are working to the detriment of beneficiaries or the plan itself, and thus market forces go a long way towards ensuring that incentives do not rise to dangerous or undesirable levels. In order for the market to function in this context, however, sponsors and beneficiaries need information about the financial incentives that are in place. Thus, I would follow the Eighth Circuit's lead in holding that the failure to disclose financial incentives is a breach of fiduciary duty under ERISA. *See Shea v. Esensten,* 107 F.3d 625 (8th Cir. 1997).

Until the Majority's expansion of liability in today's case, *Shea* stood at the frontier in terms of imposing liability under ERISA on health plans that seek to control costs by providing financial incentives to limit patient care. The *Shea* decision has proven to be controversial. . . .

Even when disclosures have been made, I would not rule out the possibility that the imposition of incentives to limit care could support a claim of breach of fiduciary duty when there is a serious flaw in the manner in which the incentive arrangement is established or a significant limitation on the ability of plan sponsors to obtain alternative arrangements in the market. Such a claim would have to make some allegation, which the plaintiffs in the instant case do not, pointing to special circumstances suggesting a breakdown in the market or in the negotiating process that led to the imposition of incentives. The complaint in this case, however, contains no allegation of nondisclosure, and it fails to make any allegations suggesting that the financial incentives to limit care are anything but the result of the bargain fairly struck between the plan's sponsor, administrator, and beneficiaries. I would affirm the decision below dismissing the complaint.

NOTES AND QUESTIONS:
Herdrich v. Pegram

1. As you can imagine, the *Herdrich* decision has been quite controversial. The case curiously suggests that the federal law that is largely blamed for creating many of the legal problems relating to managed care may well condemn many forms of managed care. Not surprisingly, the United States Supreme Court unanimously reversed the lower court's decision. *Pegram v. Herdrich*, 120 S. Ct. 2143 (2000).

2. The Supreme Court's reasoning in *Pegram* is perhaps best understood on two different levels: as a relatively narrow comment on ERISA and its preemption provisions, and as a broader comment on federal law relating to managed care.

   To understand the former, we need additional detail about how ERISA has been interpreted. As we saw in the introduction, ERISA provides a uniform federal law relating to employee benefits, including employer-provided health plans. To the extent that state laws are inconsistent with these federal laws, they are overridden ("preempted"). This is again a straightforward example of federalism.

   But not all state laws relating to health care plans *are* preempted. In particular, court decisions interpreting ERISA (including several Supreme Court opinions) appear to draw a line between eligibility determinations—deciding whether or not a person is entitled to a particular health care benefit under a plan—and the actual provision of health care services to a patient. Because eligibility determinations are felt to be at the core of ERISA's concerns, state laws that attempt to regulate them are generally preempted. In contrast, ERISA is *not* viewed as creating a federal form of malpractice law: it does not preempt state malpractice laws.

   Thus, Cynthia Herdrich had already successfully sued Dr. Pegram under Illinois medical malpractice law. This was relatively non-controversial: ERISA does not interfere with such lawsuits. Moreover, as a result of the control the HMO exercised over Dr. Pegram, Ms. Hedrich was able to successfully sue the HMO on the ground that it was responsible for the wrongdoing of the doctors who worked for it. This was a standard lawsuit based on laws that make employers responsible for the actions of employees and certain other people; it had nothing specifically to do with laws relating to providing health care or other benefits to employees. ERISA probably does not preempt this form of lawsuit.

On the other hand, had Herdrich been complaining of an eligibility determination—for example, that she told the HMO screening person of her stomach pain and that person (wrongly) told her that stomach pain was not covered—she would not have been able to sue the HMO under Illinois law; this is an eligibility determination covered by ERISA, and thus state laws would be preempted.

As Justice Souter's opinion for the Supreme Court notes, the actual events in the case presented a hybrid type of decision, relating partly to eligibility for benefits and partly to the actual health care provided:

> . . . . It will help to keep two sorts of arguably administrative acts in mind. What we will call pure "eligibility decisions" turn on the plan's coverage of a particular condition or medical procedure for its treatment. "Treatment decisions," by contrast, are choices about how to go about diagnosing and treating a patient's condition: given a patient's constellation of symptoms, what is the appropriate medical response?
>
> These decisions are often practically inextricable from one another, as *amici* on both sides agree. This is so not merely because, under a scheme like Carle's, treatment and eligibility decisions are made by the same person, the treating physician. It is so because a great many and possibly most coverage questions are not simple yes-or-no questions, like whether appendicitis is a covered condition (when there is no dispute that a patient has appendicitis), or whether acupuncture is a covered procedure for pain relief (when the claim of pain is unchallenged). The more common coverage question is a when-and-how question. Although coverage for many conditions will be clear and various treatment options will be indisputably compensable, physicians still must decide what to do in particular cases. The issue may be, say, whether one treatment option is so superior to another under the circumstances, and needed so promptly, that a decision to proceed with it would meet the medical necessity requirement that conditions the HMO's obligation to provide or pay for that particular procedure at that time in that case. The Government in its brief alludes to a similar example when it discusses an HMO's refusal to pay for emergency care on the ground that the situation giving rise to the need for care was not an emergency. In practical terms, these eligibility decisions cannot be untangled from physicians' judgments about reasonable medical treatment, and in the case before us, Dr. Pegram's decision was one of that sort. She decided (wrongly, as it turned out) that Herdrich's condition did not warrant immediate action; the consequence of that medical determination was that Carle would not cover immediate care, whereas it would have done so if Dr. Pegram had made the proper diagnosis and judgment to treat. The eligibility decision and the treatment decision were inextricably mixed, as they are in countless medical administrative decisions every day.
>
> The kinds of decisions mentioned in Herdrich's ERISA count and claimed to be fiduciary in character are just such mixed eligibility and treatment deci-

sions: physicians' conclusions about when to use diagnostic tests; about seeking consultations and making referrals to physicians and facilities other than Carle's; about proper standards of care, the experimental character of a proposed course of treatment, the reasonableness of a certain treatment, and the emergency character of a medical condition. . . . .

Based on our understanding of the matters just discussed, we think Congress did not intend Carle or any other HMO to be treated as a fiduciary to the extent that it makes mixed eligibility decisions acting through its physicians. We begin with doubt that Congress would ever have thought of a mixed eligibility decision as fiduciary in nature. At common law, fiduciary duties characteristically attach to decisions about managing assets and distributing property to beneficiaries. Trustees buy, sell, and lease investment property, lend and borrow, and do other things to conserve and nurture assets. They pay out income, choose beneficiaries, and distribute remainders at termination. Thus, the common law trustee's most defining concern historically has been the payment of money in the interest of the beneficiary.

Mixed eligibility decisions by an HMO acting through its physicians have, however, only a limited resemblance to the usual business of traditional trustees. To be sure, the physicians (like regular trustees) draw on resources held for others and make decisions to distribute them in accordance with entitlements expressed in a written instrument (embodying the terms of an ERISA plan). It is also true that the objects of many traditional private and public trusts are ultimately the same as the ERISA plans that contract with HMOs. Private trusts provide medical care to the poor; thousands of independent hospitals are privately held and publicly accountable trusts, and charitable foundations make grants to stimulate the provision of health services. But beyond this point the resemblance rapidly wanes. Traditional trustees administer a medical trust by paying out money to buy medical care, whereas physicians making mixed eligibility decisions consume the money as well. Private trustees do not make treatment judgments, whereas treatment judgments are what physicians reaching mixed decisions do make, by definition. Indeed, the physicians through whom HMOs act make just the sorts of decisions made by licensed medical practitioners millions of times every day, in every possible medical setting: HMOs, fee-for-service proprietorships, public and private hospitals, military field hospitals, and so on. The settings bear no more resemblance to trust departments than a decision to operate turns on the factors controlling the amount of a quarterly income distribution. Thus, it is at least questionable whether Congress would have had mixed eligibility decisions in mind when it provided that decisions administering a plan were fiduciary in nature. Indeed, when Congress took up the subject of fiduciary responsibility under ERISA, it concentrated on fiduciaries' financial decisions, focusing on pension plans, the difficulty many retirees faced in getting the payments they expected, and the financial mismanagement that had too often deprived employees of their benefits. Its focus was far from the subject of Herdrich's claim.

Our doubt that Congress intended the category of fiduciary administrative functions to encompass the mixed determinations at issue here hardens into conviction when we consider the consequences that would follow from Herdrich's contrary view. . . .

First, we need to ask how this fiduciary standard would affect HMOs if it applied as Herdrich claims it should be applied, not directed against any particular mixed decision that injured a patient, but against HMOs that make mixed decisions in the course of providing medical care for profit. Recovery would be warranted simply upon showing that the profit incentive to ration care would generally affect mixed decisions, in derogation of the fiduciary standard to act solely in the interest of the patient without possibility of conflict. Although Herdrich is vague about the mechanics of relief, the one point that seems clear is that she seeks the return of profit from the pockets of the Carle HMO's owners, with the money to be given to the plan for the benefit of the participants. Since the provision for profit is what makes the HMO a proprietary organization, her remedy in effect would be nothing less than elimination of the for-profit HMO. Her remedy might entail even more than that, although we are in no position to tell whether and to what extent nonprofit HMO schemes would ultimately survive the recognition of Herdrich's theory. It is enough to recognize that the Judiciary has no warrant to precipitate the upheaval that would follow a refusal to dismiss Herdrich's ERISA claim. The fact is that for over 27 years the Congress of the United States has promoted the formation of HMO practices.

3. In addition to deciding this rather specific question about the extent to which ERISA applies to mixed eligibility decisions, the Supreme Court also provided some interesting observations on the fundamental nature of HMOs:

> Traditionally, medical care in the United States has been provided on a "fee-for-service" basis. A physician charges so much for a general physical exam, a vaccination, a tonsillectomy, and so on. The physician bills the patient for services provided or, if there is insurance and the doctor is willing, submits the bill for the patient's care to the insurer, for payment subject to the terms of the insurance agreement. In a fee-for-service system, a physician's financial incentive is to provide more care, not less, so long as payment is forthcoming. The check on this incentive is a physician's obligation to exercise reasonable medical skill and judgment in the patient's interest.
>
> Beginning in the late 1960's, insurers and others developed new models for health-care delivery, including HMOs. The defining feature of an HMO is receipt of a fixed fee for each patient enrolled under the terms of a contract to provide specified health care if needed. The HMO thus assumes the financial risk of providing the benefits promised: if a participant never gets sick, the HMO keeps the money regardless, and if a participant becomes expensively ill, the HMO is responsible for the treatment agreed upon even if its cost exceeds the participant's premiums.
>
> Like other risk-bearing organizations, HMOs take steps to control costs. At the least, HMOs, like traditional insurers, will in some fashion make coverage determinations, scrutinizing requested services against the contractual provisions to make sure that a request for care falls within the scope of covered circumstances (pregnancy, for example), or that a given treatment falls within the scope of the care promised (surgery, for instance). They customarily issue gen-

eral guidelines for their physicians about appropriate levels of care. And they commonly require utilization review (in which specific treatment decisions are reviewed by a decisionmaker other than the treating physician) and approval in advance (precertification) for many types of care, keyed to standards of medical necessity or the reasonableness of the proposed treatment. These cost-controlling measures are commonly complemented by specific financial incentives to physicians, rewarding them for decreasing utilization of health-care services, and penalizing them for what may be found to be excessive treatment. Hence, in an HMO system, a physician's financial interest lies in providing less care, not more. The check on this influence (like that on the converse, fee-for-service incentive) is the professional obligation to provide covered services with a reasonable degree of skill and judgment in the patient's interest.

The adequacy of professional obligation to counter financial self-interest has been challenged no matter what the form of medical organization. HMOs became popular because fee-for-service physicians were thought to be providing unnecessary or useless services; today, many doctors and other observers argue that HMOs often ignore the individual needs of a patient in order to improve the HMOs' bottom lines. In this case, for instance, one could argue that Pegram's decision to wait before getting an ultrasound for Herdrich, and her insistence that the ultrasound be done at a distant facility owned by Carle, reflected an interest in limiting the HMO's expenses, which blinded her to the need for immediate diagnosis and treatment. . . .

Herdrich focuses on the Carle scheme's provision for a "year-end distribution" to the HMO's physician owners. She argues that this particular incentive device of annually paying physician owners the profit resulting from their own decisions rationing care can distinguish Carle's organization from HMOs generally, so that reviewing Carle's decisions under a fiduciary standard as pleaded in Herdrich's complaint would not open the door to like claims about other HMO structures. While the Court of Appeals agreed, we think otherwise, under the law as now written.

Although it is true that the relationship between sparing medical treatment and physician reward is not a subtle one under the Carle scheme, no HMO organization could survive without some incentive connecting physician reward with treatment rationing. The essence of an HMO is that salaries and profits are limited by the HMO's fixed membership fees. This is not to suggest that the Carle provisions are as socially desirable as some other HMO organizational schemes; they may not be. But whatever the HMO, there must be rationing and inducement to ration.

Since inducement to ration care goes to the very point of any HMO scheme, and rationing necessarily raises some risks while reducing others (ruptured appendixes are more likely; unnecessary appendectomies are less so), any legal principle purporting to draw a line between good and bad HMOs would embody, in effect, a judgment about socially acceptable medical risk. A valid conclusion of this sort would, however, necessarily turn on facts to which courts would probably not have ready access: correlations between malpractice rates and various HMO models, similar correlations involving fee-for-service models, and so on. And, of course, assuming such material could be obtained by courts in litigation like this, any standard defining the unacceptably risky HMO structure (and consequent vulnerability to claims like Herdrich's) would depend on a judgment about the appropriate level of expenditure for health care in light of the associated malpractice risk. But such complicated factfinding and such a debatable social judgment are not wisely required of courts unless for some reason resort cannot be had to the legislative process, with its preferable forum for comprehensive investigations and judgments of social value, such as optimum treatment levels and health care expenditure.

4. Compare the language of Justice Souter in the preceding excerpt with the issues raised in the notes following *Helling v. Carey* in chapter 7. Does the attempt to categorize physician incentive plans as either good or bad involve the sort of weighing of values that is involved in determining where to draw the limits on a standard of care?

5. According to the Supreme Court, because physician incentive plans are a basic element of an HMO, it would be too difficult for the judicial system to create and police rules distinguishing between good and bad HMOs. That conclusion does not mean it would not be appropriate for Congress to pass a law that set up such rules. Do you think that would be a good idea? In particular, what sorts of incentives might be forbidden? Should we, for example, limit the percentage of a physician's salary that might be subject to such incentives? What criteria should we use to distinguish good incentives from bad ones?

6. The Supreme Court's endorsement of the rationing aspects of an HMO is significant. Many people might think that HMOs save money by merely getting rid of "needless waste"—for example, by replacing the use of an old, costly test with a newer, more efficient test. Such actions improve the care for everyone.

   In fact, however, much of what an HMO does is to ration care, and this can involve a very different type of action: costs are often saved by reducing the amount of care some patients receive. Patients like Cynthia Herdrich end up getting an ultrasound at a later date, and thus having a greater risk of a ruptured appendix.[4]

7. Traditional medical ethics prescribes that a doctor should always do all that she can for the patient in front of her at the time. Is that concept necessarily inconsistent with managed care, assuming that most patients are interested not only in getting good care but also in not paying for inefficient medical care?

   Assume that there is a generic medication for asthma patients that costs $2 a dose. It causes occasional nausea in most patients. A new medication has identical benefits to the old medication but eliminates the nausea. The new medication costs $20 a dose. A doctor is working for an HMO that pays for all medications for the patients. Her salary is not influenced by what medications she prescribes for a particular patient. On the other hand, she knows that the organization has a fixed budget, and money spent for some patients will not be available for other patients. And if too much money is spent this year, rates may have to be raised next year, causing some patients to drop their coverage.

Is it appropriate for the doctor to consider the cost of the new medication in deciding whether to give it to a patient? Might it be relevant for her to determine whether her asthma patients would have been willing to pay the extra $18 out of their own pockets?[5]

8. The HMO discussed in item 7 might have discovered that an increasingly large portion of its budget was being spent on new medications, such as the new asthma drug, that were far costlier than previous drugs but had only marginally better effects. It might remove the new drugs from the formulary and not allow a doctor to prescribe them, absent proof that for a particular patient, the new drug was especially beneficial. Alternatively, it might provide each doctor with a budget of, say, $10,000 for prescribing costly new drugs. Once the doctor uses up that budget, then 10 percent of the costs of the prescriptions she writes for such drugs will come out of her salary. What are the positive and negative aspects of these two plans?

9. How does informed consent factor into this discussion? Disclosure of a doctor's compensation has never been a required element of informed consent. One of the few cases to raise this issue is the *Shea* case, discussed in Judge Flaum's dissenting opinion in *Herdrich*. Shea, 40, had visited his doctor several times complaining of chest pains and shortness of breath, and concerned that he might have a heart problem. He asked for a referral to a cardiologist but was assured by the doctor that he was too young and had too few symptoms to require a work-up by a cardiologist. Shea died a few months later of a heart attack. His wife sued the HMO (which provided care to Shea through his employer's health plan), and a federal court determined that ERISA required the plan to disclose that primary care doctors earned less if they made referrals to specialists.

In *Pegram*, the Supreme Court appeared to endorse the use of the informed consent process as a way of limiting physician incentives. A footnote to the opinion observed that Ms. Herdrich had initially complained of a "breach of a fiduciary obligation to disclose physician incentives to limit care." That argument was no longer before the Supreme Court, so it did not directly address it, but it did observe that under ERISA the HMO "is obligated to disclose characteristics of the plan."

10. If we require disclosure of financial conflicts of interest, *when* should that disclosure be required? Will it be sufficient for the managed care plan to lay out all its financial arrangements in the documents given when the person joins the plan? Or will a doctor be required also to disclose such conflicts at specific times when the doctor's income might be "substantially" influenced by a particular decision (as when referring—or refusing to refer—Mr. Shea to a specialist)?[6]

Endnotes

1. For more on the possible implications of *Johnson v. Kokemoor*, see, e.g., Aaron D. Twerski and Neil B. Cohen, "The Second Revolution in Informed Consent: Comparing Physicians to Each Other," 94 *Nw. U.L. Rev.* 1 (1999).
2. For a recent case discussing this issue, see *Duttry v. Patterson*, 741 A.2d 199 (Pa. Super. Ct. 1999), which the Pennsylvania Supreme Court has agreed to review.
3. For more on this issue, see, e.g., Margaret G. Farrell, "ERISA Preemption and Regulation of Managed Health Care: The Case for Managed Federalism," 23 *Am. J.L. & Med.* 251 (1997).
4. The issues raised by the Supreme Court's opinion are a subset of the broader questions relating to the rationing of health care. For more on these issues, see, e.g., Mark A. Hall, *Making Medical Spending Decisions: The Law, Ethics & Economics of Rationing Mechanisms* (New York: Oxford University Press, 1997); Peter A. Ubel, *Pricing Life: Why It's Time for Health Care Rationing* (Cambridge, Mass: MIT Press, 2000).
5. For more on this issue and a discussion of how such dilemmas are really a variant of the game theory problem known as the prisoner's dilemma, see Jerry Menikoff, "The Role of the Physician in Cost Control," 10(2) *Ophthalmology Clinics N. Am.* 191 (1997).
6. See, e.g., Mark A. Hall, "A Theory of Economic Informed Consent," 31 *Ga. L. Rev.* 511 (1997); David Mechanic, "Trust and Informed Consent to Rationing," 72 *Milbank Quarterly* 217 (1994).

9

Beyond "Standard Care": Alternative Medicine, Experimentation, and Research

In chapter 7 we saw that the very existence of tort law represents an element of paternalism in the law: we do not allow people unlimited discretion to choose what medical treatment they wish. The law protects them from making "poor" choices, on the theory that people are vulnerable to making such choices when it comes to health matters. Consider the case of Barbara Rojas, 52, an overweight woman who could not afford standard cosmetic surgery. She hired a bargain-rate doctor, Guillermo Falconi, who was licensed as a physician in Ecuador but not in the United States. After Falconi performed cosmetic surgery on Rojas in her bedroom, she died of post-operative complications. Falconi was convicted of second-degree murder.[1]

Presumably, we can agree that Falconi should not have been permitted to operate on Rojas. But what if we make the facts less outrageous? Assume that Falconi was a U.S.-licensed plastic surgeon, and Rojas still could not afford his fee. Could he then have operated in her bedroom, assuming he fully informed her of the increased risk? How different is this from the residency programs for plastic surgeons that offer discounts to patients who are operated on by relatively inexperienced physicians? How do we determine if the extra risk imposed by care that is not standard is something we will allow a person to consent to? Such issues are most squarely presented when we talk about certain categories of more legitimate non-standard care: alternative and experimental therapies. Unfortunately, it is not always easy to draw the line between appropriate governmental paternalism and inappropriate restrictions on individual autonomy.

In re Guess

Supreme Court of North Carolina

393 S.E.2d 833 (N.C. 1990)

OPINION BY JUSTICE MITCHELL:

. . . The facts of this case are essentially uncontested. The record evidence tends to show that Dr. George Albert Guess is a licensed physician practicing family medicine in Asheville. In his practice, Guess regularly administers homeopathic medical treatments to his patients. Homeopathy has been defined as:

> A system of therapy developed by Samuel Hahnemann on the theory that large doses of a certain drug given to a healthy person will produce certain conditions which, when occurring spontaneously as symptoms of a disease, are relieved by the same drug in small doses. This [is] . . . a sort of "fighting fire with fire" therapy.

Homeopathy thus differs from what is referred to as the conventional or allopathic system of medical treatment. . . .

The Board of Medical Examiners of the State of North Carolina (herein Board) is a legislatively created body established "to properly regulate the practice of medicine and surgery." On 25 June 1985, the Board charged Dr. Guess with unprofessional conduct, . . . specifically based upon his practice of homeopathy. In a subsequent Bill of Particulars, the Board alleged that in his practice of medicine, Guess utilized "so-called 'homeopathic medicines' prepared from substances including, but not limited to, moss, the night shade plant and various other animal, vegetable and mineral substances." The Board further alleged that the use of homeopathic medicines "departs from and does not conform to the standards of acceptable and prevailing medical practice in the State of North Carolina."

Following notice, a hearing was held by the Board on the charge against Dr. Guess. The hearing evidence chiefly consisted of testimony by a number of physicians. Several physicians licensed to practice in North Carolina testified that homeopathy was not an acceptable and prevailing system of medical practice in North Carolina. In fact, there was evidence indicating that Guess is the only homeopath openly practicing in the State. Guess presented evidence that homeopathy is a recognized system of practice in at least three other states and many foreign countries. There was no evidence that Guess' homeopathic treatment had ever harmed a patient, and there was anecdotal evidence that Guess' homeopathic remedies had provided relief to several patients who were apparently unable to obtain relief through allopathic medicine.

Following its hearing, the Board revoked Dr. Guess' license to practice medicine in North Carolina, based upon findings and conclusions that Guess' practice of homeopathy "departs from and does not conform to the standards of acceptable and prevailing medical practice in this State," thus constituting unprofessional conduct as defined and prohibited by [North Carolina law]. The Board, however, stayed the revocation of Guess' license for so long as he refrained from practicing homeopathy. . . .

The statute central to the resolution of this case provides in relevant part:

§ 90-14. Revocation, suspension, annulment or denial of license.

(a) The Board shall have the power to deny, annul, suspend, or revoke a license . . . issued by the Board to any person who has been found by the Board to have committed any of the following acts or conduct, or for any of the following reasons:

. . .

(6) Unprofessional conduct, including, but not limited to, any departure from, or the failure to conform to, the standards of acceptable and prevailing medical practice, or the ethics of the medical profession, irrespective of whether or not a patient is injured thereby. . . .

The Board argues, and we agree, that the Court of Appeals erred in construing the statute to add a requirement that each particular practice prohibited by the statute must pose an actual threat of harm. Our analysis begins with a basic constitutional principle: the General Assembly, in exercising the state's police power, may legislate to protect the public health, safety and general welfare. When a statute is challenged as being beyond the scope of the police power, the statute will be upheld unless it has no rational relationship to such a legitimate public purpose.

Turning to the subject of this case, regulation of the medical profession is plainly related to the legitimate public purpose of protecting the public health and safety. State regulation of the medical profession has long been recognized as a legitimate exercise of the police power. . . .

The provision of the statute in question here is reasonably related to the public health. We conclude that the legislature . . . reasonably believed that a general risk of endangering the public is inherent in any practices which fail to conform to the standards of "acceptable and prevailing" medical practice in North Carolina. We further conclude that the legislative intent was to prohibit any practice departing from acceptable and prevailing medical standards without regard to whether the particular practice itself could be shown to endanger the public. Our conclusion is buttressed by the plain language of [the statute], which allows the Board to act against any departure from acceptable medical practice "irrespective of whether or not a patient is injured thereby." By authorizing the Board to prevent or punish any medical practice departing from acceptable and prevailing standards, irrespective of whether a patient is injured thereby, the statute works as a regulation which "tend[s] to secure" the public generally "against the consequences of ignorance and incapacity as well as of deception and fraud," even though it may not immediately have that direct effect in a particular case. Therefore, the statute is a valid exercise of the police power. . . .

Dr. Guess strenuously argues that many countries and at least three states recognize the legitimacy of homeopathy. While some physicians may value the homeopathic system of practice, it seems that others consider homeopathy an outmoded and ineffective system of practice. This conflict, however interesting, simply is irrelevant here in light of the uncontroverted evidence and the Board's findings and conclusion that homeopathy is not currently an "acceptable and prevailing" system of medical practice in North Carolina.

While questions as to the efficacy of homeopathy and whether its practice should be allowed in North Carolina may be open to valid debate among members of the medical profession, the courts are not the proper forum for that debate. The legislature may one day choose to recognize the homeopathic system of treatment, or homeopathy may evolve by proper experimentation and research to the point of being recognized by the medical profession as an acceptable and prevailing form of medical practice in our state; such choices, however, are not for the courts to make.

We stress that we do not intend for our opinion in this case to retard the ongoing research and development of the healing arts in any way. The Board argues, and we agree within our admittedly limited scope of medical knowledge, that preventing the practice of homeopathy will not restrict the development and acceptance of new and beneficial medical practices. Instead, the development and acceptance of such new practices simply must be achieved by "acceptable and prevailing" methods of medical research, experimentation, testing, and approval by the appropriate regulatory or professional bodies. . . .

Dr. Guess next contends that the Board's decision unconstitutionally invades his and his patients' privacy rights, by invading Guess' right to select his method of practice and invading his patients' rights to their choice of treatments. We disagree on both points. Regarding Guess' ability to select his method of practice, "there is no right to practice medicine which is not subordinate to the police power of the states." Further, the Board's decision does not deprive Guess of his privilege to practice medicine, it simply limits his methods of treating patients to those which conform to the acceptable and prevailing standards of medical practice in North Carolina. Regarding Guess' claim that the Board's decision invades his patients' right to select the treatment of their choice, we initially note that he has no standing to raise his patients' privacy interests in this regard. Further, we have recognized no fundamental right to receive unorthodox medical treatment, and we decline to do so now. . . .

NOTES AND QUESTIONS:
In re Guess

1. Dr. Guess then went to the federal courts in an attempt to overturn the state court decision. Some of his patients also asked the federal courts for

relief, claiming that the North Carolina decision violated their constitutional right to obtain care from him. All of these claims were ultimately rejected. *Guess v. Board of Medical Examiners of North Carolina*, 967 F.2d 998 (4th Cir. 1992).

2. The North Carolina legislature did, however, change the state law with regard to the "patient harm" issue. As it is now written, the relevant statute denies the Board of Medical Examiners the power to discipline a doctor "solely because of that person's practice of a therapy that is experimental, nontraditional, or that departs from acceptable and prevailing medical practices unless, by competent evidence, the Board can establish that the treatment has a safety risk greater than the prevailing treatment or that the treatment is generally not effective." N.C. Gen. Stat. § 90-14 (a)(6) (1999).

3. The *Guess* opinion is consistent with most other court decisions, which generally support the power of a state to deny patients access to a particular form of therapy or a particular type of practitioner. Thus, for example, in *Mitchell v. Clayton*, 995 F.2d 772 (7th Cir. 1993), a federal appellate court upheld an Illinois law that categorized acupuncture as being within the practice of medicine, and therefore required that only a graduate of a medical, osteopathic or chiropractic college could provide it:

> Finally, we reach the claims of the prospective patients of the aggrieved acupuncturists. They argue that the MPA deprives them of their constitutional right to have acupuncturists who have not been to chiropractic school treat their ailments. . . . [M]ost federal courts have held that a patient does not have a constitutional right to obtain a particular type of treatment or to obtain treatment from a particular provider if the government has reasonably prohibited that type of treatment or provider.
>
> As we have said, when no fundamental right is implicated, the challenged statute passes constitutional muster as long as the legislature had a rational basis for its enactment.

Even the U.S. Supreme Court has played a role in this debate. In *United States v. Rutherford*, 442 U.S. 544 (1979), it affirmed the authority of the Food and Drug Administration to ban the use of Laetrile, a substance that was being promoted as an anti-cancer agent. End-stage cancer patients had argued that the FDA had no authority to prevent dying patients from getting access to a substance that had not been proven to be harmful. An appellate court accepted that argument, concluding that the "safety" and "effectiveness" requirements in the law had no relevance to terminally ill cancer patients, since they were going to die no matter what was done to them. Here is an excerpt from what the Supreme Court said in reversing that court:

> An otherwise harmless drug can be dangerous to any patient if it does not produce its purported therapeutic effect. But if an individual suffering from a potentially fatal disease rejects conventional therapy in favor of a drug with no demonstrable curative properties, the consequences can be irreversible. . . . The FDA's practice also reflects the recognition, amply supported by expert medi-

cal testimony in this case, that with diseases such as cancer it is often impossible to identify a patient as terminally ill except in retrospect. Cancers vary considerably in behavior and in responsiveness to different forms of therapy. Even critically ill individuals may have unexpected remissions and may respond to conventional treatment. Thus, as the Commissioner concluded, to exempt from the Act drugs with no proved effectiveness in the treatment of cancer "would lead to needless deaths and suffering among . . . patients characterized as 'terminal' who could actually be helped by legitimate therapy."

It bears emphasis that although the Court of Appeals' ruling was limited to Laetrile, its reasoning cannot be so readily confined. To accept the proposition that the safety and efficacy standards of the Act have no relevance for terminal patients is to deny the Commissioner's authority over all drugs, however toxic or ineffectual, for such individuals. If history is any guide, this new market would not be long overlooked. Since the turn of the century, resourceful entrepreneurs have advertised a wide variety of purportedly simple and painless cures for cancer, including liniments of turpentine, mustard, oil, eggs, and ammonia; peat moss; arrangements of colored floodlamps; pastes made from glycerin and limburger cheese; mineral tablets; and "Fountain of Youth" mixtures of spices, oil, and suet. In citing these examples, we do not, of course, intend to deprecate the sincerity of Laetrile's current proponents, or to imply any opinion on whether that drug may ultimately prove safe and effective for cancer treatment. But this historical experience does suggest why Congress could reasonably have determined to protect the terminally ill, no less than other patients, from the vast range of self-styled panaceas that inventive minds can devise.

4. In *Rutherford*, the Supreme Court was determining whether Congress had authorized the FDA to create a rule that denied terminally ill patients access to safe drugs with unproven efficacy. As you saw, the Court answered yes.

There is, however, a second and more important issue: even if Congress did grant that power to the FDA, is that unconstitutional? We know that the right of privacy created by the Fourteenth Amendment prevents the government from inappropriately interfering in various aspects of a person's life (such as a woman's attempt to get an abortion). Isn't it possible that the right of privacy would protect a terminally ill person's right to take a safe, though unproven, drug? It's that person's life on the line, and perhaps should be that person's choice to spend money on something unproven.

The federal district court that heard the *Rutherford* case concluded that the right of privacy did prevent the government from denying a patient access to Laetrile. But this constitutional argument was not formally addressed by the appeals court, and the Supreme Court thus did not have to comment on whether it was right or wrong. Nonetheless, given other court decisions on similar issues (such as *Mitchell*, quoted in note 3), it seems unlikely that the Supreme Court would have concluded that the Laetrile ban violated the Constitution.

5. The constitutional issues were also indirectly addressed in *Guess*. Note the final line from the excerpted opinion: "we have recognized no fundamental

right to receive unorthodox medical treatment, and we decline to do so now." If the Fourteenth Amendment did protect a person's right to choose a particular form of health care, what form of scrutiny would the court have been required to apply in evaluating the actions of the medical board? (Recall the discussion of equal protection in chapter 2, and the standards of review that a court must apply when a law might impinge on a fundamental right.) What standard of review did the *Guess* court apply?

6. A related question is whether the Constitution guarantees anyone access to needed health care. Surprisingly, the settled answer is no, there is no "constitutional right to health care." The national government has no obligation to make sure that anyone gets appropriate (or even less than appropriate) health care, or to pay for such care. See, e.g., *Harris v. McRae*, 448 U.S. 297 (1980). While Congress has passed laws that create specific rights in certain settings, such as the right to stabilizing treatment in an emergency room (EMTALA, discussed in the *Baby K* case in chapter 12), the Constitution mandates none of these rights.

7. As a matter of policy, which do you think was more appropriate: the North Carolina law that was applied to Dr. Guess, or the revised version that required the Board to prove that the treatment was either unsafe or ineffective?

8. Issues relating to alternatives to conventional medicine can arise in two ways. While licensed practitioners like Dr. Guess can be disciplined for not providing standard care, persons who are unlicensed are also subject to discipline, since they would probably be practicing medicine without a license. This issue is raised in the *Mitchell* case, discussed in note 3, where persons performing acupuncture were required to have some sort of medical degree. The laws in different states vary on who can perform what type of therapy. For example, some states have specific statutory requirements for who can practice massage therapy, homeopathy and naturopathy.

  If a state legislature has not enacted a statute that deals with a certain type of therapy, it may not be clear whether such a practitioner is illegally practicing medicine without a license. One of the groups that has curiously benefited from such a statutory "hole" is midwives. Most recently, the Supreme Court of Kansas determined that under existing statutes midwifery constituted the practice neither of medicine nor of nursing, and thus was not subject to the regulatory authority of either of the state boards for those two fields. *State Board of Nursing v. Ruebke*, 913 P.2d 142 (Kan. 1996).

9. Deciding who has the burden of proof—a regulator or the person who wants to use a particular treatment—can play a crucial role in determining what types of care are or are not permitted. The burden to prove safety, efficacy, or both can be placed on either the proponent of a therapy or on the regulatory agency itself. Obviously, from the point of view of a governmental agency with limited resources, if the burden is put on the agency, far more treatments will be permitted.

In general, federal law requires that persons wanting to market drugs must prove both their efficacy and their safety, as the *Rutherford* opinion noted. However, there is a major relatively recent exception to that rule. In 1994, a new federal law, the Dietary Supplement Health and Education Act, went into effect. This law, viewed by many as Congress's response to powerful lobbying efforts by the dietary supplement industry, exempted various "natural substances" from the usual rules requiring proof of safety and efficacy for drugs. The change led to the variety of television advertisements telling you, for example, that ginkgo biloba would do wonders for your memory. Similar regulatory considerations lie behind the attempt of some manufacturers to promote "herbal fen-phen" after the FDA restricted the use of the diet drug combination of fenfluramine and phentermine.[2]

EXPERIMENTATION AND RESEARCH

One of the types of nonstandard care we might have good reason to encourage is experimental care. Standard care is just not very effective for many medical problems. Thus, it might be quite reasonable to allow certain patients considerable discretion in opting for experimental care. But to what extent should a patient's ability to opt for experimental care be circumscribed by the existence of effective standard care? And are there special concerns when the health care provider is not merely experimenting on the patient, but also attempting to prove the superiority of a new treatment?

Consider the hypothetical case of Dr. Claudia Creative, ophthalmologist extraordinaire. While staring at a carved-out pumpkin one recent Halloween, she comes up with a new idea for how to make the initial cut in cataract surgery: the toothy-grin incision. Dr. Creative immediately starts trying out this idea on cadaver human eyes in the laboratory, and discovers that use of the toothy-grin incision produces self-sealing wounds that are much better than those produced by usual cataract incisions (including the well-known "frown" incision).

She might find these laboratory studies so convincing that she decides to begin using the new incision on patients. Can she do that? Obviously, the incision is not yet standard care. Yet for care to evolve, someone somewhere has to attempt something new and untried. At this point, we might describe Dr. Creative's technique as experimental, since it is not yet accepted by mainstream medicine. Given that the new technique is not a very great departure from standard care, the law might well determine that it is reasonable for Dr. Creative to offer this change, and equally reasonable for a patient to be given the opportunity to consent to having it tried on him. Were a patient to sue after having a bad outcome from the new procedure these issues of reasonableness may have to be resolved by state malpractice laws. (And, as with Dr. Guess, the licensing board might make its own determinations.) One of the most important points in such a case would relate to informed consent: it would obviously be crucial to determine if the experimental nature of the treatment and the standard-care alternatives were fully explained to the patient.

Let us vary the facts slightly. We have assumed up to now that Dr. Creative wanted to use the new technique solely to benefit her patients. But that will rarely be the case with legitimate experimental treatments. Presumably, she also wants to collect data and convince other ophthalmologists how great this new technique is. Under this slightly different set of facts, Dr. Creative is now pursuing two goals—treating her patient and evaluating the effectiveness of her new technique—and the two goals might conflict. In order to statistically prove the efficacy of her technique, for example, she might have to treat a number of patients in a uniform way that prevents her from individualizing their treatment and doing what is best for them. Thus, we might well conclude that she has a conflict of interest, and that the law must protect her patients from untoward consequences of that conflict of interest.

In the cases that follow, we will explore the tension between the search for medical knowledge and the responsibility to do what is best for a particular patient.

STEWART V. CLEVELAND CLINIC FOUNDATION
Court of Appeals of Ohio
736 N.E.2d 491 (Ohio Ct. App. 1999)

OPINION BY JUDGE SWEENEY:

. . . Mr. Daniel Klais utilized the Cleveland Clinic Foundation ("Cleveland Clinic") as his medical care provider. During Mr. Klais' annual physical examination in March of 1990, his primary family practice physician at the Cleveland Clinic, Dr. Cheryl Weinstein, diagnosed as a cyst a 2 cm by 2 cm nodule found on his neck. During a subsequent visit on May 21, 1990, Dr. Weinstein observed further swelling on the patient's neck and two additional nodules. At this point, Dr. Weinstein suspected a cancerous condition and referred the patient to the Cleveland Clinic's Dr. Pierre LaVertu, who specialized in head and neck oncology. The biopsy of the suspect site ordered by Dr. LaVertu on Mr. Klais' neck indicated Stage IV squamous cell carcinoma originating at the base of the tongue (an oropharyngeal tumor). Stage IV of this type of cancer is considered an advanced stage of the disease. This test result was given to Mr. Klais and he was informed that he had a 25 percent chance of living five additional years.

Dr. LaVertu then referred Mr. Klais to Dr. Adelstein of the Cleveland Clinic's Oncology Department. Mr. Klais' first meeting with Dr. Adelstein was on June 4, 1990. During this meeting, Dr. Adelstein explained to the patient and the patient's wife that there was a Phase III clinical trial at the Cleveland

Clinic studying the treatment of squamous cell head and neck cancer using experimental preoperative chemotherapy in addition to the standard treatment of radiation and surgery. Research subjects within the clinical study were to be randomly assigned between two subject groups. The "Arm A" subjects were to receive only radiation therapy and surgery, the customary, standard treatment; no chemotherapy. The "Arm B" subjects were to receive preoperative chemotherapy coupled with radiation and surgery. No matter to which Arm a subject was assigned, that subject was informed as to what treatment protocol they were to receive within the trial. Thus, it was not a blind study and it did not utilize placebos. Dr. Adelstein informed the couple that the patient was an ideal candidate to be included in the clinical study and sought the patient's consent to include him as a research subject. Dr. Adelstein, in addition to informing the patient of procedures, alternative therapies, and the risks and benefits of the clinical trial, informed the patient that he had two options. First, the patient could elect not to participate in the clinical trial and be treated with the standard treatment protocol of radiation and surgery or, second, the patient could elect to join the clinical trial where at least he had a fifty percent chance of receiving chemotherapy. Dr. Adelstein considered the effects of chemotherapy, at that point in time, to be speculative. The patient and his wife also met with Oncology Nurse Marjorie Larto, R.N., Dr. Adelstein's oncology research nurse, who further discussed the clinical trial and exchanged information and answers with the couple. While testifying about the treatment he received, Mr. Klais stated the following in response to questioning:

> Q. °°° Now, Dan, before you began your cancer treatment in 1990 did anyone at The Cleveland Clinic inform you about any studies that had already been done evaluating the effects of radiation and chemotherapy on persons having head and neck squamous cell cancer, like you were diagnosed with?
> . . .

THE WITNESS: No.

BY MR. CUNNINGHAM:

> Q. Now, before you began your cancer treatment in 1990 did anyone at The Cleveland Clinic inform you that prior evaluation studies indicated that your chance of survival were better by being treated with radiation and chemotherapy than just radiation alone? . . .

THE WITNESS: No.

BY MR. CUNNINGHAM:

> Q. Dan, before you began your cancer treatment in 1990 did anyone at The Cleveland Clinic inform you that you had a right to be treated with radiation and chemotherapy?

A. No.

Q. And before you began your treatment for cancer—cancer treatment in 1990 did anyone at The Cleveland Clinic give you the names of all or any hospital and/or cancer center which were at that time treating persons having head and neck squamous cell cancer, like you had, with radiation and chemotherapy? . . .

THE WITNESS: No.

BY MR. CUNNINGHAM:

Q. Before you began, Dan, your cancer treatment in 1990 if any of your attending physicians at The Cleveland Clinic had suggested to you that your personal chances of survival were better with treatment of radiation and chemotherapy rather than radiation alone and if you were then asked which therapy you wanted, radiation and chemotherapy or radiation alone, how would you have responded? . . .

THE WITNESS: The last of the combination of the two, going for a cure.

BY MR. CUNNINGHAM:

Q. Why was that—why would you have wanted both?

A. It was the most opportune, opportunity for a cure. . . .

The patient was given a five-page informed consent form and some other cancer treatment related literature to review at the end of this meeting. In part, this consent form provided that the patient could discontinue participation within the trial "at any time without fears (sic) of penalty or loss of medical care." The patient, who was forty-five years old at the time, executed the consent form and enrolled in the Phase III clinical trial on June 7, 1990.

As a subject in the clinical trial, Mr. Klais was assigned to Arm A; he would receive no chemotherapy. Mr. Klais' participation in the clinical trial occurred during the Summer and Fall of 1990. Over a period of fifty-nine days, Mr. Klais received radiation therapy by Dr. Sexton. Surgery to Mr. Klais's neck also was performed to remove cancerous lymph nodes.

On August 1, 1990, with his radiation treatments having concluded, Mr. Klais was examined by Dr. Adelstein. The examination indicated that the radiation had eradicated the cancer at the primary tumor site and two enlarged lymph nodes. At that examination, Dr. Adelstein discouraged the patient from pursuing chemotherapy. Thereafter, Mr. Klais was examined periodically at the Cleveland Clinic to monitor his condition and to determine if the cancer had returned.

On July 28, 1995, Mr. Klais was considered by his treating physicians to be cured of cancer because his cancer had apparently not returned for a five-year period since its diagnosis.

On January 2, 1996, Mr. Klais, at the request of Dr. Adelstein, met with Dr. Adelstein at the Cleveland Clinic. Dr. Adelstein informed the patient that his

X-ray taken on July 28, 1995, indicated that the cancer had metastasized to the lungs and that the condition was terminal, giving the patient between two to twelve months of life expectancy.

On July 8, 1996, Mr. Klais and his wife, Linda, filed suit against the Cleveland Clinic and Drs. Weinstein, LaVertu, Adelstein and Sexton, concisely alleging in a two-paragraph pleading, medical negligence in misdiagnosing and mistreating Mr. Klais. . . .

Mr. Klais died on March 22, 1997, approximately seven years after the original diagnosis and six-and-one-half years following his radiation/surgery treatments in the clinical trial. The cause of death was the metastasized cancer. . . .

On August 31 and September 2, 1998, the defendants filed motions for summary judgment. The defendants' joint motion for summary judgment was supported by unauthenticated copies of the following: (1) excerpts from the August 16, 1996, plaintiffs' deposition of Mr. Klais; (2) a photocopy of a letter, dated August 25, 1998, from Charles McCarthy, Ph.D. to defense counsel in which the author opines that, based on the limited materials he reviewed, the Phase III clinical trial complied with federal regulations and the informed consent was in compliance with FDA and HHS regulations; . . . and, (8) a copy of 45 C.F.R. 46.116, which details HHS's general requirements for informed consent. . . . The brief in opposition to the joint motion for summary judgment was supported by voluminous documentary evidence, including the following: . . . (4) an expert report prepared by Oncologist Malin Dollinger, M.D., in which the expert opines, at pages 2–4 of that report, that:

> His physicians did not disclose, verbally or as part of the written information and consent form, that a prior phase II study, at the same institution [the Cleveland Clinic], of similar treatment had shown very favorable differences and benefits if chemotherapy were added to radiation therapy (expected three-year event-free survival 70–80% vs 50%). They were ethically required to make such disclosure. Thus, these physicians violated their informed consent obligations to their patient. In addition, they did not discuss with him the option of receiving such combined treatment "off study." It has been stated that such "off study" treatment was not available at the Cleveland Clinic. However substantially similar treatment was available elsewhere, at other cancer treatment centers as well as in private oncology facilities. He was not made aware of such availability. °°° Thus, his physicians were required to function as "patient advocates" and inform him of the treatment options and possibilities that were available to patient, other than the phase III investigational protocol in which we (sic) was eventually enrolled. The affidavit of Jay Katz, M.D., also discusses this issue, and this reviewer agrees with such discussion and opinion. If such combined treatment had been given patient in 1990, it is medically probable that he would be cured or disease-free today.
>
> °°°

Based upon a reasonable medical certainty, it is my opinion that had Daniel V. Klais been treated with chemotherapy plus radiotherapy, he would have lived, disease free for several more years; and further, he would have had a substantial chance of living out his normal life expectancy, disease free, to the approximate year of 2022. [Explanation added.] . . .

. . . [G]iven the competing expert testimony and documentary evidence provided in the record on appeal, we conclude that there exist genuine issues of material fact on whether Mr. Klais gave informed consent to be a participant in the Phase III clinical trial and receive the treatment he was afforded by the Clinic and Drs. LaVertu, Adelstein and Sexton. Accordingly, the trial court erred in granting summary judgment for these four defendants. . . .

NOTES AND QUESTIONS:
Stewart v. Cleveland Clinic Foundation

1. In this case, there is no dispute that the doctors were conducting research. Because of that circumstance, they were subject to a variety of rules that regulate how research on human beings may be conducted. Most of these rules are imposed by the federal government.

   In particular, the references to the "phases" of studies relate to the rules created by the federal Food and Drug Administration for studying a new drug before it can be marketed. A drug has to successfully pass through Phase I, II, and III testing. Phase I studies are primarily designed to determine the side effects associated with increasing doses. 21 C.F.R. § 312.21. Before wasting time studying whether a drug has any good effects, we first want to make sure that it does not produce too many bad effects. Thus, in a Phase I study, a research subject may perhaps be given only a single dose of a drug. The earliest subjects will get very low doses and, if the side effects are not too great, later subjects will be given higher and higher doses. Indeed, the purpose is to keep increasing the dose until some subjects *do* begin to have significant problems caused by the drug. Only from 20 to 80 subjects will participate in the average such study. Determining whether or not the drug works is usually *not* a major purpose of a Phase I study.

   As this description should suggest, participants in a Phase I study are very unlikely to benefit from being in the study. They are far more likely to be *harmed* by their participation. Nonetheless, the possibility of a benefit is probably a motivating factor for many patients, particularly for end-stage cancer patients who have exhausted all other forms of therapy.

2. Phase II studies are where the effectiveness of the drug is first rigorously tested. These are often *controlled* studies, which means that subjects are randomly assigned to get either the drug being studied or some other drug, usually either the drug currently used for their illness or, if there is no such

drug, a placebo (an inactive substance such as a sugar pill). Randomization assures that the researchers do not, consciously or subconsciously, give patients with certain characteristics one treatment and other patients a different treatment. In addition, such studies are often double-blind: neither the researchers nor the subjects know which medication a particular subject is getting. That information is not revealed until after the study is completed. A Phase II study "usually involves no more than several hundred subjects." 21 C.F.R. § 312.21(b).

3. In *Stewart*, the combination of chemotherapy and radiation had indeed been through a Phase II study, which demonstrated it to be superior to radiation alone. To complete testing this mode of treatment, however, a Phase III trial was necessary. As the FDA notes, the results of a Phase II study can provide "preliminary evidence suggesting effectiveness" of a drug but further testing is needed to "gather the additional information about effectiveness and safety that is needed to evaluate the overall benefit-risk relationship of the drug." Phase III studies can include "from several hundred to several thousand subjects." 21 C.F.R. § 312.21(c). Such studies, like Phase II studies, are often randomized and double-blind.

4. A researcher can enroll someone in a research study only after that person has given informed consent. In essence, this is just like the informed consent that is required before a person consents to treatment, but because of the dual interests of the researcher—not just treating the patient, but also gaining research data—consent to enter into a research study is subject to special regulation. In particular, a branch of the federal government, the Office for Human Research Protections (OHRP), imposes detailed rules about how such consent takes place. For most research in the United States, a local committee known as an Institutional Review Board (IRB), often affiliated with the institution where the research takes place, must review the research proposal and the consent form.

Often, the major concern of an IRB is with the adequacy of the consent form and making sure that a subject knows what he is getting into and is familiar with the alternatives (such as standard care). But the IRB also has a blatantly paternalistic mandate. It can approve a study only when "[r]isks to subjects are reasonable in relation to anticipated benefits, if any, to subjects, and the importance of the knowledge that may reasonably be expected to result." 45 C.F.R. § 46.111(a)(2) (1999).

Consider the researchers in Nazi Germany who conducted numerous medical experiments on prisoners of war. One response to those events was the Nuremberg Code, which is a forerunner of the current American rules regulating research. The major ethical problem with the Nazi experiments was that the subjects did not voluntarily consent to the research. On the other hand, imagine that a current researcher chose to repeat some of those experiments but limited participation to consenting volunteers. Thus, to learn how to better treat victims of frostbite, a protocol might immerse healthy volunteers in freezing water for hours at a time. Such a protocol would likely be rejected by the IRB on the ground that the huge risks it imposes on the subjects are not balanced by either benefit to the subjects or sufficiently likely contribution to medical knowledge. The IRB can thus override personal autonomy by preventing subjects from even being offered the option of participating in inappropriate research studies.

5. As the *Stewart* court notes, as part of the informed consent process, Daniel Klais was entitled to know all the information that a person in his situation would want to know in deciding whether to enter the Phase III trial. He was not told about the results of the earlier Phase II trial. Indeed, in the words of another doctor who was an expert witness for his side, "[It was] clear that in 1990 there was a great deal of evidence, some of it conflicting, but most of which showed that combining chemotherapy with radiation produced a definite benefit in terms of long-term survival in patients with head and neck cancer."

6. Klais says that he was "going for a cure," and thus would not have participated in the trial had he known both (a) the earlier Phase II results, and (b) that he could get a doctor to give him the combination of chemotherapy and radiation without participating in a research trial that gave him only a chance of getting that therapy.

   Do you think there are many patients who would have views different from those of Klais? Are many patients likely to enroll in such a research protocol, assuming they are adequately informed? Would subjects who enrolled in this Phase III study, assuming they were properly informed about the prior studies, be merely stupid? Or far more altruistic than the average human being, in that they wouldn't be just "going for a cure"?

7. Was it ethical for the researchers to be doing the Phase III study? Should the local IRB not have approved the study? There was some evidence suggesting that the new combination was better than treatment without chemotherapy. On the other hand, the prior studies were not adequate to meet the strict needs for fully demonstrating the effectiveness and safety of the combination of chemotherapy and radiation.

   The term "clinical equipoise" is often used to describe a legitimate disagreement among clinicians regarding which of two therapies is truly superior. If two therapies are still in clinical equipoise, it is considered perfectly ethical—indeed appropriate—to conduct a clinical trial in which subjects are randomized between the two therapies. Doesn't the very fact that there was insufficient statistical evidence to justify the federal government's validating the use of the new therapy for head and neck cancer (and allowing the drug company to advertise that new use) go a long way toward demonstrating that there was a state of clinical equipoise?[3] There is nothing exceptionally unusual about a Phase III study taking place after results in a Phase II study demonstrate the effectiveness of a particular treatment. Indeed, had there been no demonstration of effectiveness in Phase II, there would not even be a Phase III study. Thus, it is inherent in the system that we have "some" effectiveness information—but not enough to be "certain"—when we conduct a Phase III study. (The case that follows provides an opportunity to further explore clinical equipoise and Phase III studies.)

8. Does the *Stewart* case merely highlight a problem that is inherent in conducting research: that to reach certainty about which of two therapies is best, we must continue to randomize patients even after interim results may suggest one or the other is better? And thus subjects who are adequately informed should be thinking twice about participating in such trials?

Might one solution be to not allow the new therapy to be performed outside of a research protocol? Would a federal law imposing such a requirement be constitutional? (See the notes following *Guess* earlier in this chapter.) If this had been the law, Daniel Klais would have had a choice between (a) getting the old, nonexperimental treatment, and (b) participating in the research study he in fact did participate in, which gave him a 50–50 shot at the new, promising experimental therapy. Given this choice, what do you think Klais (and most other patients) would choose?

For brand-new drugs, the law does impose such a requirement: they are only available in research protocols that are supervised by the FDA. But those regulations do not apply to medical procedures (such as surgery), nor to new uses of previously approved drugs. In the next case, we will see how these questions play out in a related but different situation: determining whether a particular therapy is experimental, and thus whether an insurance company must pay for it.

9. Ultimately, only the subject can decide whether he wishes to expose himself to the extra risks inherent in a study, recognizing that his welfare is no longer the sole motivation of the investigator (often also his doctor). This circumstance creates problems when the subject is not capable of making such a decision (children and incompetent adults) or is subject to constraints that may make it questionable whether consent is freely given (prisoners).

Specific regulations apply to the participation of children and prisoners in research. For children, it is generally required that the parent or guardian give consent and that the child, if old enough to understand, provide "assent" indicating a wish to participate. In addition, most research studies involving children need to demonstrate to the IRB that the study falls into one of three categories: (1) it will not subject the child to greater than minimal risk (e.g., getting a blood sample), (2) it involves more than minimal risk but the risk "is justified by the anticipated benefit to the subject," or (3) it involves greater than minimal risk, but the risk is only a "minor increase" over minimal risk, and the study is "likely" to produce results that are of "vital importance" to understanding the disorder that the child has. 45 C.F.R. § 46.404-406 (1999). As you might imagine, IRBs have great difficulty interpreting these vague rules.

There are no specific regulations dealing with the entry of incompetent adults into a research protocol, although the consent of a person who has appropriate legal authority to make health care decisions for the patient is required. With recent increases in research on demented subjects, there is now a great deal of debate on these issues. Should a surrogate decision-maker be authorized to enroll a subject in a protocol that cannot benefit the subject? Should such protocols be limited to incompetent persons who, while competent, agreed to allow their future enrollment in nonbeneficial protocols? Should rules similar to those used for children instead be applied?[4]

10. Another very controversial area where final regulations have yet to be approved relates to the enrollment of pregnant women in research protocols. As you can surmise, all of the issues that arose in chapter 6 are resurrected here: Should a pregnant woman be permitted to enroll in a research protocol that will not directly benefit her, assuming we do not yet know if the drug might harm a fetus? What are the arguments in favor of and against this? An additional factor is the current federal policy requiring researchers to enroll a diversity of subjects so that no group (e.g., women) is deprived of medical information that may relate to its special biological characteristics. Should the government be *requiring* that investigators enroll pregnant women in most studies? If so, under what conditions would it be appropriate to allow researchers to exclude them?[5]

11. While informed consent is at the core of current research guidelines, there are circumstances in which such consent may be waived. In particular, an IRB can allow a study to be conducted without the informed consent of the participants if it concludes, among other things, that (1) the study involves no more than minimal risk to the subjects, (2) the waiver will not adversely affect the rights of the subjects, and (3) "the research could not practicably be carried out without the waiver or alteration." 45 C.F.R. § 46.116(d) (1999).

A group of investigators want to determine whether or not "intercessory prayer"—praying for someone to get well—works. (They are interested in the effectiveness of the prayer itself, distinct from the benefit subjects may get from knowing they are being prayed for.) They propose to randomly assign all persons admitted to a hospital's cardiac care unit to either a prayer group (individuals in the hospital are given the person's name and told to pray for them) or a non-prayer group. They want to do the study without informing the subjects. In particular, they note that "the very process of obtaining informed consent could conceivably have caused increased anxiety in some patients. For example, had they known about the study, the possibility of being in the non-prayer group might have greatly distressed some patients."[6]

Does this study meet the waiver criteria? Would the results be equally useful even if the subjects were told about the design of the study? How

would you apply the waiver criteria to a similar study in which the researchers were trying to demonstrate that voodoo "curses" have no direct effect
on a person's well-being other than through the person's own reaction to
being cursed, and they argued that telling subjects they might have been
cursed imposed a significant risk of harm to them?

12. Surgery is an area of medical care that has traditionally not been subjected
to the rigorous review criteria applied to drugs. One reason is that if one
were to truly do a randomized, double-blind study of a surgical procedure,
some subjects in the control group would be exposed to the risk of surgery
unnecessarily. For example, to test whether injecting growth hormone into
a person's brain can help control Parkinson's disease, a group of research
subjects would all undergo surgery in which portions of their skulls were removed and catheters were implanted. Then, half of the subjects would have
a saline solution (a placebo) flowing through the catheters, while the other
half would get the growth hormone. The federal government has recently
been requiring such studies in certain circumstances, noting that many current surgical procedures may be "working" solely due to the "placebo response": because persons who have undergone surgery are convinced that
something will happen, their minds may physiologically alter the rest of
their bodies so that they do in fact get better.

Is it ethical to conduct "sham surgery" studies? How should an IRB (or
society in general) determine when the risk imposed on the subject getting
the placebo is too great?[7]

13. Should American rules apply to research conducted by Americans in an undeveloped nation? HIV infection is an enormous problem in many parts of
Asia and Africa. One way to combat that problem is to give pregnant
women certain drugs, such as AZT, that dramatically reduce the likelihood
of their passing the infection on to their children. Unfortunately, given the
paltry health care budgets of such nations, the costs of such drugs are
prohibitive.

One possible solution is to find a much cheaper way of preventing
transmission of HIV from a woman to her fetus. For example, instead of
treating the woman for several weeks with AZT, it might be possible to treat
her with a single, small dose. Assume that you are a health care official in an
undeveloped nation, and are considering such a course of action. You
would want to know if this low-dose AZT was actually effective in reducing
HIV transmission, so you might propose a research study in which women
were randomized between getting a placebo or getting the low-dose AZT.
The results would tell you how effective the low-dose AZT was.

Such studies, sponsored by the U.S. National Institutes of Health and
the Centers for Disease Control and Prevention, were in fact carried out in
a number of developing countries, with the encouragement of public
health officials of those countries. They were, however, highly criticized in
this country because such a study would not be ethical if conducted in the

U.S. Given that there is an effective method of preventing transmission of HIV to a fetus—the long course AZT treatment—any American research study would need to give a subject either that treatment, or one that theoretically might be as good as it (in clinical equipoise with it). Thus, it would be perfectly acceptable in this country to randomize subjects between long-course and low-dose AZT, assuming that there was good evidence to suggest that the low-dose treatment might work as well as the longer treatment. On the other hand, because a placebo does not work as well as the long course treatment, a patient could not be randomized to a placebo in an American study. In effect, you would be sitting by and watching that person remain untreated, which would be unethical.

Advocates of the studies involving placebos noted that a study that randomized patients between the long course treatment and the low-dose treatment is likely to not be very useful. It might demonstrate the two treatments are equally effective, but it also might show that the low-dose treatment is not as good. If that did indeed happen, the researchers would still not know what they wanted to know: how does the low-dose treatment compare to no treatment (i.e., placebo), which effectively is the existing standard of care in the developing countries, since patients could in general not afford any care.

What do you think? Should trials with a placebo be permitted in developing countries?[8]

14. A great deal of information about the regulation of research on human subjects is available on the web. A good starting point is OHRP's site (*ohrp.osophs.dhhs.gov*), which contains all applicable laws and regulations and includes an on-line version of the *IRB Guidebook*.

ADAMS V. BLUE CROSS/BLUE SHIELD OF MARYLAND, INC.

United States District Court for the District of Maryland

757 F. Supp. 661 (D. Md. 1991)

OPINION BY JUDGE GARBIS:

In 1990, Plaintiffs Alexandra Adams and Kelly Whittington were diagnosed as having advanced breast cancer, a potentially fatal disease. Both women were advised by their treating physicians that High Dose Chemotherapy with Autologous Bone Marrow Transplant (hereinafter "HDCT-ABMT") would be the best available care for them. Because the treatment is very expensive, costing approximately $100,000.00, Plaintiffs requested their insurance carrier Blue Cross-Blue Shield of Maryland (hereinafter "Blue Cross") to confirm in advance that it would pay for the treatment. However, Blue Cross denied coverage for both, relying upon a policy provision which excluded coverage for "experimental and investigative" treatments. While acknowledging that the policy would cover the use of HDCT-ABMT for several other diseases, Blue Cross took the position that the treatment was "experimental" when used to treat breast cancer, and that Plaintiffs were not eligible for coverage. This Court is asked to decide whether under the benefit plan Blue Cross must pay for Plaintiffs' treatment. . . .

The Treatment at Issue

Breast cancer is frequently treated with chemotherapy drugs which are designed to kill cancer cells. Administered in low doses, chemotherapy can be given to patients on an outpatient basis and is usually administered in several cycles of continuing treatment. However, the effectiveness of low-dose chemotherapy for more advanced forms of breast cancer is limited because the dosage frequently is not toxic enough to kill the more aggressive cancer cells.

Currently, doctors use a variety of dosages and drug mixtures, or "cocktails," in administering low-dose therapy (sometimes called "conventional chemotherapy"). To date, no standard dosages or preparative regimens exist for low-dose chemotherapy. Indeed, ongoing research continues to evaluate the effectiveness of different dosages and preparative regimens.

[HDCT-ABMT] is a procedure in which physicians administer relatively high doses of chemotherapy drugs in conjunction with a bone marrow "transplant." In addition to destroying cancer cells, high doses of chemotherapy also destroy the patient's bone marrow and blood cells, both of which play an essential role in immunity to disease and infection. Stripped of her bone marrow and certain blood cells, the patient is open to opportunistic infection and disease following treatment with high-dose chemotherapy. To counteract this potentially lethal side effect, a portion of the patient's bone marrow is harvested from the patient prior to her treatment with toxic chemotherapy drugs. After chemotherapy treatment is completed, the healthy marrow is then reinfused to "rescue" the patient. The marrow quickly multiplies to replace the marrow destroyed during high-dose chemotherapy. . . .

Plan Term Definitions

The pertinent contract plainly sets forth the definition for "experimental and investigative"—an experimental procedure is a procedure "not generally acknowledged as accepted medical practice by the suitable practicing medical specialty in Maryland." . . .

The parties debate the meaning of the term "accepted medical practice." Blue Cross argues that "accepted medical practice" is a "standard practice" which has (1) proven itself through a rigorous process of clinical testing and amassing of scientific evidence, (2) has known risks and benefits, and (3) is a practice not in the process of being tested to gather generalizable knowledge. . . .

This Court interprets the term "accepted medical practice" consistently with the focus of the contractual language on the Maryland medical community standards. . . .

. . . Thus, the question before the Court becomes whether, at the relevant times, a consensus of Maryland oncologists considered HDCT-ABMT to be an appropriate treatment option offered by the ordinary prudent and reasonable medical oncologist exercising due care for his or her patient. As previously noted, this definition requires the Court to look to expert testimony regarding the judgment and customary practices of oncologists practicing in Maryland. . . .

Coverage Was Incorrectly Denied

Having defined the pertinent contract terms and determined the appropriate standard for judicial review, the Court must now determine de novo whether Blue Cross' denial of coverage for Plaintiffs' treatment with HDCT-ABMT was correct under the contract language. In this regard, Blue Cross' decision to deny benefits to Mrs. Adams and Mrs. Whittington is incorrect if the Court finds that the treatment for those particular patients was, as of April or July of 1990, "generally acknowledged as accepted medical practice by the suitable medical specialty practicing in Maryland."

Blue Cross acknowledges from the outset and throughout trial that Dr. Keefe did not consult, or consulted minimally, Maryland medical oncologists in arriving at his decision to deny coverage for Plaintiffs' claims. At trial, Dr. Arthur Keefe testified that as corporate Medical Director in charge of medical policy, he alone was responsible for the decision to deny coverage to Mrs. Adams and Mrs. Whittington. Dr. Keefe testified that in deciding to deny coverage, he relied heavily on a 1988 technical evaluation prepared by the Technical Evaluation Committee (TEC) in association with the National Blue Cross-Blue Shield Association. . . . Rather than relying on local expert medical opinion, Dr. Keefe relied on Blue Cross' evaluation of scientific data, as well as his own independent review.

Despite the fact that Dr. Keefe did not consult Maryland medical oncologists, Blue Cross nevertheless maintains that Dr. Keefe in fact made the correct decision. In particular, Blue Cross seems to argue that the Blue Cross TEC evaluation reflected a national consensus, which coincided with the consensus in Maryland, that HDCT-ABMT was not yet accepted medical practice. At trial, Blue Cross presented five experts in support of its contention that HDCT-ABMT was, as of April and July of 1990, still experimental and investigational.

Blue Cross relied most heavily on Dr. David Eddy, a biostatistician hired by Blue Cross to prepare the 1990 National Association Report, which he did after reviewing the newest scientific literature on the subject. At trial, Dr. Eddy defined an "experimental" technique as a technique about which there exists a number of unanswered fundamental questions, including questions about benefits and about potential harm from the treatment. Dr. Eddy gave his opinion that based on his review of the data, HDCT-ABMT was still experimental because a number of questions remained unanswered with regard to potential benefits, in particular overall survival rates, as well as potential harm, namely, toxicity rates. In his testimony regarding the nature of the Blue Cross decision to classify the treatment as experimental, Dr. Eddy testified, as did Dr. Keefe, that Blue Cross considered it improper to rely on practitioner opinions to determine whether a procedure was experimental; instead, independent Blue Cross analysis of the scientific data was necessary. As a result, most of Dr. Eddy's testimony focused on a review of the published scientific research results.

Like several other Blue Cross experts, Dr. Eddy also found it highly significant that Phase III randomized clinical trials had not yet been completed for HDCT-ABMT, but were in the process of being conducted. Dr. Eddy acknowledged that Phase III studies were not necessary in all cases, and pointed to the use of HDCT-ABMT for non-Hodgkins lymphoma as an example of a "home-run" treatment, i.e., a treatment which had produced such dramatic results in Phase II studies that Phase III results were not required in order to classify the treatment as "accepted medical practice." However, Dr. Eddy testified that Phase I and II studies for HDCT-ABMT in the treatment of breast cancer had not achieved such "home-run" results. In particular, Dr. Eddy noted several times that significant long-term survival rates in breast cancer patients treated with HDCT-ABMT had not yet been demonstrated, at least not in studies which he considered to be reliable. Dr. Eddy found fault with studies which used historical controls, in part because he believed the historical controls to be poorly matched with experimental subjects.

Finally, Dr. Eddy testified that no consensus existed in the medical community with regard to the use of HDCT-ABMT in the treatment of breast cancer. In support of his opinion, Dr. Eddy pointed to the scientific literature in which authors had concluded their articles with a statement that more research was needed to confirm their results. Dr. Eddy also noted that when administering the procedure, physicians told patients that their treatment was part of a research project, as is required by informed consent law. . . .

Most if not all of the Blue Cross experts testified only peripherally about the opinion of members of the Maryland oncological community. . . .

The Court does not accept the opinions of the Blue Cross experts because they based their opinion on a definition of the term "accepted medical practice" which is inconsistent with the contract language. Instead of focusing testimony on the opinion of members of the Maryland oncological community, the Blue Cross experts concentrated on their own independent evaluations of the scientific data. Indeed, Blue Cross' primary expert, Dr. Eddy, is not a practicing physician but is an expert in biostatistics. However, scientific data only provides statistical results from research. After reviewing the relevant scientific data, the practicing medical community must make an overall value judgment about whether a treatment is accepted, that is, has a sufficiently acceptable risk-benefit ratio to justify offering, or indeed recommending, the treatment as an option. According to the contract, Blue Cross must defer to that practical medical judgment if a consensus among Maryland oncologists agrees that the treatment is accepted medical practice. Thus, the Court accords little weight to the opinion of the Blue Cross experts.

In contrast to the Blue Cross experts, Plaintiffs' expert witnesses utilized a practical definition of what constitutes "accepted medical treatment," one which is both consistent with the standard legal definition discussed earlier and, most importantly, consistent with the contract language. Appropriately, Plaintiffs' experts focused on whether a majority of Maryland oncologists viewed the treatment as accepted medical practice, or were in fact referring their patients for the procedure. Based on Plaintiffs' experts' testimony, this Court finds that a consensus existed as of April and July of 1990 among Maryland oncologists that HDCT-ABMT for breast cancer was an "accepted medical practice." . . .

Scientific Criteria

Although it is not necessary to support the preceding conclusion, the Court determines that even if it were to accept the Blue Cross definition of the term "accepted medical practice," which turns on scientific criteria, HDCT-ABMT would satisfy Blue Cross' purely scientific criteria. . . .

[W]ith regard to the Blue Cross experts' concern about long-term survival rates, this Court is persuaded by Plaintiffs' experts' testimony that at the time Blue Cross decided to deny benefits to Plaintiffs, HDCT-ABMT had already demonstrated dramatic increases in complete and overall response rates, that is, the rate of tumor shrinkage, as well as significant improvement in disease-free survival.

In supporting Mrs. Adams' plea for Blue Cross payment, Dr. Peters submitted a package of material in April of 1990 for Dr. Keefe to review, which included graphs of results from the Duke clinical trials illustrating survival rates for women with Stage IV and Stage II/III breast cancer, which are, respectively, the prognoses for Mrs. Whittington and Mrs. Adams. The data illustrated that for women with Stage IV metastatic breast cancer who are treated early in the disease with induction therapy (standard low-dose therapy) followed by high-dose therapy with bone marrow support, studies had demonstrated that 70% had achieved total remission as compared to a 15% to 20% "complete response" rate under standard low-dose therapy alone. Of those women treated with prior chemotherapy and high-dose therapy with bone marrow support, 25% remained disease free at a 3 and 1/2 year follow-up, versus a 20% rate for standard therapy. Dr. Peters testified that his conclusions were supported by data from the Dana Farber Cancer Institute at Harvard, and the M.D. Anderson Institute in Houston.

While overall survival rates may be similar between low-dose therapy and HDCT-ABMT for Stage IV patients, the Court nevertheless notes a significant benefit in disease-free survival to be gained from using HDCT-ABMT. That is, even if a substantial number of those women were to die tomorrow and the overall survival rate were to drop to the level of low-dose therapy, at any one point in time more women will have lived longer free of disease than if they had been treated with low-dose therapy. The Court considers it highly unreasonable for Blue Cross to ignore the benefits of disease-free survival in favor of concentrating only on long-term survival rates.

For women with Stage II/III primary breast cancer involving 10 or more lymph nodes, the data published by Duke, made available to Blue Cross in Dr. Peters' package, was even more promising. . . .

Beyond dramatically increased complete response rates and increased disease-free survival rates, the Court notes that women undergoing HDCT-ABMT spend far less time "on therapy," that is, receiving the treatment, than do their counterparts on low-dose therapy. Dr. Karen Antman, an expert in oncology at the Dana Farber Institute affiliated with Harvard University Medical Center, testified that a woman with Stage IV disease may receive low-dose treatments every 3 to 4 weeks until she dies, compared to the single treatment administered for HDCT-ABMT. Dr. Peters also testified that "off therapy" time translates into less time in which the patient experiences the toxic side effects associated with chemotherapy, such as nausea and hair loss, and a corresponding better quality of life for the patient. The Court is persuaded by expert testimony that the increase in off-therapy time, when coupled with the dramatic increase in complete response and disease-free survival rates, may serve to offset whatever increase in toxicity may result from using HDCT-ABMT.

In addition to the statistics outlined above, Dr. Peters and Dr. Antman testified that Dr. Eddy's review of the scientific literature was seriously flawed. . . .

With respect to the Blue Cross expert witnesses' concern over the incomplete Phase III studies, the Court finds such concern to be of no moment. Both sides agree that completed Phase III research is not always necessary in order to judge a treatment to be accepted medical practice. In particular, for some treatments, earlier Phase I and Phase II studies may have produced such dramatic positive results, the so-called "home-run" results, that Phase III studies are not required. For example, both Blue Cross and Plaintiffs agree that HDCT-ABMT as a treatment for lymphoma was just such an instance. The parties disagree on whether the research on HDCT-ABMT as used to treat breast cancer produced "home-run" results.

However, Dr. Antman testified for Plaintiffs, and the Court was convinced, that the data produced in Phase I and II research studying the use of HDCT-ABMT to treat breast cancer is as dramatic and convincing as was the data for lymphomas. Specifically, data on toxicity rates, complete response rates, and most importantly, rates for two-year disease-free survival, are strikingly similar for HDCT-ABMT as treatment for breast cancer and as treatment for lymphomas.

Of additional significant import is the testimony from Dr. Peters and Dr. Antman that conducting a Phase III random clinical trial would be ethically acceptable, as evaluated by institutional review boards, only if the treatment was potentially as good as, if not better than, low-dose therapy. Investigators could not ethically conduct randomized clinical trials if HDCT-ABMT was known with any certainty to be less effective than low-dose chemotherapy. Contrary to Dr. Eddy's assertions, then, the fact that Phase III studies are being conducted to determine if HDCT-ABMT is better than low-dose therapy indicates that the treatment is anticipated by an institutional review board to be at least as good as low-dose therapy, as evidenced by the results from Phase I and Phase II studies. The Court heard testimony from Dr. Peters that, contrary to the Blue Cross argument, the very fact that Phase III trials are being conducted indicates a general consensus that the treatment appears potentially to be as effective as low-dose chemotherapy, may be better, and in any event, is probably an acceptable treatment option. In fact, Dr. Peters testified that to make Phase III studies ethically acceptable, researchers have had to offer HDCT-ABMT to those patients who relapse on low-dose therapy, precisely because data demonstrates HDCT-ABMT's superiority. . . .

The Court recognizes that questions remain with respect to overall survival, but notes that research need not prove a treatment completely curative in order for it to have sufficient merit to be judged an "accepted medical practice." . . .

Furthermore, many of today's accepted medical treatments are offered under a research protocol. Given the definition of "experimental" under the plan, the fact that the treatment is administered as part of an experimental protocol designed to facilitate the collection of data does not necessarily mean that the treatment is by definition experimental.

Thus, even if one accepts the Blue Cross definition of "accepted medical practice" as dependent upon scientific criteria, the Court finds that Blue Cross's determination that HDCT-ABMT was experimental and investigative runs counter to the evidence presented at trial in this case. Questions with regard to the net health benefits of the procedure, in particular, response rates and disease-free survival, have been sufficiently answered so as to allow Maryland oncologists to choose HDCT-ABMT as an appropriate treatment alternative, and to justify the conclusion that the treatment is an accepted medical practice. The Court finds it necessary to defer, as Blue Cross should have done under the terms of its own plan, to the opinion of the consensus of Maryland oncologists. . . .

NOTES AND QUESTIONS:
Adams v. Blue Cross/Blue Shield of Maryland, Inc.

1. The *Adams* case is one of many in which insurers tried to avoid paying for high-dose chemotherapy with autologous bone marrow transplantation as a last-resort therapy for a woman with breast cancer. The results of these cases

were mixed, but in most of them (particularly the earlier ones), as in *Adams*, the insurer was ultimately required to pay. Indeed, often judges went to great lengths to find insurers liable even in the face of very explicit language in a policy that appeared to exclude coverage for such therapy.

A good example of that is *Bailey v. Blue Cross & Blue Shield of Virginia*, 67 F.3d 53 (4th Cir. 1995), where the insurance contract specifically denied coverage for "autologous bone marrow transplants or other forms of stem cell rescue (with high dose chemotherapy and/or radiation)" when used to treat breast cancer. The court nonetheless determined that since the policy covered chemotherapy in general, the insurer had to pay for the high dose chemotherapy portion of the treatment. In effect, it concluded that the exclusionary language only applied to the "rescue" portion of the therapy, and not to the initial chemotherapy that, without the "rescue," would itself have been lethal to the patient.

Other courts, more explicitly prevented by the law from finding a way to order payment for the therapy, decried their own impotence: "Although moved by the tragic circumstances of this case and the seemingly needless loss of life that resulted, we conclude the law gives us no choice but to [affirm the insurer's right to refuse to pay]." *Cannon v. Group Health Service of Oklahoma, Inc.*, 77 F.3d 1270 (10th Cir. 1996).

2. The court notes testimony from doctors that "a Phase III random clinical trial would be ethically acceptable, as evaluated by institutional review boards, only if the treatment was potentially as good as, if not better than," the existing therapy. This is, in essence, the clinical equipoise requirement discussed in the notes following *Stewart*. The *Adams* court states that the existence of the Phase III clinical trials supports the conclusion that the use of the high-dose chemotherapy to treat breast cancer is no longer experimental. Does that make sense? Any therapy, to be proven effective, must go through a Phase III clinical trial, and the results of that trial must *demonstrate* that efficacy. As the opinion notes, the fact that the new treatment is in a Phase III trial means only that there is "potential" efficacy. Is it not odd to use the fact that a therapy is still in a required part of the process of proving efficacy to demonstrate that a therapy is *no longer* experimental?

3. Here is part of an opinion that found that the treatment *was* experimental, *Glauser-Nagy v. Medical Mutual of Ohio*, 987 F. Supp. 1002 (N.D. Ohio 1997):

> On the undisputed facts before the Court, [HDCT-ABMT] meets both of the above criteria for "experimental/investigational" as applied to individuals with nonmetastatic breast cancer. The witnesses for both sides agreed, and all of the journal articles submitted by both sides indicate, that [HDCT-ABMT] is presently the subject of ongoing phase III clinical trials to determine its efficacy and safety as compared with standard-dose chemotherapy for patients with Stage II and III breast cancer. Every expert witness, every oncologist to review plaintiff's file, and every journal article submitted by either side concluded that

while [HDCT-ABMT] shows promise as a treatment for adjuvant Stage II and III breast cancer, completed phase III studies are needed before it will be possible to conclude with certainty that high dose chemotherapy is superior to standard chemotherapy for patients in plaintiff's clinical category.

4. Note that the legal issue in all of these cases is merely a contract issue of interpreting the insurance policy, a contract between the company and the insured. There were no laws requiring that insurers cover these therapies. Indeed, insurance contracts often have extensive lists of types of therapy that are excluded. In the HDCT-ABMT cases, however, the insurers were often relying on somewhat vague language excluding "experimental therapies."

5. Was it wrong of the insurance companies to try to avoid paying for these allegedly experimental treatments, requiring that their efficacy be proven in the "gold standard" randomized clinical trial? Note that Blue Cross/Blue Shield associations that were the target of many of the lawsuits are not-for-profit entities, so there were no shareholders pushing for profits. Would you want your insurance company to write a policy that allowed it to pay for *any* treatment, no matter how experimental? What would this mean for your policy costs in future years? Might your answer to this question depend on whether you are the average policyholder, or the person asking for the treatment?

   It is not uncommon for state laws to require that health insurance contracts cover certain costs. For example, they might require coverage of chiropractic services, or in vitro fertilization costs for infertile women. Are such laws a good thing? What are the arguments for and against them? How would you determine whether a particular medical service should be included in such a law?

6. As a result of the numerous lawsuits, many of which they lost, and the bad publicity from denying this therapy to women dying of breast cancer, most insurers agreed to pay for HDCT-ABMT as a treatment for breast cancer. Indeed, providing this therapy has become a big business. Here is how a front-page article in the *New York Times* describes it:[9]

> For-profit corporations offering bone marrow transplants emerged by the late 1980's. Response Oncology, one of the first, started offering the procedure in 1989 as part of what it called a "clinical trials program."
>
> That program involved only trials that gave everybody the procedure and watched how they fared. These studies cannot be used to demonstrate whether the procedure is any better than the standard treatment, because there is no comparison group of similar patients. . . .
>
> But the trials did help Response Oncology earn profits. . . .
>
> [And] the academic medical centers—even those trying to recruit patients for clinical trials—did not stand aside and let all the profits go elsewhere. . . .
>
> At academic medical centers, bone marrow transplant programs quickly became "the cash cow for the cancer service" . . . .

7. Results from a number of Phase III studies of HDCT-ABMT, in which patients had been randomly assigned to either get the therapy or not get it, finally were released in 1998. The *Washington Post* reported:[10]

> Since the early 1990's bone marrow transplants have been regarded as the best of treatments and the worst of treatments for aggressive or advanced breast cancer. Thousands of desperate women, clinging to a glimmer of hope that the procedure might cure them—or buy them significantly more time—have been willing to risk their lives and mortgage their families' futures to undergo one of the most harrowing, dangerous and expensive procedures in modern medicine.
>
> Now it seems that for most of these women, the life-threatening treatment may not have made much difference. . . .
>
> Four of the five studies involving a total of 2,000 women found that for those newly diagnosed with aggressive cancers or for those whose cancers have recurred and spread far outside the breast, transplants appear to be no better than conventional chemotherapy in prolonging life.

8. Imagine that you are a woman dying of advanced breast cancer, and you are offered a choice like that in *Stewart*:

   a. Participation in a randomized trial in which you have a 50 percent chance of getting HDCT-ABMT, and a 50 percent chance of getting the standard chemotherapy (which has already been shown to be of minimal benefit in patients with very advanced disease).

   b. A 100 percent guarantee of getting HDCT-ABMT, paid for by your insurance company.

   Do you think many women would have chosen option (a)? In fact, it was extremely hard to recruit subjects for the Phase III randomized clinical trials. Here is a further excerpt from the *New York Times* article:

> For years, Dr. Larry Norton tried to conduct a medical study to determine, once and for all, whether bone marrow transplants could really save the lives of women desperately ill with breast cancer.
>
> His effort—and those of dozens of other doctors—were largely futile. Year after year, few women were willing to participate in the clinical tests, which, to be scientifically valid, required patients to be randomly assigned to either the experimental treatment or standard chemotherapy.

9. Had the insurance companies been more successful in court in categorizing HDCT-ABMT as an experimental therapy, might more women have opted for choice (a) because they would have been unable to afford the approximately $100,000 cost of option (b)? Would it be wrong to have used such economic incentives to help recruit subjects for the clinical trials? What about the alternative suggested in the notes after *Stewart*: enact a law preventing health care providers from providing experimental treatments such as HDCT-ABMT other than in a randomized clinical trial?

   As the *Stewart* case demonstrates, there is nothing unique about the HDCT-ABMT situation. In a world of sophisticated medical consumers, the tension between patients pursuing their own self-interest and the need for subjects in randomized clinical trials will no doubt worsen over time.

10. An appropriate closing comment to this discussion about courts and science is provided by the remarks of Marsha Pechman a day after being appointed to be a federal judge:[11]

> King County Superior Court Judge Marsha Pechman knows how to weigh evidence.
>
> Recently, some medical experts have claimed that new scientific findings provide evidence that stem-cell transplantation as a treatment for advanced breast cancer is no better than standard chemotherapy.
>
> Pechman, along with her Seattle physicians, disagrees. "You can do all the studies you want," she said. "I don't have any doubt the procedure saved my life."

Endnotes

1. "Under the Knife," *Dateline NBC*, November 8, 1999.
2. For more on these issues, see, e.g., Margaret Gilhooley, "Herbal Remedies and Dietary Supplements: The Boundaries of Drug Claims and Freedom of Choice," 49 *Fla. L. Rev.* 669 (1997); Steven R. Salbu, "The FDA and Public Access to New Drugs: Appropriate Levels of Scrutiny in the Wake of HIV, AIDS, and the Diet Drug Debacle," 79 *B.U. L. Rev.* 93 (1999). For more on how the legal system deals with alternative forms of health care, see, e.g., Kathleen M. Boozang, "Western Medicine Opens the Door to Alternative Medicine," 24 Am. *J. L. & Med.* 185 (1998); Lori B. Andrews, "The Shadow Health Care System: Regulation of Alternative Health Care Providers," 32 *Hous. L. Rev.* 1273 (1996); Michael H. Cohen, "Holistic Health Care: Including Alternative and Complementary Medicine in Insurance and Regulatory Schemes," 38 *Ariz. L. Rev.* 83 (1996).
3. See, e.g., Benjamin Freedman, "A Response to a Purported Ethical Difficulty with Randomized Clinical Trials Involving Cancer Patients," 3 *J. Clin. Ethics* 231 (1992).
4. For one set of detailed recommendations, and an introduction to the literature, see the 1998 report by the National Bioethics Advisory Commission, *Research Involving Persons with Mental Disorders that May Affect Decisionmaking Capacity* (available on the web at *bioethics.gov*).
5. For guidance on how existing antidiscrimination laws might apply to these problems, see *International Union, UAW v. Johnson Controls*, 499 U.S. 187 (1991) (private employers cannot exclude fertile women from jobs that might impose risks to the health of a fetus).
6. William S. Harris et al., "A Randomized, Controlled Trial of the Effects of Remote, Intercessory Prayer on Outcomes in Patients Admitted to the Coronary Care Unit," 159 *Arch. Int. Med.* 2273 (1999).
7. See, e.g., L. Johannes, "Sham Surgery Is Used to Test Effectiveness of Novel Operations," *Wall Street Journal*, 11 December 1998 at A1; Thomas B. Freeman et al., "Use of Placebo Surgery in Controlled Trials of a Cellular-Based Therapy for Parkinson's Disease," 341 *New Eng. J. Med.* 988 (1999); Ruth Macklin, "The Ethical Problems with Sham Surgery in Clinical Research," 341 *New Eng. J. Med.* 992 (1999).

8. See, e.g., Peter Lurie and Sidney M. Wolfe, "Unethical Trials of Interventions to Reduce Perinatal Transmission of the Human Immunodeficiency Virus in Developing Countries," 337 *New Eng. J. Med.* 853 (1997); Harold Varmus and David Satcher, "Ethical Complexities of Conducting Research in Developing Countries," 337 *New Eng. J. Med.* 1003 (1997); Marcia Angell, "Investigators' Responsibilities for Human Subjects in Developing Countries," 342 *New Eng. J. Med.* 907 (2000).

9. Gina Kolata and Kurt Eichenwald, "Hope for Sale: Business Thrives on Unproven Care," *New York Times*, 3 October 1999.

10. Sandra G. Boodman, "Breast Cancer Roulette," *Washington Post*, 27 April 1999, Z12.

11. Tom Paulson, "Stem Cells 'Saved My Life,' Says Judge," *Seattle Post-Intelligencer*, 9 September 1999, G4.

End-of-Life Decisions

10

The Right to Refuse Care

In previous chapters, we saw how tort law—in particular, the right to be free from battery and the right to informed consent—created at least the beginning of the notion that a patient has the right to choose among medical care alternatives. But creating a right and determining when that right can effectively be exercised are two different things. It is the latter problem to which we now turn.

As we saw in the abortion and maternal-fetal conflict cases, a person wishing to exercise a right may find that the interests of others—in those cases, the interest in preserving fetal life—may trump that right. A major new theme in the cases that follow relates to determining what interests might conflict with a person's interest in refusing care. Often it is the "state"—representing society at large—that advances such interests. The government's position may sometimes strike you as somewhat alien to your view of modern American society. It may indeed remind you of Orwell's *1984*, where the individual is relatively unimportant, except to the extent that he or she can contribute to society.

This view of the world—that the patient's interests are secondary to those of society—rarely wins out in the cases. Nonetheless, it is important to recognize it when it comes up, and to contrast it with the very different situations where the government is "merely" claiming that its concern is the patient's own interests. Moreover, as you will see in the next chapter, it may well be that considerations relating to what is best for society do play a substantial role in determining the extent of our constitutional rights.

The *Quinlan* case is a landmark. If nothing else, the publicity it generated brought the issue of terminating life-sustaining care to the attention of the general public. It is somewhat surprising to realize that this case took place barely 25 years ago. Consider how many parties were lined up to oppose the attempt of Karen Ann Quinlan's family to withdraw care and allow her to die: her doctors, the hospital, the local prosecutor, the State of New Jersey, and even the court-appointed guardian who was supposed to represent her best interests. Given that David-Goliath aspect of the dispute, it is not surprising that the court's decision in favor of the family was considered of major consequence.

In re Quinlan

Supreme Court of New Jersey
355 A.2d 647 (N.J. 1976)

OPINION BY CHIEF JUSTICE HUGHES:

The Litigation

The central figure in this tragic case is Karen Ann Quinlan, a New Jersey resident. At the age of 22, she lies in a debilitated and allegedly moribund state at Saint Clare's Hospital in Denville, New Jersey. The litigation has to do, in final analysis, with her life—its continuance or cessation—and the responsibilities, rights and duties, with regard to any fateful decision concerning it, of her family, her guardian, her doctors, the hospital, the State through its law enforcement authorities, and finally the courts of justice. . . .

Essentially then, appealing to the power of equity, and relying on claimed constitutional rights of free exercise of religion, of privacy and of protection against cruel and unusual punishment, Karen Quinlan's father sought judicial authority to withdraw the life-sustaining mechanisms temporarily preserving his daughter's life, and his appointment as guardian of her person to that end. His request was opposed by her doctors, the hospital, the Morris County Prosecutor, the State of New Jersey, and her guardian *ad litem*.

The Factual Base

An understanding of the issues in their basic perspective suggests a brief review of the factual base developed in the testimony and documented in greater detail in the opinion of the trial judge.

On the night of April 15, 1975, for reasons still unclear, Karen Quinlan ceased breathing for at least two 15 minute periods. She received some ineffectual mouth-to-mouth resuscitation from friends. She was taken by ambulance to Newton Memorial Hospital. There she had a temperature of 100 degrees, her pupils were unreactive and she was unresponsive even to deep pain. The history at the time of her admission to that hospital was essentially incomplete and uninformative.

Three days later, Dr. Morse examined Karen at the request of the Newton admitting physician, Dr. McGee. He found her comatose with evidence of decortication, a condition relating to derangement of the cortex of the brain causing a physical posture in which the upper extremities are flexed and the lower extremities are extended. She required a respirator to assist her breathing. . . . Dr. Morse testified that Karen has been in a state of coma, lack of consciousness, since he began treating her. He explained that there are basically two types of coma, sleep-like unresponsiveness and awake unresponsiveness. Karen was originally in a sleep-like unresponsive condition but soon developed "sleep-wake" cycles, apparently a normal improvement for comatose patients occurring within three to four weeks. In the awake cycle she blinks, cries out and does things of that sort but is still totally unaware of anyone or anything around her.

Dr. Morse and other expert physicians who examined her characterized Karen as being in a "chronic persistent vegetative state." Dr. Fred Plum, one of such expert witnesses, defined this as a "subject who remains with the capacity to maintain the vegetative parts of neurological function but who ° ° ° no longer has any cognitive function."

Dr. Morse, as well as the several other medical and neurological experts who testified in this case, believed with certainty that Karen Quinlan is not "brain dead." They identified the Ad Hoc Committee of Harvard Medical School report as the ordinary medical standard for determining brain death, and all of them were satisfied that Karen met none of the criteria specified in that report and was therefore not "brain dead" within its contemplation.

In this respect it was indicated by Dr. Plum that the brain works in essentially two ways, the vegetative and the sapient. He testified:

> We have an internal vegetative regulation which controls body temperature, which controls breathing, which controls to a considerable degree blood pressure, which controls to some degree heart rate, which controls chewing, swallowing and which controls sleeping and waking. We have a more highly developed brain which is uniquely human which controls our relation to the outside world, our capacity to talk, to see, to feel, to sing, to think. Brain death necessarily must mean the death of both of these functions of the brain, vegetative and the sapient. Therefore, the presence of any function which is regulated or governed or controlled by the deeper parts of the brain which in laymen's terms might be considered purely vegetative would mean that the brain is not biologically dead.

Because Karen's neurological condition affects her respiratory ability (the respiratory system being a brain stem function) she requires a respirator to assist her breathing. From the time of her admission to Saint Clare's Hospital Karen has been assisted by an MA-1 respirator, a sophisticated machine which delivers a given volume of air at a certain rate and periodically provides a "sigh" volume, a relatively large measured volume of air designed to purge the lungs of excretions. Attempts to "wean" her from the respirator were unsuccessful and have been abandoned.

The experts believe that Karen cannot now survive without the assistance of the respirator; that exactly how long she would live without it is unknown; that the strong likelihood is that death would follow soon after its removal, and that removal would also risk further brain damage and would curtail the assistance the respirator presently provides in warding off infection.

It seemed to be the consensus not only of the treating physicians but also of the several qualified experts who testified in the case, that removal from the respirator would not conform to medical practices, standards and traditions.

The further medical consensus was that Karen in addition to being comatose is in a chronic and persistent "vegetative" state, having no awareness of anything or anyone around her and existing at a primitive reflex level. Although she does have some brain stem function (ineffective for respiration) and has other reactions one normally associates with being alive, such as moving, reacting to light, sound and noxious stimuli, blinking her eyes, and the like, the quality of her feeling impulses is unknown. She grimaces, makes stereotyped cries and sounds and has chewing motions. Her blood pressure is normal.

Karen remains in the intensive care unit at Saint Clare's Hospital, receiving 24-hour care by a team of four nurses characterized, as was the medical attention, as "excellent." She is nourished by feeding by way of a nasal-gastro tube and is routinely examined for infection, which under these circumstances is a serious life threat. The result is that her condition is considered remarkable under the unhappy circumstances involved.

Karen is described as emaciated, having suffered a weight loss of at least 40 pounds, and undergoing a continuing deteriorative process. Her posture is described as fetal-like and grotesque; there is extreme flexion-rigidity of the arms, legs and related muscles and her joints are severely rigid and deformed.

From all of this evidence, and including the whole testimonial record, several basic findings in the physical area are mandated. Severe brain and associated damage, albeit of uncertain etiology, has left Karen in a chronic and persistent vegetative state. No form of treatment which can cure or improve that condition is known or available. As nearly as may be determined, considering the guarded area of remote uncertainties characteristic of most medical science predictions, she can *never* be restored to cognitive or sapient life. Even with regard to the vegetative level and improvement therein (if such it may be called) the prognosis is extremely poor and the extent unknown if it should in fact occur.

She is debilitated and moribund and although fairly stable at the time of argument before us (no new information having been filed in the meanwhile in expansion of the record), no physician risked the opinion that she could live more than a year and indeed she may die much earlier. Excellent medical and nursing care so far has been able to ward off the constant threat of infection, to which she is peculiarly susceptible because of the respirator, the tracheal tube and other incidents of care in her vulnerable condition. Her life accordingly is sustained by the respirator and tubal feeding, and removal from the respirator would cause her death soon, although the time cannot be stated with more precision. . . .

. . . When plaintiff and his family, finally reconciled to the certainty of Karen's impending death, requested the withdrawal of life support mechanisms, [Dr. Morse] demurred. His refusal was based upon his conception of medical standards, practice and ethics described in the medical testimony, such as in the evidence given by another neurologist, Dr. Sidney Diamond, a witness for the State. Dr. Diamond asserted that no physician would have failed to provide respirator support at the outset, and none would interrupt its life-saving course thereafter, except in the case of cerebral death. In the latter case, he thought the respirator would in effect be disconnected from one already dead, entitling the physician under medical standards and, he thought, legal concepts, to terminate the supportive measures. We note Dr. Diamond's distinction of major surgical or transfusion procedures in a terminal case not involving cerebral death, such as here:

> The subject has lost human qualities. It would be incredible, and I think unlikely, that any physician would respond to a sudden hemorrhage, massive hemorrhage or a loss of all her defensive blood cells, by giving her large quantities of blood. I think that ° ° ° major surgical procedures would be out of the question even if they were known to be essential for continued physical existence.

This distinction is adverted to also in the testimony of Dr. Julius Korein, a neurologist called by plaintiff. Dr. Korein described a medical practice concept of "judicious neglect" under which the physician will say:

> Don't treat this patient anymore, ° ° ° it does not serve either the patient, the family, or society in any meaningful way to continue treatment with this patient.

Dr. Korein also told of the unwritten and unspoken standard of medical practice implied in the foreboding initials DNR (do not resuscitate), as applied to the extraordinary terminal case:

> Cancer, metastatic cancer, involving the lungs, the liver, the brain, multiple involvements, the physician may or may not write: Do not resuscitate. ° ° ° [I]t could be said to the nurse: if this man stops breathing don't resuscitate him. ° ° ° No physician that I know personally is going to try and resuscitate a man riddled with cancer and in agony and he stops breathing. They are

not going to put him on a respirator. ° ° ° I think that would be the height of misuse of technology.

While the thread of logic in such distinctions may be elusive to the non-medical lay mind, in relation to the supposed imperative to sustain life at all costs, they nevertheless relate to medical decisions, such as the decision of Dr. Morse in the present case. We agree with the trial court that that decision was in accord with Dr. Morse's conception of medical standards and practice. . . .

Constitutional and Legal Issues

At the outset we note the dual role in which plaintiff comes before the Court. He not only raises, derivatively, what he perceives to be the constitutional and legal rights of his daughter Karen, but he also claims certain rights independently as parent. . . .

I. THE FREE EXERCISE OF RELIGION

We think the contention as to interference with religious beliefs or rights may be considered and dealt with without extended discussion, given the acceptance of distinctions so clear and simple in their precedential definition as to be dispositive on their face.

Simply stated, the right to religious beliefs is absolute but conduct in pursuance thereof is not wholly immune from governmental restraint. So it is that, for the sake of life, courts sometimes (but not always) order blood transfusions for Jehovah's Witnesses (whose religious beliefs abhor such procedure); and protect the public health as in the case of compulsory vaccination (over the strongest of religious objections). The public interest is thus considered paramount, without essential dissolution of respect for religious beliefs.

We think, without further examples, that, ranged against the State's interest in the preservation of life, the impingement of religious belief, much less religious "neutrality" as here, does not reflect a constitutional question, in the circumstances at least of the case presently before the Court. Moreover, like the trial court, we do not recognize an independent parental right of religious freedom to support the relief requested. . . .

III. THE RIGHT OF PRIVACY

It is the issue of the constitutional right of privacy that has given us most concern, in the exceptional circumstances of this case. Here a loving parent, *qua* parent and raising the rights of his incompetent and profoundly damaged daughter, probably irreversibly doomed to no more than a biologically vegetative remnant of life, is before the court. He seeks authorization to abandon specialized technological procedures which can only maintain for a time a body having no potential for resumption or continuance of other than a "vegetative" existence.

We have no doubt, in these unhappy circumstances, that if Karen were herself miraculously lucid for an interval (not altering the existing prognosis of the condition to which she would soon return) and perceptive of her irreversible condition, she could effectively decide upon discontinuance of the life-support apparatus, even if it meant the prospect of natural death. To this extent we may distinguish [a prior decision] which concerned a severely injured young woman whose life depended on surgery and blood transfusion; and who was in such extreme shock that she was unable to express an informed choice (although the Court apparently considered the case as if the patient's own religious decision to resist transfusion were at stake), but most importantly a patient apparently salvable to long life and vibrant health;—a situation not at all like the present case.

We have no hesitancy in deciding, in the instant diametrically opposite case, that no external compelling interest of the State could compel Karen to endure the unendurable, only to vegetate a few measurable months with no realistic possibility of returning to any semblance of cognitive or sapient life. We perceive no thread of logic distinguishing between such a choice on Karen's part and a similar choice which, under the evidence in this case, could be made by a competent patient terminally ill, riddled by cancer and suffering great pain; such a patient would not be resuscitated or put on a respirator in the example described by Dr. Korein, and *a fortiori* would not be kept *against his will* on a respirator.

Although the Constitution does not explicitly mention a right of privacy, Supreme Court decisions have recognized that a right of personal privacy exists and that certain areas of privacy are guaranteed under the Constitution. The Court has interdicted judicial intrusion into many aspects of personal decision, sometimes basing this restraint upon the conception of a limitation of judicial interest and responsibility, such as with regard to contraception and its relationship to family life and decision. *Griswold v. Connecticut.*

The Court in *Griswold* found the unwritten constitutional right of privacy to exist in the penumbra of specific guarantees of the Bill of Rights "formed by emanations from those guarantees that help give them life and substance." Presumably this right is broad enough to encompass a patient's decision to decline medical treatment under certain circumstances, in much the same way as it is broad enough to encompass a woman's decision to terminate pregnancy under certain conditions.

Nor is such right of privacy forgotten in the New Jersey Constitution.

The claimed interests of the State in this case are essentially the preservation and sanctity of human life and defense of the right of the physician to administer medical treatment according to his best judgment. In this case the doctors say that removing Karen from the respirator will conflict with their professional judgment. The plaintiff answers that Karen's present treatment serves only a maintenance function; that the respirator cannot cure or improve her condition but at best can only prolong her inevitable slow deterioration and death; and that the interests of the patient, as seen by her surrogate, the guardian, must be evaluated by the court as predominant, even in the face of an opinion *contra* by the present attending physicians. Plaintiff's distinction is significant. The nature of Karen's care and the realistic chances of her recovery are quite unlike those of the patients discussed in many of the cases where treatments were ordered. In many of those cases the medical procedure required (usually a transfusion) constituted a minimal bodily invasion and the chances of recovery and return to functioning life were very good. We think that the State's interest *contra* weakens and the individual's right to privacy grows as the degree of bodily invasion increases and the prognosis dims. Ultimately there comes a point at which the individual's rights overcome the State interest. It is for that reason that we believe Karen's choice, if she were competent to make it, would be vindicated by the law. Her prognosis is extremely poor—she will never resume cognitive life. And the bodily invasion is very great—she requires 24 hour intensive nursing care, antibiotics, the assistance of a respirator, a catheter and feeding tube.

Our affirmation of Karen's independent right of choice, however, would ordinarily be based upon her competency to assert it. The sad truth, however, is that she is grossly incompetent and we cannot discern her supposed choice based on the testimony of her previous conversations with friends, where such testimony is without sufficient probative weight. Nevertheless we have concluded that Karen's right of privacy may be asserted on her behalf by her guardian under the peculiar circumstances here present.

If a putative decision by Karen to permit this non-cognitive, vegetative existence to terminate by natural forces is regarded as a valuable incident of her right of privacy, as we believe it to be, then it should not be discarded solely on the basis that her condition prevents her conscious exercise of the choice. The only practical way to prevent destruction of the right is to permit the guardian and family of Karen to render their best judgment, subject to the qualifications hereinafter stated, as to whether she would exercise it in these circumstances. If their conclusion is in the affirmative this decision should be accepted by a society the overwhelming majority of whose members would, we think, in similar circumstances, exercise such a choice in the same way for themselves or for those closest to them. It is for this reason that we determine that Karen's right of privacy may be asserted in her behalf, in this respect, by her guardian and family under the particular circumstances presented by this record. . . .

IV. THE MEDICAL FACTOR

Having declared the substantive legal basis upon which plaintiff's rights as representative of Karen must be deemed predicated, we face and respond to the assertion on behalf of defendants that our premise unwarrantably offends prevailing medical standards. We thus turn to consideration of the medical decision supporting the determination made below, conscious of the paucity of pre-existing legislative and judicial guidance as to the rights and liabilities therein involved. . . .

. . . [There is] a real distinction between the self-infliction of deadly harm and a self-determination against artificial life support or radical surgery, for instance, in the face of irreversible, painful and certain imminent death. The contrasting situations mentioned are analogous to those continually faced by the medical profession. When does the institution of life-sustaining procedures, ordinarily mandatory, become the subject of medical discretion in the context of administration to persons *in extremis*? And when does the withdrawal of such procedures, from such persons already supported by them, come within the orbit of medical discretion? When does a determination as to either of the foregoing contingencies court the hazard of civil or criminal liability on the part of the physician or institution involved? . . .

The medical obligation is related to standards and practice prevailing in the profession. The physicians in charge of the case, as noted above, declined to withdraw the respirator. That decision was consistent with the proofs below as to the then existing medical standards and practices.

Under the law as it then stood, Judge Muir was correct in declining to authorize withdrawal of the respirator.

However, in relation to the matter of the declaratory relief sought by plaintiff as representative of Karen's interests, we are required to reevaluate the applicability of the medical standards projected in the court below. The question is whether there is such internal consistency and rationality in the application of such standards as should warrant their constituting an ineluctable bar to the effectuation of substantive relief for plaintiff at the hands of the court. We have concluded not. . . .

We glean from the record here that physicians distinguish between curing the ill and comforting and easing the dying; that they refuse to treat the curable as if they were dying or ought to die, and that they have sometimes refused to treat the hopeless and dying as if they were curable. In this sense, as we were reminded by the testimony of Drs. Korein and Diamond, many of them have refused to inflict an undesired prolongation of the process of dying on a patient in irreversible condition when it is clear that such "therapy" offers neither human nor humane benefit. We think these attitudes represent a balanced implementation of a profoundly realistic perspective on the meaning of life and death and that they respect the whole Judeo-Christian tradition of regard for human life. No less would they seem consistent with the moral matrix of medicine, "to heal," very much in the sense of the endless mission of the law, "to do justice."

Yet this balance, we feel, is particularly difficult to perceive and apply in the context of the development by advanced technology of sophisticated and artificial life-sustaining devices. For those possibly curable, such devices are of great value, and, as ordinary medical procedures, are essential. Consequently, as pointed out by Dr. Diamond, they are necessary because of the ethic of medical practice. But in light of the situation in the present case (while the record here is somewhat hazy in distinguishing between "ordinary" and "extraordinary" measures), one would have to think that the use of the same respirator or like support could be considered "ordinary" in the context of the possibly curable patient but "extraordinary" in the context of the forced sustaining by cardio-respiratory processes of an irreversibly doomed patient. And this dilemma is sharpened in the face of the malpractice and criminal action threat which we have mentioned. . . .

Nevertheless, there must be a way to free physicians, in the pursuit of their healing vocation, from possible contamination by self-interest or self-protection concerns which would inhibit their independent medical judgments for the well-being of their dying patients. We would hope that this opinion might be serviceable to some degree in ameliorating the professional problems under discussion.

A technique aimed at the underlying difficulty (though in a somewhat broader context) is described by Dr. Karen Teel, a pediatrician and a Director of Pediatric Education, who writes in the *Baylor Law Review* under the title "The Physician's Dilemma: A Doctor's View: What The Law Should Be." Dr. Teel recalls:

> . . . I suggest that it would be more appropriate to provide a regular forum for more input and dialogue in individual situations and to allow the responsibility of these judgments to be shared. Many hospitals have established an Ethics Committee composed of physicians, social workers, attorneys, and theologians, ° ° ° which serves to review the individual circumstances of ethical dilemma and which has provided much in the way of assistance and safeguards for patients and their medical caretakers. Generally, the authority of these committees is primarily restricted to the hospital setting and their official status is more that of an advisory body than of an enforcing body.

The most appealing factor in the technique suggested by Dr. Teel seems to us to be the diffusion of professional responsibility for decision, comparable in a way to the value of multi-judge courts in finally resolving on appeal difficult questions of law. Moreover, such a system would be protective to the hospital as well as the doctor in screening out, so to speak, a case which might be contaminated by less than worthy motivations of family or physician. In the real world and in relationship to the momentous decision contemplated, the value of additional views and diverse knowledge is apparent.

We consider that a practice of applying to a court to confirm such decisions would generally be inappropriate, not only because that would be a gratuitous encroachment upon the medical profession's field of competence, but because it would be impossibly cumbersome. Such a requirement is distinguishable from the judicial overview traditionally required in other matters such as the adjudication and commitment of mental incompetents. This is not to say that in the case of an otherwise justiciable controversy access to the courts would be foreclosed; we speak rather of a general practice and procedure. . . .

In summary of the present Point of this opinion, we conclude that the state of the pertinent medical standards and practices which guided the attending physicians in this matter is not such as would justify this Court in deeming itself bound or controlled thereby in responding to the case for declaratory relief established by the parties on the record before us.

V. ALLEGED CRIMINAL LIABILITY

Having concluded that there is a right of privacy that might permit termination of treatment in the circumstances of this case, we turn to consider the relationship of the exercise of that right to the criminal law. We are aware that such termination of treatment would accelerate Karen's death. The County Prosecutor and the Attorney General maintain that there would be criminal liability for such acceleration. Under the statutes of this State, the unlawful killing of another human being is criminal homicide. We conclude that there would be no criminal homicide in the circumstances of this case. We believe, first, that the ensuing death would not be homicide but rather expiration from existing natural causes. Secondly, even if it were to be regarded as homicide, it would not be unlawful.

These conclusions rest upon definitional and constitutional bases. The termination of treatment pursuant to the right of privacy is, within the limitations of this case, *ipso facto* lawful. Thus, a death resulting from such an act would not come within the scope of the homicide statutes proscribing only the unlawful killing of another. There is a real and in this case determinative distinction between the unlawful taking of the life of another and the ending of artificial life-support systems as a matter of self-determination.

Furthermore, the exercise of a constitutional right such as we have here found is protected from criminal prosecution. We do not question the State's undoubted power to punish the taking of human life, but that power does not encompass individuals terminating medical treatment pursuant to their right of privacy. The constitutional protection extends to third parties whose action is necessary to effectuate the exercise of that right where the individuals themselves would not be subject to prosecution or the third parties are charged as accessories to an act which could not be a crime. . . .

VI. THE GUARDIANSHIP OF THE PERSON

. . . The trial court was apparently convinced of the high character of Joseph Quinlan and his general suitability as guardian under other circumstances, describing him as "very sincere, moral, ethical and religious." The court felt, however, that the obligation to concur in the medical care and treatment of his daughter would be a source of anguish to him and would distort his "decision-making processes." We disagree, for we sense from the whole record before us that while Mr. Quinlan feels a natural grief, and understandably sorrows because of the tragedy which has befallen his daughter, his strength of purpose and character far outweighs these sentiments and qualifies him eminently for guardianship of the person as well as the property of his daughter. Hence we discern no valid reason to overrule the statutory intendment of preference to the next of kin. . . .

NOTES AND QUESTIONS:
In re Quinlan

1. When the *Quinlan* case was taking place, the diagnosis of "persistent vegetative state" was relatively new and poorly understood. As a demonstration of that fact, note the statement that "death would follow soon" after the removal of the respirator. (And the separate comment that even with the respirator, she was not likely to live more than a year.) After the court decision, and after Karen's father exercised his right to have the respirator turned off, Karen lived another ten years. In fact, it is not uncommon for people in a persistent vegetative state to live for a substantial time without a respirator. After all, the key element to the diagnosis is that what Dr. Plum called the "sapient" part of the brain—which might also be referred to as the "higher brain," responsible for our thoughts and feelings—is permanently destroyed. The rest of the body might be very healthy, as was indeed the case for Karen.

2. What Karen did require, even after the respirator was removed, was some method for feeding. At the time of the case, she had a nasogastric tube, which is merely a plastic tube inserted into her nose and threaded down into her stomach. Every person in a persistent vegetative state needs some way of getting food and fluids into them. Usually, instead of using a nasogastric tube, a tube to the stomach is surgically implanted through the wall of the abdomen. This avoids the need for anything in the person's nose or upper throat, and is of course cosmetically more acceptable.

    Without food and fluids, a person in a persistent vegetative state would die in about a week or two. Why do you think Karen was kept alive for the ten years? Why did her father not attempt to have the feedings stopped? This issue was not raised in the court case, since it was assumed that stopping the respirator would lead to her death within hours, if not minutes.

3. The court correctly notes that Karen was not legally dead. To be legally dead even though the heart is still beating (described as being "brain dead"), the person's entire brain must be permanently destroyed. A person in a persistent vegetative state has lost only the "higher brain," and still has a functioning brainstem (or "lower brain"). We will address this in detail in chapter 15. Do you think Karen should have been considered legally dead? Why or why not?

4. The court rejects the argument that, assuming Karen's religious beliefs indicated she would want to refuse the respirator, those beliefs must be followed. It claims that the "public interest is thus considered paramount" in overriding Karen's possible exercise of her religious beliefs. What "public interest" do you think the court has in mind? One might think that a state opposing a person who is refusing care on religious grounds has an especially high burden to meet, since the person has two rights at issue (right to freedom of religion in addition to right to refuse care). What is it about the medical circumstances of persons refusing care on religious grounds (such as Jehovah's Witnesses) that might distinguish their situation from that of someone like Karen? (The court notes this distinction later in the opinion.)

   In fact, this represents an area where the law has changed since *Quinlan*. It is relatively unlikely that a court would, "for the sake of life," today override the wishes of a competent adult Jehovah's Witness to refuse a blood transfusion. As noted in the introduction, this represents a gradual move away from allowing state interests to override the wishes of a competent patient. Might it make a difference if that person had young children who would no longer have a mother? (This is discussed in the notes following the *Bouvia* case.)

5. The court determines that Karen has a right to refuse care that is grounded in her right of privacy. It finds that this right exists in both the United States Constitution and the New Jersey constitution. We will discuss the former claim in more detail in the next chapter, where we review the U.S. Supreme Court's pronouncements on this issue. Under the principles of federalism, the New Jersey Supreme Court's determination that the U.S. Constitution includes a right to refuse care is *not* binding on the U.S. Supreme Court, but if the U.S. Supreme Court were to say that there is no such right embodied in the U.S. Constitution, that conclusion *would be* binding on the New Jersey Supreme Court.

   The State of New Jersey does, however, have ultimate authority to interpret its *own* laws. Thus, even the U.S. Supreme Court cannot reverse the *Quinlan* court's opinion that there is a right to refuse care under the New Jersey constitution.

6. The court acknowledges that there are state interests that might oppose allowing Karen's respirator to be turned off. What are those interests? What does the court say about the relative weight of Karen's right to privacy and the interests advanced by the state in opposing her exercise of that right?

7. The court also evaluates the interests of the medical profession. Note the court's conclusion that under "existing medical standards and practices" it was appropriate for the doctors taking care of Karen to not remove the respirator. What were those standards? Are the doctors stating that even if Karen had somehow said, ahead of time, that she did not want the respirator, it still would have been inappropriate to remove it?

8. The court quotes Dr. Diamond as noting that because Karen has "lost human qualities," it would be "incredible" and "unlikely" for a physician to do major surgery on her, or give her a major transfusion of blood. There was also discussion of the practice of limiting care to dying patients so as to avoid the "height of misuse of technology." The court accepted that these were correct statements about accepted medical practice.

Why would the medical profession refuse these actions, yet at the same time insist that Karen's respirator must be kept going? Is the court correct in its comment about the "thread of logic" in these distinctions being "elusive"? Do you agree with its conclusion to not allow the interests of the medical profession to override Karen's right to refuse care?

9. Over time, a number of efforts have been made to categorize certain kinds of care into that which can be refused and that which cannot be refused. Most of these distinctions have now been accepted as being both legally and ethically irrelevant.[1] The *Quinlan* case addressed, and rejected, the distinction between *ordinary* care and *extraordinary* care. This distinction, which originated in Catholic theological writings in the 16th century, held that people must use "ordinary" measures to preserve their lives, but need not use "extraordinary" measures. Here is what the *Conroy* case, 486 A.2d at 1235, which follows in this chapter, said about this issue:

> The terms "ordinary" and "extraordinary" have assumed too many conflicting meanings to remain useful. To draw a line on this basis for determining whether treatment should be given leads to a semantical milieu that does not advance the analysis.
>
> The distinction between ordinary and extraordinary treatment is frequently phrased as one between common and unusual, or simple and complex, treatment; "extraordinary" treatment also has been equated with elaborate, artificial, heroic, aggressive, expensive, or highly involved or invasive forms of medical intervention. Depending on the definitions applied, a particular treatment for a given patient may be considered both ordinary and extraordinary. Further, since the common/unusual and simple/complex distinctions among medical treatments "exist on continuums with no precise dividing line," and the continuum is constantly shifting due to progress in medical care, disagreement will often exist about whether a particular treatment is ordinary or extraordinary. In addition, the competent patient generally could refuse even ordinary treatment; therefore, an incompetent patient theoretically should also be able to make such a choice when the surrogate decision-making is effectuating the patient's subjective intent. In such cases, the ordinary/extraordinary distinction is irrelevant except insofar as the particular patient would have made the distinction.
>
> The ordinary/extraordinary distinction has also been discussed in terms of the benefits and burdens of treatment for the patient. If the benefits of the treatment outweigh the burdens it imposes on the patient, it is characterized as ordinary and therefore ethically required; if not, it is characterized as extraordinary and therefore optional. This formulation is extremely fact-sensitive and

would lead to different classifications of the same treatment in different situations. . . . Moreover, while the analysis may be useful in weighing the implications of the specific treatment for the patient, essentially it merely restates the question: whether the burdens of a treatment so clearly outweigh its benefits to the patient that continued treatment would be inhumane.

10. Another distinction effectively rejected by the *Quinlan* court (and by all subsequent cases) is that between *withholding* treatment and *withdrawing* treatment. It had previously been argued that it was sometimes acceptable to withhold a certain treatment—for example, to never put Karen on the respirator—but that it would be wrong to terminate the treatment after it had been started. Here is what the *Conroy* court said:

> This distinction is more psychologically compelling than logically sound. As mentioned above, the line between active and passive conduct in the context of medical decisions is far too nebulous to constitute a principled basis for decisionmaking. Whether necessary treatment is withheld at the outset or withdrawn later on, the consequence—the patient's death—is the same. Moreover, from a policy standpoint, it might well be unwise to forbid persons from discontinuing a treatment under circumstances in which the treatment could permissibly be withheld. Such a rule could discourage families and doctors from even attempting certain types of care and could thereby force them into hasty and premature decisions to allow a patient to die.

11. An important part of the court's opinion is not merely the recognition of Karen's right to refuse the respirator, but the acknowledgement that someone else—in this case, her father—must be given the authority to exercise that right on her behalf. Obviously, if no one but Karen can exercise the right, it will have little meaning. As we shall see, much of the subsequent case law is concerned with this secondary issue: how to design a system so as to effectuate the wishes of incompetent patients.

12. Another important aspect of this opinion is its encouragement of the use of ethics committees. While these are now standard in modern hospital care, this was a new concept at the time of this case. The court was also ahead of its time in concluding that "a practice of applying to a court to confirm such decisions would generally be inappropriate." Many subsequent courts have been far less willing to leave such decisions in the hands of families and doctors.

13. Was it unreasonable for Karen's doctors to be concerned about the possibility that they would have been guilty of homicide had they turned off the respirator? Note that a person cannot "consent" to being killed: if you shoot me, even if I asked you to do so, you are criminally guilty of having caused my death. We will later revisit the distinction between terminating care at a patient's request, which is not considered to be homicide (or assisted suicide), and "actively" doing something that goes beyond merely terminating care (such as injecting a lethal drug, or the steps taken by Jack Kevorkian with his various suicide machines), which may well be considered homicide

or some related crime. Nonetheless, the *Quinlan* court's statement of the law on this issue is remarkably correct, even a quarter century later.

BOUVIA V. SUPERIOR COURT
California Court of Appeals
225 Cal. Rptr. 297 (Cal. Ct. App. 1986)

OPINION BY JUSTICE BEACH:

Petitioner, Elizabeth Bouvia, a patient in a public hospital, seeks the removal from her body of a nasogastric tube inserted and maintained against her will and without her consent by physicians who so placed it for the purpose of keeping her alive through involuntary forced feeding. . . .

Petitioner is a 28-year-old woman. Since birth she has been afflicted with and suffered from severe cerebral palsy. She is quadriplegic. She is now a patient at a public hospital maintained by one of the real parties in interest, the County of Los Angeles. Other parties are physicians, nurses and the medical and support staff employed by the County of Los Angeles. Petitioner's physical handicaps of palsy and quadriplegia have progressed to the point where she is completely bedridden. Except for a few fingers of one hand and some slight head and facial movements, she is immobile. She is physically helpless and wholly unable to care for herself. She is totally dependent upon others for all of her needs. These include feeding, washing, cleaning, toileting, turning, and helping her with elimination and other bodily functions. She cannot stand or sit upright in bed or in a wheelchair. She lies flat in bed and must do so the rest of her life. She suffers also from degenerative and severely crippling arthritis. She is in continual pain. Another tube permanently attached to her chest automatically injects her with periodic doses of morphine which relieves some, but not all of her physical pain and discomfort.

She is intelligent, very mentally competent. She earned a college degree. She was married but her husband has left her. She suffered a miscarriage. She lived with her parents until her father told her that they could no longer care for her. She has stayed intermittently with friends and at public facilities. A search for a permanent place to live where she might receive the constant care which she needs has been unsuccessful. She is without financial means to support herself and, therefore, must accept public assistance for medical and other care.

She has on several occasions expressed the desire to die. In 1983 she sought the right to be cared for in a public hospital in Riverside County while she intentionally "starved herself to death." A court in that county denied her judicial assistance to accomplish that goal. She later abandoned an appeal from that ruling. Thereafter, friends took her to several different facilities, both public and private, arriving finally at her present location. Efforts by the staff of real party in interest County of Los Angeles and its social workers to find her an apartment of her own with publicly paid live-in help or regular visiting nurses to care for her, or some other suitable facility, have proved fruitless.

Petitioner must be spoon fed in order to eat. Her present medical and dietary staff have determined that she is not consuming a sufficient amount of nutrients. Petitioner stops eating when she feels she cannot orally swallow more, without nausea and vomiting. As she cannot now retain solids, she is fed soft liquid-like food. Because of her previously announced resolve to starve herself, the medical staff feared her weight loss might reach a life-threatening level. Her weight since admission to real parties' facility seems to hover between 65 and 70 pounds. Accordingly, they inserted the subject tube against her will and contrary to her express written instructions.

Petitioner's counsel argue that her weight loss was not such as to be life threatening and therefore the tube is unnecessary. However, the trial court found to the contrary as a matter of fact, a finding which we must accept. Nonetheless, the point is immaterial, for, as we will explain, a patient has the right to refuse any medical treatment or medical service, even when such treatment is labelled "furnishing nourishment and hydration." This right exists even if its exercise creates a "life threatening condition."

3. THE RIGHT TO REFUSE MEDICAL TREATMENT.

"[A] person of adult years and in sound mind has the right, in the exercise of control over his own body, to determine whether or not to submit to lawful medical treatment." It follows that such a patient has the right to refuse any medical treatment, even that which may save or prolong her life. In our view the foregoing authorities are dispositive of the case at bench. Nonetheless, the county and its medical staff contend that for reasons unique to this case Elizabeth Bouvia may not exercise the right available to others. Accordingly, we again briefly discuss the rule in the light of real parties' contentions.

The right to refuse medical treatment is basic and fundamental. It is recognized as a part of the right of privacy protected by both the state and federal constitutions. Its exercise requires no one's approval. It is not merely one vote subject to being overridden by medical opinion.

In *Barber v. Superior Court*, we considered this same issue although in a different context. Writing on behalf of this division, Justice Compton thoroughly analyzed and reviewed the issue of withdrawal of life-support systems beginning with the seminal case of the *Matter of Quinlan* and continuing on to the then recent enactment of the California Natural Death Act. His opinion clearly and repeatedly stresses the fundamental underpinning of its conclusion, i.e., the patient's right to decide: "In this state a clearly recognized legal right to control one's own medical treatment predated the Natural Death Act. A long line of cases . . . have held that where a doctor performs treatment in the absence of an informed consent, there is an actionable battery. The obvious corollary to this principle is that *a competent adult patient has the legal right to refuse medical treatment"* . . . .

For example, addressing one part of the problem, California passed the "Natural Death Act." Although addressed to terminally ill patients, the significance of this legislation is its expression as state policy "that adult persons have the fundamental right to control the decisions relating to the rendering of their own medical care . . . ." Section 7188 provides the method whereby an adult person may execute a directive for the withholding or withdrawal of life-sustaining procedures. Recognition of the right of other persons who may not be terminally ill and may wish to give other forms of direction concerning their medical care is expressed in section 7193: "Nothing in this chapter shall impair or supersede any legal right or legal responsibility which any person may have to effect the withholding or withdrawal of life-sustaining procedures in any lawful manner. In such respect the provisions of this chapter are cumulative."

Moreover, . . . there is no practical or logical reason to limit the exercise of this right to "terminal" patients. The right to refuse treatment does not need the sanction or approval by any legislative act, directing how and when it shall be exercised. . . .

A recent Presidential Commission for the Study of Ethical Problems in Medicine and Biomedical and Behavioral Research concluded in part: "The voluntary choice of a competent and informed patient should determine whether or not life-sustaining therapy will be undertaken, just as such choices provide the basis for other decisions about medical treatment. Health care institutions and professionals should try to enhance patients' abilities to make decisions on their own behalf and to promote understanding of the available treatment options. . . . Health care professionals serve patients best by maintaining a presumption in favor of sustaining life, while recognizing that competent patients are entitled to choose to forego any treatments, including those that sustain life."

. . . Significant also is the statement adopted on March 15, 1986, by the Council on Ethical and Judicial Affairs of the American Medical Association. It is entitled "Withholding or Withdrawing Life Prolonging Medical Treatment." In pertinent part, it declares: "The social commitment of the physician is to sustain life and relieve suffering. Where the performance of one duty conflicts with the other, the choice of the patient, or his family or legal representative if the patient is incompetent to act in his own behalf, should prevail. Life prolonging medical treatment includes medication and artificially or technologically supplied respiration, nutrition or hydration. In treating a terminally ill or irreversibly comatose patient, the physician should determine whether the benefits of treatment outweigh its burdens. At all times, the dignity of the patient should be maintained."

We do not believe that all of the foregoing case law and statements of policy and statutory recognition are mere lip service to a fictitious right. As noted in *Bartling*, "We do not doubt the sincerity of [the hospital and medical personnel's] moral and ethical beliefs, or their sincere belief in the position they have taken in this case. However, if the right of the patient to self-determination as to his own medical treatment is to have any meaning at all, it must be paramount to the interests of the patient's hospital and doctors. . . . The right of a competent adult patient to refuse medical treatment is a constitutionally guaranteed right which must not be abridged."

It is indisputable that petitioner is mentally competent. She is not comatose. She is quite intelligent, alert, and understands the risks involved.

4. THE CLAIMED EXCEPTIONS TO THE PATIENT'S RIGHT TO CHOOSE ARE INAPPLICABLE.

. . . [T]he real parties in interest, a county hospital, its physicians and administrators, urge that the interests of the state should prevail over the rights of Elizabeth Bouvia to refuse treatment. Advanced by real parties under this argument are the state's interests in (1) preserving life, (2) preventing suicide, (3) protecting innocent third parties, and (4) maintaining the ethical standards of the medical profession, including the right of physicians to effectively render necessary and appropriate medical service and to refuse treatment to an uncooperative and disruptive patient. Included, whether as part of the above or as separate and additional arguments, are what real parties assert as distinctive facts not present in other cases, i.e., (1) petitioner is a patient in a public facility, thereby making the state a party to the result of her conduct, (2) she is not comatose, nor incurably, nor terminally ill, nor in a vegetative state, all conditions which have justified the termination of life-support system in other instances, (3) she has asked for medical treatment, therefore, she cannot accept a part of it while cutting off the part that would be effective, and (4) she is, in truth, trying to starve herself to death and the state will not be a party to a suicide. . . .

At bench the trial court concluded that with sufficient feeding petitioner could live an additional 15 to 20 years; therefore, the preservation of petitioner's life for that period outweighed her right to decide. In so holding the trial court mistakenly attached undue importance to the amount of time possibly available to petitioner, and failed to give equal weight and consideration for the quality of that life; an equal, if not more significant, consideration.

All decisions permitting cessation of medical treatment or life-support procedures to some degree hastened the arrival of death. In part, at least, this was permitted because the quality of life during the time remaining in those cases had been terribly diminished. In Elizabeth Bouvia's view, the quality of her life has been diminished to the point of hopelessness, uselessness, unenjoyability and frustration. She, as the patient, lying helplessly in bed, unable to care for herself, may consider her existence meaningless. She cannot be faulted for so concluding. If her right to choose may not be exercised because there remains to her, in the opinion of a court, a physician or some committee, a certain arbitrary number of years, months, or days, her right will have lost its value and meaning.

Who shall say what the minimum amount of available life must be? Does it matter if it be 15 to 20 years, 15 to 20 months, or 15 to 20 days, if such life has been physically destroyed and its quality, dignity and purpose gone? As in all matters lines must be drawn at some point, somewhere, but that decision must ultimately belong to the one whose life is in issue.

Here Elizabeth Bouvia's decision to forego medical treatment or life-support through a mechanical means belongs to her. It is not a medical decision for her physicians to make. Neither is it a legal question whose soundness is to be resolved by lawyers or judges. It is not a conditional right subject to approval by ethics committees or courts of law. It is a moral and philosophical decision that, being a competent adult, is hers alone.

Adapting the language of *Satz v. Perlmutter*, "It is all very convenient to insist on continuing [Elizabeth Bouvia's] life so that there can be no question of foul play, no resulting civil liability and no possible trespass on medical ethics. However, it is quite another matter to do so at the patient's sole expense and against [her] competent will, thus inflicting never ending physical torture on [her] body until the inevitable, but artificially suspended, moment of death. Such a course of conduct invades the patient's constitutional right of privacy, removes [her] freedom of choice and invades [her] right to self-determine." Here, if force fed, petitioner faces 15 to 20 years of a painful existence, endurable only by the constant administrations of morphine. Her condition is irreversible. There is no cure for her palsy or arthritis. Petitioner would have to be fed, cleaned, turned, bedded, toileted by others for 15 to 20 years! Although alert, bright, sensitive, perhaps even brave and feisty, she must lie immobile, unable to exist except through physical acts of others. Her mind and spirit may be free to take great flights but she herself is imprisoned and must lie physically helpless subject to the ignominy, embarrassment, humiliation and dehumanizing aspects created by her helplessness. We do not believe it is the policy of this state that all and every life must be preserved against the will of the sufferer. It is incongruous, if not monstrous, for medical practitioners to assert their right to preserve a life that someone else must live, or, more accurately, endure, for "15 to 20 years." We cannot conceive it to be the policy of this state to inflict such an ordeal upon anyone.

It is, therefore, immaterial that the removal of the nasogastric tube will hasten or cause Bouvia's eventual death. Being competent she has the right to live out the remainder of her natural life in dignity and peace. It is precisely the aim and purpose of the many decisions upholding the withdrawal of life-support systems to accord and provide as large a measure of dignity, respect and comfort as possible to every patient for the remainder of his days, whatever be their number. This goal is not to hasten death, though its earlier arrival may be an expected and understood likelihood.

Real parties assert that what petitioner really wants is to "commit suicide" by starvation at their facility. The trial court in its statement of decision said:

It is fairly clear from the evidence and the court cannot close its eyes to the fact that [petitioner] during her stay in defendant hospital, and for some time prior thereto, has formed an intent to die. She has voiced this desire to a member of the staff of defendant hospital. She claims, however, she does not wish to commit suicide. On the evidence, this is but a semantic distinction. The reasonable inference to be drawn from the evidence is that [petitioner] in defendant facility has purposefully engaged in a selective rejection of medical treatment and nutritional intake to accomplish her objective and accept only treatment which gives her some degree of comfort pending her demise. Stated another way, [petitioner's] refusal of medical treatment and nutritional intake is motivated not by a bona fide exercise of her right of privacy but by a desire to terminate her life. . . . Here [petitioner] wishes to pursue her objective to die by the use of public facilities with staff standing by to furnish her medical treatment to which she consents and to refrain from that which she refuses.

Overlooking the fact that a desire to terminate one's life is probably the ultimate exercise of one's right to privacy, we find no substantial evidence to support the court's conclusion. Even if petitioner had the specific intent to commit suicide in 1983, while at Riverside, she did not carry out that plan. Then she apparently had the ability, without artificial aids, to consume sufficient nutrients to sustain herself; now she does not. That is to say, the trial court here made the following express finding, "Plaintiff, when she chooses, can orally ingest food by masticating 'finger food' *though additional nutritional intake is required intravenously and by nasogastric tube . . . .*" As a consequence of her changed condition, it is clear she has now merely resigned herself to accept an earlier death, if necessary, rather than live by feedings forced upon her by means of a nasogastric tube. Her decision to allow nature to take its course is not equivalent to an election to commit suicide with real parties aiding and abetting therein.

Moreover, the trial court seriously erred by basing its decision on the "motives" behind Elizabeth Bouvia's decision to exercise her rights. If a right exists, it matters not what "motivates" its exercise. We find nothing in the law to suggest the right to refuse medical treatment may be exercised only if the patient's *motives* meet someone else's approval. It certainly is not illegal or immoral to prefer a natural, albeit sooner, death than a drugged life attached to a mechanical device.

It is not necessary to here define or dwell at length upon what constitutes suicide. Our Supreme Court dealt with the matter in the case of *In re Joseph G.* wherein, declaring that the state has an interest in preserving and recognizing the sanctity of life, it observed that it is a crime to aid in suicide. But it is significant that the instances and the means there discussed all involved affirmative, assertive, proximate, direct conduct such as furnishing a gun, poison, knife, or other instrumentality or usable means by which another could physically and immediately inflict some death-producing injury upon himself. Such situations are far different than the mere presence of a doctor during the exercise of his patient's constitutional rights. . . .

We do not purport to establish what will constitute proper medical practice in all other cases or even other aspects of the care to be provided petitioner. We hold only that her right to refuse medical treatment, even of the life-sustaining variety, entitles her to the immediate removal of the nasogastric tube that has been involuntarily inserted into her body. The hospital and medical staff are still free to perform a substantial if not the greater part of their duty, i.e., that of trying to alleviate Bouvia's pain and suffering.

Petitioner is without means to go to a private hospital and, apparently, real parties' hospital as a public facility was required to accept her. Having done so it may not deny her relief from pain and suffering merely because she has chosen to exercise her fundamental right to protect what little privacy remains to her. . . .

NOTES AND QUESTIONS:
Bouvia v. Superior Court

1. After she won the case, and the right to end her life, Elizabeth Bouvia chose not to do so. She explained her decision during a *60 Minutes* segment broadcast on September 7, 1997, eleven years after she had first appeared on that show:

    > Mike Wallace: (*Voiceover*) After several attempts at starvation, Elizabeth told us, it just became physically too difficult to do. She didn't want to die a slow, agonizing death, nor to do it in the spotlight of public scrutiny. And so she told us, with great regret, she quietly chose to live.
    >
    > Ms. Bouvia: Starvation is not an easy way to go.
    >
    > Wallace: Oh, no.
    >
    > Ms. Bouvia: You can't just keep doing it and keep doing it. It really messes up your body. And my body was already messed up.

    During this interview, Ms. Bouvia indicated that she viewed herself as a burden on society (costing $150,000 a year). She was still interested in ending her life, but remained physically unable to do it on her own. She was concerned that if she asked someone to put a lethal medication in her mouth, that person might be liable for causing her death. She told Wallace that she didn't want to be alive 10 years in the future to do a third interview, and that "she simply wants to stay out of the headlines and away from the never-ending debate over the right to die."

2. A case like *Bouvia* is relatively rare in that it involves a competent patient who is trying to refuse care. The great majority of the court cases involving refusals of care concern incompetent patients like Karen Ann Quinlan.

Thus, those cases need to address both the extent of the right to refuse care, and how to decide if the patient would want to exercise that right.

3. What facts relating to Ms. Bouvia's condition have made this case more difficult to resolve than *Quinlan*?

4. The *Bouvia* case highlights another one of the "rejected" distinctions (like that between *ordinary* and *extraordinary* care or between *withholding* and *withdrawing* care) between care that could be refused and care that could not. Here, the distinction was between medical care in general and artificially administered nutrition and hydration. Here is what the *Conroy* case (which follows in this chapter) said about this distinction:

> Certainly, feeding has an emotional significance. As infants we could breathe without assistance, but we were dependent on others for our lifeline of nourishment. Even more, feeding is an expression of nurturing and caring, certainly for infants and children, and in many cases for adults as well.
>
> Once one enters the realm of complex, high-technology medical care, it is hard to shed the "emotional symbolism" of food. However, artificial feedings such as nasogastric tubes, gastrostomies, and intravenous infusions are significantly different from bottle-feeding or spoonfeeding—they are medical procedures with inherent risks and possible side effects, instituted by skilled health-care providers to compensate for impaired physical functioning. Analytically, artificial feeding by means of a nasogastric tube or intravenous infusion can be seen as equivalent to artificial breathing by means of a respirator. Both prolong life through mechanical means when the body is no longer able to perform a vital bodily function on its own.

5. Note the similarity between the basic arguments in *Quinlan* and in this case: determining whether the patient has a right to refuse care, and then deciding what state interests might override that right. The state interests raised in *Quinlan* were refined and expanded, in subsequent cases, to the "standard" four interests that are discussed in *Bouvia*. Here is what the *Conroy* court said about those four interests:

> Whether based on common-law doctrines or on constitutional theory, the right to decline life-sustaining medical treatment is not absolute. In some cases, it may yield to countervailing societal interests in sustaining the person's life. Courts and commentators have commonly identified four state interests that may limit a person's right to refuse medical treatment: preserving life, preventing suicide, safeguarding the integrity of the medical profession, and protecting innocent third parties.
>
> The state's interest in preserving life is commonly considered the most significant of the four state interests. It may be seen as embracing two separate but related concerns: an interest in preserving the life of the particular patient, and an interest in preserving the sanctity of all life.
>
> While both of these state interests in life are certainly strong, in themselves they will usually not foreclose a competent person from declining life-sustaining medical treatment for himself. This is because the life that the state is seeking to protect in such a situation is the life of the same person who has compe-

tently decided to forego the medical intervention; it is not some other actual or potential life that cannot adequately protect itself. *Cf. Roe v. Wade* (authorizing state restrictions or proscriptions of woman's right to abortion in final trimester of pregnancy to protect viable fetal life); *Muhlenberg Hosp. v. Patterson* (authorizing blood transfusion to save infant's life over parents' religious objections).

In cases that do not involve the protection of the actual or potential life of someone other than the decisionmaker, the state's indirect and abstract interest in preserving the life of the competent patient generally gives way to the patient's much stronger personal interest in directing the course of his own life. Indeed, insofar as the "sanctity of individual free choice and self-determination [are] fundamental constituents of life," the value of life may be lessened rather than increased "by the failure to allow a competent human being the right of choice."

It may be contended that in conjunction with its general interest in preserving life, this state has a particular legislative policy of preventing suicide. This state interest in protecting people from direct and purposeful self-destruction is motivated by, if not encompassed within, the state's more basic interest in preserving life. Thus, it is questionable whether it is a distinct state interest worthy of independent consideration.

In any event, declining life-sustaining medical treatment may not properly be viewed as an attempt to commit suicide. Refusing medical intervention merely allows the disease to take its natural course; if death were eventually to occur, it would be the result, primarily, of the underlying disease, and not the result of a self-inflicted injury. *But cf. In re Caulk*, 480 A.2d 93 (1984) (stating that attempt of an otherwise healthy prisoner to starve himself to death because he preferred death to life in prison was tantamount to attempted suicide, and that the state, to prevent such suicide, could force him to eat). In addition, people who refuse life-sustaining medical treatment may not harbor a specific intent to die; rather, they may fervently wish to live, but to do so free of unwanted medical technology, surgery, or drugs, and without protracted suffering.

Recognizing the right of a terminally ill person to reject medical treatment respects that person's intent, not to die, but to suspend medical intervention at a point consonant with the "individual's view respecting a personally preferred manner of concluding life." The difference is between self-infliction or self-destruction and self-determination. . . .

The third state interest that is frequently asserted as a limitation on a competent patient's right to refuse medical treatment is the interest in safeguarding the integrity of the medical profession. This interest, like the interest in preventing suicide, is not particularly threatened by permitting competent patients to refuse life-sustaining medical treatment. Medical ethics do not require medical intervention in disease at all costs. As long ago as 1624, Francis Bacon wrote, "I esteem it the office of a physician not only to restore health, but to mitigate pain and dolours; and not only when such mitigation may conduce to recovery, but when it may serve to make a fair and easy passage." More recently, we wrote in *Quinlan* that modern-day "physicians distinguish between curing the ill and comforting and easing the dying; that they refuse to

treat the curable as if they were dying or ought to die, and that they have sometimes refused to treat the hopeless and dying as if they were curable." Indeed,
recent surveys have suggested that a majority of practicing doctors now approve of passive euthanasia and believe that it is being practiced by members
of the profession.

Moreover, even if doctors were exhorted to attempt to cure or sustain their
patients under all circumstances, that moral and professional imperative, at
least in cases of patients who were clearly competent, presumably would not
require doctors to go beyond advising the patient of the risks of foregoing
treatment and urging the patient to accept the medical intervention. If the patient rejected the doctor's advice, the onus of that decision would rest on the
patient, not the doctor. Indeed, if the patient's right to informed consent is to
have any meaning at all, it must be accorded respect even when it conflicts
with the advice of the doctor or the values of the medical profession as a whole.

The fourth asserted state interest in overriding a patient's decision about his
medical treatment is the interest in protecting innocent third parties who may
be harmed by the patient's treatment decision. When the patient's exercise of
his free choice could adversely and directly affect the health, safety, or security
of others, the patient's right of self-determination must frequently give way.
Thus, for example, courts have required competent adults to undergo medical
procedures against their will if necessary to protect the public health, *Jacobson
v. Massachusetts* (recognizing enforceability of compulsory smallpox vaccination law); to prevent a serious risk to prison security, *Myers* (compelling prisoner with kidney disease to submit to dialysis over his protest rather than ac-
quiescing in his demand to be transferred to a lower-security prison); or to
prevent the emotional and financial abandonment of the patient's minor children, *Application of President & Directors of Georgetown College, Inc.* (ordering mother of seven-month-old infant to submit to blood transfusion over her
religious objections because of the mother's "responsibility to the community
to care for her infant"); *Holmes v. Silver Cross Hosp.*, (indicating that patient's
status as father of minor child might justify authorizing blood transfusion to
save his life despite his religious objections).

On balance, the right to self-determination ordinarily outweighs any countervailing state interests, and competent persons generally are permitted to refuse medical treatment, even at the risk of death. Most of the cases that have
held otherwise, unless they involved the interest in protecting innocent third
parties, have concerned the patient's competency to make a rational and considered choice of treatment.

6. These four interests have never been found to override a competent person's choice (on nonreligious grounds) to refuse care. As noted above,
however, there are few such cases, and it may merely be that the right case
has not yet come along. What sort of fact pattern do you think might perhaps lead a court to decide against allowing a competent patient to refuse
care?

7. Note that when the state claims it wants to "preserve life," it is not claiming
it wants to do this to help Ms. Bouvia. Rather, it is claiming that preserving

(human) life is itself a good thing, and something that the state, on behalf of society, can try to do. In general, the courts have not given this state interest very much weight. Why do you think that is so? Might it have something to do with the medical circumstances of the patients in these disputes? (Recall what the *Quinlan* court said about the relevance of Karen Quinlan's condition.) What does the *Bouvia* court say about this factor in this case? Note how the *Conroy* court seems to have a somewhat different view from that expressed in *Quinlan* and *Bouvia*.

Do not assume that this factor might not be significant in the right case. You might wish to revisit this issue after reading the U.S. Supreme Court opinions in *Cruzan* and the physician-assisted suicide cases in chapter 11.

8. The *Bouvia* court concludes that the state interest in preventing suicide is not relevant. Ms. Bouvia's "decision to allow nature to take its course is not equivalent to an election to commit suicide."

How much of that determination turns on very specific facts? What constitutes "allowing nature" (a pre-existing illness?) to take its course? Given "her previously announced resolve to starve herself to death," can you be certain that the amount she eats is not partially determined by her desire to accelerate her death? Consider the following two possibilities:

a. Elizabeth Bouvia is eating as much as she can, and only stopping when she can eat no more without suffering. Nonetheless, she is not getting enough nutrition to sustain her life, and will die shortly from malnutrition if a nasogastric tube is not used.

b. Elizabeth Bouvia could very comfortably eat more, but is intentionally limiting the amount she consumes because she wants to die. Again, without the use of a nasogastric tube, she will shortly die from malnutrition.

Does the trial court's finding about the need for the nasogastric tube answer the question of whether we are dealing with situation (a) or (b)?

And should it matter if the facts of this case fit situation (a) or (b)? What do you think the *Bouvia* court would say? It did, after all, specifically conclude that "now she does not [have the ability] without artificial aids" to sustain herself. Is that determination crucial to the court's conclusion? Or is it saying that, even in situation (b), it is all right to let nature take its course?

If you conclude that it does not matter which scenario we are dealing with, (a) or (b), how do you justify that conclusion? Isn't this more complicated than the court suggests? Try to come up with a consistent rationale for categorizing what to do about the following scenarios, in addition to (a) and (b). In each case, assume the person has been determined to be competent and is not suffering from clinical depression:

c. A healthy person chooses to stop eating, having concluded that life is not worth living after the death of a spouse. A court must decide whether to force the use of a nasogastric tube.

d. Same situation as in (d), except that the person is a diabetic, and is refusing to use insulin.

e. A person who is very sick and suffering (like Ms. Bouvia), but who nonetheless has a healthy appetite and no difficulty eating, chooses to stop eating and die. The court is being asked to order the use of a feeding tube.

f. A person who has terminal cancer has swallowed a fatal dose of barbiturates. He has been brought to the emergency room and before the drugs began to take effect was refusing treatment. A court is being asked to force him to have his stomach pumped.

g. An otherwise healthy woman who is hemorrhaging after delivering a child refuses a lifesaving blood transfusion because she is a Jehovah's Witness.

h. An otherwise healthy person refuses antibiotics that would easily cure an infection that might become life-threatening because she knows that plants were killed in making the antibiotics and does not want to have any involvement in the misuse of God's creatures.

The *Bouvia* court observed that the "trial court erred by basing its decision on the 'motives' behind Elizabeth Bouvia's decision to exercise her rights. If a right exists, it matters not what 'motivates' its exercise. We find nothing in the law to suggest the right to refuse treatment may be exercised only if the patient's motives meet someone else's approval." Do you agree? If so, what remains of the state's alleged interest in preventing suicide? (For further discussion of these issues, see the notes following *Washington v. Glucksberg* in Chapter 11, including the comments on terminal sedation.)

9. The state interest in protecting third parties is given little weight in this case, as is generally true in similar cases. Like the state interest in preserving life, this interest seems something of a throwback to a view of society where the state has the right to use people to serve its own interests, even to the extent of preventing them from choosing to die. For example, in some of the cases where Jehovah's Witnesses have refused blood transfusions, there has been discussion of whether the patient has children who would become wards of the state. *See, e.g., Application of President & Directors of Georgetown College, Inc.*, 331 F.2d 1000 (D.C. Cir. 1964) ("The state . . . will not allow a parent to abandon a child, and so it should not allow this most ultimate of voluntary abandonments. The patient had a responsibility to the community to care for her infant. Thus the people had an interest in preserving the life of her mother."). Thus, under this view, a single, childless person would have more freedom to end her life than someone with children (especially, a single parent with children). It is questionable whether a modern court would accept this reasoning.

Oddly, those most likely to object to this view are not so much advocates for the rights of the parent—the one being denied a right, namely the right to end her life—as advocates for disabled persons. If we give substantial weight to the "protecting third parties" argument, we are effectively legally endorsing the proposition that certain persons—particularly, the able-bodied—are worth more to society than others, and should therefore be treated differently under the law. This argument can lead to greater acceptance of the "reasonableness" of allowing the disabled to end their lives, and perhaps even society's encouragement of such actions, given their alleged lack of contributions to the community.

MAKING DECISIONS FOR INCOMPETENT PATIENTS

One of the consequences of the *Quinlan* decision was increasing attention toward how to make health care decisions for incompetent persons. To understand later developments in the law, it is helpful to first ask what goals we are trying to accomplish in these situations. To help us better articulate these goals, consider the following hypothetical dilemma of an involuntary tourist:

> You have learned that some time in the next year you are going to be kidnapped and dropped by parachute from an airplane into a very hazardous and remote area in an Amazonian rain forest. There is nothing you can do to prevent this. However, you will be dropped into the forest with appropriate survival equipment. In addition, you will be given high-tech communications equipment, including devices to allow you to transmit real-time video images of your surroundings. The remoteness of your location will not permit rescuers to come to you, but you will be able to use your communications equipment to get whatever assistance you might wish from people who are expert in survival skills for this type of forest.
>
> You have had no experience with Amazonian rain forests, nor have you had any particular desire to learn about them.

There are two very different ways that our involuntary tourist might respond to this situation:

1. She might try to educate herself about Amazonian rain forests, becoming an expert in the hazards that will confront her. She would then rely primarily on her own survival skills. Of course, taking this course of action would require an investment of time and effort that might take her away from doing things that she would prefer.
2. A quite different, and equally plausible, response would be to choose not to learn anything about Amazonian rain forests. She will have her communication equipment, and she can rely on others to direct her out of the rain forest. If she chooses this option, she can to some extent avoid allowing her dreaded unavoidable trip to unduly affect her current life.

Finally, there is no reason to choose solely one option or the other. Our tourist might spend a bit of time educating herself about the upcoming *terra incognita* but also recognize that there are still many hazards about which she has not learned. She could hope to combine her own skills with those of the experts whom she will reach through her communications equipment.

The metaphor of the involuntary tourist is obviously inadequate for the dilemma of the unconscious patient. The biggest difference is that the goal of our tourist is relatively well-defined—getting out of the forest alive and in good condition—while that of the patient is far more nebulous—is it perhaps better to die, for example, than live in a persistent vegetative state?—and perhaps depends more on the patient's own wishes. Nonetheless, the metaphor does illustrate two very distinct themes that have flavored the evolution of the law relating to decision-making for incompetent patients: *substantive* versus *procedural* aspects of decision-making.

Advance Directives

In response to *Quinlan,* states began to pass laws providing for the use of "advance directives"— written documents in which people state what should be done if they became incompetent. Although the exact design and content of these documents have changed over time and there are problems with their use, many still believe that the use of advance directives represents the gold standard in respecting a patient's autonomy. Only if there is an advance directive are you (relatively) sure that you are doing what the patient wanted.

The first such documents were "living wills." The Natural Death Act mentioned in the *Bouvia* case represented California's early effort at allowing for such a document. Here is an excerpt from the language of Illinois's living will law (Ill. Rev. Stat. 1989, Ch. 110 ½ par. 703):

> If at any time I should have an incurable and irreversible injury, disease or illness judged to be a terminal condition by my attending physician who has personally examined me and has determined that my death is imminent except for death-delaying procedures, I direct that such procedures which would only prolong the dying process be withheld or withdrawn, and that I be permitted to die naturally with only the administration of medication, sustenance, or the performance of any medical procedure deemed necessary by my attending physician to provide me with comfort care.

Living wills are generally relevant in only very narrow circumstances, and for that reason are disfavored by many. Most living wills apply only if the patient is in a "terminal condition," which is commonly understood to mean that even if given aggressive care she will be dead in six months. Because doctors are often unable or unwilling to predict when a patient will likely die, it can be difficult to find one willing to determine that the conditions of the living will have been met. Some conditions in which many people might want to have care withheld—for example, a persistent vegetative state—do not constitute terminal conditions. In addition, there may be restrictions on what types of care may be withheld (for example, not allowing refusal of feeding through a nasogastric tube).

Returning to our involuntary tourist analogy, notice how the living will corresponds to the tourist who wishes to educate herself about the rain forest, or at least about some small subenvironment of it. She has chosen the substantive route, being willing to make her own choices about a particular outcome. Of course, if she doesn't land in that particular subenvironment, her education—like the living will—is relatively useless.

Efforts have been made to produce advance directives that are more comprehensive than the usual living will. A good example of such a document is the medical directive designed by Linda and Ezekiel Emanuel.[2] This document is not formally authorized as an advance directive by the laws of any state. On the other hand, it remains unclear to what extent state laws could constitutionally exclude legitimate evidence of a patient's end-of-life wishes merely because the patient chose to use a form of documentation that differed from the type of document specified in the state statutes.

The medical directive describes six hypothetical medical situations—e.g., having irreversible brain damage "that makes me unable to think or have feelings" but not necessarily any terminal illness—and asks signers to describe whether they would or would not want a number of specific therapies in each situation. This is a good analogy to the tourist who chooses to become an expert on almost everything about the rain forest.

In response to the inadequacy of living wills, an alternative approach has evolved, reflecting the views of the involuntary tourist who chooses not to learn about the rain forest. This is to appoint a person to make decisions when the patient is incompetent. These types of documents are referred to as durable powers of attorney for health care. The person filling out this form of directive need not give specific guidance to the person they appointed. Indeed, one can imagine someone filling out an advance directive that specifically contradicts any obligation on the part of the surrogate to try to determine what the patient would have wanted done, e.g.: "I want my surrogate to make all decisions relating to my health care based on what they think is best, regardless of whether such decisions are in agreement with any prediction of what I would have chosen in the circumstances."

Finally, it is now common to find very flexible hybrid documents that let signers designate a surrogate decision-maker and also let them list conditions that limit the powers of that surrogate, for example by indicating when care should be withheld. This comports with the tourist who wants to be making her own decisions about some aspects of the rain forest, but is willing to let others be the decision-makers outside of those situations.

Beyond Advance Directives

Relatively few people have filled out an advance directive. In an effort to improve this situation, the federal government passed the Patient Self-Determination Act in 1990. This act requires certain entities, such as hospitals, nursing homes, and health maintenance organizations, to inform patients about any rights they have to refuse care under state law, and to ask for a copy of any advance directive the patient may have already completed. In hospitals, this process usually takes place when the patient is being admitted. Some studies suggest that the act has had some effect on encouraging more patients to complete advance directives, but not a huge one. Most people still have not completed such forms.

A further legal development has dealt with the situation of persons who fail to complete advance directives. As you will see from the cases that follow, it is difficult to decide what should be done for them. Moreover, as a legal matter, there is no single person who is authorized to make decisions for them. For example, absent specific legislation, a wife has no particular authority to make health care decisions for her unconscious husband. (Indeed, the general rule is that no person has any authority to make any decision—health care or other— for any other person. The only broad exception is parents, who have the legal authority to make binding decisions for their children.) The wife could get that authority by a court proceeding in which she is appointed as his legal guardian with specific authority over health care decisions. This takes money and effort that few family members choose or can afford to invest.

To simplify matters, states have begun passing statutes that, somewhat arbitrarily, appoint a particular person as a decision-maker for someone who is incompetent. These surrogacy laws now exist in over two-thirds of the states. An edited version of the Illinois law follows.

ILLINOIS HEALTH CARE SURROGATE ACT

(Ill. Ann. Stat. ch 755, para. 40/1 et seq.)

Sec. 5. Legislative findings and purposes. (a) Findings. . . . Lack of decisional capacity, alone, should not prevent decisions to forgo life-sustaining treatment from being made on behalf of persons who lack decisional capacity and have no known applicable living will or power of attorney for health care.

Uncertainty and lack of clarity in the law concerning the making of private decisions concerning medical treatment and to forgo life-sustaining treatment, without judicial involvement, causes unnecessary emotional distress to the individuals involved and unduly impedes upon the individual right to forgo life-sustaining treatment.

The enactment of statutory guidelines for private decision making will bring improved clarity and certainty to the process for implementing decisions concerning medical treatment and to forgo life-sustaining treatment and will substantially reduce the associated emotional distress for involved parties.

Sec. 10. Definitions. . . .

"Qualifying condition" means the existence of one or more of the following conditions in a patient certified in writing in the patient's medical record by the attending physician and by at least one other qualified physician:

(1) "Terminal condition" means an illness or injury for which there is no reasonable prospect of cure or recovery, death is imminent, and the application of life-sustaining treatment would only prolong the dying process.

(2) "Permanent unconsciousness" means a condition that, to a high degree of certainty, (i) will last permanently, without improvement, (ii) in which thought, sensation, purposeful action, social interaction, and awareness of self and environment are absent, and (iii) for which initiating or continuing life-sustaining treatment, in light of the patient's medical condition, provides only minimal medical benefit.

(3) "Incurable or irreversible condition" means an illness or injury (i) for which there is no reasonable prospect of cure or recovery, (ii) that ultimately will cause the patient's death even if life-sustaining treatment is initiated or continued, (iii) that imposes severe pain or otherwise imposes an inhumane burden on the patient, and (iv) for which initiating or continuing life-sustaining treatment, in light of the patient's medical condition, provides only minimal medical benefit.

The determination that a patient has a qualifying condition creates no presumption regarding the application or non-application of life-sustaining treatment. It is only after a determination by the attending physician that the patient has a qualifying condition that the surrogate decision maker may consider whether or not to forgo life-sustaining treatment. . . .

Sec. 15. Applicability. This Act applies to patients who lack decisional capacity or who have a qualifying condition. This Act does not apply to instances in which the patient has an operative and unrevoked living will . . . or an authorized agent under a power of attorney for health care . . . and the patient's condition falls within the coverage of the [living will or power of attorney]. . . .

Sec. 20. Private decision making process. . . (b) Decisions whether to forgo life-sustaining treatment on behalf of a patient without decisional capacity are lawful, without resort to the courts or legal process, if the patient has a qualifying condition and if the decisions are made in accordance with one of the following paragraphs in this subsection and otherwise meet the requirements of this Act:

(1) Decisions whether to forgo life-sustaining treatment on behalf of a minor or adult patient who lacks decisional capacity may be made by a surrogate decision maker or makers in consultation with the attending physician, in the order and priority provided in Section 25. A surrogate decision maker shall make decisions for the adult patient conforming as closely as possible to what the patient would have done or intended under the circumstances, taking into account evidence that includes, but is not limited to, the patient's personal, philosophical, religious and moral beliefs and ethical values relative to the pur-

pose of life, sickness, medical procedures, suffering, and death. Where possible, the surrogate shall determine how the patient would have weighed the burdens and benefits of initiating or continuing life-sustaining treatment against the burdens and benefits of that treatment. . . . If the adult patient's wishes are unknown and remain unknown after reasonable efforts to discern them or if the patient is a minor, the decision shall be made on the basis of the patient's best interests as determined by the surrogate decision maker. In determining the patient's best interests, the surrogate shall weigh the burdens on and benefits to the patient of initiating or continuing life-sustaining treatment against the burdens and benefits of that treatment and shall take into account any other information, including the views of family and friends, that the surrogate decision maker believes the patient would have considered if able to act for herself or himself. . . .

    Sec. 25. Surrogate decision making. (a) When a patient lacks decisional capacity, the health care provider must make a reasonable inquiry as to the availability and authority of a health care agent [under a power of attorney previously filled out by the patient]. When no health care agent is authorized and available, the health care provider must make a reasonable inquiry as to the availability of possible surrogates listed in items (1) through (8) of this subsection. The surrogate decision makers, as identified by the attending physician, are then authorized to make decisions as follows: . . . (ii) for patients who lack decisional capacity and have a qualifying condition, medical treatment decisions including whether to forgo life-sustaining treatment on behalf of the patient may be made without court order or judicial involvement in the following order of priority:

(1) the patient's guardian of the person;
(2) the patient's spouse;
(3) any adult son or daughter of the patient;
(4) either parent of the patient;
(5) any adult brother or sister of the patient;
(6) any adult grandchild of the patient;
(7) a close friend of the patient;
(8) the patient's guardian of the estate.

    The health care provider shall have the right to rely on any of the above surrogates if the provider believes after reasonable inquiry that neither a health care agent [under a power of attorney] nor a surrogate of higher priority is available.

    Where there are multiple surrogate decision makers at the same priority level in the hierarchy, it shall be the responsibility of those surrogates to make reasonable efforts to reach a consensus as to their decision on behalf of the patient regarding the forgoing of life-sustaining treatment. If 2 or more surrogates who are in the same category and have equal priority indicate to the attending physician that they disagree about the health care matter at issue, a majority of the available persons in that category . . . shall control. . . .

Of course, even with advance directives and laws that automatically appoint surrogates, there are still numerous issues that remain in deciding care for incompetent persons. One issue that will always remain relates to determining when a person is incompetent, and is addressed in the case that follows. The complex issues relating to how a surrogate decision maker should determine what to do are explored later in this chapter.

NOTES AND QUESTIONS:
Advance Directives

1. There are a variety of places to locate advance directives on the web. One is the site for Choice in Dying, which has created its own versions of advance directives for each of the states, at *www.choices.org*. Look up the advance directives for your state. Is there a classic living will? Is there a form that lets you give broad instructions about the care you want without having to appoint a surrogate decision-maker? Decide what kind of care you would want, and complete the form. (Note that your completed document might now be legally effective, even if you do not fully meet the technicalities relating to getting witnesses or notarization that the statute might require. Does this make you take the task somewhat more seriously?)

2. Why do you think relatively few people have completed advance directives? How did you feel when you completed the form yourself?

3. Do you think the approach taken by the Patient Self-Determination Act, to have issues about advance directives addressed when a patient is admitted to a hospital, is a good one? What problems might you foresee in such an approach? Can you think of any better time to have a discussion about advance directives? Who might best discuss these documents with the patient? Might there have been political reasons for the approach taken in the Act, with Congress not willing to impose a burden upon a politically powerful group of professionals?[3]

4. In several studies people have been asked questions about specific kinds of care they might want in certain settings (like the scenarios above for the medical directive), and the surrogate decision-makers they had appointed were asked what care they would have chosen for the patient in those situations. Often, there is not a great deal of agreement between the patient and the surrogate. Should we be concerned about that? Does it demonstrate that the process of using advance directives is less useful than previously assumed? Or might the involuntary tourist analogy suggest a different conclusion, based on a different premise about what makes a particular decision by a surrogate "right"?

5. How do you think the Illinois legislature came up with the specific ordering of persons who might be appointed surrogates? Does the use of such a list make sense to you?

6. How useful is it to both appoint a surrogate decision-maker and also put language in the advance directive that imposes specific substantive criteria for how the surrogate must make decisions? Given the nearly infinite variety of ways people die, how likely is it that a person will be able to come up with language that unequivocally states that a particular element of care must be withheld or provided in whatever circumstance that person ends up in? Note that so long as there is ambiguity, a health care provider might be able to use the substantive language to claim that the surrogate was denied the right to take the action proposed. In contrast, if there were no substantive language in the form, there would be less ground for anyone to oppose the surrogate.

Assuming that a person truly trusts the surrogate he is appointing, it might be better not to limit the surrogate's authority in the advance directive itself. Specific wishes the person wishes to communicate to the surrogate can be provided in discussions or in informal writings given to the surrogate (which might specifically state that they are not meant to limit the surrogate's powers).[4]

7. Assume that a person did fill out a durable power of attorney for health care, appointing a surrogate and specifically mentioning the power to withhold life-sustaining treatment, but with no guidance on how that power should be exercised. What substantive rules should limit the exercise of that power? Given how few advance directives have been litigated, there is very little guidance from the courts.

No doubt there are many circumstances in which it would be inappropriate to allow a surrogate to exercise a power to refuse life-sustaining care. For example, if an otherwise healthy diabetic ends up in a coma, which can easily be treated by fluids given over a period of hours, it would be reasonable for health care providers to contest a surrogate's attempt to refuse consent for the treatment. Assume, however, that the patient has a significant medical problem such that competent patients in a similar situation might themselves think about refusing care. In such a circumstance, should the surrogate be required to prove with at least some minimal amount of evidence that the patient would have wanted care withdrawn? Would imposing such a requirement at least partially subvert the purpose of an advance directive, which is to allow the decision to be made by the agent?

8. Can an agent make decisions that are not necessarily in the narrow "best interests" of the patient? Imagine, for example, that a patient is in a persistent vegetative state after an automobile accident. There is evidence that the patient had stated a desire not to be kept alive in such a condition. However, there is a lawsuit pending against the driver of the other car, and the patient's lawyer advises that it would be highly desirable for the patient to be

kept alive for the jury to see him at trial. The trial is not expected to take place for another year or two. The proceeds of the lawsuit would benefit the patient's wife and children, whom he loved.

Can the surrogate decide to keep the patient alive? In doing so, the surrogate might be viewed as acting against the expressed wishes of the patient, or, even if there were no such expressed wishes, the best interests of the patient. To avoid this problem, should patients add language to advance directives that specifically tries to override any duty on the part of the surrogate to follow any "best interest" rules, at least to the extent that such rules do not recognize the possibility of altruistic behavior?

9. In the Illinois statute, note how statutorily appointed surrogates are given only limited authority to withdraw life-sustaining care. Under what clinical situations will a surrogate have such power? Do you agree with the concept of limiting such a grant of power by defining the specific circumstances? (Note how this directly deals with some of the problems raised in note 7, such as withdrawing care on the healthy diabetic.) Assuming you agree with the general concept, do you agree with the categories created ? Would you allow life-sustaining care to be withdrawn in a broader or narrower set of circumstances? What are they?

10. Assuming that a patient in Illinois is in one of the categories that allows the surrogate to withdraw life-sustaining care, what substantive rules control the exercise of that discretion by the surrogate? Review the issues raised in notes 7 and 8. Are there reasons for filling out an advance directive and perhaps giving a surrogate greater discretion than is provided by the statute?

LANE V. CANDURA

Appeals Court of Massachusetts

376 N.E.2d 1232 (Mass. App. Ct. 1978)

OPINION BY THE COURT:

This case concerns a 77-year old widow, Mrs. Rosaria Candura, of Arlington, who is presently a patient at the Symmes Hospital in Arlington suffering from gangrene in the right foot and lower leg. Her attending physicians recommended in April that the leg be amputated without delay. After some vacillation, she refused to consent to the operation, and she persists in that refusal. Her daughter, Grace R. Lane of Medford, filed a petition in the Probate Court for Middlesex County seeking appointment of herself as temporary guardian with authority to consent to the operation on behalf of her mother. An order and a judgment were entered in the Probate Court to that effect, from which the guardian ad litem appointed to represent Mrs. Candura has appealed.

We hold that Mrs. Candura has the right under the law to refuse to submit either to medical treatment or a surgical operation, that on the evidence and findings in this case the decision is one that she may determine for herself, and that therefore her leg may not be amputated unless she consents to that course of action.

The right of a person in most circumstances to decline treatment is clearly recognized in the important recent case of *Superintendent of Belchertown State Sch. v. Saikewicz.* "The constitutional right to privacy, as we conceive it, is an expression of the sanctity of individual free choice and self-determination as fundamental constituents of life. The value of life as so perceived is lessened not by a decision to refuse treatment, but by the failure to allow a competent human being the right of choice." Although the *Saikewicz* case also recognizes certain countervailing interests of the State which may in some cases outweigh the right of a competent individual to refuse life saving or life prolonging treatment, the case before us does not involve factors which would bring it within those lines of cases and thus warrant a court's overriding the will of a competent person.

The principal question arising on the record before us, therefore, is whether Mrs. Candura has the legally requisite competence of mind and will to make the choice for herself. We look first to the findings of fact made by the judge who heard the testimony, including that of Mrs. Candura herself. His decision does not include a clear-cut finding that Mrs. Candura lacks the requisite legal competence. The nearest approach to such a finding is contained in the following passage from his decision:

"It is fair to conclude—without necessarily finding that the ward is mentally ill for all purposes—that she is incapable of making a rational and competent choice to undergo or reject the proposed surgery to her right leg. To this extent, at least, her behavior is irrational. She has closed her mind to the entire issue to the extent that the Court cannot conclude that her decision to reject further treatment is rational and informed. . . . In the absence of substantial evidence that the ward has come to her current position as a result of a rational process after careful consideration of the medical alternatives, the Court finds that her confused mental condition resulting from her underlying senility and depression warrants the exercise of the jurisdiction of this Court and the application of a substitute choice for the ward as enunciated in the [*Saikewicz*] case. . . ."

In context, the quoted passage means only that, given some indications of a degree of senility and confusion on some subjects, the judge was not satisfied that Mrs. Candura arrived at her decision in a rational manner, i.e., "after careful consideration of the medical alternatives." We do not think that the passage can be construed as a finding of legal incompetence, and we do not think that the evidence in the case would have warranted such a finding.

The facts found by the judge or established by uncontradicted evidence are as follows. . . . She originally agreed to amputation of the leg, but she withdrew her consent on the morning scheduled for the operation. . . . She has discussed with some persons the reasons for her decision: that she has been unhappy since the death of her husband; that she does not wish to be a burden to her children; that she does not believe that the operation will cure her; that she does not wish to live as an invalid or in a nursing home; and that she does not fear death but welcomes it. She is discouraged by the failure of the earlier operations to arrest the advance of the gangrene. She tends to be stubborn and somewhat irascible. In her own testimony before the judge she expressed a desire to get well but indicated that she was resigned to death and was adamantly against the operation. Her testimony (corroborated by that of several of the witnesses) showed that she is lucid on some matters and confused on others. Her train of thought sometimes wanders. Her conception of time is distorted. She is hostile to certain doctors. She is on occasion defensive and sometimes combative in her responses to questioning. But she has exhibited a high degree of awareness and acuity when responding to questions concerning the proposed operation. She has made it clear that she does not wish to have the operation even though that decision will in all likelihood lead shortly to her death. We find no indication in any of the testimony that that is not a choice with full appreciation of the consequences. The most that is shown is that the decision involves strong emotional factors, that she does not choose to discuss the decision with certain persons, and that occasionally her resolve against giving consent weakens.

We start with the proposition that, in a proceeding for the appointment of a guardian . . . , the burden is on the petitioner to prove that the proposed ward is incompetent. A person is presumed to be competent unless shown by the evidence not to be competent. Such evidence is lacking in this case. We recognize that Dr. Kelley, one of two psychiatrists who testified, did state that in his opinion Mrs. Candura was incompetent to make a rational choice whether to consent to the operation. His opinion appears to have been based upon (1) his inference from her unwillingness to discuss the problem with him that she was unable to face up to the problem or to understand that her refusal constituted a choice; (2) his characterization of "an unwilling[ness], for whatever reason, to consent to life saving treatment . . . as suicidal"; and (3) a possibility, not established by evidence as a reasonable probability, that her mind might be impaired by toxicity caused by the gangrenous condition. His testimony, read closely, and in the context of the questions put to him, indicates that his opinion is not one of incompetency in the legal sense, but rather that her ability to make a rational choice (by which he means the medically rational choice) is impaired by the confusion existing in her mind by virtue of her consideration of irrational and emotional factors. . . .

The decision of the judge, as well as the opinion of Dr. Kelley, predicates the necessity for the appointment of a guardian chiefly on the irrationality (in medical terms) of Mrs. Candura's decision to reject the amputation. Until she changed her original decision and withdrew her consent to the amputation, her competence was not questioned. But the irrationality of her decision does not justify a conclusion that Mrs. Candura is incompetent in the legal sense. The law protects her right to make her own decision to accept or reject treatment, whether that decision is wise or unwise.

Similarly, the fact that she has vacillated in her resolve not to submit to the operation does not justify a conclusion that her capacity to make the decision is impaired to the point of legal incompetence. Indeed, her reaction may be readily understandable in the light of her prior surgical experience and the prospect of living the remainder of her life nonambulatory. Senile symptoms, in the abstract, may, of course, justify a finding of incompetence, but the inquiry must be more particular. What is lacking in this case is evidence that Mrs. Candura's areas of forgetfulness and confusion cause, or relate in any way to, impairment of her ability to understand that in rejecting the amputation she is, in effect, choosing death over life. This is not a case, therefore, like *State v. Northern*, in which the ward elected both to live and to reject an amputation operation, not appreciating that she must choose. Rather, this case is like *In the Matter of Quackenbush*, in which an elderly person, although subject (like Mrs. Candura) to fluctuations in mental lucidity and to occasional losses of his train of thought, was held to be competent to reject a proposed operation to amputate gangrenous legs because he was capable of appreciating the nature and consequences of his decision.

Mrs. Candura's decision may be regarded by most as unfortunate, but on the record in this case it is not the uninformed decision of a person incapable of appreciating the nature and consequences of her act. We cannot anticipate whether she will reconsider and will consent to the operation, but we are all of the opinion that the operation may not be forced on her against her will.

NOTES AND QUESTIONS: *Lane v. Candura*

1. While it is commonly said that legal determinations of competency are "all-or-nothing," *Lane* represents the more correct view, especially in the health care context. It is necessary to determine exactly what decision needs to be made, and then specifically evaluate the person's capacity to understand the issues relevant to making the decision.

Here are some observations on this issue from a recent report by the National Bioethics Advisory Commission:[5]

> In practice, it is not usually difficult to determine whether a person lacks all ability to make decisions, so findings of incapacity in this global sense are not often subject to much disagreement. Much more challenging (and the subject of numerous "hard cases" in the law) is determining whether someone with limited decisional capacity has sufficient capacity to make a particular choice, thereby demonstrating a level of capacity that one, on moral principle, should honor.

Individuals who have some cognitive deficit that renders them incapable of making some treatment decisions may nevertheless be quite functional and independent in activities of daily living. Having a decisional impairment need not imply a particular social or legal status. As a functional term, decisional impairment is neutral with respect to other particular characteristics an individual may possess. Moreover, as Grisso and Appelbaum have noted, what counts as impaired decisionmaking capacity is partly determined by the standard of competence that is chosen.

Capacity refers to an ability, or set of abilities, which may be situation or context-specific. There is a growing consensus that the standards for assessing decision-making capacity include the ability to evidence a choice, the ability to understand relevant information, the ability to appreciate the situation and its consequences, and the ability to manipulate information rationally. . . . Whether the context is treatment or research, the particular standard or combination of standards selected for assessing capacity will determine what counts as impaired decision making. . . . Thus, what counts as decisional capacity is dependent on a subtle set of assumptions and evaluations.

2. Does the court accept the fact that Mrs. Candura was showing some symptoms of senility? What does it make of that fact? Does the existence of a real clinical disorder that influences one's thinking necessarily determine whether a person is competent to make a particular decision?

3. Should a psychiatric consult always be required in evaluating the competence of a patient? Why or why not?

4. Cases like *Lane* almost always involve patients who are attempting to *refuse* care. This reflects the general perception that health care providers are unlikely to question the competence of a patient who accepts the provider's recommendation about getting a certain type of care. In other words, scrutiny of a patient's competence is often applied on a sliding scale, with greater attention paid to the possible incompetence of patients who are refusing recommended care, particularly where the care is needed to sustain the patient's life.

Is it inappropriate to apply such a scale? In a world of limited resources, is it unreasonable to begin with an assumption of competence, and to use the fact that the patient is making a decision that most competent patients would view as irrational as a basis for seeking greater verification of the patient's competence?

5. A patient may be able to demonstrate competence at making particular decisions even if he is not able to speak, and even if he is not aware that he is answering a question. Bob has advanced Alzheimer's disease, such that he no longer speaks intelligibly. When he gets his lunch trays, I notice that he leaves the ice cream uneaten unless it is chocolate. Would it be appropriate to say he has the capacity to decide what type of ice cream he likes?

6. As the court notes, the starting assumption is that a person is competent until proven otherwise. This assumption is reversed for one large group:

minors (in most states, persons under the age of 18). In general, a minor lacks the authority to make a broad array of legally binding decisions, including health care decisions. Thus, for example, a doctor will usually need to get a parent's consent in order to treat a minor for a nonemergency condition. Most states do, however, have some specific categories of medical care for which a minor is given authority to consent. For example, it is not uncommon for state laws to allow minors the authority to seek and obtain care on their own for reproductive matters.

In addition, just as a competent adult can be proven incompetent, a minor can obtain the status of being "legally competent" before reaching the age of majority. The most common method is to become "emancipated." While state laws vary on what this means (and may be somewhat vague in defining it), a minor is usually considered emancipated when she is living on her own, independent of her parents, or when she has married.

Apart from being emancipated, a minor can also attempt to demonstrate that she has the maturity to make her own decisions and therefore should be declared a "mature minor." This is a subjective determination, based not on any single specific aspect of the minor's life but rather on an overall evaluation of maturity.

In bioethics, these issues are most likely to arise where a minor is attempting to refuse life-sustaining treatment. Consider the following scenarios:

a. Wendy, 16, has been getting cancer chemotherapy on and off for several years. After a relapse, she is told that another round of chemotherapy has at most a 5 percent chance of achieving remission, although no one can predict how long the remission would last. Her parents insist that she be given the therapy. She insists on refusing it and being allowed to die. Should she be permitted to make that choice?

b. Laura, 15, is a Jehovah's Witness, as are her parents. She suffers from a rare form of anemia that will lead to her death unless she receives blood transfusions. She wishes to refuse the transfusions. Her parents accept her choice. Assume that, as a legal matter, a court would generally override the parent's refusal of treatment on the ground that it is beyond the range of discretion allowed parents and so would constitute child abuse. Should a court nonetheless allow Laura's own wishes to govern, perhaps finding that she is a mature minor? How could one determine that a minor has ever had sufficient life experience to be able to knowingly end her life in furtherance of religious beliefs?

7. In March 1999, 42-year-old Georgette Smith told her 68-year-old mother, Shirley Egan, that she wanted to place her in a nursing home. Ms. Egan managed to get a gun and shot her daughter. The bullet severed Ms. Smith's spine, making her a quadraplegic. She "can speak, but only with great effort; she is unable to swallow and must be fed through a tube. She has no control of her bodily functions and is at risk, doctors said, of pneu-

monia, ulcers and bed sores." Her condition is irreversible, and a psychiatric evaluation found her to be mentally competent.[6] Ms. Smith begged a
judge to be allowed to die, and was granted that wish. Her ventilator was
turned off barely two and a half months after she was shot.

Is it absolutely clear that Ms. Smith was competent to make the decision to die? While she passed all standard tests of competence, might some
decisions require a longer time to make sure that the patient fully appreci-
ates the consequences? For patients like Ms. Smith who have recently suffered high spinal cord injuries, there is evidence that the transition from
being a healthy, fully mobile person to a quadriplegic is such a huge change
that it may take several months for the person to fully absorb the consequences.[7] Assume, for example, that one week after such a transition, 99
percent of such patients begged to be allowed to die, even though they
were told they would probably get used to their condition. After one
month, perhaps only 75 percent wanted to die. At two months and four
months, maybe the numbers are reduced to 50 percent and 25 percent. Do
these hypothetical figures suggest something about limits on the patient's
ability to make a knowing decision early after the accident? Would anyone
object to requiring the patient to wait at least a week? If not, then we are already accepting some notion of lack of competence early after the event,
and it is merely a question of determining how long to wait before following
the patient's wishes.

A similar example is the case of Dax Cowart, who was horribly burned
in a propane gas explosion and who begged to be allowed to die during the
many months of painful treatments that followed. Yet in spite of being blind
and having lost the use of his hands, Cowart went on to graduate from law
school, has a very productive life, and now describes himself as "happier
than most people." Nonetheless, he emphatically insists that it was wrong
of his doctors to have ignored his requests to die.[8]

8. Consider the following excerpt from Ronald Dworkin's *Life's Dominion*:

> When Andrew Firlik was a medical student, he met a fifty-four-year-old Alz-
> heimer's victim whom he called Margo. . . . The apartment had many locks to
> keep Margo from slipping out at night and wandering in the park in her night-
> gown, which she had done before. Margo said she knew who Firlik was each
> time he arrived, but she never used his name, and he suspected this was just
> politeness. She said she was reading mysteries, but Firlik "noticed that her
> place in the book jumps randomly from day to day. . . ." Margo attended an art
> class for Alzheimer's victims—they all, including her, painted pretty much the
> same picture every time, except near the end, just before death, when the pic-
> tures became more primitive. Firlik was confused, he said, by the fact that "de-
> spite her illness, or maybe somehow because of it, Margo is undeniably one of
> the happiest people I have ever known."[9]

Dworkin then discusses a question that has intrigued commentators: what
would we do if Margo had completed an advance directive that, according

to its terms, required the withdrawal of the care that was keeping Margo alive?

In particular, we can assume that Margo had completed an advance directive like the medical directive, which asked her to document what care she would desire under a variety of conditions, among them a brain disease that was irreversible and made her unable to recognize people. She had stated that if she was in such a condition, she wished not to be given antibiotics to fight an infection. Margo catches pneumonia, which could be easily treated with antibiotics. Do we, or do we not, give her the medication?

This situation raises a problem that could not arise in the fact patterns that led to the development of advance directives. Persons like Karen Ann Quinlan were unconscious; therefore there was no possibility of them giving us guidance that might conflict with the instructions in an advance directive. But in today's society, questions about the withdrawal of care are far more likely to arise with the huge numbers of elderly patients who become demented than with persons who are unconscious. Thus, Margo's situation is far from hypothetical. It raises fundamental questions about what we want advance directives to accomplish.

Andrew Firlik notes that Margo seems remarkably happy. We might well ask if she has the capacity to decide whether or not she wants to die. What do you think? Does the fact that she is actually enjoying life constitute a sufficient "statement" of her views to be accorded respect?

Most laws make it relatively easy for a person to revoke an advance directive. Indeed, in some cases the law makes it relatively clear that even incompetent persons can revoke advance directives if they object to something being done to them that would be required under the advance directive. Has Margo effectively revoked the advance directive under such a standard?

Even if a "yes" answer is a valid interpretation of the current law, we might well ask if we should change the law. We could rewrite it to clarify that Margo's behavior would not constitute a revocation of the advance directive, on the theory that the wishes of the fully competent Margo should override those of the later less competent demented Margo. The competent Margo would effectively sign a "Ulysses contract" designed to bind the actions of her future self. Such contracts are named after the actions of Odysseus (Ulysses) as recounted in Homer's *Odyssey*: to enable himself to listen to the seductive song of the Sirens yet resist its spell, Odysseus had his men bind him to the ship's mast so that he could not break free.

The Ulysses contract is most commonly discussed in the context of a person with mental illness who, during a period of competence, wishes to irrevocably bind himself to forced medical treatment later when (although not incompetent enough to legally require involuntary treatment) he might be vehemently refusing to consent to such treatment. Such contracts raise the complicated issue of when a court can order a person to comply with the terms of a contract, as opposed to merely awarding money damages for breaching the contract. Forced compliance is known as *specific performance*, which is often described as an "extraordinary remedy." It stems from a court's *equity* jurisdiction, the discretionary power to do what is just and fair in a very broad sense. Historically, specific performance has been a somewhat difficult remedy to obtain when dealing with personal services, such as an employment contract. While that circumstance has been changing over recent years, it is still true that the self-commitment of Ulysses contracts is controversial.

So how do you think a court might react to Margo's case? Absent a very explicit statute requiring that the wishes of the competent Margo win out, do you think it likely that a court will consider it just and fair to order a person's death, particularly where the person appears to be objecting to being allowed to die? Should a court respect the views of the competent Margo and allow her to die?[10]

In re Conroy

Supreme Court of New Jersey

486 A.2d 1209 (N.J. 1985)

OPINION BY JUSTICE SCHREIBER:

At issue here are the circumstances under which life-sustaining treatment may be withheld or withdrawn from incompetent, institutionalized, elderly patients with severe and permanent mental and physical impairments and a limited life expectancy. . . .

I

In 1979 Claire Conroy, who was suffering from an organic brain syndrome that manifested itself in her exhibiting periodic confusion, was adjudicated an incompetent, and plaintiff, her nephew, was appointed her guardian. . . .

At the time of trial, Ms. Conroy was no longer ambulatory and was confined to bed, unable to move from a semi-fetal position. She suffered from arteriosclerotic heart disease, hypertension, and diabetes mellitus; her left leg was gangrenous to her knee; she had several necrotic decubitus ulcers (bed sores) on her left foot, leg, and hip; an eye problem required irrigation; she had a urinary catheter in place and could not control her bowels; she could not speak; and her ability to swallow was very limited. On the other hand, she interacted with her environment in some limited ways: she could move her head, neck, hands, and arms to a minor extent; she was able to scratch herself, and had pulled at her bandages, tube, and catheter; she moaned occasionally when moved or fed through the tube, or when her bandages were changed; her eyes sometimes followed individuals in the room; her facial expressions were different when she was awake from when she was asleep; and she smiled on occasion when her hair was combed, or when she received a comforting rub.

Dr. Kazemi and Dr. Davidoff, a specialist in internal medicine who observed Ms. Conroy before testifying as an expert on behalf of the guardian, testified that Ms. Conroy was not brain dead, comatose, or in a chronic vegetative state. They stated, however, that her intellectual capacity was very limited, and that her mental condition probably would never improve. Dr. Davidoff characterized her as awake, but said that she was severely demented, was unable to respond to verbal stimuli, and, as far as he could tell, had no higher functioning or consciousness. Dr. Kazemi, in contrast, said that although she was confused and unaware, "she responds somehow."

The medical testimony was inconclusive as to whether, or to what extent, Ms. Conroy was capable of experiencing pain. . . .

Both doctors testified that if the nasogastric tube were removed, Ms. Conroy would die of dehydration in about a week. Dr. Davidoff believed that the resulting thirst could be painful but that Ms. Conroy would become unconscious long before she died. Dr. Kazemi concurred that such a death would be painful.

Dr. Kazemi stated that he did not think it would be acceptable medical practice to remove the tube and that he was in favor of keeping it in place. As he put it, "she's a human being and I guess she has a right to live if it's possible." Ms. Rittel, the nurse, also thought the tube should not be removed since in her view it was not an extraordinary treatment. The nursing home had taken no position on the subject.

Dr. Davidoff said that if he had been the treating physician and the case had not come to court, he would have removed the tube with the family's consent. In his opinion, although Ms. Conroy seemed to be receiving excellent care, she did not have long to live, perhaps a few months. In those circumstances, he considered nasogastric feeding an extraordinary, or optional, medical treatment, because it went "beyond the necessities of life." He analogized the nasogastric tube to a respirator that supplies oxygen and said that since Ms. Conroy was "hopelessly ill with no possibility of returning to any sort of cognitive function, in the face of possibly [sic] suffering taking place at the moment," he could recommend that the feeding tube be removed. . . .

II

This case requires us to determine the circumstances under which life-sustaining treatment may be withheld or withdrawn from an elderly nursing-home resident who is suffering from serious and permanent mental and physical impairments, who will probably die within approximately one year even with the treatment, and who, though formerly competent, is now incompetent to make decisions about her life-sustaining treatment and is unlikely to regain such competence. . . .

A tragic situation like that of Claire Conroy raises profoundly disturbing questions that do not lend themselves to easy answers or ideal solutions. As scientific advances make it possible for us to live longer than ever before, even when most of our physical and mental capacities have been irrevocably lost, patients and their families are increasingly asserting a right to die a natural death without undue dependence on medical technology or unnecessarily protracted agony—in short, a right to "die with dignity." On the other hand, all persons have a fundamental right to expect that their lives will not be foreshortened against their will. The President's Commission for the Study of Ethical Problems in Medicine and Biomedical and Behavioral Research . . . stated the problem this way: "Once someone realizes that the time and manner of death are substantially under the control of medical science, he or she wants to be protected against decisions that make death too easy and quick as well as from those that make it too agonizing and prolonged."

Deciding on a course of treatment for an incompetent patient without impinging on either of these two interests is a difficult task. To err either way—to keep a person alive under circumstances under which he would rather have been allowed to die, or to allow that person to die when he would have chosen to cling to life—would be deeply unfortunate. . . .

III

. . . In view of the case law, we have no doubt that Ms. Conroy, if competent to make the decision and if resolute in her determination, could have chosen to have her nasogastric tube withdrawn. Her interest in freedom from nonconsensual invasion of her bodily integrity would outweigh any state interest in preserving life or in safeguarding the integrity of the medical profession. In addition, rejecting her artificial means of feeding would not constitute attempted suicide, as the decision would probably be based on a wish to be free of medical intervention rather than a specific intent to die, and her death would result, if at all, from her underlying medical condition, which included her inability to swallow. Finally, removal of her feeding tube would not create a public health or safety hazard, nor would her death leave any minor dependents without care or support.

It should be noted that if she were competent, Ms. Conroy's right to self-determination would not be affected by her medical condition or prognosis. Our Legislature has recognized that an institutionalized, elderly person, whatever his physical and mental limitations and life expectancy, has the same right to receive medical treatment as a competent young person whose physical functioning is basically intact. Moreover, a young, generally healthy person, if competent, has the same right to decline life-saving medical treatment as a competent elderly person who is terminally ill. Of course, a patient's decision to accept or reject medical treatment may be influenced by his medical condition, treatment, and prognosis; nevertheless, a competent person's common-law and constitutional rights do not depend on the quality or value of his life. . . . .

IV

B.

The *Quinlan* decision dealt with a special category of patients: those in a chronic, persistent vegetative or comatose state. In a footnote, the opinion left open the question whether the principles it enunciated might be applicable to incompetent patients in "other types of terminal medical situations ° ° °, not necessarily involving the hopeless loss of cognitive or sapient life." We now are faced with one such situation: that of elderly, formerly competent nursing-home residents who, unlike Karen Quinlan, are awake and conscious and can interact with their environment to a limited extent, but whose mental and physical functioning is severely and permanently impaired and whose life expectancy, even with the treatment, is relatively short. The capacities of such people, while significantly diminished, are not as limited as those of irreversibly comatose persons, and their deaths, while no longer distant, may not be imminent. Large numbers of aged, chronically ill, institutionalized persons fall within this general category.

Such people (like newborns, mentally retarded persons, permanently comatose individuals, and members of other groups with which this case does not deal) are unable to speak for themselves on life-and-death issues concerning their medical care. This does not mean, however, that they lack a right to self-determination. . . .

Since the condition of an incompetent patient makes it impossible to ascertain definitively his present desires, a third party acting on the patient's behalf often cannot say with confidence that his treatment decision for the patient will further rather than frustrate the patient's right to control his own body. Nevertheless, the goal of decision-making for incompetent patients should be to determine and effectuate, insofar as possible, the decision that the patient would have made if competent. Ideally, both aspects of the patient's right to bodily integrity—the right to consent to medical intervention and the right to refuse it—should be respected.

In light of these rights and concerns, we hold that life-sustaining treatment may be withheld or withdrawn from an incompetent patient when it is clear that the particular patient would have refused the treatment under the circumstances involved. The standard we are enunciating is a subjective one, consistent with the notion that the right that we are seeking to effectuate is a very personal right to control one's own life. The question is not what a reasonable or average person would have chosen to do under the circumstances but what the particular patient would have done if able to choose for himself.

The patient may have expressed, in one or more ways, an intent not to have life-sustaining medical intervention. Such an intent might be embodied in a written document, or "living will," stating the person's desire not to have certain types of life-sustaining treatment administered under certain circumstances. It might also be evidenced in an oral directive that the patient gave to a family member, friend, or health care provider. It might consist of a durable power of attorney or appointment of a proxy authorizing a particular person to make the decisions on the patient's behalf if he is no longer capable of making them for himself. It might take the form of reactions that the patient voiced regarding medical treatment administered to others. It might also be deduced from a person's religious beliefs and the tenets of that religion, or from the patient's consistent pattern of conduct with respect to prior decisions about his own medical care. Of course, dealing with the matter in advance in some sort of thoughtful and explicit way is best for all concerned. . . .

Although all evidence tending to demonstrate a person's intent with respect to medical treatment should properly be considered by surrogate decision-makers, or by a court in the event of any judicial proceedings, the probative value of such evidence may vary depending on the remoteness, consistency, and thoughtfulness of the prior statements or actions and the maturity of the person at the time of the statements or acts. Thus, for example, an offhand remark about not wanting to live under certain circumstances made by a person when young and in the peak of health would not in itself constitute clear proof twenty years later that he would want life-sustaining treatment withheld under those circumstances. In contrast, a carefully considered position, especially if written, that a person had maintained over a number of years or that he had acted upon in comparable circumstances might be clear evidence of his intent.

Another factor that would affect the probative value of a person's prior statements of intent would be their specificity. Of course, no one can predict with accuracy the precise circumstances with which he ultimately might be faced. Nevertheless, any details about the level of impaired functioning and the forms of medical treatment that one would find tolerable should be incorporated into advance directives to enhance their later usefulness as evidence.

Medical evidence bearing on the patient's condition, treatment, and prognosis, like evidence of the patient's wishes, is an essential prerequisite to decision-making under the subjective test. The medical evidence must establish that the patient fits within the Claire Conroy pattern: an elderly, incompetent nursing-home resident with severe and permanent mental and physical impairments and a life expectancy of approximately one year or less. In addition, since the goal is to effectuate the patient's right of informed consent, the surrogate decision-maker must have at least as much medical information upon which to base his decision about what the patient would have chosen as one would expect a competent patient to have before consenting to or rejecting treatment. Such information might include evidence about the patient's present level of physical, sensory, emotional, and cognitive functioning; the degree of physical pain resulting from the medical condition, treatment, and termination of treatment, respectively; the degree of humiliation, dependence, and loss of dignity probably resulting from the condition and treatment; the life expectancy and prognosis for recovery with and without treatment; the various treatment options; and the risks, side effects, and benefits of each of those options. Particular care should be taken not to base a decision on a premature diagnosis or prognosis.

We recognize that for some incompetent patients it might be impossible to be clearly satisfied as to the patient's intent either to accept or reject the life-sustaining treatment. Many people may have spoken of their desires in general or casual terms, or, indeed, never considered or resolved the issue at all. In such cases, a surrogate decision-maker cannot presume that treatment decisions made by a third party on the patient's behalf will further the patient's right to self-determination, since effectuating another person's right to self-determination presupposes that the substitute decision-maker knows what the person would have wanted. Thus, in the absence of adequate proof of the patient's wishes, it is naive to pretend that the right to self-determination serves as the basis for substituted decision-making.

We hesitate, however, to foreclose the possibility of humane actions, which may involve termination of life-sustaining treatment, for persons who never clearly expressed their desires about life-sustaining treatment but who are now suffering a prolonged and painful death. An incompetent, like a minor child, is a ward of the state, and the state's *parens patriae* power supports the authority of its courts to allow decisions to be made for an incompetent that serve the incompetent's best interests, even if the person's wishes cannot be clearly established. This authority permits the state to authorize guardians to withhold or withdraw life-sustaining treatment from an incompetent patient if it is manifest that such action would further the patient's best interests in a narrow sense of the phrase, even though the subjective test that we articulated above may not be satisfied. We therefore hold that life-sustaining treatment may also be withheld or withdrawn from a patient in Claire Conroy's situation if either of two "best interests" tests—a limited-objective or a pure-objective test—is satisfied.

Under the limited-objective test, life-sustaining treatment may be withheld or withdrawn from a patient in Claire Conroy's situation when there is some trustworthy evidence that the patient would have refused the treatment, and the decision-maker is satisfied that it is clear that the burdens of the patient's continued life with the treatment outweigh the benefits of that life for him. By this we mean that the patient is suffering, and will continue to suffer throughout the expected duration of his life, unavoidable pain, and that the net burdens of his prolonged life (the pain and suffering of his life with the treatment less the amount and duration of pain that the patient would likely experience if the treatment were withdrawn) markedly outweigh any physical pleasure, emotional enjoyment, or intellectual satisfaction that the patient may still be able to derive from life. This limited-objective standard permits the termination of treatment for a patient who had not unequivocally expressed his desires before becoming incompetent, when it is clear that the treatment in question would merely prolong the patient's suffering.

Medical evidence will be essential to establish that the burdens of the treatment to the patient in terms of pain and suffering outweigh the benefits that the patient is experiencing. The medical evidence should make it clear that the treatment would merely prolong the patient's suffering and not provide him with any net benefit. Information is particularly important with respect to the degree, expected duration, and constancy of pain with and without treatment, and the possibility that the pain could be reduced by drugs or other means short of terminating the life-sustaining treatment. The same types of medical evidence that are relevant to the subjective analysis, such as the patient's life expectancy, prognosis, level of functioning, degree of humiliation and dependency, and treatment options, should also be considered.

This limited-objective test also requires some trustworthy evidence that the patient would have wanted the treatment terminated. This evidence could take any one or more of the various forms appropriate to prove the patient's intent under the subjective test. Evidence that, taken as a whole, would be too vague, casual, or remote to constitute the clear proof of the patient's subjective intent that is necessary to satisfy the subjective test—for example, informally expressed reactions to other people's medical conditions and treatment—might be sufficient to satisfy this prong of the limited-objective test.

In the absence of trustworthy evidence, or indeed any evidence at all, that the patient would have declined the treatment, life-sustaining treatment may still be withheld or withdrawn from a formerly competent person like Claire Conroy if a third, pure-objective test is satisfied. Under that test, as under the limited-objective test, the net burdens of the patient's life with the treatment should clearly and markedly outweigh the benefits that the patient derives from life. Further, the recurring, unavoidable and severe pain of the patient's life with the treatment should be such that the effect of administering life-sustaining treatment would be inhumane. Subjective evidence that the patient would not have wanted the treatment is not necessary under this pure-objective standard. Nevertheless, even in the context of severe pain, life-sustaining treatment should not be withdrawn from an incompetent patient who had previously expressed a wish to be kept alive in spite of any pain that he might experience.

Although we are condoning a restricted evaluation of the nature of a patient's life in terms of pain, suffering, and possible enjoyment under the limited-objective and pure-objective tests, we expressly decline to authorize decision-making based on assessments of the personal worth or social utility of another's life, or the value of that life to others. We do not believe that it would be appropriate for a court to designate a person with the authority to determine that someone else's life is not worth living simply because, to that person, the patient's "quality of life" or value to society seems negligible. The mere fact that a patient's functioning is limited or his prognosis dim does not mean that he is not enjoying what remains of his life or that it is in his best interests to die. More wide-ranging powers to make decisions about other people's lives, in our view, would create an intolerable risk for socially isolated and defenseless people suffering from physical or mental handicaps.

We are aware that it will frequently be difficult to conclude that the evidence is sufficient to justify termination of treatment under either of the "best interests" tests that we have described. Often, it is unclear whether and to what extent a patient such as Claire Conroy is capable of, or is in fact, experiencing pain. Similarly, medical experts are often unable to determine with any degree of certainty the extent of a nonverbal person's intellectual functioning or the depth of his emotional life. When the evidence is insufficient to satisfy either the limited-objective or pure-objective standard, however, we cannot justify the termination of life-sustaining treatment as clearly furthering the best interests of a patient like Ms. Conroy. . . .

C.

We emphasize that in making decisions whether to administer life-sustaining treatment to patients such as Claire Conroy, the primary focus should be the patient's desires and experience of pain and enjoyment—not the type of treatment involved. Thus, we reject the distinction that some have made between actively hastening death by terminating treatment and passively allowing a person to die of a disease as one of limited use in a legal analysis of such a decision-making situation.

Characterizing conduct as active or passive is often an elusive notion, even outside the context of medical decision-making. . . .The distinction is particularly nebulous, however, in the context of decisions whether to withhold or withdraw life-sustaining treatment. In a case like that of Claire Conroy, for example, would a physician who discontinued nasogastric feeding be actively causing her death by removing her primary source of nutrients; or would he merely be omitting to continue the artificial form of treatment, thus passively allowing her medical condition, which includes her inability to swallow, to take its natural course? The ambiguity inherent in this distinction is further heightened when one performs an act within an over-all plan of non-intervention, such as when a doctor writes an order not to resuscitate a patient. . . .

Furthermore, while nasogastric feeding and other medical procedures to ensure nutrition and hydration are usually well tolerated, they are not free from risks or burdens; they have complications that are sometimes serious and distressing to the patient. The volume of fluid needed to carry nutrients itself is sometimes harmful.

Finally, dehydration may well not be distressing or painful to a dying patient. For patients who are unable to sense hunger and thirst, withholding of feeding devices such as nasogastric tubes may not result in more pain than the termination of any other medical treatment. Indeed, it has been observed that patients near death who are not receiving nourishment may be more comfortable than patients in comparable conditions who are being fed and hydrated artificially. Thus, it cannot be assumed that it will always be beneficial for an incompetent patient to receive artificial feeding or harmful for him not to receive it.

Under the analysis articulated above, withdrawal or withholding of artificial feeding, like any other medical treatment, would be permissible if there is sufficient proof to satisfy the subjective, limited-objective, or pure-objective test. A competent patient has the right to decline any medical treatment, including artificial feeding, and should retain that right when and if he becomes incompetent. In addition, in the case of an incompetent patient who has given little or no trustworthy indication of an intent to decline treatment and for whom it becomes necessary to engage in balancing under the limited-objective or pure-objective test, the pain and invasiveness of an artificial feeding device, and the pain of withdrawing that device, should be treated just like the results of administering or withholding any other medical treatment. . . .

NOTES AND QUESTIONS:
In re Conroy

1. Before the case reached the New Jersey Supreme Court, Ms. Conroy had in fact died, with her feeding tube still in place. Normally, this would make the case moot—since there is no longer a controversy affecting a specific person—but the court chose to review the case because "the matter is of substantial importance and is capable of repetition but evades review."

2. In deciding that Ms. Conroy had the right to choose to refuse care, the court evaluated the four "state" interests commonly raised by the government in opposing such requests. As is usual, the court found those interests non-persuasive. (That portion of the opinion was reprinted in the notes following the *Bouvia* case, pp. 263–65.)

    With regard to the suicide issue, the court notes that "rejecting her artificial means of feeding would not constitute attempted suicide, as the decision would probably be based on a wish to be free of medical intervention rather than a specific intent to die, and her death would result, if at all, from her underlying medical condition, which included her inability to swallow." What if we knew the basis of her decision? Should her reasoning matter? What if Ms. Conroy were able to magically communicate with us, and said one of the following two things:

    a. "This life is absolutely dreadful—not because of the medical interventions, but rather just because lying in a bed, not being able to move, is a horrible way to live. I would rather be dead, and if removing the feeding tube is the way to make me dead, then let's go ahead and do it."

    b. "This life isn't so bad in itself, but I really hate having the feeding tube attached to me. I want it removed. I understand that I am going to die shortly after it is removed. Nonetheless, I do not want to remain attached to this feeding tube, since I find the tube intolerable."

Is the court saying that viewpoint (a) constitutes attempted suicide—and might *not* be allowed—whereas viewpoint (b) is more acceptable? Should this distinction matter? If so, how do you think it might affect people who are trying to refuse care? Should people who are refusing care because of the burdens of the care itself be more privileged than those who just don't want to continue the life that the care makes possible? (This issue differs from that discussed in the *Bouvia* notes—whether or not the suicide issue arises if the death occurs not because of the underlying condition but because of the patient's active attempt to starve to death, even if there is no inability to swallow. We will confront both of these aspects of suicide again in chapter 11.)

3. Note the court's comment that "if she were competent, Ms. Conroy's right to self-determination would not be affected by her medical condition or prognosis." In particular, it goes to great pains to observe that a "young, generally healthy person" and an elderly person have the same right to refuse care. Yet in the discussion of the state's interests (pp. 263–65, 286) the court spends quite a bit of time on the state interest in protecting third parties, and specifically comments on the fact that her death would not "leave any minor dependents without care or support." Are these two points consistent? If we are going to give any weight to the state interest in protecting third parties (and maybe we aren't), can we still claim that healthy people and the elderly have the same right to refuse care? Aren't healthy young people far more likely to have dependents (e.g., young children), and thus less likely to be allowed to die? (Recall the views of disability rights advocates, discussed in the notes after *Bouvia*.)

4. As we shall see in the next chapter, the Constitution places very few limits on the mechanisms that a state might adopt to make decisions for incompetent patients. The result is a variety of largely court-made rules used to determine when life-sustaining treatment can be removed from a person who has failed to give substantial guidance about health care modalities and for whom no decision-maker has been appointed either by the person or by statute. (Fortunately, many state statutes now automatically appoint a decision-maker, thus substantially alleviating this problem, since such decision-makers are often given relatively broad discretion.) *Conroy,* one of the most influential cases on this issue, is significant for the impact its reasoning has had on other courts.

5. One of the more important aspects of the *Conroy* opinion is its discussion of the distinction between what might be called "substitute decision-making" and "best interests" analysis. With regard to the former, it notes that life-sustaining treatment may be withheld "when it is clear that the particular patient would have refused the treatment under the circumstances involved." There is general agreement that if it is possible to determine what a patient would have wanted, such a "substituted decision" should be followed, rather than doing a "best interests" analysis.

On the other hand, in some circumstances, though we do not have very good information about what this particular person would have wanted done, a decision still has to be made about whether or not to have care terminated. The court notes that in such a circumstance, "it is naive to pretend that the right to self-determination serves as the basis for substituted decision-making." Rather, *we* (e.g., the judges or the appointed decision-maker) are making a decision with regard to what *we* think is best for that person. This is generally called "best interests" analysis.

6. Does it matter whether we are doing substitute decision-making rather than best interests analysis, apart from knowing which rule we are applying? Note the court's comment that when best interests analysis is applied, we are no longer fulfilling the patient's right to self-determination. If that is the case, does that mean we have greater discretion in making such decisions? For example, are we no longer bound by the need to respect the person's right to refuse care under the U.S. or a state constitution, since the person has not given us any useful guidance?

7. Assuming there is a difference between the standards involved in substitute decision-making and in best interests analysis, do you agree with how the *Conroy* court draws the line where one ends and the other begins? A major element in the court's analysis appears to be that substitute decision-making can be used only when there is "subjective" evidence of the patient's desires. This appears to refer to rather specific comments by that patient about what kind of care she would want. If there is no such evidence, the court seems to suggest that a best interests test is being applied.

Do we need specific evidence of a patient's wishes to conclude that we are furthering the patient's autonomy? Assume a patient never said a word about the kind of care that he would want, but he ends up in a condition in which there is good evidence about what the average person would want done. For example, he might be in a persistent vegetative state, with surveys demonstrating (hypothetically) that 99.9 percent of the public would want to be allowed to die under such circumstances. Why should we not view a decision to terminate care for that person as a way of effectuating a very good guess about what the person wanted? Does the fact that the evidence of the person's views comes from general knowledge about what others want make it less credible? After all, even when we use the specific subjective evidence that the court wants, there is still a possibility that we have guessed wrongly. (We will return to this issue with *Cruzan* in chapter 11.)

This question—to what extent should we be making decisions using merely naked statistical evidence?—raises issues that have been extensively debated in the legal literature. A man is hit by a bus that he never got a good look at. Some 80 percent of the buses traveling on that route at that time are owned by a single company. Is that enough evidence to allow a jury to conclude that, based on a legal standard requiring proof only of "more likely than not" (>50%), this company is liable for the man's injuries?[11] In general, a court would not find liability based solely on this evidence. Why do you think that rule was adopted? Is it relevant to the issues in *Conroy* and similar cases?

8. What are the two best interests tests announced by the court? When are they to be used? How would they apply to the actual case of Ms. Conroy? Given that she had never indicated her wishes, do you think that, had she not died before the case was resolved, either of them could have been met? (For the answer given by one of the judges in that case, see Justice Handler's opinion, partly concurring with and partly dissenting from the majority, at 486 A.2d 1245.)

Do you agree with these tests, and their outcome in this case? If not, do you think the tests should be refashioned to make it easier or harder to withdraw life-sustaining treatment?

9. The case of a formerly competent patient like Ms. Conroy is not especially helpful in demonstrating the difference between best interests analysis and substitute decision-making. On the other hand, there are cases in which it is clear we are required to do a best interests analysis. These involve persons who were never competent, such as infants or older persons with life-long cognitive disorders. Such patients never had the ability to tell us what they wanted, and thus there is no real possibility of doing the preferred method, substitute decision-making.

One of the more famous of these cases is *Superintendent of Belchertown State School v. Saikewicz*, 370 N.E.2d 417 (1977), decided almost a decade before *Conroy*. Joseph Saikewicz, 67, was profoundly mentally retarded. He had the mental age of an infant of two years and eight months. When he developed leukemia, a decision had to be made about whether or not to treat him with chemotherapy. The chemotherapy would have made him sicker, causing pain and discomfort in addition to a variety of other medical problems. Without the chemotherapy, he would perhaps live only for a matter of weeks. With it, he had a 30 percent to 50 percent chance of achieving a remission of the cancer for two to thirteen months.

The Supreme Judicial Court of Massachusetts first evaluated the state interests that might override Saikewicz's right to refuse care, and, as in *Conroy*, found them unpersuasive. The court then reasoned as follows:

> The "best interests" of an incompetent person are not necessarily served by imposing on such persons results not mandated as to competent persons similarly situated. It does not advance the interest of the State or the ward to treat the ward as a person of lesser status or dignity than others. To protect the incompetent person within its power, the State must recognize the dignity and worth of such a person and afford to that person the same panoply of rights and choices it recognizes in competent persons. If a competent person faced with death may choose to decline treatment which not only will not cure the person but which substantially may increase suffering in exchange for a possible yet brief prolongation of life, then it cannot be said that it is always in the "best in-

terests" of the ward to require submission to such treatment. Nor do statistical factors indicating that a majority of competent persons similarly situated choose treatment resolve the issue. The significant decisions of life are more complex than statistical determinations. Individual choice is determined not by the vote of the majority but by the complexities of the singular situation viewed from the unique perspective of the person called on to make the decision. To presume that the incompetent person must always be subjected to what many rational and intelligent persons may decline is to downgrade the status of the incompetent person by placing a lesser value on his intrinsic human worth and vitality. . . .

. . . Evidence that most people choose to accept the rigors of chemotherapy has no direct bearing on the likely choice that Joseph Saikewicz would have made. Unlike most people, Saikewicz had no capacity to understand his present situation or his prognosis. The guardian ad litem gave expression to this important distinction in coming to grips with this "most troubling aspect" of withholding treatment from Saikewicz: "If he is treated with toxic drugs he will be involuntarily immersed in a state of painful suffering, the reason for which he will never understand. Patients who request treatment know the risks involved and can appreciate the painful side-effects when they arrive. They know the reason for the pain and their hope makes it tolerable." To make a worthwhile comparison, one would have to ask whether a majority of people would choose chemotherapy if they were told merely that something outside of their previous experience was going to be done to them, that this something would cause them pain and discomfort, that they would be removed to strange surroundings and possibly restrained for extended periods of time, and that the advantages of this course of action were measured by concepts of time and mortality beyond their ability to comprehend.

To put the above discussion in proper perspective, we realize that an inquiry into what a majority of people would do in circumstances that truly were similar assumes an objective viewpoint not far removed from a "reasonable person" inquiry. While we recognize the value of this kind of indirect evidence, we should make it plain that the primary test is subjective in nature—that is, the goal is to determine with as much accuracy as possible the wants and needs of the individual involved. This may or may not conform to what is thought wise or prudent by most people. The problems of arriving at an accurate substituted judgment in matters of life and death vary greatly in degree, if not in kind, in different circumstances. For example, the responsibility of Karen Quinlan's father to act as she would have wanted could be discharged by drawing on many years of what was apparently an affectionate and close relationship. In contrast, Joseph Saikewicz was profoundly retarded and noncommunicative his entire life, which was spent largely in the highly restrictive atmosphere of an institution. While it may thus be necessary to rely to a greater degree on objective criteria, such as the supposed inability of profoundly retarded persons to conceptualize or fear death, the effort to bring the substituted judgment into step with the values and desires of the affected individual must not, and need not, be abandoned. . . .

[W]e now reiterate the substituted judgment doctrine as we apply it in the instant case. We believe that both the guardian ad litem in his recommendation and the judge in his decision should have attempted (as they did) to ascertain the incompetent person's actual interests and preferences. In short, the decision in cases such as this should be that which would be made by the incompetent person, if that person were competent, but taking into account the present and future incompetency of the individual as one of the factors which would necessarily enter into the decision-making process of the competent person. Having recognized the right of a competent person to make for himself the same decision as the court made in this case, the question is, do the facts on the record support the proposition that Saikewicz himself would have made the decision under the standard set forth. We believe they do.

The two factors considered by the probate judge to weigh in favor of administering chemotherapy were: (1) the fact that most people elect chemotherapy and (2) the chance of a longer life. Both are appropriate indicators of what Saikewicz himself would have wanted, provided that due allowance is taken for this individual's present and future incompetency. . . .

The probate judge identified six factors weighing against administration of chemotherapy. Four of these—Saikewicz's age, the probable side effects of treatment, the low chance of producing remission, and the certainty that treatment will cause immediate suffering—were clearly established by the medical testimony to be considerations that any individual would weigh carefully. A fifth factor—Saikewicz's inability to cooperate with the treatment—introduces those considerations that are unique to this individual and which therefore are essential to the proper exercise of substituted judgment. The judge heard testimony that Saikewicz would have no comprehension of the reasons for the severe disruption of his formerly secure and stable environment occasioned by the chemotherapy. He therefore would experience fear without the understanding from which other patients draw strength. The inability to anticipate and prepare for the severe side effects of the drugs leaves room only for confusion and disorientation. The possibility that such a naturally uncooperative patient would have to be physically restrained to allow the slow intravenous administration of drugs could only compound his pain and fear, as well as possibly jeopardize the ability of his body to withstand the toxic effects of the drugs.

The sixth factor identified by the judge as weighing against chemotherapy was "the quality of life possible for him even if the treatment does bring about remission." To the extent that this formulation equates the value of life with any measure of the quality of life, we firmly reject it.

Note how the *Saikewicz* court initially is talking about best interests, yet later says it is applying the substituted judgment doctrine. Which interpretation of what it did makes more sense? Note also how the court talks about the "subjective" nature of the decision it is making. Would the *Conroy* court use that adjective to describe what happened in *Saikewicz*?

In *Saikewicz*, the court approved the decision not to give the patient chemotherapy. What do you think would have happened to *Saikewicz* under the *Conroy* court's analysis? Which do you think is the better result? Why?

10. Another obvious category of persons for whom substituted judgment decision-making is impossible is young children, particularly newborn infants. In

general, the law authorizes parents to make all decisions for their children, including those relating to health care. In spite of that, a great deal of attention has been paid to limiting the general rule in the case of parents who choose to withhold life-sustaining treatment from a handicapped newborn child. Why might the general presumption that parents are strong protectors of a child's best interests not necessarily apply in such circumstances?

The recent history of decision-making for newborns starts in 1982, when a child was born in Indiana with Down's syndrome. As was noted in chapter 3, such infants almost always have some mental retardation, although the severity is highly variable. Such infants often have a variety of other medical problems. In this instance, the child had an opening between its esophagus and its trachea (a "tracheoesophageal fistula") that prevented it from being fed naturally. Because the child was likely to be retarded to some extent, the parents refused to give consent for the surgical repair. A state court judge refused to overturn the parents' decision. The child, who became known as Baby Doe in the ensuing publicity, was moved to the back of the nursery and the baby died several days later.

In a direct response to these events, the United States Department of Health and Human Services in 1984 promulgated a set of rules commonly known as the "Baby Doe" regulations. These rules required that most hospitals post notices stating that it is illegal to withhold nourishment or medical treatment from handicapped infants solely in response to anticipated physical or mental handicaps. The notices were to include a phone number for a 24-hour toll-free hotline. Numerous court challenges were brought against these regulations, and the Supreme Court ultimately struck them down on the ground that they were not authorized by the statute under which they were promulgated (i.e., Congress had not given the agency authority to write such regulations). *Bowen v. American Hospital Association*, 476 U.S. 610 (1986).

The regulations were later reissued in a substantially revised and "weakened" form. The current rules are relatively flexible and vague. It is unclear to what extent they have any substantial effect on current day-to-day practices in hospitals. Here is the current wording, 45 C.F.R. § 1340.15(b)(1)-(2):

> (1) The term "medical neglect" means the failure to provide adequate medical care. . . . The term "medical neglect" includes, but is not limited to, the withholding of medically indicated treatment from a disabled infant with a life-threatening condition.
>
> (2) The term "withholding of medically indicated treatment" means the failure to respond to the infant's life-threatening conditions by providing treatment (including appropriate nutrition, hydration, and medication) which, in the treating physician's (or physicians') reasonable medical judgment, will be most likely to be effective in ameliorating or correcting all such conditions, except that the term does not include the failure to provide treatment (other than

appropriate nutrition, hydration, or medication) to an infant when, in the treating physician's (or physicians') reasonable medical judgment any of the following circumstances apply:

    (i) The infant is chronically and irreversibly comatose;

    (ii) The provision of such treatment would merely prolong dying, not be effective in ameliorating or correcting all of the infant's life-threatening conditions, or otherwise be futile in terms of the survival of the infant; or

    (iii) The provision of such treatment would be virtually futile in terms of the survival of the infant and the treatment itself under such circumstances would be inhumane.

11. Do you think the current Baby Doe rules provide a good description of circumstances in which reasonable people might differ about whether or not it is in a child's best interests to allow it to die, and so the parents (consulting with the doctors) should have the discretion to make the decision? (You might compare them to the rules for adults who have not given prior guidance about what to do, such as the "pure objective" rule created by the *Conroy* court, or the categories created by the Illinois Health Care Surrogate Act.) Do you think parents should be given greater discretion? Less discretion?

How would the Baby Doe rules apply in these circumstances:

    a. An infant that had the same handicaps as the original Baby Doe.

    b. An infant that had a genetic defect that assured very severe mental retardation, with a maximal I.Q. that would never exceed that of a one-year-old.

    c. An infant with the same defect as in (b), but also blind and deaf.[12]

12. The most recent high-visibility case involving an infant is that of Sidney Miller. She was born in August 1990, seventeen weeks premature. The parents had been told by doctors before the delivery that the infant was likely not to survive, and even if she did survive, she would suffer from severe abnormalities. The parents then asked that the child not be given aggressive medical care, and instead be allowed to die "peacefully." However, the hospital had a policy of aggressively treating infants that weighed at least 500 grams (one pound, twelve ounces). Because Sidney exceeded that weight, she was kept alive against her parents' wishes. In 1998, at the age of seven, she weighed 30 pounds, had the mental capacity of a 6-month old, and suffered from poor vision, cerebral palsy, and seizures. She could not walk or talk, and her left arm was the only part of the body she could control.[13] The Millers sued Women's Hospital of Texas, where Sidney was born, for failing to comply with their wishes to withhold care, and in 1998 a jury awarded them $29 million for the costs of Sidney's care and $13.5 million in punitive damages. As of this writing, the hospital is appealing the case.[14]

13. The rules created by *Conroy* usually tip the balance in favor of life, at least where there is no very clear evidence that the patient wanted to have life-sustaining treatment withdrawn. As the U.S. Supreme Court says of

Conroy in the *Cruzan* opinion, if neither the subjective test nor either of the two objective tests was met, "the [Conroy] court [determined] it was best to err in favor of preserving life." Are the *Conroy* tests consistent with the court's observation earlier in the opinion that to "err either way—to keep a person alive under circumstances under which he would rather have been allowed to die, or to allow that person to die when he would have chosen to cling to life—would be deeply unfortunate"? Or are they merely an appropriate attempt to decide which error is more acceptable?

Note that the court was in something of a dilemma once it started trying to delineate an objective rule that would allow life-sustaining treatment to be withdrawn on patients who had given no good prior evidence of their wishes. Imagine that a patient's medical condition met the standards of the court's "pure-objective" test. That patient will have care withdrawn and will be allowed to die. *All* such patients would be allowed to die. Can you understand the court's reluctance to define such a category in a broad way, to make a broad-brush determination that a group of people should die?

Given the court's analysis, what should be done with patients in a persistent vegetative state who previously gave no indication of their wishes? Do they meet the pure-objective test? Note that all such patients with this condition are presumably suffering (or not suffering) equally. An objective rule would presumably either conclude they *all* should be kept alive or they *all* should be allowed to die (or, under a different view of the facts, be condemned to death). Is this a decision that a court should have to make? Or is it more appropriate for a legislature? For the New Jersey Supreme Court's later determination that the *Conroy* rules should not be used in the case of such patients, see *In re Jobes*, 529 A.2d 434 (N.J. 1987).

14. Is the *Conroy* court looking for too much certainty in an area that will never lend itself to total certainty? Should the role of the courts (and legislatures) be merely to delineate, for patients who have not provided guidance, conditions in which there is substantial genuine disagreement about whether it is better for that person to live or die (a zone of legitimate uncertainty), and then to allow some appropriate decision-maker to make a (perhaps somewhat arbitrary) choice one way or the other? (See the previous comments with respect to decision-making for newborns, in note 11.)

Perhaps Justice Handler, in his partially dissenting and partially concurring opinion in *Conroy*, was moving in such a direction when he criticized the narrow criteria set up by the majority opinion:

> In my opinion, the Court's objective tests too narrowly define the interests of people like Miss Conroy. While the basic standard purports to account for several concerns, it ultimately focuses on pain as the critical factor. The presence of significant pain in effect becomes the sole measure of such a person's best interests. "Pain" thus eclipses a whole cluster of other human values that have a proper place in the subtle weighing that will ultimately determine how life should end. . . .

The person should be terminally ill and facing imminent death. There should also be present the permanent loss of conscious thought processes in the form of a comatose state or profound unconsciousness. Further, there should be the irreparable failure of at least one major and essential bodily organ or system. Obviously the presence or absence of significant pain is highly relevant.

In addition, the person's general physical condition must be of great concern. The presence of progressive, irreversible, extensive, and extreme physical deterioration, such as ulcers, lesions, gangrene, infection, incontinence and the like, which frequently afflict the bed-ridden terminally ill, should be considered in the formulation of an appropriate standard. . . . Eventually, pervasive bodily intrusions, even for the best motives, will arouse feelings akin to humiliation and mortification for the helpless patient. When cherished values of human dignity and personal privacy, which belong to every person living or dying, are sufficiently transgressed by what is being done to the individual, we should be ready to say: enough.

In my view, our understanding as to how life should end must be infused with the fundamental human moral values that serve us while we live. As we have faced life, so should we be able to face death. When an individual's personal philosophy or moral values cannot otherwise be brought to bear to resolve the dilemma of whether to live or die, then factors that generally and normally shape basic human moral values should be taken into account. These factors should be assessed reasonably and fairly from the patient's perspective. They should be weighed and balanced by an appropriate, responsible surrogate decision-maker in reaching the final awesome decision whether to withdraw life-prolonging treatment from the unfortunate and hapless patient. I believe that a decision informed by these considerations would be conducive to the humane, dignified, and decent ending of life.

How do Justice Handler's criteria fit with your own views of what might represent such a zone of legitimate uncertainty? How do they compare to the criteria established by the Illinois Health Care Surrogate Act?

15. Though *Conroy* is an influential case, there remains a great deal of diversity among the states with regard to when life support can be removed from patients who have provided little or no evidence of their wishes. Some of that diversity will be discussed in the Supreme Court's *Cruzan* opinion in chapter 11, and there is already an extensive literature.[15]

16. In the final portion of the *Conroy* opinion (not reprinted here), the court determines that because of the "special vulnerability" of the elderly residents of nursing homes, special procedures are required before deciding to terminate life-sustaining treatment. In such circumstances, a decision mutually reached between the family, the doctors, and the institution's ethics committee would not sufficiently protect the patient's interests. Rather, there had to be a judicial determination of the patient's incompetence, together with appointment of a guardian, plus the concurrence of a state ombudsman in the decision to allow the patient to die. These provisions are far stricter than those created by many other courts, which usually have not

imposed any special rules (such as the need for review by a court) for nursing home residents or any other similar categories.

Endnotes

1. See generally President's Commission for the Study of Ethical Problems in Medicine and Biomedical and Behavioral Research, *Deciding to Forego Life-Sustaining
Treatment* (1983) at 60–90 (Washington, D.C.: U.S. Government Printing Office,
1983).
2. Linda L. Emanuel and Ezekiel J. Emanuel, "The Medical Directive: A New Comprehensive Advance Care Document," 261 *JAMA* 3288 (1989).
3. See, e.g., Susan Wolf et al., "Sources of Concern about the Patient Self-Determination Act," 325 *New Eng. J. Med.* 1666 (1991).
4. See, e.g., George J. Annas, "The Health Care Proxy and the Living Will," 324 *New
Eng. J. Med.* 1210 (1991); Joanne Lynn, "Why I Don't Have a Living Will," 19 *Law,
Med. & Health Care* 101 (1991).
5. National Bioethics Advisory Commission, *Research Involving Persons with Mental
Disorders that May Affect Decisionmaking Capacity*, Vol. 1: 18–19 (1998). The entire report is available on the web at *bioethics.gov*.
6. Rick Bragg, "A Family Shooting and a Twist Like No Other," *New York Times*, 19
May 1999, A-1.
7. See, e.g., David R. Patterson et al., "When Life Support Is Questioned Early in the
Care of Patients with Cervical-Level Quadriplegia," 328 *New Eng. J. Med.* 506
(1993).
8. See "Confronting Death: Who Chooses, Who Controls? A Dialogue between Dax
Cowart and Robert Burt," 28(1) *Hastings Ctr. Rep.* 14 (1998).
9. Ronald Dworkin, *Life's Dominion* at 220–21 (New York: Random House, Inc.,
1993).
10. For more on these issues, and Ulysses contracts in general, see, e.g., Rebecca
Dresser, "Bound to Treatment: The Ulysses Contract," 13 *Hastings Ctr Rep.* (June
1984); Rebecca Dresser, "Missing Persons: Legal Perceptions of Incompetent Persons," 609 *Rutgers L. Rev.* 636 (1994); Jon Elster, *Ulysses and the Sirens: Studies in
Rationality and Irrationality* at 38–47 (Cambridge: Cambridge University Press,
rev. ed., 1984).
11. For an introduction to these highly controversial issues, see Laurence Tribe's classic
article, "Trial by Mathematics: Precision and Ritual in the Legal Process," 84 *Harv.
L. Rev.* 1329 (1971). See also Charles Nesson, "The Evidence or the Event? On Judicial Proof and the Acceptability of Verdicts," 98 *Harv. L. Rev.* 1357 (1985); Daniel
Shaviro, "Statistical-Probability Evidence and the Appearance of Justice," 103 *Harv.
L. Rev.* 530 (1989).
12. There is an extensive literature on issues relating to the treatment of handicapped
infants. See, e.g., Martha A. Field, "Killing 'the Handicapped'—before and after
Birth," 16 *Harv. Women's L. J.* 79 (1993); Martha Minow, "Beyond State Intervention in the Family: For Baby Jane Doe," 18 *Univ. Mich. J. L. Ref.* 933 (1985); Mary
A. Crossley, "Of Diagnoses and Discrimination: Discriminatory Nontreatment of Infants with HIV Infection," 93 *Colum. L. Rev.* 1581 (1993).

13. See Brian Wallstin, "A Question of Life," *Houston Press*, 5 February 1998; "The Smallest of the Small," *60 Minutes*, CBS News, 12 April 1998.

14. For more on the social issues being raised by aggressive treatment of premature infants, see Elizabeth Rosenthal, "As More Tiny Infants Live, Choices and Burdens Grow," *New York Times*, 29 September 1991 at A1 (first of a three-part series, followed by front-page articles on September 30 and October 1 by Gina Kolata and Jane E. Brody).

15. For an extensive survey of state laws with respect to such decisions, and to advance directives generally, see Alan Meisel's two-volume *The Right to Die* (New York: John Wiley & Sons, 2nd ed., 1995). For other views on the dilemma of making decisions for patients such as Claire Conroy, see, e.g., Nancy K. Rhoden, "Litigating Life and Death," 105 *Harv. L. Rev.* 1426 (1992); Norman L. Cantor, "Discarding Substituted Judgment and Best Interests: Toward a Constructive Preference Standard for Dying, Previously Competent Patients without Advance Directives," 48 *Rutgers L. Rev.* 1193 (1996).

11

The Constitution and the Right to Die

Several of the cases in the preceding chapter concluded that there was a constitutional right to refuse care, under the United States Constitution, a particular state constitution, or both. Only the U.S. Supreme Court can authoritatively define federal constitutional rights, and only it can determine how the existence of such a right might restrict a state's ability to pass laws relating to "end-of-life" decision-making. We again turn to issues at the heart of federalism with the Supreme Court's pronouncements on "the right to die": the complex concurring and dissenting opinions in both *Cruzan* and the physician-assisted suicide cases.

CRUZAN V. DIRECTOR, MISSOURI DEPARTMENT OF HEALTH
Supreme Court of the United States
497 U.S. 261 (1990)

OPINION BY CHIEF JUSTICE REHNQUIST:

Petitioner Nancy Beth Cruzan was rendered incompetent as a result of severe injuries sustained during an automobile accident. Copetitioners Lester and Joyce Cruzan, Nancy's parents and coguardians, sought a court order directing the withdrawal of their daughter's artificial feeding and hydration equipment after it became apparent that she had virtually no chance of recovering her cognitive faculties. The Supreme Court of Missouri held that because there was no clear and convincing evidence of Nancy's desire to have life-sustaining treatment withdrawn under such circumstances, her parents lacked authority to effectuate such a request. We granted certiorari, and now affirm.

On the night of January 11, 1983, Nancy Cruzan lost control of her car as she traveled down Elm Road in Jasper County, Missouri. The vehicle overturned, and Cruzan was discovered lying face down in a ditch without detectable respiratory or cardiac function. Paramedics were able to restore her breathing and heartbeat at the accident site, and she was transported to a hospital in an unconscious state. An attending neurosurgeon diagnosed her as having sustained probable cerebral contusions compounded by significant anoxia (lack of oxygen). The Missouri trial court in this case found that permanent brain damage generally results after 6 minutes in an anoxic state; it was estimated that Cruzan was deprived of oxygen from 12 to 14 minutes. She remained in a coma for approximately three weeks and then progressed to an unconscious state in which she was able to orally ingest some nutrition. In order to ease feeding and further the recovery, surgeons implanted a gastrostomy feeding and hydration tube in Cruzan with the consent of her then husband. Subsequent rehabilitative efforts proved unavailing. She now lies in a Missouri state hospital in what is commonly referred to as a persistent vegetative state: generally, a condition in which a person exhibits motor reflexes but evinces no indications of significant cognitive function. The State of Missouri is bearing the cost of her care.

After it had become apparent that Nancy Cruzan had virtually no chance of regaining her mental faculties, her parents asked hospital employees to terminate the artificial nutrition and hydration procedures. All agree that such a removal would cause her death. The employees refused to honor the request without court approval. The parents then sought and received authorization from the state trial court for termination. The court found that a person in Nancy's condition had a fundamental right under the State and Federal Constitutions to refuse or direct the withdrawal of "death prolonging procedures." The court also found that Nancy's "expressed thoughts at age twenty-five in somewhat serious conversation with a housemate friend that if sick or injured she would not wish to continue her life unless she could live at least halfway normally suggests that given her present condition she would not wish to continue on with her nutrition and hydration."

The Supreme Court of Missouri reversed by a divided vote. The court recognized a right to refuse treatment embodied in the common-law doctrine of informed consent, but expressed skepticism about the application of that doctrine in the circumstances of this case. The court also declined to read a broad right of privacy into the State Constitution which would "support the right of a person to refuse medical treatment in every circumstance," and expressed doubt as to whether such a right existed under the United States Constitution. It then decided that the Missouri Living Will statute embodied a state policy strongly favoring the preservation of life. The court found that Cruzan's statements to her roommate regarding her desire to live or die under certain conditions were "unreliable for the purpose of determining her intent," "and thus insufficient to support the co-guardians['] claim to exercise substituted judgment on Nancy's behalf." It rejected the argument that Cruzan's parents were entitled to order the termination of her medical treatment, concluding that "no person can assume that choice for an incompetent in the absence of the formalities required under Missouri's Living Will statutes or the clear and convincing, inherently reliable evidence absent here." The court also expressed its view that "broad policy questions bearing on life and death are more properly addressed by representative assemblies" than judicial bodies.

We granted certiorari to consider the question whether Cruzan has a right under the United States Constitution which would require the hospital to withdraw life-sustaining treatment from her under these circumstances.

At common law, even the touching of one person by another without consent and without legal justification was a battery. Before the turn of the century, this Court observed that "no right is held more sacred, or is more carefully guarded, by the common law, than the right of every individual to the possession and control of his own person, free from all restraint or interference of others, unless by clear and unquestionable authority of law." This notion of bodily integrity has been embodied in the requirement that informed consent is generally required for medical treatment. Justice Cardozo, while on the Court of Appeals of New York, aptly described this doctrine: "Every human being of adult years and sound mind has a right to determine what shall be done with his own body; and a surgeon who performs an operation without his patient's consent commits an assault, for which he is liable in damages." The informed consent doctrine has become firmly entrenched in American tort law.

The logical corollary of the doctrine of informed consent is that the patient generally possesses the right not to consent, that is, to refuse treatment. Until about 15 years ago and the seminal decision in *In re Quinlan*, the number of right-to-refuse-treatment decisions was relatively few. Most of the earlier cases involved patients who refused medical treatment forbidden by their religious beliefs, thus implicating First Amendment rights as well as common-law rights of self-determination. More recently, however, with the advance of medical technology capable of sustaining life well past the point where natural forces would have brought certain death in earlier times, cases involving the right to refuse life-sustaining treatment have burgeoned.

In the *Quinlan* case, young Karen Quinlan suffered severe brain damage as the result of anoxia and entered a persistent vegetative state. Karen's father sought judicial approval to disconnect his daughter's respirator. The New Jersey Supreme Court granted the relief, holding that Karen had a right of privacy grounded in the Federal Constitution to terminate treatment. Recognizing that this right was not absolute, however, the court balanced it against asserted state interests. Noting that the State's interest "weakens and the individual's right to privacy grows as the degree of bodily invasion increases and the prognosis dims," the court concluded that the state interests had to give way in that case. The court also concluded that the "only practical way" to prevent the loss of Karen's privacy right due to her incompetence was to allow her guardian and family to decide "whether she would exercise it in these circumstances."

After *Quinlan*, however, most courts have based a right to refuse treatment either solely on the common-law right to informed consent or on both the common-law right and a constitutional privacy right. In *Superintendent of Belchertown State School v. Saikewicz* (1977), the Supreme Judicial Court of Massachusetts relied on both the right of privacy and the right of informed consent to permit the withholding of chemotherapy from a profoundly retarded 67-year-old man suffering from leukemia. Reasoning that an incompetent person retains the same rights as a competent individual "because the value of human dignity extends to both," the court adopted a "substituted judgment" standard whereby courts were to determine what an incompetent individual's decision would have been under the circumstances. Distilling certain state interests from prior case law—the preservation of life, the protection of the interests of innocent third parties, the prevention of suicide, and the maintenance of the ethical integrity of the medical profession—the court recognized the first interest as paramount and noted it was greatest when an affliction was curable, "as opposed to the State interest where, as here, the issue is not whether, but when, for how long, and at what cost to the individual [a] life may be briefly extended."

In *In re Storar* (1981), the New York Court of Appeals declined to base a right to refuse treatment on a constitutional privacy right. Instead, it found such a right "adequately supported" by the informed consent doctrine. In *In re Eichner* (decided with *In re Storar*), an 83-year-old man who had suffered brain damage from anoxia entered a vegetative state and was thus incompetent to consent to the removal of his respirator. The court, however, found it unnecessary to reach the question whether his rights could be exercised by others since it found the evidence clear and convincing from statements made by the patient when competent that he "did not want to be maintained in a vegetative coma by use of a respirator." In the companion *Storar* case, a 52-year-old man suffering from bladder cancer had been profoundly retarded during most of his life. Implicitly rejecting the approach taken in *Saikewicz, supra,* the court reasoned that due to such life-long incompetency, "it is unrealistic to attempt to determine whether he would want to continue potentially life prolonging treatment if he were competent." As the evidence showed that the patient's required blood transfusions did not involve excessive pain and without them his mental and physical abilities would deteriorate, the court concluded that it should not "allow an incompetent patient to bleed to death because someone, even someone as close as a parent or sibling, feels that this is best for one with an incurable disease."

Many of the later cases build on the principles established in *Quinlan, Saikewicz,* and *Storar/Eichner.* For instance, in *In re Conroy,* the same court that decided *Quinlan* considered whether a nasogastric feeding tube could be removed from an 84-year-old incompetent nursing-home resident suffering irreversible mental and physical ailments. [The Court then discusses the *Conroy* case in detail, commenting on its use of the subjective, limited-objective, and pure-objective tests.]

In contrast to *Conroy*, the Court of Appeals of New York recently refused to accept less than the clearly expressed wishes of a patient before permitting the exercise of her right to refuse treatment by a surrogate decisionmaker. *In re Westchester County Medical Center on behalf of O'Connor* (1988). There, the court, over the objection of the patient's family members, granted an order to insert a feeding tube into a 77-year-old woman rendered incompetent as a result of several strokes. While continuing to recognize a common-law right to refuse treatment, the court rejected the substituted judgment approach for asserting it "because it is inconsistent with our fundamental commitment to the notion that no person or court should substitute its judgment as to what would be an acceptable quality of life for another. Consequently, we adhere to the view that, despite its pitfalls and inevitable uncertainties, the inquiry must always be narrowed to the patient's expressed intent, with every effort made to minimize the opportunity for error." The court held that the record lacked the requisite clear and convincing evidence of the patient's expressed intent to withhold life-sustaining treatment. . . .

As these cases demonstrate, the common-law doctrine of informed consent is viewed as generally encompassing the right of a competent individual to refuse medical treatment. Beyond that, these cases demonstrate both similarity and diversity in their approaches to decision of what all agree is a perplexing question with unusually strong moral and ethical overtones. State courts have available to them for decision a number of sources—state constitutions, statutes, and common law—which are not available to us. In this Court, the question is simply and starkly whether the United States Constitution prohibits Missouri from choosing the rule of decision which it did. This is the first case in which we have been squarely presented with the issue whether the United States Constitution grants what is in common parlance referred to as a "right to die." We follow the judicious counsel of [a prior decision] where we said that in deciding "a question of such magnitude and importance . . . it is the [better] part of wisdom not to attempt, by any general statement, to cover every possible phase of the subject."

The Fourteenth Amendment provides that no State shall "deprive any person of life, liberty, or property, without due process of law." The principle that a competent person has a constitutionally protected liberty interest in refusing unwanted medical treatment may be inferred from our prior decisions. In *Jacobson v. Massachusetts* (1905), for instance, the Court balanced an individual's liberty interest in declining an unwanted smallpox vaccine against the State's interest in preventing disease. . . .

Just this Term, in the course of holding that a State's procedures for administering antipsychotic medication to prisoners were sufficient to satisfy due process concerns, we recognized that prisoners possess "a significant liberty interest in avoiding the unwanted administration of antipsychotic drugs under the Due Process Clause of the Fourteenth Amendment." *Washington v. Harper* ("The forcible injection of medication into a nonconsenting person's body represents a substantial interference with that person's liberty"). Still other cases support the recognition of a general liberty interest in refusing medical treatment. *Vitek v. Jones* (1980) (transfer to mental hospital coupled with mandatory behavior modification treatment implicated liberty interests); *Parham v. J. R.* (1979) ("[A] child, in common with adults, has a substantial liberty interest in not being confined unnecessarily for medical treatment"). But determining that a person has a "liberty interest" under the Due Process Clause does not end the inquiry; "whether respondent's constitutional rights have been violated must be determined by balancing his liberty interests against the relevant state interests."

Petitioners insist that under the general holdings of our cases, the forced administration of life-sustaining medical treatment, and even of artificially delivered food and water essential to life, would implicate a competent person's liberty interest. Although we think the logic of the cases discussed above would embrace such a liberty interest, the dramatic consequences involved in refusal of such treatment would inform the inquiry as to whether the deprivation of that interest is constitutionally permissible. But for purposes of this case, we assume that the United States Constitution would grant a competent person a constitutionally protected right to refuse lifesaving hydration and nutrition.

Petitioners go on to assert that an incompetent person should possess the same right in this respect as is possessed by a competent person. . . . The difficulty with petitioners' claim is that in a sense it begs the question: An incompetent person is not able to make an informed and voluntary choice to exercise a hypothetical right to refuse treatment or any other right. Such a "right" must be exercised for her, if at all, by some sort of surrogate. Here, Missouri has in effect recognized that under certain circumstances a surrogate may act for the patient in electing to have hydration and nutrition withdrawn in such a way as to cause death, but it has established a procedural safeguard to assure that the action of the surrogate conforms as best it may to the wishes expressed by the patient while competent. Missouri requires that evidence of the incompetent's wishes as to the withdrawal of treatment be proved by clear and convincing evidence. The question, then, is whether the United States Constitution forbids the establishment of this procedural requirement by the State. We hold that it does not.

Whether or not Missouri's clear and convincing evidence requirement comports with the United States Constitution depends in part on what interests the State may properly seek to protect in this situation. Missouri relies on its interest in the protection and preservation of human life, and there can be no gainsaying this interest. As a general matter, the States—indeed, all civilized nations—demonstrate their commitment to life by treating homicide as a serious crime. Moreover, the majority of States in this country have laws imposing criminal penalties on one who assists another to commit suicide. We do not think a State is required to remain neutral in the face of an informed and voluntary decision by a physically able adult to starve to death.

But in the context presented here, a State has more particular interests at stake. The choice between life and death is a deeply personal decision of obvious and overwhelming finality. We believe Missouri may legitimately seek to safeguard the personal element of this choice through the imposition of heightened evidentiary requirements. It cannot be disputed that the Due Process Clause protects an interest in life as well as an interest in refusing life-sustaining medical treatment. Not all incompetent patients will have loved ones available to serve as surrogate decisionmakers. And even where family members are present, "there will, of course, be some unfortunate situations in which family members will not act to protect a patient." A State is entitled to guard against potential abuses in such situations. Similarly, a State is entitled to consider that a judicial proceeding to make a determination regarding an incompetent's wishes may very well not be an adversarial one, with the added guarantee of accurate factfinding that the adversary process brings with it. Finally, we think a State may properly decline to make judgments about the "quality" of life that a particular individual may enjoy, and simply assert an unqualified interest in the preservation of human life to be weighed against the constitutionally protected interests of the individual.

In our view, Missouri has permissibly sought to advance these interests through the adoption of a "clear and convincing" standard of proof to govern such proceedings. "The function of a standard of proof, as that concept is embodied in the Due Process Clause and in the realm of factfinding, is to 'instruct the factfinder concerning the degree of confidence our society thinks he should have in the correctness of factual conclusions for a particular type of adjudication.'" "This Court has mandated an intermediate standard of proof —'clear and convincing evidence'—when the individual interests at stake in a state proceeding are both 'particularly important' and 'more substantial than mere loss of money.'" . . .

We think it self-evident that the interests at stake in the instant proceedings are more substantial, both on an individual and societal level, than those involved in a run-of-the-mine civil dispute. But not only does the standard of proof reflect the importance of a particular adjudication, it also serves as "a societal judgment about how the risk of error should be distributed between the litigants." The more stringent the burden of proof a party must bear, the more that party bears the risk of an erroneous decision. We believe that Missouri may permissibly place an increased risk of an erroneous decision on those seeking to terminate an incompetent individual's life-sustaining treatment. An erroneous decision not to terminate results in a maintenance of the status quo; the possibility of subsequent developments such as advancements in medical science, the discovery of new evidence regarding the patient's intent, changes in the law, or simply the unexpected death of the patient despite the administration of life-sustaining treatment at least create the potential that a wrong decision will eventually be corrected or its impact mitigated. An erroneous decision to withdraw life-sustaining treatment, however, is not susceptible of correction. . . .

It is also worth noting that most, if not all, States simply forbid oral testimony entirely in determining the wishes of parties in transactions which, while important, simply do not have the consequences that a decision to terminate a person's life does. . . . There is no doubt that statutes requiring wills to be in writing, and statutes of frauds which require that a contract to make a will be in writing, on occasion frustrate the effectuation of the intent of a particular decedent, just as Missouri's requirement of proof in this case may have frustrated the effectuation of the not-fully-expressed desires of Nancy Cruzan. But the Constitution does not require general rules to work faultlessly; no general rule can.

In sum, we conclude that a State may apply a clear and convincing evidence standard in proceedings where a guardian seeks to discontinue nutrition and hydration of a person diagnosed to be in a persistent vegetative state. We note that many courts which have adopted some sort of substituted judgment procedure in situations like this, whether they limit consideration of evidence to the prior expressed wishes of the incompetent individual, or whether they allow more general proof of what the individual's decision would have been, require a clear and convincing standard of proof for such evidence.

The Supreme Court of Missouri held that in this case the testimony adduced at trial did not amount to clear and convincing proof of the patient's desire to have hydration and nutrition withdrawn. In so doing, it reversed a decision of the Missouri trial court which had found that the evidence "suggested" Nancy Cruzan would not have desired to continue such measures, but which had not adopted the standard of "clear and convincing evidence" enunciated by the Supreme Court. The testimony adduced at trial consisted primarily of Nancy Cruzan's statements made to a housemate about a year before her accident that she would not want to live should she face life as a "vegetable," and other observations to the same effect. The observations did not deal in terms with withdrawal of medical treatment or of hydration and nutrition. We cannot say that the Supreme Court of Missouri committed constitutional error in reaching the conclusion that it did. . . .

CONCURRING OPINION BY JUSTICE O'CONNOR:

I agree that a protected liberty interest in refusing unwanted medical treatment may be inferred from our prior decisions, and that the refusal of artificially delivered food and water is encompassed within that liberty interest. I write separately to clarify why I believe this to be so.

As the Court notes, the liberty interest in refusing medical treatment flows from decisions involving the State's invasions into the body. Because our notions of liberty are inextricably entwined with our idea of physical freedom and self-determination, the Court has often deemed state incursions into the body repugnant to the interests protected by the Due Process Clause. . . . The State's imposition of medical treatment on an unwilling competent adult necessarily involves some form of restraint and intrusion. A seriously ill or dying patient whose wishes are not honored may feel a captive of the machinery required for life-sustaining measures or other medical interventions. Such forced treatment may burden that individual's liberty interests as much as any state coercion.

The State's artificial provision of nutrition and hydration implicates identical concerns. Artificial feeding cannot readily be distinguished from other forms of medical treatment. Whether or not the techniques used to pass food and water into the patient's alimentary tract are termed "medical treatment," it is clear they all involve some degree of intrusion and restraint. Feeding a patient by means of a nasogastric tube requires a physician to pass a long flexible tube through the patient's nose, throat, and esophagus and into the stomach. Because of the discomfort such a tube causes, "many patients need to be restrained forcibly and their hands put into large mittens to prevent them from removing the tube." A gastrostomy tube (as was used to provide food and water to Nancy Cruzan) or jejunostomy tube must be surgically implanted into the stomach or small intestine. Requiring a competent adult to endure such procedures against her will burdens the patient's liberty, dignity, and freedom to determine the course of her own treatment. Accordingly, the liberty guaranteed by the Due Process Clause must protect, if it protects anything, an individual's deeply personal decision to reject medical treatment, including the artificial delivery of food and water.

I also write separately to emphasize that the Court does not today decide the issue whether a State must also give effect to the decisions of a surrogate decisionmaker. In my view, such a duty may well be constitutionally required to protect the patient's liberty interest in refusing medical treatment. Few individuals provide explicit oral or written instructions regarding their intent to refuse medical treatment should they become incompetent. States which decline to consider any evidence other than such instructions may frequently fail to honor a patient's intent. Such failures might be avoided if the State considered an equally probative source of evidence: the patient's appointment of a proxy to make health care decisions on her behalf. Delegating the authority to make medical decisions to a family member or friend is becoming a common method of planning for the future. Several States have recognized the practical wisdom of such a procedure by enacting durable power of attorney statutes that specifically authorize an individual to appoint a surrogate to make medical treatment decisions. Some state courts have suggested that an agent appointed pursuant to a general durable power of attorney statute would also be empowered to make health care decisions on behalf of the patient. Other States allow an individual to designate a proxy to carry out the intent of a living will. These procedures for surrogate decisionmaking, which appear to be rapidly gaining in acceptance, may be a valuable additional safeguard of the patient's interest in directing his medical care. Moreover, as patients are likely to select a family member as a surrogate, giving effect to a proxy's decisions may also protect the "freedom of personal choice in matters of . . . family life."

Today's decision, holding only that the Constitution permits a State to require clear and convincing evidence of Nancy Cruzan's desire to have artificial hydration and nutrition withdrawn, does not preclude a future determination that the Constitution requires the States to implement the decisions of a patient's duly appointed surrogate. Nor does it prevent States from developing other approaches for protecting an incompetent individual's liberty interest in refusing medical treatment. As is evident from the Court's survey of state court decisions, no national consensus has yet emerged on the best solution for this difficult and sensitive problem. Today we decide only that one State's practice does not violate the Constitution; the more challenging task of crafting appropriate procedures for safeguarding incompetents' liberty interests is entrusted to the "laboratory" of the States in the first instance.

CONCURRING OPINION BY JUSTICE SCALIA:

The various opinions in this case portray quite clearly the difficult, indeed agonizing, questions that are presented by the constantly increasing power of science to keep the human body alive for longer than any reasonable person would want to inhabit it. The States have begun to grapple with these problems through legislation. I am concerned, from the tenor of today's opinions, that we are poised to confuse that enterprise as successfully as we have confused the enterprise of legislating concerning abortion—requiring it to be conducted against a background of federal constitutional imperatives that are unknown because they are being newly crafted from Term to Term. That would be a great misfortune.

While I agree with the Court's analysis today, and therefore join in its opinion, I would have preferred that we announce, clearly and promptly, that the federal courts have no business in this field; that American law has always accorded the State the power to prevent, by force if necessary, suicide—including suicide by refusing to take appropriate measures necessary to preserve one's life; that the point at which life becomes "worthless," and the point at which the means necessary to preserve it become "extraordinary" or "inappropriate," are neither set forth in the Constitution nor known to the nine Justices of this Court any better than they are known to nine people picked at random from the Kansas City telephone directory; and hence, that even when it is demonstrated by clear and convincing evidence that a patient no longer wishes certain measures to be taken to preserve his or her life, it is up to the citizens of Missouri to decide, through their elected representatives, whether that wish will be honored. It is quite impossible (because the Constitution says nothing about the matter) that those citizens will decide upon a line less lawful than the one we would choose; and it is unlikely (because we know no more about "life and death" than they do) that they will decide upon a line less reasonable.

The text of the Due Process Clause does not protect individuals against deprivations of liberty *simpliciter*. It protects them against deprivations of liberty "without due process of law." To determine that such a deprivation would not occur if Nancy Cruzan were forced to take nourishment against her will, it is unnecessary to reopen the historically recurrent debate over whether "due process" includes substantive restrictions. It is at least true that no "substantive due process" claim can be maintained unless the claimant demonstrates that the State has deprived him of a right historically and traditionally protected against state interference. That cannot possibly be established here.

At common law in England, a suicide—defined as one who "deliberately puts an end to his own existence, or commits any unlawful malicious act, the consequence of which is his own death"— was criminally liable. Although the States abolished the penalties imposed by the common law (i.e., forfeiture and ignominious burial), they did so to spare the innocent family and not to legitimize the act. Case law at the time of the adoption of the Fourteenth Amendment generally held that assisting suicide was a criminal offense. . . . And most States that did not explicitly prohibit assisted suicide in 1868 recognized, when the issue arose in the 50 years following the Fourteenth Amendment's ratification, that assisted and (in some cases) attempted suicide were unlawful. Thus, "there is no significant support for the claim that a right to suicide is so rooted in our tradition that it may be deemed 'fundamental' or 'implicit in the concept of ordered liberty.' "

Petitioners rely on three distinctions to separate Nancy Cruzan's case from ordinary suicide: (1) that she is permanently incapacitated and in pain; (2) that she would bring on her death not by any affirmative act but by merely declining treatment that provides nourishment; and (3) that preventing her from effectuating her presumed wish to die requires violation of her bodily integrity. None of these suffices. Suicide was not excused even when committed "to avoid those ills which [persons] had not the fortitude to endure." "The life of those to whom life has become a burden—of those who are hopelessly diseased or fatally wounded—nay, even the lives of criminals condemned to death, are under the protection of the law, equally as the lives of those who are in the full tide of life's enjoyment, and anxious to continue to live." Thus, a man who prepared a poison, and placed it within reach of his wife, "to put an end to her suffering" from a terminal illness was convicted of murder; the "incurable suffering of the suicide, as a legal question, could hardly affect the degree of criminality. . . ." Nor would the imminence of the patient's death have affected liability. "The lives of all are equally under the protection of the law, and under that protection to their last moment. . . . [Assisted suicide] is declared by the law to be murder, irrespective of the wishes or the condition of the party to whom the poison is administered. . . ."

The second asserted distinction—suggested by the recent cases canvassed by the Court concerning the right to refuse treatment—relies on the dichotomy between action and inaction. Suicide, it is said, consists of an affirmative act to end one's life; refusing treatment is not an affirmative act "causing" death, but merely a passive acceptance of the natural process of dying. I readily acknowledge that the distinction between action and inaction has some bearing upon the legislative judgment of what ought to be prevented as suicide—though even there it would seem to me unreasonable to draw the line precisely between action and inaction, rather than between various forms of inaction. It would not make much sense to say that one may not kill oneself by walking into the sea, but may sit on the beach until submerged by the incoming tide; or that one may not intentionally lock oneself into a cold storage locker, but may refrain from coming indoors when the temperature drops below freezing. Even as a legislative matter, in other words, the intelligent line does not fall between action and inaction but between those forms of inaction that consist of abstaining from "ordinary" care and those that consist of abstaining from "excessive" or "heroic" measures. Unlike action versus inaction, that is not a line to be discerned by logic or legal analysis, and we should not pretend that it is.

But to return to the principal point for present purposes: the irrelevance of the action-inaction distinction. Starving oneself to death is no different from putting a gun to one's temple as far as the common-law definition of suicide is concerned; the cause of death in both cases is the suicide's conscious decision to "put an end to his own existence." Of course the common law rejected the action-inaction distinction in other contexts involving the taking of human life as well. In the prosecution of a parent for the starvation death of her infant, it was no defense that the infant's death was "caused" by no action of the parent but by the natural process of starvation, or by the infant's natural inability to provide for itself. A physician, moreover, could be criminally liable for failure to provide care that could have extended the patient's life, even if death was immediately caused by the underlying disease that the physician failed to treat.

It is not surprising, therefore, that the early cases considering the claimed right to refuse medical treatment dismissed as specious the nice distinction between "passively submitting to death and actively seeking it. The distinction may be merely verbal, as it would be if an adult sought death by starvation instead of a drug. If the State may interrupt one mode of self-destruction, it may with equal authority interfere with the other."

The third asserted basis of distinction—that frustrating Nancy Cruzan's wish to die in the present case requires interference with her bodily integrity— is likewise inadequate, because such interference is impermissible only if one begs the question whether her refusal to undergo the treatment on her own is suicide. It has always been lawful not only for the State, but even for private citizens, to interfere with bodily integrity to prevent a felony. That general rule has of course been applied to suicide. At common law, even a private person's use of force to prevent suicide was privileged. It is not even reasonable, much less required by the Constitution, to maintain that although the State has the right to prevent a person from slashing his wrists, it does not have the power to apply physical force to prevent him from doing so, nor the power, should he succeed, to apply, coercively if necessary, medical measures to stop the flow of blood. The state-run hospital, I am certain, is not liable under [federal civil rights laws] for violation of constitutional rights, nor the private hospital liable under general tort law, if, in a State where suicide is unlawful, it pumps out the stomach of a person who has intentionally taken an overdose of barbiturates, despite that person's wishes to the contrary.

The dissents of Justices Brennan and Stevens make a plausible case for our intervention here only by embracing—the latter explicitly and the former by implication—a political principle that the States are free to adopt, but that is demonstrably not imposed by the Constitution. "The State," says Justice Brennan, "has no legitimate general interest in someone's life, completely abstracted from the interest of the person living that life, that could outweigh the person's choice *to avoid medical treatment.*" The italicized phrase sounds moderate enough and is all that is needed to cover the present case—but the proposition cannot logically be so limited. One who accepts it must also accept, I think, that the State has no such legitimate interest that could outweigh "the person's choice to put an end to her life." Similarly, if one agrees with Justice Brennan that "the State's general interest in life must accede to Nancy Cruzan's particularized and intense interest in self-determination in her choice of medical treatment," he must also believe that the State must accede to her "particularized and intense interest in self-determination in her choice whether to continue living or to die." For insofar as balancing the relative interests of the State and the individual is concerned, there is nothing distinctive about accepting death through the refusal of "medical treatment," as opposed to accepting it through the refusal of food, or through the failure to shut off the engine and get out of the car after parking in one's garage after work. Suppose that Nancy Cruzan were in precisely the condition she is in today, except that she could be fed and digest food and water without artificial assistance. How is the State's "interest" in keeping her alive thereby increased, or her interest in deciding whether she wants to continue living reduced? It seems to me, in other words, that Justice Brennan's position ultimately rests upon the proposition that it is none of the State's business if a person wants to commit suicide. Justice Stevens is explicit on the point: "Choices about death touch the core of liberty. . . . Not much may be said with confidence about death unless it is said from faith, and that alone is reason enough to protect the freedom to conform choices about death to individual conscience." This is a view that some societies have held, and that our States are free to adopt if they wish. But it is not a view imposed by our constitutional traditions, in which the power of the State to prohibit suicide is unquestionable.

What I have said above is not meant to suggest that I would think it desirable, if we were sure that Nancy Cruzan wanted to die, to keep her alive by the means at issue here. I assert only that the Constitution has nothing to say about the subject. To raise up a constitutional right here we would have to create out of nothing (for it exists neither in text nor tradition) some constitutional principle whereby, although the State may insist that an individual come in out of the cold and eat food, it may not insist that he take medicine; and although it may pump his stomach empty of poison he has ingested, it may not fill his stomach with food he has failed to ingest. Are there, then, no reasonable and humane limits that ought not to be exceeded in requiring an individual to preserve his own life? There obviously are, but they are not set forth in the Due Process Clause. What assures us that those limits will not be exceeded is the same constitutional guarantee that is the source of most of our protection—what protects us, for example, from being assessed a tax of 100% of our income above the subsistence level, from being forbidden to drive cars, or from being required to send our children to school for 10 hours a day, none of which horribles are categorically prohibited by the Constitution. Our salvation is the Equal Protection Clause, which requires the democratic majority to accept for themselves and their loved ones what they impose on you and me. This Court need not, and has no authority to, inject itself into every field of human activity where irrationality and oppression may theoretically occur, and if it tries to do so it will destroy itself.

DISSENTING OPINION BY JUSTICE BRENNAN:

. . . Today the Court, while tentatively accepting that there is some degree of constitutionally protected liberty interest in avoiding unwanted medical treatment, including life-sustaining medical treatment such as artificial nutrition and hydration, affirms the decision of the Missouri Supreme Court. The majority opinion, as I read it, would affirm that decision on the ground that a State may require "clear and convincing" evidence of Nancy Cruzan's prior decision to forgo life-sustaining treatment under circumstances such as hers in order to ensure that her actual wishes are honored. Because I believe that Nancy Cruzan has a fundamental right to be free of unwanted artificial nutrition and hydration, which right is not outweighed by any interests of the State, and because I find that the improperly biased procedural obstacles imposed by the Missouri Supreme Court impermissibly burden that right, I respectfully dissent. Nancy Cruzan is entitled to choose to die with dignity. . . .

Although the right to be free of unwanted medical intervention, like other constitutionally protected interests, may not be absolute, no state interest could outweigh the rights of an individual in Nancy Cruzan's position. Whatever a State's possible interests in mandating life-support treatment under other circumstances, there is no good to be obtained here by Missouri's insistence that Nancy Cruzan remain on life-support systems if it is indeed her wish not to do so. Missouri does not claim, nor could it, that society as a whole will be benefited by Nancy's receiving medical treatment. No third party's situation will be improved and no harm to others will be averted.

The only state interest asserted here is a general interest in the preservation of life. But the State has no legitimate general interest in someone's life, completely abstracted from the interest of the person living that life, that could outweigh the person's choice to avoid medical treatment. "The regulation of constitutionally protected decisions . . . must be predicated on legitimate state concerns other than disagreement with the choice the individual has made. . . .

Otherwise, the interest in liberty protected by the Due Process Clause would be a nullity." Thus, the State's general interest in life must accede to Nancy Cruzan's particularized and intense interest in self-determination in her choice of medical treatment. There is simply nothing legitimately within the State's purview to be gained by superseding her decision.

This is not to say that the State has no legitimate interests to assert here. As the majority recognizes, Missouri has a *parens patriae* interest in providing Nancy Cruzan, now incompetent, with as accurate as possible a determination of how she would exercise her rights under these circumstances. Second, if and when it is determined that Nancy Cruzan would want to continue treatment, the State may legitimately assert an interest in providing that treatment. But until Nancy's wishes have been determined, the only state interest that may be asserted is an interest in safeguarding the accuracy of that determination.

Accuracy, therefore, must be our touchstone. Missouri may constitutionally impose only those procedural requirements that serve to enhance the accuracy of a determination of Nancy Cruzan's wishes or are at least consistent with an accurate determination. The Missouri "safeguard" that the Court upholds today does not meet that standard. The determination needed in this context is whether the incompetent person would choose to live in a persistent vegetative state on life support or to avoid this medical treatment. Missouri's rule of decision imposes a markedly asymmetrical evidentiary burden. Only evidence of specific statements of treatment choice made by the patient when competent is admissible to support a finding that the patient, now in a persistent vegetative state, would wish to avoid further medical treatment. Moreover, this evidence must be clear and convincing. No proof is required to support a finding that the incompetent person would wish to continue treatment. . . .

The majority . . . argues that where, as here, important individual rights are at stake, a clear and convincing evidence standard has long been held to be an appropriate means of enhancing accuracy, citing decisions concerning what process an individual is due before he can be deprived of a liberty interest. In those cases, however, this Court imposed a clear and convincing standard as a constitutional minimum on the basis of its evaluation that one side's interests clearly outweighed the second side's interests and therefore the second side should bear the risk of error. See *Santosky v. Kramer* (1982) (requiring a clear and convincing evidence standard for termination of parental rights because the parent's interest is fundamental but the State has no legitimate interest in termination unless the parent is unfit, and finding that the State's interest in finding the best home for the child does not arise until the parent has been found unfit); *Addington v. Texas* (1979) (requiring clear and convincing evidence in an involuntary commitment hearing because the interest of the individual far outweighs that of a State, which has no legitimate interest in confining individuals who are not mentally ill and do not pose a danger to themselves or others). Moreover, we have always recognized that shifting the risk of error reduces the likelihood of errors in one direction at the cost of increasing the likelihood of errors in the other. In the cases cited by the majority, the imbalance imposed by a heightened evidentiary standard was not only acceptable but required because the standard was deployed to protect an individual's exercise of a fundamental right, as the majority admits. In contrast, the Missouri court imposed a clear and convincing evidence standard as an obstacle to the exercise of a fundamental right.

The majority claims that the allocation of the risk of error is justified because it is more important not to terminate life support for someone who would wish it continued than to honor the wishes of someone who would not. An erroneous decision to terminate life support is irrevocable, says the majority, while an erroneous decision not to terminate "results in a maintenance of the status quo." But, from the point of view of the patient, an erroneous decision in either direction is irrevocable. An erroneous decision to terminate artificial nutrition and hydration, to be sure, will lead to failure of that last remnant of physiological life, the brain stem, and result in complete brain death. An erroneous decision not to terminate life support, however, robs a patient of the very qualities protected by the right to avoid unwanted medical treatment. His own degraded existence is perpetuated; his family's suffering is protracted; the memory he leaves behind becomes more and more distorted.

Even a later decision to grant him his wish cannot undo the intervening harm. But a later decision is unlikely in any event. "The discovery of new evidence," to which the majority refers is more hypothetical than plausible. The majority also misconceives the relevance of the possibility of "advancements in medical science," by treating it as a reason to force someone to continue medical treatment against his will. The possibility of a medical miracle is indeed part of the calculus, but it is a part of the patient's calculus. If current research suggests that some hope for cure or even moderate improvement is possible within the lifespan projected, this is a factor that should be and would be accorded significant weight in assessing what the patient himself would choose. . . .

I do not suggest that States must sit by helplessly if the choices of incompetent patients are in danger of being ignored. Even if the Court had ruled that Missouri's rule of decision is unconstitutional, as I believe it should have, States would nevertheless remain free to fashion procedural protections to safeguard the interests of incompetents under these circumstances. The Constitution provides merely a framework here: Protections must be genuinely aimed at ensuring decisions commensurate with the will of the patient, and must be reliable as instruments to that end. Of the many States which have instituted such protections, Missouri is virtually the only one to have fashioned a rule that lessens the likelihood of accurate determinations. In contrast, nothing in the Constitution prevents States from reviewing the advisability of a family decision, by requiring a court proceeding or by appointing an impartial guardian ad litem. . . .

As many as 10,000 patients are being maintained in persistent vegetative states in the United States, and the number is expected to increase significantly in the near future. Medical technology, developed over the past 20 or so years, is often capable of resuscitating people after they have stopped breathing or their hearts have stopped beating. Some of those people are brought fully back to life. Two decades ago, those who were not and could not swallow and digest food, died. Intravenous solutions could not provide sufficient calories to maintain people for more than a short time. Today, various forms of artificial feeding have been developed that are able to keep people metabolically alive for years, even decades. In addition, in this century, chronic or degenerative ailments have replaced communicable diseases as the primary causes of death. The 80% of Americans who die in hospitals are "likely to meet their end . . . 'in a sedated or comatose state; betubed nasally, abdominally and intravenously; and far more like manipulated objects than like moral subjects.' " A fifth of all adults surviving to age 80 will suffer a progressive dementing disorder prior to death. . . .

. . . Missouri and this Court have displaced Nancy's own assessment of the processes associated with dying. They have discarded evidence of her will, ignored her values, and deprived her of the right to a decision as closely approximating her own choice as humanly possible. They have done so disingenuously in her name and openly in Missouri's own. That Missouri and this Court may truly be motivated only by concern for incompetent patients makes no matter. As one of our most prominent jurists warned us decades ago: "Experience should teach us to be most on our guard to protect liberty when the government's purposes are beneficent. . . . The greatest dangers to liberty lurk in insidious encroachment by men of zeal, well meaning but without understanding."

DISSENTING OPINION BY JUSTICE STEVENS:

. . . This case is the first in which we consider whether, and how, the Constitution protects the liberty of seriously ill patients to be free from life-sustaining medical treatment. So put, the question is both general and profound. We need not, however, resolve the question in the abstract. Our responsibility as judges both enables and compels us to treat the problem as it is illuminated by the facts of the controversy before us.

The most important of those facts are these: "Clear and convincing evidence" established that Nancy Cruzan is "oblivious to her environment except for reflexive responses to sound and perhaps to painful stimuli"; that "she has no cognitive or reflexive ability to swallow food or water"; that "she will never recover" these abilities; and that her "cerebral cortical atrophy is irreversible, permanent, progressive and ongoing." Recovery and consciousness are impossible; the highest cognitive brain function that can be hoped for is a grimace in "recognition of ordinarily painful stimuli" or an "apparent response to sound." . . .

[Nancy Cruzan's guardian ad litem] endorsed the critical finding that "it was in [her] best interests to have the tube feeding discontinued."

That important conclusion thus was not disputed by the litigants. One might reasonably suppose that it would be dispositive: If Nancy Cruzan has no interest in continued treatment, and if she has a liberty interest in being free from unwanted treatment, and if the cessation of treatment would have no adverse impact on third parties, and if no reason exists to doubt the good faith of Nancy's parents, then what possible basis could the State have for insisting upon continued medical treatment? Yet, instead of questioning or endorsing the trial court's conclusions about Nancy Cruzan's interests, the State Supreme Court largely ignored them. . . .

To be constitutionally permissible, Missouri's intrusion upon . . . fundamental liberties must, at a minimum, bear a reasonable relationship to a legitimate state end. Missouri asserts that its policy is related to a state interest in the protection of life. In my view, however, it is an effort to define life, rather than to protect it, that is the heart of Missouri's policy. Missouri insists, without regard to Nancy Cruzan's own interests, upon equating her life with the biological persistence of her bodily functions. Nancy Cruzan, it must be remembered, is not now simply incompetent. She is in a persistent vegetative state and has been so for seven years. The trial court found, and no party contested, that Nancy has no possibility of recovery and no consciousness.

It seems to me that the Court errs insofar as it characterizes this case as involving "judgments about the 'quality' of life that a particular individual may enjoy." Nancy Cruzan is obviously "alive" in a physiological sense. But for patients like Nancy Cruzan, who have no consciousness and no chance of recovery, there is a serious question as to whether the mere persistence of their bodies is "life" as that word is commonly understood, or as it is used in both the Constitution and the Declaration of Independence. The State's unflagging determination to perpetuate Nancy Cruzan's physical existence is comprehensible only as an effort to define life's meaning, not as an attempt to preserve its sanctity.

This much should be clear from the oddity of Missouri's definition alone. Life, particularly human life, is not commonly thought of as a merely physiological condition or function. Its sanctity is often thought to derive from the impossibility of any such reduction. When people speak of life, they often mean to describe the experiences that comprise a person's history, as when it is said that somebody "led a good life." They may also mean to refer to the practical manifestation of the human spirit, a meaning captured by the familiar observation that somebody "added life" to an assembly. If there is a shared thread among the various opinions on this subject, it may be that life is an activity which is at once the matrix for, and an integration of, a person's interests. In any event, absent some theological abstraction, the idea of life is not conceived separately from the idea of a living person. Yet, it is by precisely such a separation that Missouri asserts an interest in Nancy Cruzan's life in opposition to Nancy Cruzan's own interests. The resulting definition is uncommon indeed. . . .

My disagreement with the Court is thus unrelated to its endorsement of the clear and convincing standard of proof for cases of this kind. Indeed, I agree that the controlling facts must be established with unmistakable clarity. The critical question, however, is not how to prove the controlling facts but rather what proven facts should be controlling. In my view, the constitutional answer is clear: The best interests of the individual, especially when buttressed by the interests of all related third parties, must prevail over any general state policy that simply ignores those interests. Indeed, the only apparent secular basis for the State's interest in life is the policy's persuasive impact upon people other than Nancy and her family. Yet, "although the State may properly perform a teaching function," and although that teaching may foster respect for the sanctity of life, the State may not pursue its project by infringing constitutionally protected interests for "symbolic effect." The failure of Missouri's policy to heed the interests of a dying individual with respect to matters so private is ample evidence of the policy's illegitimacy.

Only because Missouri has arrogated to itself the power to define life, and only because the Court permits this usurpation, are Nancy Cruzan's life and liberty put into disquieting conflict. If Nancy Cruzan's life were defined by reference to her own interests, so that her life expired when her biological existence ceased serving any of her own interests, then her constitutionally protected interest in freedom from unwanted treatment would not come into conflict with her constitutionally protected interest in life. Conversely, if there were any evidence that Nancy Cruzan herself defined life to encompass every form of biological persistence by a human being, so that the continuation of treatment would serve Nancy's own liberty, then once again there would be no conflict between life and liberty. The opposition of life and liberty in this case are thus not the result of Nancy Cruzan's tragic accident, but are instead the artificial consequence of Missouri's effort, and this Court's willingness, to abstract Nancy Cruzan's life from Nancy Cruzan's person.

NOTES AND QUESTIONS:
Cruzan v. Director, Missouri Department of Health

1. What are Nancy Cruzan's parents seeking from the court? How does their request differ from what happened in the *Quinlan* case?
2. What rule was Missouri applying in deciding when life-sustaining care could be stopped in the case of a person in a persistent vegetative state?
3. The Missouri Supreme Court found that there was no right of privacy in that state's constitution which "would support the right of a person to refuse medical treatment in every circumstance." Do you think the Missouri court would have reached a different result if it had found such a right? How did the nonexistence of such a right factor into the Missouri court's reasoning?

   In particular, could Missouri still "adopt a state policy favoring the preservation of life" even if there were such a right? Are the two inconsistent? Why or why not? (The majority opinion in *Cruzan*—especially what it says about the U.S. Constitution—should help you in answering this question.)
4. This case divided the court, with only five of the nine Justices voting to support the Missouri law. There are five opinions in this case: the majority

opinion (by Rehnquist), two concurring opinions (by O'Connor and Scalia), and two dissenting opinions (by Brennan and Stevens). Not only do these opinions represent a wide range of views, even the opinions on the same side are often very far apart. Which two opinions are the best examples of that?

5. The majority opinion states that "[t]his is the first case in which we have been squarely presented with the issue whether the United States Constitution grants what is in common parlance referred to as a 'right to die.'" Is this case really about the "right to die"? What is the most accurate description of the right that the court is talking about?

6. Rehnquist notes that the Court "assumes" that Nancy Cruzan had a constitutional interest at stake in this case. Is the majority actually determining that there really is such a right—as opposed to "assuming" there might be such a right? What is it about this case that might permit the Court to not conclusively resolve this issue? (If your reasoning leads to the same result whether a particular statement is true or false, can you avoid deciding whether that statement is true? As a general rule, courts try not to answer a question unless that question *must* be answered in order to resolve the case before them.)

7. What evidence does Rehnquist marshal in concluding that there might be a constitutional interest at stake here? Based upon that evidence, and what you know about constitutional rights in general, do you think that Nancy Cruzan did have a constitutional right?

8. Rehnquist notes that "[w]e do not think a State is required to remain neutral in the face of an informed and voluntary decision by a physically able adult to starve to death." What is he talking about? What state interest is at stake? Does this state interest have anything to do with helping make a decision consistent with what Nancy Cruzan would have wanted?

9. As we noted in the discussion of *Michael H.* in chapter 5, the constitutionality of a statute often depends on the purpose of the statute. Consider the following alternative statements of what Missouri was trying to accomplish with its rule:

   a. To best make sure that the decision whether or not to withdraw life-sustaining care from an incompetent person is based on that person's wishes.

   b. To "generally" make sure that such wishes are followed, but also to try to limit the number of instances in which a mistake might be made in which care is withdrawn from a person who did not wish to refuse care.

   If the legislature's purpose had been (a), did the Missouri rule serve that purpose well? Might it have been subject to attack under the procedural due process rules of the Fourteenth Amendment: if we want to determine what a patient wanted done, is it reasonable to exclude the only evidence of the patient's wishes? On the other hand, if (b) is the legislative purpose, does it make greater sense to exclude "good" but not "great" evidence?

10. Another way to describe the issue raised by option (b) in note 9 is to compare it to what happens with medical tests. No test is perfect, and thus it is always important to determine how often the test will be wrong. But a test can be wrong in two different ways.

Consider, for example, the pressure test used to detect glaucoma that was discussed in *Helling* in chapter 7. Assume we applied that test to 100 people who in fact do have glaucoma, and it was positive in only 85 instances. Thus, it erred in not finding the illness in 15 percent of the cases. This is described as a *false negative* problem, since the test incorrectly (and thus falsely) described these patients as not having glaucoma.

On the other hand, imagine the test was applied to 100 people who do not have glaucoma. A perfect test would have a negative result in all 100 cases. Assume, however, that our test is not perfect, and that it says that 5 of the people do in fact have glaucoma. These are *false positives*; the test incorrectly comes up with a positive result.

Most real-world tests are imperfect, and thus have a non-zero likelihood of producing both false positives and false negatives. Moreover, attempts to improve one of these error rates will usually increase the other one. For example, if we attempt to reduce the false negative rate of a test for glaucoma, we will likely have to loosen our criteria for concluding that someone has glaucoma. As a result, we would likely increase the number of false positive results. Determining what constitutes the "best" test requires comparing the harm caused by a false negative result with that of a false positive result.

For an example of this phenomenon in the law, we can turn to the rules relating to a determination of guilt or innocence in a criminal trial. A person is to be assumed innocent; guilt must be proven "beyond a reasonable doubt." In line with those principles, it is often said that it would be better if 100 guilty people went free than if one innocent person were wrongly convicted. Note that convicting an innocent person would in effect be making a false positive determination of guilt, while letting a guilty person go free would be a false negative. Thus, we are saying that because the wrong resulting from a false positive far outweighs that of a false negative, we are willing to accept a system of proof that is highly inaccurate: we recognize that we will be finding too many people innocent, but conclude that this result is necessary to prevent false positives.

11. Which of the two interpretations of the underlying purpose of the Missouri law does Justice Rehnquist adopt? Note his comment that "Missouri may permissibly place an increased risk of an erroneous decision on those seeking to terminate an incompetent individual's life-sustaining treatment. An erroneous decision not to terminate results in a maintenance of the status quo. . . An erroneous decision to withdraw life-sustaining treatment, however, is not susceptible of correction."

Assuming you agree with the majority about what the state of Missouri was attempting to do with this law, do you agree with the conclusion that such a tipping of the scales against "wrongly" allowing a person to die is constitutionally permissible? Is it acceptable to create a rule that intentionally ignores the best information regarding a person's desire to exercise the right to refuse care? If we are accepting that a person assumedly has a fundamental, constitutionally protected interest in refusing unwanted care, what standard must be met by a state law that might impinge on that right? (Recall the discussion of equal protection in chapter 2: what must a state demonstrate in order to discriminate between those persons who have given "good" evidence of their wish to refuse care, and those who have given "clear and convincing evidence"?) Has the state of Missouri met that standard? Is the harm from wrongly allowing a person in a persistent vegetative state to die even though the person really wanted to live sufficient to counterbalance the harm from keeping, for example, 100 people in persistent vegetative states alive for many years even though they wanted to be allowed to die?

In balancing these two harms, might it be relevant that the constitutional right under discussion is the right to *refuse* care? As was noted in chapter 9, there is no constitutional right to *get* medical care. Might this circumstance be relevant in interpreting the legitimacy of the Missouri law?

12. Justice Brennan in his dissent takes issue with much of what Rehnquist says. In particular, looking at the two possible purposes that Missouri might have had in justifying its law (see note 9), he rejects purpose (b), and concludes that "the only state interest that may be asserted is an interest in safeguarding the accuracy of that determination." Why does he reach this conclusion? Do you agree with his reasoning?

    Assuming that Brennan was correct in concluding that the only permissible purpose for the state of Missouri is to determine, most accurately, what a person's wishes are, is the Missouri rule acceptable? What arguments does Brennan advance in concluding that it is not? How convincing are they?

13. Justice O'Connor in concurring is somewhat more definite than Rehnquist in concluding that Nancy Cruzan did have a constitutional right to refuse care and, in particular, to refuse the artificial delivery of food and water. She also comments on "the issue whether a State must also give effect to the decisions of a surrogate decisionmaker." What does she say about that issue, and what type of fact pattern does she have in mind? How might the majority opinion reach a result different from the one she favors?

14. According to Justice Scalia, how does the U.S. Constitution limit a state's choice of laws relating to when a person can refuse life-sustaining treatment? How does he justify his conclusions? What does he say about the existence of a constitutional right to refuse care?

    Much of his concurrence is spent in discussing the meaning of suicide. Does he think a state has a right, should it choose to do so, to prevent a person from committing suicide? On what side of the line—suicide or not suicide—would he place a person's decision to refuse care? Whether or not you agree with his interpretation of the Constitution's restriction on state power, what do you think of his arguments about the differences between refusing care and other ways of committing suicide? (Compare his views to the discussion of suicide in the notes following *Bouvia*, 266–67.)

15. Justice Stevens makes a very different argument from any of his colleagues. What is his view of Nancy's condition? How does that view alter his interpretation of the interests the state of Missouri might advance?

In particular, what if Nancy had said absolutely nothing about what she wanted to be done? What does Stevens think should then have been done with regard to feeding her? What assumption is he making about the wishes of the average person with regard to being maintained in a persistent vegetative state? This fact pattern is not a minor issue; many if not the great majority of us are likely to die without having given much guidance about our wishes in such a situation. Would Brennan reach the same result for such a patient?

16. Would either of the following state laws be constitutional? Why or why not?

a. A state law that says that life-sustaining treatment *must* be withheld from an incompetent person if there is evidence demonstrating that it is more likely than not that the person would have wanted the treatment withheld.

b. A state law that says that life-sustaining treatment *must* be withheld from an incompetent person *unless* there is clear and convincing evidence that the patient would have wanted to receive the treatment.

17. Evaluate the likely constitutionality of each of the following laws under each of the five opinions in *Cruzan*:

a. A state law that denies a patient the right to refuse any form of life-sustaining care necessary to keep him alive.

b. A state law that denies a patient the right to refuse life-sustaining care unless the patient is "sufficiently sick," based on a particular definition.

18. Assume that Nancy Cruzan had, a day before her accident, filled out a valid durable power of attorney for health care, appointing her mother as her surrogate decision-maker. The document itself gave no substantive guidance about how her mother should exercise that authority. Consider the following two situations:

a. Mom states that Nancy never gave her any indication of her views about whether or not she wanted to be kept alive in a persistent vegetative state.

b. Mom states that Nancy had once made remarks, in a casual conversation, that suggested she might not want to be kept alive in a persistent vegetative state.

Assume that there was no other evidence of Nancy's wishes, and that the state of Missouri was opposing Mom's efforts to have the respirator turned off, noting that there was no clear and convincing evidence of her desire to be allowed to die in these circumstances. What conclusion would a majority of the Justices on the *Cruzan* court have come to on these facts?

PHYSICIAN-ASSISTED SUICIDE

Based upon both *Cruzan* and the cases discussed in chapter 10, we can be relatively comfortable that the United States Constitution and many state constitutions likely recognize some form of right to refuse medical care. While a state might perhaps be able to come up with sufficient reasons to justify limitations on that right in unique circumstances, these reasons are likely not to apply in the situation of a terminally ill, suffering patient. Thus, in almost all such circumstances, the patient who is being kept alive by some form of medical treatment will have a right to end his life by requesting that the treatment be discontinued.

Many times, however, a person may be terminally ill and suffering yet not be dependent on any form of life-sustaining medical treatment. The patient may not need a respirator, and may not require artificial hydration or nutrition. Such persons thus obtain no benefit from the "negative" right to be free from unwanted care. They may want someone's assistance to help them die, assuming they are unwilling to use a gun, or stop eating and drinking. It was just such circumstances that created Dr. Jack Kevorkian's "clientele." These people needed Kevorkian's help precisely because there was no machine that could be conveniently turned off. So Kevorkian would step in and hook them up to a device that would allow them to press a button, for example, and effectively inject themselves with a lethal drug. It is this act of assistance beyond merely terminating treatment that placed Kevorkian's actions in the category of physician-assisted suicide. Many states have specific statutes that criminalize such actions. Even in the states where this is not clearly defined as a crime, it may nonetheless be considered a form of homicide.

It is certainly not obvious why a person's ability to end her life with the assistance of her doctor should be determined by the "luck" of having the type of disease that conveniently makes her dependent on some form of life-sustaining treatment. The tenuousness of that very distinction led several patients to bring lawsuits in the states of Washington and New York to overturn state laws criminalizing physician-assisted suicide. In each of these cases there were three patients, all of whom died before the cases made their way through the trial and appellate levels of the federal court system, let alone reached the U.S. Supreme Court. Their stories are recounted in the opinions of the two federal courts of appeal but did not make it into the Supreme Court's opinions.

The statements of the three patient-plaintiffs in the New York case, *Quill v. Vacco*, 80 F.3d 716, 720-21 (2d Cir. 1996), are representative:

[**Jane Doe:**] I have a large cancerous tumor which is wrapped around the right carotid artery in my neck and is collapsing my esophagus and invading my voice box. The tumor has significantly reduced my ability to swallow and prevents me from eating anything but very thin liquids in extremely small amounts. The cancer has metastasized to my plural [sic] cavity and it is painful to yawn or cough. . . . In early July 1994 I had the [feeding] tube implanted and have suffered serious problems as a result. . . . I take a variety of medications to manage the pain. . . . It is not possible for me to reduce my pain to an acceptable level of comfort and to retain an alert state. . . . At this time, it is clear to me, based on the advice of my doctors, that I am in the terminal phase of this disease. . . . At the point at which I can no longer endure the pain and suffering associated with my cancer, I want to have drugs available for the purpose of hastening my death in a humane and certain manner. I want to be able to discuss freely with my treating physician my intention of hastening my death through the consumption of drugs prescribed for that purpose.

[**Mr. Kingsley:**] At this time I have almost no immune system function. . . . My first major illness associated with AIDS was cryptosporidiosis, a parasitic infection which caused me severe fevers and diarrhea and associated pain, suffering and exhaustion. . . . I also suffer from cytomegalovirus ("CMV") retinitis, an AIDS-related virus which attacks the retina and causes blindness. To date I have become almost completely blind in my left eye. I am at risk of losing my sight altogether from this condition. . . . I also suffer from toxoplasmosis, a parasitic infection which has caused lesions to develop on my brain. . . . I . . . take daily infusions of cytovene for the . . . retinitis condition. This medication, administered for an hour through a Hickman tube which is connected to an artery in my chest, prevents me from ever taking showers and makes simple routine functions burdensome. In addition, I inject my leg daily with neupogen to combat the deficient white cell count in my blood. The daily injection of this medication is extremely painful. . . . At this point it is clear to me, based on the advice of my doctors, that I am in the terminal phase of [AIDS]. . . . It is my desire that my physician prescribe suitable drugs for me to consume for the purpose of hastening my death when and if my suffering becomes intolerable.

[**Mr. Barth:**] In May 1992, I developed a Kaposi's sarcoma skin lesion. This was my first major illness associated with AIDS. I underwent radiation and chemotherapy to treat this cancer. . . . In September 1993, I was diagnosed with cytomegalovirus ("CMV") in my stomach and colon which caused severe diarrhea, fevers and wasting. . . . In February 1994, I was diagnosed with microsporidiosis, a parasitic infection for which there is effectively no treatment. . . . At approximately the same time, I contracted AIDS-related pneumonia. The pneumonia's infusion therapy treatment was so extremely toxic that I vomited with each infusion. . . . In March 1994, I was diagnosed with cryptosporidiosis, a parasitic infection which has caused severe diarrhea, sometimes producing 20 stools a day, extreme abdominal pain, nausea and additional significant wasting. I have begun to lose bowel control . . . . For each of these conditions I have undergone a variety of medical treatments, each of which has had significant adverse side effects. . . . While I have tolerated some [nightly intravenous] feedings, I am unwilling to accept this for an extended period of time. . . . I understand that there are no cures. . . . I can no longer endure the pain and suffering . . . and I want to have drugs available for the purpose of hastening my death.

The issues raised in both the Washington and New York cases were identical. Oddly enough, even though both federal appellate courts struck down the state laws that restricted a patient's access to "physician-assisted suicide," the two courts did so for different reasons. In the Washington case, the court determined that the state law unconstitutionally burdened a patient's right to privacy. The court therefore chose not to address a second argument of the plaintiffs: that in treating differently people who are being kept alive by medical treatment and those who can live without such treatment, the law violated the equal protection clause of the Fourteenth Amendment.

In contrast, the New York federal appellate court found there was an equal protection violation, but also concluded that there was *no* right of privacy violation. Thus, the two federal court opinions reached the same decision, but were at least partly inconsistent in reaching different conclusions on the privacy issue. Because of the different conclusions by the two appellate courts, the Supreme Court provides two different opinions.

WASHINGTON V. GLUCKSBERG
Supreme Court of the United States
521 U.S. 702 (1997)

OPINION BY CHIEF JUSTICE REHNQUIST:

The question presented in this case is whether Washington's prohibition against "causing" or "aiding" a suicide offends the Fourteenth Amendment to the United States Constitution. We hold that it does not.

It has always been a crime to assist a suicide in the State of Washington. In 1854, Washington's first Territorial Legislature outlawed "assisting another in the commission of self-murder." Today, Washington law provides: "A person is guilty of promoting a suicide attempt when he knowingly causes or aids another person to attempt suicide." "Promoting a suicide attempt" is a felony, punishable by up to five years' imprisonment and up to a $10,000 fine. At the same time, Washington's Natural Death Act, enacted in 1979, states that the "withholding or withdrawal of life-sustaining treatment" at a patient's direction "shall not, for any purpose, constitute a suicide."

The plaintiffs asserted "the existence of a liberty interest protected by the Fourteenth Amendment which extends to a personal choice by a mentally competent, terminally ill adult to commit physician-assisted suicide." . . .

I

We begin, as we do in all due-process cases, by examining our Nation's history, legal traditions, and practices. In almost every State—indeed, in almost every western democracy—it is a crime to assist a suicide. The States' assisted-suicide bans are not innovations. Rather, they are longstanding expressions of the States' commitment to the protection and preservation of all human life. Indeed, opposition to and condemnation of suicide—and, therefore, of assisting suicide—are consistent and enduring themes of our philosophical, legal, and cultural heritages.

More specifically, for over 700 years, the Anglo-American common-law tradition has punished or otherwise disapproved of both suicide and assisting suicide. In the 13th century, Henry de Bracton, one of the first legal-treatise writers, observed that "just as a man may commit felony by slaying another so may he do so by slaying himself." The real and personal property of one who killed himself to avoid conviction and punishment for a crime were forfeit to the king; however, thought Bracton, "if a man slays himself in weariness of life or because he is unwilling to endure further bodily pain . . . [only] his movable goods [were] confiscated." Thus, "the principle that suicide of a sane person, for whatever reason, was a punishable felony was . . . introduced into English common law." Centuries later, Sir William Blackstone, whose Commentaries on the Laws of England not only provided a definitive summary of the common law but was also a primary legal authority for 18th and 19th century American lawyers, referred to suicide as "self-murder" and "the pretended heroism, but real cowardice, of the Stoic philosophers, who destroyed themselves to avoid those ills which they had not the fortitude to endure . . . ." Blackstone emphasized that "the law has . . . ranked [suicide] among the highest crimes," although, anticipating later developments, he conceded that the harsh and shameful punishments imposed for suicide "border a little upon severity." . . .

Over time, however, the American colonies abolished these harsh common-law penalties. . . . [T]he movement away from the common law's harsh sanctions did not represent an acceptance of suicide; rather, . . . this change reflected the growing consensus that it was unfair to punish the suicide's family for his wrongdoing. . . . That suicide remained a grievous, though nonfelonious, wrong is confirmed by the fact that colonial and early state legislatures and courts did not retreat from prohibiting assisting suicide. . . . And the prohibitions against assisting suicide never contained exceptions for those who were near death. Rather, "the life of those to whom life had become a burden—of those who [were] hopelessly diseased or fatally wounded—nay, even the lives of criminals condemned to death, [were] under the protection of law, equally as the lives of those who [were] in the full tide of life's enjoyment, and anxious to continue to live."

The earliest American statute explicitly to outlaw assisting suicide was enacted in New York in 1828, and many of the new States and Territories followed New York's example. . . . By the time the Fourteenth Amendment was ratified, it was a crime in most States to assist a suicide. . . . In this century, the Model Penal Code also prohibited "aiding" suicide, prompting many States to enact or revise their assisted-suicide bans. The Code's drafters observed that "the interests in the sanctity of life that are represented by the criminal homicide laws are threatened by one who expresses a willingness to participate in taking the life of another, even though the act may be accomplished with the consent, or at the request, of the suicide victim."

Though deeply rooted, the States' assisted-suicide bans have in recent years been reexamined and, generally, reaffirmed. Because of advances in medicine and technology, Americans today are increasingly likely to die in institutions, from chronic illnesses. Public concern and democratic action are therefore sharply focused on how best to protect dignity and independence at the end of life, with the result that there have been many significant changes in state laws and in the attitudes these laws reflect. Many States, for example, now permit "living wills," surrogate health-care decisionmaking, and the withdrawal or refusal of life-sustaining medical treatment. At the same time, however, voters and legislators continue for the most part to reaffirm their States' prohibitions on assisting suicide.

The Washington statute at issue in this case was enacted in 1975 as part of a revision of that State's criminal code. Four years later, Washington passed its Natural Death Act, which specifically stated that the "withholding or withdrawal of life-sustaining treatment . . . shall not, for any purpose, constitute a suicide" and that "nothing in this chapter shall be construed to condone, authorize, or approve mercy killing . . . ." In 1991, Washington voters rejected a ballot initiative which, had it passed, would have permitted a form of physician-assisted suicide. Washington then added a provision to the Natural Death Act expressly excluding physician-assisted suicide.

California voters rejected an assisted-suicide initiative similar to Washington's in 1993. On the other hand, in 1994, voters in Oregon enacted, also through ballot initiative, that State's "Death With Dignity Act," which legalized physician-assisted suicide for competent, terminally ill adults. Since the Oregon vote, many proposals to legalize assisted-suicide have been and continue to be introduced in the States' legislatures, but none has been enacted. And just last year, Iowa and Rhode Island joined the overwhelming majority of States explicitly prohibiting assisted suicide. Also, on April 30, 1997, President Clinton signed the Federal Assisted Suicide Funding Restriction Act of 1997, which prohibits the use of federal funds in support of physician-assisted suicide.

Attitudes toward suicide itself have changed since Bracton, but our laws have consistently condemned, and continue to prohibit, assisting suicide. De-

spite changes in medical technology and notwithstanding an increased emphasis on the importance of end-of-life decisionmaking, we have not retreated from
this prohibition. Against this backdrop of history, tradition, and practice, we
now turn to respondents' constitutional claim.

II

The Due Process Clause guarantees more than fair process, and the "liberty" it
protects includes more than the absence of physical restraint. The Clause also
provides heightened protection against government interference with certain
fundamental rights and liberty interests. In a long line of cases, we have held
that, in addition to the specific freedoms protected by the Bill of Rights, the
"liberty" specially protected by the Due Process Clause includes the rights to
marry; to have children; to direct the education and upbringing of one's children; to marital privacy; to use contraception; to bodily integrity, and to abortion. We have also assumed, and strongly suggested, that the Due Process
Clause protects the traditional right to refuse unwanted lifesaving medical
treatment. But we "have always been reluctant to expand the concept of substantive due process because guideposts for responsible decisionmaking in this
unchartered area are scarce and open-ended." . . . Our established method of
substantive-due-process analysis has two primary features: First, we have regularly observed that the Due Process Clause specially protects those fundamental rights and liberties which are, objectively, "deeply rooted in this Nation's history and tradition." Second, we have required in substantive-due-process cases
a "careful description" of the asserted fundamental liberty interest. Our Nation's history, legal traditions, and practices thus provide the crucial "guideposts
for responsible decisionmaking," that direct and restrain our exposition of the
Due Process Clause. As we stated recently . . . the Fourteenth Amendment
"forbids the government to infringe . . . 'fundamental' liberty interests at all, no
matter what process is provided, unless the infringement is narrowly tailored to
serve a compelling state interest."

  Turning to the claim at issue here, the Court of Appeals stated that "properly analyzed, the first issue to be resolved is whether there is a liberty interest
in determining the time and manner of one's death," or, in other words, "is there
a right to die?" Similarly, respondents assert a "liberty to choose how to die" and
a right to "control of one's final days," and describe the asserted liberty as "the
right to choose a humane, dignified death," and "the liberty to shape death." As
noted above, we have a tradition of carefully formulating the interest at stake in
substantive-due-process cases. For example, although *Cruzan* is often described as a "right to die" case, we were, in fact, more precise: we assumed that
the Constitution granted competent persons a "constitutionally protected right
to refuse lifesaving hydration and nutrition." The Washington statute at issue in
this case prohibits "aiding another person to attempt suicide," and, thus, the
question before us is whether the "liberty" specially protected by the Due Pro-

cess Clause includes a right to commit suicide which itself includes a right to assistance in doing so.

We now inquire whether this asserted right has any place in our Nation's
traditions. Here, as discussed above, we are confronted with a consistent and almost universal tradition that has long rejected the asserted right, and continues
explicitly to reject it today, even for terminally ill, mentally competent adults. To
hold for respondents, we would have to reverse centuries of legal doctrine and
practice, and strike down the considered policy choice of almost every State.

Respondents contend, however, that the liberty interest they assert is consistent with this Court's substantive-due-process line of cases, if not with this Nation's history and practice. Pointing to *Casey* and *Cruzan*, respondents read our
jurisprudence in this area as reflecting a general tradition of "self-sovereignty,"
and as teaching that the "liberty" protected by the Due Process Clause includes
"basic and intimate exercises of personal autonomy." According to respondents,
our liberty jurisprudence, and the broad, individualistic principles it reflects,
protects the "liberty of competent, terminally ill adults to make end-of-life decisions free of undue government interference." The question presented in this
case, however, is whether the protections of the Due Process Clause include a
right to commit suicide with another's assistance. With this "careful description"
of respondents' claim in mind, we turn to *Casey* and *Cruzan*.

In *Cruzan*, we considered whether Nancy Beth Cruzan, who had been severely injured in an automobile accident and was in a persistent vegetative state,
"had a right under the United States Constitution which would require the hospital to withdraw life-sustaining treatment" at her parents' request. We began
with the observation that "at common law, even the touching of one person by
another without consent and without legal justification was a battery." We then
discussed the related rule that "informed consent is generally required for medical treatment." After reviewing a long line of relevant state cases, we concluded
that "the common-law doctrine of informed consent is viewed as generally encompassing the right of a competent individual to refuse medical treatment."
Next, we reviewed our own cases on the subject, and stated that "the principle
that a competent person has a constitutionally protected liberty interest in refusing unwanted medical treatment may be inferred from our prior decisions."
Therefore, "for purposes of [that] case, we assumed that the United States Constitution would grant a competent person a constitutionally protected right to
refuse lifesaving hydration and nutrition." We concluded that, notwithstanding
this right, the Constitution permitted Missouri to require clear and convincing
evidence of an incompetent patient's wishes concerning the withdrawal of
life-sustaining treatment.

Respondents contend that in *Cruzan* we "acknowledged that competent,
dying persons have the right to direct the removal of life-sustaining medical
treatment and thus hasten death," and that "the constitutional principle behind
recognizing the patient's liberty to direct the withdrawal of artificial life support
applies at least as strongly to the choice to hasten impending death by consum-

ing lethal medication." Similarly, the Court of Appeals concluded that "*Cruzan*, by recognizing a liberty interest that includes the refusal of artificial provision of life-sustaining food and water, necessarily recognized a liberty interest in hastening one's own death."

The right assumed in *Cruzan*, however, was not simply deduced from abstract concepts of personal autonomy. Given the common-law rule that forced medication was a battery, and the long legal tradition protecting the decision to refuse unwanted medical treatment, our assumption was entirely consistent with this Nation's history and constitutional traditions. The decision to commit suicide with the assistance of another may be just as personal and profound as the decision to refuse unwanted medical treatment, but it has never enjoyed similar legal protection. Indeed, the two acts are widely and reasonably regarded as quite distinct. In *Cruzan* itself, we recognized that most States outlawed assisted suicide—and even more do today—and we certainly gave no intimation that the right to refuse unwanted medical treatment could be somehow transmuted into a right to assistance in committing suicide.

Respondents also rely on *Casey*. There, the Court's opinion concluded that "the essential holding of *Roe v. Wade* should be retained and once again reaffirmed." We held, first, that a woman has a right, before her fetus is viable, to an abortion "without undue interference from the State"; second, that States may restrict post-viability abortions, so long as exceptions are made to protect a woman's life and health; and third, that the State has legitimate interests throughout a pregnancy in protecting the health of the woman and the life of the unborn child. In reaching this conclusion, the opinion discussed in some detail this Court's substantive-due-process tradition of interpreting the Due Process Clause to protect certain fundamental rights and "personal decisions relating to marriage, procreation, contraception, family relationships, child rearing, and education," and noted that many of those rights and liberties "involve the most intimate and personal choices a person may make in a lifetime." The Court of Appeals, like the District Court, found *Casey* " 'highly instructive' " and " 'almost prescriptive' " for determining " 'what liberty interest may inhere in a terminally ill person's choice to commit suicide' ":

> Like the decision of whether or not to have an abortion, the decision how and when to die is one of 'the most intimate and personal choices a person may make in a lifetime,' a choice 'central to personal dignity and autonomy.'

Similarly, respondents emphasize the statement in *Casey* that:

> "At the heart of liberty is the right to define one's own concept of existence, of meaning, of the universe, and of the mystery of human life. Beliefs about these matters could not define the attributes of personhood were they formed under compulsion of the State."

By choosing this language, the Court's opinion in *Casey* described, in a general way and in light of our prior cases, those personal activities and decisions that this Court has identified as so deeply rooted in our history and traditions, or so fundamental to our concept of constitutionally ordered liberty, that they are protected by the Fourteenth Amendment. The opinion moved from the recognition that liberty necessarily includes freedom of conscience and belief about ultimate considerations to the observation that "though the abortion decision may originate within the zone of conscience and belief, it is more than a philosophic exercise." That many of the rights and liberties protected by the Due Process Clause sound in personal autonomy does not warrant the sweeping conclusion that any and all important, intimate, and personal decisions are so protected, and *Casey* did not suggest otherwise.

The history of the law's treatment of assisted suicide in this country has been and continues to be one of the rejection of nearly all efforts to permit it. That being the case, our decisions lead us to conclude that the asserted "right" to assistance in committing suicide is not a fundamental liberty interest protected by the Due Process Clause. The Constitution also requires, however, that Washington's assisted-suicide ban be rationally related to legitimate government interests. This requirement is unquestionably met here. As the court below recognized, Washington's assisted-suicide ban implicates a number of state interests.

First, Washington has an "unqualified interest in the preservation of human life." The State's prohibition on assisted suicide, like all homicide laws, both reflects and advances its commitment to this interest. This interest is symbolic and aspirational as well as practical:

> "While suicide is no longer prohibited or penalized, the ban against assisted suicide and euthanasia shores up the notion of limits in human relationships. It reflects the gravity with which we view the decision to take one's own life or the life of another, and our reluctance to encourage or promote these decisions."

Respondents admit that "the State has a real interest in preserving the lives of those who can still contribute to society and enjoy life." The Court of Appeals also recognized Washington's interest in protecting life, but held that the "weight" of this interest depends on the "medical condition and the wishes of the person whose life is at stake." Washington, however, has rejected this sliding-scale approach and, through its assisted-suicide ban, insists that all persons' lives, from beginning to end, regardless of physical or mental condition, are under the full protection of the law. As we have previously affirmed, the States "may properly decline to make judgments about the 'quality' of life that a particular individual may enjoy." This remains true, as *Cruzan* makes clear, even for those who are near death. Relatedly, all admit that suicide is a serious public-health problem, especially among persons in otherwise vulnerable groups. The State has an interest in preventing suicide, and in studying, identifying, and treating its causes.

Those who attempt suicide—terminally ill or not—often suffer from depression or other mental disorders. Research indicates, however, that many people who request physician-assisted suicide withdraw that request if their depression and pain are treated. The New York Task Force, however, expressed its concern that, because depression is difficult to diagnose, physicians and medical professionals often fail to respond adequately to seriously ill patients' needs. Thus, legal physician-assisted suicide could make it more difficult for the State to protect depressed or mentally ill persons, or those who are suffering from untreated pain, from suicidal impulses.

The State also has an interest in protecting the integrity and ethics of the medical profession. In contrast to the Court of Appeals' conclusion that "the integrity of the medical profession would [not] be threatened in any way by [physician-assisted suicide]," the American Medical Association, like many other medical and physicians' groups, has concluded that "physician-assisted suicide is fundamentally incompatible with the physician's role as healer." And physician-assisted suicide could, it is argued, undermine the trust that is essential to the doctor-patient relationship by blurring the time-honored line between healing and harming.

Next, the State has an interest in protecting vulnerable groups—including the poor, the elderly, and disabled persons—from abuse, neglect, and mistakes. The Court of Appeals dismissed the State's concern that disadvantaged persons might be pressured into physician-assisted suicide as "ludicrous on its face." We have recognized, however, the real risk of subtle coercion and undue influence in end-of-life situations. Similarly, the New York Task Force warned that "legalizing physician-assisted suicide would pose profound risks to many individuals who are ill and vulnerable. . . . The risk of harm is greatest for the many individuals in our society whose autonomy and well-being are already compromised by poverty, lack of access to good medical care, advanced age, or membership in a stigmatized social group." If physician-assisted suicide were permitted, many might resort to it to spare their families the substantial financial burden of end-of-life health-care costs.

Finally, the State may fear that permitting assisted suicide will start it down the path to voluntary and perhaps even involuntary euthanasia. The Court of Appeals struck down Washington's assisted-suicide ban only "as applied to competent, terminally ill adults who wish to hasten their deaths by obtaining medication prescribed by their doctors." Washington insists, however, that the impact of the court's decision will not and cannot be so limited. If suicide is protected as a matter of constitutional right, it is argued, "every man and woman in the United States must enjoy it." The Court of Appeals' decision, and its expansive reasoning, provide ample support for the State's concerns. The court noted, for example, that the "decision of a duly appointed surrogate decision maker is for all legal purposes the decision of the patient himself," that "in some instances, the patient may be unable to self-administer the drugs and . . . administration by the physician . . . may be the only way the patient may be able to receive them," and that not only physicians, but also family members and loved ones, will inevitably participate in assisting suicide. Thus, it turns out that what is couched as a limited right to "physician-assisted suicide" is likely, in effect, a much broader license, which could prove extremely difficult to police and contain. Washington's ban on assisting suicide prevents such erosion.

This concern is further supported by evidence about the practice of euthanasia in the Netherlands. The Dutch government's own study revealed that in 1990, there were 2,300 cases of voluntary euthanasia (defined as "the deliberate termination of another's life at his request"), 400 cases of assisted suicide, and more than 1,000 cases of euthanasia without an explicit request. In addition to these latter 1,000 cases, the study found an additional 4,941 cases where physicians administered lethal morphine overdoses without the patients' explicit consent. This study suggests that, despite the existence of various reporting procedures, euthanasia in the Netherlands has not been limited to competent, terminally ill adults who are enduring physical suffering, and that regulation of the practice may not have prevented abuses in cases involving vulnerable persons, including severely disabled neonates and elderly persons suffering from dementia. . . .

Throughout the Nation, Americans are engaged in an earnest and profound debate about the morality, legality, and practicality of physician-assisted suicide. Our holding permits this debate to continue, as it should in a democratic society. . . .

OPINION BY JUSTICE O'CONNOR, CONCURRING:

Death will be different for each of us. For many, the last days will be spent in physical pain and perhaps the despair that accompanies physical deterioration and a loss of control of basic bodily and mental functions. Some will seek medication to alleviate that pain and other symptoms.

The Court frames the issue in this case as whether the Due Process Clause of the Constitution protects a "right to commit suicide which itself includes a right to assistance in doing so," and concludes that our Nation's history, legal traditions, and practices do not support the existence of such a right. I join the Court's opinions because I agree that there is no generalized right to "commit suicide." But respondents urge us to address the narrower question whether a mentally competent person who is experiencing great suffering has a constitutionally cognizable interest in controlling the circumstances of his or her imminent death. I see no need to reach that question in the context of the facial challenges to the New York and Washington laws at issue here. The parties and *amici* agree that in these States a patient who is suffering from a terminal illness and who is experiencing great pain has no legal barriers to obtaining medication, from qualified physicians, to alleviate that suffering, even to the point of causing unconsciousness and hastening death. In this light, even assuming that we would recognize such an interest, I agree that the State's interests in protecting those who are not truly competent or facing imminent death, or those whose decisions to hasten death would not truly be voluntary, are sufficiently weighty to justify a prohibition against physician-assisted suicide.

Every one of us at some point may be affected by our own or a family member's terminal illness. There is no reason to think the democratic process will not strike the proper balance between the interests of terminally ill, mentally competent individuals who would seek to end their suffering and the State's interests in protecting those who might seek to end life mistakenly or under pressure. As the Court recognizes, States are presently undertaking extensive and serious evaluation of physician-assisted suicide and other related issues. In such circumstances, "the . . . challenging task of crafting appropriate procedures for safeguarding . . . liberty interests is entrusted to the 'laboratory' of the States . . . in the first instance."

In sum, there is no need to address the question whether suffering patients have a constitutionally cognizable interest in obtaining relief from the suffering that they may experience in the last days of their lives. There is no dispute that dying patients in Washington and New York can obtain palliative care, even when doing so would hasten their deaths. The difficulty in defining terminal illness and the risk that a dying patient's request for assistance in ending his or her life might not be truly voluntary justifies the prohibitions on assisted suicide we uphold here.

OPINION BY JUSTICE STEVENS,
CONCURRING IN THE JUDGMENTS:

The Court ends its opinion with the important observation that our holding today is fully consistent with a continuation of the vigorous debate about the "morality, legality, and practicality of physician-assisted suicide" in a democratic society. I write separately to make it clear that there is also room for further debate about the limits that the Constitution places on the power of the States to punish the practice.

I

History and tradition provide ample support for refusing to recognize an open-ended constitutional right to commit suicide. Much more than the State's paternalistic interest in protecting the individual from the irrevocable consequences of an ill-advised decision motivated by temporary concerns is at stake. There is truth in John Donne's observation that "No man is an island." The State has an interest in preserving and fostering the benefits that every human being may provide to the community—a community that thrives on the exchange of ideas, expressions of affection, shared memories and humorous incidents as well as on the material contributions that its members create and support. The value to others of a person's life is far too precious to allow the individual to claim a constitutional entitlement to complete autonomy in making a decision to end that life. Thus, I fully agree with the Court that the "liberty" protected by the Due Process Clause does not include a categorical "right to commit suicide which itself includes a right to assistance in doing so."

But just as our conclusion that capital punishment is not always unconstitutional did not preclude later decisions holding that it is sometimes impermissibly cruel, so is it equally clear that a decision upholding a general statutory prohibition of assisted suicide does not mean that every possible application of the statute would be valid. A State, like Washington, that has authorized the death penalty and thereby has concluded that the sanctity of human life does not require that it always be preserved, must acknowledge that there are situations in which an interest in hastening death is legitimate. Indeed, not only is that interest sometimes legitimate, I am also convinced that there are times when it is entitled to constitutional protection.

II

In *Cruzan*, the Court assumed that the interest in liberty protected by the Fourteenth Amendment encompassed the right of a terminally ill patient to direct the withdrawal of life-sustaining treatment. As the Court correctly observes today, that assumption "was not simply deduced from abstract concepts of personal autonomy." Instead, it was supported by the common-law tradition protecting the individual's general right to refuse unwanted medical treatment. We have recognized, however, that this common-law right to refuse treatment is neither absolute nor always sufficiently weighty to overcome valid countervailing state interests. . . .

. . . I insist that the source of Nancy Cruzan's right to refuse treatment was not just a common-law rule. Rather, this right is an aspect of a far broader and more basic concept of freedom that is even older than the common law. This freedom embraces, not merely a person's right to refuse a particular kind of unwanted treatment, but also her interest in dignity, and in determining the character of the memories that will survive long after her death. In recognizing that the State's interests did not outweigh Nancy Cruzan's liberty interest in refusing medical treatment, *Cruzan* rested not simply on the common-law right to refuse medical treatment, but—at least implicitly—on the even more fundamental right to make this "deeply personal decision."

While I agree with the Court that *Cruzan* does not decide the issue presented by these cases, *Cruzan* did give recognition, not just to vague, unbridled notions of autonomy, but to the more specific interest in making decisions about how to confront an imminent death. Although there is no absolute right to physician-assisted suicide, *Cruzan* makes it clear that some individuals who no longer have the option of deciding whether to live or to die because they are already on the threshold of death have a constitutionally protected interest that may outweigh the State's interest in preserving life at all costs. The liberty interest at stake in a case like this differs from, and is stronger than, both the com-

mon-law right to refuse medical treatment and the unbridled interest in deciding whether to live or die. It is an interest in deciding how, rather than whether,
a critical threshold shall be crossed.

III

The state interests supporting a general rule banning the practice of physician-assisted suicide do not have the same force in all cases. . . .

As the New York State Task Force on Life and the Law recognized, a State's
prohibition of assisted suicide is justified by the fact that the "ideal" case in
which "patients would be screened for depression and offered treatment, effective pain medication would be available, and all patients would have a supportive committed family and doctor" is not the usual case. Although, as the Court
concludes today, these potential harms are sufficient to support the State's general public policy against assisted suicide, they will not always outweigh the individual liberty interest of a particular patient. Unlike the Court of Appeals, I
would not say as a categorical matter that these state interests are invalid as to
the entire class of terminally ill, mentally competent patients. I do not, however,
foreclose the possibility that an individual plaintiff seeking to hasten her death,
or a doctor whose assistance was sought, could prevail in a more particularized
challenge. Future cases will determine whether such a challenge may succeed.

NOTES AND QUESTIONS:
Washington v. Glucksberg

1. The historical treatment of suicide plays an important role in the Court's
   decision. How is that history crucial to the legal analysis? What question
   does it help answer?
2. What does the Court say about the historical treatment in this country of
   suicide, as opposed to assisted suicide? How much of its conclusions with
   regard to assisted suicide depends on what it says about suicide?
3. Do you agree with the Court's conclusions about the history of suicide?
   Does that history square with your own views and what you think the public's views are? Justice Rehnquist observes that "opposition to and condemnation of suicide . . . are consistent and enduring themes of our philosophical, legal and cultural heritages." Is "condemnation" a fair description of
   how the average American feels about someone who commits suicide, let
   alone an "enduring theme" of our heritage? (Do you think more people
   condemn suicide than condemn abortion?)

   Would you be surprised to learn that in no state is suicide (or even attempted suicide, whose perpetrators it is obviously easier to punish) now a
   crime?[1] Moreover, this circumstance did *not* result from any relatively recent burst of legislative activity among the various states. Does this fact tell
   you anything? If we do not believe suicide is itself a criminal act (albeit per-

haps difficult to punish), how does that alter, if at all, the validity of the Court's reasoning?

Consider also the following comments by Judge Calabresi in his concurrence in the appellate court opinion that the Supreme Court reversed in *Vacco v. Quill* (80 F.3d 732-35):

> There once was a time when the law and its judges were not called upon to make choices for human beings lying in the twilight between life and death. In the past, many of these decisions were left to individual doctors and their patients. Sometimes, easing of pain melded, not quite imperceptibly, into more. While doctors did not advertise their availability, there often was an understanding (perhaps unspoken), as patients entered into what usually were long-term relationships with physicians, that when the time came doctors would do what was expected of them. Laws prohibiting assisted suicide were on the books. But whether they were ever meant to apply to a treating physician, or whether such doctors were even slightly concerned about them, is unclear and lost in the shadows of time. And despite a web of statutes, and doctors who, understandably, have become increasingly averse to taking risks and responsibilities, that tradition undoubtedly continues today. . . .
>
> The statutes at issue were born in another age. New York enacted its first prohibition of assisted suicide in 1828. . . .
>
> From this historical survey, I conclude that 1) what petitioners seek is nominally still forbidden by New York statutes; 2) the bases of these statutes have been deeply eroded over the last hundred and fifty years; and 3) few of their foundations remain in place today.

Specifically:

- The original reason for the statutes—criminalizing conduct that aided or abetted other crimes—is long since gone.
- The distinction that has evolved over the years between conduct currently permitted (suicide, and aiding someone who wishes to die to do so by removing hydration, feeding, and life support systems) and conduct still prohibited (giving a competent, terminally ill patient lethal drugs, which he or she can self-administer) is tenuous at best.
- The Legislature—for many, many years—has not taken any recognizably affirmative step reaffirming the prohibition of what petitioners seek.
- The enforcement of the laws themselves has fallen into virtual desuetude—not so much as to render the case before us nonjusticiable, but enough to cast doubt on whether, in a case like that which the petitioners present, a prosecutor would prosecute or a jury would convict. And this fact by itself inevitably raises doubts about the current support for these laws.

4. What "right" is it that the plaintiffs are claiming? Consider the various formulations of the right listed below. Describe how these various formulations are either narrower or broader than the right at issue in this case:

> A right to die.
> A right to control one's final days.
> A right to choose how to die.

A right to physician-assisted suicide.

A right to prevent the government from interfering in one's chosen way to die.

What formulation does the Court choose?

5. The plaintiffs were arguing that the right they sought came from what provision of the Constitution? What does the Court conclude about whether there is such a constitutionally protected "right" at stake in this case? Based on the cases you have previously read regarding similar constitutional rights, do you agree with the Court's resolution?

6. How does the Court attempt to distinguish *Cruzan*, where it did at least "assume" that there might be a constitutional right involved, from the situation in this case? Do you think it is on solid ground in making this distinction?

7. Answer the same question with regard to how the Court distinguishes *Casey*, another case in which it had found a constitutionally protected interest. Is it on weaker or more solid ground here than it was in distinguishing *Cruzan*?

8. As a result of the Court's conclusions that there was no constitutional right at stake, what did the state of Washington then have to demonstrate to have its law upheld? Do you think the Court was correct in concluding that Washington had met that standard for justifying its law?

9. What if the Court had instead determined that there was indeed a constitutional right that the Washington law infringed? What would Washington have had to demonstrate to get the law upheld? Do you think the outcome—whether the law was found constitutional—would have been any different?

10. Justice O'Connor notes that "in these States a patient who is suffering from a terminal illness and who is experiencing great pain has no legal barriers to obtaining medication, from qualified physicians, to alleviate that suffering, even to the point of causing unconsciousness and hastening death." This comment is directed at the circumstance that high dosages of some pain medications, such as morphine, might in some circumstances hasten a patient's death (by, for example, causing the patient to stop breathing). Doctors frequently voice fears that they might be prosecuted for murder if, in using a sufficiently high dose of pain medication to relieve a patient's pain, the patient dies as a result of the side effects of the drug.

In fact, such prosecutions are exceedingly rare, and the doctor's action should not constitute murder. (Is the doctor's action any different than that of an oncologist who gives a high dose of chemotherapy knowing that there is a not insignificant risk that the medications may hasten the patient's death?) Under these facts, the doctor is neither acting negligently, nor attempting to kill the patient. Here is what a Kansas appellate court said in reversing the attempted murder conviction of a doctor who was alleged to have misused morphine in treating a patient, *Kansas v. Naramore*, 965 P.2d 211, 213-14 (Kan. Ct. App. 1998):

> We can find no criminal conviction of a physician for the attempted murder or murder of a patient which has ever been sustained on appeal based on evidence of the kind presented here. . . .
>
> One of the key issues involved in this case involves what is known as "palliative care." The [Kansas Medical Society] makes the following observation regarding palliative care:
>
> ". . . Pain management for patients in the later stages of cancer presents a particular challenge for physicians. Palliative care refers to medical intervention in which the primary purpose is to alleviate pain and suffering. It is sometimes referred to as having a 'double effect,' however, because in addition to relieving pain and suffering, the level of pain medication necessary to relieve pain may have the consequence of shortening life. Thus, the health care provider's role as healer conflicts with his or her role as reliever of suffering when increasing amounts of pain medication are required to provide comfort care, but these increasing doses may have the effect of slowing respirations and thereby hastening death. . . . [A] health care provider is ethically permitted, and perhaps even required, to implement pain medication and palliative care, with the consent of the patient or the patient's family, notwithstanding the potential for hastening death. This position recognizes that there is an ethical distinction between providing palliative care which may have fatal side effects and providing euthanasia. Whereas the goal in palliative care is providing comfort care to relieve suffering even though death may occur, the goal of euthanasia is itself to cause death and through death relieve the suffering. Perhaps a subtle distinction, but an important one, for in providing palliative care the intent is to relieve suffering, not to kill."

11. The issue of possibly hastening a patient's death while attempting to control pain is sometimes analyzed using a Catholic moral rule known as the "doctrine of double effect." This doctrine has had little direct effect on legal analysis, being cited in only a handful of court opinions. It is a highly technical doctrine, and it is far from clear how useful it is in distinguishing between permissible and impermissible actions. Here is one description of the doctrine, from the New York State Task Force report:

> It is widely recognized that the provision of pain medication is ethically and professionally acceptable even when the treatment may hasten the patient's death, if the medication is intended to alleviate pain and severe discomfort, not to cause death. . . .
>
> According to [the principle of double effect], an action with both good and evil effects is permitted if the action is not intrinsically wrong, the agent intends only the good and not the evil effect, the evil effect is not the means to the good effect, and there is a favorable balance between the good and evil effects. . . . The administration of medication is not intrinsically wrong and is intended to alleviate the patient's pain, not to hasten the patient's death, although

the risk of death could be anticipated. Respiratory failure is not intended, nor is it necessary to relieve pain. In addition, because the patient is terminally ill and experiencing severe pain, the good achieved would outweigh the risk of harm.[2]

12. Suppose that New York amended its law to expand the definition of physician-assisted suicide to include instances in which a doctor gives a patient a dose of pain medication (even if solely to relieve the patient's pain) that is so high that it is likely to hasten the patient's death. (For example, the patient stops breathing due to a high dose of morphine.) Would this be constitutional? Why or why not?

13. The principle of double effect is discussed in a footnote to the majority opinion in *Vacco*, the companion case to *Glucksberg* that follows these notes. The discussion centers on the practice known as "terminal sedation." Instead of giving a patient pain medication, a doctor might instead give that person sedatives that put them to sleep. This is an alternative way to make sure the patient is no longer suffering. Having done that, however, the patient will obviously no longer be eating or drinking. Thus, unless artificial (e.g., using intravenous lines) hydration and nutrition is started, the patient will die as a result of dehydration within a week or two. (Assume that, contrary to what is often likely to be the case, the patient still has a good appetite and would find it uncomfortable to just stop eating.)

Here is what Chief Justice Rehnquist says about terminal sedation, a practice that is apparently legal in New York (521 U.S. 808, n. 11):

> Respondents also argue that the State irrationally distinguishes between physician-assisted suicide and "terminal sedation," a process respondents characterize as "inducing barbiturate coma and then starving the person to death." Petitioners insist, however, that "'although proponents of physician-assisted suicide and euthanasia contend that terminal sedation is covert physician-assisted suicide or euthanasia, the concept of sedating pharmacotherapy is based on informed consent and the principle of double effect.'" Just as a State may prohibit assisting suicide while permitting patients to refuse unwanted lifesaving treatment, it may permit palliative care related to that refusal, which has the foreseen but unintended "double effect" of hastening the patient's death.

Is Rehnquist correct in apparently accepting the characterization that terminal sedation is no different than giving pain medication that may, in some circumstances, hasten death? In particular, is he correct in noting that the hastening of the patient's death is "foreseen but unintended"? Consider the following scenarios:

a. A patient with an untreatable cancer and severe pain is offered the option of sedation. He is told he can also choose whether or not to receive artificial hydration or nutrition. If he chooses not to receive it, he will surely die within one to two weeks. The patient refuses the artificial hydration and nutrition.

b. The same patient chooses to get both the sedation and the artificial hydration and nutrition.

Is the death of the patient in (a) unintended? In what sense? (See the further discussion of intent in the notes following the *Vacco* case.)

14. Assume that California passed a law to the effect that, whenever a person is given sedation who was able to eat or drink normally before sedation, the person must be given artificial hydration and nutrition regardless of the person's desires, and failure to do so will constitute physician-assisted suicide. The law is challenged as unconstitutional based on the following argument: "This law deprives a person of the constitutionally protected fundamental right to refuse care. The exercise of that fundamental right cannot be turned into a criminal act. Such a law is no more constitutional than a state law that says, for example, that a person who needs a respirator to be kept alive must be put on such a machine, regardless of the person's wishes."

Do you think that this argument should be accepted, and the hypothetical California law declared unconstitutional? (And is the observation about the constitutionality of the respirator law correct?)

15. Assume that for some patients who are put on respirators, their own attempts to breathe sometimes lead to an uncomfortable situation in which they inadvertently fight the operation of the respirator—e.g., a person tries to exhale while the machine is trying to force air into his lungs. Assume further that there is a long-acting drug that selectively paralyzes the breathing muscles, and that giving this drug increases the comfort of such patients. Before stopping the use of the respirator (and allowing a patient to begin breathing on his own), a fast-acting "reversal" drug would normally be given that ended the paralysis within a minute or two.

A hypothetical patient named Robert, who is 40 years old, has had AIDS for several years. He recently developed pneumonia, has been in the hospital getting antibiotics, and has been put on a respirator. To increase his comfort, he has been receiving the paralysis drug. His doctor tells Robert that his lungs are almost fully healed, and that tomorrow he intends to turn off the respirator and allow Robert to breathe on his own.

Robert is still relatively healthy and could live for quite a few years with current anti-AIDS therapy. Nonetheless, he is tired of the continued fight against the disease and wishes to die. He tells the doctor to go ahead and turn off the respirator the following day, but that he is refusing the reversal drug. He would, of course, die within a few minutes after the respirator is turned off, since his muscles would still be paralyzed.

The doctor is concerned that he might be guilty of physician-assisted suicide. What is your advice to him? How does this situation compare to terminal sedation?

16. Whether or not a state can constitutionally ban terminal sedation, what is the answer to the question raised by the patients who were challenging the New York law in *Vacco* quoted in note 13: Is a state that allows terminal se-

dation effectively endorsing physician-assisted suicide? (Or, perhaps, a practice that goes beyond mere assistance, in that the physician is "actively" causing the person's death. See the notes following the Oregon Death with Dignity Act for a discussion of the distinction between "voluntary euthanasia" and assisted suicide.)[3]

17. Justice Stevens says that he cannot "foreclose the possibility that an individual plaintiff seeking to hasten her death, or a doctor whose assistance was sought, could prevail in a more particularized challenge." Can you think of possible circumstances that might fit this category?

18. Both Justices Ginsburg and Breyer joined Justice O'Connor's concurring opinion. In addition, Justice Souter wrote a concurring opinion in which he acknowledged that in a future physician-assisted suicide case he might determine that there is indeed a constitutional right at issue. Thus, five of the nine Supreme Court Justices acknowledged some willingness, in a future case, to find some form of constitutional right that might limit a state's ability to enforce laws limiting access to physician-assisted suicide.

VACCO V. QUILL

Supreme Court of the United States

521 U.S. 793 (1997)

OPINION BY CHIEF JUSTICE REHNQUIST:

In New York, as in most States, it is a crime to aid another to commit or attempt suicide, but patients may refuse even lifesaving medical treatment. The question presented by this case is whether New York's prohibition on assisting suicide therefore violates the Equal Protection Clause of the Fourteenth Amendment. We hold that it does not. . . .

The Equal Protection Clause commands that no State shall "deny to any person within its jurisdiction the equal protection of the laws." This provision creates no substantive rights. Instead, it embodies a general rule that States must treat like cases alike but may treat unlike cases accordingly. If a legislative classification or distinction "neither burdens a fundamental right nor targets a suspect class, we will uphold [it] so long as it bears a rational relation to some legitimate end."

New York's statutes outlawing assisting suicide affect and address matters of profound significance to all New Yorkers alike. They neither infringe fundamental rights nor involve suspect classifications. These laws are therefore entitled to a "strong presumption of validity."

On their faces, neither New York's ban on assisting suicide nor its statutes permitting patients to refuse medical treatment treat anyone differently than anyone else or draw any distinctions between persons. *Everyone*, regardless of physical condition, is entitled, if competent, to refuse unwanted lifesaving medical treatment; *no one* is permitted to assist a suicide. Generally speaking, laws that apply evenhandedly to all "unquestionably comply" with the Equal Protection Clause.

The Court of Appeals, however, concluded that some terminally ill people—those who are on life-support systems—are treated differently than those who are not, in that the former may "hasten death" by ending treatment, but the latter may not "hasten death" through physician-assisted suicide. This conclusion depends on the submission that ending or refusing lifesaving medical treatment "is nothing more nor less than assisted suicide." Unlike the Court of Appeals, we think the distinction between assisting suicide and withdrawing life-sustaining treatment, a distinction widely recognized and endorsed in the medical profession and in our legal traditions, is both important and logical; it is certainly rational.

The distinction comports with fundamental legal principles of causation and intent. First, when a patient refuses life-sustaining medical treatment, he dies from an underlying fatal disease or pathology; but if a patient ingests lethal medication prescribed by a physician, he is killed by that medication.

Furthermore, a physician who withdraws, or honors a patient's refusal to begin, life-sustaining medical treatment purposefully intends, or may so intend, only to respect his patient's wishes and "to cease doing useless and futile or degrading things to the patient when [the patient] no longer stands to benefit from them." The same is true when a doctor provides aggressive palliative care; in some cases, painkilling drugs may hasten a patient's death, but the physician's purpose and intent is, or may be, only to ease his patient's pain. A doctor who assists a suicide, however, "must, necessarily and indubitably, intend primarily that the patient be made dead." Similarly, a patient who commits suicide with a doctor's aid necessarily has the specific intent to end his or her own life, while a patient who refuses or discontinues treatment might not.

The law has long used actors' intent or purpose to distinguish between two acts that may have the same result. Put differently, the law distinguishes actions taken "because of" a given end from actions taken "in spite of" their unintended but foreseen consequences.

Given these general principles, it is not surprising that many courts, including New York courts, have carefully distinguished refusing life-sustaining treatment from suicide. In fact, the first state-court decision explicitly to authorize withdrawing lifesaving treatment noted the "real distinction between the self-infliction of deadly harm and a self-determination against artificial life support." *In re Quinlan.* And recently, the Michigan Supreme Court also rejected the argument that the distinction "between acts that artificially sustain life and acts that artificially curtail life" is merely a "distinction without constitutional significance—a meaningless exercise in semantic gymnastics," insisting that "the *Cruzan* majority disagreed and so do we." *Kevorkian*, 527 N. W. 2d, at 728.

Similarly, the overwhelming majority of state legislatures have drawn a clear line between assisting suicide and withdrawing or permitting the refusal of unwanted lifesaving medical treatment by prohibiting the former and permitting the latter. And "nearly all states expressly disapprove of suicide and assisted suicide either in statutes dealing with durable powers of attorney in health-care situations, or in 'living will' statutes." Thus, even as the States move to protect and promote patients' dignity at the end of life, they remain opposed to physician-assisted suicide. . . .

This Court has also recognized, at least implicitly, the distinction between letting a patient die and making that patient die. In *Cruzan*, we concluded that "the principle that a competent person has a constitutionally protected liberty interest in refusing unwanted medical treatment may be inferred from our prior decisions," and we assumed the existence of such a right for purposes of that case. But our assumption of a right to refuse treatment was grounded not, as the Court of Appeals supposed, on the proposition that patients have a general and abstract "right to hasten death," but on well established, traditional rights to bodily integrity and freedom from unwanted touching. In fact, we observed that "the majority of States in this country have laws imposing criminal penalties on one who assists another to commit suicide." *Cruzan* therefore provides no support for the notion that refusing life-sustaining medical treatment is "nothing more nor less than suicide."

For all these reasons, we disagree with respondents' claim that the distinction between refusing lifesaving medical treatment and assisted suicide is "arbitrary" and "irrational." Granted, in some cases, the line between the two may not be clear, but certainty is not required, even were it possible. Logic and contemporary practice support New York's judgment that the two acts are different, and New York may therefore, consistent with the Constitution, treat them differently. By permitting everyone to refuse unwanted medical treatment while prohibiting anyone from assisting a suicide, New York law follows a longstanding and rational distinction.

New York's reasons for recognizing and acting on this distinction—including prohibiting intentional killing and preserving life; preventing suicide; maintaining physicians' role as their patients' healers; protecting vulnerable people from indifference, prejudice, and psychological and financial pressure to end their lives; and avoiding a possible slide towards euthanasia—are discussed in greater detail in our opinion in *Glucksberg, ante*. These valid and important public interests easily satisfy the constitutional requirement that a legislative classification bear a rational relation to some legitimate end.

OPINION BY JUSTICE STEVENS,
CONCURRING IN THE JUDGMENTS:

. . . In New York, a doctor must respect a competent person's decision to refuse or to discontinue medical treatment even though death will thereby ensue, but the same doctor would be guilty of a felony if she provided her patient assistance in committing suicide. Today we hold that the Equal Protection Clause is not violated by the resulting disparate treatment of two classes of terminally ill people who may have the same interest in hastening death. I agree that the distinction between permitting death to ensue from an underlying fatal disease and causing it to occur by the administration of medication or other means provides a constitutionally sufficient basis for the State's classification. Unlike the Court, however, I am not persuaded that in all cases there will in fact be a significant difference between the intent of the physicians, the patients or the families in the two situations.

There may be little distinction between the intent of a terminally-ill patient who decides to remove her life-support and one who seeks the assistance of a doctor in ending her life; in both situations, the patient is seeking to hasten a certain, impending death. The doctor's intent might also be the same in prescribing lethal medication as it is in terminating life support. A doctor who fails to administer medical treatment to one who is dying from a disease could be doing so with an intent to harm or kill that patient. Conversely, a doctor who prescribes lethal medication does not necessarily intend the patient's death—rather that doctor may seek simply to ease the patient's suffering and to comply with her wishes. The illusory character of any differences in intent or causation is confirmed by the fact that the American Medical Association unequivocally endorses the practice of terminal sedation—the administration of sufficient dosages of pain-killing medication to terminally ill patients to protect them from excruciating pain even when it is clear that the time of death will be advanced. The purpose of terminal sedation is to ease the suffering of the patient and comply with her wishes, and the actual cause of death is the administration of heavy doses of lethal sedatives. This same intent and causation may exist when a doctor complies with a patient's request for lethal medication to hasten her death.

Thus, although the differences the majority notes in causation and intent between terminating life-support and assisting in suicide support the Court's rejection of the respondents' facial challenge, these distinctions may be inapplicable to particular terminally ill patients and their doctors. Our holding today in *Vacco v. Quill* that the Equal Protection Clause is not violated by New York's classification, just like our holding in *Washington v. Glucksberg* that the Washington statute is not invalid on its face, does not foreclose the possibility that some applications of the New York statute may impose an intolerable intrusion on the patient's freedom. . . .

NOTES AND QUESTIONS:
Vacco v. Quill

1. An equal protection claim is always based on differences in treatment between two groups of people. What are the two groups in this case?
2. The equal protection clause of the Constitution plays its most significant role when one or both of two conditions are met. What are these two conditions, and how does their existence alter the analysis of a case?

3. Why does the resolution of *Vacco* depend in part on the Court's decision in *Glucksberg*?

4. Assuming that the Court is correct in determining that there is no constitutional right at issue in these cases, is it correct in its resolution of the equal protection claim?

5. What if there was indeed a constitutional right at issue here (as, indeed, five of the nine justices think there may be, in at least some situations)? If that were indeed the case, how would the equal protection analysis be changed, if at all?

6. Compare the two majority opinions—*Glucksberg's* discussion of the right to physician-assisted suicide (the substantive due process issue), and *Vacco's* discussion of the equal protection issue. Which do you find to be on more solid ground?

7. The Court discusses a number of differences between refusing treatment and asking for a lethal medication. One of those differences is said to be the "intent" of the physician.

   Intent can be defined in a number of ways. A person can intend a particular result because she desires that outcome. On the other hand, in the law, a person is often viewed as intending the foreseeable consequences of her actions, whether or not she desired them to take place. The latter view of intent often makes more sense if we wish to hold people responsible for the consequences of their actions. Thus, two people might be jogging on a narrow path on the side of a mountain, and one of them, in a hurry, pushes the other off the path to an inevitable death. The impatient jogger might not have cared whether or not the other person died; he merely wanted the person out of his way. Nonetheless, he would be found guilty of murdering that person, since he knowingly (and thus *intentionally*, under one interpretation of that concept) caused the person's death.

   How do these concepts fit with the distinction that the Court wishes to make? Which definition of "intent" is the Court using? Consider the following situations, assuming in each case that the patient requested that the doctor take the specified actions:

   a. A doctor turns off the respirator that is keeping the patient alive.

   b. A doctor gives a patient a high dose of a pain-killing drug (but one necessary to control the pain)—a dose so high that it has a 50 percent chance of causing the patient to die within a few hours as a result of side effects.

   c. A doctor gives a different patient an even higher dose of such a drug (also necessary to control the pain), but in this case there is a 100 percent chance of causing the patient's death.

   d. A doctor injects a lethal medication into the patient solely because the patient wishes to die in order to end his emotional suffering.

   In which of these scenarios does the doctor intend the patient's death using the "desire" definition of intent? How about using the "foreseeable" definition? Is there a difference, under either definition, in the doctor's intent in cases (a) and (d)? Is the Court correct in using the claim that a "doctor who assists a suicide . . . 'must, necessarily and indubitably intend primarily that the patient be made dead'" to distinguish what happens when a doctor turns off a life-supporting machine at the patient's request? Note Justice Stevens's comments in his concurrence.

8. Is physician-assisted suicide a good name for what these cases are about? Whether or not we want to legalize the conduct at issue, is there nonetheless a difference between the conduct of the plaintiffs in this case and what we ordinarily view as suicide? Review the discussion of similar issues in the *Bouvia* case. Is the person who seeks physician-assisted suicide that different from the person who refuses life-sustaining care? The latter person is less frequently described as committing suicide. Does that distinction, in terms of which is a true suicide, hold up?

Oregon Death with Dignity Act

Or. Rev. Stat. §§ 127.800-.897

[In 1994, as a result of a voter initiative, Oregon enacted a law that legalizes certain forms of physician-assisted suicide. Excerpts from that law are provided here.]

Section 1.01 *Definitions* . . .

(12) "Terminal disease" means an incurable and irreversible disease that has been medically confirmed and will, within reasonable medical judgment, produce death within six (6) months. . . .

Section 2.01. *Who may initiate a written request for medication.*

An adult who is capable, is a resident of Oregon, and has been determined by the attending physician and consulting physician to be suffering from a terminal disease, and who has voluntarily expressed his or her wish to die, may make a written request for medication for the purpose of ending his or her life in a humane and dignified manner. . . .

Section 2.02. *Form of the written request.*

(1) A valid request for medication . . . shall be in substantially the form described in ORS 127.897, signed and dated by the patient and witnessed by at least two individuals who, in the presence of the patient, attest that to the best of their knowledge and belief the patient is capable, acting voluntarily, and is not being coerced to sign the request. . . .

Section 3.01. *Attending physician responsibilities.*

The attending physician shall:

(1) Make the initial determination of whether a patient has a terminal disease, is capable, and has made the request voluntarily;

(2) Inform the patient of:
  (a) His or her medical diagnosis;
  (b) His or her prognosis;
  (c) The potential risks associated with taking the medication to be prescribed;
  (d) The probable result of taking the medication to be prescribed;
  (e) The feasible alternatives, including, but not limited to, comfort care, hospice care and pain control.

(3) Refer the patient to a consulting physician for medical confirmation of the diagnosis, and for a determination that the patient is capable and acting voluntarily. . . .

Section 3.06. *Written and oral requests.*

In order to receive a prescription for medication to end his or her life in a humane and dignified manner, a qualified patient shall have made an oral request and a written request, and reiterate the oral request to his or her attending physician no less than fifteen (15) days after making the initial oral request. At the time the qualified patient makes his or her second oral request, the attending physician shall offer the patient an opportunity to rescind the request.

Section 3.07. *Right to rescind request.*

A patient may rescind his or her request at any time and in any manner without regard to his or her mental state. . . .

Section 3.08. *Waiting periods.*

No less than fifteen (15) days shall elapse between the patient's initial oral request and the writing of a prescription. . . . No less than 48 hours shall elapse between the patient's written request and the writing of a prescription. . . .

Section 6.01. *Form of the request.*

A request for a medication . . . shall be in substantially the following form:

REQUEST FOR MEDICATION TO END MY LIFE IN A HUMANE AND DIGNIFIED MANNER

I, —————————————————————, am an adult of sound mind.

I am suffering from ————————, which my attending physician has determined is a terminal disease and which has been medically confirmed by a consulting physician.

I have been fully informed of my diagnosis, prognosis, the nature of medication to be prescribed and potential associated risks, the expected result, and the feasible alternatives, including comfort care, hospice care and pain control.

I request that my attending physician prescribe medication that will end my life in a humane and dignified manner.

INITIAL ONE:

———————— I have informed my family of my decision and taken their opinions into consideration.

———————— I have decided not to inform my family of my decision.

———————— I have no family to inform of my decision.

I understand that I have the right to rescind this request at any time.

I understand the full import of this request and I expect to die when I take the medication to be prescribed.

I make this request voluntarily and without reservation, and I accept full moral responsibility for my actions.

Signed: ————————————————

Dated: ————————————————

DECLARATION OF WITNESSES

We declare that the person signing this request:

(a) Is personally known to us or has provided proof of identity;

(b) Signed this request in our presence;

(c) Appears to be of sound mind and not under duress, fraud or undue influence;

(d) Is not a patient for whom either of us is attending physician. . . .

NOTE: One witness shall not be a relative (by blood, marriage or adoption) of the person signing this request, shall not be entitled to any portion of the person's estate upon death and shall not own, operate or be employed at a health care facility where the person is a patient or resident. If the patient is an inpatient at a health care facility, one of the witnesses shall be an individual designated by the facility.

NOTES AND QUESTIONS:
Oregon Death with Dignity Act

1. Although the voter initiative approving the Oregon law took place in 1994, the law did not become effective for over three years. (In part, it had to survive an attempt to repeal it through another initiative in 1997.) A primary reason for the delay involved court challenges to its constitutionality. In 1995, a federal court held it to be unconstitutional, accepting an interesting argument. *Lee v. Oregon*, 891 F. Supp. 1429 (D. Ore. 1995). The persons

challenging the law were terminally ill persons who did *not* want the right to physician-assisted suicide. Specifically, they claimed that by providing that right, Oregon had violated the equal protection clause of the Fourteenth Amendment to the Constitution.

Every equal protection claim requires disparate treatment of two groups, and in this case, the alleged two groups were the terminally ill and those who were not terminally ill. The plaintiffs claimed that because the Oregon law had inadequate safeguards to protect those terminally ill persons who did not want physician-assisted suicide from inadvertently getting that "service," it denied them protections provided to persons who were not terminally ill. The alleged defects in the law were, for example, the fact that a physician could choose the second doctor who was brought in to confirm a diagnosis, and that a physician was not required to be present at the time the medication was actually used.

Based on what you know about equal protection law, what standard of review would the State of Oregon have had to meet to demonstrate that such a law was constitutional? Do you think it could have met such a standard? What arguments might it have made?

While a federal appellate court did overturn the earlier decision invalidating the law, it did not address the equal protection argument. It merely concluded that the plaintiff's case was too hypothetical (technically, she lacked standing to sue), since for her to be harmed by the law, she would have to become so clinically depressed that she was unable to meaningfully decide about physician-assisted suicide, she would then have to request a lethal medication under the Oregon law, and then two doctors would both have to fail to recognize that her depression was influencing her ability to make an informed decision. *Lee v. Oregon*, 107 F.3d 1382 (9th Cir. 1997).

2. The Oregon law was evaluated by the state after its first year of operation.[4] The study reports that 23 patients obtained lethal medication under the law in that first year, and that 15 of those patients died after using such medications. The authors concluded that the law is working well. This report has itself been criticized, primarily on the ground that the reporting system did little to truly find out what was going on in the minds of the persons who requested the medication.[5] Does the fact that so few people used the law help you decide whether or not it makes sense? Might the fact that a patient knows she can get a lethal medication itself be reassurance enough that she does not need the medication?

Take a look at the report. Assuming you agree with the criticism that the information collected is not very useful in evaluating the law, is it futile to attempt to collect information that would be very helpful in such an evaluation? How might you suggest collecting such information?

3. Dr. Jack Kevorkian was finally convicted of physician-assisted suicide for assisting in the death of a patient, Thomas Youk, who had amyotrophic lat-

eral sclerosis (Lou Gehrig's disease). This illness gradually causes a patient to be unable to move his body. As it gets worse, the patient would need a ventilator, and thus would effectively have a right to die by merely refusing the continued use of the ventilator.

Mr. Youk's disease had not yet progressed to the stage where he required a ventilator, but since he could not move his arms and legs, Kevorkian had to give him the lethal injection. (With Kevorkian's previous patients, the patient would in each case trigger the device that led to death.) Since the patient was not causing his own death, this is sometimes referred to as "voluntary euthanasia," as distinguished from physician-assisted suicide. (Justice Rehnquist raised this distinction in his *Glucksberg* opinion in discussing the practices in the Netherlands, where certain forms of euthanasia are not prosecuted.) The distinction is that the physician has gone beyond merely assisting and is himself causing the patient's death. Kevorkian had videotaped the death of Mr. Youk, and on November 22, 1998 that video was televised on the CBS newsmagazine "60 Minutes."

Assuming that Mr. Youk was likely to die within the next six months, would he have been able to take advantage of the Oregon law, had he been an Oregon resident? Consider the following possibilities:

a. He was able to swallow, but could not otherwise move his arms or legs. His doctor took some pills and placed them in Mr. Youk's mouth. Is the doctor protected by the Oregon law?

b. He is no longer able to swallow.

4. Assume that you are a lawyer representing a group of people like Mr. Youk who are unable to benefit from the Oregon law. What arguments might you make with regard to the equal protection clause of the Fourteenth Amendment? Do you think you have any better case than the plaintiffs in *Vacco*?

Endnotes

1. New York State Task Force on Life and the Law, *When Death is Sought: Assisted Suicide and Euthanasia in the Medical Context* at 55 (Albany: Health Education Series, 1994).
2. Ibid., p. 163.
3. See, e.g., Robert A. Burt, "The Supreme Court Speaks: Not Assisted Suicide but a Constitutional Right to Palliative Care," 337 *New Eng. J. Med.* 1234 (1997); David Orentlicher, "The Supreme Court and Physician-Assisted Suicide: Rejecting Assisted Suicide but Embracing Euthanasia," 337 *New Eng. J. Med.* 1236 (1997); John A. Robertson, "Respect for Life in Bioethical Dilemmas: The Case of Physician-Assisted Suicide," 45 *Clev. St. L. Rev.* 329 (1997).
4. See Arthur E. Chin et al., "Oregon's Death with Dignity Act: The First Year's Experience" (1999), on the web at *www.ohd.hr.state.or.us/chs/pas/year1/ar–index.htm*.
5. Kathleen Foley and Herbert Hendin, "The Oregon Report: Don't Ask, Don't Tell," 29 *Hastings Ctr. Rep.* 37 (May-June 1999).

1 2

"Futile" Medical Care

The previous two chapters dealt with patients who were refusing care that they did not want. A growing problem in health care, given the attention to cutting costs, is quite the opposite: patients who are demanding care that health providers choose not to give them. This issue is commonly referred to as "medical futility," because providers tend to claim that the reason for not providing the requested care is that it is futile.

To frame this issue, we need to return to how the legal system deals with the relationship between doctors and patients. In particular, we need to further examine the legal role of *patient autonomy*, that leading principle in the philosopher's world of bioethics. To do this, let us visit a hypothetical Patient Autonomy World, where the law gives full reign to this concept, and see how much it resembles our current world.

Before visualizing that world, we should first note that there are parts of today's legal framework where consumer autonomy is a leading principle. An excellent example is the stock market. The government does very little to prevent people from buying stocks and bonds as they choose. Indeed, the primary form of regulation in this area is to make sure that sellers provide a certain amount of truthful information to the buyers. Apart from that, however, the government usually does not try to rate securities, tell us which are good or bad, or tell us which to buy or not buy. If you wish to invest your meager amount of savings in a very shaky company though you are poor, that's your prerogative. The fact that it is risky may suggest greater upside potential. The investor's right to make that (possibly stupid) choice is respected by the law. Autonomy rules!

Medical care, as you can surmise, is quite different. As patients, our autonomy is restricted in numerous ways. Indeed, an underlying theme in our society is that as patients we are vulnerable and can easily fall prey to those who would sell us useless or even harmful treatments.

The legal restrictions on our autonomy to choose among types of health care are openly paternalistic, and openly opposed to the notion that an informed patient should be free to pick whatever care he desires. These restrictions, which are comprehensive and long-standing, have been validated at the highest levels of our legal system. For example, as we saw in chapter 9, federal rules limiting access to drugs not yet demonstrated to be effective have been upheld by the U.S. Supreme Court. The federal government denies a patient the option of taking a drug of unknown efficacy even if it has been proven safe and even if the patient is dying of an otherwise untreatable illness.

This effort to protect patients, as opposed to letting well-informed patients exercise their autonomy, finds equal expression in state law. Only licensed practitioners can practice medicine, and "practice" is often broadly defined. The poor woman who wants liposuction and cannot afford to pay a licensed practitioner does not have the option of having an unlicensed foreign-trained physician do the procedure in her bedroom; freedom of contract does not extend to permitting the patient to take that much risk. The physician who wants to provide an alternative therapy such as homeopathy to patients who are not benefiting from traditional therapy may risk losing his license, even in spite of strong support from his patients. The homeopathy practitioner who is *not* a physician may find himself committing a crime because he is practicing medicine without a license. (Is this a catch-22 or what?) The very premise of malpractice law is highly paternalistic and anti-autonomy in that it requires patients to get, and doctors to provide, care that meets a certain level of efficacy and safety.

We could certainly *imagine* a Patient Autonomy World in which adequately informed patients could freely decide what elements of care they wish to get. The doctor's role, apart from hands-on skills (both diagnostic and therapeutic) would be largely to make sure the patient has adequate information. Thus, the patient who demonstrated a thorough knowledge of a particular prescription drug could force the doctor to prescribe it, even though the doctor thought that this drug was not the best for this condition.

But we do not yet live in this imaginary world. With that as a given, is it likely that the law would *force* a doctor to give a patient a particular kind of care that is not considered standard care? This is the broad issue at the heart of the debate about futility.

IN RE WANGLIE

Minnesota District Court, Hennepin County, Probate Court Division

No. PX-91-283, July 1, 1991

[*The case of Helga Wanglie is relatively famous in bioethics even though there was no real judicial resolution of the underlying issues. To explain the case, we will present excerpts from the legal proceedings, together with comments published by one of the major participants in the case. The following is from the stipulation of facts.]*

    1. Helga Wanglie is eighty-six years old, having been born on October 20, 1904;

    2. In December, 1989, Mrs. Wanglie sustained a hip fracture, causing her to be hospitalized at North Memorial Hospital and subsequently placed at a nursing home;

    3. On January 1, 1990, while being transferred from a nursing home to Hennepin County Medical Center (HCMC) by ambulance, she suffered an acute respiratory arrest;

    4. Following the respiratory arrest, she was placed on a respirator at HCMC, and over time it was determined that she was ventilator dependent;

    5. On May 7, 1990, Mrs. Wanglie was transferred to Bethesda Lutheran Hospital in St. Paul, Minnesota;

    6. On May 23, 1990, Mrs. Wanglie suffered a cardiorespiratory arrest and was transferred to St. Joseph's Hospital in St. Paul after being resuscitated;

    7. On May 31, 1990, Mrs. Wanglie was transferred to HCMC, where she has remained until the present time;

    8. As a result of the cardiorespiratory arrest on May 23, 1990, Mrs. Wanglie suffered severe anoxic encephalopathy and has not regained consciousness since that time;

    9. Since readmission to HCMC on May 31, 1990, Mrs. Wanglie has been respirator dependent (via tracheotomy tube); has been given nourishment only by intubation; has been on a Kinn-Air bed, which shifts her position and weight periodically because she cannot move herself, in order to prevent decubitus ulcers; and has received repeated courses of antibiotics for recurrent lung infections;

    10. Mrs. Wanglie has the following medical conditions: . . .

        e. Chronic respiratory insufficiency with dependence on mechanical ventilation, which her physicians have concluded is irreversible;

        f. Persistent vegetative state with no change in one year, i.e., unconsciousness since her cardiorespiratory arrest on May 23, 1990, which her physicians have concluded is irreversible.

[Steven Miles is a prominent physician-ethicist consulted by the doctors who were treating Helga Wanglie. He initiated the legal proceeding, asking the court to appoint someone other than Wanglie's husband to make health care decisions for her. In particular, Miles objected to the husband's demand that, in spite of her being in a persistent vegetative state, she continue to be kept on a respirator. All parties agreed that Ms. Wanglie would die if the respirator was turned off,

and that she would need to be on the respirator for the rest of her life. This is how Miles described this situation:[1]]

In June and July of 1990, physicians suggested that life-sustaining treatment be withdrawn since it was not benefiting the patient. Her husband, daughter and son insisted on continued treatment. They stated their view that physicians should not play God, that the patient would not be better off dead, that removing life support showed moral decay in our civilization, and that a miracle could occur. Her husband told a physician that his wife has never stated her preferences concerning life-sustaining treatment. . . .

In October 1990, a new attending physician . . . concluded that she was at the end of her life and that the respirator was "non-beneficial," in that it could not heal her lungs, palliate her suffering, or enable this unconscious and permanently respirator-dependent woman to experience the benefit of the life afforded by respirator support. Because the respirator could prolong life, it was not characterized as "futile." . . .

The hospital [went to court to resolve the dispute], first asking for the appointment of an independent conservator to decide whether the respirator was beneficial to the patient and second, if the conservator found it was not, for a second hearing on whether it was obliged to provide the respirator.

[The court rejected the hospital's request in the following Memorandum opinion by Judge Belois:]

The court is asked whether it is in the best interest of an elderly woman who is comatose, gravely ill, and ventilator-dependent to have decisions about her medical care made by her husband of fifty-three years or by a stranger. . . .

. . . Miles believes that Oliver Wanglie is not competent to be Helga Wanglie's conservator with regard to making decisions about her shelter, medical care, and religious requirements. Oliver Wanglie disagrees.

Except for unconvincing testimony from some physicians and health care providers at the Hennepin County Medical Center, there is no evidence that Oliver Wanglie is unable to perform the duties and responsibilities of a guardian. The evidence overwhelmingly supports the conclusion that Oliver Wanglie can understand the medical issues involving his wife. . . .

Oliver Wanglie has shown himself to be dedicated to his wife's proper medical care. He visits her regularly, although the frequency is in dispute. He expresses the belief that the nurses caring for his wife are skilled professionals and compassionate people. Except with regard to the issue of removing the ventilator, he has thoughtfully agreed with the treating physicians about every major decision in his wife's care. . . .

No Court order to continue or stop any medical treatment for Helga Wanglie has been made or requested at this time. Whether such a request will be made, or such an order is proper, or this Court would make such an order, and whether Oliver Wanglie would execute such an order are speculative matters not now before the Court.

Oliver Wanglie believes that he is the best person to be the guardian for his wife. Their children agree with him. The evidence clearly and convincingly supports their position.

NOTES AND QUESTIONS:
In re Wanglie

1. Helga Wanglie died shortly after the court issued its determination that her husband had the authority to make health care decisions on her behalf. Had she not died, the hospital intended to bring a second action claiming it was not required to provide the respirator.
2. There are a number of arguments that one might make in opposing Mr. Wanglie's request to keep his wife alive:
   a. Mr. Wanglie was wrong in claiming that his wife would have wanted to be kept alive under these circumstances.
   b. Mr. Wanglie was wrong in claiming that it was in his wife's best interests to be kept alive under these circumstances.
   c. Even if Mr. Wanglie was correct in claiming his wife would have wanted to be kept alive under these circumstances (e.g., she believed in the value of life itself, even for a person who had permanently lost consciousness), the hospital did not have an obligation to provide the requested services.

   Which of these arguments best presents the issues that are at stake in the futility debate?
3. Note that Miles and the hospital were not claiming that Ms. Wanglie's artificial nutrition and hydration should be stopped. (Recall from *Quinlan* and *Cruzan* that any patient in a persistent vegetative state needs such care to be kept alive.) Nor were they arguing that every patient in a persistent vegetative state should be denied all life-sustaining care in Hennepin County Medical Center. What was different about Ms. Wanglie and the respirator? Was it relevant that most other doctors would have offered artificial nutrition and hydration to Ms. Wanglie—i.e., it was standard care to offer those therapies to a person in a persistent vegetative state? Perhaps the debate is not about futile care at all but about a much broader category, namely all care that is beyond that required by the standard of care. We will explore this issue further in the case that follows.
4. Miles says that the *Wanglie* case is not about futility but rather about "non-beneficial" care. Is this distinction helpful? Is there any doubt that the respirator benefited Ms. Wanglie, at least to the extent of keeping her alive? If a patient is not entitled to "non-beneficial" care, why were the doctors not arguing that no patient in a persistent vegetative state is entitled to

artificial hydration and nutrition? Isn't such treatment equally non-beneficial to such patients?

5. It is helpful to consider the following method for categorizing futility cases:[2]

Physiologic Futility: A patient is requesting a treatment that is known, from a purely scientific viewpoint, not to be effective in achieving the patient's goal. An example is a patient with an upper-respiratory infection (a cold) of proven viral etiology who requests an antibiotic, which would be effective only against bacteria, not a virus. Most people, considering this the easy case, have little difficulty in concluding that a patient has no right to get care that is physiologically futile.

Qualitative Futility: A patient is requesting a treatment that is effective in achieving the patient's goals, but the doctors believe that because of the patient's poor condition, the treatment will provide insufficient benefit to the patient. The *Wanglie* case is often described as an example of qualitatitive futility.

Quantitative Futility: A patient is requesting a treatment that has a chance of achieving the patient's goals, but that chance is so low that the doctors think the treatment need not be provided. Assume, for example, that doing a bone marrow transplant on patients with a particular form of otherwise incurable cancer has been demonstrated to have one chance in a thousand of eliminating the cancer. This treatment is relatively expensive—about $60,000. Is the small possibility of cure sufficient to warrant the costs?

6. In thinking about futility issues, it is important to ask who is paying for the care. Assume, for example, that the patient is covered by an insurance plan or is part of a managed care organization. Would it be wrong for that organization to create rules to assure that the fees paid by the participants are used in a particular way? Dollars spent on keeping Helga Wanglie alive obviously are not available to take care of other patients. Thus, where the patient is in effect using someone else's money, the issue may be less whether the care is futile as whether the group of participants had agreed in advance that this was an appropriate use of their money.[3] The core futility case would involve a patient paying for medical care out of her own resources. In that circumstance, no argument can be made that it is an improper use of someone else's money. The argument against forcing the doctor to provide the care must be more subtle, dealing with the extent to which the government should force doctors to provide care that is not deemed sufficiently worth doing. We will explore this further in the notes after the *Causey* case.

In *Wanglie*, Medicare had paid $200,000 for one hospitalization, while a private insurer picked up the bill for $500,000 in a second hospitalization. Based on this, might financing issues, as opposed to futility arguments, be more relevant to determining what care Helga Wanglie should have gotten?

7. The more difficult issues in the futility debate come down to disagreements about how to value things that are not easily valued. Ms. Wanglie's family

was claiming that a life without consciousness was valuable enough to be worth the extra effort and costs of using the respirator. The doctors treating her disagreed. Is it unusual for decisions about the value of such intangibles to be required in the medical realm? As a legal matter, how do you think we resolve such disputes? As you read the next case, ask yourself how any decision about the medical standard of care is determined, and recall the discussion of this issue in the context of *Helling v. Carey* in chapter 7.

CAUSEY V. ST. FRANCIS MEDICAL CENTER
Court of Appeal of Louisiana
719 So. 2d 1072 (La. Ct. App. 1998)

OPINION BY JUDGE BROWN:

The facts of this end of life drama are not materially disputed. Believing it medically and ethically inappropriate, a physician and hospital withdrew life-sustaining care to a 31-year-old, quadriplegic, end-stage renal failure, comatose patient over the strongly expressed objections of the patient's family. As filed, this action was premised as an intentional battery-based tort. The trial court, however, found that defendants "acted in accordance with professional opinions and professional judgment" and thus this action was covered by the medical malpractice act, which required that it first be presented to a medical review panel. Accordingly, the trial court dismissed the action as premature.

FACTS

Having suffered cardiorespiratory arrest, Sonya Causey was transferred to St. Francis Medical Center (SFMC) from a nursing home. She was comatose, quadriplegic and in end-stage renal failure. Her treating physician, Dr. Herschel R. Harter, believed that continuing dialysis would have no benefit. Although Dr. Harter agreed that with dialysis and a ventilator Mrs. Causey could live for another two years, he believed that she would have only a slight (1% to 5%) chance of regaining consciousness. Because Mrs. Causey's family demanded aggressive life-sustaining care, Dr. Harter sought unsuccessfully to transfer her to another medical facility willing to provide this care.

Dr. Harter enlisted support from SFMC's Morals and Ethics Board. The Board agreed with Dr. Harter's opinion to discontinue dialysis, life-support procedures, and to enter a "no-code" status (do not resuscitate). Mrs. Causey was taken off a feeding tube and other similar devices. The day the ventilator was removed, Mrs. Causey died of respiratory and cardiac failure.

Plaintiffs, the husband, father and mother of Sonya Causey, brought this petition for damages against SFMC and Dr. Harter. . . . Plaintiffs claim that to discontinue dialysis, remove life-support systems and enter a "no code" order was treatment without consent and an intentional tort not covered by the malpractice act. . . .

DISCUSSION

Patient participation in medical decision-making is now well-established. Recognizing individual autonomy and the right to self-determination, our state legislature enacted a statute granting a competent, terminally ill person the right to refuse medical treatment.

In the Karen Quinlan case the court rejected a physician's adamant stand that he had a moral duty to treat to the last gasp. In that case, the father, not the physician, was given the power to decide whether his comatose daughter's life-prolonging care was beneficial. The legal basis for individual autonomy is the requirement of informed consent. *Cruzan.* Implicitly, the decision to refuse care is based on the patient's personal values. If a patient is incompetent, then the responsibility or authority to make decisions falls to the next of kin. The court as the protector of incompetents, however, can override an intolerable choice by a surrogate decision-maker.

Now the roles are reversed. Patients or, if incompetent, their surrogate decision-makers, are demanding life-sustaining treatment regardless of its perceived futility, while physicians are objecting to being compelled to prolong life with procedures they consider futile. The right or autonomy of the patient to refuse treatment is simply a severing of the relationship with the physician. In this case, however, the patient (through her surrogate) is not severing a relationship, but demanding treatment the physician believes is "inappropriate."

The problem is not with care that the physician believes is harmful or literally has no effect. For example, radiation treatment for Mrs. Causey's condition would not have been appropriate. This is arguably based on medical science. Rather, the problem is with care that has an effect on the dying process, but which the physician believes has no benefit. Such life-prolonging care is grounded in beliefs and values about which people disagree. Strictly speaking, if a physician can keep the patient alive, such care is not medically or physiologically "futile;" however, it may be "futile" on philosophical, religious or practical grounds.

Placement of statistical cut-off points for futile treatment involves subjective value judgments. The difference in opinion as to whether a 2% or 9% probability of success is the critical point for determining futility can be explained in terms of personal values, not in terms of medical science. When the medical professional and the patient, through a surrogate, disagree on the worth of pursuing life, this is a conflict over values, i.e., whether extra days obtained through medical intervention are worth the burden and costs.

SFMC had in place a Futile Care Policy which allowed for the discontinuance of medical care over and above that necessary for comfort and support if the probability of improving the patient's condition was slight and would serve only to prolong life in that condition. The inclusion of non-medical persons on the Morals and Ethics Board signals that this is not strictly a physiological or medical futility policy, but a policy asserting values and beliefs on the worth of sustaining life, even in a vegetative condition.

Futility is a subjective and nebulous concept which, except in the strictest physiological sense, incorporates value judgments. Obviously, in this case, subjective personal values of the benefit of prolonging life with only a slight possibility of improvement dictated SFMC's and Dr. Harter's decision.

To focus on a definition of "futility" is confusing and generates polemical discussions. We turn instead to an approach emphasizing the standard of medical care.

Physicians are professionals and occupy a special place in our community. They are licensed by society to perform this special role. No one else is permitted to use life-prolonging technology, which is considered by many as "fundamental" health care. The physician has an obligation to present all medically acceptable treatment options for the patient or her surrogate to consider and either choose or reject; however, this does not compel a physician to provide interventions that in his view would be harmful, without effect or "medically inappropriate." In recognizing a terminal patient's right to refuse care, [the relevant Louisiana statute] states that [it] is not to be construed "to require the application of medically inappropriate treatment or life-sustaining procedures to any patient or to interfere with medical judgment with respect to the application of medical treatment or life-sustaining procedures." Unfortunately, "medically inappropriate" and "medical judgment" are not defined.

A physician's obligation to obtain informed consent is both an ethical requirement and a legal standard of care derived from principles of individual integrity and self-determination. Informed consent implicates the disclosure and explanation of all material information of the nature, purpose, expected benefit and foreseeable risks of any treatment. In the present case, Dr. Harter fully explained to Mrs. Causey's family the situation. The family rejected the proposed withdrawal of treatment. Despite the lack of any consent, defendants proceeded to withdraw what they considered to be "medically inappropriate" treatment....

Standards of medical malpractice require a physician to act with the degree of skill and care ordinarily possessed by those in that same medical speciality acting under the same or similar circumstances. Departure from this prevailing standard of care, coupled with harm, may result in professional malpractice liability. A finding that treatment is "medically inappropriate" by a consensus of physicians practicing in that speciality translates into a standard of care. Thus, in this case, whether Dr. Harter and SFMC met the standard of care concerning the withdrawal of dialysis, life-support procedures and the entering of a "no code" status must be determined. If the withdrawal of or the refusal to provide care is considered a "medical procedure," then it may be that the circumstances of this case present an exception to the [Louisiana] supreme court's statement . . . that "one can hardly argue that it is not below the appropriate standard of care for a doctor or nurse to perform a medical procedure without obtaining any kind of consent." In any event, the Medical Malpractice Act is applicable and the matter should first be submitted to a medical review panel. . . .

NOTES AND QUESTIONS:
Causey v. St. Francis Medical Center

1. Dr. Harter seems to be of a like mind to Dr. Miles (from the *Wanglie* case), finding that Ms. Causey would get no benefit from the dialysis. Do you agree? What benefits were possible to Ms. Causey?
2. Dr. Harter claimed that the "1% to 5% chance" of regaining consciousness was "slight." Do you agree? How does one decide?
3. In a survey about futility, two researchers asked physicians to complete the statement, "Regarding terminally ill patients, I consider a treatment to be futile if the probability of success is __ percent or below"; 20 percent of the physicians gave "zero percent" as the answer. The authors interpreted this to mean that these physicians were denying the concept of medical futility.[4]

   Do you agree? How does one decide that something is medically futile? Is an important piece of information missing from the question posed to the physicians: What if there was one chance in 100,000 that the patient's illness could be cured by administering a 1-cent aspirin? Would it be futile to give that to the patient? What if there was 1 chance in 100 that the patient could be cured, but it would require spending $10 million?
4. The court suggests that instead of determining whether something is futile or not futile, one should instead determine whether something meets the standard of medical care. Would shifting the question in this way get rid of the problem of making determinations that incorporate value judgments about the worth of sustaining life in a particular circumstance?
5. On the other hand, is the claim that futility judgments are based on values a red herring? Aren't value judgments about the worth of a life already built into the current tort law, by means of the standard of care? To determine *any* standard of care, the medical profession must explicitly or implicitly make determinations about how to put a value on various medical conditions (such as loss of vision, loss of a breast, or loss of virility). Theoretically, we could be testing every person, every day, for every imaginable medical condition, but we do not. Partly, that is because the tests themselves might be somewhat harmful, but more likely a balance has been struck between the cost of the test and the likelihood of detecting any pathology. For most cancers, the risk increases with age, and we begin screening at the age where we are more likely to detect the condition. By doing so, we acknowledge that some people, below that cut-off—like Barbara Helling and her glaucoma (chapter 7)—will not have their condition detected until they have suffered irreparable damage.
6. *Causey* is in essence posing the question whether the law gives a patient the right to force a doctor to provide any medical care that is beyond the standard of care—what we might call extra-standard care. If the answer to this question is "no," we also have an answer to the debate about futile care, since all futile care, under any definition, will be subsumed under the much

broader category of extra-standard care. (Any care within the standard of care is already required by the legal system since the doctor who fails to provide it is committing malpractice.)

7. Is it not possible that a person's own valuation of a particular condition—say, how much it would be worth to avoid losing eyesight—differs from the average judgment built into the medical profession's determination of the standard of care? Thus, even though an element of care is not standard care, the patient might reasonably want that element. (We have said nothing about such care being futile—to the contrary, it might be very useful to the patient.)

Nothing in the law prevents the doctor from complying with such a request. On the other hand, should the patient's request for the treatment be sufficient that the legal system force the doctor to provide that treatment? To answer this question, we might draw on the overall thrust of legal regulation in the medical area, which attempts to balance both elements of paternalism (e.g., in protecting patients from inappropriate care) and elements of respect for patient autonomy (e.g., in allowing patients broad discretion to refuse care). Which of the following options appears most reasonable when we are talking about such extra-standard care:[5]

a. The law should *forbid* doctors from providing such care, on the theory that since it is not included within the standard of care, it is inappropriate care.

b. The law should give doctors discretion to provide such care on the theory that the standard of care is the minimum level of care that all patients must get, and that care beyond that minimum is within the realm of contract, to be freely decided by mutual agreement between doctors and patients.

c. The law should *require* doctors to provide such care whenever a patient requests it, on the theory that the law should protect the autonomous choice of a patient to get care beyond the minimum guaranteed by the law.

IN RE BABY K

United States Court of Appeals for the Fourth Circuit

16 F.3d 590 (4th Cir. 1994)

OPINION BY JUDGE WILKINS:

The Hospital instituted this action against Ms. H, Mr. K, and Baby K, seeking a declaratory judgment that it is not required under the Emergency Medical Treatment and Active Labor Act (EMTALA) to provide treatment other than warmth, nutrition, and hydration to Baby K, an anencephalic infant. Because we agree with the district court that EMTALA gives rise to a duty on the part of the Hospital to provide respiratory support to Baby K when she is presented at the Hospital in respiratory distress and treatment is requested for her, we affirm.

I.

Baby K was born at the Hospital in October of 1992 with anencephaly, a congenital malformation in which a major portion of the brain, skull, and scalp are missing. While the presence of a brain stem does support her autonomic functions and reflex actions, because Baby K lacks a cerebrum, she is permanently unconscious. Thus, she has no cognitive abilities or awareness. She cannot see, hear, or otherwise interact with her environment.

When Baby K had difficulty breathing on her own at birth, Hospital physicians placed her on a mechanical ventilator. This respiratory support allowed the doctors to confirm the diagnosis and gave Ms. H, the mother, an opportunity to fully understand the diagnosis and prognosis of Baby K's condition. The physicians explained to Ms. H that most anencephalic infants die within a few days of birth due to breathing difficulties and other complications. Because aggressive treatment would serve no therapeutic or palliative purpose, they recommended that Baby K only be provided with supportive care in the form of nutrition, hydration, and warmth. Physicians at the Hospital also discussed with Ms. H the possibility of a "Do Not Resuscitate Order" that would provide for the withholding of lifesaving measures in the future.

The treating physicians and Ms. H failed to reach an agreement as to the appropriate care. Ms. H insisted that Baby K be provided with mechanical breathing assistance whenever the infant developed difficulty breathing on her own, while the physicians maintained that such care was inappropriate. As a result of this impasse, the Hospital sought to transfer Baby K to another hospital. This attempt failed when all of the hospitals in the area with pediatric intensive care units declined to accept the infant. In November of 1992, when Baby K no longer needed the services of an acute-care hospital, she was transferred to a nearby nursing home.

Since being transferred to the nursing home, Baby K has been readmitted to the Hospital three times due to breathing difficulties. Each time she has been provided with breathing assistance and, after stabilization, has been discharged to the nursing home. Following Baby K's second admission, the Hospital filed this action to resolve the issue of whether it is obligated to provide emergency medical treatment to Baby K that it deems medically and ethically inappropriate. Baby K's guardian *ad litem* and her father, Mr. K, joined in the Hospital's request for a declaration that the Hospital is not required to provide respiratory support or other aggressive treatments. Ms. H contested the Hospital's request for declaratory relief. After the district court issued its findings of fact and conclusions of law denying the requested relief, the Hospital, Mr. K, and Baby K's guardian *ad litem* (collectively referred to as the "Hospital") noticed this appeal.

II.

Congress enacted EMTALA in response to its "concern that hospitals were 'dumping' patients [who were] unable to pay, by either refusing to provide emergency medical treatment or transferring patients before their emergency conditions were stabilized." Through EMTALA, Congress sought "to provide an 'adequate first response to a medical crisis' for all patients," by imposing two duties on hospitals that have entered into Medicare provider agreements.

First, those hospitals with an emergency medical department must provide an appropriate medical screening to determine whether an emergency medical condition exists for any individual who comes to the emergency medical department requesting treatment. A hospital fulfills this duty if it utilizes identical screening procedures for all patients complaining of the same condition or exhibiting the same symptoms.

An additional duty arises if an emergency medical condition is discovered during the screening process. . . . [O]nce an individual has been diagnosed as presenting an emergency medical condition, the hospital must provide that treatment necessary to prevent the material deterioration of the individual's condition or provide for an appropriate transfer to another facility.

In the application of these provisions to Baby K, the Hospital concedes that when Baby K is presented in respiratory distress a failure to provide "immediate medical attention" would reasonably be expected to cause serious impairment of her bodily functions. Thus, her breathing difficulty qualifies as an emergency medical condition, and the diagnosis of this emergency medical condition triggers the duty of the hospital to provide Baby K with stabilizing treatment or to transfer her in accordance with the provisions of EMTALA. Since transfer is not an option available to the Hospital at this juncture, the Hospital must stabilize Baby K's condition.

The Hospital acknowledged in its complaint that aggressive treatment, including mechanical ventilation, is necessary to "assure within a reasonable medical probability, that no material deterioration of Baby K's condition is likely to occur." Thus, stabilization of her condition requires the Hospital to provide respiratory support through the use of a respirator or other means necessary to ensure adequate ventilation. In sum, a straightforward application of the statute obligates the Hospital to provide respiratory support to Baby K when she arrives at the emergency department of the Hospital in respiratory distress and treatment is requested on her behalf.

In an effort to avoid the result that follows from the plain language of EMTALA, the Hospital offers four arguments. The Hospital claims: (1) that this court has previously interpreted EMTALA as only requiring uniform treatment of all patients exhibiting the same condition; [and] (2) that in prohibiting disparate emergency medical treatment Congress did not intend to require physicians to provide treatment outside the prevailing standard of medical care. . . . We find these arguments unavailing.

A.

. . . [T]he Hospital contends that it is only required to provide Baby K with the same treatment that it would provide other anencephalic infants—supportive care in the form of warmth, nutrition, and hydration. . . . Advancing the proposition that anencephaly, as opposed to respiratory distress, is the emergency medical condition at issue, the Hospital concludes that it is only required to provide uniform treatment to all anencephalic infants. We disagree.

. . . If, as the Hospital suggests, it were only required to provide uniform treatment, it could provide any level of treatment to Baby K, including a level of treatment that would allow her condition to materially deteriorate, so long as the care she was provided was consistent with the care provided to other individuals. The definition of stabilizing treatment advocated by the Hospital directly conflicts with the plain language of EMTALA.

As we have previously stated, "it is not our role to rewrite legislation passed by Congress. When a statute is clear and unambiguous, we must apply its terms as written." The terms of EMTALA as written do not allow the Hospital to fulfill its duty to provide stabilizing treatment by simply dispensing uniform treatment. Rather, the Hospital must provide that treatment necessary to prevent the material deterioration of each patient's emergency medical condition. In the case of Baby K, the treatment necessary to prevent the material deterioration of her condition when she is in respiratory distress includes respiratory support.

Even if this court were to interpret EMTALA as requiring hospitals to provide uniform treatment for emergency medical conditions, we could not find that the Hospital is only required to provide Baby K with warmth, nutrition, and hydration. As the Hospital acknowledged during oral argument, Baby K resides at the nursing home for months at a time without requiring emergency medical attention. Only when she has experienced episodes of bradypnea or apnea has Baby K required respiratory support to prevent serious impairment of her bodily functions. It is bradypnea or apnea, not anencephaly, that is the emergency medical condition that brings Baby K to the Hospital for treatment. Uniform treatment of emergency medical conditions would require the Hospital to provide Baby K with the same treatment that the Hospital provides all other patients experiencing bradypnea or apnea. The Hospital does not allege that it would refuse to provide respiratory support to infants experiencing bradypnea or apnea who do not have anencephaly. Indeed, a refusal to provide such treatment would likely be considered as providing no emergency medical treatment.

B.

The second argument of the Hospital is that, in redressing the problem of disparate emergency medical treatment, Congress did not intend to require physicians to provide medical treatment outside the prevailing standard of medical care. The Hospital asserts that, because of their extremely limited life expectancy and because any treatment of their condition is futile, the prevailing standard of medical care for infants with anencephaly is to provide only warmth, nutrition, and hydration. Thus, it maintains that a requirement to provide respiratory assistance would exceed the prevailing standard of medical care. However, the plain language of EMTALA requires stabilizing treatment for any individual who comes to a participating hospital, is diagnosed as having an emergency medical condition, and cannot be transferred. . . . The Hospital has been unable to identify, nor has our research revealed, any statutory language or legislative history evincing a Congressional intent to create an exception to the duty to provide stabilizing treatment when the required treatment would exceed the prevailing standard of medical care. We recognize the dilemma facing physicians who are requested to provide treatment they consider morally and ethically inappropriate, but we cannot ignore the plain language of the statute because "to do so would 'transcend our judicial function.'" The appropriate branch to redress the policy concerns of the Hospital is Congress. . . .

Notes and Questions:
In re Baby K

1. The *Baby K* case is best viewed as an introduction to some of the specific federal laws that relate to medical futility in particular situations. Thus, for example, if the patient is being treated in an emergency room, EMTALA may be relevant to whether or not certain forms of possibly futile care must be offered.
2. The doctors treating Baby K claimed that "aggressive treatment would serve no therapeutic or palliative purpose." Do you agree?
3. Do you agree with the court's conclusion that the EMTALA law was intended to require doctors to provide medical care that was "outside the prevailing standard of care"? (No other court has directly addressed this issue since the *Baby K* opinion.) The primary problem addressed by EMTALA was the situation in which people were being turned away from emergency rooms due to lack of funds and not receiving any care. Does remedying that problem suggest the need to require the provision of care above standard care?
4. The *Baby K* case was discussed in a footnote to *Causey*. Here is what that footnote said, 719 So.2d 1075 n.2:

> This matter is further complicated by federal legislation, such as the Americans with Disability Act (ADA) and Emergency Medical Treatment and Active Labor Act (EMTALA), that preempts state law and does not recognize a health care provider's right to withdraw life-sustaining care deemed medically inappropriate. Mrs. Causey was both disabled and an emergency patient.

In re Baby K presents facts similar to this case. The court in *In re Baby K* found that to the extent that state law exempted physicians from providing care they considered medically inappropriate, it conflicted with EMTALA provisions requiring continuous stabilizing treatment for emergency patients and was thus preempted by EMTALA. See, however, distinguishing opinion of *Bryan v. Rectors and Visitors of University of Virginia*, 95 F.3d 349 (4th Cir. 1996).

In *Bryan*, the Fourth Circuit backed off the sweeping statement made in the Baby K case that EMTALA imposed upon the hospital an obligation not only to admit a patient for treatment of an emergency condition, which was done, but thereafter to continuously stabilize her condition, no matter how long required. Instead, the court in *Bryan* stated that EMTALA was a limited "anti-dumping" statute, not a federal malpractice law. "Its core purpose is to get patients into the system who might otherwise go untreated and be left without a remedy because traditional medical malpractice law affords no claim for failure to treat." The court recognized that EMTALA imposed a duty on hospitals to provide emergency care and created a new cause of action "generally unavailable under state tort law, for what amounts to a failure to treat." However, EMTALA was found to regulate the hospital's care of the patient only in the immediate aftermath of the act of admitting her for emergency treatment and while it considered whether it would undertake longer-term full treatment. In this respect, *In re Baby K* was not followed. Agreeing with *Bryan*, we find that EMTALA provisions are not applicable to the present case.

As the *Causey* court suggests, the *Bryan* opinion is often viewed as an attempt by the Fourth Circuit Court of Appeals to cut back on the impact of its earlier *Baby K* opinion. In *Bryan*, Shirley Robinson had been transferred to the University of Virginia Medical Center in respiratory distress. Her family made it clear that they wanted the hospital to "take all necessary measures to keep her alive and trust in God's wisdom." During that hospitalization, and against the wishes of the family, the doctors entered a "do not resuscitate" order in her chart. This meant that if she was found in her bed, not breathing and without a pulse, no effort would be made to revive her.

Mrs. Robinson did in fact die during the hospitalization, and never received the resuscitative efforts that might have kept her alive. The appellate court determined that this was not an EMTALA violation, since EMTALA does not restrict the conduct of the hospital after it has succeeded in stabilizing the patient. Other courts have reached different conclusions about how long a hospital must keep a patient stabilized under EMTALA. What arguments are there for reading EMTALA to impose a particular duty of care only in the emergency room, and not with regard to care the patient receives after they are transferred to other portions of the hospital? (Recall the basic purpose of EMTALA.)

Some of these issues suggest the difficulty of trying to resolve questions relating to a broad topic like medical futility through statutes designed to deal with relatively narrow problems.

5. Also relevant to the futility debate are federal and state laws relating to discrimination against the handicapped. In fact, the trial court in the *Baby K* case had held that the hospital's withholding of treatment from the child would violate two federal antidiscrimination laws, the Rehabilitation Act of 1973 and the Americans with Disabilities Act. (The appellate court chose not to rule on these issues, since it had already determined that EMTALA required that the ventilator be provided.) Here is what the trial court said about the latter act, 832 F. Supp. 1028-29:

> Section 302 of the Americans with Disabilities Act ("ADA") prohibits discrimination against disabled individuals by "public accommodations." A "disability" is "a physical or mental impairment that substantially limits one or more of the major life activities" of an individual. This includes any physiological disorder or condition affecting the neurological system, musculoskeletal system, or sense organs, among others. Anencephaly is a disability, because it affects the baby's neurological functioning, ability to walk, and ability to see or talk. "Public accommodation" is defined to include a "professional office of a health care provider, hospital, or other service establishment." The Hospital is a public accommodation under the ADA.
>
> Section 302(a) of the ADA states a general rule of nondiscrimination against the disabled:
>
>> General rule. No individual shall be discriminated against on the basis of disability in the full and equal enjoyment of the goods, services, facilities, privileges, advantages, or accommodation of any place of public accommodations by any person who owns, leases (or leases to), or operates a place of public accommodation.
>
> . . . [S]ection 302(b)(1)(A) of the ADA states that "it shall be discriminatory to subject an individual or class of individuals on the basis of a disability . . . to a denial of the opportunity of the individual or class to participate in or benefit from the goods, services, facilities, privileges, advantages, or accommodations of an entity."
>
> The Hospital asks this court for authorization to deny the benefits of ventilator services to Baby K by reason of her anencephaly. The Hospital's claim is that it is "futile" to keep alive an anencephalic baby, even though the mother has requested such treatment. But the plain language of the ADA does not permit the denial of ventilator services that would keep alive an anencephalic baby when those life-saving services would otherwise be provided to a baby without disabilities at the parent's request. The Hospital's reasoning would lead to the denial of medical services to anencephalic babies as a class of disabled individuals. Such discrimination against a vulnerable population class is exactly what the American with Disabilities Act was enacted to prohibit. The Hospital would therefore violate the ADA if it were to withhold ventilator treatment from Baby K.

6. Apply the ADA to Helga Wanglie's case. Would refusal to keep her on the ventilator be a violation of the act?

7. The application of antidiscrimination laws to medical treatment decisions is much debated. Often, medical decisions—including a determination of

what constitutes the standard care a patient is entitled to—turn on how sick the person is. That very sickness may constitute a disability under such a law, so it may seem impermissible to consider the sickness in treating the person.

There are certainly cases where it is easy to agree that inappropriate discrimination is taking place. If 80-year-olds Karen and Mary both need gall bladder surgery, the fact that Mary is blind should be irrelevant in determining what care she is entitled to. On the other hand, assume both are in renal failure, and Karen is otherwise healthy, while Mary has a terminal cancer that will likely cause her death within weeks. Can this distinction be taken into account in concluding that Mary should not start on dialysis treatment? (In Great Britain, for example, it is accepted that patients above a certain age are not offered dialysis.)[6]

Endnotes

1. Steven Miles, "Informed Demand for 'Non-Beneficial' Medical Treatment," 325 *New Eng. J. Med.* 512 (1991).
2. See, e.g., Steven H. Miles, "Medical Futility," 20 *Law, Med. & Health Care* 310 (1992).
3. See, e.g., E. Haavi Morreim, "Profoundly Diminished Life: The Casualties of Coercion," 24(1) *Hastings Ctr. Rep.* 33 (1994).
4. Jeffrey W. Swanson & S. Van McCrary, "Doing All They Can: Physicians Who Deny Medical Futility," 22 *J. Law Med. & Ethics* 318 (1994).
5. For more on the relationship between "medical futility" arguments and the right to extra-standard care, see Jerry Menikoff, "Demanded Medical Care," 30 *Ariz. St. L. J.* 1091 (1998).
6. See, e.g., Philip G. Peters, "When Physicians Balk at Futile Care: Implications of the Disability Rights Laws," 91 *Nw. U. L. Rev.* 798 (1997).

PART V

New Technologies

13

The "Uniqueness" of Genetics

An important part of celebrating the Jewish holiday of Passover is to repeatedly ask (and answer) the question, Why is this night different from all other nights? A similar process is often used to evaluate the legal issues that arise in dealing with genetics questions. As the materials that follow suggest, the topic can arise in a variety of contexts, from insurance coverage to the types of human genetic manipulation that should be permitted. In each instance, ask yourself if the introduction of the genetics issue substantially alters the question, or if we are merely dealing with a minor variation on a question that is adequately dealt with in other areas of law and bioethics.

KATSKEE V. BLUE CROSS/BLUE SHIELD OF NEBRASKA

Supreme Court of Nebraska

515 N.W.2d 645 (Neb. 1994)

OPINION BY JUSTICE WHITE:

This appeal arises from a summary judgment issued by the Douglas County District Court dismissing appellant Sindie Katskee's action for breach of contract. This action concerns the determination of what constitutes an illness within the meaning of a health insurance policy issued by appellee, Blue Cross/Blue Shield of Nebraska. We reverse the decision of the district court and remand the cause for further proceedings.

In January 1990, upon the recommendation of her gynecologist, Dr. Larry E. Roffman, appellant consulted with Dr. Henry T. Lynch regarding her family's history of breast and ovarian cancer, and particularly her health in relation to such a history. After examining appellant and investigating her family's medical history, Dr. Lynch diagnosed her as suffering from a genetic condition known as breast-ovarian carcinoma syndrome. Dr. Lynch then recommended that appellant have a total abdominal hysterectomy and bilateral salpingo-oophorectomy, which involves the removal of the uterus, the ovaries, and the fallopian tubes. Dr. Roffman concurred in Dr. Lynch's diagnosis and agreed that the recommended surgery was the most medically appropriate treatment available.

After considering the diagnosis and recommended treatment, appellant decided to have the surgery. In preparation for the surgery, appellant filed a claim with Blue Cross/Blue Shield. Both Drs. Lynch and Roffman wrote to Blue Cross/Blue Shield and explained the diagnosis and their basis for recommending the surgery. Initially, Blue Cross/Blue Shield sent a letter to appellant and indicated that it might pay for the surgery. Two weeks before the surgery, Dr. Roger Mason, the chief medical officer for Blue Cross/Blue Shield, wrote to appellant and stated that Blue Cross/Blue Shield would not cover the cost of the surgery. Nonetheless, appellant had the surgery in November 1990. . . .

Blue Cross/Blue Shield contends that appellant's costs are not covered by the insurance policy. The policy provides coverage for services which are medically necessary. The policy defines "medically necessary" as follows:

> The services, procedures, drugs, supplies or Durable Medical Equipment provided by the Physician, Hospital or other health care provider, in the diagnosis *or treatment of the Covered Person's Illness*, Injury, or Pregnancy, which are:
>
> 1. Appropriate for the symptoms and diagnosis of the patient's Illness, Injury or Pregnancy; . . .
>
> We shall determine whether services provided are Medically Necessary. Services will not automatically be considered Medically Necessary because they have been ordered or provided by a Physician.

. . . Blue Cross/Blue Shield denied coverage because it concluded that appellant's condition does not constitute an illness, and thus the treatment she received was not medically necessary. Blue Cross/Blue Shield has not raised any other basis for its denial, and we therefore will limit our consideration to whether appellant's condition constituted an illness within the meaning of the policy.

The policy broadly defines "illness" as a "bodily disorder or disease." The policy does not provide definitions for either bodily disorder or disease.

An insurance policy is to be construed as any other contract to give effect to the parties' intentions at the time the contract was made. When the terms of the contract are clear, a court may not resort to rules of construction, and the terms are to be accorded their plain and ordinary meaning as the ordinary or reasonable person would understand them. In such a case, a court shall seek to ascertain the intention of the parties from the plain language of the policy.

Whether a policy is ambiguous is a matter of law for the court to determine. If a court finds that the policy is ambiguous, then the court may employ rules of construction and look beyond the language of the policy to ascertain the intention of the parties. A general principle of construction, which we have applied to ambiguous insurance policies, holds that an ambiguous policy will be construed in favor of the insured. . . .

Applying these principles, our interpretation of the language of the terms employed in the policy is guided by definitions found in dictionaries, and additionally by judicial opinions rendered by other courts which have considered the meaning of these terms. Webster's Third New International Dictionary, Unabridged 648 (1981), defines disease as

> an impairment of the normal state of the living animal or plant body or of any of its components that interrupts or modifies the performance of the vital functions, being a response to environmental factors . . . to specific infective agents . . . to inherent defects of the organism (as various genetic anomalies), or to combinations of these factors: Sickness, Illness.

The same dictionary defines disorder as "a derangement of function: an abnormal physical or mental condition: Sickness, Ailment, Malady."

These lay definitions are consistent with the general definitions provided in Dorland's Illustrated Medical Dictionary (27th ed. 1988). Dorland's defines disease as

> any deviation from or interruption of the normal structure or function of any part, organ, or system . . . of the body that is manifested by a characteristic set of symptoms and signs and whose etiology [theory of origin or cause], pathology [origin or cause], and prognosis may be known or unknown.

In *Cheney v. Bell National Life* (1989), the Court of Appeals for Maryland considered whether hemophilia was a disease or sickness in the context of an exclusionary clause of an accidental death insurance policy. The insurer argued that hemophilia is not a disease because it is a genetic or hereditary condition of the body which tends to make the individual susceptible to certain diseases, but the court disagreed. The court recognized that the scientific community is not unanimous in its descriptions and characterizations of hemophilia. The court, however, stated that its interpretation of the term "disease" should be controlled by its ordinary and common meaning. Relying on definitions found in several dictionaries and reference materials, the court broadly interpreted disease to encompass an abnormal condition of such a degree that in its natural progression would be expected to be a source of trouble; a condition which has impaired, or will impair if it progresses, the working of bodily functions; a significant condition which would be commonly referred to as a disease; or an inherent defect which impairs the normal state of the body. Applying the commonly accepted meaning of the term "disease," the court concluded that hemophilia is a disease as that term is used in the insurance policy.

We find that the language used in the policy at issue in the present case is not reasonably susceptible of differing interpretations and thus not ambiguous.

The plain and ordinary meaning of the terms "bodily disorder" and "disease," as they are used in the policy to define illness, encompasses any abnormal condition of the body or its components of such a degree that in its natural progression would be expected to be problematic; a deviation from the healthy or normal state affecting the functions or tissues of the body; an inherent defect of the body; or a morbid physical or mental state which deviates from or interrupts the normal structure or function of any part, organ, or system of the body and which is manifested by a characteristic set of symptoms and signs.

The issue then becomes whether appellant's condition—breast-ovarian carcinoma syndrome—constitutes an illness.

Blue Cross/Blue Shield argues that appellant did not suffer from an illness because she did not have cancer. Blue Cross/Blue Shield characterizes appellant's condition only as a "predisposition to an illness (cancer)" and fails to address whether the condition itself constitutes an illness. . . .

According to Dr. Lynch, some forms of cancer occur on a hereditary basis. Breast and ovarian cancer are such hereditary forms of cancer which may occur on a hereditary basis. It is our understanding that the hereditary occurrence of this form of cancer is related to the genetic makeup of the woman. In this regard, the genetic deviation has conferred changes which are manifest in the individual's body and at some time become capable of being diagnosed.

At the time that he gave his deposition, Dr. Lynch explained that the state of medical research was such that detecting and diagnosing the syndrome was achieved by tracing the occurrences of hereditary cancer throughout the patient's family. Dr. Lynch stated that at the time of appellant's diagnosis, no conclusive physical test existed which would demonstrate the presence of the condition. However, Dr. Lynch stated that this area of research is progressing toward the development of a more determinative method of identifying and tracing a particular gene throughout a particular family, thus providing a physical method of diagnosing the condition.

Women diagnosed with the syndrome have at least a 50-percent chance of developing breast and/or ovarian cancer, whereas unaffected women have only a 1.4-percent risk of developing breast or ovarian cancer. In addition to the genetic deviation, the family history, and the significant risks associated with this condition, the diagnosis also may encompass symptoms of anxiety and stress, which some women experience because of their knowledge of the substantial likelihood of developing cancer.

The procedures for detecting the onset of ovarian cancer are ineffective. Generally, by the time ovarian cancer is capable of being detected, it has already developed to a very advanced stage, making treatment relatively unsuccessful. Drs. Lynch and Roffman agreed that the standard of care for treating women with breast carcinoma syndrome ordinarily involves surveillance methods. However, for women at an inordinately high risk for ovarian cancer, such as appellant, the standard of care may require radical surgery which involves the removal of the uterus, ovaries, and fallopian tubes.

Dr. Lynch explained that the surgery is labeled "prophylactic" and that the surgery is prophylactic as to the prevention of the onset of cancer. Dr. Lynch also stated that appellant's condition itself is the result of a genetic deviation from the normal, healthy state and that the recommended surgery treats that condition by eliminating or significantly reducing the presence of the condition and its likely development.

Blue Cross/Blue Shield has not proffered any evidence disputing the premise that the origin of this condition is in the genetic makeup of the individual and that in its natural development it is likely to produce devastating results. Although handicapped by his limited knowledge of the syndrome, Dr. Mason did not dispute the nature of the syndrome as explained by Dr. Lynch and supported by Dr. Roffman, nor did Dr. Mason dispute the fact that the surgery falls within the standard of care for many women afflicted with this syndrome.

In light of the plain and ordinary meaning of the terms "illness," "bodily disorder," and "disease," we find that appellant's condition constitutes an illness within the meaning of the policy. Appellant's condition is a deviation from what is considered a normal, healthy physical state or structure. The abnormality or deviation from a normal state arises, in part, from the genetic makeup of the woman. The existence of this unhealthy state results in the woman's being at substantial risk of developing cancer. The recommended surgery is intended to correct that morbid state by reducing or eliminating that risk.

Although appellant's condition was not detectable by physical evidence or a physical examination, it does not necessarily follow that appellant does not suffer from an illness. The record establishes that a woman who suffers from breast-ovarian carcinoma syndrome does have a physical state which significantly deviates from the physical state of a normal, healthy woman. Specifically, appellant suffered from a different or abnormal genetic constitution which, when combined with a particular family history of hereditary cancer, significantly increases the risk of a devastating outcome.

We are mindful that not every condition which itself constitutes a predisposition to another illness is necessarily an illness within the meaning of an insurance policy. There exists a fine distinction between such conditions, which was recognized by Chief Justice Cardozo in *Silverstein v. Metropolitan Life Ins. Co.* (1930). Writing for the court, Chief Justice Cardozo explained that when a condition is such that in its probable and natural progression it may be expected to be a source of mischief, it may reasonably be described as a disease or an illness. On the other hand, he stated that if the condition is abnormal when tested by a standard of perfection, but so remote in its potential mischief that common speech would not label it a disease or infirmity, such a condition is at most a predisposing tendency. The *Silverstein* court found that a pea-size ulcer, which was located at the site of damage caused by a severe blow to the deceased's stomach, was not a disease or infirmity within the meaning of an exclusionary clause of an accident insurance policy because if left unattended, the ulcer would have been only as harmful as a tiny scratch. . . .

NOTES AND QUESTIONS:
Katskee v. Blue Cross/Blue Shield of Nebraska

1. The court concludes that Ms. Katskee did indeed have an illness. Do you agree? Why or why not?
2. Why did Blue Cross/Blue Shield determine that she did not have an illness? What about Ms. Katskee's condition distinguishes it from most other things that we might claim to be illnesses? Consider that:
   a. Her condition does not create a present medical problem, in that she can do anything she wants and thus is not now sick. (Is being sick different from having an illness?) Compare this situation to someone with high blood pressure, which does not alter the person's present life style, nor make them currently sick. Do you think Blue Cross/Blue Shield covers treatment for high blood pressure? Can you think of other medical conditions that do not make the person currently sick?
   b. Her condition only creates a possibility of a medical problem in the future. Again, compare her to a person with high blood pressure. Do all people with high blood pressure die from the complications of that condition (e.g., a stroke or a heart attack)?
   c. Some genetic conditions create a *certainty* of a future medical problem. For example, a person may inherit a gene for Huntington's Disease, which leads to neurological degeneration when a person is a young adult. Assuming that there was a therapy that the person could take as a child that would correct the genetic problem, do you think insurers such as Blue Cross/Blue Shield would refuse to pay for it?
3. Does the ability to detect genetic problems in fact make it easier to categorize something as a disease? Is alcoholism a disease, or merely a behavioral weakness? What scientific information might you want to know?
4. In an episode of the television show *Ally McBeal*, the intrepid lawyers are asked to defend a man who cheated on his wife. His defense is that he was addicted to sex. If you were the judge in that case, what additional information about his condition might you want to know?
5. Is homosexuality a disease? According to the current medical guidelines of the psychiatric profession, it is not. Do you agree with that? Why or why not?
   Assume that researchers discover a certain protein that, when present in a developing male fetus, causes changes in the brain that lead to the resulting child having a sexual attraction to the opposite sex. Furthermore, on doing research on a subset of male homosexuals, they discover that there is a point mutation in the gene for that protein. Should persons with that genetic mutation be considered to have an illness? What would your answer be if it were shown that for a particular person homosexuality was a learned behavior that had nothing to do with genetic makeup?
6. Why do homosexuals normally not want to be labeled as having an illness? Is the problem with the label, or how people treat them as a result of that

label? In fact, are there laws that might prevent someone from being mistreated on the grounds of having an illness? (A person who was not labeled as having an illness might not have the protection of such laws.)

Why might a person want to be considered to have an illness? Would Ms. Katskee have wanted to be considered illness-free? Assume that Robert is a male homosexual who possesses the genetic mutation discussed in item 5, and wants to receive a treatment that would convert him to being a heterosexual. Should an insurance company have to pay for that? Will that decision turn on whether or not he has an illness?

7. To what extent does culture and not science determine what is or is not an illness? Is the determination that attraction to the opposite sex is not an "ordinary" or "natural" function for human beings, and therefore the lack of such attraction not an illness, ultimately a *social* determination? If we make that determination, how do we consistently draw a line between things that are or are not illnesses? Large segments of the public are infertile. Is infertility an illness? Can't an infertile person function perfectly well in society? Why is it not a normal variation, like being a particular height?

8. Is deafness an illness? Some members of the deaf community claim that they have a distinct society, which is merely different (no better and no worse) than that of the hearing society. Assuming there was an effective treatment for certain genetic causes of deafness, should it be considered child abuse to not treat a child's deafness?

   The desire among some deaf parents to have a deaf child is very real. A good illustration of how far that might go is the occasionally discussed scenario of deaf parents wanting to have a fetus tested for deafness. The purpose of such testing would be to allow a decision to abort the fetus if it was discovered not to have inherited a gene that causes deafness.[1]

9. There is an aspect of Ms. Katskee's medical condition that is not discussed in the opinion. What is it, and why do you think she was not raising this with the insurance company? You might ask yourself, recalling our discussion of standard care, what determines that a particular treatment is medically appropriate? When this case took place, presumably doctors often advised patients with Ms. Katskee's condition to have a hysterectomy. What were they probably not bothering to recommend?

10. Although the *Katskee* case represents a scenario in which the insurance company wants to treat a genetic condition *differently* than other medical problems, the far more common scenario is just the opposite: insurers wants to use genetic information about a person to deny coverage or charge a higher premium because it is a "pre-existing condition." While in that scenario the insurer is looking for equality of treatment, the law is rapidly moving toward an approach that treats genetic information differently from other kinds of medical problems.

    In particular, a majority of states have enacted at least some restriciton on the ability of insurance companies to use genetic information (which is defined in various ways) in making coverage or pricing decisions. The Connecticut statute, Conn. Gen. Stat. § 38a-816, describing an "unfair and deceptive practice in the business of insurance," is fairly typical:

> (19) With respect to an insurance company, . . . refusing to insure, refusing to continue to insure or limiting the amount, extent or kind of coverage available to an individual or charging an individual a different rate for the same coverage because of genetic information. Genetic information indicating a predisposition to a disease or condition shall not be deemed a preexisting condition in the absence of a diagnosis of such disease or condition that is based on other medical information. An insurance company . . . shall not be prohibited from refusing to insure or applying a preexisting condition limitation, to the extent permitted by law, to an individual who has been diagnosed with a disease or condition based on medical information other than genetic information and has exhibited symptoms of such disease or condition. For the purposes of this subsection, "genetic information" means the information about genes, gene products or inherited characteristics that may derive from an individual or family member.

11. Consider the following scenarios:
    a. Ten years ago, while getting a routine mammogram, the machine malfunctioned and exposed Ashley to a very high dose of radiation. As a result, she has appproximately a 90 percent lifetime chance of developing breast cancer.
    b. Beth comes from a family in which a number of relatives have died at an early age from breast cancer. She recently underwent genetic testing, and it demonstrates that she has approximately a 90 percent lifetime chance of developing breast cancer.

    In Connecticut, can an insurance company charge Ashley a higher premium based on her risk of breast cancer? How about Beth? What arguments might justify a distinction? If we are troubled about the use of information relating to pre-existing conditions, is there a reason to distinguish between genetic and nongenetic pre-existing conditions?[2]

SAFER v. PACK

Superior Court of New Jersey, Appellate Division

677 A.2d 1188 (N.J. Super. Ct. App. Div. 1996)

OPINION BY JUDGE KESTIN:

. . . Donna Safer's claim arises from the patient-physician relationship in the 1950s and 1960s between her father, Robert Batkin, a resident of New Jersey, and Dr. George T. Pack, also a resident of New Jersey, who practiced medicine and surgery in New York City and treated Mr. Batkin there. It is alleged that Dr. Pack specialized in the treatment and removal of cancerous tumors and growths.

In November 1956, Mr. Batkin was admitted to the hospital with a pre-operative diagnosis of retroperitoneal cancer. A week later, Dr. Pack performed a total colectomy and an ileosigmoidectomy for multiple polyposis of the colon with malignant degeneration in one area. The discharge summary noted the finding in a pathology report of the existence of adenocarcinoma developing in an intestinal polyp, and diffuse intestinal polyposis "from one end of the colon to the other." Dr. Pack continued to treat Mr. Batkin postoperatively. . . .

. . . After some treatment, Mr. Batkin died on January 3, 1964, at forty-five years of age. Donna was ten years old at the time of her father's death. Her sister was seventeen.

In February 1990, Donna Safer, then thirty-six years of age and newly married, residing in Connecticut, began to experience lower abdominal pain. Examinations and tests revealed a cancerous blockage of the colon and multiple polyposis. In March, Ms. Safer underwent a total abdominal colectomy with ileorectal anastamosis. A primary carcinoma in the sigmoid colon was found to extend through the serosa of the bowel and multiple polyps were seen throughout the entire bowel. Because of the detection of additional metastatic adenocarcinoma and carcinoma, plaintiff's left ovary was also removed. Between April 1990 and mid-1991, Ms. Safer underwent chemotherapy treatment.

In September 1991, plaintiffs obtained Robert Batkin's medical records, from which they learned that he had suffered from polyposis. Their complaint was filed in March 1992, alleging a violation of duty (professional negligence) on the part of Dr. Pack in his failure to warn of the risk to Donna Safer's health.

Plaintiffs contend that multiple polyposis is a hereditary condition that, if undiscovered and untreated, invariably leads to metastatic colorectal cancer. They contend, further, that the hereditary nature of the disease was known at the time Dr. Pack was treating Mr. Batkin and that the physician was required, by medical standards then prevailing, to warn those at risk so that they might have the benefits of early examination, monitoring, detection and treatment, that would provide opportunity to avoid the most baneful consequences of the condition.

. . . Ida Batkin, Donna Safer's mother, had also given a deposition in which she testified, among other details, that neither her husband nor Dr. Pack had ever told her that Mr. Batkin suffered from cancer; and that, throughout the courses of surgery and treatment, Dr. Pack advised her that he was treating a "blockage" or an unspecified "infection." On the one or two occasions when Mrs. Batkin inquired of Dr. Pack whether the "infection" would affect her children, she was told not to worry.

In dismissing, the trial court held that a physician had no "legal duty to warn a child of a patient of a genetic risk[.]" In the absence of any evidence whether Dr. Pack had warned Mr. Batkin to provide information concerning his disease for the benefit of his children, the motion judge "assumed that Dr. Pack did not tell Robert Batkin of the genetic disease."

The motion judge's reasoning proceeded from the following legal premise: "in order for a doctor to have a duty to warn, there must be a patient/physician relationship or circumstances requiring the protection of the public health or the community [at] large." Finding no physician-patient relationship between Dr. Pack and his patient's daughter Donna, the court then held genetically transmissible diseases to differ from contagious or infectious diseases or threats of harm in respect of the duty to warn, because "the harm is already present within the non-patient child, as opposed to being introduced, by a patient who was not warned to stay away. The patient is taking no action in which to cause the child harm." . . .

Whether a legal duty exists is . . . a matter of law. We see no impediment, legal or otherwise, to recognizing a physician's duty to warn those known to be at risk of avoidable harm from a genetically transmissible condition. In terms of foreseeability especially, there is no essential difference between the type of genetic threat at issue here and the menace of infection, contagion or a threat of physical harm. The individual or group at risk is easily identified, and substantial future harm may be averted or minimized by a timely and effective warning.

The motion judge's view of this case as one involving an unavoidable genetic condition gave too little significance to the proferred expert view that early monitoring of those at risk can effectively avert some of the more serious consequences a person with multiple polyposis might otherwise experience. We cannot conclude either, as the trial court did, that Dr. Pack breached no duty because avoidable harm to Donna was not foreseeable, i.e., "that Dr. Pack's conduct did not create a 'foreseeable zone of risk.'" Such a determination would ignore the presumed state of medical knowledge at the time. It would also tend to undervalue the concepts that inform our case law establishing a cause of action for increased risk of harm, as well as the underlying rationale of our rules of law on foreseeability, heretofore held to be specifically applicable in professional negligence cases involving genetic torts.

Although an overly broad and general application of the physician's duty to warn might lead to confusion, conflict or unfairness in many types of circumstances, we are confident that the duty to warn of avertible risk from genetic causes, by definition a matter of familial concern, is sufficiently narrow to serve the interests of justice. Further, it is appropriate, for reasons already expressed by our Supreme Court, that the duty be seen as owed not only to the patient himself but that it also "extends beyond the interests of a patient to members of the immediate family of the patient who may be adversely affected by a breach of that duty." We need not decide, in the present posture of this case, how, precisely, that duty is to be discharged, especially with respect to young children who may be at risk, except to require that reasonable steps be taken to assure that the information reaches those likely to be affected or is made available for their benefit. We are aware of no direct evidence that has been developed concerning the nature of the communications between physician and patient regarding Mr. Batkin's disease: what Dr. Pack did or did not disclose; the advice he gave to Mr. Batkin, if any, concerning genetic factors and what ought to have been done in respect of those at risk; and the conduct or expressed preferences of Mr. Batkin in response thereto. There may be enough from Mrs. Batkin's testimony and other evidence for inferences to be drawn, however.

We decline to hold as the Florida Supreme Court did in *Pate v. Thelkel* that, in all circumstances, the duty to warn will be satisfied by informing the patient. It may be necessary, at some stage, to resolve a conflict between the physician's broader duty to warn and his fidelity to an expressed preference of the patient that nothing be said to family members about the details of the disease. We cannot know presently, however, whether there is any likelihood that such a conflict may be shown to have existed in this matter or, if it did, what its qualities might have been. As the matter is currently constituted, it is as likely as not that no such conflict will be shown to have existed and that the only evidence on the issue will be Mrs. Batkin's testimony, including that she received no information, despite specific inquiry, that her children were at risk. We note, in addition, the possible existence of some offsetting evidence that Donna was rectally examined as a young child, suggesting that the risk to her had been disclosed.

This case implicates serious and conflicting medical, social and legal policies. . . . Some such policy considerations may need to be addressed in ultimately resolving this case. For example, if evidence is produced that will permit the jury to find that Dr. Pack received instructions from his patient not to disclose details of the illness or the fact of genetic risk, the court will be required to determine whether, as a matter of law, there are or ought to be any limits on physician-patient confidentiality, especially after the patient's death where a risk of harm survives the patient, as in the case of genetic consequences.

NOTES AND QUESTIONS:
Safer v. Pack

1. When this case went to trial, Ms. Safer lost on factual grounds. There was evidence that she had a medical examination of her colon as a child, strongly suggesting that the doctor had informed her parents of the fact that she had a high risk of getting cancer.
2. The issue raised in this case—on whom to impose an obligation to disclose certain information—is very similar to that raised in what other case in this book?
3. Do you agree with the court that it was appropriate to impose a duty to warn on the doctor? Why or why not?
4. As discussed in the notes to *Katskee*, many states are passing laws specifically designed to protect the confidentiality of genetic information. To what extent do the concerns that motivated such laws apply to the facts of this case?
5. What exactly does the court want the doctor to do in fulfilling his duty to his patient's daughter? Note its comment that it need not decide "how, pre-

cisely, that duty is to be discharged, especially with respect to young children who may be at risk, except to require that reasonable steps be taken to assure that the information reaches those likely to be affected or is made available for their benefit." Because Donna Safer was a minor at the time her father was being treated, her parents had the legal authority to make decisions for her. Normally it would be appropriate to deal with them with regard to fulfilling duties toward the child. Should Dr. Pack have been required to:

a. Inform Donna's father about the fact that this was a genetic condition, and that his daughter was at risk. (Dr. Pack may in fact have done this.)

b. Inform both of Donna's parents about that fact.

c. Inform both of Donna's parents and in addition tell Donna.

Assuming that in general the law concludes that notice to one parent is sufficient, is there a reason to alter that rule if there is a duty to disclose in cases such as this? Should the law be assuming that parents will be so concerned about the confidentiality of their medical condition that they will act in a way that harms a child? And once the doctor tells the patient about the risk to the children, does the parent have a duty to use that information to protect the health of the children? If there is such a duty, why impose an additional duty on the doctor?

6. Why limit the rationale of *Safer* to children? Presumably, that sort of genetic information might be relevant to quite a few blood relatives of the patient, including brother and sisters, cousins, nieces, and nephews. Is it the doctor's duty to inform them all ? If we want to impose a duty to share relevant genetic information, should the duty be imposed on the person who has the closest relationship to such persons, namely the patient himself? Or should we not impose such a duty on anyone?

FOUNDATION ON ECONOMIC TRENDS V. HECKLER

United States Court of Appeals for the District of Columbia Circuit

756 F.2d 143 (D.C. Cir. 1985)

OPINION BY JUDGE WRIGHT:

Almost 14 years ago, soon after passage of the National Environmental Policy Act, this court faced the challenge of ensuring that the Act's "important legislative purposes, heralded in the halls of Congress, [were] not lost or misdirected in the vast hallways of the federal bureaucracy." This case poses a no less formidable challenge: to ensure that the bold words and vigorous spirit of NEPA are not similarly lost or misdirected in the brisk frontiers of science.

For this appeal presents an important question at the dawn of the genetic engineering age: what is the appropriate level of environmental review required of the National Institutes of Health (NIH) before it approves the deliberate release of genetically engineered, recombinant-DNA-containing organisms into the open environment? More precisely, in the context of this case, the question is whether to affirm an injunction temporarily enjoining NIH from approving deliberate release experiments without a greater level of environmental concern than the agency has shown thus far. . . .

This case arises against a backdrop of the National Environmental Policy Act, the emergence of genetic engineering, and federal attempts to regulate genetic engineering.

A. NATIONAL ENVIRONMENTAL POLICY ACT

On January 1, 1970 the National Environmental Policy Act became law. Recognizing "the profound impact of man's activity on the interrelation of all components of the natural environment," Congress sought to "fulfill the responsibilities of each generation as trustee of the environment for succeeding generations." The major "action-forcing" provision of NEPA is the requirement that "all agencies of the Federal government" prepare a detailed environmental analysis for "major Federal actions significantly affecting the quality of the human environment." Congress mandated that this detailed statement, long known as an Environmental Impact Statement (EIS), include such considerations as "the environmental impact of the proposed action," "any adverse environmental effects which cannot be avoided should the proposal be implemented," and "alternatives to the proposed action." . . .

B. GENETIC ENGINEERING

Genetic engineering is an important development at the very cusp of scientific advances. More than a decade ago scientists discovered a method for transplanting deoxyribonucleic acid (DNA), the principal substance of genes. Although exchanges and mutations of DNA occur in nature, genetic engineering provides the ability to control these fundamental processes of life and evolution. DNA segments can be recovered and cloned from one organism and inserted into another. The result is known as "recombinant DNA."

Recombinant DNA technology has been limited primarily to small organisms, usually bacteria. This production of new bacteria through altering genetic material has been confined to the laboratory; organisms with recombinant DNA have never been released into the general environment.

Broad claims are made about both the potential benefits and the potential hazards of genetically engineered organisms. Use of recombinant DNA may lead to welcome advances in such areas as food production and disease control. At the same time, however, the environmental consequences of dispersion of genetically engineered organisms are far from clear. According to a recent report by a

House of Representatives subcommittee, "The potential environmental risks associated with the deliberate release of genetically engineered organisms or the translocation of any new organism into an ecosystem are best described as 'low probability, high consequence risk'; that is, while there is only a small possibility that damage could occur, the damage that could occur is great."

C. FEDERAL OVERSIGHT OF GENETIC ENGINEERING

Spurred by scientists involved in genetic research, NIH began efforts to oversee genetic engineering in the mid-1970's. . . .

1. NIH's 1976 standards: prohibition on deliberate release. In 1976 the NIH Director issued "Guidelines for Research on Recombinant DNA Molecules." The Guidelines were an historic development, representing the first major federal effort to oversee genetic research and the culmination of intense scientific attention to the possible hazards of genetic research.

In 1974 scientists working in genetic research voluntarily called for a moratorium on certain kinds of experiments until an international meeting could be convened to consider the potential hazards of recombinant DNA molecules. On October 7, 1974 NIH established the Recombinant DNA Advisory Committee (RAC) to consider genetic research issues. . . .

Finally, in the summer of 1976 the NIH Director announced the Guidelines that would govern NIH-supported genetic research experiments. In broad terms, the Guidelines permitted certain laboratory experiments to go forward under carefully specified conditions; certain other types of experiments were flatly prohibited. Deliberate release—"deliberate release into the environment of any organism containing a recombinant DNA molecule"—was one of five categories explicitly banned. In announcing the Guidelines the Director noted that deliberate release of organisms with recombinant DNA was not yet feasible and that, if it became feasible, the ban could be reconsidered. But he stressed that, if such reconsideration occurred, environmental concerns should be paramount: "It is most important that the potential environmental impact of the release be considered."

Significantly, NIH prepared an EIS to accompany its Guidelines—the only EIS NIH has ever completed on the subject of genetic engineering. The EIS did not specifically refer to deliberate release experiments; such experiments were banned. The EIS did, however, note that dispersion of organisms with recombinant DNA molecules loomed as a potential environmental hazard from the permitted experiments:

> Should organisms containing recombined DNA be dispersed into the environment, they might, depending on their fitness relative to naturally occuring [sic] organisms, find a suitable ecological niche for their own reproduction. A potentially dangerous organism might then multiply and spread. Subsequent cessation of experiments would not stop the diffusion of the hazardous agent.

Thus in 1976 the NIH Guidelines prohibited deliberate release; the Director emphasized the importance of full environmental consideration of any possible future release; and the EIS identified dispersion of organisms with recombinant DNA as a possible environmental hazard.

2. The 1978 revision: permission to waive the prohibition against deliberate release. In 1978 the NIH Director undertook an effort to revise the Guidelines "in light of NIH's experience operating under them and in light of [NIH's] increasing knowledge about the potential risks and benefits of this research technique." . . . [T]he 1978 revision allowed the NIH Director authority to grant exceptions to the five absolute prohibitions in the Guidelines—including the prohibition on deliberate release of organisms containing recombinant DNA into the environment.

NIH announced that the standard governing the use of this waiver authority would be the standard generally applicable to the Director's exercise of his duties: "The Director shall weigh each proposed action, through appropriate analysis and consultation, to determine that it complies with the Guidelines and presents no significant risk to health or the environment." NIH also declared that the Director would exercise his authority "with the advice of the Recombinant DNA Advisory Committee after appropriate notice and opportunity for public comment." The Director further stated that his "waiver decisions [would] include a careful consideration of the potential environmental impact, and certain decisions may be accompanied by a formal assessment or statement. This must be determined on a case-by-case basis."

On the subject of deliberate release experiments in particular, the Director suggested that clear standards might be necessary to guide his waiver discretion: "Recognizing the need expressed by ° ° ° commentators for more definitive standards [to govern deliberate release waiver decision], I will refer the matter to the Recombinant Advisory Committee (RAC) for its consideration. ° ° ° The RAC will be asked to address conditions under which exceptions to various prohibited categories of experiments may be granted." Thus the Director perceived a possible need for more definitive standards and suggested that such standards might be forthcoming. . . .

3. Approval of deliberate release experiments. The 1978 revision was the last significant revision of NIH's guidelines regarding deliberate release experiments. . . . The "more definitive standards" suggested by the Director never emerged.

Although the guidelines have not changed, NIH's role has begun to change dramatically. For, with the maturation of genetic engineering technology, NIH has been faced with applications for approval of deliberate release experiments.

The NIH Director, acting on the advice of RAC, has approved three deliberate release experiments at institutions receiving NIH funds for recombinant DNA research. On August 7, 1981 the Director approved a request by Dr. Ronald Davis of Stanford University to field-test corn plants containing recombinant DNA molecules. The goal was to increase the corn's dietary value by improving its ability to store protein. However, the field tests were never conducted because feasibility problems developed.

On April 15, 1983 the Director approved a request by Dr. John Sanford of Cornell University to field-test tomato and tobacco plants with recombinant DNA. The goal was to prove that pollen could serve as a "vector" for insertion of recombinant DNA. Again, however, due to feasibility problems, the experiment never went forward.

On June 1, 1983 the Director gave final approval to the experiment at issue on appeal—the request by Drs. Nickolas Panopoulos and Steven Lindow of the University of California at Berkeley to apply genetically altered bacteria to plots of potatoes, tomatoes, and beans in northern California. As discussed in greater detail below, the goal was to increase the crops' frost resistance. Because of the cancellation of the previous two experiments, the Panopoulos-Lindow experiment would be the first NIH-approved deliberate release experiment actually to be conducted.

In February 1984 a congressional subcommittee report sharply criticized NIH's method of reviewing deliberate release experiments. The report concluded that "the current regulatory framework does not guarantee that adequate consideration will be given to the potential environmental effects of a deliberate release." In particular, "the RAC's ability to adequately evaluate the environmental hazards posed by deliberate releases is limited by both its expertise and its jurisdiction." The subcommittee report recommended a moratorium on deliberate release approvals until an interagency review panel was established to consider the potential environmental effects of each deliberate release experiment. "Each [deliberate release experiment] could result in major environmental damage or adverse public health effects." . . .

III. The University of California Experiment

. . . 1. The proposed experiment. On September 17, 1982 Drs. Lindow and Panopoulos, scientists at Berkeley, submitted a request for NIH approval of an experiment that would involve deliberate release of genetically altered organisms in the open environment. . . . Lindow and Panopoulos proposed to apply the genetically altered bacteria to various crops, including potatoes, tomatoes, and beans. By changing the bacteria's genetic composition, Lindow and Panopoulos hoped that the bacteria would change from frost-triggering bacteria to non-frost-triggering bacteria; they further hoped that the engineered non-frost-triggering bacteria would displace the natural frost-triggering bacteria. The ultimate goal was to protect the crops from frost and thus to extend their growing season. Such non-frost-triggering bacteria occur in nature as products of natural mutation, but Lindow and Panopoulos apparently hoped that the genetically engineered organisms would be more stable than the natural mutants. They sought to treat crops at six sites; the workers applying the recombinant-DNA-containing bacteria would wear respirators to reduce the risk of inhalation.

2. NIH review. NIH announced the Lindow-Panopoulos request for approval, the RAC meeting at which it would be considered, and the opportunity to comment. No comments were received. At the RAC meeting on October 25, 1982 RAC members raised questions about the number of sites, the lack of adequate information, and the possible effects on rainfall. . . . The Director decided to postpone approval and suggested further consideration.

Lindow and Panopoulos resubmitted their proposal with some modifications, including a reduction of experiment sites from six to one. On April 11, 1983, after some discussion, RAC voted to recommend approving the proposal by a vote of 19-0, with no abstentions. The Director then approved the experiment.

3. NEPA compliance. NIH's consideration of the Lindow-Panopoulos experiment falls far short of the NEPA requirements. And, despite the government's apparent belief, the deficiency is not a question of which document contains the environmental analysis. Rather, the deficiency rests in NIH's complete failure to consider the possibility of various environmental effects. . . .

The most glaring deficiency in NIH's review of the Lindow-Panopoulos experiment is its treatment of the possibility of dispersion of recombinant-DNA-containing organisms. As noted, NIH's only EIS on genetic engineering specifically identified dispersion as one of the major environmental concerns associated with recombinant DNA research. The consequences of dispersion of genetically altered organisms are uncertain. Some observers believe that such dispersion would affect the environment and the climate in harmful ways.

Thus the problem of dispersion would seem to be one of the major concerns associated with the Lindow-Panopoulos experiment, the first experiment that would actually release genetically engineered organisms in the open environment. Yet in the minutes of the RAC meeting—the only document on appeal that records any NIH consideration of the environmental impact of dispersion—the entirety of the consideration of dispersion is the following statement: according to a RAC evaluator, "Although some movement of bacteria toward sites near treatment locations by insect or aerial transport is possible, the number of viable cells transported has been shown to be very small; and these cells are subject to biological and physical processes limiting survival." In this sentence, which was taken almost verbatim from the Lindow-Panopoulos proposal, the RAC evaluator thus conceded the possibility of aerial or insect transport, but merely commented that the number of viable cells would be small, and that they were subject to processes limiting survival. Remarkably, therefore, RAC completely failed to consider the possible environmental impact from dispersion of genetically altered bacteria, however small the number and however subject to procedures limiting survival.

In light of this complete failure to address a major environmental concern, NIH's environmental assessment utterly fails to meet the standard of environmental review necessary before an agency decides not to prepare an EIS. . . .

NIH, no less than any other federal agency, must ensure that its decisions meet the standards of environmental concern and reasoned decisionmaking required by law. The complexity and uncertainty of the issues before NIH do not diminish these responsibilities one iota. Indeed, "one of the functions of a NEPA statement is to indicate the extent to which environmental effects are essentially unknown. * * * We must reject any attempt by agencies to shirk their responsibilities under NEPA by labeling any and all discussion of future environmental effects as 'crystal ball inquiry.'

We affirm the injunction as it applies to the University of California experiment. We vacate the injunction as it applies to NIH's approval of all other deliberate release experiments, but we share and support the District Court's concern that NIH has not yet given adequate consideration to broad and important issues relating to its role in approving deliberate release experiments.

Recombinant DNA Research: Notice of Intent to Propose Amendments to NIH Guidelines
National Institutes of Health
61 Fed. Reg. 35774 (July 8, 1996)

. . . I. Background

In 1974, the National Academy of Sciences (NAS) established a Committee on Recombinant DNA Molecules which was charged with examining the risks associated with recombinant DNA research and recommending specific actions or guidelines. The NAS Committee report requested: (1) that certain experiments be voluntarily deferred; (2) that plans to construct recombinants with animal DNA should be carefully weighed; (3) that the NIH Director establish a committee to oversee a program to evaluate hypothetical risks, to develop procedures to minimize the spread of recombinant DNA molecules, and to recommend guidelines to be followed by investigators; and (4) that an international meeting be convened to review progress and discuss ways to deal with potential hazards.

In that same year, the Department of Health, Education, and Welfare (currently the Department of Health and Human Services (DHHS)) chartered a committee (later identified as the RAC) in response to the NAS report. In 1975, RAC held its first meeting to establish appropriate biological and physical containment practices and procedures that were later developed into a set of guidelines for the safe conduct of recombinant DNA research (the NIH Guidelines). Subsequently, the NIH created [the Office of Recombinant DNA Activities, also called ORDA,] to provide administrative support to the RAC.

In 1982, an in-depth examination of the broad ethical implications of human gene therapy research, *The Social and Ethical Issues of Genetic Engineering with Human Beings (Splicing Life)*, was published by the President's Commission for the Study of Ethical Problems in Medicine and Biomedical and Behavioral Research. *Splicing Life* proposed that, " . . . since laboratory biohazards related to recombinant DNA research were no longer regarded as urgent matters, the NIH should extend its purview over recombinant DNA research beyond environmental issues to human gene therapy."

They recommended that the membership of the RAC should be broadened to include a combination of Federal and non-Federal scientists, lay public participants, and ethicists. In response to Splicing Life, the NIH established the RAC Human Gene Therapy Subcommittee which was subsequently merged with the parent committee to become the current RAC.

II. Rationale for Change

In recognition of the committee's critical role in maintaining public accountability for recombinant DNA research, the NIH Director weighed a variety of factors prior to announcing NIH's intent to change and enhance its current oversight responsibilities for recombinant DNA research. In order to clarify the rationale for the proposed changes described herein, a series of questions and answers are provided below.

1. On what basis does the NIH conclude that this is the optimal time to eliminate the RAC and realign NIH's responsibilities to public discussion and data management of human gene therapy clinical trials?

Since its inception, the NIH has continuously relinquished oversight of various elements in the field of recombinant DNA research, as such elements reached maturity. From 1979–1983, several major revisions were made to the NIH Guidelines when putative risks to the public did not materialize and the initial restrictions were deemed unnecessary. In 1991, the NIH's oversight of environmental release of genetically modified organisms was relinquished and these responsibilities were ceded to the U.S. Department of Agriculture and the Environmental Protection Agency. These changes were, in part, motivated by the recognition that NIH did not have the statutory authority or the "tools" to function as a regulatory agency.

In 1995, a similar devolution of NIH oversight of human gene therapy occurred. By this time, the RAC had reviewed and approved 113 gene therapy protocols and over 1,000 patients had been enrolled in world-wide trials. The RAC, the scientific community, and the public had a substantial base of information regarding the use and safety of many of the vectors employed in, and target diseases addressed by, human gene therapy. Subsequent analyses revealed that the human health and environmental safety concerns expressed at the inception of gene therapy clinical trials had not materialized. Absent evidence for substantial safety concerns for gene therapy protocols which have been previously tested, on

March 6, 1995, the RAC voted to recommend approval of amendments to the NIH Guidelines that would eliminate RAC review and approval of human gene therapy experiments not considered to be novel. Under this mechanism, all protocols determined not to represent a novel gene therapy delivery strategy or target disease that could adversely affect human health were considered exempt from RAC review and approval and were forwarded directly to the FDA. This streamlined process, which became known as the NIH and FDA "Consolidated Review," eliminated unnecessary and time consuming duplication of effort by the NIH and the FDA. On April 17, 1995, the NIH Director approved these amendments to the NIH Guidelines. Once again, the NIH relinquished a portion of its oversight of recombinant DNA research to the agency (FDA) with statutory responsibility to approve such protocols.

Since the implementation of consolidated review in July 1995, only six of the 36 protocols submitted to ORDA required RAC review and approval; and five of those six protocols were already in the system before consolidated review. The consolidated review process proved to be so successful in eliminating the need for RAC review and approval, that NIH canceled both the March and June 1996 RAC meetings due to the lack of novel protocols requiring RAC attention.

The NIH Director has concluded that the current proposal to enhance NIH oversight of recombinant DNA activities is timely and appropriate based on the current base of knowledge, the need for substantial discussion of gene therapy techniques which are not yet being tested in humans, and the duplication of review and approval by the NIH while the FDA holds the statutory authority. Thus, the NIH Director proposes the termination of the RAC, relinquishing of all protocol approval to the FDA and the creation of two new entities to enhance the depth and breadth of public discussion of gene therapy issues.

2. Why does the NIH propose to replace the RAC?

The proposed actions regarding the RAC should not be viewed narrowly as "eliminating" the RAC. Rather, these actions were developed in a timely and appropriate response to a series of publicly debated discussions over a period of several years. The NIH Director maintains that the establishment of the [Office for Recombinant DNA Activities Advisory Committee (OAC)] and the convening of the [Gene Therapy Policy Conferences (GTPC)] are effective and innovative responses to this rapidly changing area of biomedical research based on the foundation of scientific knowledge that has been gained over the last six years and overlapping responsibilities of other Federal agencies. This proposal optimizes current Federal resources, maintains public access to information, and facilitates public discussion of novel issues relevant to human gene therapy research. NIH concludes that it is not the RAC per se that is critical for public accountability, but the system by which NIH continues to provide public discussion of the scientific, safety, and ethical/legal issues related to human gene therapy.

As proposed, the OAC will provide a smaller, but fully representational, standing committee with a range of advisory and administrative oversight responsibilities similar, but not identical to, the RAC. In contrast, participation in the proposed GTPC will be subject to recommendations by the OAC and ORDA and, as such, will provide the necessary flexibility to engender in-depth, expert discussion of scientific issues and societal implications that cannot be achieved under current mechanisms. The GTPC will continue to maintain favorable RAC attributes such as continued public access to conference discussions and recommendations, publication of scheduled meeting dates and proposed agendas in the Federal Register, and publication of official conference minutes. Eliminating RAC protocol approval reduces duplication of effort with the FDA while enhancing the time and effort devoted to both ongoing and anticipated gene therapy policy issues deserving of substantial public discussion.

3. *Why not continue RAC review and approval of gene therapy protocols?*

In 1990, when the RAC first turned its attention to human gene therapy, the NIH was the sole source of the substantial expertise necessary to review the relatively new field of human gene therapy. Since that time, the FDA has created a new Division of Cellular and Gene Therapies and has committed substantial resources to the development of review capabilities in this arena. At its inception, it was critical for the RAC to conduct a case-by-case review of human gene transfer protocols, since each new protocol invariably set a new precedent. Six years later, the RAC has relinquished most of its review and approval activities under the "consolidated" review plan which forwards all but novel protocols directly to the FDA for consideration.

During the six years of RAC review and approval, there has been considerable discussion of the juxtaposition of the NIH mandate to oversee the most meritorious medical research and the RAC mission to approve or disapprove individual protocols based predominantly on issues of safety. By adopting a new model of public discussion that does not require approval, the NIH can, through the proposed policy conferences, engage in substantive critique of the scientific merit of a line of research without having to give an NIH stamp of approval on the basis of limited threat to human health or safety.

. . .

5. *Will there be a mechanism for continuing to review gene therapy informed consent documents?*

As needs dictate, both OAC and the GTPC will provide a forum for the oversight of human gene therapy informed consent. It is expected that an entire conference may be devoted to such informed consent issues in the context of gene therapy. The NIH Director will continue, when appropriate, to make amendments to sections of the NIH Guidelines, Points to Consider relevant to informed consent procedures during gene therapy clinical trials. Investigators and IRBs engaged in, or reviewing, human gene therapy trials are expected to employ the NIH Guidelines, Points to Consider for this purpose. However, under the proposal contained herein, neither the OAC nor the GTPC will engage in protocol-by-protocol review of informed consent documents.

The sixteen Federal agencies that engage in human subjects research reference the Common Rule and, thus, abide by the principle of giving full authority of individual approval of informed consent documents to locally constituted Institutional Review Boards (IRBs). These responsibilities remain solely within the regulatory framework of OPRR through the local IRBs. . . . OPRR requires each institution that conducts or supports research involving human subjects to set forth the procedures it will use to protect human subjects in a policy statement called an Assurance of Compliance.

Finally, there is no other disease, disability, or methodology that, at present, requires a Federal review of individual informed consent documents. It is the proposal of the NIH Director that human gene therapy informed consent documents be subject to the same procedures as all other forms of human subject research. . . .

RECOMBINANT DNA RESEARCH: ACTIONS UNDER THE GUIDELINES
National Institutes of Health
62 Fed. Reg. 59032 (Oct. 31, 1997)

. . . On July 8, 1996, the NIH Director published a Notice of Intent to Propose Amendments to the NIH Guidelines for Research Involving Recombinant DNA Molecules Regarding Enhanced Oversight of Recombinant DNA Activities. This Notice of Intent proposed modifications in the NIH oversight of human gene transfer research. Specifically, it was proposed that [the Recombinant DNA Advisory Committee (RAC)] would be terminated and that all approval responsibilities for recombinant DNA experiments involving human gene transfer would be relinquished to the Food and Drug Administration (FDA), which retains statutory authority for such approval. Under this revised structure, a newly created [advisory committee] would preserve continued public accountability for recombinant DNA research. To ensure quality and efficiency of public discussion of the scientific merit and the ethical issues relevant to gene therapy clinical trials, it was proposed that the NIH Director implement a regular series of Gene Therapy Policy Conferences (GTPCs). Finally, the proposal assured the continuation of the publicly available comprehensive NIH database of clinical trials with human gene transfer, including reporting of adverse events.

In response to the Notice of Intent, NIH received 71 written comments (90 signatures) reflecting a broad spectrum of public opinion on the proposed changes. Comments were received from a variety of stakeholders, including individuals representing academia, industry, patient advocacy organizations, consumer advocacy organizations, professional scientific societies, ethicists, other

Federal agencies, NIH-funded investigators, past and present RAC members, and private citizens. . . .

On November 22, 1996, the NIH Director published the Notice of Proposed Actions. . . .

In the Proposed Actions, the NIH Director proposed to: (1) Retain RAC, while modifying its roles and responsibilities relevant to human gene therapy research, (2) continue RAC discussion of novel human gene transfer experiments, without RAC approval of individual human gene transfer experiments; (3) regularly convene GTPCs; and (4) maintain public access to human gene transfer clinical trial information. . . .

Appendix M is amended to read:

"Appendix M. Points To Consider in the Design and Submission of Protocols for the Transfer of Recombinant DNA Molecules Into One or More Human Subjects (Points to Consider)

"Appendix M applies to research conducted at or sponsored by an institution that receives any support for recombinant DNA research from NIH. Researchers not covered by the NIH Guidelines are encouraged to use Appendix M.

"The acceptability of human somatic cell gene therapy has been addressed in several public documents as well as in numerous academic studies. In November 1982, the President's Commission for the Study of Ethical Problems in Medicine and Biomedical and Behavioral Research published a report, Splicing Life, which resulted from a two-year process of public deliberation and hearings. Upon release of that report, a U.S. House of Representatives subcommittee held three days of public hearings with witnesses from a wide range of fields from the biomedical and social sciences to theology, philosophy, and law. In December 1984, the Office of Technology Assessment released a background paper, Human Gene Therapy, which concluded that civic, religious, scientific, and medical groups have all accepted, in principle, the appropriateness of gene therapy of somatic cells in humans for specific genetic diseases. Somatic cell gene therapy is seen as an extension of present methods of therapy that might be preferable to other technologies. In light of this public support, RAC is prepared to consider proposals for somatic cell gene transfer.

"RAC will not at present entertain proposals for germ line alterations but will consider proposals involving somatic cell gene transfer. The purpose of somatic cell gene therapy is to treat an individual patient, e.g., by inserting a properly functioning gene into the subject's somatic cells. Germ line alteration involves a specific attempt to introduce genetic changes into the germ (reproductive) cells of an individual, with the aim of changing the set of genes passed on to the individual's offspring. . . .

"Public discussion of human gene transfer experiments (and access to relevant information) shall serve to inform the public about the technical aspects of the proposals, meaning and significance of the research, and significant safety, social, and ethical implications of the research. RAC discussion is intended to ensure safe and ethical conduct of gene therapy experiments and facilitate public understanding of this novel area of biomedical research.

"In its evaluation of human gene transfer proposals, RAC will consider whether the design of such experiments offers adequate assurance that their consequences will not go beyond their purpose, which is the same as the traditional purpose of clinical investigation, namely, to protect the health and well being of human subjects being treated while at the same time gathering generalizable knowledge. Two possible undesirable consequences of the transfer of recombinant DNA would be unintentional: (i) Vertical transmission of genetic changes from an individual to his/her offspring, or (ii) horizontal transmission of viral infection to other persons with whom the individual comes in contact. Accordingly, [appendices] request information that will enable RAC and NIH/ORDA to assess the possibility that the proposed experiment(s) will inadvertently affect reproductive cells or lead to infection of other people (e.g., medical personnel or relatives). . . ."

NOTES AND QUESTIONS:
Recombinant DNA Research

1. The use of recombinant DNA technology in human beings is still very much experimental. The law relating to it largely concerns itself with research rather than established therapy. The *Heckler* case and the NIH comments are provided to give you a sense of recent regulation in this area.

2. The Foundation for Economic Trends was a public interest organization that often challenged governmental actions in the biotechnology area. Its president was Jeremy Rifkin, a well-known environmental activist.

3. *Heckler* represents what may be called the high water mark of success by a public interest organization in challenging the adequacy of governmental regulation of technology. In later lawsuits, such organizations almost always lost in court, largely on the ground that since the harm to them was in no way different from the harm to members of the public generally, they lacked standing to bring a lawsuit. (Courts do not in general resolve theoretical disputes; they must have a specific case or controversy brought by a party suffering distinct harm from a challenged action.) See, for example, *Foundation on Economic Trends v. Watkins*, 794 F. Supp. 395 (D.D.C. 1992) (failed challenge to federal government's rules relating to global warming).

    Recently there has been a growing concern—particularly in Europe—about exactly the kinds of issues that Rifkin and his organization were raising. Consider these statements:

    > While fears that [genetically altered] crops are unsafe to eat have raised public alarm in Europe, and to a lesser extent in the United States, some biologists say

the more immediate concern is this: that genetically modified plants could interact with the environment in hazardous ways, and that regulators are not demanding the proper studies to assess the risks. [3]

> Since genetically engineered crops came on the American agricultural scene in 1992, farmers have enthusiastically adopted these plants, last year harvesting [them on] an area one and a half times the size of New York State.... A major concern is that foreign genes from these plants could escape into wild plants by interbreeding. The fear is that wild plants endowed with new genes and potent new abilities, for example, to produce insecticide or withstand herbicide, might spread quickly, becoming difficult or costly to remove. Previously, researchers talked about the movement of foreign genes into wild plants as unlikely, but the picture emerging today is that with many crops it will be inevitable.[4]

Does your review of regulation in this area suggest that the existing legal structures may not give adequate attention to unknown risks in the biotechnology area? Should we perhaps be allowing more of these issues to be addressed in court, as in *Heckler*?

4. As the readings indicate, there has been a gradual shift in regulatory authority away from the National Institutes of Health, and its Recombinant DNA Advisory Committee (the RAC), and toward other governmental agencies that deal with more specific areas of regulation.[5] Consistent with that shift, it is noteworthy that the RAC has only been mentioned twice (and briefly at that) in all the federal and state court opinions written in the fifteen years since *Heckler*.

5. Note the distinction the NIH made between "somatic cell gene therapy," which alters the body chromosomes of a person but not their eggs or sperm cells, and "germ line alteration," which changes a person's egg or sperm cells and thus creates a change that is transmitted to the person's offspring. The possibility of altering the genes of innumerable future generations has led to the long-recognized distinction that the latter forms of therapy are far more risky.

6. Recent events suggest the possibility that, like genetically engineered crops, genetic research in humans (even just the somatic kind) may soon be given greater scrutiny. This change stems from the September 1999 death of Jesse Gelsinger, an 18-year-old who suffered from ornithine transcarbamylase deficiency, a rare metabolic disorder. Gelsinger had a mild form of this disorder, and was able to avoid adverse consequences by strictly controlling his diet and taking medications. Nonetheless, he volunteered for an experiment at the University of Pennsylvania in which a weakened cold virus was introduced into his body to alter genes so that it would perhaps correct the defect. He unexpectedly died within four days of beginning the therapy.[6]

7. Gelsinger's sudden death prompted activity on a number of fronts. On November 22, 1999, the director of the NIH Office of Recombinant DNA Activities sent a memorandum to "all institutions conducting human gene

transfer research," asking them to conduct internal reviews to make sure they were in compliance with federal regulations regarding the reporting of adverse events during research. The little-known RAC suddenly began to get front-page headlines when it held a December 8, 1999, hearing. Questions were also raised about the existing regulatory structures. Here is what the *New York Times* said:

> [I]n mid-1995, after seeking the advice of an expert panel, [NIH director Harold] Varmus reorganized the RAC, slashing its membership from 25 to 15 and stripping it of its approval authority—a decision that, some say, has enabled gene-therapy researchers to ignore the panel and keep information about safety to themselves. "The RAC," complains Dr. Robert Erickson, a University of Arizona medical geneticist who served on the panel, "became a debating society."[7]

Did you find the reasons given in the readings for removing power from the RAC adequate? Is the response to Gelsinger's death appropriate?

8. A great deal of material relating to the regulation of genetic research can be found on the web. In particular, the NIH Office of Biotechnology Activities (the current reincarnation of the Office of Recombinant DNA Activities) has a page at *www.nih.gov/od/oba*. It claims that it will eventually list all on-going human recombinant DNA research protocols at that location. Additional information can be found at the NIH web page for the Human Genome Project (which, as discussed in chapter 14, has been mapping all of the human genes), at *www.nhgri.nih.gov*.

9. While most attention these days is directed at the possibility of gene therapy[8]—which has thus far cured only a single disease—people are also looking ahead to when we will be able to use genetic manipulation to enhance ourselves and our children. We might well ask how this will differ from other types of non-genetic enhancement that society currently permits. For example, adults and children often undergo procedures for aesthetic enhancement, ranging from tooth straightening and whitening to skin lasering and breast enlargement. The use of growth hormone to possibly increase the height of a borderline short child continues to generate debate. Because of how we respond to an attractive person, all of these interventions have the possibility of improving the person's success.

Should we allow parents-to-be to make such enhancing genetic changes in a fertilized egg? If not, why not? Should a line be drawn between cosmetic changes and functional changes (e.g., improving a child's intellect or athletic ability)?[9]

Endnotes

1. See, e.g., Dena S. Davis, "Genetic Dilemmas and the Child's Right to an Open Future," 27(2) *Hastings Ctr. Rep.* 7 (1997); Bonnie Poitras Tucker, "Deaf Culture, Cochlear Implants, and Elective Disability," 28(4) *Hastings Ctr. Rep.* 6 (1998).

2. The literature about the use of genetic information for insurance and other purposes is vast. See, e.g., Mark A. Rothstein, ed., *Genetic Secrets: Protecting Privacy and Confidentiality in the Genetic Era* (New Haven, CT: Yale University Press, 1997); the proceedings from a symposium on the Human Genome Project published in the *Journal of Law, Medicine and Ethics* 26(3) (1998); Eric Mills Holmes, "Solving the Insurance/Genetic Fair/Unfair Discrimination Dilemma in Light of the Human Genome Project," 85 *Ky. L. J.* 503 (1996); Paul A. Lombardo, "Genetic Confidentiality: What's the Big Secret?" 3 *U. Chi. Law Sch. Roundtable* 589 (1996); Ronald M. Green and A. Mathew Thomas, "DNA: Five Distinguishing Features for Policy Analysis," 11 *Harv. J. Law & Tech.* 571 (1998); Anne Lawton, "Regulating Genetic Destiny: A Comparative Study of Legal Constraints in Europe and the United States," 11 *Emory Int'l L. Rev.* 365 (1997).

3. Carol Kaesuk Yoon, "Reassessing Ecological Risks of Genetically Altered Crops," *New York Times*, 3 November 1999, A1.

4. Carol Kaesuk Yoon, "Studies Raise Concern about Genetically Engineered Crops," *New York Times*, 3 November 1999, A22.

5. Judith E. Beach, "The New RAC: Restructuring of the National Institutes of Health Recombinant DNA Advisory Committee," 54 *Food & Drug L. J.* 49 (1999).

6. Sheryl Gay Stolberg, "The Biotech Death of Jesse Gelsinger," *New York Times*, 28 November 1999, Section 6, 137.

7. Ibid.

8. For a skeptical view of the extent to which increasing knowledge about genetics will lead to better therapies for disease, see Neil A. Holtzman and Theresa M. Marteau, "Will Genetics Revolutionize Medicine?" 343 *New Eng. J. Med.* 141 (2000).

9. See, e.g., Maxwell J. Mehlman, "How Will We Regulate Genetic Enhancement?" 34 *Wake Forest L. Rev.* 671 (1999).

14

The Ownership of Life

The United States has a capitalist economy. We encourage the ownership of stuff. People who own things are more likely to take care of them, and thus benefit themselves and (possibly) others: witness the well-cared-for neighborhood of owner-occupied homes, as contrasted with the nearby run-down neighborhood where renters have no incentive to improve things.

Tied in with the concept of ownership is a recognition of the value of markets, where willing sellers get together with willing buyers, improving the welfare of both sets of parties with each trade. As Martha Stewart might have noted following the billion-dollar offering of stock in her company, "It's a good thing."

From a legal viewpoint, this entire system is merely one application of freedom of contract. But as we have already seen, there are values that our society respects that can override that freedom; thus we at times restrict the ability to own things and buy and sell them. In 1865, the Thirteenth Amendment to the U.S. Constitution banned the ownership of people by outlawing slavery. As we discussed in chapter 5, in spite of Richard Posner's arguments, we have yet to allow children to be sold.

On the other hand, we do allow people to own (and buy and sell) many types of non-human living things, from plants to pets. And in an effort to encourage the creative scientific process, we even allow the ownership of entire new varieties of living things. In *Diamond v. Chakrabarty*, 447 U.S. 303 (1980), a microbiologist was attempting to get a patent on a new genetically engineered version of the bacterium *Pseudomonas* that could break down components of crude oil and thus help control oil spills. The patent examiner had refused to grant the patent, claiming that the bacterium was a "product of nature" and that one cannot obtain a patent on a living thing.

The Supreme Court rejected both of those objections. As a starting point, the Court noted that patent law gives inventors a limited period of exclusive rights to their inventions in order that "[the] productive effort thereby fostered will have a positive effect on society through the introduction of new products and processes of manufacture into the economy, and the emanations by way of increased employment and better lives for our citizens." It then proceeded to clarify which "things of nature" are or are not patentable:

This is not to suggest that [the patent law] has no limits or that it embraces every discovery. The laws of nature, physical phenomena, and abstract ideas have been held not patentable. Thus, a new mineral discovered in the earth or a new plant found in the wild is not patentable subject matter. Likewise, Einstein could not patent his celebrated law that $E=mc^2$; nor could Newton have patented the law of gravity. Such discoveries are "manifestations of . . . nature, free to all men and reserved exclusively to none." Judged in this light, respondent's micro-organism plainly qualifies as patentable subject matter. His claim is not to a hitherto unknown natural phenomenon, but to a nonnaturally occurring manufacture or composition of matter—a product of human ingenuity "having a distinctive name, character [and] use." . . . [In contrast to previous cases, here] the patentee has produced a new bacterium with markedly different characteristics from any found in nature and one having the potential for significant utility. His discovery is not nature's handiwork, but his own; accordingly it is patentable subject matter under [the patent law].

Chakrabarty's bacteria were indeed new genetic creations. Nonetheless, there remained unanswered questions about the exact limits on what is a nonpatentable product of nature, rather than something that represents the product of human intervention. One of the most interesting questions related to the status of discoveries about naturally occurring genetic sequences, including those that are part of the human genome.[1] Court decisions since *Diamond v. Chakrabarty* have determined that naturally occurring DNA sequences are indeed patentable, once the complex and detailed criteria of the patent law, requiring demonstrations of *utility*, *novelty*, and *nonobviousness*, have been met. Thus, for example, biotechnology giant Amgen, Inc. obtained a patent for the DNA sequence for erythropoietin, the protein that regulates the production of red blood cells in all human beings. *Amgen, Inc. v. Chugai Pharmaceutical Co.*, 927 F.2d 1200 (Fed. Cir. 1991).

The controversy over patenting genes has grown during the course of the Human Genome Project, the attempt to "map" the entire human genome. While this project announced initial success in the summer of 2000, it is important to understand what this map does and does not involve.

The 23 pairs of human chromosomes are composed of deoxyribonucleic acid, or DNA, which is in turn made up of long strings of four nucleotides: adenine (A), cytosine (C), guanine (G) and thymine (T). There are approximately three billion such nucleotide "letters" that compose the information in a person's DNA. That set of letters is broken up into shorter units, known as genes, which usually spell out the directions for producing a specific protein.

As a result of the Human Genome Project, we now have a complete list of these three billion nucleotides—very long sequences of letters, such as ATTGCTATAGC . . . and so forth, with information on where these sequences show up on each of the chromosomes. The complete map will be extraordinarily useful in future research to learn more about the function of human genes.

On the other hand, it is important to understand what this map does *not* tell us. It does not alone tell us much about the proteins that our genes produce, such as what role a particular protein plays in our functioning. The map is like a book in a foreign language that gives instructions for building some complicated object: until we translate the words in the book, we cannot understand the information the book contains. Translating the information contained in the nucleotide sequences will require years of future research.

To what extent, then, should a genetic sequence be patentable even before anyone has much of an idea what role the protein produced by the gene plays in a human being's functioning? For a time, the National Institutes of Health were attempting to patent large numbers of DNA segments being discovered as part of the Human Genome Project, even when there was no idea what the segments coded for. Those actions led to high-level international disputes about U.S. patent policies. With the success of the project, many private companies have begun to file patents on thousands of genes, again often without much understanding of the function of those genes.

Recall that in order to patent something, you need to demonstrate utility, novelty, and nonobviousness. The most controversial element in current attempts to patent naked (and incompletely understood) gene sequences is how to prove the sequences are useful. Companies patenting genetic sequences attempt to rely on demonstrations that the sequences are useful in current research. It remains to be seen whether this is an appropriate extension of patent protection.

Similar issues relating to the "ownership of life" can raise legal questions that go beyond the somewhat arcane and technical realm of patent law. It was just such a question that developed out of a routine patient encounter between John Moore and his doctors. And later in this chapter, we will visit the special issues that arise when the living matter at issue has the potential of a new human life.

MOORE V. REGENTS OF THE UNIVERSITY OF CALIFORNIA

Supreme Court of California

793 P.2d 479 (Cal. 1990)

OPINION BY JUSTICE PANELLI:

I. Introduction

We granted review in this case to determine whether plaintiff has stated a cause of action against his physician and other defendants for using his cells in potentially lucrative medical research without his permission. Plaintiff alleges that his physician failed to disclose preexisting research and economic interests in the cells before obtaining consent to the medical procedures by which they were extracted. . . .We hold that the complaint states a cause of action for breach of the physician's disclosure obligations, but not for conversion.

II. Facts

. . . [Plaintiff John] Moore first visited UCLA Medical Center on October 5, 1976, shortly after he learned that he had hairy-cell leukemia. After hospitalizing Moore and "withdr[awing] extensive amounts of blood, bone marrow aspirate, and other bodily substances," [his attending physician, Dr. David] Golde confirmed that diagnosis. At this time all defendants, including Golde, were aware that "certain blood products and blood components were of great value in a number of commercial and scientific efforts" and that access to a patient whose blood contained these substances would provide "competitive, commercial, and scientific advantages."

On October 8, 1976, Golde recommended that Moore's spleen be removed. Golde informed Moore "that he had reason to fear for his life, and that the proposed splenectomy operation . . . was necessary to slow down the progress of his disease." Based upon Golde's representations, Moore signed a written consent form authorizing the splenectomy.

Before the operation, Golde . . . "formed the intent and made arrangements to obtain portions of [Moore's] spleen following its removal" and to take them to a separate research unit. Golde gave written instructions to this effect on October 18 and 19, 1976. These research activities "were not intended to have . . . any relation to [Moore's] medical . . . care." However, neither Golde nor [the other researchers] informed Moore of their plans to conduct this research or requested his permission. Surgeons at UCLA Medical Center, whom the complaint does not name as defendants, removed Moore's spleen on October 20, 1976.

Moore returned to the UCLA Medical Center several times between November 1976 and September 1983. He did so at Golde's direction and based upon representations "that such visits were necessary and required for his health and well-being, and based upon the trust inherent in and by virtue of the physician-patient relationship . . . ." On each of these visits Golde withdrew additional samples of "blood, blood serum, skin, bone marrow aspirate, and sperm." On each occasion Moore travelled to the UCLA Medical Center from his home in Seattle because he had been told that the procedures were to be performed only there and only under Golde's direction.

"In fact, [however,] throughout the period of time that [Moore] was under [Golde's] care and treatment, . . . the defendants were actively involved in a number of activities which they concealed from [Moore]. . . ." Specifically, defendants were conducting research on Moore's cells and planned to "benefit financially and competitively . . . [by exploiting the cells] and [their] exclusive access to [the cells] by virtue of [Golde's] ongoing physician-patient relationship. . . ."

Sometime before August 1979, Golde established a cell line from Moore's T-lymphocytes. On January 30, 1981, the Regents applied for a patent on the cell line, listing Golde and Quan as inventors. "[B]y virtue of an established policy . . . , [the] Regents, Golde, and Quan would share in any royalties or profits . . . arising out of [the] patent." The patent issued on March 20, 1984, naming Golde and Quan as the inventors of the cell line and the Regents as the assignee of the patent.

The Regent's patent also covers various methods for using the cell line to produce lymphokines. Moore admits in his complaint that "the true clinical potential of each of the lymphokines . . . [is] difficult to predict, [but] . . . competing commercial firms in these relevant fields have published reports in biotechnology industry periodicals predicting a potential market of approximately $3.01 Billion Dollars by the year 1990 for a whole range of [such lymphokines] . . . ."

III. Discussion

A. BREACH OF FIDUCIARY DUTY AND LACK OF INFORMED CONSENT

Moore repeatedly alleges that Golde failed to disclose the extent of his research and economic interests in Moore's cells before obtaining consent to the medical procedures by which the cells were extracted. These allegations, in our view, state a cause of action against Golde for invading a legally protected interest of his patient. This cause of action can properly be characterized either as the breach of a fiduciary duty to disclose facts material to the patient's consent or, alternatively, as the performance of medical procedures without first having obtained the patient's informed consent.

Our analysis begins with three well-established principles. First, "a person of adult years and in sound mind has the right, in the exercise of control over his own body, to determine whether or not to submit to lawful medical treatment." Second, "the patient's consent to treatment, to be effective, must be an informed consent." Third, in soliciting the patient's consent, a physician has a fiduciary duty to disclose all information material to the patient's decision.

These principles lead to the following conclusions: (1) a physician must disclose personal interests unrelated to the patient's health, whether research or economic, that may affect the physician's professional judgment; and (2) a physician's failure to disclose such interests may give rise to a cause of action for performing medical procedures without informed consent or breach of fiduciary duty.

To be sure, questions about the validity of a patient's consent to a procedure typically arise when the patient alleges that the physician failed to disclose medical risks, as in malpractice cases, and not when the patient alleges that the physician had a personal interest, as in this case. The concept of informed consent, however, is broad enough to encompass the latter. "The scope of the physician's communication to the patient . . . must be measured by the patient's need, and that need is whatever information is material to the decision."

Indeed, the law already recognizes that a reasonable patient would want to know whether a physician has an economic interest that might affect the physician's professional judgment. As the Court of Appeal has said, "[c]ertainly a sick patient deserves to be free of any reasonable suspicion that his doctor's judgment is influenced by a profit motive." . . .

It is important to note that no law prohibits a physician from conducting research in the same area in which he practices. Progress in medicine often depends upon physicians, such as those practicing at the university hospital where Moore received treatment, who conduct research while caring for their patients.

Yet a physician who treats a patient in whom he also has a research interest has potentially conflicting loyalties. This is because medical treatment decisions are made on the basis of proportionality—weighing the benefits *to the patient* against the risks *to the patient*. As another court has said, "the determination as to whether the burdens of treatment are worth enduring for any individual patient depends upon the facts unique in each case," and "the patient's interests and desires are the key ingredients of the decision-making process." A physician who adds his own research interests to this balance may be tempted to order a scientifically useful procedure or test that offers marginal, or no, benefits to the patient. The possibility that an interest extraneous to the patient's health has affected the physician's judgment is something that a reasonable patient would want to know in deciding whether to consent to a proposed course of treatment. It is material to the patient's decision and, thus, a prerequisite to informed consent.

Golde argues that the scientific use of cells that have already been removed cannot possibly affect the patient's medical interests. The argument is correct in one instance but not in another. If a physician has no plans to conduct research on a patient's cells at the time he recommends the medical procedure by which they are taken, then the patient's medical interests have not been impaired. In that instance the argument is correct. On the other hand, a physician who does have a preexisting research interest might, consciously or unconsciously, take that into consideration in recommending the procedure. In that instance the argument is incorrect: the physician's extraneous motivation may affect his judgment and is, thus, material to the patient's consent. . . .

Accordingly, we hold that a physician who is seeking a patient's consent for a medical procedure must, in order to satisfy his fiduciary duty and to obtain the patient's informed consent, disclose personal interests unrelated to the patient's health, whether research or economic, that may affect his medical judgment. . . .

B. CONVERSION

Moore also attempts to characterize the invasion of his rights as a conversion—a tort that protects against interference with possessory and ownership interests in personal property. He theorizes that he continued to own his cells following their removal from his body, at least for the purpose of directing their use, and that he never consented to their use in potentially lucrative medical research. Thus, to complete Moore's argument, defendants' unauthorized use of his cells constitutes a conversion. As a result of the alleged conversion, Moore claims a proprietary interest in each of the products that any of the defendants might ever create from his cells or the patented cell line.

No court, however, has ever in a reported decision imposed conversion liability for the use of human cells in medical research. While that fact does not end our inquiry, it raises a flag of caution. In effect, what Moore is asking us to do is to impose a tort duty on scientists to investigate the consensual pedigree of each human cell sample used in research. To impose such a duty, which would affect medical research of importance to all of society, implicates policy concerns far removed from the traditional, two-party ownership disputes in which the law of conversion arose. Invoking a tort theory originally used to determine whether the loser or the finder of a horse had the better title, Moore claims ownership of the results of socially important medical research, including the genetic code for chemicals that regulate the functions of every human being's immune system. . . .

. . .[W]e first consider whether the tort of conversion clearly gives Moore a cause of action under existing law. We do not believe it does. Because of the novelty of Moore's claim to own the biological materials at issue, to apply the theory of conversion in this context would frankly have to be recognized as an extension of the theory. Therefore, we consider next whether it is advisable to extend the tort to this context.

1. Moore's Claim Under Existing Law

"To establish a conversion, plaintiff must establish an actual interference with his ownership or right of possession. . . . Where plaintiff neither has title to the property alleged to have been converted, nor possession thereof, he cannot maintain an action for conversion."

Since Moore clearly did not expect to retain possession of his cells following their removal, to sue for their conversion he must have retained an ownership interest in them. But there are several reasons to doubt that he did retain any such interest. First, no reported judicial decision supports Moore's claim, either directly or by close analogy. Second, California statutory law drastically limits any continuing interest of a patient in excised cells. Third, the subject matters of the Regents' patent—the patented cell line and the products derived from it—cannot be Moore's property.

Neither the Court of Appeal's opinion, the parties' briefs, nor our research discloses a case holding that a person retains a sufficient interest in excised cells to support a cause of action for conversion. We do not find this surprising, since the laws governing such things as human tissues, transplantable organs, blood, fetuses, pituitary glands, corneal tissue, and dead bodies deal with human biological materials as objects sui generis, regulating their disposition to achieve policy goals rather than abandoning them to the general law of personal property. It is these specialized statutes, not the law of conversion, to which courts ordinarily should and do look for guidance on the disposition of human biological materials.

Lacking direct authority for importing the law of conversion into this context, Moore relies, as did the Court of Appeal, primarily on decisions addressing privacy rights. One line of cases involves unwanted publicity. These opinions hold that every person has a proprietary interest in his own likeness and that unauthorized, business use of a likeness is redressible as a tort. But in neither opinion did the authoring court expressly base its holding on property law. Each court stated . . . that it was "pointless" to debate the proper characterization of the proprietary interest in a likeness. For purposes of determining whether the tort of conversion lies, however, the characterization of the right in question is far from pointless. Only property can be converted.

Not only are the wrongful-publicity cases irrelevant to the issue of conversion, but the analogy to them seriously misconceives the nature of the genetic materials and research involved in this case. Moore, adopting the analogy originally advanced by the Court of Appeal, argues that "[i]f the courts have found a sufficient proprietary interest in one's persona, how could one not have a right in one's own genetic material, something far more profoundly the essence of one's human uniqueness than a name or a face?" However, as the defendants' patent makes clear—and the complaint, too, if read with an understanding of the scientific terms which it has borrowed from the patent—the goal and result of defendants' efforts has been to manufacture lymphokines. Lymphokines, unlike a name or a face, have the same molecular structure in every human being and the same, important functions in every human being's immune system. Moreover, the particular genetic material which is responsible for the natural production of lymphokines, and which defendants use to manufacture lymphokines in the laboratory, is also the same in every person; it is no more unique to Moore than the number of vertebrae in the spine or the chemical formula of hemoglobin. . . .

Finally, the subject matter of the Regents' patent—the patented cell line and the products derived from it—cannot be Moore's property. This is because the patented cell line is both factually and legally distinct from the cells taken from Moore's body. Federal law permits the patenting of organisms that represent the product of "human ingenuity," but not naturally occurring organisms. (*Diamond v. Chakrabarty.*) Human cell lines are patentable because "[l]ong-term adaptation and growth of human tissues and cells in culture is difficult—often considered an art . . . ," and the probability of success is low. It is this inventive effort that patent law rewards, not the discovery of naturally occurring raw materials. Thus, Moore's allegations that he owns the cell line and the products derived from it are inconsistent with the patent, which constitutes an authoritative determination that the cell line is the product of invention. Since such allegations are nothing more than arguments or conclusions of law, they of course do not bind us.

2. Should Conversion Liability Be Extended?

As we have discussed, Moore's novel claim to own the biological materials at issue in this case is problematic, at best. Accordingly, his attempt to apply the theory of conversion within this context must frankly be recognized as a request to extend that theory. While we do not purport to hold that excised cells can never be property for any purpose whatsoever, the novelty of Moore's claim demands express consideration of the policies to be served by extending liability rather than blind deference to a complaint alleging as a legal conclusion the existence of a cause of action.

There are three reasons why it is inappropriate to impose liability for conversion based upon the allegations of Moore's complaint. First, a fair balancing of the relevant policy considerations counsels against extending the tort. Second, problems in this area are better suited to legislative resolution. Third, the tort of conversion is not necessary to protect patients' rights. For these reasons, we conclude that the use of excised human cells in medical research does not amount to a conversion.

Of the relevant policy considerations, two are of overriding importance. The first is protection of a competent patient's right to make autonomous medical decisions. That right, as already discussed, is grounded in well-recognized and long-standing principles of fiduciary duty and informed consent. This policy weighs in favor of providing a remedy to patients when physicians act with undisclosed motives that may affect their professional judgment. The second important policy consideration is that we not threaten with disabling civil liability innocent parties who are engaged in socially useful activities, such as researchers who have no reason to believe that their use of a particular cell sample is, or may be, against a donor's wishes.

To reach an appropriate balance of these policy considerations is extremely important. In its report to Congress, the Office of Technology Assessment emphasized that "[u]ncertainty about how courts will resolve disputes between specimen sources and specimen users could be detrimental to both academic researchers and the infant biotechnology industry, particularly when the rights are asserted long after the specimen was obtained. The assertion of rights by sources would affect not only the researcher who obtained the original specimen, but perhaps other researchers as well. . . ."

We need not, however, make an arbitrary choice between liability and nonliability. Instead, an examination of the relevant policy considerations suggests an appropriate balance: Liability based upon existing disclosure obligations, rather than an unprecedented extension of the conversion theory, protects patients' rights of privacy and autonomy without unnecessarily hindering research. . . .

Research on human cells plays a critical role in medical research. This is so because researchers are increasingly able to isolate naturally occurring, medically useful biological substances and to produce useful quantities of such substances through genetic engineering. These efforts are beginning to bear fruit. Products developed through biotechnology that have already been approved for marketing in this country include treatments and tests for leukemia, cancer, diabetes, dwarfism, hepatitis-B, kidney transplant rejection, emphysema, osteoporosis, ulcers, anemia, infertility, and gynecological tumors, to name but a few.

The extension of conversion law into this area will hinder research by restricting access to the necessary raw materials. Thousands of human cell lines already exist in tissue repositories. . . . These repositories respond to tens of thousands of requests for samples annually. Since the patent office requires the holders of patents on cell lines to make samples available to anyone, many patent holders place their cell lines in repositories to avoid the administrative burden of responding to requests. At present, human cell lines are routinely copied and distributed to other researchers for experimental purposes, usually free of charge. This exchange of scientific materials, which still is relatively free and efficient, will surely be compromised if each cell sample becomes the potential subject matter of a lawsuit. . . .

Finally, there is no pressing need to impose a judicially created rule of strict liability, since enforcement of physicians' disclosure obligations will protect patients against the very type of harm with which Moore was threatened. So long as a physician discloses research and economic interests that may affect his judgment, the patient is protected from conflicts of interest. Aware of any conflicts, the patient can make an informed decision to consent to treatment, or to withhold consent and look elsewhere for medical assistance. As already discussed, enforcement of physicians' disclosure obligations protects patients directly, without hindering the socially useful activities of innocent researchers.

For these reasons, we hold that the allegations of Moore's third amended complaint state a cause of action for breach of fiduciary duty or lack of informed consent, but not conversion.

NOTES AND QUESTIONS:
Moore v. Regents of the University of California

1. Dr. Golde and others involved in this case did in fact make millions of dollars from the manufacture of the lymphokines that were produced using John Moore's cells.
2. What were the two causes of action addressed by the court, and what conclusions did it reach on each of them?
3. Review the discussion of informed consent in chapter 7, in particular the "professional standard" and "reasonable patient" rules used in different states. Based on what happened in *Moore*, which of these rules represents the law in California? What would have been the result of the informed consent claim in *Moore* if the other rule had applied? What additional information might you need to know to answer that question?
4. When does the Moore court think that a conflict of interest exists? Note its comment that "[i]f a physician has no plans to conduct research on a patient's cells at the time he recommends the medical procedure by which they are taken, then the patient's medical interests have not been impaired." Consider if there would be any breach of fiduciary duty in the following scenarios:
   a. Assume that the very first blood sample taken from John Moore both demonstrated that he had the interesting form of leukemia and also gave the doctors sufficient cells that they could produce a cell line and do everything else they needed to do to manufacture lymphokines. In other words, assume they did not need any more of Moore's cells or need to do any other tests on his body. Under the *Moore* opinion, would the doctors have done anything wrong?
   b. Assume a hospital has a policy of doing tests on tissues removed from the bodies of patients in standard surgical procedures, looking for new products that might be made. These tests are done by the pathology department. If new products are derived, no portion of the profits is given directly to the patient's surgeon.

   Does getting informed consent based on revealing such conflicts of interest fully protect all of a patient's interests? (Compare the discussion about disclosure of financial conflicts of interest for HMO doctors in the notes following *Herdrich v. Pegram* in chapter 8.) Have any interests of the patient been violated in these scenarios? If not, might there be a reason to rethink the court's conclusions on the second issue, the conversion cause of action? Do you agree that "the tort of conversion is not necessary to protect patients' rights"?
5. The court makes a number of arguments about why there is no conversion of Moore's property. What are they?
6. The court rejects the analogy accepted by the lower court, that if a person has a property interest in one's persona or likeness, then "how could one

not have a right in one's own genetic material, something far more profoundly the essence of one's human uniqueness than a name or face?" The court rejects it on the ground that the products being sold by the defendants are lymphokines, which are the same for all people.

Does that observation address Moore's complaint? If someone had a patent on a new way to manufacture chocolate, could others use that process without paying the discoverer, on the ground that the chocolate they are manufacturing is no different than any other form of chocolate? To manufacture the lymphokines, the defendants had to use cells derived from Moore's cancer, and those cells were indeed unique.

7. The court similarly concludes that the "patented cell line and the products derived from it" cannot be Moore's property, because they are "distinct from the cells taken from Moore's body." Again, is there a missing link in the court's argument? Isn't the underlying issue that the defendants had to use Moore's cells to derive the patented cell line, and whether that use of those cells was proper? Presumably it would be improper to use stolen matter, or a patent owned by someone else (without compensation), in producing a new patentable product.

8. John and Judy Smith want to maximize the likelihood that their future daughter will have a happy and successful life. Accordingly, one day John shakes supermodel Christie Brinkley's hand, and manages to isolate some of her skin cells that rub off. He intends to use the DNA from these cells to produce a clone of Ms. Brinkley. The Smiths of course want their daughter to be a unique person—and understand that even with this cloning process, she still will be—but they want her to get the enormous benefits that come from being physically attractive.

   Following the reasoning in *Moore*, have the Smiths done anything wrong? Presumably, Ms. Brinkley does not own the cells that rub off when she shakes hands, and so they were not stolen from her. The cells of the resulting child will not be the actual cells from Ms. Brinkley, just as the cells reproducing in the laboratory of the defendants in *Moore* were not the actual cells taken from Moore, but rather "descendants" of those cells.

9. Does the degree to which a purpose is worthwhile affect its legitimacy? For example, the *Moore court* emphasized the importance of medical research. What if we varied the Christie Brinkley example and instead were dealing with a research team that had, in the same less than forthcoming manner, obtained cells from a world-famous scientist in order to see if they could produce a brilliant child?

10. Ed Entrepreneur begins contracting with barber shops and hair salons around the country to get hair samples and names of their customers. Most of those samples have some hairs that were pulled out, not cut, and thus have hair root cells with usable DNA. Ed intends to process the DNA and determine what genetic defects or disease predispositions each person might have. He will create a huge database and sell this information to

health insurance companies. (He is careful to do transactions only in states where no statutes prevent insurers from using genetic information.) Under the reasoning in *Moore*, is he doing anything wrong?

11. Isn't the wrong that Moore is ultimately complaining about in the conversion action not the actual taking of his cells, but the use of the *information* contained in the DNA of those cancerous cells? In that sense, is his claim really all that different than that of the person whose face is used on an ad without her permission?

   The law devotes an entire field, intellectual property, to the protection of certain types of information. That law is intended to protect the discoverer or creator of the information, so as to encourage similar discovery. (Patent law is a part of intellectual property law.) That rationale does not apply to a person's own genetic code, since he neither discovered nor created it. Nonetheless, should a person have a right to control the use of that code, just as he has the right to control the use of his image?

12. The court concludes that requiring the consent of a person for the use of their cells in a commercial process would have a "broad impact" on important medical research. Do you think it is right? Participants in research studies are in fact increasingly demanding a share in any commercial profits from the research.[2] If you were a legislator, how would you vote on a law that required such consent? (Note that the law could be prospective in effect, "grandfathering" the use of preexisting cells lines where the patient's consent had not been obtained before the law was passed.)

13. Justice Arabian in his concurring opinion in *Moore* wrote:

   > I join in the views cogently expounded by the majority. I write separately to give voice to a concern that I believe informs much of that opinion but finds little or no expression therein. I speak of the moral issue.
   >
   > Plaintiff has asked us to recognize and enforce a right to sell one's own body tissue *for profit*. He entreats us to regard the human vessel—the single most venerated and protected subject in any civilized society—as equal with the basest commercial commodity. He urges us to commingle the sacred with the profane. He asks much. . . .
   >
   > . . . Does it uplift or degrade the "unique human persona" to treat human tissue as a fungible article of commerce? . . . I do not know the answers to these troubling questions, nor am I willing . . . to treat them simply as issues of "tort" law, susceptible of *judicial* resolution.

Are you convinced? These are arguments commonly made against commodification of the human body. If you object to such commodification, is what the doctors are doing any less objectionable than what Moore was asking for? As noted earlier, Dr. Golde and his colleagues were not working for purely altruistic reasons—nor even just to get their usual salaries. They earned millions of dollars in corporate stock as a result of turning Moore's cells into a commercial process for producing lymphokines. Is Moore's attempt to get a cut of those profits "commingling the sacred with the profane" any more than the actions of everyone else around him? Might it be relevant that since *Moore*, there has been an explosion in the commercial use of biotechnological information, as evidenced by such phenomena as the patenting of genes, increased involvement of academic researchers in for-profit companies,[3] and even the growing sale of processed human body parts (discussed in chapter 16)?

14. A different issue that raises similar questions about what things can be owned and commercialized relates to the patentability of medical procedures. Much of modern medicine is permeated by business-like practices and, as you have probably surmised by now, patent protection plays a major role in many of those practices. That protection is considered a sine qua non by companies that invest millions of dollars in research to create new drugs and medical devices.

   For over a century and a half, it had been generally believed that medical "procedures," as opposed to drugs or devices, could not be patented. Thus, in the early case of *Morton v. New York Eye Infirmary*, 17 F. Cas. 869 (C.C.S.D.N.Y. 1862) (No. 9,865), it was determined that the use of ether for purposes of surgical anesthesia could not be patented. In recent years, however, the nonpatentability of medical procedures has been questioned, and patent applications have been filed for hundreds of such procedures. The practice gained widespread attention in 1993 when Arizona ophthalmologist Samuel Pallin came across a cataract surgery article written by Dartmouth ophthalmologist Jack Singer (discussing the well-known "frown" incision), and sued him for violation of the patent Pallin had filed relating to the shape of the incision. Pallin lost his lawsuit, on the ground that others had been using that particular incision before his attempt to patent it. As a result of the controversy, however, in 1996 a federal law was passed that eliminated any possibility of patenting a medical procedure.[4] Should medical procedures not be patentable? What are the lines that determine which ideas should or should not be patentable?

DAVIS V. DAVIS

Supreme Court of Tennessee

842 S.W.2d 588 (Tenn. 1992)

OPINION BY JUSTICE DAUGHTREY:

This appeal presents a question of first impression, involving the disposition of the cryogenically-preserved product of *in vitro* fertilization (IVF), commonly referred to in the popular press and the legal journals as "frozen embryos." The case began as a divorce action, filed by the appellee, Junior Lewis Davis, against his then wife, appellant Mary Sue Davis. The parties were able to agree upon all terms of dissolution, except one: who was to have "custody" of the seven "frozen embryos" stored in a Knoxville fertility clinic that had attempted to assist the Davises in achieving a much-wanted pregnancy during a happier period in their relationship.

I. INTRODUCTION

Mary Sue Davis originally asked for control of the "frozen embryos" with the intent to have them transferred to her own uterus, in a post-divorce effort to become pregnant. Junior Davis objected, saying that he preferred to leave the embryos in their frozen state until he decided whether or not he wanted to become a parent outside the bounds of marriage. . . .

. . . [T]heir positions have . . . shifted: both have remarried and Mary Sue Davis (now Mary Sue Stowe) has moved out of state. She no longer wishes to utilize the "frozen embryos" herself, but wants authority to donate them to a childless couple. Junior Davis is adamantly opposed to such donation and would prefer to see the "frozen embryos" discarded. The result is, once again, an impasse, but the parties' current legal position does have an effect on the probable outcome of the case, as discussed below.

At the outset, it is important to note the absence of two critical factors that might otherwise influence or control the result of this litigation: When the Davises signed up for the IVF program at the Knoxville clinic, they did not execute a written agreement specifying what disposition should be made of any unused embryos that might result from the cryopreservation process. Moreover, there was at that time no Tennessee statute governing such disposition, nor has one been enacted in the meantime. . . .

But, if we have no statutory authority or common law precedents to guide us, we do have the benefit of extensive comment and analysis in the legal journals. In those articles, medical-legal scholars and ethicists have proposed various models for the disposition of "frozen embryos" when unanticipated contingencies arise, such as divorce, death of one or both of the parties, financial reversals, or simple disenchantment with the IVF process. Those models range from a rule requiring, at one extreme, that all embryos be used by the gamete-providers or donated for uterine transfer, and, at the other extreme, that any unused embryos be automatically discarded. Other formulations would vest control in the female gamete-provider—in every case, because of her greater physical and emotional contribution to the IVF process, or perhaps only in the event that she wishes to use them herself. There are also two "implied contract" models: one would infer from enrollment in an IVF program that the IVF clinic has authority to decide in the event of an impasse whether to donate, discard, or use the "frozen embryos" for research; the other would infer from the parties' participation in the creation of the embryos that they had made an irrevocable commitment to reproduction and would require transfer either to the female provider or to a donee. There are also the so-called "equity models": one would avoid the conflict altogether by dividing the "frozen embryos" equally between the parties, to do with as they wish; the other would award veto power to the party wishing to avoid parenthood, whether it be the female or the male progenitor.

Each of these possible models has the virtue of ease of application. Adoption of any of them would establish a bright-line test that would dispose of disputes like the one we have before us in a clear and predictable manner. As appealing as that possibility might seem, we conclude that given the relevant principles of constitutional law, the existing public policy of Tennessee with regard to unborn life, the current state of scientific knowledge giving rise to the emerging reproductive technologies, and the ethical considerations that have developed in response to that scientific knowledge, there can be no easy answer to the question we now face. We conclude, instead, that we must weigh the interests of each party to the dispute, in terms of the facts and analysis set out below, in order to resolve that dispute in a fair and responsible manner.

II. THE FACTS

. . . As explained at trial, IVF involves the aspiration of ova from the follicles of a woman's ovaries, fertilization of these ova in a petri dish using the sperm provided by a man, and the transfer of the product of this procedure into the uterus of the woman from whom the ova were taken. Implantation may then occur, resulting in a pregnancy and, it is hoped, the birth of a child.

Beginning in 1985, the Davises went through six attempts at IVF, at a total cost of $35,000, but the hoped-for pregnancy never occurred. Despite her fear of needles, at each IVF attempt Mary Sue underwent the month of subcutaneous injections necessary to shut down her pituitary gland and the eight days of intermuscular injections necessary to stimulate her ovaries to produce ova. She was anesthetized five times for the aspiration procedure to be performed. Forty-eight to 72 hours after each aspiration, she returned for transfer back to her uterus, only to receive a negative pregnancy test result each time.

The Davises then opted to postpone another round of IVF until after the clinic with which they were working was prepared to offer them cryogenic preservation, scheduled for November 1988. Using this process, if more ova are aspirated and fertilized than needed, the conceptive product may be cryogenically preserved (frozen in nitrogen and stored at sub-zero temperatures) for later transfer if the transfer performed immediately does not result in a pregnancy. The unavailability of this procedure had not been a hinderance to previous IVF attempts by the Davises because Mary Sue had produced at most only three or four ova, despite hormonal stimulation. However, on their last attempt, on December 8, 1988, the gynecologist who performed the procedure was able to retrieve nine ova for fertilization. The resulting one-celled entities, referred to before division as zygotes, were then allowed to develop in petri dishes in the laboratory until they reached the four- to eight-cell stage.

Needless to say, the Davises were pleased at the initial success of the procedure. At the time, they had no thoughts of divorce and the abundance of ova for fertilization offered them a better chance at parenthood, because Mary Sue Davis could attempt to achieve a pregnancy without additional rounds of hormonal stimulation and aspiration. They both testified that although the process of cryogenic preservation was described to them, no one explained the ways in which it would change the nature of IVF for them. There is, for example, no indication that they ever considered the implications of storage beyond the few months it would take to transfer the remaining "frozen embryos," if necessary. There was no discussion, let alone an agreement, concerning disposition in the event of a contingency such as divorce. . . .

IV. THE "PERSON" VS. "PROPERTY" DICHOTOMY

One of the fundamental issues the inquiry poses is whether the preembryos in this case should be considered "persons" or "property" in the contemplation of the law. The Court of Appeals held, correctly, that they cannot be considered "persons" under Tennessee law. . . .

Nor do preembryos enjoy protection as "persons" under federal law. In *Roe v. Wade*, the United States Supreme Court explicitly refused to hold that the fetus possesses independent rights under law, based upon a thorough examination of the federal constitution, relevant common law principles, and the lack of scientific consensus as to when life begins. . . .

To our way of thinking, the most helpful discussion on this point is found not in the minuscule number of legal opinions that have involved "frozen embryos," but in the ethical standards set by The American Fertility Society, as follows:

> Three major ethical positions have been articulated in the debate over preembryo status. At one extreme is the view of the preembryo as a human subject after fertilization, which requires that it be accorded the rights of a person. This position entails an obligation to provide an opportunity for implantation to occur and tends to ban any action before transfer that might harm the preembryo or that is not immediately therapeutic, such as freezing and some preembryo research.
>
> At the opposite extreme is the view that the preembryo has a status no different from any other human tissue. With the consent of those who have decision-making authority over the preembryo, no limits should be imposed on actions taken with preembryos.
>
> A third view—one that is most widely held—takes an intermediate position between the other two. It holds that the preembryo deserves respect greater than that accorded to human tissue but not the respect accorded to actual persons. The preembryo is due greater respect than other human tissue because of its potential to become a person and because of its symbolic meaning for many people. Yet, it should not be treated as a person, because

it has not yet developed the features of personhood, is not yet established as developmentally individual, and may never realize its biologic potential. . . . Within the limits set by institutional policies, decision-making authority regarding preembryos should reside with the persons who have provided the gametes. . . . As a matter of law, it is reasonable to assume that the gamete providers have primary decision-making authority regarding preembryos in the absence of specific legislation on the subject. A person's liberty to procreate or to avoid procreation is directly involved in most decisions involving preembryos.

We conclude that preembryos are not, strictly speaking, either "persons" or "property," but occupy an interim category that entitles them to special respect because of their potential for human life. It follows that any interest that Mary Sue Davis and Junior Davis have in the preembryos in this case is not a true property interest. However, they do have an interest in the nature of ownership, to the extent that they have decision-making authority concerning disposition of the preembryos, within the scope of policy set by law.

V. THE ENFORCEABILITY OF CONTRACT

Establishing the locus of the decision-making authority in this context is crucial to deciding whether the parties could have made a valid contingency agreement prior to undergoing the IVF procedures and whether such an agreement would now be enforceable on the question of disposition. . . .

We believe, as a starting point, that an agreement regarding disposition of any untransferred preembryos in the event of contingencies (such as the death of one or more of the parties, divorce, financial reversals, or abandonment of the program) should be presumed valid and should be enforced as between the progenitors. This conclusion is in keeping with the proposition that the progenitors, having provided the gametic material giving rise to the preembryos, retain decision-making authority as to their disposition.

At the same time, we recognize that life is not static, and that human emotions run particularly high when a married couple is attempting to overcome infertility problems. It follows that the parties' initial "informed consent" to IVF procedures will often not be truly informed because of the near impossibility of anticipating, emotionally and psychologically, all the turns that events may take as the IVF process unfolds. Providing that the initial agreements may later be modified by agreement will, we think, protect the parties against some of the risks they face in this regard. But, in the absence of such agreed modification, we conclude that their prior agreements should be considered binding.

It might be argued in this case that the parties had an implied contract to reproduce using in vitro fertilization, that Mary Sue Davis relied on that agreement in undergoing IVF procedures, and that the court should enforce an implied contract against Junior Davis, allowing Mary Sue to dispose of the preembryos in a manner calculated to result in reproduction. The problem with such an analysis is that there is no indication in the record that disposition in the event of contingencies other than Mary Sue Davis's pregnancy was ever considered by the parties, or that Junior Davis intended to pursue reproduction outside the confines of a continuing marital relationship with Mary Sue. We therefore decline to decide this case on the basis of implied contract or the reliance doctrine. . . .

VI. THE RIGHT OF PROCREATIONAL AUTONOMY

Although an understanding of the legal status of preembryos is necessary in order to determine the enforceability of agreements about their disposition, asking whether or not they constitute "property" is not an altogether helpful question. As the appellee points out in his brief, "[as] two or eight cell tiny lumps of complex protein, the embryos have no [intrinsic] value to either party." Their value lies in the "potential to become, after implantation, growth and birth, children." Thus, the essential dispute here is not where or how or how long to store the preembryos, but whether the parties will become parents. . . .

Here, the specific individual freedom in dispute is the right to procreate. In terms of the Tennessee state constitution, we hold that the right of procreation is a vital part of an individual's right to privacy. Federal law is to the same effect.

In construing the reach of the federal constitution, the United States Supreme Court has addressed the affirmative right to procreate in only two cases. In *Buck v. Bell* (1927), the Court upheld the sterilization of a "feebleminded white woman." However, in *Skinner v. Oklahoma* (1942), the Supreme Court struck down a statute that authorized the sterilization of certain categories of criminals. The Court described the right to procreate as "one of the basic civil rights of man [sic]," and stated that "marriage and procreation are fundamental to the very existence and survival of the race." . . .

That a right to procreational autonomy is inherent in our most basic concepts of liberty is also indicated by the reproductive freedom cases, *see, e.g., Griswold v. Connecticut*, and *Roe v. Wade*, and by cases concerning parental rights and responsibilities with respect to children. . . .

The United States Supreme Court has never addressed the issue of procreation in the context of in vitro fertilization. Moreover, the extent to which procreational autonomy is protected by the United States Constitution is no longer entirely clear. Justice Blackmun noted, in his dissent, that the plurality opinion in *Webster v. Reproductive Health Services*, "turns a stone face to anyone in search of what the plurality conceives as the scope of a woman's right under the Due Process Clause to terminate a pregnancy free from the coercive and brooding influence of the State." The *Webster* opinion lends even less guidance to those seeking the bounds of constitutional protection of other aspects of procreational autonomy.

For the purposes of this litigation it is sufficient to note that, whatever its ultimate constitutional boundaries, the right of procreational autonomy is composed of two rights of equal significance—the right to procreate and the right to avoid procreation. Undoubtedly, both are subject to protections and limitations.

The equivalence of and inherent tension between these two interests are nowhere more evident than in the context of in vitro fertilization. None of the concerns about a woman's bodily integrity that have previously precluded men from controlling abortion decisions is applicable here. We are not unmindful of the fact that the trauma (including both emotional stress and physical discomfort) to which women are subjected in the IVF process is more severe than is the impact of the procedure on men. In this sense, it is fair to say that women contribute more to the IVF process than men. Their experience, however, must be viewed in light of the joys of parenthood that is desired or the relative anguish of a lifetime of unwanted parenthood. As they stand on the brink of potential parenthood, Mary Sue Davis and Junior Lewis Davis must be seen as entirely equivalent gamete-providers.

It is further evident that, however far the protection of procreational autonomy extends, the existence of the right itself dictates that decisional authority rests in the gamete-providers alone, at least to the extent that their decisions have an impact upon their individual reproductive status. As discussed in Section V above, no other person or entity has an interest sufficient to permit interference with the gamete-providers' decision to continue or terminate the IVF process, because no one else bears the consequences of these decisions in the way that the gamete-providers do.

Further, at least with respect to Tennessee's public policy and its constitutional right of privacy, the state's interest in potential human life is insufficient to justify an infringement on the gamete-providers' procreational autonomy. The United States Supreme Court has indicated in *Webster*, and even in *Roe*, that the state's interest in potential human life may justify statutes or regulations that have an impact upon a person's exercise of procreational autonomy. This potential for sufficiently weighty state's interests is not, however, at issue here, because Tennessee's statutes contain no statement of public policy which reveals an interest that could justify infringing on gamete-providers' decisional authority over the preembryos to which they have contributed. . . .

Certainly, if the state's interests do not become sufficiently compelling in the abortion context until the end of the first trimester, after very significant developmental stages have passed, then surely there is no state interest in these preembryos which could suffice to overcome the interests of the gamete-providers. The abortion statute reveals that the increase in the state's interest is marked by each successive developmental stage such that, toward the end of a pregnancy, this interest is so compelling that abortion is almost strictly forbidden. This scheme supports the conclusion that the state's interest in the potential life embodied by these four- to eight-cell preembryos (which may or may not be able to achieve implantation in a uterine wall and which, if implanted, may or may not begin to develop into fetuses, subject to possible miscarriage) is at best slight. When weighed against the interests of the individuals and the burdens inherent in parenthood, the state's interest in the potential life of these preembryos is not sufficient to justify any infringement upon the freedom of these individuals to make their own decisions as to whether to allow a process to continue that may result in such a dramatic change in their lives as becoming parents.

The unique nature of this case requires us to note that the interests of these parties in parenthood are different in scope than the parental interest considered in other cases. Previously, courts have dealt with the childbearing and child-rearing aspects of parenthood. Abortion cases have dealt with gestational parenthood. In this case, the Court must deal with the question of genetic parenthood. We conclude, moreover, that an interest in avoiding genetic parenthood can be significant enough to trigger the protections afforded to all other aspects of parenthood. The technological fact that someone unknown to these parties could gestate these preembryos does not alter the fact that these parties, the gamete-providers, would become parents in that event, at least in the genetic sense. The profound impact this would have on them supports their right to sole decisional authority as to whether the process of attempting to gestate these preembryos should continue. This brings us directly to the question of how to resolve the dispute that arises when one party wishes to continue the IVF process and the other does not.

VII. BALANCING THE PARTIES' INTERESTS

Resolving disputes over conflicting interests of constitutional import is a task familiar to the courts. One way of resolving these disputes is to consider the positions of the parties, the significance of their interests, and the relative burdens that will be imposed by differing resolutions. In this case, the issue centers on the two aspects of procreational autonomy—the right to procreate and the right to avoid procreation. We start by considering the burdens imposed on the parties by solutions that would have the effect of disallowing the exercise of individual procreational autonomy with respect to these particular preembryos.

Beginning with the burden imposed on Junior Davis, we note that the consequences are obvious. Any disposition which results in the gestation of the preembryos would impose unwanted parenthood on him, with all of its possible financial and psychological consequences. The impact that this unwanted parenthood would have on Junior Davis can only be understood by considering his particular circumstances, as revealed in the record.

Junior Davis testified that he was the fifth youngest of six children. When he was five years old, his parents divorced, his mother had a nervous break-down, and he and three of his brothers went to live at a home for boys run by the Lutheran Church. Another brother was taken in by an aunt, and his sister stayed with their mother. From that day forward, he had monthly visits with his mother but saw his father only three more times before he died in 1976. Junior Davis testified that, as a boy, he had severe problems caused by separation from his parents. He said that it was especially hard to leave his mother after each monthly visit. He clearly feels that he has suffered because of his lack of opportunity to establish a relationship with his parents and particularly because of the absence of his father.

In light of his boyhood experiences, Junior Davis is vehemently opposed to fathering a child that would not live with both parents. Regardless of whether he or Mary Sue had custody, he feels that the child's bond with the non-custodial parent would not be satisfactory. He testified very clearly that his concern was for the psychological obstacles a child in such a situation would face, as well as the burdens it would impose on him. Likewise, he is opposed to donation because the recipient couple might divorce, leaving the child (which he definitely would consider his own) in a single-parent setting.

Balanced against Junior Davis's interest in avoiding parenthood is Mary Sue Davis's interest in donating the preembryos to another couple for implantation. Refusal to permit donation of the preembryos would impose on her the burden of knowing that the lengthy IVF procedures she underwent were futile, and that the preembryos to which she contributed genetic material would never become children. While this is not an insubstantial emotional burden, we can only conclude that Mary Sue Davis's interest in donation is not as significant as the interest Junior Davis has in avoiding parenthood. If she were allowed to donate these preembryos, he would face a lifetime of either wondering about his parental status or knowing about his parental status but having no control over it. He testified quite clearly that if these preembryos were brought to term he would fight for custody of his child or children. Donation, if a child came of it, would rob him twice—his procreational autonomy would be defeated and his relationship with his offspring would be prohibited.

The case would be closer if Mary Sue Davis were seeking to use the preembryos herself, but only if she could not achieve parenthood by any other reasonable means. We recognize the trauma that Mary Sue has already experienced and the additional discomfort to which she would be subjected if she opts to attempt IVF again. Still, she would have a reasonable opportunity, through IVF, to try once again to achieve parenthood in all its aspects—genetic, gestational, bearing, and rearing.

Further, we note that if Mary Sue Davis were unable to undergo another round of IVF, or opted not to try, she could still achieve the child-rearing aspects of parenthood through adoption. The fact that she and Junior Davis pursued adoption indicates that, at least at one time, she was willing to forego genetic parenthood and would have been satisfied by the child-rearing aspects of parenthood alone. . . .

NOTES AND QUESTIONS:
Davis v. Davis

1. The court notes that the preembryos are not persons under either Tennessee or federal law. Do you agree, at least with regard to federal law? What if the court had reached a different conclusion with regard to (a) Tennessee

law alone, or (b) federal law alone? What does the court say about the outcome that might then have been required?

With regard to possibility (a), compare Louisiana law, La. R.S. 9:123 (1999), which states that an "in vitro fertilized human ovum exists as a juridical person until such time as the in vitro fertilized human is implanted in the womb." La. R.S. 9:131 further provides that "[i]n disputes arising between any parties regarding the in vitro fertilized ovum, the judicial standard for resolving such disputes is to be the best interest of the in vitro fertilized ovum."

2. How does the court categorize preembryos? As a result of its categorization, the court concludes that the Davises have an interest that "is not a true property interest" but which is an "interest in the nature of ownership, to the extent that they have decision-making authority concerning disposition of the preembryos." If this is not a true property interest, exactly how does it differ from one? What can the Davises not do with the preembryos that they would be able to do with ordinary property? Is the court talking about rules for the protection of the well-being of the preembryos, the same way we have rules relating to the protection of other living things, such as pets?

On the other hand, the court is willing to allow the Davises to have the preembryos destroyed, so how concerned is it about protection of the preembryos? Is the court perhaps referring to concepts related to the well-being not of the preembryos, but rather of society, such as limitations on the ability to sell living material, as discussed in *Moore*?

3. How does the court's analysis of the case turn on how it categorized the preembryos? (Look at how it deals with the possible interests of the state.) In particular, what if it had concluded that the preembryos were "ordinary" property? Do you think it would have reached a different result?

4. What does the court say about the role of contract law in disputes like this? Would the desires of the parties control if they were clearly laid out in a contract? Do you think there are likely to be many similar disputes in the future? If you were a lawyer working for a reproductive clinic, what advice would you give it? (See also notes 12 and 13 below.)

5. The court finds a "right to procreation" under both the Tennessee and United States constitutions, although it is not clear what the scope of the right is. How does that right play a role in the rest of the analysis?

6. Would the following state laws be consistent with the United States Constitution? Why or why not?

    a. A law that required all "unused" preembryos produced during in vitro fertilization to be destroyed.

    b. A law that required all such preembryos to be offered to other infertile couples.

    c. A law that required that all such preembryos be destroyed, unless one of the parties can demonstrate an inability to produce any more genetic children, in which case that party has the right to that embryo.

d. A law that required all such preembryos, if the parties divorce, to be given to the woman, who would have absolute discretion to decide what would be done with them (e.g., destruction, donation for research, or implantation in herself or another woman). (Should it matter whether the law would then make the former husband the legal father of the resulting child?)

(Recall the discussion of the constitutional aspects of the "right to procreation" in the Cloning section of chapter 5, pp. 118–26.)

7. The court resolves the conflict between the Davises by balancing the interests of the two parties, noting that each of them has an interest of "constitutional import." Given the nature of the protection given to these rights by the U.S. Constitution, does categorizing these rights this way really add anything to the analysis? Once the court has determined that the government is not attempting to infringe on the rights of either Junior or Mary Sue, how does the fact that "constitutional rights" are at issue change things?

8. How, exactly, does the court balance the interests? How might the court resolve the case if the facts were different:

   a. Assume that Junior had had a happy childhood and a good relationship with his father, but nonetheless just did not want a child with Mary Sue now.

   b. Assume that Mary Sue wanted to gestate and raise the child herself.

   c. Assume that both (a) and (b) were true.

9. The court notes that the "case would be closer if Mary Sue Davis were seeking to use the preembryos herself, but only if she could not achieve parenthood by any other reasonable means." How important should this latter factor be? Should it really matter very much that she could not become pregnant by other means?

10. How crucial to the analysis is the fact that we are dealing with a preembryo that already represents the union of genetic material contributed by each of the Davises? What if Mary Sue and Junior were still married, and she wanted another child (to be raised by both of them) but he did not? Under what circumstances, if any, should a court be willing to force Junior to contribute his sperm for artificial insemination? Should it be willing to force him to have sexual intercourse with her? If not, why not? Is her "right to procreate" any less compelling in this scenario?

11. Is balancing an appropriate way to resolve this conflict, absent a statute that tells the court to do it? Isn't Mary Sue basically asking to do something that should require Junior's consent? (Recall that the court was willing to treat this as a purely contractual issue, had the parties stated in the contract what they wanted done.) So long as he is unwilling to consent, why should the importance of the result to Mary Sue matter?

Try to place this case in the context of more general legal principles. Recall the common law assumption that as a general rule, each individual is autonomous, and has no particular duty to help out anyone else. (Recall the discussions about women making decisions that might harm a fetus.) Transactions take place when they are freely entered into with the consent of both parties. Does anything in these contractual battles over frozen preembryos suggest that courts should read in a duty on the part of one spouse to help another, overriding the principles of freedom to contract?

In chapter 16, we will further delve into the "no duty" assumption, and find that a patient's blood relative cannot be forced to undergo a relatively benign medical procedure (bone marrow donation) even if that is the only way to save the patient's life. If that is so, are you comfortable with forcing one person involuntarily to become a parent just to allow another person to have a genetically related child?

12. The *Davis* court said that "an agreement regarding disposition of any untransferred premebryos in the event of contingencies . . . should be presumed valid and should be enforced." At least with regard to an agreement to *not* use frozen embryos to produce additional children, *Davis* is being followed by other courts. In *Kass v. Kass*, 696 N.E.2d 174 (N.Y. 1998), for example, Maureen and Steven Kass had signed a contract that unused preembryos would be donated for research purposes. After their divorce, Maureen sought to have the preembryos implanted, claiming it would be her only chance for genetic motherhood. New York State's highest court rejected her claim:

> [W]e conclude that disposition of these [preembryos] does not implicate a woman's right of privacy or bodily integrity in the area of reproductive choice; nor are the [preembryos] recognized as "persons" for constitutional purposes. The relevant inquiry thus becomes who has dispositional authority over them. Because that question is answered in this case by the parties' agreement, for purposes of resolving the present appeal we have no cause to decide whether the [preembryos] are entitled to "special respect" (*cf., Davis v. Davis*).

13. Is the solution to the problem raised in *Davis* merely to make sure that fertility clinics write better contracts that cover all possible contingencies? Are you content with resolving disagreements by having the parties abide by the terms of a contract, assuming the contract discusses the contingency that took place?

Assume in *Davis*, for example, that Mary Sue and Junior had signed an agreement when they created the embryos stating that Mary Sue could have the embryos implanted in herself after a divorce if she so desired. Assume that she now wanted to do so, but Junior was objecting: he could not stand the thought of the two of them being linked by a biological child, of which he would be the legal father.

Should a court enforce such an agreement? Should a frozen embryo ever be implanted in anyone without the *contemporaneous* agreement of both the parties who contributed genes to that embryo? (Recall the discussion in chapter 10 of Margo's case, and the reluctance of the law to enforce certain types of contracts by means of specific performance.) Is creating a new human being something that should ever take place based on the enforcement of earlier contractual promises? Imagine, for example, that Mary Sue and Junior had, when happily married, signed a contract agreeing that if they ever divorced without having children, either could require the other to later engage in intercourse in order to produce such a child. Do you think that a court would enforce such an agreement—even in a jurisdiction where prostitution was legal? If not, which should we consider the greater wrong: forcing one of them to undergo unwilling sexual relations, or forcing the creation of a child that was unwanted by at least one of them?[5]

The Massachusetts Supreme Judicial Court (the highest court in the state) recently addressed these issues in *A.Z. v. B.Z.*, 725 N.E.2d 1051 (Mass. 2000). B.Z. (wife) and A.Z. (husband) married in 1977. In 1988 the wife, after three years of in vitro fertilization treatments, gave birth to twin daughters. During the treatments, extra embryos were frozen for possible future use. The fertility clinic gave the parties forms that required them to specify what should be done with the embryos in various circumstances, including a marital separation. It appeared from the testimony that each time, the husband would sign a blank form and the wife would fill in the blanks, indicating that the frozen embryos should be given to her.

The couple did separate and then divorce, and the husband opposed the wife's later attempt to use the frozen embryos to produce another child. The Massachusetts court concluded that it was unclear whether, given the actual circumstances, the written agreement correctly reflected the true earlier wishes of both husband and wife. But the court decided that the answer was ultimately irrelevant:

> With this said, we conclude that, even had the husband and the wife entered into an unambiguous agreement between themselves regarding the disposition of the frozen preembryos, we would not enforce an agreement that would compel one donor to become a parent against his or her will. As a matter of public policy, we conclude that forced procreation is not an area amenable to judicial enforcement. It is well-established that courts will not enforce contracts that violate public policy. While courts are hesitant to invalidate contracts on these public policy grounds, the public interest in freedom of contract is sometimes outweighed by other public policy considerations; in those cases the contract will not be enforced. To determine public policy, we look to the expressions of the Legislature and to those of this court.
>
> The Legislature has already determined by statute that individuals should not be bound by certain agreements binding them to enter or not enter into familial relationships. [T]he Legislature abolished the cause of action for the breach of a promise to marry. [T]he Legislature provided that no mother may agree to surrender her child "sooner than the fourth calendar day after the date of birth of the child to be adopted" regardless of any prior agreement.
>
> Similarly, this court has expressed its hesitancy to become involved in intimate questions inherent in the marriage relationship. "Except in cases involv-

ing divorce or separation, our law has not in general undertaken to resolve the many delicate questions inherent in the marriage relationship. We would not order either a husband or a wife to do what is necessary to conceive a child or to prevent conception, any more than we would order either party to do what is necessary to make the other happy."

In our decisions, we have also indicated a reluctance to enforce prior agreements that bind individuals to future family relationships. In *R. R. v. M. H.* (1998), we held that a surrogacy agreement in which the surrogate mother agreed to give up the child on its birth is unenforceable unless the agreement contained, inter alia, a "reasonable" waiting period during which the mother could change her mind. In *Capazzoli v. Holzwasser*, we determined, as an expression of public policy, that a contract requiring an individual to abandon a marriage is unenforceable. . . . .

We glean from these statutes and judicial decisions that prior agreements to enter into familial relationships (marriage or parenthood) should not be enforced against individuals who subsequently reconsider their decisions. This enhances the "freedom of personal choice in matters of marriage and family life."

. . . . This policy is grounded in the notion that respect for liberty and privacy requires that individuals be accorded the freedom to decide whether to enter into a family relationship. "There are 'personal rights of such delicate and intimate character that direct enforcement of them by any process of the court should never be attempted.'"

In this case, we are asked to decide whether the law of the Commonwealth may compel an individual to become a parent over his or her contemporaneous objection. The husband signed this consent form in 1991. Enforcing the form against him would require him to become a parent over his present objection to such an undertaking. We decline to do so.

A New Jersey court adopted this reasoning in a similar case, but one where the husband wanted to keep the embryos for possible implantation in a woman with whom he might develop a relationship. *J.B. v. M.B.*, 751 A.2d 613 (N.J. Super. Ct. App. Div. 2000).

HECHT V. SUPERIOR COURT (HECHT 1)
Court of Appeal of California
20 Cal. Rptr. 2d 275 (Cal. Ct. App. 1993)

OPINION BY PRESIDING JUSTICE LILLIE:

. . . This proceeding presents several matters of first impression involving the disposition of cryogenically preserved sperm of a deceased. . . .

At the age of 48, William E. Kane took his own life on October 30, 1991, in a Las Vegas hotel. For about five years prior to his death, he had been living with petitioner, thirty-eight-year-old Deborah E. Hecht. Kane was survived by two college-age children of his former wife whom he had divorced in 1976.

In October 1991, decedent deposited 15 vials of his sperm in an account at California Cryobank, Inc., a Los Angeles sperm bank (hereinafter sperm bank). On September 24, 1991, he signed a "Specimen Storage Agreement" with sperm bank which provided in pertinent part that "In the event of the death of the client [William E. Kane], the client instructs the Cryobank to: . . . [¶] Continue to store [the specimens] upon request of the executor of the estate [or] [r]elease the specimens to the executor of the estate." A provision captioned "Authorization to Release Specimens" states, "I, William Everett Kane, . . . authorize the [sperm bank] to release my semen specimens (vials) to Deborah Ellen Hecht. I am also authorizing specimens to be released to recipient's physician Dr. Kathryn Moyer." . . .

An October 21, 1991, letter signed by Kane and addressed to his children stated: "I address this to my children, because, although I have only two, Everett and Katy, it may be that Deborah will decide—as I hope she will—to have a child by me after my death. I've been assiduously generating frozen sperm samples for that eventuality. If she does, then this letter is for my posthumous offspring, as well, with the thought that I have loved you in my dreams, even though I never got to see you born. [¶] If you are receiving this letter, it means that I am dead—whether by my own hand or that of another makes very little difference. I feel that my time has come; and I wanted to leave you with something more than a dead enigma that was your father. [¶] . . . I am inordinately proud of who I have been—what I made of me. I'm so proud of that that I would rather take my own life now than be ground into a mediocre existence by my enemies—who, because of my mistakes and bravado have gained the power to finish me." . . .

[The administrator of Kane's estate] requested the [probate] court to select one of four alternative dispositions: (1) order destruction of the sperm; (2) order distribution of the sperm to decedent's children; (3) order distribution of 80 percent of the sperm to decedent's children and 20 percent to Hecht, and determine whether any children subsequently conceived by use of the sperm shall be entitled to distribution of estate assets; and (4) order distribution of the sperm to Hecht, but reserve one or two vials for future DNA/paternity testing, and determine to what extent any children subsequently conceived shall be entitled to estate assets.

[Kane's adult son and daughter] filed a statement of interested parties in which they argued that ordering destruction of decedent's sperm would "help guard the family unit in two different ways": First, such an order would prevent the birth of children who will never know their father and "never even have the slightest hope of being raised in a traditional family." Second, such an order would "prevent the disruption of existing families by after-born children," and would "prevent additional emotional, psychological and financial stress on those family members already in existence." They characterized the desire to father children after one's death as "egotistic and irresponsible," and stated that they "have lost their father to a tragic death which Hecht could easily have prevented; they do not wish to suffer any more at her hands. Further, they do not wish to be troubled for the rest of their lives with worries about the fate of their half-sibling(s)." . . .

II

Nature of Rights in Semen

"The present legal position toward property rights in the human body is unsettled and reflects no consistent philosophy or approach. Until recently, the common law either refused to recognize a property right in human bodies or recognized only a quasi-property right. . . . [The court in *Moore v. Regents of University of California*] did not resolve the debate over the existence or extent of a property interest in one's body. Nor does the existing statutory scheme quiet the debate. The statutes that address individuals' control over their bodies delineate the extent of that control in specific situations, but do not establish a general principle." . . .

One commentator recently noted that although some sperm banks operate as commercial enterprises, they are virtually free from state licensing and other regulation. The various state statutes modeled after the Uniform Parentage Act address the issue of the legal relationship between the sperm donor and the child born by artificial insemination. However, "[n]one of the statutes on artificial insemination indicate who owns the sperm donation, but sperm banks generally require those donors who are to be anonymous to sign a written waiver of any rights to the deposit and any paternity claims to children born from it. In return, the sperm bank guarantees the donor's anonymity. Thus, according to the contract between the parties, the donor no longer 'owns' the sperm. [¶] Men who use sperm banks to store their sperm for their own future use, however, do own their donation(s) of sperm and are required to pay for its maintenance and its later withdrawal. Upon notice of the death of the donor, however, many storage agreements authorize the sperm bank to dispose of the deposit. Requests from the widow of the donor to be inseminated with the sperm, as a matter of practice, are denied absent express instructions in the donor's will or a court order."

The American Fertility Society, in its ethical statement on in vitro fertilization, has written that "It is understood that the gametes and concepti are the property of the donors. The donors therefore have the right to decide at their sole discretion the disposition of these items, provided such disposition is within medical and ethical guidelines." . . .

In this case, the trial court could not have properly ordered the sperm destroyed by applying the provisions of the will; . . . the will evidences the decedent's intent that Hecht, should she so desire, is to receive his sperm stored in the sperm bank to bear his child posthumously. . . .

We thus proceed to address the argument that public policy forbids the artificial insemination of Hecht because she is an unmarried woman.

III

Artificial Insemination and Unmarried Women

Although artificial insemination in itself is not new, having been performed on animals for centuries, the first recorded successful human artificial insemination was performed in England in 1770. Although the practice was slow to be accepted in the United States until the mid-20th century, artificial insemination has now gained widespread acceptance as "medical technology has made it increasingly available and inexpensive to the estimated fifteen percent of all married couples who are infertile." Artificial insemination was made available to the astronauts in 1961 so they could still father healthy children using stored sperm even if space travel were to harm their reproductive systems. . . .

[We] find without merit the argument of [Kane's children] that "The state's interest in protecting the institutions of family and marriage dictates petitioner should be denied access to the sperm." Clearly the institution of marriage is not implicated in this case, especially where there was no existing marriage relationship involving decedent at the time of his death and obviously there can be none after his death. It is also premature for us to address the issue of family integrity and, in any case, there is no factual basis in this record to support any contention that the artificial insemination of Hecht would have an impact on any other family, including any family involving decedent's surviving adult children. . . .

IV

Postmortem Artificial Insemination

. . . [Kane's children] argue that "this court should adopt a state policy against posthumous conception," because it is "in truth, the creation of orphaned children by artificial means with state authorization," a result which they characterize as "tragic." However, [they] do not cite any authority establishing the propriety of this court, or any court, to make the value judgment as to whether it is better for such a potential child not to be born, assuming that both gamete providers wish to conceive the child. In other words, assuming that both Hecht and decedent desired to conceive a child using decedent's sperm, [they] fail to establish a state interest sufficient to justify interference with that decision. . . .

We also disagree with [their] claim that any order other than destruction of the sperm is tantamount to "state authorization" of posthumous conception of children, i.e., the creation of a public policy in favor of such conception. In such a case, the state is simply acknowledging that "no other person or entity has an interest sufficient to permit interference with the gamete-providers' decision. . . because no one else bears the consequences of these decisions in the way that the gamete-providers do." *Davis v. Davis.*

Citing *Davis*, [Kane's children] also urge this court to uphold the trial court's order on the ground that Hecht "can easily procreate by a variety of other means," and she "cannot bear a child using [decedent's] sperm without encroaching upon the family integrity of [decedent's] existing children." As pointed out above, our record is inadequate to address the issue of [their] "family integrity." . . .

As recently stated by our Supreme Court in a case involving a surrogacy contract: "It is not the role of the judiciary to inhibit the use of reproductive technology when the Legislature has not seen fit to do so; any such effort would raise serious questions in light of the fundamental nature of the rights of procreation and privacy." (*Johnson v. Calvert.*)

For the foregoing reasons we conclude that the trial court abused its discretion in ordering decedent's sperm destroyed.

HECHT V. SUPERIOR COURT (HECHT 2)
Court of Appeal of California
59 Cal. Rptr. 2d 222 (Cal. Ct. App. 1996)

OPINION BY JUSTICE JOHNSON:

For several years now, the decedent's adult children, William Everett Kane, Jr., and Katherine Kane, have been attempting to frustrate the petitioner, Deborah Ellen Hecht (Hecht), from conceiving a child using their deceased father's sperm. . . .

On April 26, 1994, another probate judge, the Honorable Arnold Gold, decided Hecht at a minimum was entitled to the 20 percent of the sperm she would receive as "assets" of the estate under the terms of the property settlement. Accordingly, he ordered a preliminary distribution of three (of the fifteen) sperm vials to Hecht. . . .

Hecht received the three sperm vials. The first two attempts to conceive proved unsuccessful. Before trying again, her gynecologist wanted to know whether there was only one more vial available, which would dictate usage of a riskier technique, or whether they could gain possession of the remaining 12 vials and use normal procedures.

. . . After ordering a settlement conference, which proved unsuccessful, the probate judge denied the petition on grounds the property settlement governed disposition of the sperm vials as well as the real and personal property of the estate. Finding the property settlement gave Hecht 20 percent of the estate's residual "assets," the court ruled Hecht was only entitled to the three vials (out of fifteen) she already had received in the preliminary distribution. . . .

The principles enunciated in our first opinion in this case, authored by Presiding Justice Lillie, largely resolve this fundamental issue. As that opinion highlighted, the genetic material involved here is a unique form of "property." It is not subject to division through an agreement among the decedent's potential beneficiaries which is inconsistent with decedent's manifest intent about its disposition. A man's sperm or a woman's ova or a couple's embryos are not the same as a quarter of land, a cache of cash, or a favorite limousine. Rules appropriate to the disposition of the latter are not necessarily appropriate for the former. If we are to honor decedent's intent as expressed in several written documents, his sperm can only be used by and thus only has value to one person, the petitioner in this case. . . .

From decedent's clear expressions of intent, it is apparent he created these vials of sperm for one purpose, to produce a child with this woman. Not to produce a child with any other specific woman or with an anonymous female. Not to produce a descendant with any other genetic makeup than would result from a combination of his sperm and this woman's ovum. Even Hecht lacks the legal entitlement to give, sell, or otherwise dispose of decedent's sperm. She and she alone can use it. Even she cannot allow its use by others, if the law is to honor the decedent's clearly expressed intent. Thus, in a very real sense, to the extent this sperm is "property" it is only "property" for that one person. As such it is not an "asset" of the estate subject to allocation, in whole or in part, to any other person whether through agreement or otherwise.

The unanimous opinion Justice Lillie authored establishes the principle the intent of the sperm donor—and no one else's—controls the disposition and use of the sperm. This opinion quotes at length and with approval from an account of a decision of a French court. That decision "characterized sperms . . . as" "'the seed of life . . . tied to the fundamental liberty of a human being to conceive or not to conceive.' This fundamental right must be jealously protected, and is not to be subjected to the rules of contracts. Rather the fate of the sperm must be decided by the person from whom it is drawn. Therefore, the sole issue becomes that of intent." Applying this principle to the present case, the decedent's right to procreate with whom he chooses cannot be defeated by some contract third persons—including his chosen donee—construct and sign. His "fundamental right" must be "jealously guarded." It is true the chosen donee may voluntarily elect not to become impregnated with the descendant's sperm. But she may not sell or contract away the decedent's "fundamental right" to other persons.

So even assuming, as decedent's adult children do, that Hecht intended to sign away 80 percent of decedent's sperm to those adult children in order to achieve a resolution of the property issues implicated in this will contest, she lacked the right and legal power to do so under the principles enunciated in this court's first opinion. Such a term, even if explicit in the settlement agreement, would violate not only the decedent's express intent but also his most "fundamental right"—to choose the genetic inheritance he leaves on this earth. The only reasonable reading of the opinion Justice Lillie wrote for this court is that the law should not permit anyone, including even Hecht, to treat the decedent's "fundamental interest" in procreation as an item for negotiation and trade among the claimants for decedent's estate. The only way for the law to ensure the decedent's "fundamental interest" is not so used is to remove it from the negotiating table. And, the only way to remove it from the table is to refuse to enforce any contract term which purports to impair realization of the decedent's intent his sperm be used to produce a child with the woman he wanted to bear that child. . . .

This court hopes and expects this is the last in the series of cases over Hecht's right to these vials of sperm. This has never been a dispute over whether women shall be allowed to produce children through sperm donated by now dead fathers. Under current law and technology Hecht could have gone to this same cryobank and obtained sperm from an anonymous donor, including one who is no longer alive. All we decided was her entitlement to the sperm of a particular donor, the man she had loved and lived with for five years. It became an issue only because of an unusual, and perhaps unique, configuration of personalities and motivations. Unfortunately, it also took three years of litigation and three trips to this court to finally resolve the question.

We also emphasize another set of issues we did not decide in this opinion. We do not have before us the many legal questions raised by the possible birth of a child to Hecht through use of Kane's sperm. Thus, we do not decide, for instance, whether that child would be entitled to inherit any property as Kane's heir. . . .

CONCURRING OPINION BY JUSTICE WOODS:

I am concurring separately over concern for possible misinterpretation of language that appears in this opinion . . .

On second reflection, when we held in *Hecht v. Superior Court* (1993) that "no other person or *entity* has an interest sufficient to permit interference with the gamete-providers' decision . . . because no one else bears the consequences of these decisions in the way that the gamete-providers do" (emphasis added), I become apprehensive that the reader might construe the language to mean that no "entity," state or otherwise, can ever have sufficient interest to interfere with donations of human gametal material. I do not perceive this to be the intention of our initial decision, nor a desirable result thereof.

Although I possess a good dose of Orwellian caution when it comes to governmental interference in such intimate matters as the Hecht/Kane arrangement in this instance, I am not convinced that the state as an entity is devoid of "any" sufficient interest to justify interference in such matters. I would caution that our initial opinion and this opinion should not be construed beyond the facts of the instant matter. It is beyond the capacity of this court to speculate on all of the consequences that might be spawned should our initial opinion and the opinion herein be construed too broadly.

For instance, and only by way of one example among many conceivable examples, can it be said that a state entity can never have a sufficient interest to interfere with reproduction by persons capable of producing only severely imbecilic offspring? Oliver Wendell Holmes Jr. certainly thought so when he spoke his famous words on behalf of the majority of the Justices of the United States Supreme Court, "three generations of imbeciles are enough." I am convinced that a state entity may have a sufficient interest to intercede and prevent donations of gametical materials in very extreme instances under carefully regulated statutes. . . .

NOTES AND QUESTIONS:
Hecht v. Superior Court

1. What reasons did Kane's children give for opposing Deborah Hecht's attempt to use their father's sperm? What did the court (in *Hecht 1*) say about those reasons? Do you think the children were really quite so concerned with possible worries about "the fate of their half-sibling(s)"? Might they have had somewhat less altruistic concerns? (What legal question does the court in *Hecht 2* specifically say it is *not* deciding?)

2. Note the difference between the issues raised in *Davis* and those raised in *Hecht*. In *Hecht*, both of the parties to the proposed "transaction"—William Kane and Deborah Hecht—had allegedly consented to that transaction. Kane's children were asking the courts to interfere with that consensual arrangement. In contrast, in *Davis*, Mary Sue was asking the courts to force Junior to allow the use of the preembryo in a way that he objected to. Might this difference in the cases alter the relevance of any constitutional "right to procreate"? Which case is more likely to implicate such a right? (Remember to ask, Whose actions does the constitutional right restrict?)

3. The court concludes that it has not been shown any state interest that is inconsistent with allowing Hecht to use the sperm. It notes that it is "not the role of the judiciary to inhibit the use of reproductive technology when the Legislature has not seen fit to do so; any such effort would raise serious questions in light of the fundamental nature of the rights of procreation and privacy." Of course, that raises the question of possible legislative action on this issue. Would a state law that banned the use of any sperm or eggs of a dead person (for purposes of creating an embryo) be consistent with the Constitution? Assuming there is indeed a right to procreate protected by the Constitution, does it necessarily survive the death of a person? (Some of the issues relating to the rights of dead persons are discussed in chapter 16.)

Even assuming such a right did in fact apply after a person's death, might a state nonetheless be able to ban such use of the sperm or eggs? What legal standard would apply in judging the sufficiency of the state's claimed purpose? What reasons might a state use to justify such a ban? (Note the comments by Justice Woods in his concurrence in *Hecht 2*.)

4. *Hecht 1* specifically addresses the fact that Deborah Hecht was not married. What does it conclude? Would a state law banning such posthumous use of gametes based on the legislature's determination that it is inappropriate to have children born into one-parent households be constitutional? (What U.S. Supreme Court cases are most relevant? For a discussion of similar issues, see the notes following Cloning in chapter 5.)

   Suppose Morality in Fertility, a private clinic providing reproductive services, adopted a policy that it would provide services only to married, heterosexual couples. Would that violate the U.S. Constitution? (A somewhat related fact pattern in *Walker v. Pierce*, 560 F.2d 609 (4th Cir. 1977), involved an obstetrician who refused to treat poor pregnant women unless they agreed to be sterilized after the birth of their third child.)

5. What does the *Hecht 1* opinion say about the nature of the ownership interest in a person's sperm or eggs? How does it differ from other property? Do you agree with the court?

   What does *Hecht 2* add? Do you agree, for example, with its conclusion that Hecht should not be allowed to transfer Kane's sperm to another woman?

6. In *Hecht*, William Kane had clearly expressed his desire to have another child. What should we do where there is no such expression? Do you think most people would want a child to be conceived posthumously? Does it matter what most people would want? What outcome would be appropriate in the following cases (and why)?[6]

   a. John and Mary, both in their mid-twenties, were married several months ago. John has just had a sudden heart attack that has left him brain dead (and therefore legally dead). They never got around to discussing whether or not they wanted to have children. Mary is asking the doctors to collect some of his sperm so that she can have his child.

   b. Same facts as (a), except that they both very much wanted children. However, they had never discussed the possibility of a child being conceived after John's death.

7. Would it be constitutional for a state to ban the use of a person's sperm or eggs for purposes of posthumous conception unless that person had stated, in writing, a desire to have such a conception take place? What cases would you cite in analyzing this law?

Endnotes

1. See, e.g., Rebecca S. Eisenberg, "Patenting the Human Genome," 39 *Emory L. J.* 721 (1990).

2. Gina Kolata, "Sharing of Profits Is Debated as the Value of Tissue Rises," *New York Times,* 15 May 2000, A1.

3. See, e.g., Marcia Angell, "Is Academic Medicine for Sale?" 342 *New Eng. J. Med.* 1516 (2000).

4. See, e.g., Robert M. Portman, "Legislative Restriction on Medical and Surgical Procedure Patents Removes Impediment to Medical Progress," 4 *U. Baltimore Intell. Prop. J.* 91 (1996) (including an interesting discussion of recent attempts to patent medical procedures, such as the use of ultrasound to identify the sex of a fetus, and a Kansas company's attempt to patent the use of direct penile injections of vasodilating drugs as a treatment for impotence); Council on Ethical and Judicial Affairs, American Medical Association, "Ethical Issues in the Patenting of Medical Procedures," 53 *Food & Drug L. J.* 341(1998); Chris J. Katopis, "Patients v. Patents: Policy Implications of Recent Patent Legislation," 71 *St. John's L. Rev.* 329 (1997).

5. See New York State Task Force on Life and the Law, *Assisted Reproductive Technologies: Analysis and Recommendations for Public Policy* at 315–26 (1998); Carl H. Coleman, "Procreative Liberty and Contemporaneous Choice: An Inalienable Rights Approach to Frozen Embryo Disputes," 84 *Minn. L. Rev.* 55 (1999).

6. See, e.g., Susan Kerr, "Post-Mortem Sperm Procurement: Is It Legal?" 3 *DePaul J. Health Care L.* 39 (1999).

Death and Transplantation

15

The Definition of Death

"You see," Max explained as he pumped, "there's different kinds of dead: there's sort of dead, mostly dead, and all dead. This fella here, he's only sort of dead, which means there's still a memory inside, there's still bits of brain."

William Goldman, *The Princess Bride*

People often say that life used to be simpler. Whether or not that is the case, it certainly is true that *death* used to be simpler. If we go back more than a few decades, determining whether or not someone was dead was, appropriately enough, a no-brainer: a dead person would not be breathing. As a result of that circumstance, other confirming changes in the person's body—becoming cold and gray, for example—would soon follow. By the time, hours if not days later, that any actions were taken that were incompatible with the person being alive—for example, embalming the body or burying it—it was certain that virtually every organ in the body was "dead."

To understand how death has become so complicated, we must review some physiology. Our brains, in very simple terms, can be imagined as composed of two very distinct portions. (You might review what Dr. Plum, one of the experts quoted in *Quinlan* in chapter 10, said about this.) The "higher brain," or cerebral hemispheres, is responsible for our ability to think and feel. The "lower brain," or brainstem, is responsible for keeping the rest of our body functioning (like the control systems in a building that regulate heating, ventilation, and air conditioning). In particular, our lower brain controls the impulses that trigger the muscles that keep us breathing. Thus, in the past, when our brain was sufficiently injured, we would stop breathing and, due to lack of oxygen going to any of the tissues of our body, our entire body would soon be dead.

This cascade of death through the human body can now be stopped in midstream, largely as a result of the invention several decades ago of a single machine: the respirator (sometimes called a ventilator), a relatively low-tech machine that pumps air into and out of a person's lungs. This raises an obvious question: if a person is still breathing, albeit with the help of a respirator, how can we consider him dead? Do we need to wait until the machine is turned off, and the rest of the body is dead, as has been the case throughout history (a "whole body" or "non-brain-based" concept of death)? Alternatively, on what basis can we declare the person dead while the machine is still working? One argument has been to base the declaration on the fact the person's entire brain was dead, both the higher and the lower brain; this is known as the "whole brain" concept of death. An alternative position is that a person should be dead when the higher brain alone has been permanently destroyed—the "higher brain" concept of death.

Thus, there are effectively three major positions on how much of a person's body must be dead in order to declare that the *person* is legally dead. Those positions, in simplified terms, are:

Higher Brain Concept: Only the higher brain

Whole Brain Concept: Entire brain (both higher brain and brainstem)

Whole Body Concept: Entire body (entire brain *and* essentially all other organs)

The cases that follow reveal the history of the debate over these concepts in the United States, and how it has turned out. As you read them, try to figure out why the courts are concerned about determining when a person is dead. When you have answers to that question, ask yourself if "death" is the right concept for addressing those concerns. Does the way death is defined by the law fit with your own notions of what death is about?

In particular, how do the issues discussed in this chapter relate to the mirror image question we addressed earlier in dealing with fetuses and the beginning of a human life? As you may recall, the legal resolution depended in large part on when a human being gained "personhood." The Supreme Court itself ducked the question of when life began. Is the death debate really about the *loss of personhood*? If so, why aren't we using that terminology, instead of talking about death?

IN RE BOWMAN

Supreme Court of Washington

617 P.2d 731 (Wash. 1980)

OPINION BY JUSTICE UTTER:

This is an appeal by the guardian ad litem appointed for William Matthew Bowman (Matthew) prior to Matthew's death, from the decision of the Snohomish County Superior Court ruling that because he had suffered irreversible loss of brain activity, he was in fact dead on October 17, 1979. Issues raised on appeal are: (1) whether law or medicine should define the standards establishing when death occurs; (2) if law is to define those standards, should the brain death standard be adopted; and (3) if that standard is adopted, what role should medicine have in defining the criteria for determining whether the standard has been met. We hold that it is for law to define the standard of death, that the brain death standard should be adopted, and that it is for the medical profession to determine the applicable criteria—in accordance with accepted medical standards—for deciding whether brain death is present. Our action affirms the judgment of the trial court.

Matthew Bowman, age 5, was admitted to Stevens Memorial Hospital on September 30, 1979, after suffering massive physical injuries inflicted by a nonfamily member who was caring for him. . . .

That testimony indicated that Matthew had been unconscious since admission to Stevens Hospital, and except for a brief period of increased neurological activity, had gradually weakened. He was being maintained on a ventilator, which enabled him to breathe and provided oxygen to his heart, and various other life support mechanisms. Numerous tests had been performed during his hospitalization to measure Matthew's brain functions.

The physician testified that on the date of the hearing Matthew showed no brain activity. An electroencephalogram (EEG) gave no reading and a radionuclide scan, which shows whether blood is getting to and through the brain, found a total absence of blood flow. No cornea reflex was present and Matthew's pupils were dilated and nonreactive to any stimuli. There were also no deep tendon reflexes or other signs of brain stem action, nor responses to deep pain or signs of spontaneous breathing. Body temperature and drug intake had been controlled to avoid adverse influence on these tests. The testifying physician indicated that he believed Matthew's brain was dead under the most rigid criteria available, called the "Harvard criteria," and that his cardiovascular system would, despite the life support systems, fail in 14 to 60 days. He further testified that all physicians in the Children's Orthopedic Hospital intensive care unit agreed that Matthew was no longer alive by October 17 and recommended that he be removed from the ventilator, a recommendation consented to by his mother. According to the physician, brain death is operative as a definition of death in the state of Washington, and medically accepted criteria exist in the state for determining when brain death occurs. These generally require coma, lack of electrical activity, and lack of blood flow to the brain.

Findings of fact entered by the trial court and supported by substantial evidence establish the following:

> The prevailing practice of the medical community, both in the State of Washington and nationwide, is to regard "brain death" as the death of the person. The medical profession has established several criteria by which to determine if brain death has occurred, and under the most stringent crite-

ria offered by the medical profession, Matthew has suffered brain death. There is no possibility that Matthew's brain will resume functioning.

The trial judge then held, based on the findings of fact that:

> The legal definition of death in the State of Washington must coincide with the prevailing medical opinion within the State as to when death occurs. Since the prevailing medical opinion recognizes that a person dies when an irreversible loss of brain function occurs, the irreversible cessation of brain activity constitutes death under Washington law.
>
> Under Washington law, William Matthew Bowman is dead. The fact that modern medical technology can keep his heart beating and his blood circulating for a finite period of time after brain death does not make him a living being in the eyes of the law. . . .

I

Death is both a legal and medical question. Traditionally, the law has regarded the question of at what moment a person died as a question of fact to be determined by expert medical testimony. However, recognizing that the law has independent interests in defining death which may be lost when deference to medicine is complete, courts have established standards which, although based on medical knowledge, define death as a matter of law. Thus, the law has adopted standards of death but has turned to physicians for the criteria by which a particular standard is met.

Until recently, the definition of death was both medically and legally a relatively simple matter. When the heart stopped beating and the lungs stopped breathing, the individual was dead according to physicians and according to the law. The traditional definition did not include the criterion of lack of brain activity because no method existed for diagnosing brain death. Moreover, until recently, no mechanical means have been available to maintain heart and lung action; and respiration, heart action, and brain function are so closely related that without artificial support, the cessation of any one of them will bring the other two to a halt within a very few minutes. Thus, Black's Law Dictionary 488 (4th ed. 1951), based upon older medical technology, defines death as:

> The cessation of life; the ceasing to exist; defined by physicians as a total stoppage of the circulation of the blood, and a cessation of the animal and vital functions consequent thereon, such as respiration, pulsation, etc.

With the recent advancement of medical science, the traditional common law "heart and lungs" definition is no longer adequate. Some of the specific factors compelling a more refined definition are: (1) modern medicine's technological ability to sustain life in the absence of spontaneous heartbeat or respiration, (2) the advent of successful organ transplantation capabilities which creates a demand for viable organs from recently deceased donors, (3) the enormous expenditure of resources potentially wasted if persons in fact dead are being treated medically as though they were alive, and (4) the need for a precise time of death so that persons who have died may be treated appropriately.

The numerous legal issues which look to the time and presence of death as determining factors require a legal response to these new developments. Inheritance, liability for death claims under an insurance contract, proximate cause and time of death in homicide cases, and termination of life support efforts are but a few of the areas in which legal consequences follow from a determination of whether death has occurred.

Recognizing that the former common law definition of death is no longer universally applicable, respondents maintain that brain death is also death under Washington law such that life supports may be terminated. Appellants, on the other hand, argue that there is an insufficient basis for the law to move away from the traditional "heart and lungs" definition, and to do so, as the trial court did, is tantamount to depriving persons of life.

The specific issue in this case is whether or not Matthew was legally dead on October 17, 1979, when the physicians declared that he had suffered brain death. We are not presented with the much more difficult question of whether life support mechanisms may be terminated while a person is still alive but in that condition known as a "persistent vegetative state," in which some brain functioning continues to exist. We are concerned here only with whether brain death, identified as the irreversible destruction of the entire brain from which cardiorespiratory death inevitably follows, is a recognized standard of death in this state.

II

With the ability of modern medical techniques to restore the function of vital organs or compensate for their nonfunction, medical decisions may be made based not on "scientific" fact but on the physician's concept of life and death. The decision by a physician as to whether a person is dead is thus not merely a medical, biological, or physical conclusion. It is, in part, a philosophical decision about what conditions define human life, combined with an empirical determination that those conditions are absent and not latent in a given case. The determination involves differentiating between human life and biological life, marking the dividing line between what constitutes human life and that which is purely mechanical. . . .

While 20 years ago a victim of cardiac arrest had little chance of survival, now, however, up to one in five victims returns to productive life. This advance in technology has produced a tragic problem not known before, of those whose cardiorespiratory systems may be kept functioning but whose brains have suffered massive and irreversible damage resulting in brain death.

Society does not require physicians to be experts on the philosophical aspects of these questions, or to define which physiological functions decisively identify a living human organism. Society does turn to physicians, like other scientists, to suggest which "vital signs" have what significance for which human functions. They may, for example, show that a person in an irreversible coma exhibits total unawareness to externally applied stimuli and biological needs and complete unresponsiveness, and they may project that when tests for this condition yield the same results over a 24-hour period, there is only a very minute chance that the coma will be "reversed." However, the judgment that total unawareness and complete unresponsiveness are the equivalent of death addresses questions more related to philosophy and law and is not the exclusive domain of medicine.

The determination by a physician that the symptoms of brain death are present, in accordance with acceptable medical standards, emphasizes that cessation of brain function is a symptom of the loss that makes a person dead, rather than the loss itself. It is the law's determination that brain death is the legal equivalent of death because—under current medical science—the capacity for life is irretrievably lost when the entire brain, including the brain stem, has ceased functioning.

III

To fully understand the precise contentions of both parties, it is necessary to review what occurs to patients who suffer brain damage.

The most frequent causes of brain death are massive head injuries, massive spontaneous brain hemorrhage secondary to complications of hypertension or rupture of a congenital berry aneurysm, and lack of blood pumped into the brain because of cardiac arrest or systemic hypotension. Brain death occurs when the swelling is so severe that the pressure within the cranial cavity exceeds the pressure of blood flowing into the brain and the brain stem, causing cerebral circulation to cease. In this condition, there is no clinical evidence of brain function. Intense stimulation may bring no response or voluntary motor movements, and there are no eye movements at the brain stem level. Spontaneous respiration ceases because the vital respiratory centers of the brain have been destroyed. The patient depends entirely on mechanical support to maintain cardiorespiratory function. Normal cardiac functioning can be achieved, mechanically, even in the presence of total brain destruction, and can continue for as long as an hour after a patient is pronounced dead and the respirator discontinued.

However, mechanical maintenance of heartbeat and circulation can be continued only for a limited period of time when the brain stem has been destroyed. It is this limited survival period that distinguishes between brain death and the persistent vegetative state. In the latter state, irreversible damage occurs to the cerebral cortex, but the brain stem continues to function. Considerations involved in dealing with this condition are entirely different from those involved in brain death and require the drawing of a line between severe dysfunction and no function at all. That is not the case now before this court.

Determination of whether cessation of brain function has occurred may be made in a matter of minutes. The decision as to whether it is irreversible may require several days. Ingestion of suppressant drugs and low body temperature may cause a reversible loss of brain function, so these possibilities must be screened out before a person is pronounced brain dead.

The medical profession has established criteria by which to measure whether brain death has occurred. . . . In 1968, a Harvard Medical School committee developed criteria which now constitute the basis of accepted medical standards for the determination of brain death. Ad Hoc Committee of the Harvard Medical School to Examine the Definition of Brain Death, *A Definition of Irreversible Coma*, 205 J.A.M.A. 337 (1968). These "Harvard criteria" require (1) unreceptivity and unresponsivity to even the most intensely painful stimuli; (2) no spontaneous movements or spontaneous breathing for at least 1 hour; (3) no reflexes, as shown by no ocular movement, no blinking, no swallowing, and fixed and dilated pupils. The report further recommended flat electroencephalograms (EEG's) as a confirmatory test, and that hypothermia and use of central nervous system depressants as causes be eliminated. . . . We defer to the medical profession for further refinement of the criteria.

IV

Both courts and legislatures have responded to these medical advances and adopted brain death as a standard of death. At least 25 state legislatures have enacted brain death statutes. Kansas, the first state to adopt such legislation, established a 2-tier definition of death. Their 1971 act provides that a person is dead where there is an absence of spontaneous respiration and cardiac function and attempts at resuscitation are considered hopeless; or, when there is an absence of spontaneous brain function and it appears that further attempts at resuscitation will not succeed. In 1972, a model statute was proposed by Professor Alexander Morgan Capron of the University of Pennsylvania and Dr. Leon R. Kass. Adopted by at least eight states, this version differs from the Kansas statute in that it recognizes brain death only when "heart and lungs" death cannot be determined because of the use of artificial life supports.

In 1975, the American Bar Association sought to simplify earlier brain death legislation. It approved a model which is now used by two states, but also asked the Uniform Law Commissioners to refine the proposal. The American Medical Association's Board of Trustees has also approved a model bill. The essential difference between this model and other proposals is that the other proposals include brain stem death, which thus draws a clear legal line between brain death and the persistent vegetative state.

In other states, brain death has been approved by judicial ruling. . . . In [a 1979 case, the Colorado Supreme Court] adopted the language then proposed by the National Conference of Commissioners on Uniform State Laws for the Uniform Brain Death Act. That act provided:

> For legal and medical purposes, an individual who has sustained irreversible cessation of all functioning of the brain, including the brain stem, is dead. A determination under this section must be made in accordance with reasonable medical standards.

As was the case in Colorado and Massachusetts, no statute in this state has been enacted to define what constitutes death as posed by the facts now before us. It is both appropriate and proper, therefore, that this court decide that question. The definition adopted [by the Colorado Supreme Court] does not clarify how the concept of brain death is interrelated with the more traditional definition of death as the cessation of respiration and circulation. A revised act was submitted to the National Conference of Commissioners on Uniform State Laws on July 26, 1980. That act, approved and recommended for enactment in all states, harmonizes the two concepts, clarifying possible ambiguity previously existing.

Adoption of this standard will alleviate concern among medical practitioners that legal liability might be imposed when life support systems are withdrawn, even though the brain is irreversibly dead and circulation and respiration will inevitably cease. It will also permit discontinuation of artificial means of life support in a manner where even those most morally and emotionally committed to the preservation of life will not be offended. We do not address what are acceptable diagnostic tests and medical procedures for determining when brain death has occurred. It is left to the medical profession to define the acceptable practices, taking into account new knowledge of brain function and new diagnostic procedures.

We therefore adopt the provisions of the Uniform Determination of Death Act which state:

> An individual who has sustained either (1) irreversible cessation of circulatory and respiratory functions, or (2) irreversible cessation of all functions of the entire brain, including the brain stem, is dead. A determination of death must be made in accordance with accepted medical standards.

Uniform Determination of Death Act (August 7, 1980 recommendation). This standard reflects both the former common law standard and the evolutionary change in medical technology. . . .

NOTES AND QUESTIONS:
In re Bowman

1. The use of brain-death criteria as a method for declaring a person dead, as an alternative to the traditional heart-lung criteria, has been uniformly accepted throughout all of the fifty states, either by the enactment of laws

that are versions of the Uniform Determination of Death Act, or through court decisions such as *In re Bowman* itself.

2. Why do you think there was such a uniform and (relatively) rapid acceptance of the new brain death criteria? Usually a change takes place because there is an important need for it, and there are powerful interests pushing for it.

    The court describes four factors requiring that there be a more accurate definition of death. What are those four factors? Which two of them merely argue for accurately knowing when death occurs, as opposed to arguing in favor of one or another of the three possible concepts of death (whole body, whole brain, or higher brain death)?

3. Do you think the money spent on keeping brain-dead people alive was an important issue for members of the medical profession when the debate about brain death began in earnest? The Harvard criteria, which played a major role in getting the definition of death changed, came out in 1968. Was cost control likely to be an argument that physicians were concerned about? Review the *Quinlan* opinion, which came out in 1976, several years after the Harvard criteria. In *Quinlan*, the doctors were arguing in favor of continuing very expensive care, even though the family wanted to terminate that care. Do you see anything in that opinion suggesting that physicians viewed cost control as even a minor issue?

4. The struggle for giving patients the right to refuse care largely took place because of lawsuits such as *Quinlan*, *Bouvia*, and *Cruzan*, in which patients and their representatives were the protagonists for change. Would it surprise you to know that no lawsuits were brought in the early days of the debate arguing for a change in the definition of death (e.g., claiming that a relative who was "brain dead" should be declared legally dead)? Might it be relevant that it was hard at that time to keep a brain-dead person's body alive very long? Even if the person was on a respirator, after a few days the heart would usually stop, and the person would shortly be dead even under the traditional criteria. Given this fact, even if people were concerned about cost control, was declaring people dead by using brain death criteria likely to save large amounts of money?

5. As the court notes, the growing success of organ transplantation was creating a demand for organs at the very time when the debate about the definition of death was taking place. Do you think this was a coincidence? If a person who meets the brain-death criteria is not determined to be legally dead, what legal problem would you run into if you took out their organs (their kidneys, lungs, etc.) shortly after they suffer the initial injury that damages their brain? On the other hand, if doctors waited the several days until the brain-dead person's heart stopped, and the person was declared dead under the traditional heart-lung criteria, by that time the other organs would have been damaged by changes in the person's metabolism during the waiting period. They would be less useful for transplantation.

Currently, almost all the organs for transplantation that are taken from people at the time of their deaths (*cadaveric* donors) are taken from those who are declared brain-dead. (As discussed in chapter 16, a substantial number of organs for transplantation are actually taken from *living* donors, as when someone donates a kidney or part of a liver.) These are very healthy organs, since even though the person is legally dead, the organs are still receiving blood-carrying oxygen. In contrast, when a person is declared dead the traditional way, the heart is not beating and the lungs are not functioning, so the rest of the body's organs degenerate rapidly.

6. Whether or not the definition of death was modified primarily to allow greater harvesting of organs for transplantation, there is still a question of whether that change fits in with underlying notions of what it "means" to be dead. In fact, the committee that announced the Harvard criteria stated that it was not in fact changing the definition of death, but rather recognizing that even the traditional criteria of death were followed only as a means of determining whether a person's brain still functioned. Is that conclusion obvious to you? Do you think, if we went back several hundred years and asked the average woman-about-town, she would have said, "Sure, the brain is the only thing that matters when a person is declared dead"? If we had shown that woman a person with a dead brain, but with the rest of the body functioning quite nicely, would she be comfortable declaring him dead? As opposed to saying, "This person—with a dead brain in a living body—is not dead until you turn off the machines, and the entire body is dead."

7. The court says that the determination of death is not merely a biological question but also a philosophical decision. Do you agree? Is the court's description of the change consistent with what the Harvard Committee said it was doing? Who is being more honest: the *Bowman* court or the Harvard Committee?

   Do you think the public in general understands that the adoption of brain death as a component of the legal definition of death was a philosophical decision, not just a refinement of scientific criteria that was required by new technology such as respirators?

8. To return to the issues raised at the beginning of the chapter, does the legal adoption of brain death criteria create confusion between loss of personhood and death? Death is a concept most of us are relatively familiar with, at least in terms of its biological (nonphilosophical) sense. It happens not just to human beings but to all living things. If we accept the brain-death criteria, we are declaring a human being dead when our pet dog or cat, for example, would, if in identical physiological circumstances, not be declared dead. Should we be respecting the life left in a brain-dead person's body the same way we respect other forms of life? For example, current technology would permit us to create a pacemaker that triggers a brain-dead person's breathing mechanism, so that she need not be hooked up to a ventilator. Assuming that

the person's organs were not being donated, would you be comfortable burying her while she is still breathing, with a heartbeat? If not, why not? Should we perhaps have a separate legal category for loss of personhood (just as we have a category, birth, that determines the start of personhood) that would allow donation of organs, loss of various legal rights, but not declare that to be the equivalent of death?

In spite of the uniform acceptance of brain death by all fifty states, proposals to return to the older definition (and thus declare a brain-dead person legally alive until the respirator is turned off and the entire body dies) still generate substantial debate.[1] Moreover, even medical personnel who regularly deal with these issues in their jobs often apply personal concepts of death that are incoherent.[2]

9. A late colleague of mine, Bill Bartholome, told the following story about a parent's encounter with death (the child's name has been changed from the original, which appeared in the internet bioethics discussion group run by the Medical College of Wisconsin):

> I think every pediatric resident remembers his/her first death. Mine was Susan T. She was a beautiful little girl . . . [and] was dying of cystic fibrosis. Her dying was not acknowledged by any person involved in her care other than her mother and I. . . . We became very close over the long days and nights we spent together with Susan. We worked out a plan for her death bed scene. When Susan died, I was to stand guard at the door of her room and protect Mrs. T.'s private time with Susan. On the day of her death, I was standing outside Susan's room keeping nurses and students and others out of the room. We had agreed that I would not "pronounce" or "announce" Susan's death until after her mother had had this special time alone with her body sans tubes and oxygen mask and I.V.s. I stood there until I heard Susan's mother screaming for me. When I entered the room, she was trying to get up out of the chair and hand Susan's body to me at the same time. She was crying and screaming. I will never forget what she was screaming and why she was so angry with me. She was screaming: "You didn't tell me that she would get cold!" In fact, I had not warned Susan's mother that her daughter's body would get cold and strangely very heavy as she sat there holding her.

Does the mother's natural reaction tell us something about the importance we place on the biological dividing line between life and death, even apart from philosophical views about personhood? Did she correctly feel closer to her daughter while her body was warm? Is this a distinction we should perhaps maintain even when a body is being kept alive by the use of a respirator?

10. Some religions do not accept that a person who meets the whole-brain-death criteria is in fact dead. Should the law be changed to allow for such views? The First Amendment to the Constitution provides that Congress "shall make no law respecting an establishment of religion, or prohibiting the free exercise thereof." It is often difficult to determine when a neutral law (one

not directed at religious beliefs in general or a specific religion) must provide for religious exemptions because otherwise it would unduly burden the free exercise of a religion. Thus, for example, the Supreme Court has held that the federal government could ban the practice of polygamy, even though this was an important part of Mormon religious duties, *Reynolds v. United States*, 98 U.S. 145 (1878):

> Laws are made for the government of actions, and while they cannot interfere with mere religious belief and opinions, they may with practices. Suppose one believed that human sacrifices were a necessary part of religious worship, would it be seriously contended that the civil government under which he lived could not interfere to prevent a sacrifice? Or if a wife religiously believed it was her duty to burn herself upon the funeral pile of her dead husband, would it be beyond the power of the civil government to prevent her carrying her belief into practice? So here, as a law of the organization of society under the exclusive dominion of the United States, it is provided that plural marriages shall not be allowed. Can a man excuse his practices to the contrary because of this religious belief? To permit this would be to make the professed doctrines of religious belief superior to the law of the land, and in effect to permit every citizen to become a law unto himself.

On the other hand, secular laws have at times been found to interfere inappropriately with religious practices. In *Wisconsin v. Yoder*, 406 U.S. 205 (1972), the Supreme Court determined that the Amish need not comply with a Wisconsin law that required children to attend school until age 16. The Court observed that it was necessary to balance the state interest against the religious interests being asserted, and that "only those [governmental] interests of the highest order . . . can overbalance legitimate claims of free exercise."

What outcome would you expect if a state brain-death law were challenged on religious grounds? Two states (New Jersey by statute and New York by regulations) have specifically provided that a person who did not believe in the concept of brain death cannot be declared dead using brain death criteria. Here is an excerpt from the New Jersey law, N.J. Rev. Stat. § 26:6A-5 (1999):

> The death of an individual shall not be declared upon the basis of neurological criteria . . . when the licensed physician authorized to declare death, has reason to believe . . . that such a declaration would violate the personal religious beliefs of the individual. In these cases, death shall be declared, and the time of death fixed, solely upon the basis of cardio-respiratory criteria pursuant to section 2 of this act.

Is it appropriate to allow religious exceptions to the secular definition of death? Should determining when somebody is dead be considered an important core value of the society that cannot be overridden by religious practices?[3]

In any event, is there really any need to modify the definition of death in order to accommodate the religious views of those who do not accept brain death?

What if we merely said that such persons are dead, but it is permissible for their bodies to be kept alive using life-sustaining treatment? In this way the state would be maintaining the integrity of the definition of death, yet the religious practitioners could conduct themselves in exactly the way they desired.

IN RE T.A.C.P.

Supreme Court of Florida

609 So. 2d 588 (Fla. 1992)

OPINION BY JUSTICE KOGAN:

. . . At or about the eighth month of pregnancy, the parents of the child T.A.C.P. were informed that she would be born with anencephaly. This is a birth defect invariably fatal, in which the child typically is born with only a "brain stem" but otherwise lacks a human brain. In T.A.C.P.'s case, the back of the skull was entirely missing and the brain stem was exposed to the air, except for medical bandaging. The risk of infection to the brain stem was considered very high. Anencephalic infants sometimes can survive several days after birth because the brain stem has a limited capacity to maintain autonomic bodily functions such as breathing and heartbeat. This ability soon ceases, however, in the absence of regulation from the missing brain.

In this case, T.A.C.P. actually survived only a few days after birth. The medical evidence in the record shows that the child T.A.C.P. was incapable of developing any sort of cognitive process, may have been unable to feel pain or experience sensation due to the absence of the upper brain, and at least for part of the time was placed on a mechanical ventilator to assist her breathing. At the time of the hearing below, however, the child was breathing unaided, although she died soon thereafter.

On the advice of physicians, the parents continued the pregnancy to term and agreed that the mother would undergo caesarean section during birth. The parents agreed to the caesarean procedure with the express hope that the infant's organs would be less damaged and could be used for transplant in other sick children. Although T.A.C.P. had no hope of life herself, the parents both testified in court that they wanted to use this opportunity to give life to others. However, when the parents requested that T.A.C.P. be declared legally dead for this purpose, her health care providers refused out of concern that they thereby might incur civil or criminal liability.

The parents then filed a petition in the circuit court asking for a judicial determination. . . . We have accepted jurisdiction to resolve this case of first impression.

II. THE MEDICAL NATURE OF ANENCEPHALY

Although appellate courts appear never to have confronted the issue, there already is an impressive body of published medical scholarship on anencephaly. From our review of this material, we find that anencephaly is a variable but fairly well defined medical condition. Experts in the field have written that anencephaly is the most common severe birth defect of the central nervous system seen in the United States, although it apparently has existed throughout human history.

A statement by the Medical Task Force on Anencephaly ("Task Force") printed in the New England Journal of Medicine generally described "anencephaly" as "a congenital absence of major portions of the brain, skull, and scalp, with its genesis in the first month of gestation." The large opening in the skull accompanied by the absence or severe congenital disruption of the cerebral hemispheres is the characteristic feature of the condition. . . .

The Task Force defined anencephaly as diagnosable only when all of the following four criteria are present:

(1) A large portion of the skull is absent. (2) The scalp, which extends to the margin of the bone, is absent over the skull defect. (3) Hemorrhagic, fibrotic tissue is exposed because of defects in the skull and scalp. (4) Recognizable cerebral hemispheres are absent.

Anencephaly is often, though not always, accompanied by defects in various other body organs and systems, some of which may render the child unsuitable for organ transplantation.

Thus, it is clear that anencephaly is distinguishable from some other congenital conditions because its extremity renders it uniformly lethal. . . . We emphasize that the child T.A.C.P. clearly met the four criteria described above. . . .

The Task Force stated that most reported anencephalic children die within the first few days after birth, with survival any longer being rare. After reviewing all available medical literature, the Task Force found no study in which survival beyond a week exceeded nine percent of children meeting the four criteria. Two months was the longest confirmed survival of an anencephalic, although there are unconfirmed reports of one surviving three months and another surviving fourteen months. The Task Force reported, however, that these survival rates are confounded somewhat by the variable degrees of medical care afforded to anencephalics. Some such infants may be given considerable life support while others may be given much less care.

The Task Force reported that the medical consequences of anencephaly can be established with some certainty. All anencephalics by definition are permanently unconscious because they lack the cerebral cortex necessary for conscious thought. Their condition thus is quite similar to that of persons in a persistent vegetative state. Where the brain stem is functioning, as it was here, spontaneous breathing and heartbeat can occur. In addition, such infants may show spontaneous movements of the extremities, "startle" reflexes, and pupils that respond to light. Some may show feeding reflexes, may cough, hiccup, or exhibit eye movements, and may produce facial expressions.

The question of whether such infants actually suffer from pain is somewhat more complex. It involves a distinction between "pain" and "suffering." The Task Force indicated that anencephaly in some ways is analogous to persons with cerebral brain lesions. Such lesions may not actually eliminate the reflexive response to a painful condition, but they can eliminate any capacity to "suffer" as a result of the condition. Likewise, anencephalic infants may reflexively avoid painful stimuli where the brain stem is functioning and thus is able to command an innate, unconscious withdrawal response; but the infants presumably lack the capacity to suffer. It is clear, however, that this incapacity to suffer has not been established beyond all doubt.

After the advent of new transplant methods in the past few decades, anencephalic infants have successfully been used as a source of organs for donation. However, the Task Force was able to identify only twelve successful transplants using anencephalic organs by 1990. Transplants were most successful when the anencephalic immediately was placed on life support and its organs used as soon as possible, without regard to the existence of brain-stem activity. However, this only accounted for a total of four reported transplants.

There appears to be general agreement that anencephalics usually have ceased to be suitable organ donors by the time they meet all the criteria for "whole brain death," i.e., the complete absence of brain-stem function. There also is no doubt that a need exists for infant organs for transplantation. Nationally, between thirty and fifty percent of children under two years of age who need transplants die while waiting for organs to become available.

III. LEGAL DEFINITIONS OF "DEATH" & "LIFE"

As the parties and *amici* have argued, the common law in some American jurisdictions recognized a cardiopulmonary definition of "death": A human being was not considered dead until breathing and heartbeat had stopped entirely, without possibility of resuscitation.

However, there is some doubt about the exact method by which this definition was imported into the law of some states. Apparently the definition was taken from earlier editions of *Black's Law Dictionary*, which itself did not cite to an original source. The definition thus may only have been the opinion of Black's earlier editors.

We have found no authority showing that Florida ever recognized the original *Black's Law Dictionary* definition or any other definition of "death" as a matter of our own common law. Even if we had adopted such a standard, however, it is equally clear that modern medical technology has rendered the earlier Black's definition of "death" seriously inadequate. With the invention of life-support devices and procedures, human bodies can be made to breathe and blood to circulate even in the utter absence of brain function.

As a result, the ability to withhold or discontinue such life support created distinct legal problems in light of the "cardiopulmonary" definition of death originally used by Black's Dictionary. For example, health care providers might be civilly or criminally liable for removing transplantable organs from a person sustained by life support, or defendants charged with homicide might argue that their victim's death actually was caused when life support was discontinued.

In light of the inadequacies of a cardiopulmonary definition of "death," a number of jurisdictions began altering their laws in an attempt to address the medical community's changing conceptions of the point in time at which life ceases. An effort was made to synthesize many of the new concerns into a Uniform Determination of Death Act issued by the National Conference of Commissioners on Uniform State Laws. The uniform statute states:

> An individual who has sustained either (1) irreversible cessation of circulatory and respiratory functions, or (2) irreversible cessation of all functions of the entire brain, including the brain stem, is dead. A determination of death must be made in accordance with accepted medical standards.

Unif. Determination of Death Act §1, 12 U.L.A. 340 (Supp. 1991). Thus, the uniform act both codified the earlier common law standard and extended it to deal with the specific problem of "whole brain death." While some American jurisdictions appear to have adopted substantially the same language, Florida is not among these.

Indeed, Florida appears to have struck out on its own. The statute cited as controlling by the trial court does not actually address itself to the problem of anencephalic infants, nor indeed to *any* situation other than patients actually being sustained by artificial life support. The statute provides:

> For legal and medical purposes, *where respiratory and circulatory functions are maintained by artificial means of support* so as to preclude a determination that these functions have ceased, the occurrence of death *may* be determined where there is the irreversible cessation of the functioning of the entire brain, including the brain stem, determined in accordance with this section.

A later subsection goes on to declare:

> Except for a diagnosis of brain death, the standard set forth in this section is not the exclusive standard for determining death or for the withdrawal of life-support systems.

This language is highly significant for two reasons.

First, the statute does not purport to codify the common law standard applied in some other jurisdictions, as does the uniform act. The use of the permissive word "may" in the statute in tandem with the savings clause of [this section] buttresses the conclusion that the legislature envisioned other ways of defining "death." Second, the statutory framers clearly did not intend to apply the statute's language to the anencephalic infant not being kept alive by life support. To the contrary, the framers expressly limited the statute to that situation in which "respiratory and circulatory functions are maintained by artificial means of support." . . .

From [other Florida statutory] definitions, it is clear that T.A.C.P. was a "live birth" and not a "fetal death," at least for purposes of the collection of vital statistics in Florida. These definitions obviously are inapplicable to the issues at hand today, but they do shed some light on the Florida legislature's thoughts regarding a definition of "life" and "death."

Similarly, an analogous (if distinguishable) problem has arisen in Florida tort law. In cases alleging wrongful death, our courts have held that fetuses are not "persons" and are not "born alive" until they acquire an existence separate and independent from the mother. We believe the height of the evidence supports the conclusion that T.A.C.P. was "alive" in this sense because she was separated from the womb, and was capable of breathing and maintaining a heartbeat independently of her mother's body for some duration of time thereafter. Once again, however, this conclusion arises from law that is only analogous and is not dispositive of the issue at hand.

We also note that the 1988 Florida Legislature considered a bill that would have defined "death" to include anencephaly. The bill died in committee. While the failure of legislation in committee does not establish legislative intent, it nevertheless supports the conclusion that as recently as 1988 no consensus existed among Florida's lawmakers regarding the issue we confront today.

The parties have cited to no authorities directly dealing with the question of whether anencephalics are "alive" or "dead." Our own research has disclosed no other federal or Florida law or precedent arguably on point or applicable by analogy. We thus are led to the conclusion that no legal authority binding upon this Court has decided whether an anencephalic child is alive for purposes of organ donation. In the absence of applicable legal authority, this Court must weigh and consider the public policy considerations at stake here.

IV. COMMON LAW & POLICY

Initially, we must start by recognizing that [a Florida statute] provides a method for determining death in those cases in which a person's respiratory and circulatory functions are maintained artificially. Likewise, we agree that a cardiopulmonary definition of death must be accepted in Florida as a matter of our common law, applicable whenever [that statute] does not govern. Thus, if cardiopulmonary function is not being maintained artificially as stated in [that statute], a person is dead who has sustained irreversible cessation of circulatory and respiratory functions as determined in accordance with accepted medical standards. We have found no credible authority arguing that this definition is inconsistent with the existence of death, and we therefore need not labor the point further.

The question remaining is whether there is good reason in public policy for this Court to create an additional common law standard applicable to anencephalics. Alterations of the common law, while rarely entertained or allowed, are within this Court's prerogative. However, the rule we follow is that the common law will not be altered or expanded unless demanded by public necessity, or where required to vindicate fundamental rights. We believe, for example, that our adoption of the cardiopulmonary definition of death today is required by public necessity and, in any event, merely formalizes what has been the common practice in this state for well over a century.

Such is not the case with petitioners' request. Our review of the medical, ethical, and legal literature on anencephaly discloses absolutely no consensus that public necessity or fundamental rights will be better served by granting this request.

We are not persuaded that a public necessity exists to justify this action, in light of the other factors in this case—although we acknowledge much ambivalence about this particular question. We have been deeply touched by the altruism and unquestioned motives of the parents of T.A.C.P. The parents have shown great humanity, compassion, and concern for others. The problem we as a Court must face, however, is that the medical literature shows unresolved controversy over the extent to which anencephalic organs can or should be used in transplants.

There is an unquestioned need for transplantable infant organs. Yet some medical commentators suggest that the organs of anencephalics are seldom usable, for a variety of reasons, and that so few organ transplants will be possible from anencephalics as to render the enterprise questionable in light of the ethical problems at stake—even if legal restrictions were lifted.

Others note that prenatal screening now is substantially reducing the number of anencephalics born each year in the United States and that, consequently, anencephalics are unlikely to be a significant source of organs as time passes. And still others have frankly acknowledged that there is no consensus and that redefinition of death in this content should await the emergence of a consensus. . . .

Some legal commentators have urged that treating anencephalics as dead equates them with "nonpersons," presenting a "slippery slope" problem with regard to all other persons who lack cognition for whatever reason. Others have quoted physicians involved in infant-organ transplants as stating, "[T]he slippery slope is real," because some physicians have proposed transplants from infants with defects less severe than anencephaly.

We express no opinion today about who is right and who is wrong on these issues—if any "right" or "wrong" can be found here. The salient point is that no consensus exists as to: (a) the utility of organ transplants of the type at issue here; (b) the ethical issues involved; or (c) the legal and constitutional problems implicated.

V. CONCLUSIONS

Accordingly, we find no basis to expand the common law to equate anencephaly with death. We acknowledge the possibility that some infants' lives might be saved by using organs from anencephalics who do not meet the traditional definition of "death" we reaffirm today. But weighed against this is the utter lack of consensus, and the questions about the overall utility of such organ donations. The scales clearly tip in favor of not extending the common law in this instance.

NOTES AND QUESTIONS:
In re T.A.C.P.

1. This case, like *Bowman*, clearly represents the uniform legal conclusion on this issue. No court has ever declared that anencephalics can be considered dead, nor has any state passed such a statute.
2. As the court notes, the anencephalic is very much like what other category of brain-damaged person that you should be very familiar with by now? Why are these two groups so similar?
3. Can you understand why legislatures have been so reluctant to declare anencephalics dead? Find the passage where the court describes how these infants "behave." What does that description remind you of? You might again ask yourself, to what extent do we have a natural instinct to value the miracle of life—and, more specifically, human life—even in the absence of personhood?
4. This court is no doubt correct in its conclusion that it would be inappropriate for it to rewrite the definition of death. As a court, it merely interprets the law. Changing the law, and making policy, is left to the legislature.

   But assuming you were the legislature, should anencephalics be declared dead? To answer this question, you will need to revisit the issues raised in *Bowman*. Assuming that you choose to reject a whole body definition of death, there are still two remaining options: whole brain or higher brain. Which of these is truer to the philosophical reasons for deciding to look at the brain in determining when a human being is dead? Are there other reasons for choosing one of these over the other?
5. Does this case, and the arguments discussed above, have any relevance to what definition of death we should apply to persons who are not anencephalics? What are the arguments for moving to a higher brain definition of death? Which persons would be declared dead under that standard who are now considered to be alive? What negative consequences might take place as a result of that change? If we wanted to make such a change, does it make sense to first limit it to anencephalics?
6. Do we need to change the definition of death to accomplish the goals of both the parents of T.A.C.P. and those who are in favor of transplanting the

organs of anencephalics? Could we recognize that a child like T.A.C.P. is alive, but nonetheless that it might be appropriate—given her medical condition—to accelerate her inevitable death in a way that allows her life to have additional meaning? What criminal laws might we have to change to allow this practice?

This type of change would be highly controversial among many in the organ transplant community. Currently, there is an informal practice known as the "dead donor" rule; it states that organs should not be removed from a donor before death, but only after death has been declared. The fear is that if this rule is not followed, the number of organ donors might decrease, since patients might worry that organs are being removed from them before their deaths.[4]

THE HEART-LUNG CRITERIA FOR DEATH: EVERYTHING OLD IS NEW AGAIN

In *Bowman* the court observed: "Until recently, the definition of death was both medically and legally a relatively simple matter. When the heart stopped beating and the lungs stopped breathing, the individual was dead according to physicians and according to the law." In fact, however, even this "relatively simple matter" is now generating a great deal of controversy.

Historically, after a person was found without a heartbeat and not breathing, there was usually no need to ascertain the *exact* moment of death. Typically, the person might be found in a bedroom or a hospital room. Then a doctor would be called who would "pronounce" death minutes or even hours later.

Recently, however, there have been efforts to have persons who die in this usual manner serve as organ donors. Presently, the majority of people who give organs at the time of their deaths are pronounced dead using brain-death, not heart-lung (cardiopulmonary), criteria. Allowing organs to be donated by people who die when their hearts and lungs stop functioning ("non-heart-beating donors") could substantially increase the number of organs available for transplantation.

There is a difficulty in getting usable organs from these people, however. When a person's heart stops beating, the blood is no longer circulating, and therefore the rest of the organs are not receiving any oxygen. These organs then begin to deteriorate. If we wish to use these organs for transplantation purposes, we would like to declare the person dead as soon as possible, before the deterioration becomes irreversible. (We are assuming that it would not be possible to take the organs out *before* the person is pronounced dead. What legal problem might we need to address if we did not wait?) Thus, it has become extremely important to specify *exactly how long we must wait* after a person's heart has stopped beating and the person has stopped breathing before concluding the person is dead.

The person whose heart stops while home alone will obviously not be found in time for her organs to be useful for transplantation. Organs deteriorate in minutes without blood flow, so the only possible donors are people who die in hospitals, with doctors ready to begin removing the organs immediately. The ideal candidate is someone for whom we can control the moment of death. Consider a person—call him Fred—who has a terminal illness and has decided to die by refusing medical care (like Ms. Bouvia). For example, Fred might have Lou Gehrig's disease (also known as amyotrophic lateral sclerosis), which gradually decreases his ability to control his muscles. After a time, such a person cannot breathe on his own, and would need to be put on a respirator to be kept alive. But after months or years on the respirator, as the disease continues to progress, that person might choose to die by having the respirator turned off. He might also wish, however, to have some good come of his death by donating his organs.

So we might arrange to take Fred to an operating room in preparation for this procedure. The respirator will be turned off. The following events will then take place, in this order:

1. Fred will immediately stop breathing, since the respirator was the only thing that enabled him to breathe.
2. After several minutes, due to a lack of oxygen, his heart will stop beating.
3. After a few minutes more, the heart not only will have stopped, but it will not be able to restart on its own. (After point 2 has been reached, a heart will occasionally try to begin beating again on its own, which is called "auto-resuscitation.") On the other hand, there is still a significant possibility at this time that the heart could be restarted by medical intervention, such as by using electrical stimulation via the crash cart paddles that you see in television shows like *E.R.*
4. A few minutes later, the heart will be so damaged (due to continued lack of oxygen) that even with medical intervention, it would be impossible to start it beating again. However, even at this point, portions of Fred's brain might not be irreversibly damaged: if one were to begin passing oxygenated blood through them, they might begin functioning again (though in a very damaged way, most likely).
5. A few minutes after that, the entire brain—both upper and lower portions—will be irreversibly damaged.

At which of these times is Fred dead? In response to controversy about whether organs were being removed from people like Fred before they were truly dead (including a segment on *60 Minutes* broadcast on April 13, 1997), the General Counsel's office of the United States Department of Health and Human Services commissioned a not-for-profit organization that advises the federal government on medical issues, the Institute of Medicine, to determine when such people are both legally and ethically dead under the Uniform Determination of Death Act. This is the law that the *Bowman* court chose to adopt for Washington state. It has also been adopted by legislatures in a majority of states.

The relevant part of this act states that a person can be declared dead when he or she has sustained "irreversible cessation of circulatory and respiratory function." The Institute, using that definition, concluded that a person like Fred could be declared dead at time (3), the time after which the heart will not begin beating on its own.[5] It determined that the ability to medically intervene to restart the heart was not relevant in determining irreversible cessation of function, since the patient did not want anyone to do that: restarting the heart would have been morally and legally wrong based on the patient's wishes, and thus these options should not be considered in evaluating irreversibility. The Institute also determined that it was irrelevant that the person might not have suffered irreversible loss of all brain function at time (3), since he was being declared dead based on a definition that only referred to heart and lung functions.

The federal government commissioned a second report from the Institute, which was issued in 1999, so that states can begin to implement the Institute's recommendations and obtain more organs from such donors.

NOTES AND QUESTIONS:
The Heart-Lung Criteria for Death

1. How should the irreversibility requirement in the Uniform Determination of Death Act be interpreted? Should it refer to "moral" reversibility, as argued by the Institute: circulation has irreversibly been lost so long as the patient does not want anyone to restart the heart? (In a real sense, these patients are permitted to "wish themselves" to death, since their desires, independent of what happens to them, control whether or not they are dead.) Or should it refer to "scientific" reversibility: so long as we can restart the heart, loss of circulation is not irreversible? Which of these definitions fits with our understanding of the dividing line between being alive and being dead?

2. Is it appropriate to have a definition of death that permits a person to be declared legally dead, and then to have the person come back to life? Imagine that Fred's heart has stopped, and we have waited enough minutes so that we are certain the heart will not restart on its own. Under the Institute definition of irreversibility, Fred can be declared legally dead.

    Fred's wife then barges into the operating room, distraught, waving a gun and demanding that he be brought back to life. The doctors are able to restart his heart, and they turn on the ventilator again. He has suffered some brain damage, but he is certainly now alive by virtually anyone's definition.

Comment on whether this type of scenario has any bearing on the acceptability of the Institute's interpretation of irreversibility.
3. One of the organs that can be donated is a heart. Thus, after declaring Fred dead, his heart might be quickly removed and later used to replace the failing heart of some other person. Is it consistent to claim that Fred has died due to "irreversible" cessation of cardiac function when the source of that cardiac function—his heart—may well function for years in someone else's body?
4. A separate issue raised by the use of non-heart-beating donors relates to whether a person can ever be declared dead—even by the classic heart-lung criteria—if all of that person's brain has not yet irreversibly ceased functioning. In other words, can a person be declared dead at a point when, if we restarted heart and lung function, portions of the brain might be brought back to normal functioning?

To understand why this is a problem, let us reexamine the Uniform Determination of Death Act:

An individual who has sustained either
(1) irreversible cessation of circulatory and respiratory functions, or
(2) irreversible cessation of all functions of the entire brain, including the brain stem, is dead.

We are talking about declaring a person dead under clause (1), which only refers to heart and lung function, and says nothing about the brain. Thus, from the wording alone, there is a good argument in favor of the Institute's conclusion that brain function is irrelevant for purposes of clause (1).

However, the history behind the drafting of the Uniform Act—which was partially reviewed in *Bowman*—suggests otherwise. The early statutes that first recognized brain death (as in Kansas) suggested that there were two distinct concepts of death, heart-lung death and brain death, and they had nothing to do with one another. Later statutes went in a very different direction, suggesting that both prongs for determining death were merely different ways to measure a single underlying condition. The extreme of this view was the language in an early (1979) version of a proposed uniform law, as discussed in *Bowman*:

For legal and medical purposes, an individual who has sustained irreversible cessation of all functioning of the brain, including the brain stem, is dead. A determination under this section must be made in accordance with reasonable medical standards.

This language makes it very clear that the underlying concept determining whether a person is dead or not is whether brain function still exists.

Ultimately, that version of the uniform law was rejected, largely because it was too cryptic in not mentioning the classic heart and lung criteria for declaring someone dead. (Those details were subsumed in the second sentence, which left it to the medical profession to determine the medical standards.) As the *Bowman* court noted, that definition "does not clarify how the concept of brain death is interrelated with the more traditional definition of death as the cessation of respiration and circulation." In contrast, it felt that the current language in the Uniform Determination of Death Act "harmonizes" the two sets of criteria.

Based on this history, one might argue the current language of the Uniform Act is intended to mean the following:

> An individual who has sustained irreversible cessation of all functions of the entire brain is dead. This may be demonstrated by either of two sets of criteria:
>
> (1) Irreversible loss of heart and lung function *for a long enough period* so that we are certain that the cessation of brain function is irreversible.
>
> (2) Direct measurement of brain function so as to demonstrate the irreversible loss of brain function.

Indeed, only such an interpretation can fully harmonize the two criteria in the statute and make it clear that they are referring to a single underlying concept of death.

5. The *60 Minutes* segment noted that a number of protocols for using non-heart-beating donors suggest that "if there is doubt about the patient's ability to experience pain," it might be appropriate to provide pain medication even after the patient has been declared dead. This provision in such a protocol actually makes sense, so long as a person can be declared dead in a way that does not assure that the brain had fully and irreversibly stopped functioning. Of course, the fact that it makes sense to provide such medication to a dead person might equally suggest that there is something wrong with such a definition of death.

6. It is not just the legislative history of the Uniform Determination of Death Act that supports the need for looking to brain function when declaring someone dead using heart-lung criteria. Consider the following heretofore unchallenged statement from an editorial in the New England Journal of Medicine:[6]

> Indeed, it is clear that a person is not dead unless his brain is dead. The time-honored criteria of stoppage of the heartbeat and circulation are indicative of death only when they persist long enough for the brain to die.

7. Do you agree with the definition of death currently being promulgated by the federal government and the Institute? Is the definition of death being gerrymandered to allow the use of non-heart-beating donors?

There is an alternative solution to this dilemma that would allow the use of organs from non-heart-beating donors. As suggested in the discussion of anencephalics, we could acknowledge that the donors are not yet dead at the time we begin organ removal, and modify the law so that it is permissible to remove the organs at such a time. Do you think such a solution is likely to be accepted? Why or why not?[7]

Endnotes

1. See, e.g., Robert D. Truog, "Is It Time to Abandon Brain Death?" 27(1) *Hastings Ctr. Rep.* 29 (1997); James L. Bernat, "A Defense of the Whole-Brain Concept of Death," 28(2) *Hastings Ctr. Rep.* 14 (1998).
2. See Stuart J. Youngner et al., " 'Brain Death' and Organ Retrieval: A Cross-sectional Survey of Knowledge and Concepts among Health Professionals," 261 *JAMA* 2205 (1989).
3. See, e.g., Robert S. Olick, "Brain Death, Religious Freedom, and Public Policy: New Jersey's Landmark Legislative Initiative," 1 *Kennedy Inst. of Ethics J.* 275 (1991); Robert M. Veatch, "The Conscience Clause: How Much Individual Choice in Defining Death Can Our Society Tolerate?", in *The Definition of Death: Contemporary Controversies*, Stuart J. Youngner et al., eds. (Baltimore: Johns Hopkins University Press, 1999), at 137.
4. See, e.g., Robert M. Arnold and Stuart J. Youngner, "The Dead Donor Rule: Should We Stretch It, Bend It, or Abandon It?", 3 *Kennedy Inst. of Ethics J.* 263 (1993).
5. Institute of Medicine, *Non-heart-beating Organ Transplantation: Medical and Ethical Issues in Procurement* at 58–59 (Washington, D.C.: National Academy Press, 1997).
6. W.H. Sweet, "Brain Death," 299 *New Eng. J. Med.* 410 (1978).
7. For more on these issues, see *Kennedy Institute of Ethics Journal*, 3(2) (1993), devoted entirely to the question of the non-heart-beating donor; Jerry Menikoff, "Doubts about Death: The Silence of the Institute of Medicine," 26 *J. Law, Med. & Ethics* 157 (1998); John T. Potts, Jr. et al., "Commentary: Clear Thinking and Open Discussion Guide IOM's Report on Organ Donation," 26 *J. Law, Med. & Ethics* 166 (1998).

16

Organ Transplantation

The last thing the traveler remembers until they wake up in a hotel room bathtub, their body submerged to their neck in ice, is sipping that drink. There is a note taped to the wall instructing them not to move and to call 911. . . . The business traveler is instructed by the 911 operator to very slowly and carefully reach behind them and feel if there is a tube protruding from their lower back. The business traveler finds the tube and answers, "Yes." . . . The operator knows that both of the business traveler's kidneys have been harvested.

An "urban legend"

The field of organ transplantation allows us to visit—in a very stark, life-or-death arena—some of the most challenging issues in law and bioethics. How should we obtain organs for transplantation? To answer this question we must reexamine how the law determines the extent of a person's obligation to others. Who should get the organs? To answer this question we must deal with the tragic choice of allocating a scarce resource, knowing that our conclusions will sentence some people to certain death.

As you read the cases in this chapter, pay particular attention to the distinct issues raised by these two very different questions. Think also about how different ways to obtain organs may or may not have consequences for who gets organs. Is it possible to design systems that fully separate these two functions? Why might we want to do that?

McFall v. Shimp

Allegheny County Court (Pennsylvania)

10 Pa. D. & C. 3d 90 (1978)

OPINION BY JUDGE FLAHERTY:

Plaintiff, Robert McFall, suffers from a rare bone marrow disease and the prognosis for his survival is very dim, unless he receives a bone marrow transplant from a compatible donor. Finding a compatible donor is a very difficult task and limited to a selection among close relatives. After a search and certain tests, it has been determined that only defendant is suitable as a donor. Defendant refuses to submit to the necessary transplant, and before the court is a request for a preliminary injunction which seeks to compel defendant to submit to further tests, and, eventually, the bone marrow transplant.

. . . The question posed by plaintiff is that, in order to save the life of one of its members by the only means available, may society infringe upon one's absolute right to his "bodily security"?

The common law has consistently held to a rule which provides that one human being is under no legal compulsion to give aid or take action to save another human being or to rescue. A great deal has been written regarding this rule which, on the surface, appears to be revolting in a moral sense. Introspection, however, will demonstrate that the rule is founded upon the very essence of our free society. It is noteworthy that counsel for plaintiff has cited authority which has developed in other societies in support of plaintiff's request in this instance. Our society, contrary to many others, has as its first principle, the respect for the individual, and that society and government exist to protect the individual from being invaded and hurt by another. Many societies adopt a contrary view which has the individual existing to serve the society as a whole. In preserving such a society as we have, it is bound to happen that great moral conflicts will arise and will appear harsh in a given instance. In this case, the chancellor is being asked to force one member of society to undergo a medical procedure which would provide that part of that individual's body would be removed from him and given to another so that the other could live. Morally, this decision rests with the defendant, and, in the view of the court, the refusal of defendant is morally indefensible. For our law to *compel* defendant to submit to an intrusion of his body would change every concept and principle upon which our society is founded. To do so would defeat the sanctity of the individual, and would impose a rule which would know no limits, and one could not imagine where the line would be drawn.

The request is not to be compared with an action at law for damages, but rather is an action in equity before a chancellor, which, in the ultimate, if granted, would require the forcible submission to the medical procedure. For a society which respects the rights of *one* individual, to sink its teeth into the jugular vein or neck of one of its members and suck from it sustenance for *another* member, is revolting to our hard-wrought concepts of jurisprudence. Forcible extraction of living tissue causes revulsion to the judicial mind. Such would raise the spectre of the swastika and the Inquisition, reminiscent of the horrors this portends. . . .

NOTES AND QUESTIONS:
McFall v. Shimp

1. Living donation (as opposed to cadaveric donation, at the time of a patient's death) plays an increasingly large role in organ transplantation. During 1998 there were 4,122 living donors, nearly equaling the 5,791 cadaveric donors.[1] Of course, a living donor usually donates only a single organ, whereas multiple organs are obtained from most cadaveric donors, so that the latter group generates a much higher percentage of the total organs. In addition, vital organs—such as hearts—can only come from cadaveric donors. (Why can't a living person donate his heart? What legal problem would arise? An episode of the *Ally McBeal* television show attempted to get around this difficulty by having the donor swap his healthy heart for the diseased heart of the recipient. For the possible problems with an organ swap, see the notes after *Wilson v. Adkins*, below.)

2. David Shimp was Robert McFall's first cousin. McFall died of his aplastic anemia within three weeks of the court's decision, noting that he forgave his cousin. As a result of the publicity given to the case, thousands of people had volunteered to be tested as possible donors for McFall.

3. Based on what we have already covered in this book, do you think the court is right in concluding that the common law "has consistently held that one human being is under no legal compulsion to give aid or take action to save another human being or to rescue?" Where did we previously come across a reference to the *McFall* case, with regard to this very issue?

   As noted in chapter 6, most good Samaritan laws merely provide that a person who goes to the aid of another cannot be sued for acting negligently. Suppose a state wrote a more stringent law, making it a crime for someone not to go the aid of another in circumstances where there would be no risk to the Samaritan. Would it be constitutional?

4. The conclusion reached by the judge in *McFall* with regard to organ donation represents the generally accepted law in this country. There do not appear to be any court decisions, nor any statutes, that require people to donate organs against their will.

5. Whatever the common law might be, a legislature can pass a statute that changes the law. What would happen if a legislature passed a statute that did require a person to "use parts of his body" to help someone else? Would

such a law be constitutional? Do the cases dealing with abortion and maternal-fetal conflict help answer this question?

Another area that might lend some insight involves attempts to gain bodily evidence of crimes from criminal defendants. The Supreme Court has addressed this issue a number of times. In one case, *Winston v. Lee*, 470 U.S. 753 (1985), the Court concluded that a defendant could not be forced to undergo a surgical procedure to have a bullet removed. A major issue in the case was the Fourth Amendment, which protects the "right of the people to be secure in their persons . . . against unreasonable searches and seizures." Whether or not that is relevant to what we are discussing, the Court also spoke of the broader concerns relating to an individual's privacy interests, concluding that "[t]he reasonableness of any surgical intrusion beneath the skin depends on a case-by-case approach, in which the individual's interests in privacy and security are weighed against society's interests in conducting the procedure." Does this rejection of a bright-line ban on mandated procedures in favor of a balancing of interests seem consistent with the themes developed by this Court and others in the abortion and maternal-fetal conflict areas?

6. Evaluate the constitutionality of the following laws:
   a. A new medical procedure allows certain cancers of the immune system to be cured. It requires, however, cells from a healthy person who has a particular genetic pattern similar to that of the sick person. The cells can be obtained just by gently wiping the inside of a person's mouth with a swab. A state passes a law that requires such a person to consent to the collection and use of cells in this manner. (Assume that the healthy person has been identified in a manner that does not otherwise violate that person's rights.)
   b. Assume the same facts as in example (a), except that to collect the cells a single blood drawing is required, of the same amount of blood given if someone were donating blood.
   c. The state passes a law that certain blood relatives of a person with cancers affecting the bone marrow must undergo testing and, based on that testing, may be required to consent to being a bone marrow donor. Donating bone marrow is somewhat uncomfortable, but the donor's bone marrow will regenerate, and the risk to the donor's health is minimal. (The law excludes persons for whom donation might indeed be a health risk.)
   d. Assume the same facts as in (c), except that the law relates to persons with kidney failure and requires the donor to give up a kidney. While the risks are low, the donation itself requires a major intraabdominal surgical procedure. In addition, although a person can usually live a perfectly healthy life with just one kidney, any injury to the remaining kidney would cause a major health problem.

STRUNK V. STRUNK

Court of Appeals of Kentucky

445 S.W.2d 145 (Ky. 1969)

OPINION BY JUDGE OSBORNE:

The specific question involved upon this appeal is: Does a court of equity have the power to permit a kidney to be removed from an incompetent ward of the state upon petition of his committee, who is also his mother, for the purpose of being transplanted into the body of his brother, who is dying of a fatal kidney disease? We are of the opinion it does.

The facts of the case are as follows: Arthur L. Strunk, 54 years of age, and Ava Strunk, 52 years of age, of Williamstown, Kentucky, are the parents of two sons. Tommy Strunk is 28 years of age, married, an employee of the Penn State Railroad and a part-time student at the University of Cincinnati. Tommy is now suffering from chronic glomerulus nephritis, a fatal kidney disease. He is now being kept alive by frequent treatment on an artificial kidney, a procedure which cannot be continued much longer.

Jerry Strunk is 27 years of age, incompetent, and through proper legal proceedings has been committed to the Frankfort State Hospital and School, which is a state institution maintained for the feebleminded. He has an I.Q. of approximately 35, which corresponds with the mental age of approximately six years. He is further handicapped by a speech defect, which makes it difficult for him to communicate with persons who are not well acquainted with him. When it was determined that Tommy, in order to survive, would have to have a kidney the doctors considered the possibility of using a kidney from a cadaver if and when one became available or one from a live donor if this could be made available. The entire family, his mother, father and a number of collateral relatives were tested. Because of incompatibility of blood type or tissue none were medically acceptable as live donors. As a last resort, Jerry was tested and found to be highly acceptable. This immediately presented the legal problem as to what, if anything, could be done by the family, especially the mother and the father to procure a transplant from Jerry to Tommy. The mother as a committee petitioned the county court for authority to proceed with the operation. The court found that the operation was necessary, that under the peculiar circumstances of this case it would not only be beneficial to Tommy but also beneficial to Jerry because Jerry was greatly dependent upon Tommy, emotionally and psychologically, and that his well-being would be jeopardized more severely by the loss of his brother than by the removal of a kidney. . . .

Upon this appeal we are faced with the fact that all members of the immediate family have recommended the transplant. The Department of Mental Health has likewise made its recommendation. The county court has given its approval. The circuit court has found that it would be to the best interest of the ward of the state that the procedure be carried out. Throughout the legal proceedings, Jerry has been represented by a guardian ad litem, who has continually questioned the power of the state to authorize the removal of an organ from the body of an incompetent who is a ward of the state. . . .

The right to act for the incompetent in all cases has become recognized in this country as the doctrine of substituted judgment and is broad enough not only to cover property but also to cover all matters touching on the well-being of the ward. The doctrine has been recognized in American courts since 1844. . . .

We are of the opinion that a chancery court does have sufficient inherent power to authorize the operation. The circuit court having found that the operative procedures in this instance are to the best interest of Jerry Strunk and this finding having been based upon substantial evidence, we are of the opinion the judgment should be affirmed. . . .

NOTES AND QUESTIONS:
Strunk v. Strunk

1. What is the theory under which the court decides to allow the transplant? Is it consistent with the reasoning of the court in *McFall v. Shimp*?
2. This case is ultimately about making a decision for an incompetent person. Is the court very clear about what rule it is applying in determining how that decision is made? At one point, it says that it is using the doctrine of substituted judgment, while at another point it concludes that the procedure will be in the best interest of the incompetent person. Based on what we covered in chapter 10, which of these rules is more appropriate here? (Be sure to comment on issues relating to whether we are basing our decision on objective or subjective criteria.)
3. The opinion indicates that Strunk had a mental age of approximately six years. Might a 6-year-old understand some of the issues in this case? We are told that Strunk was emotionally dependent on his brother, but it is not clear if he was explicitly asked about whether he wanted to undergo the transplant. Should his feelings be relevant to the decision, even apart from their relevance to the best interests analysis? When, if ever, should they influence the outcome? Should his reluctance to undergo the procedure prevent it even if his family thinks it is good for him? On the other hand, what if other family members were not in favor of the procedure, yet he was very fond of his brother and specifically indicated his willingness to participate? Again, note the issue of subjective and objective criteria.
4. Most courts that have addressed fact patterns similar to *Strunk* have also approved the organ donation. Occasionally, however, courts have concluded that they lack the authority to approve a medical procedure that will not affirmatively benefit the incompetent's health. *See, e.g., In re Pescinski*, 226 N.W.2d 180 (Wis. 1975).

5. In *Strunk*, we were dealing with a donor who would perhaps never understand the consequences of his actions. When the proposed donor is an otherwise healthy child, however, that person will eventually (over time) become competent and be able in retrospect to evaluate what happened.
How might this change the analysis? Imagine, for example, that Strunk was
not a retarded 27-year-old with the mind of a 6-year-old, but rather a
healthy 6-year-old.

Consider the case of Tamas Bosze and Nancy Curran, who were living
together in 1987 when she gave birth to twins Alison and James. The parents had a falling out, and Nancy was awarded custody. Tamas later met another woman and Jean Pierre was born. Jean Pierre soon developed acute
undifferentiated leukemia, and his doctor felt that a bone marrow transplant was his only hope. After finding that other relatives were not suitable
donors, Tamas asked Nancy to have Jean Pierre's half-siblings tested. She
refused, and Tamas brought a legal action. In a lengthy opinion, the Supreme Court of Illinois supported Nancy's right to refuse having the twins
tested. *Curran v. Bosze*, 566 N.E.2d 1319 (Ill. 1990).

Much of the court's conclusion was based on the low likelihood that a
transplant was going to help Jean Pierre, given the severity of his condition.
It also extensively reviewed other cases in which similar issues arose, concluding that in "each of the foregoing cases where consent to the kidney
transplant was authorized . . . the key inquiry was the presence or absence
of a benefit to the potential donor. . . . [T]he standard . . . was whether the
transplant would be in the best interest of the child or incompetent person," and that benefit "arises from the relationship existing between the donor and recipient." The court noted that, due to animosity between the two
parents, the twins had rarely if ever met Jean Pierre, let alone developed a
relationship with him. Testimony was also provided by the director of child
psychiatry at the University of Chicago, who noted that the children would
suffer "adverse psychological consequences" if forced to undergo the transplant, since their mother was opposed to it and they would therefore lack
her emotional support as they went through the process. On the other
hand, he concluded that there would not be any psychological benefits to
the twins 10 to 20 years in the future from learning that, for example, they
saved the life of their half-brother. Do you agree? How might you feel if
you learned that your very existence saved the life of someone else, even if
you were not very close to that person?

Might it be relevant that due to the extremely low risks, almost all
adults who are asked to be donors consent to donating? (David Shimp was
apparently a rare, though highly visible, exception.) A newspaper article
commenting on the *Curran* case noted that a bone marrow donation causes
"pain in the hip for several days," and "causes death in 1 out of 10,000
cases" as a result of the need for general anesthesia. " 'I don't feel that I'm
killing this boy,' Ms. Curran, a 34-year-old accounting clerk, said. 'I could

be killing my own children if I let this happen. Why should they go into the hospital when there's nothing wrong with them?' "[2]

6. In June 1991, 19-year-old Anissa Ayala received a bone marrow transplant from her 14-month-old sister, Marissa. This case received national attention for highlighting a phenomenon that was not uncommon but had not yet been publicly discussed: parents conceiving a child in the hope that the child might be a compatible bone marrow donor for someone else.[3] Some criticized the parents for conceiving the child. On the other hand, parents have children for many trivial reasons. Is it wrong to have a child in the hope that it could save another person's life?

Given that the parents agreed to the donation, there was apparently no court review of their giving consent to the procedure on behalf of Marissa. Assuming we were talking about a somewhat more risky procedure, such as a kidney donation, should it have been allowed? (The donation was successful, and a year later Marissa served as a flower girl at her big sister's wedding.)

7. Assume that at a future date, cloning technology has been perfected and it is considered a routine reproductive option. John has kidney failure and has had difficulty in finding a compatible kidney donor. His wife agrees to gestate a child cloned from his cells. Such a child, due to its nearly identical genetic background, would be an ideal kidney donor. Assuming that a transplant of one of the child's kidneys would otherwise be considered beneficial to John (which, due to its small size, would likely not be the case in reality), could the reasoning in *Strunk* justify the transplant? If not, why not? Would it be more compelling if John were single, and thus the child's only parent? (Note how the reasoning of *Strunk* would *not* justify cloning oneself and keeping the clone in suspended animation, to be used solely as a source for organs. Why not?)

8. Any number of alternatives to the use of donated organs are being explored. One option is xenotransplantation, the use of organs from animals, such as pigs. A major concern is that this may lead to a new epidemic like AIDS as animal viruses get transferred to human beings.

Another promising alternative is to grow new organs for people from their own cells. Scientists are discovering that certain cells in a young human embryo—*stem cells*—can be manipulated to develop into different kinds of specialized tissues. The hope is that we will eventually learn how to direct stem cells to form whole new organs, such as a liver or a kidney. Since these organs would be produced by a person's own cells, there would likely be no danger of the body ever rejecting the organ, as it does organs from another person.

The major current stem cell research controversy relates to the fact that such cells are found only in young embryos. Thus, they have to be obtained either from embryos specially created for research purposes, from embryos created in in vitro fertilization that are no longer needed for that purpose, or from aborted fetuses. The issues this raises—including the role of the federal government in funding such studies—are discussed at length in a report by the National Bioethics Advisory Commission, *Ethical Issues in Human Stem Cell Research* (1999), which is available on the web at *www.bioethics.gov.*

STATE V. POWELL

Supreme Court of Florida

497 So. 2d 1188 (Fla. 1986)

OPINION BY JUSTICE OVERTON:

This is a petition to review a circuit court order finding unconstitutional section 732.9185, Florida Statutes (1983), which authorizes medical examiners to remove corneal tissue from decedents during statutorily required autopsies when such tissue is needed for transplantation. The statute prohibits the removal of the corneal tissue if the next of kin objects, but does not require that the decedent's next of kin be notified of the procedure. . . .

The challenged statute provides:

Corneal removal by medical examiners.—

(1) In any case in which a patient is in need of corneal tissue for a transplant, a district medical examiner or an appropriately qualified designee with training in ophthalmologic techniques may, upon request of any eye bank authorized under s. 732.918, provide the cornea of a decedent whenever all of the following conditions are met:

(a) A decedent who may provide a suitable cornea for the transplant is under the jurisdiction of the medical examiner and an autopsy is required in accordance with s. 406.11.

(b) No objection by the next of kin of the decedent is known by the medical examiner.

(c) The removal of the cornea will not interfere with the subsequent course of an investigation or autopsy. . . .

The trial court decided this case by summary judgment. The facts are not in dispute. On June 15, 1983, James White drowned while swimming at the city beach in Dunellon, Florida. Associate Medical Examiner Dr. Thomas Techman, who is an appellant in this cause, performed an autopsy on James' body at Leesburg Community Hospital. On July 11, 1983, Anthony Powell died in a motor vehicle accident in Marion County. Medical Examiner Dr. William H. Shutze, who is also an appellant in this cause, performed an autopsy on Anthony's body. In each instance, under the authority of section 732.9185, the medical examiner removed corneal tissue from the decedent without giving notice to or obtaining consent from the parents of the decedent.

James' and Anthony's parents, who are the appellees in this case, each brought an action claiming damages for the alleged wrongful removal of their sons' corneas and seeking a judgment declaring section 732.9185 unconstitutional. The actions were subsequently consolidated.

In its judgment, the trial court noted that section 732.9185 "has as its purpose the commendable and laudable objective of providing high quality cornea tissue to those in need of same," but declared the statute unconstitutional on the grounds that it (1) deprives survivors of their fundamental personal and property right to dispose of their deceased next of kin in the same condition as lawful autopsies left them, without procedural or substantive due process of law; (2) creates an invidious classification which deprives survivors of their right to equal protection; and (3) permits a taking of private property by state action for a non-public purpose, in violation of article X, section 6(a), of the Florida Constitution. The court concluded that the state has no compelling interest in non-consensual removal of appellees' decedents' corneal tissue that outweighs the survivors' right to dispose of their sons' bodies in the condition death left them. For the reasons expressed below, we reject these findings.

In addressing the issue of the statute's constitutionality, we begin with the premise that a person's constitutional rights terminate at death. *See Roe v. Wade.* If any rights exist, they belong to the decedent's next of kin.

Next, we recognize that a legislative act carries with it the presumption of validity and the party challenging a statute's constitutionality must carry the burden of establishing that the statute bears no reasonable relation to a permissible legislative objective. In determining whether a permissible legislative objective exists, we must review the evidence arising from the record in this case.

The unrebutted evidence in this record establishes that the State of Florida spends approximately $138 million each year to provide its blind with the basic necessities of life. At present, approximately ten percent of Florida's blind citizens are candidates for cornea transplantation, which has become a highly effective procedure for restoring sight to the functionally blind. As advances are made in the field, the number of surgical candidates will increase, thereby raising the demand for suitable corneal tissue. The increasing number of elderly persons in our population has also created a great demand for corneas because corneal blindness often is age-related. . . . The record reflects that the key to successful corneal transplantation is the availability of high-quality corneal tissue and that corneal tissue removed more than ten hours after death is generally unsuitable for transplantation. The implementation of section 732.9185 in 1977 has, indisputably, increased both the supply and quality of tissue available for transplantation. Statistics show that, in 1976, only 500 corneas were obtained in Florida for transplantation while, in 1985, more than 3,000 persons in Florida had their sight restored through corneal transplantation surgery. . . .

An autopsy is a surgical dissection of the body; it necessarily results in a massive intrusion into the decedent. This record reflects that cornea removal, by comparison, requires an infinitesimally small intrusion which does not affect the decedent's appearance. With or without cornea removal, the decedent's eyes must be capped to maintain a normal appearance.

Our review of section 732.9185 reveals certain safeguards which are apparently designed to limit cornea removal to instances in which the public's interest is greatest and the impact on the next of kin the least: corneas may be removed only if the decedent is under the jurisdiction of the medical examiner; an autopsy is mandated by Florida law; and the removal will not interfere with the autopsy or an investigation of the death. Further, medical examiners may not automatically remove tissue from all decedents subject to autopsy; rather, a request must be made by an eye bank based on a present need for the tissue.

We conclude that this record clearly establishes that this statute reasonably achieves the permissible legislative objective of providing sight to many of Florida's blind citizens.

We next address the trial court's finding that section 732.9185 deprives appellees of a fundamental property right. All authorities generally agree that the next of kin have no property right in the remains of a decedent. . . . More recently, we affirmed the district court's determination that the next of kin's right in a decedent's remains is based upon "the personal right of the decedent's next of kin to bury the body rather than any property right in the body itself." . . .

Appellees also assert that their right to control the disposition of their decedents' remains is a fundamental right of personal liberty protected against unreasonable governmental intrusion by the due process clause. Appellees argue that, because the statute permits the removal of a decedent's corneas without reference to his family's preferences, it infringes upon a right, characterized as one of religion, family, or privacy, which is fundamental and must be subjected to strict scrutiny. Appellees rely upon a line of decisions from the United States Supreme Court which recognize the freedom of personal choice in matters of family life as one of the liberties protected by the due process clause. Appellees also point out that the United States Supreme Court has found rights to personal privacy in connection with activities relating to marriage; procreation; contraception; abortion; and child-rearing and education. According to appellees, the theme which runs through these cases, and which compels the invalidation of section 732.9185, is the protection from governmental interference of the right of free choice in decisions of fundamental importance to the family.

We reject appellees' argument. The cases cited recognize only freedom of choice concerning personal matters involved in existing, ongoing relationships among living persons as fundamental or essential to the pursuit of happiness by free persons. . . .

We also reject the trial court's finding that section 732.9185 creates an invidious classification regarding the next of kin of deceased persons. "Legislatures have wide discretion in passing laws that have the inevitable effect of treating some people differently from others." We find that the statute's effect on the next of kin is incidental and does not offend equal protection. . . .

NOTES AND QUESTIONS:
State v. Powell

1. What is the theory under which the *Powell* court determines that it was appropriate to allow the corneas to be removed from Anthony and James? What are the rights of a deceased person, and that person's family, with regard to what happens to the body?

2. The Florida statute is somewhat unusual in not requiring that the coroner's office make an attempt to contact relatives of the deceased person. More commonly, such laws do require such an attempt, although it is not clear that this requirement changes the outcome very much. Oddly enough, this issue did not receive widespread publicity until 1998, a full thirteen years after *Powell*, when it was covered as a segment on the ABC television newsmagazine *20/20* for March 2, 1998. As Barbara Walters noted at the start, "In morgues across the country, technicians are helping themselves and harvesting from the dead a part of the eye called the cornea, without so much as a word to the grieving family." Reporter Connie Chung commented later in the show, "A nationwide 20/20 survey found that laws in California and thirteen other states allow the removal of corneas during an autopsy without notifying the next of kin. An additional twenty-two states allow corneas to be taken without consent if some reasonable effort is made to contact the families. But the bottom line in all the laws is that corneas can be taken if there is 'no known objection.' The trouble is, how can you object if you aren't even asked?"

3. In effect, the Florida statute is creating a strong presumption of consent to donation, and making it very difficult for that presumption to be rebutted, at least in the case of persons whose bodies end up in a coroner's office. The default assumption that donation will take place, absent a specific rebuttal, is in fact the law for organ donation generally (not just for coroners' cases) throughout much of Europe. What does the *Powell* case suggest about the constitutionality of such an arrangement, were a state to enact that as the law? (Assume, for example, a new Florida statute said that when a person dies in Florida—in a hospital, or anywhere else, and whether or not the coroner becomes involved—that person will be assumed to have consented to organ donation in the absence of explicit proof of a desire not to donate.)

4. The law relating to organ donation is another area in which most or all state statutes are one version or another of a uniform law from the private body that creates such model laws. Here is an excerpt from the most recent version of the Uniform Anatomical Gift Act (UAGA) of 1987:

§ 2. Making, Amending, Revoking, And Refusing To Make Anatomical Gifts By Individual.

(a) An individual who is at least [18] years of age may (i) make an anatomical gift for any of the purposes stated in Section 6(a), (ii) limit an anatomical gift to one or more of those purposes, or (iii) refuse to make an anatomical gift.

(b) An anatomical gift may be made only by a document of gift signed by the donor. If the donor cannot sign, the document of gift must be signed by another individual and by two witnesses, all of whom have signed at the direction and in the presence of the donor and of each other, and state that it has been so signed. . . .

(h) An anatomical gift that is not revoked by the donor before death is irrevocable and does not require the consent or concurrence of any person after the donor's death.

(i) An individual may refuse to make an anatomical gift of the individual's body or part by (i) a writing signed in the same manner as a document of gift, (ii) a statement attached to or imprinted on a donor's motor vehicle operator's or chauffeur's license, or (iii) any other writing used to identify the individual as refusing to make an anatomical gift. During a terminal illness or injury, the refusal may be an oral statement or other form of communication. . . .

§ 3. Making, Revoking, And Objecting To Anatomical Gifts, By Others.

(a) Any member of the following classes of persons, in the order of priority listed, may make an anatomical gift of all or a part of the decedent's body for an authorized purpose, unless the decedent, at the time of death, has made an unrevoked refusal to make that anatomical gift:

(1) the spouse of the decedent;

(2) an adult son or daughter of the decedent;

(3) either parent of the decedent;

(4) an adult brother or sister of the decedent;

(5) a grandparent of the decedent; and

(6) a guardian of the person of the decedent at the time of death.

(b) An anatomical gift may not be made by a person listed in subsection (a) if:

(1) a person in a prior class is available at the time of death to make an anatomical gift;

(2) the person proposing to make an anatomical gift knows of a refusal or contrary indications by the decedent; or

(3) the person proposing to make an anatomical gift knows of an objection to making an anatomical gift by a member of the person's class or a prior class. . . .

5. After a person dies, medical personnel will often find evidence indicating that the deceased did want to donate organs. For example, they may come across a signed statement on the back of the person's driver's license. At that point, it is a standard practice to ask the person's relatives whether or not they are willing to permit organ donation. If the relatives say no, usually there is no donation. Based on the excerpt from the UAGA in (4), comment on this practice.

6. Examine section 3 of the UAGA closely. Under what conditions does it allow family members to consent to donation of the organs of a deceased individual? Note that the list of family members is very similar to the lists that appear in the health care surrogacy acts (chapter 10) that determine who can make health care decisions on behalf of an incompetent patient. Do you recall the standards that were imposed upon a surrogate decision-maker under such acts?

What standards are imposed on a family member under the UAGA? In particular, is there a requirement that the family member consent to donation only if there is a certain amount of evidence (e.g., clear and convincing evidence, as discussed in *Cruzan*) that the deceased would want to donate? Assume, for example, that the family member is totally clueless about what the deceased would have wanted because the deceased never spoke about organ donation. Can the family member say, "Well, I don't know what Joe would have wanted, but I certainly think organ donation is a good thing, so I'm going to consent to donation on Joe's behalf"?

At its core, is the portion of the UAGA relating to consent by relatives really attempting to further the autonomy of the deceased? Or is its purpose—unlike the procedures relating to health care decision-making for incompetent patients—fundamentally different? If the latter, does *Powell* suggest why the UAGA does not run into problems relating to its constitutionality?

7. What is the purpose of section 2(i) of the UAGA? Have you ever heard of anyone taking advantage of this section? After thinking about the issues raised in note 6, can you appreciate the importance of this section? Does the relatively low public awareness of this section further demonstrate how the UAGA is not primarily intended to further a person's autonomy in making decisions about organ donation—at least when that autonomy might be exercised *against* donation?

8. We have been sidestepping the obvious question, so let us go whole hog and ask: Would a state law be constitutional that enabled usable organs to be removed from every person at death, regardless of that person's previously expressed objections? (Compare the issues raised in *Powell* with those raised in *McFall* and *Strunk*.)

9. The quotation beginning this chapter, about people waking up in ice-filled bathtubs after having their organs stolen, reflects a persistent but totally unfounded rumor. There are, however, occasional legitimate stories about organ thefts. In May, 1998, the Associated Press carried a story about the arrest of three surgeons in India for participating in an organ theft ring. "A mechanic, Shaukat Ali, had filed a complaint that he had been robbed of a kidney after having been taken to the Noida center, one of the few in the country that performs kidney transplants, for a medical examination. Solicitors promised him a lucrative job in Singapore and told him that he needed the exam to obtain a visa, Mr. Ali said."[4]

10. Many of the statutes that authorize organ removal by coroners do not refer just to corneas. Yet virtually all of the disputes about such removal do relate to corneas. Why do you think that this is so?

WILSON V. ADKINS

Court of Appeals of Arkansas, Division 1

941 S.W.2d 440 (Ark. Ct. App. 1997)

OPINION BY JUDGE CRABTREE:

Appellant Alta Wilson, a resident of Florida, sued her nephew, Ronnie Adkins, in chancery court for detrimental reliance, breach of contract, and fraud stemming from an alleged agreement in which the appellant agreed to donate bone marrow to her ailing sister in exchange for $101,500.00 as compensation for risk in the procedure. . . .

Here, the complaint states in paragraph II:

That on or about the 1st day of April 1992, the Plaintiff, Alta Wilson and the Defendant Ronnie Adkins and the Defendant Georgia Adkins, now deceased, entered into an agreement whereby the Plaintiff would elect and act as a bone marrow donor for the benefit of the Defendant, Georgia Adkins.

The complaint artfully characterizes the agreement as an exchange of $101,500.00 for the risk, difficulties, and insurance consequences of appellant's marrow donation. While appellants' attorney goes to great lengths to disguise the nature of the contract, it is, as the trial court noted, "so intertwined and commingled that [it] cannot be separated," and clearly falls under the rubric of federal law on the sale of human organs. Here, the complaint essentially admits that the parties contracted for an illegal sale of organs. No matter how the appellants' attorney characterizes the transaction, the dollar amount and the consideration are telling signs that the contract is one for the sale of an organ in violation of federal law.

Title 42 of the United States Code section 274(e) provides the following:

(a) Prohibition

It shall be unlawful for any person to knowingly acquire, receive, or otherwise transfer any human organ for valuable consideration for use in human transplantation if the transfer affects interstate commerce.

(b) Penalties

Any person who violates subsection (a) of this section shall be fined not more than $50,000 or imprisoned not more than five years, or both.

(c) Definitions

For purposes of subsection (a) of this section:

(1) The term "human organ" means the human (including fetal) kidney, liver, heart, lung, pancreas, bone marrow, cornea, eye, bone, and skin or any subpart thereof and any other human organ (or any subpart thereof, including that derived from a fetus) specified by the Secretary of Health and Human Services by regulation.

(2) The term "valuable consideration" does not include the reasonable payments associated with the removal, transportation, implantation, processing, preservation, quality control, and storage of a human organ or the expenses of travel, housing, and lost wages incurred by the donor of a human organ in connection with the donation of the organ. . . .

While this statute does allow "reasonable payments" for the cost of the procedure and incidental expenses, it is clear that $101,500.00 is not payment for reasonable incidental expenses incurred in the organ donation, but is an illegal sale of an organ specifically prohibited by federal law. . . .

Here, while the contract the appellants seek to enforce is not a bribe, the act of selling one's organs is equally offensive, and just as clearly illegal as bribery. While the statute regarding organ sales is relatively modern (1986), its genesis is in a clear public policy based on long standing attitudes about transplantation of organs. "Laws regarding the removal of human tissues for transplantation implicate moral, ethical, theological, philosophical, and economic concerns which do not readily lend themselves to analysis within a traditional legal framework." *State v. Powell*. In commenting on *Powell*, another court noted:

> For that reason, the courts should look instead to the particular statutes that were written on those subjects in an effort to balance the peculiar interests involved. Recently, the California Supreme Court said that courts should not look to conversion law but to the specialized statutes dealing "with human biological materials as objects sui generis, regulating their disposition to achieve policy goals rather than abandoning them to the general law of personal property." Moore v. Regents of the University of California. The same could be said for resorting strictly to contract law when there is an alleged agreement for the transfer of human remains. *Perry v. Saint Francis Hosp. & Medical Ctr.* (D. Kan. 1995).

In *Perry*, the court addressed the issue of an alleged contract between a hospital nurse and a grieving family for the donation of tissues from a deceased patient. While the family did recover on other grounds for the hospital's overreaching organ harvesting, the court rejected a contract approach to the communication between the family and the hospital, stating, "A contract approach is not reconcilable with societal beliefs and values on this subject." . . . Further, the court cited commentary on both the uniform law and the federal act that these laws "embody a commitment to the belief that organs should be given as a gift, either to a specific individual or to society at large." Based on the reasoning in Perry, . . . it is wholly appropriate for a trial court to refuse to meddle in the illegal dealings of parties when the subject matter of their agreement is so clearly repulsive to public policy and federal law. . . .

NOTES AND QUESTIONS:
Wilson v. Adkins

1. Not all parts of our bodies are included in the federal law's definition of human organs. For example, it does not include sperm or eggs. What other part of human bodies is commonly sold? Why do you think the statute has these exclusions? Do you agree with them?

    Sales of eggs have been getting increasing attention recently, particularly as the prices have escalated. One of the more legitimate offers came in an advertisement that ran in elite college newspapers, stating that $50,000 would be paid for an egg from a healthy, tall, athletic woman who had scored at least 1400 on her SATs. (This price was a major step up from the previous going rate, which was closer to $5,000.[5]) If it is acceptable to sell eggs, should it matter how much is paid for them?

2. Section (c)(2) of the federal law provides an exception for "reasonable payments" relating to the processing of human tissue. This exception has allowed a growing business in the sale of processed human body parts. The *Orange County Register* provoked controversy in April 2000 when it featured a series of articles on the practices of some of these businesses:[6]

    > Families are led to think they are giving the gift of life. They are not told that skin goes to enlarge penises or smooth out wrinkles, or that executives of tissue banks—nonprofit groups that obtain body parts—routinely earn six-figure salaries. The products are rarely life-saving as advertised.
    >
    > "I thought I was donating to a nonprofit. I didn't know I was lining someone's pocket," said Sandra Shadwick of Burbank, Calif., whose brother died two years ago. Ms. Shadwick gave her brother's remains to a Los Angeles tissue bank. "It makes me angry. It makes me appalled. If it's not illegal, it ought to be. It's certainly immoral."
    >
    > Industry leaders say donations would plummet if families knew their gifts generate profits. One consequence would be a potential drop in the supply of vital organs.
    >
    > "If donors were told at the time about profits, they wouldn't donate," said Jan Pierce, director of the Intermountain Tissue Center, a Salt Lake City nonprofit bank.

    Should the tens of thousands of dollars of profit generated by the parts of a person's body be encompassed by the "reasonable payments" exception? Should the law be rewritten to more clearly limit the amount of such payments, or at least require greater disclosure of such practices to donors? Note the similarities of these issues to the discussion in the notes following *Moore* in chapter 14.

3. What are the reasons for the ban on organ sales? Do you agree with it?

4. Pennsylvania has passed a law that provides for a $300 payment to the families of organ donors for funeral expenses.[7] Does this payment violate the federal ban?

5. One of the primary concerns about the sale of body parts is that a poor person might sell an organ while still alive.[8] Many people would view this as inappropriate exploitation of the poor. One way to increase the supply of organs is to create a "futures" market, in which people get paid while alive for agreeing to donate organs when they die.[9] (This is a gamble on the part of the buyer of the organs, because most sellers will not die in a way that allows their organs to be used.) Should we enact such a plan? Even if it does not quite so explicitly harm poor people, is it nonetheless inappropriate because it treats human parts as commodities, thus diminishing our societal values?

6. Another incentive proposal for increasing the supply of organs gives priority as organ recipients to family members of persons who become organ donors when they die. Do you think such a plan would violate the federal ban on organ sales? Whether or not it does, do you think such a plan would increase the number of people who sign organ donor cards? Is this plan a good idea?

7. Richard McNutt, who suffered from kidney failure, was engaged to marry Dorothy Zauhar. Dorothy convinced her brother to donate a kidney to Richard. Shortly after the donation was completed, Richard broke off the engagement, and told Dorothy that he had now fallen in love with someone else. She sued him for breach of contract, claiming that her brother had given the kidney in exchange for his binding promise to marry her.[10]

   Does this transaction violate federal law? Why or why not?

8. It is not uncommon for a patient's relative to want to donate an organ, only to discover that the donation cannot go through because the recipient's immune system would reject the donor's kidney. In an effort to take advantage of the willingness of such donors, a type of barter arrangement has been proposed. Imagine, for example, that Mrs. Doe is willing to give a kidney to her husband, Mr. Doe, but there is a compatibility problem. The doctors would find another couple in a similar situation—for example, Mr. Smith, who similarly cannot give his kidney to Mrs. Smith. They could then check for cross-compatibility, making sure that Mr. Doe would not reject Mr. Smith's kidney, and that Mrs. Smith would not reject Mrs. Doe's. The two donations and two transplants would take place simultaneously, in a single hospital.

   Might this arrangement run afoul of the federal law? Why? Is it reasonable for such arrangements to be banned, given the intent of the law? Consider the possible relationship to the issues raised in note 6.[11]

ALLOCATING ORGANS

Having reviewed the ways organs are obtained, we now turn to the question of who gets the organs. From a practical viewpoint, it is helpful to distinguish organs obtained from living donors from those obtained from cadaveric donors. In both cases, the donor can choose to designate a specific recipient. This practice is known as "directed donation." Virtually all living donors do indeed designate someone, since that person's illness is usually the motivation for the donation in the first place. Thus, determining who gets the organs donated by living donors is easy.

In contrast, donations that take place at a person's death rarely make use of directed donation. (Can you see why?) Such organs are therefore viewed as belonging to the public. The recipients of these organs are generally determined pursuant to rules implemented under a 1984 federal law, the National Organ Transplant Act. (This is the same federal law that created the ban on organ sales discussed in *Wilson.*) The authority to run the organ distribution system (formally called the Organ Procurement and Transplantation Network or OPTN) has been delegated by the government to a private not-for-profit corporation called the United Network for Organ Sharing, or UNOS. UNOS rules for determining who gets a particular organ have come under heavy criticism in recent years, as discussed in the following statements by the federal agency charged with regulating organ transplantation.

ORGAN PROCUREMENT AND TRANSPLANTATION NETWORK: FINAL RULE

Health Resources and Services Administration

63 Fed. Reg. 16296 (April 2, 1998)

. . . (c) Liver Allocation Policies. The OPTN has wrestled with liver allocation issues for a decade. A brief summary of this history helps in understanding both the current OPTN policy and the Department's approach in this regulation. . . .

UNOS adopted a liver allocation policy in 1986, the first year of OPTN operations. The allocation policy featured a point system assigning relative weights for medical urgency, blood group compatibility and waiting time to patients within distinct distribution units. This initial system allocated organs first among all patients locally (with "local" waiting lists meaning [an area] ranging from a single transplant hospital's list to the combined lists of all transplant hospitals in an entire State), then to patients in the OPTN region. At the time this policy was adopted, the country was divided into nine regions. Eventually, the number of regions was expanded to the current eleven to reduce differences in population size among the regions. Major differences still remain, however. . . .

[In 1991, waiting] time accrual under the liver allocation criteria was also modified to give greater priority to the most urgent patients. Status 1 (originally Status 4; in the discussion the sickest patients will always be referred to as Status 1, the current definition) patients were assigned the highest priority within the same distribution unit by only allowing waiting time accrued by a patient while listed as Status 1 to count for liver allocation. The Status 1 criteria specified until recently that such patients have a life expectancy of less than 7 days without a liver transplant. Patients who are listed as Status 1 automatically revert to Status 2 after 7 days unless they are relisted as Status 1 by an attending physician. Prior to this policy change, it was possible for a patient who had been waiting a long time in a lower status to accumulate enough waiting time points to give that patient enough total points to be ranked higher than a patient who was a Status 1. The definitions of Status 2, 3, and 4 patients were, until changed, as described below:

Status 2: Patients are continuously hospitalized in an acute care bed for at least 5 days, or are in the intensive care unit. Continuous hospitalization is required.

Status 3: Patients require continuous medical care but may be followed at home or near the transplant hospital.

Status 4: Patients at home, functioning normally.

However, because the system allocates organs first locally, then regionally or nationally only if no local patients are a good match for the organ, and because at any time it is [un]likely that the relatively few (or no) local patients in Status 1 will match, many organs go to Status 2 and 3 patients despite their being ranked lower in medical priority. In the mid 1990s, about two thirds of liver transplants were received by patients waiting in the "local" area, about one fifth by patients in the region and outside of the "local" area, and about one eighth by patients outside the region. Therefore, the preference for "local" plays a significant role in determining a patient's likelihood of receiving an organ. Under the current system, there is a wide range among . . . regions in the number of patients on the waiting list, the number of donor livers available, and the ratio of patients per donor. Consequently, patients in different locations have disproportionate probabilities of being offered a liver under this arrangement. Further, because fixed boundaries are used in local and regional distribution, some patients nearest the site of the donor who are otherwise highly ranked according to urgency or waiting time continue to wait while less sick patients in the "local" region are transplanted. As a result, some patients with higher medical urgency die waiting for a liver while other patients with less medical urgency receive a transplant.

Between 1990 and 1996, the number of liver transplant hospitals performing at least one liver transplant increased from 75 to 110, and the number of liver transplant programs performing 35 or more liver transplants per year increased from 18 to 41. Liver transplants increased from 2,676 to 4,012. Thus, patients have more transplant hospitals from which to choose, but at the same time competition among liver transplant programs for available livers has increased. During 1996, there were 8,026 registrations for a liver transplant.

Some people criticize this policy because livers are allocated "local first" to whomever is highest ranked in the local area of procurement. Thus, less sick patients can be transplanted before sicker patients in other local allocation areas. They believe that the sickest patients should always be transplanted first regardless of their location, because their lives are most at risk. In 1996, about 21 percent of liver patients transplanted were Status 1 and about 30 percent were Status 2. Almost 48 percent of transplanted patients were Status 3, and less than 1 percent were Status 4.

The counter argument to this criticism is that, if sickest patients are always given preference, there is a less efficient use of the available livers, because the sickest patients (Status 1) have lower survival rates than transplant recipients with other statuses. Others say that if less sick patients receive lower preference than under the current policy, more of them will become sicker while waiting and then will have lower survival rates when they are eventually transplanted. Optimally, patients should be transplanted at a time when they are sick enough to benefit from a transplant, but not so sick that the risk of losing the graft is heightened. OPTN data show, however, that at one year after transplant there is about an 11 percentage point difference in patient survival rates and 13 percentage point difference in graft survival rates between former Status 1 and 2. Some argue that part of this difference is due to a side effect of local preference rather than greater risk of graft loss: Status 1 patients, they assert, often get an inferior organ that was made available only after it was turned down for use for any patient in another local procurement area. . . .

Another frequent criticism of the current policy is that there is wide variation in waiting times from one geographic area to another. A counter argument is that this variation cannot be attributed entirely to the allocation policy, because it may also be a function of patient selection decisions and the number of organs procured locally. However, the allocation policy, particularly as it relates to the size of the initial allocation area, is a major determinant of variation in waiting times. For livers, waiting time differentials among transplant hospitals and among organ allocation areas vary by a factor of five or more.

A third criticism of the "local first" policy is that it greatly limits patient choice. If some non-local transplant hospitals do a better job and attract more patients, these patients come to those hospitals only at the price of a reduced chance for a transplant and compete with each other for the limited supply of organs available locally. A counter argument is that some patients prefer to list at local hospitals and that an assured supply of local organs facilitates this particular choice. . . .

[From an earlier section of this document:]

Over the past two decades, the safety and survival rates for transplantation of human organs have improved markedly, and the number of transplants has increased. In 1996, about 20,000 transplants were performed in the United

States. At the same time, the rapid development of transplant techniques and the growth of the Nation's transplant system present new challenges:

1. The demand for organs for transplantation exceeds the supply, and this gap is growing. About 4,000 persons died in 1996 while awaiting transplantation.

2. The Nation's organ allocation system remains heavily weighted to the local use of organs instead of making organs available on a broader regional or national basis for patients with the greatest medical need consistent with sound medical judgment. Technological advances have made it possible to preserve organs longer and share them more widely, but the allocation system does not yet take full advantage of this capacity. Instead, some patients with less urgent medical need receive transplants before other patients with greater medical need whether listed locally or away from home.

3. The criteria used in listing those who need transplantation vary from one transplant center to another, as do the criteria used to determine the medical status of a patient. This lack of uniform, medically objective criteria makes it difficult to compare the medical need of patients in different centers.

4. As a result of both the local preference in allocation and the lack of standard medical criteria, waiting times for organs are much longer in some geographic areas than in others. The statute envisions a national allocation system, based on medical criteria, which results in the equitable treatment of transplant patients. But equitable treatment cannot be assured if medical criteria vary from one transplant center to another and if allocation policies prevent suitable organs from being offered first to those with the greatest medical need. . . .

In order to improve allocation of organs for transplantation, this final rule establishes performance goals to be achieved by the OPTN. Actions already underway in the OPTN are consistent with several of these goals. The rule does not establish specific allocation policies, but instead looks to the organ transplant community to take action to meet the performance goals. The goals include:

- Minimum Listing Criteria–The OPTN is required to define objective and measurable medical criteria to be used by all transplant centers in determining whether a patient is appropriate to be listed for a transplant. In this way, patients with essentially the same medical need will be listed in the same way at all transplant centers.

- Status Categories–The OPTN is required to determine objective medical criteria to be used nationwide in determining the medical status of those awaiting transplantation. This will provide a common measurement for use by all transplant centers in determining the urgency of an individual's medical condition, and it will facilitate OPTN efforts to direct organs to those with greatest medical need, in accordance with sound medical judgment.

- Equitable Allocation–The OPTN is required to develop equitable allocation policies that provide organs to those with the greatest medical urgency, in accordance with sound medical judgment. This increases the likelihood of patients obtaining matching organs, and gives all patients equal chances to obtain organs compared to other patients of equal medical status, wherever they live or list.

By requiring common criteria for listing eligibility and medical status, and by requiring that organs be directed so as to equalize waiting times, especially for those with greatest medical need, this rule is designed to provide patients awaiting transplants with equal access to organs and to provide organs to sickest patients first, consistent with sound medical judgment. While present OPTN policies give weight to medical need, the "local first" practice thwarts organ allocation over a broad area and thus prevents medical need from being the dominant factor in allocation decisions.

Under the provisions of this rule, it is intended that the area where a person lives or the transplant center where he or she is listed will not be primary factors in how quickly he or she receives a transplant. Instead, organs will be allocated according to objective standards of medical status and need. In this way, suitable organs will reach patients with the greatest medical need, both when they are procured locally and when they are procured outside the listed patients' areas. This objective reflects the views of many commenters on the proposed regulations, as well as the finding of the American Medical Association in its Code of Medical Ethics: "Organs should be considered a national, rather than a local or regional resource. Geographical priorities in the allocation of organs should be prohibited except when transportation of organs would threaten their suitability for transplantation." . . .

NOTES AND QUESTIONS:
Allocating Organs

1. The proposed change in organ allocation rules was at least partially motivated by money and politics. Liver transplantation in this country was pioneered at the University of Pittsburgh, but as that program became successful in training more and more doctors, those doctors went out and set up transplant programs elsewhere. While Pittsburgh has maintained an excellent reputation and has plenty of patients, the locality rule for allocating livers has meant that these patients had to wait longer and longer to get a liver. Pittsburgh also lost the lucrative profits from those deferred transplants. The program enlisted the help of a local real estate developer who was a friend of President Clinton, and who met with the president on several occasions. Those efffforts may have played a role in the eventual move by Secretary of Health and Human Services Donna Shalala to pro-

pose the new rule, accompanied by a letter from her to many members of Congress.[12]

2. Although the change in the federal regulation finally went into effect in March 2000, it was only after a rocky two years of hardball politics. During that period Congress passed a law preventing Shalala's department from implementing the new rule until a study of the issue was completed. In addition, a number of states passed laws stating that organs that came from donors in the state had to be given to a recipient living in that state. Louisiana, which enacted such a law, began a lawsuit, claiming that the federal regulation exceeded the department's authority and that only Congress could override state laws. The Governor of Wisconsin indicated that his state, too, might sue: "This rule is unconstitutional. . . . It pre-empts state's rights."[13] As of summer 2000, the dispute was still simmering, with bills in Congress that would return to UNOS the authority to make its own decisions about the geographic distribution of organs.

   Assume that Congress did in fact pass a law affirming its support of the new regulations, requiring that organs be distributed on a national basis, and that Louisiana attempted to enforce its law requiring local use of organs. What outcome would you expect from a court that tried to resolve the conflict?

3. An unusual letter Secretary Shalala sent to 181 members of Congress on June 1, 1998, in which she harshly criticized UNOS (the government's own subcontractor), gives a sense of the emotions generated by the controversy. That letter read in part:

   > . . . I am deeply concerned about recent efforts by the contractor that manages the network, [UNOS], to misrepresent the provisions of the regulation. I have received numerous letters from Members of Congress, transplant professionals, patients and the public that reflect the inaccuracies published by UNOS. I am especially distressed that UNOS is needlessly frightening transplant patients about the HHS regulation.

   The full text of her letter, which further takes issue with UNOS's claims that the change in organ allocation will require a single national waiting list (as opposed to just larger areas for distributing organs), and that the new rule will lead to fewer transplants and fewer lives being saved, is on the web (*www.hrsa.gov/osp/DSLETTER.htm*).

4. Two of the major changes discussed in these readings—allocating organs on a national basis, and making sure that the sickest person generally gets an organ—interact in an interesting way. Under the prior rules, where organs were generally given to someone in the region where the donor was located, the recipient might well not be as sick as prospective recipients elsewhere in the country. Thus, by allocating organs nationally, the system can better make sure that the sickest person gets the organ.

Might someone be in favor of one of these goals but not the other? What if you were in favor of a national system for allocating organs but did *not* believe that it was necessarily appropriate that the sickest person get an organ? Is that combination of beliefs reasonable? If you had those beliefs, how would you react to the changes proposed by the federal government?[14]

5. Do you agree with the recommendations for using larger geographic areas in determining who is eligible to receive an organ? What are the arguments for and against this change?

6. Should livers or other organs be given first to the sickest patients? As discussed in the reading, this issue continues to engender heated debate. There are certainly circumstances in which the sickest patients might not benefit from the transplant (depending on how we define "benefit") as much as healthier patients. Consider in each of the following cases whether it is appropriate to use the listed criteria for selecting between the two patients. Are there any general conclusions you can reach about why some criteria might appear more acceptable than others? (You might review the issues raised in the *Baby K* case in chapter 12 to see if any of these criteria should be considered inappropriate discrimination. Or should that concept not apply, or apply in an altered manner, to allocating a scarce resource?)

> **Immediate Transplantation Survival**: Alan and Bob are both age 40. Both have liver failure due to a virus. Bob is still weak due to having been in a car wreck several weeks ago; he has only a 60 percent chance of living through the transplant and postoperative care, compared to Alan's 80 percent chance. However, should they both live through the transplant, their post-transplant life expectancy is expected to be the same.

> **Post-Transplantation Survival #1**: Carol and Diane, both 35, also have liver failure due to a virus. While Carol is healthy, Diane has diabetes. They are both given an equal chance of surviving the transplant. However, Carol is given a 35-year post-transplant life expectancy, while Diane has a 20-year life expectancy.

> **Post-Transplantation Survival #2**: Ed is 35. Frank is 50. They both have liver failure due to a virus, and have equal chances of living through the transplant. However, because of the age difference, Ed has a 30-year post-transplant life expectancy, while Frank has a 15-year life expectancy. (If you choose not to give priority to Ed, is there any age for Frank that would make you change your answer? Or is the only relevant issue how likely it is that the patient can live through the transplant itself?)

7. Should we ever take account of nonmedical factors in allocating organs? The current organ allocation rules attempt to exclude such criteria. When Mickey Mantle received a liver, some people suggested that he had somehow been given special priority. Whether or not that was true, should he have gotten priority? Is it inappropriate to allow the use of subjective criteria relating to a person's merit?

Interestingly, a variety of criteria that you might otherwise think irrelevant can enter into a transplant program's decision to list a person as eligible to receive an organ. For example, as part of determining that the transplant will be a medical success, it is necessary to assure that the patient will have adequate post-operative care in a stable environment. Thus, a person who is living alone, with no caretaker and minimal access to transportation, may be considered a poor candidate for a transplant. This is apart from the usual requirement that the patient needs to come up with a way to pay for the transplant: unless insurance covers the transplant, or there is a state program that will pay for someone in that situation, the patient will likely be out of luck.

Of course, this is merely a specific, high-visibility instance of the fact that there is no general right to health care in this country. (Oddly enough, kidney transplants *are* paid for by the government, due to the political quirk that a law dealing with end-stage renal disease was passed by Congress early in the evolution of transplantation. Renal failure remains the only disease for which the federal government effectively provides universal insurance to all Americans, rich and poor.)

8. If we are uncomfortable with giving someone bonus points for personal merit, should we be equally uncomfortable with denying certain people a transplant? Should prisoners be denied a liver transplant? How about prisoners who were convicted for first degree murder? How about a prisoner who has received a death sentence? (Note that, with appeals, it is not uncommon for years to pass before a person actually is executed.)

9. A great deal of material relating to transplantation issues is found on the UNOS web site, *www.unos.org*. By clicking on About UNOS, and then following the Policies/Bylaws links on the left, you can get to the full detailed criteria for determining a person's rank on transplant lists. In addition, the 1999 report by the Institute of Medicine commissioned by the federal government, *Organ Procurement and Transplantation: Current Policies and the Potential Impact of the DHHS Final Rule*, can be found on the web at *books.nap.edu/catalog/9628.html*.

10. One of the classic works discussing the difficulty of deciding how to allocate a scarce resource is *Tragic Choices* by Guido Calabresi (who later became a federal appellate judge, and whose opinion in one of the physician-assisted-suicide cases was excerpted in chapter 11) and Philip Bobbitt. That work does not attempt to resolve the problems but rather discusses how societies might use different approaches to working out acceptable solutions. As the final paragraph in this discussion, it is appropriate to reprint the first paragraph of *Tragic Choices*:

> We cannot know why the world suffers. But we can know how the world decides that suffering shall come to some persons and not to others. While the world permits sufferers to be chosen, something beyond their agony is earned,

something even beyond the satisfaction of the world's needs and desires. For it is in the choosing that enduring societies preserve or destroy those values that suffering and necessity expose. In this way societies are defined, for it is by the values that are foregone no less than by those that are preserved at tremendous cost that we know a society's characteristics.[15]

Endnotes

1. U.S. Department of Health and Human Services, *1999 Report to Congress on the Scientific and Clinical Status of Organ Transplantation*, at 1 (Washington, D.C.: U.S. Dept. of Health and Human Services, 1999).

2. Isabel Wilkerson, "In Marrow Donor Lawsuit, Altruism Collides with Right to Protect Child," *New York Times*, 30 July 1990, A8.

3. Gina Kolata, "More Babies being Born to be Donors of Tissue," *New York Times*, June 4, 1991, A1.

4. Associated Press, "India Holds 10 in Plot to Steal Kidneys," *New York Times*, 12 May 1998, A8.

5. Gina Kolata, "$50,000 Offer for Egg Donor Sharpens the Debate," *New York Times*, 3 March 1999, A10; see also Rebecca Mead, "Annals of Reproduction: Eggs for Sale," *New Yorker*, 9 August 1999, 56.

6. Mark Katches, William Heisel and Ronald Campbell, "The Body Brokers: Donors Don't Realize They Are Fueling a Lucrative Business," *Orange County Register*, 16 April 2000. The entire series of articles, including full-color charts detailing what happens with various portions of a person's body, can be found on the web at *www.ocregister.com/health/body*.

7. Sheryl Gay Stolberg, "Pennsylvania Set to Break Taboo on Reward for Organ Donation," *New York Times*, 6 May 1999, A1.

8. For a discussion of some of the problems that result from a black market in organs, see Chris Hedges, "Egypt's Desperate Trade: Body Parts for Sale," *New York Times*, 23 September 1991, A1. For a discussion by a court of an unusual alleged plot to sell organs of executed Chinese prisoners, including lengthy transcriptions of conversations among the conspirators, see *Unites States v. Wang*, 1999 U.S. Dist. LEXIS 2913 (S.D.N.Y. 1999).

9. See, e.g., Lloyd R. Cohen, "Increasing the Supply of Transplant Organs: The Virtues of a Futures Market," 58 *Geo. Wash. L. Rev.* 1 (1989).

10. Amy Goldstein, "Woman Alleges Fiancé Stole Her Heart, Brother's Kidney; Lawsuit Highlights Ethical Complications of Organ Donation," *Washington Post*, 21 October 1997.

11. See Jerry Menikoff, "Organ Swapping," 29(6) *Hastings Ctr. Rep.* 28 (1999).

12. Sheryl Gay Stolberg, "Patients' Lives on the Line in Battle over Transplants," *New York Times*, 25 March 1998, A1.

13. Sheryl Gay Stolberg, "Fight over Organs Shifts to States from Washington," *New York Times*, 11 March 1999, A1.

14. See, e.g., Peter A. Ubel and Arthur L. Caplan, "Geographic Favoritism in Liver Transplantation: Unfortunate or Unfair?" 339 *New Eng. J. Med.* 1322 (1998).

15. Guido Calabresi and Philip Bobbitt, *Tragic Choices*, at 17 (New York: W.W. Norton & Co., 1978).

GLOSSARY

Amicus curiae (plural, *amici*): Literally, a friend of the court. This is a person or entity that is not directly involved in a controversy—neither a plaintiff nor a defendant—but who has reason to be concerned about the outcome of the case and wants to submit its arguments to the court. Prominent bioethics cases tend to produce many *amici*, as you can tell by the Supreme Court's occasional references to their arguments.

Appellant: The person or entity appealing the case to a higher court. It may be either the plaintiff or the defendant from the lower court proceedings, depending on who lost that case.

Appellee: When a case is appealed to a higher court, the person or entity against whom the appeal is taken. In other words, the appellee is the party that did *not* want to appeal the case (probably having won in the lower court).

Civil Law: The law relating to private interactions between individuals, as distinguished from the criminal law. Thus, both contract and tort law are part of civil law.

Common Law: The law created by court decisions, as distinguished from the law created by a legislature when it enacts statutes. Common law is the "background" law that judges were creating before there were any statutes. Much of the law in the United States is derived from English common law.

Criminal Law: Laws designed to deal with certain defined serious wrongs committed against society. Such laws serve a variety of purposes, including punishing the wrongdoer and perhaps also preventing that person from committing further crimes. In contrast to civil law (tort law, in particular), the criminal law generally does not seek to provide compensation to victims of crimes.

Defendant: The person against whom a lawsuit is brought.

Due Process: The first of the two major limitations on governmental actions provided by the 14th Amendment to the U.S. Constitution. It has been interpreted to provide two very different kinds of limitations: *procedural due process* and *substantive due process*.

Equal Protection: The second of two major limitations on governmental action imposed by the 14th Amendment to the U.S. Constitution (*see also Due Process*). This clause requires that when a law treats two groups of people differently, the government must provide a justification for that difference. In somewhat simplified terms, there are currently three levels of justification required, depending on the type of classification made by the law. The most demanding, *strict scrutiny*, applies to race-based classifications or laws that might impinge on the exercise of fundamental rights. An intermediate level of scrutiny applies to sex-based classifications. The loosest form of scrutiny, *rational basis*, applies to all classifications that do not fit into one of the other two categories.

Federal Courts: Courts of limited jurisdiction set up by the federal government: you must meet certain criteria before you can get your dispute into federal court. The two major sources of jurisdiction are controversies that relate to the laws of the federal government (including the Constitution), and controversies between citizens of different states (*diversity jurisdiction*).

The trial courts in the federal system are known as district courts, and a single judge generally handles each case. The losing party in the district court has the right to appeal to a federal appellate court, known as a circuit court of appeals. There, a panel of three judges usually hears the appeal.

The Supreme Court of the United States can reverse the decisions of circuit courts of appeal. For most purposes, there is no right to have a case heard by the Supreme Court, which has a great deal of discretion in deciding which cases it wishes to review. To ask the Supreme Court to review a case, a party must file a *writ of certiorari* with the Court.

Guardian ad Litem: A guardian appointed by a court. When a court has to decide an issue that will affect the welfare of an incompetent person, it may decide to appoint such a person so that it knows there is someone acting as an advocate for that person's best interests.

Moot: A lawsuit that is no longer of any practical significance to the parties that brought it, for example, a dispute about withdrawing care from a person who dies before there is a decision. In general, courts prefer to have a real (non-moot) controversy before them, and will often decline to give an opinion in a moot case. However, a court might choose to issue an opinion so that future parties in similar circumstances will have guidance. See, for example, the *Conroy* case.

Plaintiff: The person who begins a lawsuit.

Procedural Due Process: One of the two aspects of due process under the 14th Amendment, this is the requirement that the procedures established to accomplish a governmental purpose must be appropriate.

Respondent: In appellate court proceedings, the party challenging (and thus responding to) the appeal brought by the appellant.

Standing: In order to bring a lawsuit before a court, a person or entity must demonstrate a direct stake in the controversy. If there is no such stake, the lawsuit will be dismissed for lack of standing. This requirement is designed to make sure that courts resolve only real and current controversies. Standing is often an issue in cases brought by public interest organizations, as in *Foundation on Economic Trends v. Heckler*.

Stare Decisis: The requirement that courts pay respect to the decisions of prior courts, commonly referred to as "following precedent." This played a major role in the Supreme Court's decision in *Casey*, in which it chose not to overrule *Roe v. Wade*.

Statute: A law enacted by a legislature (as distinguished from the common law). More and more of today's law is statutory. Statutes that cover large areas of what used to be common law are not uncommon. This is known as *codifying* an area of the law: taking the general principles that have grown from numerous court decisions over many years, making them more consistent with one another, and rewriting them as a single (often lengthy) statute or code.

Substantive Due Process: The more controversial (though well-entrenched) aspect of the due process clause of the 14th Amendment, this refers to specific substantive limitations on government actions that are derived from the due process clause. The right of privacy created in *Griswold v. Connecticut* is a well-known application of substantive due process.

Uniform Acts: Model laws drafted by a private organization, the National Conference of Commissioners on Uniform State Laws. These model laws are then sent to the legislatures of the states, which are encouraged to adopt them. As a result of this process, in many areas states tend to have laws that are very similar to one another. In particular, state laws relating to organ donation (Uniform Anatomical Gift Act) and the definition of death (Uniform Determination of Death Act) closely follow these model laws. When you hear the term uniform act or uniform law, it usually refers to one of the model laws drafted by this organization. All of the uniform acts (which are often extensively debated and modified before receiving the organization's final approval) can be found on the web at *www.law. upenn.edu/bll/ulc/ulc_frame.htm*

TABLE OF CASES

INDEX